Lone Star Politics

Lone Star Politics

Second Edition

Paul Benson
Tarrant County College

David Clinkscale
Tarrant County College

Anthony Giardino
Tarrant County College

PEARSON

Boston   Columbus   Indianapolis   New York   San Francisco   Upper Saddle River
Amsterdam   Cape Town   Dubai   London   Madrid   Milan   Munich   Paris   Montréal   Toronto
Delhi   Mexico City   São Paulo   Sydney   Hong Kong   Seoul   Singapore   Taipei   Tokyo

Editor in Chief: Dickson Musslewhite
Executive Editor: Vikram Mukhija
Associate Development Editor: Corey Kahn
Assistant Editor: Beverly Fong
Editorial Assistant: Isabel Schwab
Director of Marketing: Brandy Dawson
Senior Marketing Manager: Wendy Gordon
Senior Managing Editor: Ann Marie McCarthy
Project Manager: Corey Kahn
Senior Operations Supervisor: Mary Fischer
Operations Specialist: Mary Ann Gloriande

Senior Art Director: Maria Lange
Text Designer: PreMediaGlobal, Inc.
Cover Designer: DePinho Design
Media Director: Brian Hyland
Digital Media Editor: Alison Lorber
Media Project Manager: Joe Selby
Full-Service PM: Revathi Viswanathan
Composition: PreMediaGlobal, Inc.
Printer/Binder: Courier Companies
Cover Printer: Lehigh-Phoenix Color/Hagerstown
Text Font: Adobe Caslon Pro 10.5/13

Credits and acknowledgments borrowed from other sources and reproduced, with permission, in this textbook appear on appropriate page within text (or on page 361).

Library of Congress Cataloging-in-Publication Data
Benson, Paul.
   Lone star politics / Paul Benson, David Clinkscale, Anthony Giardino. — Second edition.
      p. cm
   Includes bibliographical references and index.
   ISBN-13: 978-0-205-97081-0
   ISBN-10: 0-205-97081-8
   1. Texas—Politics and government.   I. Clinkscale, David.   II. Giardino, Anthony.   III. Title.
   JK4816.B45 2013
   320.4764—dc23

                                                                        2013015630

Front cover design is based on the photograph "Stardust" by Bob Wynn's project titled Motel. **www.bobwynnphoto.com**

10 9 8 7 6 5 4 3 2 1

Student Edition
ISBN-13: 978-0-205-970810
ISBN-10: 0-205-970818

Books A La Carte
ISBN-13: 978-0-205-970957
ISBN-10: 0-205-970958

Brief Contents

Contents

Preface

s Governor Rick Perry delivered his State of the State address to the 2013 Texas Legislature, some dozen years removed from his first, one could be forgiven for seeing the Texas political landscape as essentially unchanged. The same speaker of the house and lieutenant governor sat behind him that had been there two and four years before. Republicans continued to control both the house and the senate by comfortable margins. The land commissioner was halfway through his third term, while the attorney general and comptroller were midway through their second.

Nonetheless, there was a sea of new faces in the legislature. Voluntary and involuntary retirement changed the rosters. The lieutenant governor, who had practically packed his bags for Washington, DC, was back after primary voters had rudely rejected his bid for an open U.S. Senate seat. A year earlier, Perry had dreamed of DC as well, but his presidential ambitions didn't last past the first month of the primaries. Many of the legislators who had survived challenges did so only after promising to "do better," which meant different things depending on the makeup of their constituencies. Meanwhile, the other elected executives, who had waited patiently for the higher offices to open, were growing impatient, even as Perry and Dewhurst each fueled speculation that they might run for one more term.

Another game-changer was the state's vastly improved fiscal condition. Two years prior, the legislature came into session facing a $27 billion deficit in its current services biennial budget, causing a substantial and lasting reduction in the size of government in Texas. Instead, the 2013 session opened with a budget surplus. Even conservatives, generally averse to spend, saw these new monies—much of it generated from the state's rejuvenated oil fields—as an opportunity to begin long-needed upgrades to the state's infrastructure, with a special emphasis on finally funding Texas's all-important water development program.

Given that Texas is a conservative state, news of a surplus immediately brought calls for saving some of it or sending it back to the taxpayers through a series of tax cuts. This highlights the pressure-packed environment of Texas politics. Schools, tax cut proponents, and advocates for the poor all regarded the new revenue as at least partially theirs. And therein stands a great certainty in politics in both the Lone Star State and throughout the democratic world—no one gets everything they want.

The reality of the New Texas, with its contracted budget and significant infrastructure challenges, calls out for a revised edition of *Lone Star Politics* with a renewed emphasis on public policy. This second edition addresses the policy-making challenges foisted upon a government whose actions are limited by a predominant political culture wary of—if not outright hostile to—the mere discussion of increased taxes. Getting policy right is most important when resources are limited; getting it wrong proves significantly more costly. *Lone Star Politics* brings this process to life.

It is also important to underscore our particular interest in and knowledge of Texas politics. Starting in 2013, the Texas Higher Education Coordinating Board requires that the Texas portion of the six-hour college and university government requirement be fulfilled with a course dedicated specifically to Texas government. Collectively, the authors of *Lone Star Politics* have over three-quarters of a century experience teaching Texas government as a standalone course.

The Texas Higher Education Coordinating Board outlined eight student learning outcomes that students should master through the Texas Government course. *Lone Star Politics* supports achievements toward all of these outcomes. The following are examples of how we approach each:

1. *Explain the origin and development of the Texas constitution.* Our historic approach delves in depth into the formation of the 1876 constitution, contrasting it with the previous document and underscoring how it parallels the state's earlier constitutions.

2. *Demonstrate an understanding of state and local political systems and their relationship with the federal government.* Our strong emphasis on federalism isn't confined to one chapter, but is reinforced by "Inside the Federalist System" features throughout the book.

3. *Describe separation of powers and checks and balances in both theory and practice in Texas.* We explain separation of powers and checks and balances in the first two chapters, but we describe how they work in practice as we delve into the legislative process and again as we explain the deliberate attempt to check power through the creation of the plural executive and the establishment of separate "highest courts" for civil and criminal matters.

4. *Demonstrate knowledge of the legislative, executive, and judicial branches of Texas government.* Solid scholarship on each of the branches is found through the five chapters devoted to their study. Constraints on each are explained in the constitution chapter.

5. *Evaluate the role of public opinion, interest groups, and political parties in Texas.* Separate chapters are devoted to interest groups and political parties. This new edition contains a media and public opinion chapter as well.

6. *Analyze the state and local election process.* In addition to explaining the way in which state and local elections are run, including discussion of the different types of elections, we consider other pertinent factors ranging from campaigning to redistricting.

7. *Describe the rights and responsibilities of citizens.* Citizens' rights are covered not only in the constitution chapter but due process is given a deeper, more vibrant treatment in this edition's new criminal justice chapter. Civic engagement is encouraged in the elections, interest groups and legislative chapters.

8. *Analyze the issues, policies, and political culture of Texas.* From the opening chapter's emphasis on Texas political culture through the last three policy-intensive chapters, *Lone Star Politics* intertwines how the state's unique character both influences and limits political issues and the public policy that emerges through the policy process.

New to This Edition

The second edition of *Lone Star Politics* was comprehensively revised to cover recent political events in Texas and to support the student learning outcomes for the Texas Government course. Major changes in each chapter include:

- Chapter 1, "Texas Society and Political Culture," includes a new opening that ties the Texas Revolution to contemporary Texas politics. We have a revised, thorough analysis of changing demographics highlighting policy implications, with a new focus on the state's emerging Asian population. We analyze the state's rapid recovery from last decade's economic recession.

- Chapter 2, "Federalism and the Texas Constitution," has a new opening that ties the present to the past as it analyzes the development of our state constitution. The latest U.S. Supreme Court federalism cases are weighed. Clashes between the state and the Environmental Protection Agency are examined from a policy perspective. Fresh analysis of the constitutional amendment process offers insight into the dynamics of change.

- Chapter 3, "Voting and Elections in Texas," opens with a reconsideration of voting in Texas. An extensive new analysis considers the impact of early voting laws on campaigning. The impact of new federal runoff rules is examined, and straight-ticket voting is analyzed. A new feature examines the effectiveness of campaign spending in various races.

- Chapter 4, "Political Parties in Texas," evaluates the heavy legislative turnover of the last few sessions. A new emphasis on third parties considers both their structural differences and their potential impact on politics. We consider the partisan implications of demographic change and take a fresh look at the supporters of the two major parties, with a special emphasis on the challenges facing each of these parties in the future.

- Chapter 5, "Interest Groups in Texas Politics," has a new opening that examines contemporary issues pertinent to Texas interest groups. Political Action Committees receive a revised treatment. Both movement and more traditional groups receive new analyses. The cooperative actions between state and federal interest groups are examined in light of their impact on policy outcome.

- Chapter 6, "The Media and Public Opinion in Texas," is completely new to this edition of *Lone Star Politics*. The chapter traces media from its Texas beginnings through print, radio, and television broadcasting. We explain the ties of early radio and television stations to daily newspapers. The impact of media coverage on the 1980s Texas supreme court crisis is analyzed. We consider the impact of the new media on Texas politics and examine the role of public opinion in the state's policy making. The importance of exit polling as a political device is considered.

- Chapter 7, "The Legislative Process in Texas," has a new opening that emphasizes the impact of legislation on Texans. A new treatment of redistricting and its attendant court battles analyzes its effect on the legislature. We explore the Tea Party's challenge to Speaker Joe Straus and examine the impact of the 2009 stimulus act on the state budget.

- Chapter 8, "The Governor in Texas," takes a fresh look at the governor's veto power. We analyze both Governor Perry's lengthy tenure in office and the impact of his appointees on policy. We discuss how Perry managed to remain governor for so long in a state that has traditionally been unkind to incumbent governors.

- Chapter 9, "The Plural Executive and the Bureaucracy in Texas," introduces water policy as an overarching theme. We reconsider how and why the plural executive developed in Texas. We discuss the implications of hydraulic fracking on the water supply and examine the land commissioner's plan for converting brackish water to a usable form. We offer a new examination of the Texas Water Development Board.

- Chapter 10, "The Texas Court System," offers expanded examples of different types of law. A greater emphasis is placed on court jurisdiction, and the role of the courts in public policy making is highlighted. A new comparison of judicial selection systems is paired with an expanded treatment of proposed judicial reforms.

- Chapter 11, "Local and County Governments and Special Districts Government in Texas," includes an expanded focus on urban issues. A new offering features San Antonio Mayor Julian Castro, a rising star in Texas politics. We have taken a deeper look at the policy-making role of the city manager and a revised look at the impact of local interest groups. We analyze Councils of Government as service providers.

- Chapter 12, "Public Policy in Texas," is a standalone policy chapter with a new emphasis on the policy-making model. It examines the voter ID and state guns laws as examples of how policies are shaped by many actors. A new feature differentiates public policy from private business policy. We discuss how federalism constrains state policy options.

- Chapter 13, "Criminal Justice Policy in Texas," analyzes crime data as it applies to policy-making. It includes revised analysis of the death penalty and the dropping numbers on Texas's Death Row. New analysis visits the issue of dropping crime rates. A greater emphasis is placed on due process rights.

- Chapter 14, "Finance and Budgeting in Texas," is completely rewritten and placed in its own chapter. A major point of emphasis is the long-term impact of the 2011 budget cuts. The budget-making process is explained in detail, with special attention given to the unique constraints that impact Texas fiscal policy. A new section explores the state's major dedicated budget funds, and fresh analysis of the state's tax structure provides insight into the fiscal process. The importance of nontax revenue is explained, as is the budget's role as an important factor in public policy decisions.

We have also made the following pedagogical improvements in this edition of the text:

- **Learning objectives** tied to the major headings in every chapter identify the key concepts that students should know and understand with respect to Texas politics and government; these learning objectives also structure the end-of-chapter summaries.

- **"Review the Chapter" summaries** organized around the learning objectives highlight the most important concepts covered in each chapter.

- **"Test Yourself" quizzes** at the end of each chapter assess students' comprehension and understanding of the most important terms, concepts, and ideas; an answer key is provided at the end of the book.

- A large portion of the **photos** in this edition are new. They capture major events from the last few years, of course, but to illustrate the relevancy of politics, they show political actors and processes as well as people affected by politics, creating a visual narrative that enhances rather than repeats the text.

- All of the **figures and tables** reflect the latest data.

- A new **design** simplifies the presentation of content to facilitate print *and* digital reading experiences.

Features

Our approach in writing this book is simple. First, be realistic. Texas politics is less a debate about ideology and theory than it is a pragmatic discussion of what works. We will show how different government officials use their powers to achieve their goals. Second, we want to give students the opportunity to understand the public policy process. Finally, since we think Texas politics is the most exciting game in town, we wrote this book to be as entertaining and fun as possible while still delivering all the information you need. You might even find it funny in places—that's just the nature of Texas government.

To provide greater focus and direct the reader to think about the core themes of each chapter, we have structured our analysis around learning objectives, restructured the chapter summaries and conclusions around these learning objectives, and provided test questions at the end of each chapter. The other pedagogical features not only reflect this effort to provide more targeted learning guidance but also zero in on key themes specific to studying Texas government.

- **"Inside the Federalist System"** provides insight into the state's interaction with the national government as it implements public policy.

- **"Texas Mosaic" feature boxes** provide students with an inside look at politics in Texas, whether focusing on a group, an individual, or an institution. Each of these features is accompanied by critical thinking questions.

- **"The Texas Constitution: A Closer Look"** delves into the state's governing document, highlighting its impact on both government structure and policy.

- **Explore Further** at the end of each chapter feature seminal books and articles, as well as links to significant websites that offer information beyond that contained in the textbook.

- **A running marginal glossary** clearly defines bolded key terms for students at the points in chapters when the terms are first introduced and discussed.

Lone Star Politics provides comprehensive coverage of Texas state and local politics, with a special emphasis on policy-making. Teaching Texas as a standalone course allows more opportunity to examine policy and its impact on Texans. Each chapter helps the student understand how the political, cultural, and social underpinnings of the state influence policies that flow from the various levels of government.

- **Chapter 1, "Texas Society and Political Culture,"** introduces students to the Texas political environment. Special attention is given to the historic, economic, and demographic factors that shape the state.

- **Chapter 2, "Federalism and the Texas Constitution,"** examines the legal relationship between the national and Texas governments, focusing on the limits on and the powers of each. It evaluates how previous state constitutions have impacted the current document and how the constitution limits policy choices. Additionally, we examine political forces that maintain the status quo.

- In **Chapter 3, "Voting and Elections in Texas,"** we analyze the evolution of voting rights in Texas and evaluate its impact on turnout. After careful consideration of who votes and who doesn't, we introduce the various types of elections in the state and analyze the role of money in the quest for votes.

- **Chapter 4, "Political Parties in Texas,"** explains how the state shifted from solidly Democratic to solidly Republican, and examines factors that may lead it to shift again. New analysis of third parties in Texas adds depth, and both party structure and the convention system are examined.

- **Chapter 5, "Interest Groups in Texas Politics,"** examines the role of these groups from multiple perspectives. The roles of lobbyists and campaign contributions are analyzed, as is the important role of providing information in an environment stressed for such resources and the effects of such information on policy decisions.

- **Chapter 6, "The Media and Public Opinion in Texas,"** is an all-new chapter that analyzes the way government actions are covered by the Texas press. It traces the rise of the media in 20th-century Texas and the advocacy role that many media entrepreneurs played in boosting their cities. It includes special insight into recent cutbacks in political media deployment. Additionally, the chapter examines public opinion and exit polling in the state.

- **Chapter 7, "The Legislative Process in Texas Politics,"** emphasizes the importance of legislative leadership. It illustrates the difficult process of passing a bill, with special emphasis on maneuvers employed to stop legislation. It evaluates how legislative policy making impacts Texas citizens, and it examines recently passed legislation.

- **Chapter 8, "The Governor in Texas,"** explores the ways in which a power-limited chief executive can exercise influence over both the legislative process and the bureaucracy. It examines the importance of the governor's staff and evaluates the unique circumstances associated with the longest governor's tenure in Texas history.

- **Chapter 9, "The Plural Executive and the Bureaucracy in Texas,"** explores the powers shared across the state's executive offices, boards, and commissions. It explains the deliberate decision to disperse executive power and how it affects public policy. The chapter differentiates between the cabinet form of government in operation at the national level and in many states, and the plural executive in Texas.

- **Chapter 10, "The Texas Courts System,"** explains the differences between civil and criminal law. It examines the unique structure of the Texas court system, explains the jurisdictions of Texas courts, and evaluates the role of the courts in policy making.

- **Chapter 11, "Local and County Governments and Special Districts in Texas,"** explores the various layers of local government in the state. It explains the different types of city government and the unique challenges in delivering local public policy, as well as the expanding role of the city manager as policy creator.

- **Chapter 12, "Public Policy in Texas,"** explains the stages of the policy-making model, applying it specifically to the voter ID issue and the Stand Your Ground law. The chapter differentiates among the various types of public policy and distinguishes public policy from corporate policy.

- **Chapter 13, "Criminal Justice Policy in Texas,"** analyzes law enforcement, crime, and punishment. It examines the administration of capital punishment in the state and explores due process rights. It evaluates public policy making by the Dallas County district attorney.

- **Chapter 14, "Finance and Budgeting in Texas,"** explains budget making in Texas. It identifies the main actors in the process, examines the institutions that impact its creation, and analyzes the state's tax policy and spending choices. The chapter contains an in-depth analysis of the state's radically reduced base budget and explains the difference between tax and nontax revenue, and how this impacts policy making.

MyPoliSciLab

MyPoliSciLab is an online homework, tutorial, and assessment product that improves results by helping students better master concepts and by providing educators a dynamic set of tools for gauging individual and class performance. Its immersive experiences truly engage students in learning, helping them to understand course material and improve their performance. And MyPoliSciLab comes from Pearson—your partner in providing the best digital learning experiences.

✓ **Personalize learning.** Reach every student at each stage of learning, engage students in active rather than passive learning, and measure that learning. Refined after a decade of real-world use, MyPoliSciLab is compatible with major learning management systems like Blackboard and can be customized to support each individual student's and educator's success. You can fully control what your students' course looks like; homework, applications, and more can easily be turned on or off. You can also add your own original material.

- The intuitive assignment **calendar** lets instructors drag and drop assignments to the desired date and gives students a useful course organizer.

- Automatically graded assessment flows into the gradebook, which can be used in MyPoliSciLab or exported.

✓ **Emphasize outcomes.** Keep students focused on what they need to master course concepts.

- Practice tests help students achieve this book's learning objectives by creating personalized **study plans**. Based on a pretest diagnostic, the study plan suggests reading and multimedia for practice and moves students from comprehension to critical thinking.

- Students can study key terms and concepts with their own personal set of **flashcards**.

Improve critical thinking. Students get a lot of information about politics; your challenge as an instructor is to turn them into critical consumers of that information. **Explorer** is a hands-on way to develop quantitative literacy and to move students beyond punditry and opinion. On MyPoliSciLab, guided exercises pose key questions about Texas politics and then help students use data to answer those questions. Explorer includes data from the United States Census, General Social Survey, Statistical Abstract of the United States, Gallup, American National Election Studies, and Election Data Services, with more data being regularly added.

Engage students. Every government operates on a fundamental set of principles. Learn more about these principles with Texas constitution exercises that help students analyze key passages and consider the evolution of Texas government.

Analyze current events. Prepare students for a lifetime of following political news in Texas. Coverage of current events keeps politics relevant and models how to analyze developments in the Texas political system.

- Reflect on a hypothetical case with the **simulations** in MyPoliSciLab. Easy to assign and complete in a week, each simulation is a game-like opportunity to play the role of a political actor in Texas and apply course concepts to make realistic political decisions.

- Or analyze current events by watching streaming video from the Texas Tribune.

- Get up-to-the-minute analysis by top scholars on MyPoliSciLab's **blogs,** take the weekly quiz, and register to vote.

The Pearson eText offers a full digital version of the print book and is readable on Apple iPad and Android tablets with the Pearson eText app. Like the printed text, students can highlight relevant passages and add notes. The Pearson eText also includes **primary sources** like the Texas constitution.

Chapter Audio lets students listen to the full text of this book.

Visit **www.mypoliscilab.com** to test-drive MyPoliSciLab, set up a class test of MyPoliSciLab, and read about the efficacy of Pearson's MyLabs. You can also learn more from your local Pearson representative; find them at **www.pearsonhighered.com/replocator**.

Supplements

Make more time for your students with instructor resources that offer effective learning assessments and classroom engagement. Pearson's partnership with educators does not end with the delivery of course materials; Pearson is there with you on the first day of class and beyond. A dedicated team of local Pearson representatives will work with you to not only choose course materials but also integrate them into your class and assess their effectiveness. Our goal is your goal—to improve instruction with each semester.

Pearson is pleased to offer the following resources to qualified adopters of *Lone Star Politics.* Several of these supplements are available to instantly download on the Instructor Resource Center (IRC); please visit the IRC at **www.pearsonhighered.com/irc** to register for access.

Test Bank. Evaluate learning at every level. Reviewed for clarity and accuracy, the Test Bank measures this book's learning objectives with multiple-choice, true/false, short answer, and essay questions. You can easily customize the assessment to work in any major learning management system and to match what is covered in your course. Word, BlackBoard, and WebCT versions are available on the IRC, and Respondus versions are available upon request from **www.respondus.com**.

Pearson MyTest. This powerful assessment generation program includes all of the questions in the Test Bank. Quizzes and exams can be easily authored and saved online and then printed for classroom use, giving you ultimate flexibility to manage assessments anytime and anywhere. To learn more, visit **www.pearsonhighered .com/mytest**.

Instructor's Manual. Create a comprehensive roadmap for teaching classroom, online, or hybrid courses. Designed for new and experienced instructors, the Instructor's Manual includes a sample syllabus, brief chapter outlines, detailed chapter outlines, key terms, discussion questions, out-of-class assignments, Internet activities, and annotated resource materials. Available on the IRC.

Instructor's eText. The instructor's eText offers links to relevant instructor's resources and student activities in MyPoliSciLab. You can access these resources by simply clicking on an icon at the start of each chapter. Available on MyPoliSciLab.

PowerPoint Presentation with Classroom Response System (CRS). Make lectures more enriching for students. The PowerPoint Presentation includes a full lecture script, discussion questions, and photos and figures from the book. With integrated clicker questions, get immediate feedback on what your students are learning during a lecture. Available on the IRC.

Class Preparation. Add multimedia, figures, photos, and lots more from any of our political science books to your lectures. Available on MyPoliSciLab.

Acknowledgments

We would like to acknowledge Dickson Musslewhite, Vikram Mukhija, and Corey Kahn, without whom this book would not be possible. Many people at Tarrant County College had an important role in the development of *Lone Star Politics*, including Division Dean Arrick Jackson, department chair Wanda Hill and administrative assistant Darla Hernandez; we would like to thank them for their patience and support during the writing process. The library staff, especially Sandra McCurdy, made our job much easier. Kudos to the numerous students who made valuable suggestions over the last couple of years. A special thank you to Vincent Giardino, a former student who is currently an adjunct instructor, for his extensive insight, advice, and editing of this edition's new media chapter. Finally, and most importantly, we want to thank our families. This book would not have happened without our spouses—Carolyn Benson, Karen Clinkscale, and Lisa Giardino. They all thank you for reading *Lone Star Politics*.

1

Texas Society and Political Culture

Texas: Being better than your state since 1845!

—Kate Gustafson, College freshman and native Texan

I n the first days of a cold, wet March in 1836, two groups of men considered their futures. One group, numbering slightly over 180, had taken sanctuary in an old Spanish mission popularly known as the Alamo. There, they awaited what appeared to be an inevitable and fatal attack by troops under the command of Antonio Lopez de Santa Anna, president and dictator of Mexico. These men had decided to take up arms against the Mexican government because . . . well, we can never know for sure their reasons for doing so since almost all would die within and without those crumbling walls. But we do know that they came from all parts of the United States, from Anglo and Tejano communities of Texas, and even from foreign countries, and thus were diverse in their origins, their motives, and even the color of their skin.

Another group, less than half the number of the first, assembled in the crude little village of Washington located on a bluff above the Brazos River some 150 miles east of San Antonio de Bexar and the Alamo. The reasons for their actions we know more clearly, as they declared

1.1	**1.2**	**1.3**	**1.4**	**1.5**	**1.6**
Differentiate between government and politics and show the relationship between these two elements.	Identify the key events from Texas history that have shaped the state's political landscape.	Compare and contrast the geographic regions of Texas and show how the land has shaped Texans and their politics.	Analyze the economic evolution of Texas and identify economic factors that may influence Texas public policy in the future.	Profile the current Texas population (including the major ethnic groups) and identify future demographic developments.	Discuss three political cultures in the United States and identify the dominant political cultures in Texas.

Even as one group of Texans perished at the Alamo, another gathered to the East, formally declaring independence and beginning the arduous task of crafting a new government.

1.1 politics
Who gets what, when, and how.

1.2 government
Public institutions acting with authority to levy taxes and to allocate things for society.

1.3

1.4

1.5

1.6

themselves to be independent of the Republic of Mexico and created the framework of a new government under which they and their posterity would be able to live in freedom. Like the men at the Alamo, they came from many parts of the United States and from foreign countries, although only two were native Texans. Yet despite their soaring rhetoric, the perspective of history clearly shows that they and their posterity would only slowly and with great resistance consider that "the people of Texas" of which their declaration spoke would include anyone who was not Anglo, Protestant, and American.

In these two groups we see, in microcosm, both the complexities and the contradictions of the place we call Texas and the people we call Texans. Only by understanding these myriad elements can we understand the nature and the dynamic of government and politics in the Lone Star State. This chapter will help you gain that understanding.

The Conceptual Pieces

1.1 Differentiate between government and politics and show the relationship between these two elements.

Since this is about the government and politics of Texas, we must begin by defining these concepts. Let's look first at "politics." There are probably as many definitions of this word as there are political scientists eager to establish a reputation by defining it. However, when you strip away the verbal clutter that often accompanies such efforts, a basic working definition emerges. Simply put, **politics** is who gets what, when, and how.[1]

The term *politics* and its first cousin, *politician*, aren't the most popular words around. Yet politics is an integral part of human society and the human condition. In even the most rudimentary cultures, people will want to benefit themselves by acquiring needed or desired things by seeking, gaining, and maintaining power. This process is politics, and it can occur anywhere human beings interact with each other. If you need evidence of this, watch a group of 3-year-olds on a playground. They may be complete strangers when the play period begins, but within five minutes somebody will have determined who gets what, when, and how by having achieved power.

The second basic term we must define is *government*, which (like *politics*) is one of those terms that everyone bandies about, but whose definition can prove elusive. It calls to mind the story told about U.S. Supreme Court Justice Potter Stewart, who was asked to define the term *obscene*. He remarked that while he could not, in fact, define it, he knew it when he saw it! Since we know government when we see it, we offer this working definition of the term. **Government** is composed of public institutions that have the authority to mandate the collection of revenue and to allocate valuable things for a society. Public institutions can include such disparate entities as the Texas Legislature, the Office of Governor, the Higher Education Coordinating Board, the Houston City Council, the El Paso County Commissioners Court, the 144th Criminal District Court in San Antonio, and so on. Mandatory revenues constitute money payments that must be rendered by citizens. Valuable things can include money, land, natural resources, individual freedoms—even life itself. And an allocation made with authority simply refers to a division or distribution that is recognized as legitimate. In short, government provides a structural framework within which activities (like politics) take place.

Politics and government are inextricably intertwined with one another. You will never have government without politics, but politics pervades everything we do. It's in our jobs, our churches, our civic clubs, our schools, our families, our soccer leagues—it's anywhere and everywhere humans interact with one another. Sure, it's easy to dismiss politics as unsavory and government as corrupt. But a more responsible strategy is to try to understand their dynamic interaction and to explore practical ways that you can use politics to affect government in a positive way. Rest assured that if you don't, others are going to, and they may not have your good intentions. Besides, government and politics in Texas are fascinating. Let's take a closer look.

Any study of the panorama of Texas politics must begin with an understanding of the land and its people. Texas and Texans generate strong feelings with which not everyone will agree. This should come as no surprise because Texas is many things to many people. This rather large piece of real estate has been a refuge, an escape hatch, a land of opportunity, a dream maker, and a heartbreaker for countless thousands who have called themselves "Texans" (or "Texians" or "Tejanos" or even, simply, "the People"). By turns, Native Americans, Spaniards, Africans, French, Mexicans, Germans, Irish, Italians, Asians, and scores of others have made their way to Texas and made themselves Texans in the process. This incredible ethnic and cultural diversity makes defining a "Texas" society and a uniformly "Texan" culture an exercise in futility to some extent. As the tuxedo-clad young urban professional couple sits in a Lexus awaiting valet parking before attending the opening of the "Sublime Light" photo exhibit at the San Antonio Museum of Art, Bubba, on his way to a Robert Earl Keen concert at Greune Hall outside New Braunfels, drives by in a mostly blue '92 Chevy pickup, complete with a dog of manifold and indeterminate lineage and a bumper sticker proclaiming, "Keep Honking, I'm Reloading!" Neighborhoods of abject poverty and random violence stand in stark contrast to enclaves of unimaginable wealth and political power, often in the same city, within mere miles of each other. On a given day, the temperature may be 95°F in Brownsville and 25°F in Dalhart. Yet it is this sheer diversity and variety that may, in the final analysis, define Texas and Texans more than anything else.

On reflection, it seems clear that there cannot possibly be only one Texas society and one Texas culture. This state's society and its culture constitute a **mosaic**, a picture made up of many parts and fragments. There are historical, geographic, economic, and demographic pieces. Only by attempting to understand these individual pieces and their relationship to one another can we begin to see the whole picture of Texas, its people, and its politics.

mosaic
The joining of small pieces of material, varied in shape and color, to produce a whole image; often used to describe the social and cultural diversity that defines Texas.

1.1

1.2

1.3

1.4

1.5

1.6

Cattle drives were once a major driver of the Texas economy, accounting for much of the state's accumulation of wealth.

1.1

1.2

1.3

1.4

1.5

1.6

The Historical Pieces

| 1.2 | Identify the key events from Texas history that have shaped the state's political landscape |

ome of the more interesting pieces in the Texas mosaic emerge from history. Certain historical events have helped to shape political attitudes as well as political actions in this state. While the following brief survey of Texas history can only be considered cursory, it nevertheless highlights some of these important elements.

☐ The Explorers

THE SPANISH When the first Europeans came to that part of the so-called New World now known as Texas, the land was already occupied. Numerous Native American groups—bands, tribes, even confederations—lived here, representing a wide range of social organization and lifestyle. Much of what is known about these groups is derived from reports made by some of the early European explorers. One of the first, a Spaniard named Alvar Nuñez Cabeza de Vaca, arrived in Texas (by way of Florida) in November 1528, and spent the next seven years wandering over a large portion of Texas and the American Southwest. After numerous encounters with various native people, he eventually found his way to a Spanish outpost on the Gulf of California, and thence to Mexico City, where he recounted his adventures to Spanish colonial officials.[2]

His report prompted these officials to outfit a full-scale expedition to explore systematically the area he had traveled and, in particular, to search for several "golden

Frederic Remington's famous depiction of Spanish explorer Francisco Vasquez de Coronado.

cities" that he claimed to have observed at a distance. This expedition, led by Francisco Vásquez de Coronado, spent several years wandering through parts of present-day Arizona, New Mexico, and Texas (one group made it as far as Kansas) in a fruitless search for wealth before returning to Mexico City.[3] At about the same time, a remnant of the ill-fated de Soto expedition wandered into East Texas and encountered the relatively sophisticated Caddo cultures there. Despite these early contacts, the rather pessimistic reports filed by these would-be *conquistadores*, depicting Texas as barren, inhospitable, and lacking accessible natural resources, cooled the Spanish desire to see more of Texas for the time being. However, even though these early explorations proved to be an economic disappointment for Spain, they did establish for that nation an important territorial claim to Texas that went largely unchallenged for the next century and a half.

THE FRENCH The Spanish, with their policy of benign neglect toward the empire's northern reaches, received a rude shock when a small French expedition, led by René-Robert Cavelier, Sieur de La Salle, landed on the Texas coast in 1684 and claimed the area for the king of France. La Salle had strayed from his original target (he had intended to land at the mouth of the Mississippi River), and his expedition never amounted to much, at least from the French perspective. He was murdered, and most of his compatriots died as a result of disease, starvation, or Indian attacks. This French "settlement" lasted barely three years, yet it had significant long-term consequences. As a result of the abortive La Salle expedition, Spain saw the need to reassert a more vigorous claim to the part of its empire that included Texas. The Spanish made plans to establish a permanent presence in these desolate northern provinces in order to deter future incursions by other European powers. Ironically, the greatest legacy of La Salle and his ill-fated band was to ensure Spain's continuing attempts to occupy Texas for the next 130 years.[4]

☐ The Colonists

The first tool Spain used to establish a permanent presence in Texas was the mission.

The mission system had worked well in other parts of Spain and its empire as a means of subduing conquered or indigenous peoples and converting them into both faithful Christians and loyal Spanish subjects. The results of their efforts in Texas, however, were mixed at best.

THE HISPANICS The first Spanish missions to Texas proper were established in east Texas near present-day Nacogdoches. They did not prosper because the Caddo Indians living there, among the most highly developed and sophisticated in Texas, saw no real advantage to relocating to the missions. Moreover, initial contact with the Europeans often introduced diseases among the native peoples to which they had no genetic resistance and that resulted in extremely high mortality rates. After several attempts over a period of years during the early 1700s, the east Texas mission effort was largely abandoned.

Similarly, Spanish efforts to establish missions among the Plains Indians during the middle years of the 18th century proved fruitless. Missions near present-day Brady and Menard lasted less than two years before they were attacked and destroyed by Comanche bands. The message to Spain was painfully clear: The People (or, more properly, "the only true human beings," as the Comanche called themselves) wanted no part of the Spanish or their institutions, except as a source of horses to be stolen and captives to be seized.

Only in south Texas did the missions truly prosper, and it would be here, in an area bounded by the Rio Grande River and the Gulf of Mexico, that Spanish culture would put down its deepest, most persistent roots. These south Texas colonial outposts blended the native cultures of the area's Coahuiltecan Indians with elements from Spain, the Canary Islands, and, increasingly, an emerging Mexican culture. Today we see the most obvious influence of this culture in the hundreds of Spanish place names throughout Texas, but these Hispanic colonists also made significant contributions to

1.1

1.2

1.3

1.4

1.5

1.6

1.1

1.2

1.3

1.4

1.5

1.6

Cowboys ride in front of the Alamo; a mixing of two iconic images.

Texas's legal heritage in such diverse areas as community property and water rights. In addition, vibrant communities based on free-range cattle ranching established between the Rio Grande River and San Antonio de Bexar in the second half of the 18th century provided the basis for a growing cattle trade with the Hispanic settlements to the south as well as with American communities to the north and east. This cattle culture would later provide most of the tools, terminology, and technology for an emerging Anglo cattle industry in the 19th century.

Born of the melding of Spanish and Native Indian bloodlines, the Mexican people rose up in revolution against their colonial overlords on September 16, 1810. After 10 years of bloody fighting, Spain abandoned its colonial empire and the Republic of Mexico was born. Yet even as this young country struggled to establish its place among the community of nations, a new, and ultimately divisive, force appeared in its northernmost state: Anglo settlers who began to arrive in Texas.

THE ANGLOS The first organized Anglo settlement of Texas was established under the leadership of Stephen F. Austin, whose father, Moses, had negotiated a settlement agreement with the Spanish.

After his father's death, Stephen Austin confirmed this agreement with the new government of Mexico and began issuing land grants.[5] In the 1820s, land was a precious commodity and a powerful magnet, and the deal Austin offered was too good to pass up. Farmers received 177 acres of land; ranchers, 4,428 acres. (It is truly amazing how hundreds of Southern dirt farmers were transformed into ranchers by passing through or over the waters of the Red or Sabine rivers.) This land came with relatively few restrictions. The prospective landowner had to occupy the land within two years, have it surveyed, make improvements to it, and become a Catholic (the only religion recognized as legal by the Mexican Constitution). While the typical Anglo settler, coming from the upland areas of the Old South, was not a Catholic, the possibility of possessing more than 4,400 acres of prime river bottom land acted as a powerful, if superficial, agent of conversion. In addition to Austin, other land agents (called *empresarios*), such as Green DeWitt, Sterling C. Robertson, and Ben Milam, were also permitted to give out land grants under the authority of various Mexican state governments.

So the Anglos came. They came by the hundreds and, eventually, the thousands. They brought their families, their livestock, and, most significantly, their attitudes toward society and government, attitudes that ran counter to those of the prevailing Hispanic culture. These Anglos—poor, proud, fiercely independent, and enormously intolerant of those unlike themselves—gradually became more and more estranged from the government in faraway Mexico City. And that government, in turn, became more and more concerned about the increasingly rebellious attitudes of these newcomers. In order to stem this foreign tide, Mexico enacted tough restrictions on immigration beginning in 1830, but this merely heightened the tension between these two proud cultures. In 1832, several confrontations between Anglo settlers and Mexican officials erupted, and these encounters would prove to be a harbinger of much more serious conflict in the future.

The election of Antonio López de Santa Anna as president of Mexico in 1833, and his subsequent assumption of virtually dictatorial powers, added another element to the increasingly combustible mix in Texas. Santa Anna's flaunting of democratic principles (he maintained that Mexico was not yet ready for democracy) alienated many of the old families of Hispanic Texas. These true "native Texans" (known as Tejanos) included such venerable families as the Ruizes, the Navarros, the Veramendis,

1.1

1.2

1.3

1.4

1.5

1.6

GENERAL D. ANTONIO LOPEZ DE SANTA-ANNA.
PRESIDENT OF THE REPUBLIC OF MEXICO.
By A. Hoffy, from an original likeness taken from life at Vera-Cruz.

Santa Anna would continue to move in and out of Mexican political leadership for two decades after Texas's independence.

1.1

1.2

1.3

1.4

1.5

1.6

Republic of Texas
The independent nation created by Texans that lasted from 1836 to 1846; its status as an independent country has contributed to (and continues to influence) an independent spirit in its politics.

and the Seguins, and their opposition to Santa Anna soon led them to make common cause with their Anglo neighbors to the east. In October 1835, fighting broke out between Anglo settlers near Gonzales and Mexican cavalry troops from San Antonio. The battle was soon being referred to as the "Lexington of Texas," and within weeks the Anglo colonists and their allies from the Hispanic communities were in active revolt against the government of President Santa Anna. This alliance was somewhat shaky from the start, as many of the Anglos openly manifested the typically American attitude of racial superiority common in that day. However, such underlying divisions were temporarily put aside in the face of a more immediate threat. By early 1836, Santa Anna had responded, entering Texas at the head of a large army and promising to destroy these rebellious interlopers.[6]

As wars go, the Texas Revolution was rather brief. It lasted a mere seven months and saw relatively few major battles, although the one fought at the old mission San Antonio de Valero (popularly known as the Alamo) would almost immediately become the stuff of legend and would help create a popular and persistent image of the fearless Texan standing tall against insurmountable odds. General Santa Anna's counterpart was Sam Houston, a free-spirited politico from Tennessee who had come to Texas. He had spent considerable time with his Cherokee friends, who called him the Big Drunk, in Indian Territory, before coming to Texas to start life anew. He was reluctant to fight against superior odds, but when he finally took the field against Mexican troops at San Jacinto (near present-day Houston) on the afternoon of April 21, the element of surprise, the emotional memories of the massacres of friends and compatriots at the Alamo and Goliad, and no small amount of luck led to victory for the "Texians" and defeat and capture for Santa Anna.[7]

After San Jacinto and the subsequent withdrawal of Mexican forces from Texas (brought about partly by the Texians holding Santa Anna hostage and partly by torrential rains that made it impossible for the Mexican army to maneuver), the victors found themselves in something of a dilemma. No longer a part of Mexico, they were not yet part of anything else. Popular opinion among Anglo Texans favored admission to the United States as a state, but unwilling to antagonize Mexico or to upset the free state–slave state balance that then existed in Congress, the U.S. government rebuffed Texas. In the face of these political realities, Texans did what was completely in keeping with their independent nature: Acting on the Declaration of Independence they had penned back in March, they became their own nation.

☐ The Texans

THE REPUBLIC The **Republic of Texas** existed for almost ten years. This decade was marked by a growing population, an expanding frontier, a deteriorating economy, a chronically bankrupt government, Indian attacks, Mexican invasions, European immigration, and politics that made your typical barroom brawl look like a Sunday School picnic by comparison. Despite an enormous influx of people, including, near the end of the Republic's life, a large number of Germans who settled in the Hill Country of central Texas, times were tough for this young nation and its citizens. Inflation was rampant, and the economy in many areas came to be based on barter. Cash was scarce and was usually outrageously inflated.

The economy was not the only area where controversy and confusion reigned.

Political parties did not yet exist, but the clash of egos between Sam Houston, hero of San Jacinto and first president of the Republic, and his successor, a latter-day cavalier and poet from Georgia with the colorful name of Mirabeau Buonaparte Lamar, sparked an endless series of political pyrotechnics centering on the personalities of the people involved. A growing estrangement between Anglo and Tejano further fueled the political turmoil, as public policies and cultural practices began to turn against the Tejanos. Moreover, Indians were likely to raid frontier settlements at the drop of an arrow, and Mexico sent armies to invade Texas not once but twice. Although not exactly what 17th-century English philosopher Thomas Hobbes spoke of in his description of the presocietal state of nature ("nasty, brutish, and short"), life

1.1
1.2
1.3
1.4
1.5
1.6

Texas ★ Mosaic

Rough Justice: Order in the Court

Just exactly how rough was it for government officials of the Republic of Texas? Look at what happened to the Honorable Robert McAlpin Williamson, circuit court judge for the Republic of Texas. Williamson was nicknamed "Three-Legged Willie" because a bout with childhood polio had left him with a withered left leg to which he attached a wooden peg. As a circuit judge, he would ride to various counties and hold court. One of the counties on his "circuit" was Gonzales County, known for its brazen disregard for the law. On one memorable trip to Gonzales County, Judge Williamson was attempting to hold court outdoors. His judicial bench was a board held up by two kegs of whiskey, and his seat was a keg of nails. He leaned his cane and a long rifle against a nearby tree and tried repeatedly to bring the unruly mob to order. As the crowd became more menacing, the judge leaned over, picked up his rifle, placed it before him on the bench, and loudly cocked it. "This court is coming to order," he said. "If it doesn't come to order—right now—I am by God gonna kill somebody, and I'm not particular who I kill." Court came to order.

Source: C. F. Eckhardt, *Texas Tales Your Teacher Never Told You* (Plano, TX: Wordware, 1992), p. 144.

1. What conclusions can you draw from this account regarding the state of law and order in the Republic of Texas?

2. What does this incident reveal about attitudes of the Republic's citizens toward government?

in Texas during the period of the Republic was certainly difficult, as the Texas Mosaic suggests. Thus, the failures of the Republic served to intensify a tendency by these evolving Texans to regard government and authority as superfluous at best and dangerous at worst.

Ultimately, the way out of the many dilemmas confronting the Republic lay in union with the United States.[8] By the mid-1840s, U.S. public opinion favoring territorial expansion and a political agenda based on Manifest Destiny combined to bring about the annexation of Texas, and, in February 1846, the government of the Republic of Texas ceased to exist. Yet the shadow cast by this dubious decade of nationhood would stretch far into the future, and as subsequent generations of Texans looked back on the Republic, they would tend to ignore its failures and see instead a kind of golden era during which Texas stood tall among the community of nations. This attitude of uniqueness, often labeled Texas Exceptionalism, manifests itself as an enormous sense of pride on the part of Texans that, in turn, has become an integral part of the Texas social, cultural, and political equation. However, those less generous in their evaluation would see Texas Exceptionalism as evidence of a bloated self-centeredness that has led to arrogance, violence, and racism, as well as an almost religious disdain for government, especially the federal variety.

THE CONFEDERACY Texans had hardly gotten used to calling themselves Americans before they once again shifted their political allegiance. Barely 15 years after becoming the 28th state in the Union, Texas joined 10 other Southern states in attempting to sunder that union by forming the Confederate States of America. Not all Texans favored disunion, and, reflecting the diversity that is so characteristic of this state, opposition would continue to simmer throughout the Civil War in such areas as the German Hill Country and several of the Red River counties of north central Texas. As early as the summer of 1862, opposition to the Confederacy in and around Gainesville in Cooke County was so strong that a large group of citizens plotted to remove the area from Confederate control. The scheme was uncovered, and more than 40 participants were hanged. In the same year, a cavalry troop slaughtered a number of German Texans on the Nueces River as they were making their way to Mexico and thence to join the Union army. The bodies were left where they fell as a warning to others who shared the same sentiment. However, a solid majority of Texans supported

1.1

1.2

1.3

1.4

1.5

1.6

Inside the Federalist System

A Federal Government Ally in the Texas Governor's Mansion

There are occasions when the long arm of the federal government extends unusually deep into a state through an individual whose political interests demonstrate a greater loyalty to the federal government than to the citizens he was elected to govern. Often, that governor is charged with implementing rules, regulations, and programs endorsed by the federal government but which are completely in opposition to the beliefs and sentiments of most of the state's citizens. Such was the fate—and the choice—of Edmund J. Davis, who governed the state during the highly controversial period known as Reconstruction.

Davis, Texas's first post-Civil War governor, was a former Union army officer. Like all children of wealthy families, Davis was well educated long before his family moved to Texas in 1848. He became a lawyer one year later. During the early part of his professional career, Davis served as an inspector and deputy customs collector. In 1853, he became district attorney of the Twelfth Judicial District at Brownsville. Three years later, Governor Elisha M. Pease named him a judge of the same district, where he served until 1861. Davis joined the Democratic Party in 1855, but he renounced his affiliation with the party shortly before the end of the Civil War. Because he vigorously opposed secession, the state eliminated his judgeship. After Texas voted to secede, Davis left the state in May 1862. The following October, he met with Abraham Lincoln, who commissioned Davis as a colonel responsible for recruiting cavalrymen on behalf of the Union. His leadership in a number of successful missions led to his promotion to brigadier general.

At the conclusion of the Civil War, Davis participated in state politics as a Unionist and Republican. His political exploits, however, paled in comparison with his military successes. While he served in the Constitutional Convention of 1866, he was defeated in his attempt to win a state Senate seat. However, he was chosen as the president of the Constitutional Convention of 1869. In this capacity, David favored the restriction of political rights of former secessionists and expanded rights for blacks. In addition, he supported a proposal to divide Texas into several Republican-controlled states. Clearly, Davis represented every characteristic favored by Union sympathizers and resented by Democrats who were, at the time, prohibited from voting.

In the election of 1869, Davis successfully ran for governor as a Radical Republican, but his election was highly contentious. As the state's fourteenth governor, Davis loyally served as the national government's crony and seemed intent on punishing Texas Democrats during Reconstruction. His most controversial actions included using the state's militia to intimidate political opponents; suppressing the publication of newspapers critical of his leadership; and bolstering the rights of newly free slaves. Davis's tenure in office was characterized by excessive public spending, significant property tax increases, appropriation of public funds for the benefit of the governor's political and financial allies; and strict control of voter registration by the occupying Union military. Regardless of any favorable policies or programs implemented during his administration, Davis is often considered to be the most controversial of all Texas governors.

Despite his obvious unpopularity, Davis ran for re-election in December 1873. By then, many Democrats had renounced their loyalty to the Confederacy and had, as a result, regained the right to vote. Democratic voters contributed heavily to the election of Davis's Democratic opponent, Richard Coke. Davis attributed his defeat in part to the vindictive policies of the Republican national government and the resulting strain that existed between the state and Washington. From 1875 until his death, Davis led the weakened Republican Party in Texas. However, because of his perceived but now disputed loyalty to the national government, which appeared to most Texans as oppressive during Reconstruction, he was soundly rejected by voters in every subsequent election for state and federal office. Over one hundred years would elapse before Texans elected another Republican governor.

The perceived abuses of the Davis administration have had policy implications to this day. They have acted as a reinforcing agent against both centralized government power and government power in general. Especially among members of the modern Republican Party, any expansion of government power is subject to intense scrutiny, often followed by charges of overreach. State legislators and executives have to keep this in mind as they make government policy.

The Handbook of Texas (citing Ronald N. Gray and Edmund J. Davis: Radical Republican and Reconstruction Governor of Texas (Ph.D. dissertation, Texas Tech University, 1976). William C. Nunn, *Texas under the Carpetbaggers* (Austin: University of Texas Press, 1962). Charles W. Ramsdell, *Reconstruction in Texas* (New York: Columbia University Press, 1910; rpt., Austin: Texas State Historical Association, 1970)).

1. **In what ways did Davis's actions as governor run counter to the prevailing political attitudes of Texas at this time?**

2. **How do you think the policies of Republican Governor Davis would be received by the Texas Republican Party today?**

the Confederacy, and although few major battles were actually fought on Texas soil, the state became a major supplier of men and material to the South's war effort.[9]

That effort, of course, would prove futile, and when the Confederacy finally capitulated, Texas found itself economically devastated, politically decimated, and militarily occupied. When he stepped ashore on June 19, 1865, at the head of 1,800 Federal troops, General Gordon Granger brought more than military occupation. He also brought with him a copy of the Emancipation Proclamation, which first had been issued by President Lincoln in 1863. His public pronouncement that those who had been slaves were now free spread quickly among African Americans in Texas. Eventually, black Texans began to celebrate June 19 ("Juneteenth") as a holiday, and the practice continues today in many Texas communities. The arrival of General Granger and his federal troops at Galveston in June 1865, signaled the beginning of a new and uncertain period in the history of Texas: **Reconstruction**.

Reconstruction was a time of great stress and turmoil in Texas. The withdrawal of federal troops at the beginning of the Civil War had left Texas's extensive western frontier vulnerable to repeated attacks by Plains Indians. The Union blockade of Southern ports had helped to destroy the state's economy. Wartime deaths and injuries had devastated a generation of Texans. The initial policies of Reconstruction were not terribly onerous, though they certainly aggravated many Texans who clung stubbornly to the values that had given birth to the Confederacy, primary among which was a hearty detesting of a strong (in the eyes of some, dictatorial) federal government. Yet harsher policies implemented by the Radical Republicans in Congress resulted in many Confederate supporters and wartime state officials being barred from voting and holding elective office. These laws, along with others that gave a modest measure of civil rights to those black Texans who had been slaves, helped bring about the election of the state's first Republican governor, E. J. Davis, in 1869.[10]

Davis's governorship has been much discussed by scholars. Given extraordinarily broad powers by the Texas Legislature, Davis struggled to bring order out of the economic and political chaos that confronted him. But he and the Republican-dominated legislature were forced to raise taxes (never a popular move with Texans), and his vigorous use of the state's militia and police forces to combat widespread lawlessness earned him growing hostility from a population weary of military rule.

By 1873, many former Confederates had their voting rights restored. They returned to the polls with a vengeance, bent on removing the hated Davis and his fellow Republicans from office. In an election marred by widespread voter fraud on both sides (the basic political strategy employed by the two parties seems to have been "vote early and often"), Davis was swept from office. However, he refused to go quietly and sought to overturn the election by appealing to the Texas Supreme Court and its justices, all of whom Davis had appointed. Davis won the appeal, but faced with a mostly Democratic mob that besieged him in the state capitol, he finally relented and gave up his office.

The departure of E. J. Davis marked the effective end of Reconstruction in Texas, but the legacy of this period would live on for 100 years. In truth, Davis probably wasn't as bad as his political successors made him out to be, but unfortunately, what happened in history is never as important as what people think happened. And those who came to power immediately after Davis and beyond had a low opinion of him and of all Republicans. This attitude would make the Democratic Party the only real political force in Texas for a century and would doom the Republican Party to 100 years of electoral frustration and futility. However, looks can be deceiving. The Democrats who would control Texas's political destiny for the next 100 years were not today's Democrats. Staunchly conservative and supportive of "states' rights," they would be much more comfortable with the ideology of a contemporary Republican than with that of a contemporary Democrat.

☐ The Americans

A FRONTIER STATE The last years of the 19th century in Texas were marked by expansion, recovery, and, as we've come to expect, political upheaval. The return of federal troops to the frontier in the early 1870s helped to ensure the ultimate demise of the Plains Indians as a free-roaming people. Their forced removal from the High Plains, coupled with the eradication of the buffalo herds on which their culture depended, set the stage for a rapid expansion of settlement into the western parts of the state.[11] And people weren't the only newcomers. Spreading out from the south Texas brush

Reconstruction
Post-Civil War period (1865–1877) during which former Confederate states had restrictive laws applied to them by the federal government; it (and E. J. Davis) led to Texas becoming a one-party Democratic state.

1.1

1.2

1.3

1.4

1.5

1.6

1.1

1.2

1.3

1.4

1.5

1.6

Progressive Era
A period of time (1890–1910) during which Texas enacted numerous laws designed to protect ordinary citizens and to prevent their being taken advantage of by large monopolies such as the railroads.

country came Texas longhorns numbering in the millions. By the mid-1880s, vast areas of west Texas had been divided into huge ranches, and cotton had a rival for economic dominance in Texas. Texas's long frontier experience with hostile Indians, border bandits, and a general lack of law and order contributed significantly to the development of an individualistic political culture that is so evident in the state today (as discussed in the "Individualistic" section below). It also encouraged self-reliance, the importance of land ownership, and a belief in material progress and growth as positive forces in a community. A general attitude of friendliness and a willingness to help others—even strangers—is also sometimes associated with the legacy of the frontier in Texas.

As Texas's population grew and moved westward, railroads were built and eventually spread to the farthest reaches of the state. The railroads meant life and prosperity for those communities through which they passed, and they provided Texas with a sorely needed network of dependable transportation. But many people were angered at the preferential treatment given railroads by the legislature (e.g., free public land) as well as by some of the questionable practices and tactics of these companies. Growing economic troubles and political dissatisfaction, chiefly among small farmers and shopkeepers, led to the election of Governor James Stephen Hogg in 1890 and to the beginning of the **Progressive Era** in Texas politics.[12]

After taking office, Hogg made good on a campaign promise when he persuaded the legislature to establish the Texas Railroad Commission. This act (which created one of the first state agencies in the nation to regulate an industry effectively and which the railroads vehemently opposed), was only one in a series of laws that sought to redress some of the grievances that had been festering among many ordinary Texans. Acts regulating insurance companies, restricting child labor, and restructuring the state's prisons (sound familiar?) as well as local government soon followed. The kind of activism that produced these laws runs counter to the "leave me alone" approach that most Texans take toward government, but it is an undercurrent that manifests itself on occasion. These periods of activism often muddy our attempts to analyze the waters of Texas politics. In reality, Texas at this time was a state in transition: from country to city, from farm to factory, from the 19th century to the 20th. It should come as no surprise that its society and its politics would reflect the turmoil of this transition.

A MODERN STATE Big Oil followed the 20th century into Texas by 10 days. On January 10, 1901, A. F. Lucas brought in a huge well south of Beaumont, and the Spindletop field became the most productive in the world.[13] Although there were still plenty of cattle, lots of cowboys, and the wide vistas associated with the traditional images of a frontier state, Texas would never be the same.

The early decades of the century saw an accelerated movement of people from rural to urban areas. Cheap, readily available fuel powered a growing drive toward industrialization that moved Texas farther away from its agrarian past. After all, many people found that working in an oil refinery in Texas City was vastly better than following the north end of a southbound mule down a rock-filled furrow for 16 hours a day!

In the midst of this change, Jim Ferguson leapt to the center of the political stage. In 1914, Ferguson ("Farmer Jim") won the governorship. He claimed to represent "the boys who live back at the forks of the creek." Touting programs that benefited farmers and other rural residents, he enjoyed a successful first term and growing public approval. After his reelection in 1916, however, Farmer Jim made a fatal political mistake: He crossed political swords with the University of Texas. In a feud with faculty and administration, many of whom had supported his political opponents, Ferguson rashly used the line item veto to eliminate all funding for the university from the 1917 general appropriations bill. Ferguson tried to make amends, but it was too late. After restoring the appropriation for the University of Texas, the Texas House of Representatives charged the governor with 21 articles of impeachment; the Senate convicted him on 10 counts, most related to the questionable diversion of state funds to the Temple State Bank, which Ferguson had helped establish. Farmer Jim thus became the only governor of Texas to be impeached and removed from office (though he tried to avoid this "honor" by attempting to resign prior to the delivery of the Senate's decision).[14]

Despite these antics, Ferguson remained enormously popular with rural Texans. After all, how many of those boys who lived back at the forks of the creek sent their kids to the University of Texas? Barred from holding elected office, he nevertheless moved into the governor's mansion by way of the back door in 1924, when his wife Miriam ("Ma") ran for and won the governorship. Running on the slogan "Two Governors for the Price of One," she sought vindication for her husband. Although she is sometimes cited as a kind of pioneer for women in Texas politics, "Ma" was governor in name only. Jim continued to call the shots.

While Miriam Ferguson was largely a figurehead for her husband's thwarted political ambitions, a true leader in the fight for political equality waged by Texas women was Annie Webb Blanton. Ms. Blanton lobbied long and hard to help win the vote for women in this state and was active in politics for most of her life. She was the first woman to serve as president of the Texas State Teachers Association as well as the first woman to hold a statewide elected office in her capacity as state superintendent of public instruction from 1918 to 1922.

As the Fergusons' political soap opera, as well as other issues such as Prohibition and the resurgence of the Ku Klux Klan, diverted people's attention, Texans on the national political scene were quietly gaining substantial power. Seniority led to power in the U.S. Congress, and because Texas was essentially a one-party state, its congressmen and senators were routinely reelected until they died or retired. This guaranteed them long tenure and, after the Democratic electoral victories of 1932, a growing number of key committee chairs and leadership positions in both houses. Men like John Nance Garner, Sam Rayburn, and Lyndon Johnson followed this path to prominence and power.

The Depression hit Texas hard, largely due to the collapse of farm prices, and this hastened the exodus of many rural Texans to urban areas, where they sought work. However, new oil discoveries in east Texas and the Permian Basin of west Texas eased the economic pain somewhat, and jobs in defense plants created during and after World War II made many Texans financially secure by the 1950s. This cozy relationship between the federal government and Texas defense industries would continue to be an economic mainstay throughout the 20th century.

Unfortunately, this prosperity was not uniform. A legacy of social and economic racism meant that many Texans of color did not share life in the mainstream. *De jure* (legal) segregation and other discriminatory laws and social practices prevented many African Americans from gaining access to public education, housing, and other accommodations. Moreover, a long history of *de facto* (practiced) racial prejudice against Hispanics resulted in the denial of basic rights to these citizens. However, political activism among both Hispanic and African American Texans began to increase at this time, especially under the leadership of minority veterans who returned from the war unwilling to accept the segregated status quo of the past.

One of the most important leaders of the postwar movement for civil rights among Hispanics was Dr. Hector P. Garcia, who had fought in Europe during World War II. He organized Hispanic veterans who encountered barriers to receiving the financial and medical benefits that were due to all veterans. This group, the American GI Forum, was one of the first to boldly challenge the second-class status that long had been accorded Hispanic Texans. The Forum's clash in 1949 with a funeral home in Three Rivers, Texas, over the home's refusal to bury a decorated Hispanic soldier who had been killed in the war, brought national attention to the organization and its goals.

The 1960s witnessed the accession of the first self-acknowledged Texan to the White House when Vice President Lyndon Johnson succeeded John F. Kennedy after Kennedy's assassination in Dallas.[15] Ironically, Kennedy was in Texas trying to patch up a political feud among factions within the state's Democratic Party. Johnson's tenure was controversial and was noted both for a wide-ranging agenda of domestic legislation (the programs of the Great Society) and for increasingly bitter opposition to the Vietnam War. Faced with a divided party, Johnson chose not to seek reelection in 1968 and retired to his Hill Country ranch.

1.1
1.2
1.3
1.4
1.5
1.6

1.1

1.2

1.3

1.4

1.5

1.6

The decades of the 1970s and 1980s in Texas were a veritable roller coaster of politics, economics, and demographics. Stunned by the Sharpstown Scandal of the early 1970s (which saw a number of elected state officials convicted or implicated in the stock fraud scheme of Houston financier Frank Sharp), Texas voters "threw the rascals out" in 1972.[16] Almost half of the members of the 1973 Legislature were new, but reforms enacted as a result of the scandal were modest at best. By the mid-1970s, economics began to overshadow politics as the Arab oil embargo of 1973–1974 produced a tripling of oil prices worldwide and an incredible revenue windfall for the state of Texas. A large portion of the state's revenue was generated directly or indirectly by petroleum, and as oil prices rose, so did the state's income. The biggest "problem" facing the Texas Legislature during this time was, "How are we going to spend all this money?"

Convinced that oil prices would hit $50 a barrel by the mid-1980s, Texans went crazy. Loans for oil drilling and production were as common and as readily available as prickly pear in south Texas. Profits from the "oil patch" fueled speculative real estate ventures. Many were making money hand over fist, and there seemed to be no end in sight. People migrated to Texas by the thousands each week to get in on the action. However, as Sir Isaac Newton first taught, "What goes up must come down." When the Organization of Petroleum Exporting Countries (OPEC) failed to agree on a worldwide oil price structure in early 1984, Saudi Arabia flooded the market with oil. The result was a disaster for Texas. Oil prices plunged from $36 a barrel to $10 a barrel in 18 months. The state of Texas lost billions of dollars in revenue. Soon the Texas economy was in critical condition. The effect of defaulted energy loans rippled through the real estate market, bringing down banks and other lending institutions on a weekly basis. Unemployment in the energy sector soared. U-Haul trucks heading north on I-35 and I-45 represented an exodus of biblical proportions.

These upheavals in the economic world seared the Texas psyche greatly. And as if these events weren't enough, seismic activity began to register on the political Richter scale as well. In 1978, William P. Clements became the first Republican since E. J. Davis to win the governorship of Texas, thus effectively signaling the beginning of the end of one-party rule in Texas.[17] The 1980s saw more and more Republicans being elected each year, culminating in what many consider to be the arrival of two-party politics in Texas with the election of George H. W. Bush as president in 1988. That year, for the first time, Republicans carried "down ballot" races that had been dominated by Democrats for decades. The defeat of popular Democrat Ann Richards by Republican George W. Bush in the 1994 governor's race clearly showed a state moving quickly beyond two-party politics and toward GOP domination. This trend was subsequently confirmed in the landslide reelection of Bush as governor in 1998, as well as in the continuing Republican dominance of statewide elected offices in Texas in the elections of 2002 and 2006. Although Democrats made some modest gains in 2006 and 2008, these were swept away in the Tea Party-driven Republican resurgence in 2010.

As you can see, the portrait of Texas that emerges from this admittedly selective historical survey is varied and complex. History has helped to make Texans proud, generous, abrasive, intolerant, resilient, persistent, loved, and hated—often at the same time! It has fostered conservatism and an abiding mistrust of the federal government as the hallmark of the state's politics, and yet it has also produced an occasional recurrence of populist reform. It has, in short, contributed many important pieces to the Texas mosaic.

The Geographic Pieces

1.3 Compare and contrast the geographic regions of Texas and show how the land has shaped Texans and their politics.

hat mosaic also includes pieces shaped by the land itself, and any understanding of this state must acknowledge the pivotal role that geography has played in the lives of Texans.[18]

/>

1.1
1.2
1.3
1.4
1.5
1.6

FIGURE 1.1 This map shows most of the land claimed by the Republic of Texas, which stretches a bit more to the north.

Indeed, such geographic factors often have created political issues in and of themselves. Take, for example, the annexation of Texas by the United States. The sheer size of Texas at the time (the Republic had claimed all of present-day Texas, half of New Mexico, the Oklahoma panhandle, slivers of Kansas and Colorado, and a thin slice of Wyoming) led Congress to include a unique provision in the annexation agreement. Texas was granted the right to divide itself into as many as five states whenever it wished to do so. This provision, though of dubious constitutionality, clearly shows that Congress recognized geography as a political fact of life in Texas.

Approximately 267,000 square miles are contained within its borders. The state spans 773 miles east to west and stretches 801 miles north to south. The geographic center of Texas is situated near Mercury in northeast McCulloch County. (A marker on U.S. Highway 377 between Brownwood and Brady identifies the spot, and a local entrepreneur bought the adjacent 5 acres a number of years ago and began selling title to one-inch squares of land "deep in the heart of Texas"!) Within this vast area is an enormous variety of landform, climate, and vegetation. Because for most of human history, land has dictated lifestyle and livelihood, this geographic diversity has left an indelible mark on the people of Texas. It is possible to make some generalizations about these elements (for example, as you move from east to west across Texas, elevation increases and rainfall decreases), but Texas geography is better understood by examining it in smaller pieces.

☐ The Gulf Lowlands

Texas is divided geographically by the Balcones Escarpment. Running roughly from Del Rio to San Antonio, then north through Austin to Waco, this ancient fault line separates the higher, drier areas to the west from the lower, more humid lands to the east. The eastern area, the Gulf Lowlands, contains four geographic subdivisions.

THE COASTAL PLAINS These grasslands interwoven with coastal marshes extend in an arc along the Gulf of Mexico coast from near Corpus Christi to the Louisiana border. The Gulf coast itself is sheltered by a series of barrier islands (among them is Padre Island, which is popular among college students). These islands help create a

FIGURE 1.2 The Terrain of Texas.

fertile nursery for marine life, which in turn plays a large role in the coastal economy. The Coastal Plains generally receive adequate rainfall, and the largely treeless topography is ideally suited to raising rice, cotton, and grain sorghum crops. Here, too, were found some of the earliest significant oil and natural gas fields, especially in the arc of the upper coast from Freeport to Beaumont.

THE PINEY WOODS Lying north of the Coastal Plains, this area of forested, rolling hills receives the greatest amount of annual rainfall in Texas (nearly 60 inches per year in some areas). As the name indicates, pine trees predominate in this area, which is the westernmost extension of the great pine forests that once spread across the entire South. Timber products from the Piney Woods have long been an economic mainstay in east Texas, and since the 1930s, oil and gas production have been added to that equation. This area also contains the Big Thicket, a unique meeting place of several different ecosystems and a biological and botanical treasure trove now protected by federal law.

THE POST OAKS AND PRAIRIES As you move west out of the Piney Woods, you encounter a geographic amalgam of rolling prairies and wooded areas. Pine trees give way to oaks and hickories, and the rich soils of the area's Black and Grand Prairies are where most of the state's cotton was grown in the 19th century. Some oil is found in the region, but natural gas in shale deposits is a continuing source of economic activity now. This increasingly urbanized area includes the cities of Austin, Dallas, Fort Worth, San Antonio, and Waco.

THE SOUTH TEXAS PRAIRIE This southernmost geographic area of Texas is characterized by an arid climate and extensive brush country. One 19th-century settler complained that every bush he encountered was armed! As pointed out earlier, this area did give birth to the western cattle industry when Spanish settlers between the Rio Grande and San Antonio began raising cattle here in the mid-1700s. Today, agriculture plays a major role in the area's economy. An extended growing season (nearly 11 months in some places) combined with modern irrigation techniques have made the Winter Garden area around Crystal City as well as the lower Rio Grande Valley area major centers for the production of vegetable, fruit, and cotton crops. Over the years, the area has developed a booming tourist business, playing host annually to thousands of "snowbirds" (winter visitors from the Frost Belt states) and "birders" (bird watchers), as well as to an increasing number of retirees.

☐ The Western Highlands

North and west of the Balcones Escarpment, the land becomes more rugged, more varied, and more arid. There are five geographic subdivisions in these Western Highlands.

THE EDWARDS PLATEAU This large area of central and southwest Texas is characterized by rugged limestone hills, dense thickets of mesquite and juniper, and spring-fed streams and rivers. The Edwards Plateau has never been a haven for farming, and while some cattle ranching occurs in the region, the mainstay of agribusiness here has been raising sheep and goats. As such, San Angelo has become a regional center for marketing wool and mohair. The city also is home to a major military presence in Goodfellow Air Force Base. In recent years, the cultivation of wine grapes and the breeding of exotic game animals have added diversity to the area's economic fabric.

THE LLANO UPLIFT While limestone of relatively recent geologic vintage is the most common type of rock found in Texas, much more ancient granite and marble formations characterize the Llano Uplift.

This beautiful area of scenic hills, quiet valleys, and crystal-clear rivers accounts for much of the state's solid mineral production (the state capitol in Austin is constructed of the area's distinctive pink granite). Although agriculture has always been a tough row to hoe in this part of Texas, German immigrants in the mid-19th century managed to turn some parts of the Llano Uplift into productive farm- and ranch lands, and this area of Texas remains the center of that German culture.

THE WICHITA PRAIRIE This rolling grassland rises in waves as you move westward. Good soils in the eastern portions of the area, sometimes aided by irrigation, produce wheat and cotton crops (Hall County, at the edge of the Panhandle, claims to be the "Cotton Capital" of Texas). The western portions of the Wichita Prairie are more rugged. It was here that many of the famous ranches from Texas history (such as the Four Sixes) were established.

THE HIGH PLAINS Another escarpment, the Caprock, marks the beginning of this high, flat, grassy plateau that covers most of the Texas Panhandle and the South Plains. As noted earlier, this is where the buffalo roamed (and the deer and the antelope played!). Huge ranches in the late 1800s gave way to extensive irrigated as well as dry-land farming in the 20th century. Today, the rich soils of this high plateau, irrigated with water from the Ogallala underground aquifer, produce more cotton and grain crops (so-called cash crops) than any other area in Texas. Oil production is also found throughout the area, especially in the Permian Basin region around Midland and Odessa. The eventual depletion of the region's water resources presents a thorny and potentially contentious economic and political problem in both the near and the long term, particularly for the two major urban areas of Amarillo and Lubbock. For evidence of this, one needs look no further than the activities of multimillionaire T. Boone Pickens, who in recent years has begun buying up large tracts of water rights in west Texas in anticipation of future water shortages.

THE WEST TEXAS BASINS AND RANGES This huge area, lying generally west of the Pecos River, is the most sparsely populated part of the state. The region's largest

1.1
1.2
1.3
1.4
1.5
1.6

1.1

1.2

1.3

1.4

1.5

1.6

city, El Paso, lies at the extreme western edge of the state. The rest of this vast region contains the county with the smallest population (Loving, population 94) as well as the county with the greatest area (Brewster, 6,193 square miles). It also contains numerous mountain ranges (including Guadalupe Peak, Texas's highest point at 8,749 feet), wide elevated basin areas in between, and rainfall amounts in the 10-inch-per-year range. Although some irrigated farming takes place here, notably in the Stockton Plateau area, most of the area is desolate, wild, and starkly beautiful. Big Bend National Park and its neighbor Big Bend Ranch State Natural Area draw tourists and campers from around the country, and a vibrant and growing arts community in and around Marfa attracts visitors from around the United States and even some foreign countries. An added feature has begun to pop up on the seemingly endless horizons of the landscape in recent years. Wind-powered turbines capable of generating electricity without pollution have contributed to an economic rebirth in some areas of this otherwise desolate region. However, for those Texans who think a neighbor every 40 miles or so is close enough, this remains heaven.

The Economic Pieces

1.4　Analyze the economic evolution of Texas and identify economic factors that may influence Texas public policy in the future.

☐ The First Stage—Take It

Until fairly recently, the economy of Texas was firmly grounded in activities that can best be described as extractive—that is, they involved taking something directly from the land. Specifically, Texas in the past largely depended on the three Cs (cattle, cotton, and crude)—representing livestock, cash crops, and petroleum products—to provide its basic economic underpinning. These have receded in importance today, but they were crucial during Texas's formative years.

Cattle came to Texas with the Spanish. Mission expeditions included herds of cattle and horses, and Indians living at the missions were taught the basic skills of animal husbandry. As previously noted, towns established by Spanish settlers in south Texas during the mid-1700s quickly became centers for a regional ranching culture. The social and political upheavals of the first half of the 19th century disrupted some of this ranching activity, but they didn't keep the cattle in this brush country from reproducing at a great rate. By the 1860s, it was said that there were six head of cattle for every one person in Texas.

This abundance, along with a growing American appetite for beef after the Civil War, made it possible for a lot of people in Texas to make a lot of money. Rounding up these ill-tempered, essentially wild animals, these early-day "ranchers" herded them to railheads in Kansas and elsewhere. If a steer in which you'd invested as little as $3 sold for around $30 at market, you didn't have to be Warren Buffett to figure out you could make a pile of money this way. Eventually, this cattle culture spread north and west onto the High Plains, following the demise of the Plains Indians and the buffalo. Texas cattle became the boom market in the second half of the 19th century, attracting desperately needed investment capital from all over the United States as well as from foreign countries. You could say that Texas rode these ornery animals to economic recovery following the Civil War.

The 19th century also saw the growth of agriculture as a primary economic factor throughout Texas. Crops, especially cotton, rivaled cattle and other livestock as economic mainstays. Cotton had also come to Texas with the Spanish, but it didn't gain a major foothold in the state's economy until the advent of Anglo settlement in the 1820s. These settlers came primarily from the Old South, and they brought that region's cotton culture with them and planted it deeply in the fertile soils of east central Texas and the Coastal Plains. Of course, they also developed an extensive system of slave labor to plant, cultivate, and harvest their crops, and this "peculiar

The Spindletop gusher ushered in a new economic era in Texas, beginning an industry that has rebounded significantly in the last decade.

institution" would be the root of persistent economic, social, and cultural conflict in the years to come. After the Civil War, cotton production rose drastically, increasing by more than 1,000 percent between 1860 and 1900 as the legal bondage of slavery gave way to the economic bondage of sharecropping. By the 1920s, cotton production had spread to the High Plains. There, ranching began to give way to both irrigated and dry-land farming, and today this area leads the state in the production of cash crops.

As stock raisers and farmers moved west, the railroads followed them and soon became a major agent for the state's economic growth. Thousands of miles of track were laid in Texas between 1860 and 1900, and by the turn of the century, Texas contained more railroad miles than any other state. This expansion in turn fueled the exploitation of the east Texas forests and gave rise to an immense timber industry.

The last of the great extractive economies to develop in Texas was oil. A few oil wells were drilled in Texas after the Civil War (the first at Melrose near Nacogdoches in 1866), and a fairly profitable field was developed at Corsicana in the early 1890s. But it was the discovery of the huge Spindletop field near Beaumont early in 1901 that signaled a new economic era for Texas. There, the drilling crew had stopped to take a break when, suddenly, a tremendous explosion shook the earth. Mud, rocks, drill pipe, and derrick parts shot high into the air, followed by oil, oil, and more oil. So forceful was the flow that it took workers almost two weeks to cap the well. Within a year, Spindletop had become the most productive oil field in the world.

The rapidly expanding automobile market and the shift to oil-fired (later diesel-powered) locomotives fed a growing demand for oil and its products. Other major oil fields were soon being discovered and developed all across the state, and these fields would lay the groundwork for a major shift in the Texas economy. It wasn't long before refineries appeared, particularly along the Gulf Coast where the Houston Ship Channel was in full operation by 1925. Neither was it long before Texas was home to industry leaders in the realm of oil field equipment. New technologies in oil exploration seemed to come about as frequently as did the gushers, major cities sprang up where only sleepy towns had been before, and economic opportunity seemed endless. State government came to depend increasingly on oil and the revenue derived from it as a major budgetary foundation. Oil and Texas seemed like a match made in heaven.

☐ The Second Stage—Make It

Fueled by this oil boom, the Texas economy in the middle years of the 20th century began to expand beyond its agrarian origins. By the late 1930s, manufacturing was becoming a more important part of the state's economic picture. This expansion went into full swing in the 1940s with the advent of World War II and the ensuing growth of defense manufacturing in Texas. By the end of the decade, more Texans than ever before were employed either directly or indirectly by the myriad defense contractors across the state.

After the war, Texas became a leading manufacturer of petroleum-based chemicals and compounds such as plastics and synthetic rubber. Steel production and metal smelting began to assume a larger role in the state's economy, and by the early 1970s, electronics manufacturing, led by such industry pioneers as Texas Instruments, was becoming a major economic player in Texas. Once again, the future seemed bright and limitless.

☐ The Third Stage—Serve It

The 1980s were an economic disaster for Texas. The collapse of the oil industry, coupled with severe cuts in defense spending brought about by the end of the Cold War, left Texas reeling and grasping for any kind of economic future. But the 1990s saw the

1.1

1.2

1.3

1.4

1.5

1.6

1.1

1.2

1.3

1.4

1.5

1.6

Lone Star State make a comeback, and as Texas entered the new millennium, economic optimism was widespread. By most measures of economic vitality, the last decade of the 20th century had been a good one for Texas. The state outstripped the national average in such areas as job growth, income growth, and consumer confidence. The fastest growing segment of this revitalized economy was the service sector, as reflected in such key indicators as retail and wholesale trade and general business services. A booming entertainment industry, an increasingly important film community, as well as expanding tourism also contributed to this trend. At the end of the decade, service-related employment accounted for the lion's share of the state's total nonfarm jobs.

By early 2001, however, there were signs that this unprecedented period of economic growth in both Texas and the United States was coming to a close. Terrorist attacks, corporate misdeeds such as the Enron fiasco, and a questionable government regulatory climate all combined to make the economic outlook decidedly grimmer. Eventually, investor confidence in the once-invincible stock market began to evaporate, and by the fall of 2008, the subprime mortgage crisis triggered a worldwide collapse of financial institutions the likes of which had not been seen since at least the Savings and Loan debacle of the 1980s, if not the Great Depression. Texas did not appear to feel the effects of the Great Recession to the extent of other areas of the country, such as South Florida, Las Vegas, and much of California, but growth nonetheless slowed and unemployment rose across the Lone Star State.

At the beginning of the second decade of the 21st century, members of the Texas business community, public policy makers, and the people of Texas continue to confront the daunting task of rebuilding confidence in the economy while navigating its treacherous waters. The Texas Legislature will continue to confront simultaneously an erratic flow of existing state revenues, a dearth of any new revenue sources, and a growing need for long-term revitalization and redirection of the state's economy. Yet experience has shown that easy answers to such public policy dilemmas do not abound. Add to this reality the increasingly interrelated and global aspects of the state's economy, and Texans face still more and greater challenges as well as opportunities. The cold, hard fact of 21st-century economic reality is that states and even nations can no longer exist and, perhaps more importantly, make policy in an economic vacuum.

Most scholars agree that the key to future economic growth in Texas and the United States will lie in developing an educational infrastructure that can meet the demands of a constantly evolving, interconnected, worldwide economy. The most important product of such an infrastructure will be an educated (not merely skilled) employee, able to adapt to a rapidly changing, highly competitive, increasingly global economic reality. Yet because Texans have historically favored a "small government" approach to policy making, and because the general political climate in Texas continues to fiercely oppose any increases in either taxes or governmental expenditures, the creation and maintenance of just such an infrastructure remains problematical. If such an educational infrastructure can be created, then as a college student reading this text, you can look forward to changing careers several times over the course of your work life and, in all likelihood, to retiring from a job (at age 80!) that does not even exist at this time! However, if its creation eludes Texas, you could be confronted with a decidedly less hopeful economic future.

The Demographic Pieces

 he picture of Texas becomes even clearer when you examine the various peoples collectively called Texans. The population of this state can be analyzed in terms of both size and diversity. Let's look first at the number of people in Texas.[19]

1.1

1.2

1.3

1.4

1.5

1.6

◻ Population Size

According to the U.S. Census Bureau, the estimated population of Texas in 2011 was 25,674,641, an increase of 2.1 percent over the total recorded in the 2010 Census. That figure keeps Texas the second most populous state in the union, trailing only California, and represents an almost 22 percent increase over the official 2000 Census total.

◻ Population Growth

Unlike some states in the Northeast and Midwest, Texas has enjoyed continuous growth since the first federal census was taken here in 1850. In fact, the percentage of growth each decade has never been less than 10 percent, and during the "take the money and run" period of 1970–1980, population in the Lone Star State grew at a rate in excess of 27 percent.

Much of that decade's growth was due to people moving to Texas. The 1980s saw a different pattern emerge. Growth continued at a substantial pace, but most of the thrust of that growth came in the first half of the decade before the oil bust of 1984–1986. During the second half of the decade, growth slowed considerably (less than 1 percent increase in 1987–1988, for example), and only a substantial natural increase (Texans having little Texans) was able to offset outmigration. This trend was reversed during the 1990s, which saw a return to a more robust pattern of growth. The first decade of the 21st century saw a continuation of that trend, although at a slightly lower rate after 2008. Based on these trends, demographers are confident in projecting steady, sustained population growth for Texas well into this century (see Table 1.1).

This growth will not be uniform throughout the state, however. For several decades now, a number of Texas's 254 counties have lost population, with most of the losses recorded in counties west of I-35. Even in those west Texas counties that did not lose population, the pattern of "growth" has often been stagnant at best. It appears that the hardest-hit counties in terms of population loss have been those that have depended heavily on agriculture, oil, or both. However, some areas in and to the west of the Fort Worth–Dallas Metroplex have seen a resurgence in energy exploration (primarily in the form of extensive drilling for natural gas), and continuing high prices for oil products driven by increasing worldwide demand may keep this venerable economic engine running for a while longer.

◻ Population Distribution

The popular image of Texas around the world includes the notion that all Texans live on huge ranches with wide-open spaces and that they herd cattle when they're not drilling for oil. This vision, reinforced and exaggerated in film and literature, flies in the face of reality.

In fact, the closest most Texans come to oil is when they have their cars changed at the 10-Minute Lube down the street, and their most direct contact with cattle is

TABLE 1.1 TEXAS POPULATION PROJECTIONS *(MIGRATION SCENARIO 2000–2010)*

Year	Total	Anglo	Black	Hispanic	Other
2015	27,735,444	11,687,110	3,178,604	11,118,603	1,751,127
2020	30,622,577	11,931,829	3,477,947	13,039,858	2,172,943
2025	33,827,950	12,112,325	3,780,423	15,256,812	2,678,390
2030	37,349,108	12,211,645	4,080,463	17,764,282	3,292,718
2035	41,181,159	12,232,098	4,371,981	20,533,672	3,502,388
2040	45,380,640	12,194,136	4,653,708	23,579,647	4,953,149
2045	50,023,913	12,115,728	4,926,646	26,954,058	6,027,481
2050	55,205,312	12,024,894	5,195,861	30,719,069	7,265,488

Texas State Data Center and Office of the State Demographer, *2012 Population Projections by Migration Scenario*, San Antonio, TX: University of Texas at San Antonio, 2012). http://txsdc.utsa.edu/Data/TPEPP/Projections/Data. aspx#pnl_Output0

1.1

1.2

1.3

1.4

1.5

1.6

TABLE 1.2 PROJECTED POPULATION OF LARGEST
URBAN COUNTIES IN TEXAS, 2011

County	Population
Harris	4,180,894
Dallas	2,416,014
Tarrant	1,849,815
Bexar	1,756,153
Travis	1,063,130
El Paso	820,790
Collin	812,226
Hidalgo	797,810
Denton	686,406
Fort Bend	606,953
TOTAL	14,990,191
Texas	25,674,681

U.S. Census Bureau, *State and County Quick Facts,* 2011. *http://*
quickfacts.census.gov/qfd/states/48/48201.html

when they order a Whataburger (with cheese, jalapeños, and no onions). Of course, the biggest fallacy in this image is that of Texas as a rural state. In reality, more than 80 percent of the state's population resides in metropolitan areas, and over 58 percent of all the people in Texas can be found in 10 urban counties (see Table 1.2). The fact that Texas is the only state with three cities (Houston, San Antonio, and Dallas) among the 10 largest in the nation gives further evidence of its essentially urban character, and recent census data note that the Dallas–Fort Worth metropolitan area is one of the fastest-growing such areas in the nation.

Because the overwhelming majority of Texans live in cities and suburbs, we can expect the political agenda to be dominated by issues vital to these areas. In fact, a complaint commonly voiced by state legislators from rural districts is that the needs of their constituents are increasingly overlooked in the formulation of public policy. The issues with which Texas must deal in the future—transportation and how these needs will be addressed (mass transit? toll roads?) and the related problems of air pollution, crime, and juvenile violence; as well as the continued deterioration of big-city school systems—are all related to some degree to a highly urbanized population.

☐ Population Diversity

The people of Texas are not only many in number, they are diverse in their ethnic and cultural heritage. You could spend an entire semester studying the scores of such groups found in Texas, but time and space constraints force us to look specifically at only the four largest of these: Anglos, Hispanics, African Americans, and Asian Americans.

ANGLO TEXANS By the middle of the first decade of the 21st century, Texas had reached a demographic milestone: *No* ethnic group constituted a majority of the state's population. The largest group of Texans in the population remains (for the moment) Anglos, with the 2011 Census Bureau estimates showing some 44.8 percent of the state's population in this category. However, that percentage has been steadily decreasing over the last several decades (the 1980 population was 68 percent Anglo; the 1990 population, 56 percent; the 2000 population 52 percent), and projections for the future indicate a continuation of that pattern. Demographers estimate that by the year 2050 Anglos will account for less than 22 percent of the whole population. While this group has traditionally dominated the political (and economic and social) life of Texas, these statistics seem to indicate that, in the future, Anglos will have to share this control with other Texans.

1.1
1.2
1.3
1.4
1.5
1.6

The University of Texas is ethnically diverse. Reflecting the composition of the state as a whole, the flagship university had a majority minority enrollment for the first time in 2012.

HISPANIC TEXANS The second largest ethnic group in Texas, and the largest and fastest-growing minority group in the state is made up of Hispanic Texans. In 2011, it was estimated that 38.1 percent of the state's population was Hispanic, the result of a phenomenal growth rate over the course of the previous decades. Much of the Hispanic population lives in the state's urban areas, and if you were to draw a line on a Texas map from Victoria to Odessa, a majority of the people living south and west of the line would be Hispanic.

Politically, Hispanics were present at the creation of Texas. In fact, it is ironic that the only "native Texans" to sign the Texas Declaration of Independence were José Antonio Navarro and Francisco Ruiz. Throughout the 19th and early 20th centuries, Hispanic Texans—often either were excluded from the political process or were manipulated by political bosses, but by the 1980s such practices were waning. The elections of Raul Gonzalez to the Texas Supreme Court and Dan Morales to the office of Attorney General of Texas were earlier portents. In particular, Morales, a former state legislator, seemed destined for a much larger role in Texas politics. However, his surprise announcement that he would leave office after his term expired in 1998 dealt a blow to those who had looked to him as the future standard-bearer for Hispanics in the political arena. His failure to win the Democratic Party's gubernatorial nomination against fellow Hispanic (and political novice) Tony Sanchez in 2002 and his subsequent legal woes brought to an end what appeared to be a bright political future. On the other hand, Sanchez's candidacy created a historic political contest in Texas. The first Hispanic to win a major party nomination to the office of governor, this Laredo businessman engaged in one of the most expensive campaigns in Texas history. In 2008, State Representative Rick Noriega became the Democratic Party nominee for U.S. Senate, and although he lost to incumbent John Cornyn, no doubt he will be followed by more and more Hispanics in the coming years. Moreover, the candidacies of David Medina, Eva Guzman, and Ted Cruz under the banner of the GOP are clear signals that the Republican Party in Texas intends to try and win the hearts and, more importantly, the votes of Texas Hispanics. You can see why when you realize that by 2050, Hispanics will constitute a solid majority (55.7 percent) of the state's population. These changes seem certain to be reflected in both the electoral politics and the public policy debates of Texas.

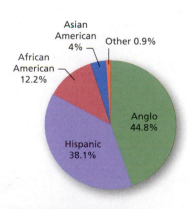

FIGURE 1.3 Estimated Texas Population, 2011.

1.1

1.2

1.3

1.4

1.5

1.6

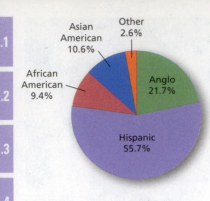

FIGURE 1.4 Estimated Texas Population, 2050.

AFRICAN AMERICAN TEXANS The third largest ethnic group in Texas is composed of African American Texans. In 2011, black Texans represented 12.2 percent of the state's population, a percentage that is little changed from 1980. Much of the state's African American population is found in the eastern half of Texas, with highest concentrations in southeast and north central Texas. Like Hispanics, a majority of African American Texans live in urban areas. Unlike Hispanics, however, the African American portion of the state's population is expected to decrease somewhat (to 9.4 percent in 2050) over the next several decades.

African American Texans have also been subjected to political, economic, and legal discrimination, but this pattern is slowly changing. When Judge Morris Overstreet was elected to the Texas Court of Criminal Appeals, he became the second African American to hold a statewide elective office in Texas. Judge Louis Sturns had been appointed to the same position a year earlier; Overstreet beat him when the seat went up for election. Notable public policy makers like Sylvester Turner, a state representative from Houston, and Royce West, a state senator from Dallas, have begun to play a more visible role in Texas politics, building on the accomplishments of predecessors like Mickey Leland, Barbara Jordan, and Wilhelmina Delco. The nomination of former Dallas mayor Ron Kirk as the Democratic candidate for the U.S. Senate in 2002 was unprecedented in Texas political annals. In the state's first general election of the 21st century, a black Texan headed a major party ticket, something unheard of in previous generations. On the Republican side, former Railroad Commissioner Michael Williams has positioned himself well for a future run at higher office, and Chief Justice Wallace Jefferson's presence on the Texas Supreme Court shows a growing willingness on the part of the Texas GOP to recruit and support African American candidates.

ASIAN AMERICAN TEXANS Growing almost as fast as Hispanics is the segment of the Texas population made up of Asian Americans. In 2011, Census Bureau estimates placed this group's share of the overall Texas population at 4 percent, and 2012 projections indicate that that percentage will more than double by 2050, rising to 10.6 percent and surpassing African Americans as a segment of the state's population. Asian Texans constitute almost 20 percent of Fort Bend County's population, almost 12 percent of Collin County's, and over 5 percent in Denton, Harris, and Dallas counties. The recent elections to the Texas House of Representatives of Angie Chen Button as a Republican from Richardson and Hubert Vo and Gene Wo as Democrats from Houston show clearly that both major parties will try to woo and win this increasingly important and politically active segment of the electorate.

Putting It Together: The Picture of Texas

1.6 Discuss three political cultures in the United States and identify the dominant political cultures in Texas.

Modern Texas is truly a multicultural state. As proof of its extraordinary diversity, no single prevailing culture or single dominant theme could serve to encompass the entire population. Yet even though this great mosaic called Texas was created by the hands of many people, we can identify some consistent similarities in the pieces from which it has been fashioned.

☐ Political Culture

For years, historians and political scientists have grappled with the concept of identifying and distinguishing the political nuances that exist among the states. They knew, as do we, that Texas is "different" from, say, New York. Although we are all Americans in terms of nationality, most Texans embrace an outlook on politics and government that is part southern, part western, and in many respects unique. Throughout this book, you will find evidence that Texas is, as the Texas Tourism Board commercials once proclaimed, "like a whole other country." The differences among the various states can best be explained in terms of variations in political culture, which take into account the many factors that make a group of people distinctive in the way they talk about, act toward, and approach politics.

Political culture, then, can be defined as the attitudes, beliefs, and behaviors that shape how people act politically. Interestingly, the political cultures of Texas have not changed much since the creation of the state. This is significant when you consider the explosive population growth and the tremendous economic and social changes this state has experienced in the past century. It tells us that political culture is a fundamental part of the makeup of a people, and that as newcomers arrive, they tend to adopt the prevailing political culture to which they are exposed. Thus, to understand any group of people, we have to understand their political culture. In a classic study of American politics, political scientist Daniel J. Elazar identified three predominant political cultures in the United States—individualistic, traditionalistic, and moralistic. Elazar's assessments are widely accepted by political scientists, and they help us gain insight into that strange and wonderful creature, the Texan.[20]

INDIVIDUALISTIC The individualistic political culture is rooted in the notions of individualism, independence, limited government, and free enterprise. This component of the Texas "psyche" emphasizes the traits associated with rugged self-reliance that many non-Texans have in mind when they think of this state. Politics is regarded as a necessary evil and politicians as generally arrogant and self-serving leeches. This doesn't mean that Texans are not a charitable people, because charity and a willingness to help your neighbor were integral parts of the frontier experience. Rather, it means that, in the minds of many Texans, the government should have no part in redistributing wealth and should generally leave folks alone. Many Texans believe that helping others should be done by the private sector, not governmental bureaucracies. The iconic (though largely mythical) image of the cowboy in many ways captures the deep-seated notion of individual achievement and self-sufficiency that is felt by many to be at the heart of what it means to be a Texan.

Examples of this individualistic political culture abound. In fact, this is one of the most widely manifested political cultures in the Lone Star State. Texas is the only state that was an independent nation. The state's constitution reflects the general distrust of government held by the framers. Legislators' salaries are low, and the governor's office is relatively weak. Even the judicial system is fragmented, presumably to prevent a single court from possessing too much power. There is, moreover, a kind of contrarian streak among Texans that such individualism breeds, which manifests itself occasionally, as in 2006 when not one but *two* independent candidates for governor made their way onto the ballot. This culture has often nurtured economic opportunity and individual initiative, but it has also engendered an attitude that assumes whatever is good for the business community is good for the greater community that is Texas. In short, Texas government is set up to be limited and to have as little impact on individual prerogative as possible.

TRADITIONALISTIC The traditionalistic political culture emphasizes maintaining the prevailing order and is extremely resistant to change. The role of government is to preserve the status quo and to refrain from innovation. Moreover, leadership tends to be restricted to a privileged few, and participation by ordinary citizens is discouraged. Politics tends to be played out in a decidedly social context, with ties among "old" families often determining the power structure. In such an atmosphere, corruption can easily flourish and often does. Moreover, the traditionalistic culture makes it very easy to ignore real human needs, which can in part account for the fact that Texas regularly ranks at or near the top in such dubious social policy categories as high school dropout rates, incidence of teenage pregnancy, number of children living in poverty, and percentage of the population without health insurance. These data mirror the reluctance of Texans to accept change of almost any kind.

political culture
The attitudes, beliefs, and behavior that shape an area's politics; often a product of various historical and social factors unique to that area.

1.1

1.2

1.3

1.4

1.5

1.6

1.1

1.2

1.3

1.4

1.5

1.6

Texas was one of the last states to introduce legalized gambling in any form and one of the last to abolish the "blue laws," which prevented individuals from purchasing a wide array of items, ranging from building materials to panty hose, on Sundays. Texas laws have also reflected this traditionalism by limiting participation in the political process in general and by attempting to keep minorities "in their place" through the use of such devices as the poll tax and the white primary. And even though Democrats ruled Texas unchallenged for 100 years, make no mistake about it—this state is and always has been conservative. Traditions and customs rightly are held in high regard by all cultures, but for Texans they often become sacred. It wouldn't be an exaggeration to say the seven most important words for many a Texan are "We just don't do things that way!"

MORALISTIC The moralistic political culture derives its basic attitudes toward politics and, in a larger sense, toward society from the viewpoint that human cultures and communities are a commonwealth. That is, our society and its component parts are interrelated, interconnected, and integrated. Because of this attitude, the role of government in a moralistic political culture is one of activism and that of politics one of inclusion. Citizens are encouraged to involve themselves in their own governance, and a plethora of activist political organizations is usually the hallmark of this culture. Along these same lines, the moralistic culture emphasizes public good over private gain and is therefore quite intolerant of governmental or political corruption. This culture is usually open to new ideas and forms of public participation.

The foregoing outline of Texas and its people clearly shows little indication of the kind of attitudes that would incubate a moralistic political culture. While this culture finds expression in many New England states as well as in certain areas of the upper Midwest (think Minnesota and Wisconsin), its basic elements simply do not fit comfortably with the beliefs and mores that characterize Texas. Some might argue that a nascent moralistic culture can be seen in places like Austin, but the fact is that the attitudes, habits, and behaviors of Texans clearly manifest themselves as expressions of the traditionalistic and individualistic cultures at the expense of the moralistic.

❑ Political Culture and Policy

Texas's individualistic political culture manifests itself in the state's public policy. Texas provides lower levels of public service than almost any other state, and even these limited benefits are usually difficult to obtain. Only three states have a lower level of union membership than Texas.[21] Voter turnout is relatively low, particularly in local elections that have the most profound impact on individual communities. Because of their strong streak of individualism, Texans are likely to be "joiners" only when it comes to church, the National Rifle Association, and in support of the local professional sports franchise, with the latter significantly influenced by the fortunes of the current season. This strong "go it alone" bent to Texas culture oddly gives government greater latitude, because the average Texan pays only limited attention to things political. On the other hand, that love of tradition that many Texans manifest has meant that such groups as the Tea Party, which advocates a "return" to the perceived traditional values of the past, have found fertile ground in the Lone Star State.

THE CHANGING FACE OF TEXAS As we write this (and as you read it), Texas continues its kaleidoscopic evolution as a society and a culture. Yet as we have seen, it probably is simplistic to speak of "a" culture when referring to this state and its people. Diversity is the hallmark of our history, our geography, our economy, and our population. Even when a certain veneer of uniformity is applied to Texas, as is the case when we somewhat arbitrarily describe its political culture as individualistic and traditionalistic, we can nevertheless rub through such a layer and uncover the rich mosaic that underlies it. And while our general political culture will continue to reflect the importance of both the individual and tradition, new people and new opportunities will challenge the way things have been. Texas politics will mirror these realities and challenges in the coming years.

Review the Chapter

🔊 **Listen** to Chapter 1

The Conceptual Pieces

1.1 Differentiate between government and politics and show the relationship between these two elements.

Government is composed of public institutions acting with authority to levy taxes and allocate things for society. Politics is a process that determines who gets what, when, and how. This process involves the seeking, gaining, and maintaining of power. While it is impossible to have government without politics, politics exists in many (if not most) areas of human activity.

The Historical Pieces

1.2 Identify the key events from Texas history that have shaped the state's political landscape.

The history of Texas is replete with clashes among and between different people, groups, and ideas. The Spanish became a permanent presence in Texas by establishing missions and ranches. Mexico gained its independence from Spain only to have Anglo settlers join Tejanos in breaking away from Mexico. After nearly a decade of independence, the Republic of Texas joined the United States. Heavily influenced by Southern values, Texas joined the Confederacy and was subjected to the rigors of Reconstruction. This experience helped cultivate an attitude of resistance to a strong federal government and made Texas a solidly Democratic state for a century. Technological developments in late 19th- and early 20th-century Texas led to its evolution from a rural, agrarian state to an urban, industrialized one by the beginning of the 21st century. This transformation was accompanied by growing Texas influence in national politics and a shift in the balance of political power from Democrat to Republican.

The Geographic Pieces

1.3 Compare and contrast the geographic regions of Texas and show how the land has shaped Texans and their politics.

The landscape of Texas is as varied as its people. For much of Texas history, land determined lifestyle for most Texans. Wetter, more humid forests and grasslands in east and east central Texas formed the center of Texas agriculture in the 19th century. In the semiarid brush country of south Texas, ranching prevailed until the early 20th century, when irrigation began to provide an almost year-round growing season. West of I-35, the land is increasingly rugged and progressively drier. The flat expanse of the High Plains, which saw the establishment of great ranching enterprises in the second half of the 19th century is the center of much of the cash crop production of Texas today. The rugged country of far west Texas has been an area where people have struggled to survive, though it does attract those who savor unlimited vistas and few neighbors.

The Economic Pieces

1.4 Analyze the economic evolution of Texas and identify economic factors that may influence Texas public policy in the future.

The Texas economy was built on extractive activities. Exploitation of a vast pool of natural resources was the engine that drove the state's economy until relatively recently. The Three Cs (cattle, cotton, and crude) fueled much of the state's economic life until the last decades of the 20th century. In the 1940s and 1950s, manufacturing became an important economic force in Texas, and later technological developments have led to the growth of the electronics and microelectronics industry. For the past several decades, the fastest growing segment of the state's economy has been the service sector. Texas' economic future is inevitably tied to an integrated global economy where change will be the norm. To address this reality, Texas public policy must help develop an educational infrastructure capable of equipping tomorrow's Texans for their role in this new economy.

The Demographic Pieces

1.5 Profile the current Texas population (including the major ethnic groups) and identify future demographic developments.

The people of Texas present a diverse and dynamic profile. The overall population of the state continues to grow, topping 25 million in the 2010 Census. Conservative growth projections envision a population in excess of 44 million by 2040. The ethnic composition of Texas is also noteworthy. No single ethnic community in Texas today comprises a majority of the state's population. However, with the percentages of Anglo population declining, African American population remaining relatively stable, and Hispanic population growing rapidly, by 2040 Hispanics will constitute over half the state's population while Anglos will account for less than 25 percent. This dynamic is sure to have significant consequences for politics and public policy in Texas.

Putting It Together: The Picture of Texas

1.6 Discuss three political cultures in the United States and identify the dominant political cultures in Texas.

The three major political cultures in the United States are the individualistic, the traditionalistic, and the moralistic.

The individualistic culture bases its values in the world of commerce and emphasizes minimal government, policies that promote economic development, and the value of the individual. The traditionalistic culture bases its values on the idea of social hierarchy and emphasizes the role of government in preserving the status quo. The moralistic culture bases its values on the notion of commonwealth and sees society as an interconnected and mutually dependent whole where the purpose of government is to actively promote the greater good. In Texas, the individualistic and the traditionalistic cultures prevail.

Learn the Terms

 Study and **Review** the **Flashcards**

government, p. 4
mosaic, p. 5
political culture, p. 27

politics, p. 4
Progressive Era, p. 14
Reconstruction, p. 13

Republic of Texas, p. 10

Test Yourself

 Study and **Review** the **Practice Tests**

1.1 Differentiate between government and politics and show the relationship between these two elements.

According to Harold Lasswell, politics can be described as
 a. the act of governing.
 b. who gets what, when, and how.
 c. mandating revenue collection.
 d. institutions that allocate valuable things.
 e. the creation of public policy.

1.2 Identify the key events from Texas history that have shaped the state's political landscape.

One result of Reconstruction in Texas was to make Texas a
 a. one-party state dominated by Republicans for the next 100 years.
 b. highly competitive two-party state for the next 100 years.
 c. state where neither major party was able to control elected offices.
 d. one-party state dominated by Democrats for the next 100 years.
 e. state controlled by the Populist Party between 1890 and 1950.

1.3 Compare and contrast the geographic regions of Texas and show how the land has shaped Texans and their politics.

The Texas geographic subregion that has an 11-month growing season is the
 a. Piney Woods.
 b. High Plains.
 c. Llano Uplift.
 d. South Texas Prairie.
 e. Wichita Prairie.

1.4 Analyze the economic evolution of Texas and identify economic factors that may influence Texas public policy in the future.

The factor that transformed the Texas economy in the early 20th century was:
 a. cotton.
 b. cattle.
 c. oil.
 d. manufacturing.
 e. electronics.

1.5 Profile the current Texas population (including the major ethnic groups) and identify future demographic developments.

By 2040, _____ are projected to make up almost 56 percent of the Texas population.
 a. Anglos
 b. African Americans
 c. Asians
 d. Hispanics
 e. Native Americans

1.6 Discuss three political cultures in the U.S. and identify the dominant political cultures in Texas.

The political culture that generally is not found in Texas is the:
 a. individualist culture.
 b. traditionalistic culture.
 c. moralistic culture.
 d. legalistic culture.
 e. popularistic culture.

Explore Further

Campbell, Randolph B. *Gone to Texas: A History of the Lone Star State*. New York: Oxford University Press, 2003.

Davis, William C. *Lone Star Rising: The Revolutionary Birth of the Texas Republic*. New York: Free Press, 2004.

Deaton, Charles. *The Year They Threw the Rascals Out*. Austin, TX: Shoal Creek Publishers, 1973.

Elazar, Daniel J. *American Federalism: A View from the States*. 3rd edition. New York: Harper and Row, 1984.

Ferguson, Keene. *The Texas Landscape: The Geographic Provinces of Texas*. Austin, TX: Texas Mosaics Publishing, 1986.

Jillson, Calvin C. *Lone Star Tarnished: A Critical Look at Texas Politics and Public Policy*. New York: Routledge, 2012.

Lasswell, Harold. *Politics: Who Gets What, When, How*. New York: Meridian Books, 1958.

Rutherford, Bruce. *Ferguson: The Impeachment of Jim Ferguson*. Austin, TX: Eakin Press, 1983.

Texas State Historical Association, *The Handbook of Texas Online*. Denton: University of North Texas. http://www.tshaonline.org/handbook/online.

2

Federalism and the Texas Constitution

Half the ballot items are ridiculous because they deal with doing away with a constable's position in Erath County or somewhere and the other half no one can understand because they involve bond financing or some arcane part of the Constitution that has to be fixed.

—*Former Texas Senator Bill Ratliff, on the Inefficiencies of the Texas Constitution*

As the 2013 legislative session opened, Democratic state representative Richard Pena Raymond launched a quixotic campaign as he introduced a constitutional amendment to require the Texas Legislature to do what their counterparts in 46 other states already do: meet in annual session. It would be a different approach for Texas, allowing the legislature to take up problems as they arise and to avoid the harried last days of the biennial legislative circus. The proposal was as dead on arrival as any single piece of legislation or proposed amendment introduced in 2013. Out of their mistrust of government, the men who crafted the current Texas constitution had deliberately limited the

2.1

Explain how state power is constrained by federalism and by the national and state constitutions.

2.2

Analyze how the national government has gained power within the federalism equation.

2.3

Explain why state constitutions tend to be long and restrictive.

2.4

Differentiate among the first six constitutions of Texas.

2.5

Analyze how Texas's current constitution is partially a reaction to the previous Reconstruction-era document and partially a return to pre–Civil War policies.

2.6

Explain why those who benefit from the current constitution will work to make comprehensive reform difficult.

Lieutenant Governor David Dewhurst gavels a special session of the Texas senate to a close. All but four states have annual legislative sessions, but the state constitution limits the legislature to one meeting every other year, and such special sessions that may be called by the governor.

2.1

2.2

2.3

2.4

2.5

2.6

federalism
A constitutional sharing of powers between the national and state governments.

frequency of legislative sessions because of their belief that the less frequently the legislature met, the less mischief in which they could engage. Many things have changed in Texas over the intervening 14 decades, but an underlying distrust of government remains.

When the delegates to the Texas Constitutional Convention convened in 1875, they had suffered through economic depression, military defeat, and a forced Reconstruction that many found humiliating and emasculating. The delegates wanted to return to a simpler time, when they controlled their lives and their destinies. This search for the familiar would lead them backward toward a framework that limited the power of the governor and the government. It was imperative, the delegates believed, to ensure that no public official ran roughshod over their rights again. In essence, they traded one form of shackle for another. In the process of severely restricting the power of government, they created a constitution that would be in perpetual amendment mode for a simple reason. In modern Texas, there are, from time to time, things that government needs to do or needs to do differently. And whether that something is significant or trivial, as the chapter-opening quote implies, that change often requires a constitutional amendment, and the strange dance among the Texas house, the Texas senate, and the voters begins. In this chapter, we consider the evolution of constitutional government in Texas. But we will start by examining the state's role in the federalist system under the United States Constitution.

Federalism

2.1 Explain how state power is constrained by federalism and by the national and state constitutions.

I
n the United States, states and the national government share power under a unique structure called **federalism**. Federalism is a dual system of government. Two systems operate concurrently, one at the national level and another within each of the states. Both levels have authority over their citizens, meaning that you have to obey the laws of both the United States and the state of Texas, as well as the ordinances of local governments, which are technically subdivisions of the state. Both the state and national governments have their own executive, judicial, and legislative branches. The president serves as the nation's chief executive; the governor holds the equivalent office in Texas. The U.S. House and U.S. Senate comprise the national Congress, while the state house and state senate serve as the Texas Legislature. The national government and the state each have their own court systems. The national court system considers alleged violations of national law and hears civil suits involving residents of different states. Texas courts handle state criminal matters and civil suits in which both parties are from Texas.

❑ Federalism Applied

Federalism is one of the most confusing aspects of American government. Citizens often find it difficult to distinguish between national and state functions. Many people are only vaguely aware that legislators and members of Congress are not the same people. It doesn't help matters that the U.S. Congress and Texas Legislature often deal with the same basic issues, such as crime control and welfare policies.

Originally, the delineation of duties between the national and state governments was clearer. The national government dealt with problems of national importance. Military and foreign policy issues are, to this day, the primary responsibility of the U.S. government. Issues with a larger local impact, such as education and aid to the poor, have traditionally fallen under the control of the state. Although the national government has taken a significant role in setting standards for education, most decision making and funding come from the state and local levels. For all the campaign rhetoric about the importance of education that you hear from national candidates,

U.S. Constitutional Limits on State Power

Article I

Section 10

No State shall enter into any Treaty, Alliance, or Confederation; grant Letters of Marque and Reprisal; coin Money; emit Bills of Credit; make any Thing but gold and silver Coin a Tender in Payment of Debts; pass any Bill of Attainder, ex post facto Law, or Law impairing the Obligation of Contracts, or grant any Title of Nobility.

No State shall, without the Consent of the Congress, lay any Imposts or Duties on Imports or Exports, except what may be absolutely necessary for executing its inspection Laws: and the net Produce of all Duties and Imposts, laid by any State on Imports or Exports, shall be for the Use of the Treasury of the United States; and all such Laws shall be subject to the Revision and Control of the Congress.

No State shall, without the Consent of Congress, lay any Duty of Tonnage, keep Troops, or Ships of War in time of Peace, enter into any Agreement or Compact with another State, or with a foreign Power, or engage in War, unless actually invaded, or in such imminent Danger as will not admit of delay.

2.1
2.2
2.3
2.4
2.5
2.6

85 percent of funding for the Texas education system is generated within the state. It is not the same in social services. Most of what Texas spends on the poor comes from federal grant programs, with the national government setting minimum standards of service that the state must provide.

An important aspect of our American system of federalism is that the delineation of power—who does what—is set out in the U.S. Constitution. This is what makes federalism "federalism," so to speak. In theory, the only way to alter that balance of power is to change the Constitution or have the U.S. Supreme Court change its interpretation of that document. In practice, the balance involves other factors, which we'll discuss later.

Federalism is a departure from the more traditional unitary or central government, where power is concentrated at the national level. Under a centralized system, the national legislature can lend power to the local level, but it retains the authority to take this power back. Real power, then, never leaves the central government. That's an important distinction. Under federalism, the U.S. government can't wake up one day and do away with the state of Texas.

☐ Constitutional Limits on States

In our system, many of the limits on states are found in Article I, Section 10 of the U.S. Constitution (see U.S. Constitutional Limits on State Power). States, for example, are prohibited from levying taxes on goods arriving from other states. A state may not enter into treaties on its own; neither may it engage in war independently unless it is attacked. States cannot issue money.

Article IV of the Constitution establishes how states must treat one another. For example, when an accused or convicted felon escapes from Texas to Oklahoma, Oklahoma is obligated to return the fugitive to Texas. Likewise, Texas must give full faith and credit to civil proceedings emanating from Oklahoma. A person cannot skip from state to state in order to avoid paying civil damages (see U.S. Constitutional Provisions Regarding Interstate Relations).

☐ Shared Powers

Under federalism, many government powers are shared. Both states and the national government collect taxes. Both work jointly to implement many programs, such as

2.1

2.2

2.3

2.4

2.5

2.6

constitution
The basic document under which a state or nation's government operates.

U.S. Constitutional Provisions Regarding Interstate Relations

Article IV

Section 1

Full Faith and Credit shall be given in each State to the public Acts, Records, and judicial Proceedings of every other State. And the Congress may by general Laws prescribe the Manner in which such Acts, Records and Proceedings shall be proved, and the Effect thereof.

Section 2

The Citizens of each State shall be entitled to all Privileges and Immunities of Citizens in the several States.

A Person charged in any State with Treason, Felony, or other Crime, who shall flee from Justice, and be found in another State, shall on Demand of the executive Authority of the State from which he fled, be delivered up, to be removed to the State having Jurisdiction of the Crime.

No Person held to Service or Labour in one State, under the Laws thereof, escaping into another, shall, in Consequence of any Law or Regulation therein, be discharged from such Service or Labour, but shall be delivered up on Claim of the Party to whom such Service or Labour may be due.

Section 3

New States may be admitted by the Congress into this Union; but no new State shall be formed or erected within the Jurisdiction of any other State; nor any State be formed by the Junction of two or more States, or Parts of States, without the Consent of the Legislatures of the States concerned as well as of the Congress.

The Congress shall have Power to dispose of and make all needful Rules and Regulations respecting the Territory or other Property belonging to the United States; and nothing in this Constitution shall be so construed as to Prejudice any Claims of the United States, or of any particular State.

Section 4

The United States shall guarantee to every State in this Union a Republican Form of Government, and shall protect each of them against Invasion; and on Application of the Legislature, or of the Executive (when the Legislature cannot be convened), against domestic Violence.

social services. Long ago, the limited social assistance programs were administered almost exclusively by state and local governments. Beginning with the economic chaos of the Great Depression, the national government assumed a larger role in welfare policy. By the 1960s and 1970s, the national government had the primary role in social services. State governments still administer most aid programs, but the national government mandates minimum standards. Many of the programs are implemented by county governments, which are an administrative subdivision of the state.

The national government provides much of the money for social programs. In Texas, federal grants generate more than half of welfare spending. Education, transportation, and health care are programs administered concurrently by federal and state governments. We traditionally think of distinct divisions between national and state powers and responsibilities, but in practice there is much overlap and interaction.

☐ Constitutions

The purpose of a **constitution** is to provide a framework in which government operates. It is, in essence, the blueprint for government. Ideally, it should specify which branch of government has what responsibilities. It should grant power to these branches but also set limits on what government can do. An important ideal of the American system of government is that a constitution should establish a system of checks and balances that keeps any branch from possessing too much power.

Most Americans learn at an early age to value democratic ideals. Politicians repeatedly proclaim that their actions reflect "the will of the people." In a pure representative democracy, the majority rules. Elected officials, in theory at least, carry the agenda of citizens forward to the legislature. The coalition that can form a majority on a particular issue will have its policy enacted.

However, we don't live in a pure democracy. We live in a constitutional republic, where constitutional law is supreme, as are acts of Congress enacted under the constitution and treaties created in accordance with the national constitution. Laws created by either the U.S. Congress or the Texas Legislature that conflict with the U.S. Constitution can be struck down, despite what the majority might want. Texas cannot, for instance, place import taxes on goods coming in from Oklahoma. Portions of a state constitution are void if courts determine that they conflict with the U.S. Constitution.

The U.S. Constitution gives 18-year-olds the right to vote; therefore Texas could not set 21 as the voting age in state elections. Similarly, a state legislature is prohibited from enacting laws that violate its state constitution. Through a process called **judicial review**, courts determine when laws are unconstitutional. Both state and national courts can exercise this power, with the U.S. Supreme Court having the last say. In 2012, for example, the Court struck down large portions of Arizona's anti-illegal immigration law because the act was preempted by existing federal law.

2.1

2.2

2.3

2.4

2.5

2.6

judicial review
The power of the courts to strike down laws that violate the state or national constitution.

amendments
Additions or deletions to the constitution; passed in a prescribed manner.

Bill of Rights
The portion of the Constitution limiting the government and empowering the individual.

National Gains

2.2 Analyze how the national government has gained power within the federalism equation.

Over the past 200 years, the balance of power has shifted significantly to the national government at the expense of the states. **Amendments** to the national constitution have played a role in this shift, but other factors have also had an impact.

◻ Constitutional Amendments

Since passage of the **Bill of Rights**, which was aimed at limiting national government power, many constitutional amendments have restricted state action. After the Civil War, the Thirteenth and Fifteenth amendments ended slavery and gave African American males the right to vote. The Fourteenth Amendment required state governments to extend due process and equal protection under the law to all their citizens. Over the past five decades, the U.S. Supreme Court has used the Fourteenth Amendment to apply significant portions of the Bill of Rights to state governments as well. In 1989, the Court threw out the state's conviction of Gregory Lee Johnson for burning the American flag, applying the First Amendment of the U.S. Constitution's free speech clause. The Seventeenth Amendment stripped state legislatures of the power to appoint U.S. senators. The Nineteenth, Twenty-fourth, and Twenty-sixth amendments prohibited states from restricting voters' rights. They respectively granted women the right to vote, ended poll taxes, and extended voting rights to 18- to 20-year-olds.

Without amending the Constitution, the national government has gained greater control over the states through its taxing and spending policies. The national budget exceeds $3.8 trillion a year. A large part of that spending is returned to the states through various grant programs. About a third of Texas's state budget comes from federal government sources.

2.1

2.2

2.3

2.4

2.5

2.6

It is important to understand that when the national government sends money to states, it comes with strings attached. The U.S. Constitution constrains Congress just as it constrains the states; limiting Congress to powers explicitly listed in Article I, Section 8 (see U.S. Congressional Powers). Congress, however, can get around this roadblock and compel the states to pass legislation by threatening to withhold federal grants.

Focusing on just one area of the budget, transportation, provides insight into the magnitude of the money and power involved. Approximately half of Texas highway funding comes from federal grants, totaling over $3 billion in both 2012 and 2013. In order to receive all of that money, the state has to abide by a series of restrictions placed on it by Congress and the U.S. Department of Transportation. In the 1970s, states were required to set maximum speed limits at 55 miles per hour in order to receive highway funds. This particular restriction has since been lifted, but the precedent for congressional control remains.

In the 1980s, states were forced to raise the drinking age to 21 in order to receive federal money for transportation. Moreover, it was in connection with the drinking age provision—in *South Dakota* v. *Dole*—that the U.S. Supreme Court explicitly upheld Congress's prerogative to withhold grant money, provided its direction was related to the "general welfare" of the nation. Later that decade, the Department of Transportation threatened to cut funds to states that did not adopt seat belt laws. Federal grants are available in most areas of state government spending, and similar restrictions affect almost every area of state government.

U.S. Congressional Powers

Article I

Section 8

The Congress shall have Power To lay and collect Taxes, Duties, Imposts and Excises, to pay the Debts and provide for the common Defence and general Welfare of the United States; but all Duties, Imposts and Excises shall be uniform throughout the United States; To borrow Money on the credit of the United States; To regulate Commerce with foreign Nations, and among the several States, and with the Indian Tribes; To establish an uniform Rule of Naturalization, and uniform Laws on the subject of Bankruptcies throughout the United States; To coin Money, regulate the Value thereof, and of foreign Coin, and fix the Standard of Weights and Measures; To provide for the Punishment of counterfeiting the Securities and current Coin of the United States; To establish Post Offices and post Roads; To promote the Progress of Science and useful Arts, by securing for limited Times to Authors and Inventors the exclusive Right to their respective Writings and Discoveries; To constitute Tribunals inferior to the supreme Court; To define and punish Piracies and Felonies committed on the high Seas, and Offences against the Law of Nations; To declare War, grant Letters of Marque and Reprisal, and make Rules concerning Captures on Land and Water; To raise and support Armies, but no Appropriation of Money to that Use shall be for a longer Term than two Years; To provide and maintain a Navy; To make Rules for the Government and Regulation of the land and naval Forces; To provide for calling forth the Militia to execute the Laws of the Union, suppress Insurrections and repel Invasions; To provide for organizing, arming, and disciplining, the Militia, and for governing such Part of them as may be employed in the Service of the United States, reserving to the States respectively, the Appointment of the Officers, and the Authority of training the Militia according to the discipline prescribed by Congress; To exercise exclusive Legislation in all Cases whatsoever, over such District (not exceeding ten Miles square) as may, by Cession of particular States, and the Acceptance of Congress, become the Seat of the Government of the United States, and to exercise like Authority over all Places purchased by the Consent of the Legislature of the State in which the Same shall be, for the Erection of Forts, Magazines, Arsenals, dock-Yards, and other needful Buildings;—And To make all Laws which shall be necessary and proper for carrying into Execution the foregoing Powers, and all other Powers vested by this Constitution in the Government of the United States, or in any Department or Officer thereof.

It is equally important, when discussing these grants, to understand that this is "Texas money" in the first place. The federal government's budget comes primarily from taxes on the income of individuals within the several states. In other words, Washington will give Texas *some* of its money back, but only if the state abides by its rules.

☐ The Federal Courts

As a result of federal laws and the Fourteenth Amendment to the U.S. Constitution, federal courts often have jurisdiction in areas once completely under state control. Over the last few decades, Texas officials have found themselves constrained by federal court orders involving areas such as prison control, mental health and retardation services, higher education funding and minority recruitment programs, and school desegregation.

☐ A Brief History of Federalism

From the beginning of the Republic through the 1920s, **dual federalism** defined the operation of the U.S. constitutional system. Under this interpretation, each level of government had its own sphere of influence, separate and distinct. States exercised great power in areas of local concern, which meant practically anything outside of national defense and trade policy. The end of dual federalism began with the advent of the Great Depression.

Citizens and politicians, desperate for economic relief, were unconcerned with philosophical questions over the nature of federalism. The problem seemed too large for states to solve independently, so power collected at and programs flowed from the national level. Under **cooperative federalism**, the role of the national government expanded significantly. Power that migrated to the national level during the depths of the Great Depression and World War II remained there after the crisis ended. Cooperative federalism was supposed to define an era under which national and state governments worked together in the administration and implementation of programs. Many state leaders, however, believed that more coercion than cooperation took place. The greatest expansion of national power, however, occurred in conjunction with President Lyndon Johnson's Great Society programs in the mid-1960s. The national government found that it could compel state and local compliance with national wishes by threatening to withhold government grants.

The significance of this approach bears reiteration. The national government found a way to enforce policy it has no constitutional power to mandate. Relevant rule-making power is clearly reserved to the states in many of these policy arenas. Nonetheless, national grants make up at least a third of most state budgets. In order to receive grant money back from Washington, states must accede to the national government's will. Often, the parameters have nothing to do with the purpose of the program. Rather, they are intended to achieve social goals deemed worthy by Washington. Proponents of national government intervention argue that the threat of sanctions has reduced discrimination, helped clean the air and water, and created a safer nation. Opponents paint the restrictions as a power play by the national government.

Several latter-day presidents, beginning with Richard Nixon, have claimed to favor a **new federalism**. Generally, new federalism entails a significant reduction in the use of categorical grants—which can only be used for narrowly defined purposes—opting for less restrictive block grants. During Ronald Reagan's administration, these block grants were used more frequently and many of the regulations that went along with grants were eased. Nonetheless, the overall size and power of the national government continued to increase.

☐ The "New" New Federalism

When the Republican Party took control of the U.S. House and Senate in 1995, members promised to reduce the scope of national government. Republican leaders

dual federalism
Well-defined divisions between national and state powers and responsibilities.

cooperative federalism
Era of expanded national government power, mandates, and funding.

new federalism
Greater discretion to state governments in the use of federal grants.

2.1

2.2

2.3

2.4

2.5

2.6

2.1
2.2
2.3
2.4
2.5
2.6

devolution
The transfer of government programs from the national to the state level.

argued that decision making should be returned to the states. However, the proponents of this "new" new federalism movement proved less than committed to substantive change. States regained some limited control. The rapid expansion of national government funding slowed, although it picked up again in the 21st century. **Devolution**, the transfer of programs from the national to the state level, occurred in some areas. Speed limits, for instance, are once again the responsibility of state governments. Federal grants may come with fewer strings attached, but the states pay for this freedom by having to pick up a larger share of many social service programs. On the other hand, restrictions may have just shifted. States that didn't adopt federal blood-alcohol levels for driving while intoxicated lost some federal transportation funds, a policy backed by some of the same Republican members of Congress who decried national interference on the issue of speed limits. If we measure government by the size of its expenditures, it grew rapidly during the George W. Bush administration. Federal grants have grown in tandem with the larger federal budget, outpacing the federal budget during the early portion of the Barack Obama administration.

Over the last two decades, however, the U.S. Supreme Court has issued decisions that have limited the power of the national government. Two major decisions have breathed life back into the Tenth Amendment to the U.S. Constitution, which reserves to the states powers not denied them by the national document. In *United States v. Lopez* (1995), the Court struck down a federal law that banned guns in the vicinity of schools. Congress argued that, because it can regulate interstate commerce, it had the power to pass the law. The Court rejected the argument, saying that if Congress is granted such a broad reading of the clause, "We are hard pressed to posit any activity by an individual that Congress is without power to regulate." In 1997, the Court

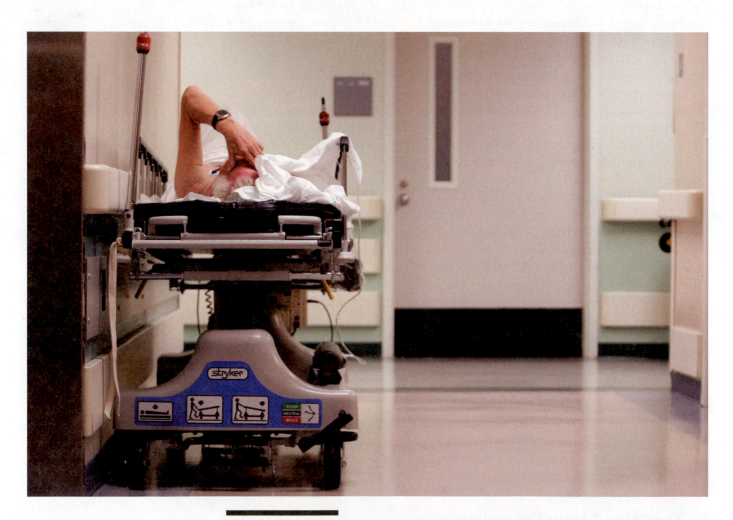

Waiting to receive care at Houston's Ben Taub Hospital, this patient is a symptom of the stresses placed upon an overburdened medical care system, exacerbated by the state's large number of uninsured residents. Those without insurance often end up in the emergency room, at taxpayers' expense, for issues that could have been treated much less expensively had they been dealt with earlier.

struck down a key provision of the Brady Bill, which required local law enforcement agencies to perform background checks on people attempting to purchase handguns. The Court ruled that Congress didn't have the power to force these governments to help administer this federal program. In the 2000 case of *United States* v. *Morrison*, a divided Court took a second step toward narrowing the commerce clause, striking down a law that would have allowed women who had been sexually assaulted to recover damages against the perpetrator in federal civil court. Congress had used the commerce clause to justify the act, reasoning that a hostile sexual environment could damage business opportunities for women. The Court struck down the law, finding again that such an expansive reading of "commerce" would give virtually limitless power to Congress. These rulings signal a willingness on the part of the U.S. Supreme Court to cap the national government's expansion of power. Some recent decisions, however, have not sided with state rights, as evidenced by the 2005 case of *Gonzales* v. *Raich*, which affirmed the Drug Enforcement Administration's authority to prosecute medicinal marijuana cases despite state laws allowing such use. Likewise, the 2012 Arizona immigration ruling limited state power, as did *Miller v Alabama*, which struck down determinate sentencing requiring life sentences for first degree murders under the age of 18. Even the Court's decision on the health care reform act was a split decision for federalism, upholding a provision that allowed Congress to tax those without health insurance but prohibiting Congress from penalizing states that don't participate in Medicaid expansion.

The states have expressed frustration with national government **mandates**. The U.S. Congress often passes regulations that set standards for state conduct. For example, states, and the businesses that operate in them, are required to meet accessibility standards under the 1990 and 2008 Americans with Disabilities Act. Enlarging doorways, building additional wheelchair ramps, and making other such improvements cost state and local governments millions of dollars. Congress provided no money to help meet these requirements, making this an **unfunded mandate**. The national government has set such standards in areas ranging from voter registration to water quality and from hazardous waste disposal to asbestos removal. These mandates force state officials to spend funds they may wish to use elsewhere and so increase the tax burden on the state's citizens.

mandates
Regulations set by Congress that state and local government must meet.

unfunded mandates
Congressional directives that are issued without corresponding federal funding.

State Constitutions

2.3 Explain why state constitutions tend to be long and restrictive.

The U.S. Constitution is a model of brevity. At 8,500 words, it established not only the national government, but the federal system as well. State constitutions, on the other hand, tend to be lengthy. Thirty-three state constitutions exceed 20,000 words, and several others exceed 17,000. Alabama's constitution is the longest at 340,000 words. The Texas constitution contains almost 90,000 words.[1] See Table 2.1 for a comparison of selected state constitutions.

State Constitutional Structure

Most state constitutions are similar in structure. Separate articles empower the executive, legislative, and judicial branches. The legislative branch makes the laws, the executive branch carries out the laws, and the judicial branch determines the constitutionality of the laws and interprets them. Another article contains the state's Bill of Rights, which protects individuals from unreasonable government action. Most constitutions include a separate article detailing the powers of and limitations on local government.

2.1

2.2

2.3

2.4

2.5

2.6

2.1

2.2

2.3

2.4

2.5

2.6

legislative law
Law passed by the legislature.

TABLE 2.1 LENGTH AND EFFECTIVE DATE OF SELECT STATE CONSTITUTIONS

State	Effective Date	Number of Words
Alabama	1901	367,000
California	1879	67,048
Delaware	1897	125,445
Indiana	1851	11,476
Louisiana	1975	69,876
Kansas	1861	14,097
Maine	1820	16,313
Massachusetts	1780	45,283
Minnesota	1858	11,734
New York	1894	44,397
North Carolina	1971	17,116
Oklahoma	1907	81,666
Texas	1876	86,936
Vermont	1793	8565

Note: States that are in boldface are close to the national model for constitution length.

Source: The Book of the States 2011 (Lexington, KY: Council of State Governments, 2011), p. 12.

Ideally, the state constitution serves as a blueprint from which government emerges. In other words, it answers the question, Who does what? Theoretically, the structure of government should be more difficult to change than the laws governing the day-to-day operations of government. In reality, though, most states blur constitutional law and **legislative law**—the bills passed by the legislature and enacted by the governor. Many constitutions include issues that go well beyond governmental structure. Most state constitutions include policy matters as well.

This mixing of constitutional law and legislative law is quite evident in the Texas constitution. Take, for instance, the cases of parimutuel gambling and the state lottery. Both are avenues through which the state profits from gambling. Neither parimutuel gambling nor the state lottery has a role in determining the government's framework, so ideally both should be dealt within the state's statutes. However, while a state law forbids horse racing, a constitutional provision bans a lottery. Legalizing betting on the horses took a simple majority vote in the House and Senate and approval from the governor. Authorizing the lottery required the much more difficult process of amending the state constitution. The same holds true for legalizing casino gambling: It would require a constitutional amendment.

Because state constitutions contain so many legislative provisions, they tend to be restrictive. There are exceptions. Vermont's constitution, which follows the national model, has only 8,565 words. It has been in effect for 220 years.[2] More often, these documents handcuff government, giving it little room in which to operate. Because of this restriction, the typical state constitution has been amended many times. Alabama holds the record. Adopted in 1901, its constitution had already been amended 854 times by 2011. California follows close behind, exceeding 500 amendments. Twenty-seven other states have more than 100 amendments. Texas is at the high end, being one of four states with more than 300 amendments. Contrast that with Vermont's constitution, amended just 54 times in the last 215 years,[3] and the U.S. Constitution with 27 amendments, only 17 of which occurred after 1791.

Table 2.2 shows the great variance in the frequency of constitutional amendments. As already suggested, the U.S. Constitution has been amended the least frequently. Although the Texas document has been amended often, it pales in comparison to South Carolina, California, and Alabama. At the other extreme are Kentucky, Rhode Island, Vermont, and Delaware, which have averaged fewer than one amendment every two years.

TABLE 2.2 FREQUENCY OF CONSTITUTIONAL AMENDMENT IN SELECTED STATES

State	Total Amendments	Amendments Per Year*
Alabama	854	7.7
Arkansas	98	0.7
California	525	3.9
Delaware	141	1.2
Hawaii	110	1.8
Idaho	123	1.0
Kentucky	41	0.3
Massachusetts	120	0.5
Maine	171	0.9
Nebraska	228	1.7
New York	220	2.0
North Dakota	150	1.3
Rhode Island	10	0.4
South Carolina	497	4.3
Texas	467	3.5
Vermont	54	0.2
Wyoming	98	0.9
United States	27	0.1

*Number of amendments per year is derived from dividing the number of amendments adopted by the number of years the constitution has been in existence. The table includes all amendments passed through January 2011.

Note: The U.S. Constitution has been amended much less frequently than the average state document.

Source: The Book of the States 2011 (Lexington, KY: Council of State Governments, 2011), p. 12.

2.1
2.2
2.3
2.4
2.5
2.6

The Constitutions of Texas

2.4 Differentiate among the first six constitutions of Texas.

☐ Coahuila y Tejas

Texas has had seven constitutions; only Georgia and Louisiana have had more. The first of these, created in 1827, governed Texas while it was still a part of the Mexican Federation. Texas was joined with Coahuila as one state, although Coahuilan representatives dominated the legislature. Texans lobbied to have their own state within the Mexican Federation. This created tensions between Texas and Mexico. Texans twice asked Mexico for separate statehood, but Mexico denied both requests. To the Texans, it represented a simple request for self-government, understandable when viewed from their American background. To Mexico, the request was slightly short of treason. Their national constitution explicitly prohibited an area with such a small population from becoming its own state.

☐ The 1836 Constitution

The 1836 constitution of the Republic of Texas emerged between the fall of the Alamo and Sam Houston's stunning victory at San Jacinto. The constitution was written quickly because it had to be. Delegates were fleeing in the face of Santa Anna's advancing troops.

The 1836 constitution generally followed the U.S. model. It created a house of representatives, a senate, and a president. Limits were placed on the president's term—he was not allowed to succeed himself. In an effort to reduce religious influences, the

2.1

2.2

2.3

2.4

2.5

2.6

As this huge statute implies, Sam Houston is still a larger-than-life figure in Texas. He was president, governor and senator, despite having already served as governor of Tennessee before moving to Texas. Most significantly, he successfully won the Republic's revolution against Mexico.

constitution prohibited clergy from holding office. Slavery was legalized, and the head of each household was given a sizable land grant.[4]

☐ The 1845 Constitution

After a decade-long struggle as a republic, Texas reached an annexation agreement with the United States at the end of 1845. No longer independent, Texas needed a state constitution.

The legislature retained a house and a senate to make state laws. A governor headed the executive branch. Term limits prohibited the heads of state from serving for more than four years of any six-year period. The governor appointed other executive officials, such as the attorney general and the secretary of state, but not the lieutenant governor, who was independently elected.[5] The governor also appointed judges at the district court level and above. As in the current Texas constitution, limits were placed on the powers of government. State debt was severely restricted, and the legislature was scheduled to meet every other year. Slavery was permitted.

In a wave of "Jacksonian democracy," selection of the attorney general, comptroller, treasurer, and judges was transferred to the voters through an 1850 amendment.[6] Jacksonian democracy, based on the political philosophy of Andrew Jackson, asserts that power should reside with the people. As a result, citizens should elect, rather than have the governor appoint, as many government officials as possible.

☐ The 1861 Constitution

Fifteen years after its successful struggle to become part of the United States, Texas seceded from the Union and became part of the Confederate States of America.

As a part of a new nation, the state needed another constitution. In reality, changes from the amended version of the 1845 constitution were not substantive; they merely acknowledged the state's place in the Confederacy. One provision did, however, forbid slaveholders from emancipating slaves without permission from the state government.

The 1866 Constitution

After the Confederacy lost the Civil War, Texas was forced back into the Union. As a conquered power, Texas was expected to write a new constitution making slavery illegal. In essence, though, the 1866 constitution was nothing more than an amended 1846 document.

The term of the elected executives was lengthened, and government officials received pay raises.[7] The constitution denied African Americans the right to vote. Also, the newly freed slaves were not allowed to hold office or to testify in court unless African Americans were party to the case.[8] Operating under this constitution, the new Texas Legislature further restricted the rights of African Americans through passage of a series of **Black Codes**. Such legislation limited job opportunities for and social interaction of the newly freed slaves. In effect, the Texas constitution and legislature had created a caste system in the state, under which African Americans were trapped in a limbo between freedom and servitude.

The 1869 Constitution

The U.S. Congress vehemently opposed the efforts of the former Confederate states to keep African Americans downtrodden. In March 1867, all Southern state governments were disbanded, and the former Confederacy was divided into five military districts. A new constitution that guaranteed African American suffrage had to be written in each state, and each had to ratify the Fourteenth Amendment to the U.S. Constitution.

Democrats were the predominant political party in Texas at the time, but members were so angered by the federal government's action that most boycotted the elections leading to creation of the new constitution. Therefore, Republicans, both Radical and moderate, dominated the 1868 Constitutional Convention. Many of the delegates were African American, as detailed in the Texas Mosaic on African American leaders. The Radicals and moderates divided over three main issues. The first was called *ab initio* and dealt with the question of whether all actions of the state government during the time of rebellion should be made null and void. Moderates, who would prevail, believed that only those actions taken in direct rebellion should be voided. The second issue was *division*. Texas's annexation agreement with the United States allows it to divide into up to five states at any time. Although there are serious constitutional questions about the viability of this provision, Radicals launched a plan to create the separate state of West Texas. Radicals knew that they could not compile an elective majority in Texas after the Democrats returned to the political process, so they figured they would create a state out west where there weren't many people, move the Radicals and their African American brethren there, and be able to control *that* state government. Obviously, the moderates won on that issue, too. **E. J. Davis**, a Radical who served as the convention chair, succeeded in his efforts to grant African American men the right to vote. The extension of voting rights was substantial. Although Davis had among his loyal supporters the freedmen, there is evidence that his concern for racial equality was genuine. On issues other than voting rights, though, Davis saw the convention slipping away from the Radicals. Rather than submit, the chair adjourned the convention. It was left to the state's military commander to mold the document into a workable constitution and submit it to the voters.

In 1869, the new state constitution was adopted by an overwhelming margin: 72,446 to 4,928. Progressive and modern, the document centralized much power in the hands of the governor. The state's chief executive had the power to appoint not

Black Codes
Post–Civil War laws restricting the freedom of African Americans.

E. J. Davis
The Republican governor of Texas during the era of Reconstruction.

2.1

2.2

2.3

2.4

2.5

2.6

2.1
2.2
2.3
2.4
2.5
2.6

Texas ★ **Mosaic**

George Ruby was a carpetbagger, which simply means that he came South after the Civil War to seek his fortune. He came to Texas in the post–Civil War era to reconstruct the recently rebellious state and help the former slaves integrate into society. Ruby was a well-educated teacher from Maine who arrived with the occupying forces shortly after the war ended. On the way to New Orleans, Ruby had been denied first-class passage on a ship for one reason: He was African American. This blatant discrimination, a kind that he had not before encountered, was an experience he would never forget.

Ruby quickly became the dominant African American in Texas politics. Residing in Galveston, he became an active leader in both the Union League and the state's infant Republican Party. The party's leaders knew that they must reach out to the African American community in order to remain politically viable in Texas. As a result, the majority of the delegates to the party's first state convention in 1867 were African American. Ruby was named vice president of the convention.

If Anglo party leaders thought that Ruby would be content with a token position within the party, they were mistaken. Ruby effectively controlled the Galveston branch of the Union League by the fall of 1867. He used this power to win election as a delegate to the 1868 state constitutional convention. He campaigned for the convention with an unwavering promise to work for the protection of African American rights. A savvy politician, Ruby worked to keep his bloc of African American delegates positioned between the other factions, siding with whichever group best protected his interests on an issue-by-issue basis.

In June 1868, Ruby became president of the statewide Union League. The league had started as a secretive, white, pro-union organization at the beginning of Reconstruction. It aimed to galvanize the newly freed slaves behind the idea of unions. Having Ruby as its head was not what league founders had in mind, but Ruby was able to convince the African American delegates to oust the sitting white president and elect him instead.

Ruby's most important role in a busy 1868 involved splitting the state party into radical and moderate factions. The moderates controlled the regular state Republican convention. E. J. Davis led his Radicals out of the convention when it failed to address issues that he considered important. Davis knew that his band of white Radicals was not large enough to have an impact on state politics on its own. Ruby, who controlled a sizable African American faction, was the key to the Radicals' viability. When the Radicals convinced Ruby to side with them by adopting many of his pet issues, Texas in effect had two Republican parties.

Moderate Republicans, attempting to discredit Ruby, resorted to a campaign of character assassination. They accused him of taking a bribe. African Americans

George Ruby was a prominent African American Republican after the Civil War. He wielded significant power during Reconstruction-era Texas.

rallied around their leader, sensing a conspiracy. Ruby and the Radicals would back Davis in his bid for governor. Davis won a close race and rewarded those who had helped him with appointments to important offices. Davis's superintendent of schools, for instance, appointed Ruby and his protégé, Norris Wright Cuney, to the Galveston County school board. Ruby also served as a state senator during the Davis administration.

Ruby, whose time at the political forefront was coming to an end, would use his power to help Cuney ascend. With Ruby's aid, Cuney became chair of the executive committee of the National Labor Convention of the Working Men of Texas, a major African American interest group. Cuney, also an African American, was born in Texas. He was sent north prior to the Civil War to acquire an education. He later studied law in Galveston and, at the age of 26, served as a delegate to the Republican National Convention in 1872. Cuney would serve as a delegate to all Republican national conventions through 1892.

When Davis died in 1883, Cuney became chair of the state Republican Party. In 1886, Cuney would add the position of Republican National Committeeman to his resume after being elected by the African American majority at the party's state convention.

In the last two decades of the nineteenth century, the Republican Party in Texas was essentially a

2.1

2.2

2.3

2.4

2.5

2.6

patronage vessel: It dispensed federal jobs to loyal party members whenever Republicans controlled the White House. Outside of a few local positions, Republicans had no chance to win elections. Cuney exploited the patronage aspect in 1889 and obtained the position of customs collector in Galveston, a high-paying and prominent job.

By the end of the 1880s, white Republicans began a concerted effort to regain control of the party from African Americans. By organizing, they were able to control the party and garner nominations for their slate of statewide candidates in 1890. At the 1892 state convention, Cuney retained control for his faction by railroading the convention and running over the "lily white" Republicans. As a result, white Republicans held a separate "rump" convention and selected their own national delegates and gubernatorial ticket. At the national convention, Cuney's delegation was seated, and he was elected to another four-year term on the Republican National Committee.

Cuney's faction of the party chose not to run a gubernatorial ticket in 1892. In 1894, there were again two Republican state conventions. This time, each side opted to run its own gubernatorial ticket. While the Democrats easily won the governor's race, Cuney's candidate outpolled the "lily white" candidate by a 10-to-1 margin.

By 1896, however, as a result of an intraparty battle over the Republican presidential nomination, Cuney found himself left out of the process because he had backed the wrong candidate. He was shut out of the national convention, lost his national committee position, and, finally, was ousted as party chair. He would be replaced by another African American, H. C. Ferguson, but the days of African American control of the state's Republican Party were all but over.

Sources: Carl H. Moneyhon, *Republicanism in Reconstruction Texas* (Austin: University of Texas Press, 1980); Paul Douglas Casdorph, "Norris Wright Cuney and Texas Republican Politics, 1883–1896," *Southwestern Historical Quarterly* 67(1963):68, 455–464.

1. How did Ruby increase African American power during Reconstruction?

2. What was the benefit of remaining Republican once the Democrats regained control of state politics?

---

only the secretary of state and the attorney general, but judges as well. Looking toward the future, the convention created the Permanent School Fund, which earmarked money generated from public lands for education. Black men, as well as most white ex-Confederate males, were guaranteed the right to vote.[9] The document provided a framework in which a strong government could operate. The factors that led to its relatively quick demise had more to do with the actions of Governor E. J. Davis, both real and attributed, than with the constitution itself.

After the constitutional convention, Davis was elected governor, winning a hotly contested race against A. J. Hamilton, a fellow Republican. Still slow to organize, the Democrats failed to field a candidate, although many eventually supported Hamilton as the lesser of two evils. Both sides claimed their opponent participated in fraud and intimidation during the election. Despite claims of corruption by the Hamilton backers, Davis might have won by a larger margin had African Americans been granted freer access to the polls. African American turnout actually dropped from the 1868 to the 1869 elections, due to intimidation in the registration and voting process.[10]

THE DAVIS ADMINISTRATION The Davis administration is infamous in Texas for its alleged abuses. Chief among the complaints was the governor's implementation of the **Obnoxious Acts**, the name opposing Democrats gave to the cornerstone of Davis's legislative agenda.

First, the governor and the Republican legislature created a state militia and a state police force. According to Texas legend, the purpose of these forces was to intimidate and harass poor white Texans. In reality, the organizations were formed to protect the frontier from Indian incursion, to stop the lynching of African Americans, and to halt the general lawlessness that engulfed Texas. The militia and police were generally effective at achieving their goals. Three factors, however, led to the negative perceptions held by generations of white Texans. First was the enormous cost of the endeavor. Second, the forces included African American militia and policemen. Anglo Texans were not thrilled with the prospect of armed former slaves patrolling the state.[11] Finally, Davis had forced the enacting bill through the legislature in a high-handed way. When some Senate opponents of the militia bill realized they didn't have the votes to stop it through traditional methods, they skipped out on the session,

Obnoxious Acts
The derisive name given to the legislation included in E. J. Davis's agenda.

2.1

2.2

2.3

2.4

2.5

2.6

Texas ★ Mosaic

Diversity of Thought: E. J. Davis

Edmund J. Davis, the Republican governor of Texas during Reconstruction, was one of the most controversial figures in Texas history. The son of an attorney, Davis arrived in Texas when he was 20 years of age. He served as a clerk at the Galveston post office while studying law. The next year, he was admitted to the bar in Corpus Christi. He used connections within the Democratic Party to secure a job as customs inspector in Laredo. Later, he was an elected Democratic district judge and, in 1857, a delegate to the Democratic state convention. Davis, a Union officer in the war, joined the Republican Party after the rebellion ended.

Davis's wife, Anne Elizabeth Britton Davis, was the daughter of Major Forbes Britton, a powerful Jacksonian Democrat who had served in both houses of the Texas Legislature. Lizzie was a strong, influential woman. She was a driving force behind her husband's political career and, no doubt, helped shape his political outlook. She considered his election as governor to be the first step toward the White House. While he was governor, she addressed the legislature, giving a speech for her husband almost 50 years before women were granted the vote in Texas.

Davis's Programs. Despite all the controversy surrounding his administration, Davis had a vision for Texas. He believed the state needed to educate its citizens. Toward that end, the governor and his legislative supporters created a centralized and free public education system. Such a program was costly and increased the state's debt. The centralization was so complete that the governor's patronage power actually extended to hiring teachers. School employees could therefore be counted upon for their loyalty to the governor.

Similarly, the state's railroad construction program, consisting partially of monetary grants to railroad companies, was expensive. Davis was a supporter of extending the rail lines and would ultimately be blamed for the debt incurred, but the legislation authorizing the monetary grants was passed over his veto. Davis favored land grants and other innovative enticements to the railroad companies.

After his term as governor, Davis did not fade quietly from the political scene. He controlled the state Republican

E. J. Davis was the last Republican governor of Texas for almost 100 years. A controversial figure, he receives less credit and more blame than he deserves. As the leader of the state during Reconstruction, he was certain to anger many of his contemporary Texans.

Party until his death in 1883. He made one last run for the governor's office in 1880, but captured less than 25 percent of the vote. In the end, he believed that the national party had abandoned the Republicans of Texas.

Sources: Carl H. Moneyhon, *Republicanism in Reconstruction Texas* (Austin: University of Texas Press, 1980); Ronald N. Gray, "Edmund J. Davis" (Ph.D. diss., Texas Tech University, 1976).

1. Why was Davis's education plan controversial?

2. Why did Davis switch parties?

thereby preventing a quorum. The governor had the missing senators arrested for contempt. The authorities returned only four of the nine absent senators to the chamber, achieving a quorum while at the same time holding opposition to a minimum, thus guaranteeing passage of the bill.[12]

Another of the Obnoxious Acts gave the governor broad power to fill vacancies created at the state or local level. Because readmittance to the Union resulted in the removal of many officeholders of questionable loyalty, Davis had the power to fill thousands of political offices. And with the consent of the United States Congress, he also postponed elections for state and congressional offices, thereby guaranteeing extended terms for Radical officeholders. You can read more on Davis in the Texas Mosaic detailing his career.

THE DEMOCRATS RETURN TO POWER The Democrats regained control of the legislature after the 1872 elections. They immediately began to dismantle the Radical programs. Davis went along with some changes, agreeing, for instance, to decentralize the school system. When he vetoed efforts to repeal portions of the "Obnoxious Acts," Democrats found enough sympathetic Republicans to help override the vetoes.[13]

In late 1873, Davis lost his bid for reelection to Democrat Richard Coke. Some Republicans, citing an alleged technical discrepancy between the state constitution and the execution of the 1873 election, argued that the election was unconstitutional. Democrats believed that Davis, who had previously stated he would not contest the election, would use the controversy to stay in office. They demanded that the governor relinquish power immediately rather than wait until his term ended in April. The Democrats convened the legislature and inaugurated Coke as governor. Davis continued to serve in office as well. In January 1874, the Republican-controlled Texas supreme court sided with Davis, declaring the elections invalid.[14]

Davis asked for federal intervention, requesting that President Ulysses S. Grant send U.S. troops to Texas to help him keep order until the election matter could be resolved. Grant refused. On January 19, before his term officially ended, Davis resigned, determined to prevent violence, which he feared might occur should the impasse continue.

The 1876 Constitution

Grange
A populist farmers' alliance influential in the creation of the 1876 constitution.

1876 constitution
The current Texas constitution, written after Reconstruction.

2.1

2.2

2.3

2.4

2.5

2.6

2.5 Analyze how Texas's current constitution is partially a reaction to the previous Reconstruction-era document and partially a return to pre–Civil War policies.

Firmly in control of both the legislative and executive branches, the Democrats moved to consolidate power. As governor, Coke was not as enthusiastic as some other Texans to downgrade his office. The Democratic leadership in 1874 authored a series of amendments to the constitution that would have retained many governmental powers. The legislature would continue to meet each year. While state debt was limited, it was 10 times more than the debt allowed under the 1846 constitution. No ceiling was placed on state or local taxes; neither were there restrictions on the uses of state tax revenue. The governor's term of four years was retained, as was the office of state superintendent of schools.[15] While the proposed constitution differed from the 1869 document, it retained the basic tenet of centralized state power. The legislature failed to act on the proposal, however, and a constitutional convention became inevitable.

The convention changed the playing field. No longer would the process be controlled by party leaders. Instead, independently elected delegates would be free from leadership constraints. The most influential group, comprising a 38-member plurality of the 90-delegate convention, was the Texas **Grange**.[16] Grangers were a populist farmers' group whose members blamed their economic decline on railroad companies, Radical Republicans, and the newly freed slaves. They believed the government was spending too much money, and they sought to rein in state debt.

The easiest interpretation of the document produced by the 1875 convention is that it represented a simple backlash against Radical Republican rule and the perceived abuses of the Davis administration. Certainly, this was a major factor. In many vital ways, however, the **1876 constitution** would mirror the pre–Civil War document. Furthermore, the new document was in line with state constitutional development throughout the nation at the time.[17] Other constitutions enacted during that period, even those created outside of the post–Reconstruction South, sought to limit government control.

The 1846 constitution had called for biennial legislative sessions, relatively low legislative salary, a two-year term limit for the governor, and six-year terms for an elected member of the Texas supreme court. It placed strict limits on state debt and prohibited state grants to banks or railroads.[18] All these provisions reappeared in the

2.1

2.2

2.3

2.4

2.5

2.6

1876 document. The Grangers' insistence on a reduction of government power was at least partially aimed at the Democratic leadership in 1874–1875, because the 1876 constitution restricted the Democrats' power as well. Many Grangers were leery of the governor and other party leaders who pushed the 1874 revision attempt in the legislature, ignoring the traditional method of changing constitutions through the convention process. This action was viewed as an effort by those already in office to retain power for the government. The perception, of course, was correct.

LIMITS ON GOVERNMENT POWER The 1876 constitution aimed to restrict the power of the government. It did not seek to limit the executive branch alone; it limited all branches. The power of the legislature was restricted by the return to biennial sessions. The reasoning was simple: The less time the legislature was in session, the fewer opportunities it had to pass laws. The salary was low, encouraging members to limit service. Senate terms were cut from six years to four. Expense money dropped as the session went on so that legislators would finish their business quickly and go home. Any increase in legislative salary required a constitutional amendment, which required voter approval. The legislature was prohibited from calling itself into special session. By giving this responsibility exclusively to the governor, power was further dispersed.

The most significant limit on the legislature, though, was the balanced budget provision, which greatly restricted the state's ability to go into debt. This was certainly a reaction to the spending habits of the Radical Republicans. Limiting the amount of money available to the legislature limits its ability to enact programs. But it was nothing new for Texans, as it echoed similar stipulations in the 1846 document.

The governor's office was restricted through stripping his appointment powers. No longer could the governor appoint his cabinet. Rather, other executive heads, such as the attorney general, lieutenant governor, and comptroller, would be elected independently. Each executive officer would have his own constituency. His loyalty would be owed to those voters, not the governor. The governor's salary was reduced as well.

The size of the judicial branch was reduced as the number of district courts decreased. The term of judges was reduced, and they were chosen by popular election, not by appointment.

THE BILL OF RIGHTS One of the most significant portions of the 1876 Constitution was its long, detailed Bill of Rights. Texans wanted to ensure that individual liberties would never be trampled again, even if those liberties, as was the case in 1876, extended only to white males. Again, the Bill of Rights cannot be viewed entirely as a reaction to Reconstruction. Most of the key components of the 1876 document are derived directly from the 1846 constitution. Many provisions in the Bill of Rights date back to the 1836 Republic of Texas constitution.[19]

A state Bill of Rights is important for two reasons. First, the U.S. Bill of Rights does not explicitly extend protections to the relationship between a state and its citizens. It wasn't until the 1940s that the U.S. Supreme Court began applying most provisions of the U.S. Bill of Rights to state and local governments, almost 70 years after the Texas constitution was created. (See the Inside the Federalist System box.)

Second, while a state cannot give less protection to its citizens than is allowed through U.S. Supreme Court interpretations, it can give more. For instance, the effort to include an Equal Rights Amendment in the U.S. Constitution, which would have banned gender-based discrimination, was defeated in 1982. The Texas constitution, however, contains such a provision as a result of a 1972 amendment (art. 1, sec. 3a).

Whereas the national constitution's Bill of Rights contains only 10 provisions, the Texas Bill of Rights has 30. In addition to protections against unreasonable searches and seizures and double jeopardy, as well as guarantees of freedom of the press and freedom of speech, it also ensures that individuals will not be imprisoned for debt and that monopolies will not be allowed in the state. Texas may not deport a citizen from the state for any offense committed in Texas.

Two portions of the Bill of Rights seem most directly attributable to a reaction against Reconstruction. Article I, Section 1 says, "Texas is a free and independent state, subject

2.1
2.2
2.3
2.4
2.5
2.6

Inside the Federalist System

Texts and the Environmental Protection Agency

By its nature, federalism requires some level of co-operation between the national and state governments in a variety of circumstances, particularly those that are regulatory in nature. So while the national government sets most pollution standards, policy implementation has, at least until the Obama administration, been left primarily to the states. In two particular cases, and there have been several others, Texas officials believed that the Environmental Protection Agency (EPA) had so overstepped its bounds that Texas sued to stop federal action. One case involved federal takeover of the permitting process for plants that produce greenhouse gases, and the other concerned cross-state air pollution rules.

Both the state's governor and attorney general accused the EPA of overreaching. The *Wall Street Journal* went a step further, accusing the EPA of waging war on Texas after the agency stripped the state's own environmental board of the power to issue permits. The state of Texas sued the EPA, which was nothing new, as the state had ongoing lawsuits against the EPA on other matters. The EPA's justification for taking over permitting was that it suddenly found issue with a plan that had been submitted to the EPA for approval some 16 years earlier. The Fifth Circuit Court sided with Texas.

It found that the EPA's decision was "arbitrary and capricious."[20]

Just a week later, the U.S. Court of Appeals for the District of Columbia struck down the EPA's Cross-State Air Pollution Rule, holding that the agency had violated the Clean Air Act, which requires that the national and state governments work together in setting clean air standards. Texas was one of several parties to the suit. Judge Brett Cavanaugh wrote, "Congress did not authorize EPA to simply adopt limits on emissions as EPA deemed reasonable."[21]

What this means, from the perspective of federalism, is that the Texas Commission on Environmental Quality (TCEF) has a role to play in setting environmental policy in the state. That in no way means that TCEQ has unfettered leeway in how it set standards. The Fifth Circuit decision remanded the case back to the EPA, meaning that the agency can still review state standards, but they must do so in a logical and consistent manner.

1. **How much power should the states have in setting air quality standards?**
2. **Are there areas where the national government should have unlimited control? Why or why not?**

only to the Constitution of the United States." The language tries to create powers for Texas that were denied to it during Reconstruction. Its placement at the beginning of the Bill of Rights emphasizes its importance. The second item is a direct strike against Davis: It prohibits the use of state money for religious purposes. Its aim was to dismantle the education structure erected by the Republicans, which included state funding for parochial schools. Neither of these two provisions had appeared in previous Texas constitutions.[22]

The Texas Bill of Rights extends many protections to those accused of crime. A person cannot be held without charges, has the right to confront accusers, and has a right to a trial by jury. Unlike some states, no person can be tried for a felony crime without first being charged by a grand jury. On the other hand, a 1989 amendment extended rights to crime victims, including the right to confer with a representative from the prosecutor's office and the right to restitution from the perpetrator.

☐ Amending the Constitution

Amending the Texas constitution is a two-step process. First, both the house and the senate must approve the proposed amendment by at least a two-thirds vote. This is the most difficult step in the process because 51 house members or 11 senators can block an amendment. Even with today's Republican majorities, any amendment vote that divides along party lines will be defeated.

Ratification of amendments approved by the legislature requires majority approval from the voters. Most of the time, voters approve proposed amendments. From 1985 through 2009, Texans had the opportunity to vote on 227 amendments. All but 29 passed. In other words, 87 percent of all proposals that reached the voters were ratified. In 1987, when 25 amendments were offered, 8 were defeated (see Figure 2.1). In 2001, all 19 proposed amendments passed, as did all 22 in 2003, all 17 in 2007, and all 11 in 2009. In 2011, as the state's antigovernment sentiment was even more pronounced than usual, voters defeated 3 out of 10 proposed amendments.

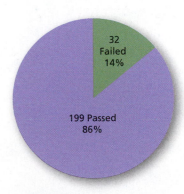

FIGURE 2.1 Proposed Constitutional Amendments, 1985–2012.

The overwhelming percentage of proposed amendments are passed by the voters.

51

| 2.1 |
| 2.2 |
| 2.3 |
| 2.4 |
| 2.5 |
| 2.6 |

The Texas Constitution

A Closer Look

The creators of the 1876 constitution wanted to restate their independence and distance themselves from Reconstruction policies. The first three sections of Article I illustrate this well.

Article I. Bill of Rights

Sec. 1. Freedom and Sovereignty of State. Texas is a free and independent State, subject only to the Constitution of the United States, and the maintenance of our free institutions and the perpetuity of the Union depend upon the preservation of the right of local self-government, unimpaired to all the States.

Sec. 2. Inherent Political Power; Republican form of Government. All political power is inherent in the people, and all free governments are founded on their authority, and instituted for their benefit. The faith of the people of Texas stands pledged to the preservation of a republican form of government, and, subject to this limitation only, they have at all times the inalienable right to alter, reform or abolish their government in such manner as they may think expedient.

Sec. 3. Equal Rights. All free men, when they form a social compact, have equal rights, and no man, or set of men, is entitled to exclusive separate public emoluments, or privileges, but in consideration of public services.

1. Why did the drafters believe it important to write that "Texas is a free and independent State"?

2. What did the drafters, who disliked the Republican Party, mean by 'a republican form of government'? Why did they consider that their only limitation in regard to altering government?

The governor has no formal role in the amendment process. Informally, he or she can use the visibility of the office to campaign for or against an amendment. The governor's support does not always help. In May 1993, Governor Ann Richards worked hard for passage of the "Robin Hood" school reform amendments, which would have redistributed money from property-rich school districts to poorer ones. The amendments went down to overwhelming defeats, foreshadowing Richards's own ouster from office a year and a half later.

The Texas constitution had been amended 474 times as of 2012. In the same amount of time, only 12 amendments were added to the U.S. Constitution.

Constitutional Revision

2.6 Explain why those who benefit from the current constitution will work to make comprehensive reform difficult.

The Texas constitution of 1876 was written for a backward, agrarian, racist state recovering from the humiliation of a military defeat and subsequent Reconstruction. The 19th-century document did not provide for an efficient governmental system in the long term, especially with myriad amendments that have served to make the constitution even bulkier and more confusing. Numerous efforts have been made to revise or rewrite the Texas constitution. Most have failed completely. Voters have shown little interest in the process.

The document itself is a model of disarray. It contains sentences that seem to go on forever. One stretches to several hundred words. This particular instance of incompetence cannot be blamed on the Grange. It was part of an amendment allowing for the creation of the Dallas/Fort Worth International Airport.

A 1999 constitutional amendment eliminated three outdated passages. First, for purposes of privilege against arrest, the original document had assumed a legislator could only travel 20 miles a day (art. 3, sec. 14). Second, the governor had been allowed to call out the militia to "protect the frontier from hostile incursions by Indians" (art. 4, sec. 7). The legislature had specifically been granted the power to give "aid to indigent and disabled confederate soldiers and sailors" (art. 3, sec. 51). But many problems remain. Article III, Section 52 contains parts a, b, and d, but not c. The legislature was confused as to the numbering sequence when it submitted the amendment to the voters. In addition, Article VII has two section 16s: one dealing with terms of office in school systems, the other pertaining to taxation of university lands.

In 1969, several obsolete provisions, such as one dealing with Spanish and Mexican land titles, were removed. Instead of renumbering the document to reflect the changes, blank sections and articles now litter the constitution. Prior to a 1991 amendment, all bond issues approved by the voters became a permanent part of the Texas constitution. Although they go through the same process for approval, new issues do not clutter the constitution.

The 1974 Constitutional Convention

The last major attempt to revise the constitution occurred in the 1970s. During a period of dissatisfaction with government in general, Texas politics entered an era of reform. The legislature embarked on an effort to give the state a new governing document. A constitutional amendment, approved by the voters in 1972, called for the creation of a revision commission that would submit its recommendations to a constitutional convention scheduled for January 1974. The convention's delegates were the elected members of the House and Senate, sitting as one body. In the wake of Watergate and the increasingly unpopular Vietnam War at the national level and the Sharpstown scandal at the state level, there was genuine hope for reform.

The revision committee produced a much shorter document, which would have drastically changed the structure of government in Texas. The proposal was only 17,500 words long. The revision would have required annual sessions of the legislature and provided for the appointment of judges.

After haggling over proposed changes from January to July 1974, the convention killed its own document. Needing two-thirds approval from the 181 members, the proposal fell three votes short. Had it succeeded, there is no guarantee that the voters would have approved the new constitution. A controversial right-to-work provision, which guaranteed that a Texan could not be required to join a union in order to get a job, contributed to the defeat. Representatives and senators from labor strongholds were pressured to vote against the document. School funding equalization, a topic that would dominate Texas's political focus from the mid-1980s through the mid-1990s, was also a factor. Delegates from property-poor areas wanted more state money devoted to education. Nonetheless, a significant majority of delegates believed that the proposed constitution was better than the present one. In 1975, reconvened as the legislature, the House and Senate submitted it to the voters in the form of eight separate propositions.

With the vocal opposition of the governor, who claimed the new document could result in a state income tax, voters overwhelmingly defeated all the provisions, with none of the eight receiving 30 percent approval. Ironically, there was no clause in the 1876 constitution at that time that would have prevented an income tax. Since then, an amendment has been added that requires voter approval before such a tax can be levied.

Prospects for Revision

For 20 years after the collapse of the last major revision effort, no serious attempt to achieve reform emerged. Given the expenditure of time, energy, and money on the

2.1
2.2
2.3
2.4
2.5
2.6

2.1

2.2

2.3

2.4

2.5

2.6

This 1974 Constitutional Convention was the last serious attempt at constitutional reform in Texas. Here, lieutenant governor William Hobby addresses the convention, which would ultimately fall three votes short of adopting a new governing document.

futile last effort, it is easy to understand why state leaders were not motivated to revisit the convention process.

There are major obstacles to revision. Any effort to change the constitution will garner opposition from groups that benefit from the way things are. The Republican Party, for instance, now confident of its ability to win statewide judicial races is likely to oppose any reform mandating judicial appointment. Likewise, the University of Texas and Texas A&M University systems, as well as their powerful alumni associations, would oppose a further division of the Permanent University Fund (PUF) revenue if they were forced to share with all public colleges and universities.

Those who would lose benefits under a new constitution are more committed to its defeat than those who might gain would be committed to its adoption. To the prospective winners under reform, promises of long-term benefit some time in the future are less tangible and less concrete. Furthermore, constitutional revision isn't a hot topic with most Texans. Families don't talk about it around the dinner table.

Many Texas political actors understand that the current constitution is ill suited for our era. Major newspapers have called for revision. Over a decade ago, Republican Senator Bill Ratliff and Democrat House Member Rob Junell collaborated on a proposed constitution that was less than a quarter of the length of the present document. It contained several significant changes for Texas government. Legislative terms would be lengthened, for instance, but terms would be limited. The governor would appoint a cabinet, including the agriculture and land commissioners, but the attorney general and comptroller would still be elected. The biggest change would be in the judiciary. The highest civil and criminal courts would be combined. Judges at the district court level and above would initially be appointed by the governor, then subjected to periodic retention elections, where voters could give a thumbs-up or thumbs-down to their continued service. Their proposal died in committee, but such is the fate of most innovative ideas on their first introduction to the Texas Legislature. Since then, both Ratliff and Junell have retired from public office, depriving the movement of its leadership, and the makeup of the legislature is less hospitable to progressive reform.

In the near future, hopes for comprehensive constitutional reform are limited. It is difficult, time-consuming, and costly, and the political rewards are limited at best. If you achieve your goal, only people who write government books will remember your name. Your reward will be a better Texas, but you're likely to make more enemies than friends simply by making the attempt.

2.1

2.2

2.3

2.4

2.5

2.6

Review the Chapter

Listen to Chapter 2

Federalism

2.1 Explain how state power is constrained by federalism and by the national and state constitutions.

Federalism is the constitutional division of power among the national and state governments. State governments are limited by both the powers given to the national government and the authority denied to the states. In addition, the powers of individual state governments are limited by their own state constitutions.

National Gains

2.2 Analyze how the national government has gained power within the federalism equation.

The national government has gained power in the equation because of a number of constitutional amendments that limit state authority. In addition, the national government has gained because of an expansive reading of the interstate commerce clause and by the enormous power of the federal purse and the national government's ability to attach strings to federal grants.

State Constitutions

2.3 Explain why state constitutions tend to be long and restrictive

Long, restrictive state constitutions are intended to limit the power of government.

The Constitutions of Texas

2.4 Differentiate among the first six constitutions of Texas.

Texas's first constitution was created while it was still part of the Mexican Federation. In 1836, the Republic of Texas had a national constitution. The 1845 document allowed Texas into the United States but was significantly amended in 1850. In 1861, Texas needed a new constitution as it joined the Confederate State of America, and another new one in 1866 to be readmitted to the Union. Congress, however, believed the state to be in de facto rebellion, so it dissolved the state government and ordered it to write a new document. The 1869 constitution both protected minority rights and centralized government power, granting extensive power to the governor and allowing the legislature to borrow money and incur debt.

The 1876 Constitution

2.5 Analyze how Texas's current constitution is partially a reaction to the previous Reconstruction-era document and partially a return to pre–Civil War policies.

Although the circumstances that led to the 1875 convention were a direct reaction to the 1869 constitution, the document that passed in 1876 provided the same basic governmental powers and restrictions that the amended 1845 document did.

Constitutional Revision

2.6 Explain why those who benefit from the current constitution will work to make comprehensive reform difficult.

Many groups benefit from provisions in the current constitution, benefits they may lose if the constitution is rewritten, The University of Texas and Texas A&M systems, for instance, share proceeds from the PUF fund with each other, but not with the rest of the state colleges and universities.

Learn the Terms

 Study and **Review** the **Flashcards**

Test Yourself

2.1 Explain how state power is constrained by federalism and by the national and state constitutions.

The most important component of the federalist system is the

   a. Supreme Court.
   b. Congress.
   c. Constitution.
   d. president.
   e. governor.

2.2 Analyze how the national government has gained power within the federalism equation.

Congress has greatly increased its control over states through

   a. taxes on state government.
   b. the judicious use of federal grants.
   c. the Civil Rights Act of 1964.
   d. veto power over state actions.
   e. treaties with other nations.

2.3 Explain why state constitutions tend to be long and restrictive.

Most states

   a. seldom amend their constitutions.
   b. cannot amend their constitutions.
   c. do not have formal constitutions.
   d. amend their constitutions more often than the national government.
   e. model their constitutions after the U. S. Constitution.

2.4 Differentiate among the first six constitutions of Texas.

Which Texas constitution was most closely modeled after the U.S. Constitution?

   a. 1836
   b. 1845
   c. 1861
   d. 1866
   e. 1869

2.5 Analyze how the current constitution is partially a reaction to the previous Reconstruction-era document and partially a return to pre–Civil War policies.

Which is true of the current Texas constitution?

   a. It is similar to the pre-Civil War constitution.
   b. It was adopted in 1975.
   c. It has been amended less than the U.S. Constitution.
   d. It carefully separates constitutional law from legislative law.
   e. Because of the Civil War, all amendments are subject to congressional approval.

2.6 Explain why those who benefit from the current constitution will work to make comprehensive reform difficult.

Which is true of the 1970s effort to revise the Texas constitution?

   a. The convention failed to meet because it lacked a quorum.
   b. The convention passed a new constitution, but it was rejected by the voters.
   c. The convention defeated the constitution, and voters rejected it when it was offered as a series of amendments.
   d. The convention defeated the constitution, but voters approved it after it was offered as a series of amendments.
   e. The governor courageously fought for the new constitution from the beginning to the end of the process.

Explore Further

Braden, George D. *Citizens' Guide to the Texas Constitution*. Austin: The Texas Advisory Commission on Intergovernmental Relations. 1972.

Bruff, Harold H. "Separation of Powers under the Texas Constitution." *Texas Law Review* 68 (1990):1337–1367.

Campbell, Randolph B. *Gone to Texas: A History of the Lone Star State*. New York: Oxford University Press, 2003.

Cnudde, Charles F., and Robert E. Crews. *Constitutional Democracy in Texas*. St Paul, MN: West, 1989.

Connor, George E., and Christopher W. Hammons. *The Constitutionalism of American States*. Columbia: University of Missouri Press, 2008.

Mauer, John Walker. "State Constitutions in a Time of Crisis," *Texas Law Review* 68 (1990):1615–1647.

May, Janice C. *The Texas State Constitution: A Reference Guide*. Westport, CT: Greenwood Press, 1996.

Tarr, G. Alan. *Understanding State Constitutions*. Princeton, NJ: Princeton University Press, 1998.

You can read the Texas Declaration of Independence at http://www.lsjunction.com/docs/tdoi.htm.

The resolution admitting Texas to the United States can be found at http://www.lsjunction.com/docs/annex.htm.

The Texas Ordinance of Secession is available at http://www.lsjunction.com/docs/secesson.htm.

3

Voting and Elections in Texas

*We will not allow political pretexts to disenfranchise
American citizens of their most precious right.*

—*Obama Administration Attorney General
Eric Holder on Texas's Voter ID*

Some people shouldn't vote; they should just go eat ice cream.

—*Paul Stockard, Texas Republican Activist,
on the Impact on Uninformed Voters*

I n the 2012 presidential election, almost 8 million Texans cast ballots. Just fewer than 59 percent of registered voters took part. Total ballots cast were near an all-time high, eclipsed only by the 2008 presidential election. But the percentage of voters paled in comparison to the modern high of 1992, when 73 percent of the state's registered voters went to the polls. There are many reasons for this discrepancy. The 1992 election took place right in the middle of the state's brief status as a

3.1	3.2	3.3	3.4	3.5
Identify past restrictions on voting rights in Texas.	Explain voter registration requirements in Texas.	Analyze causes of low voter turnout in Texas.	Differentiate among primary, general, and special elections.	Explain the obstacles to running a campaign in Texas.

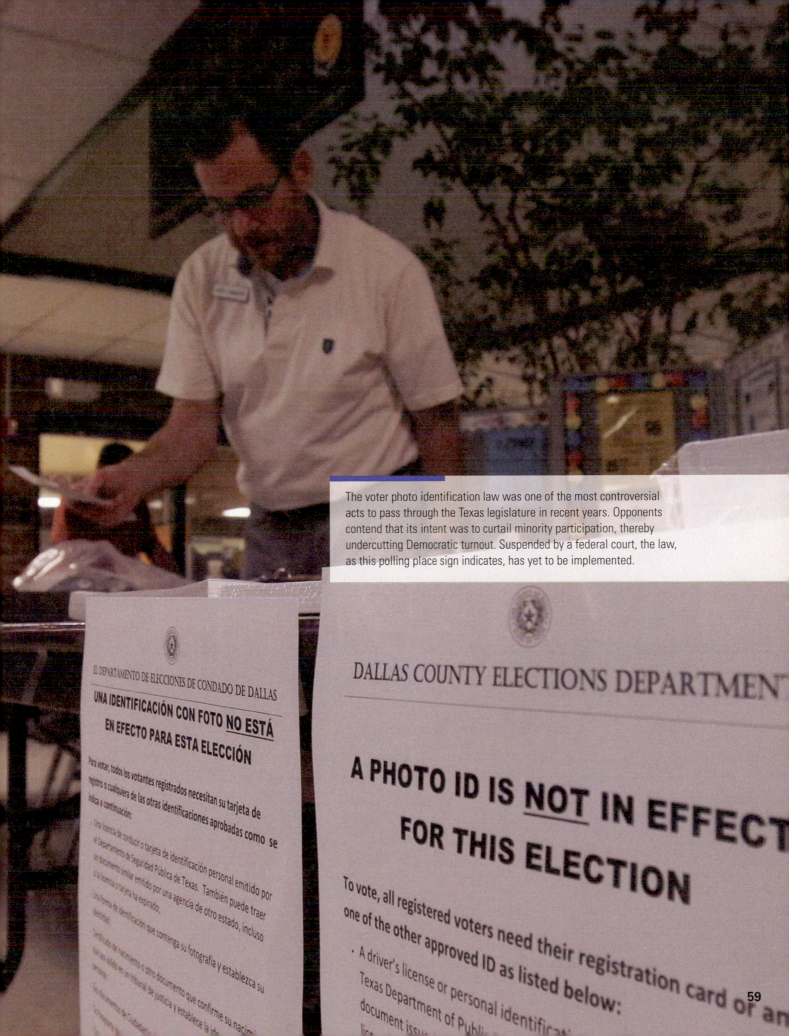

The voter photo identification law was one of the most controversial acts to pass through the Texas legislature in recent years. Opponents contend that its intent was to curtail minority participation, thereby undercutting Democratic turnout. Suspended by a federal court, the law, as this polling place sign indicates, has yet to be implemented.

EL DEPARTAMENTO DE ELECCIONES DE CONDADO DE DALLAS

UNA IDENTIFICACIÓN CON FOTO NO ESTÁ EN EFECTO PARA ESTA ELECCIÓN

Para votar, todos los votantes registrados necesitan su tarjeta de registro o cualquiera de las otras identificaciones aprobadas como se indica a continuación:

DALLAS COUNTY ELECTIONS DEPARTMENT

A PHOTO ID IS NOT IN EFFECT FOR THIS ELECTION

To vote, all registered voters need their registration card or any one of the other approved ID as listed below:

· A driver's license or personal identificati...
Texas Department of Publi...
document issu...

59

universal suffrage
The concept that holds that virtually all adult citizens (felons and illegal aliens are excluded) have the right to vote.

white primary
The practice of allowing only whites to vote in the Democratic primary (discontinued).

true two-party state. Democrats were no longer almost always victorious, but Republicans had yet to begin their dominance of statewide offices. Registration was more difficult, so a greater percentage of those who went to the trouble of going through the process were apt to cast ballots. By 2012, many political pundits questioned the motives of a state that had recently passed a voter identification law, even though its implementation had been halted by federal courts. Furthermore, presidential elections tend to overstate voter interest. Only 38 percent of those registered actually voted in the 2010 gubernatorial election, while barely 5 percent made it to the polls for ratification of a series of constitutional amendments in 2011.

It is the legacy of Texas that, during its first century as a state, it devoted far more energy to keeping citizens from voting than it did to encouraging political participation. African Americans, women, the poor, and those not wise in the ways of voting regulations found it difficult, if not impossible, to exercise any meaningful power in the elective process. It required a bloody fight, both literally and figuratively, to break down this official repression. Today, as the state has all but **universal suffrage** for its adult citizens, relatively few exercise that right on a regular basis. This chapter will help you understand why Texas turnout lags. Additionally, you will learn how the processes of the state's electoral system operate in order to comprehend how individual political participation can impact the government that emerges after the ballots have been counted.

A History of Voting Rights

3.1 Identify past restrictions on voting rights in Texas.

Before the Civil War, of course, slaves in Texas had no voting rights. When Texas fell under martial law after the Civil War, the state had to extend voting rights to African American males in order to regain full statehood. This extension was short-lived, however. After white conservatives regained control of the state, both intimidation and government action were used to restrict minority voter access. By 1900, the state had 650,000 potential African American voters, but only 25,000 were qualified to vote.[1]

Women, meanwhile, had no firm voting rights until the Nineteenth Amendment to the U.S. Constitution passed in 1920. Texas was the first Southern state to approve the amendment and had allowed women to participate in primary elections as early as 1918.

White Primary

In Texas, from the end of Reconstruction until the early 1960s, gaining the Democratic nomination was tantamount to being elected. Republicans never won. By the beginning of the 20th century, Democrats held every office in the state. Therefore, the Democratic Party made the real decisions as to who would win which office.

In 1905, under the auspices of progressive reform, the Texas Democratic Party adopted the primary system to replace the party caucus. Under the caucus method, party leaders selected Democratic nominees for elective office, choosing officeholders, not merely nominees. Under the primary system, voters chose nominees—who would be officeholders—in the Democratic primary. The so-called progressives wanted to shift nomination power to some, but not all, Texas citizens. They did not favor racial equality and so they adopted a **white primary** system, whereby African Americans were prohibited from participating. Once African Americans were excluded from the primary, they were, effectively, excluded from the political process. Even if they were permitted to vote in the general election, the winning candidate had already been chosen. By 1923, this Democratic Party rule had become state law.

African American leaders contended that such a system violated the Fifteenth Amendment to the U.S. Constitution, which guarantees that race cannot be used to prevent a person from voting. In 1924, in *Nixon* v. *Herndon*, the U.S. Supreme Court struck down a Texas law that prevented African Americans from taking part in a Democratic primary. (Note that the law did not ban Hispanics from participating. Whether Hispanics could vote in the primary was determined locally.) Texas Democrats reacted to the 1924 decision by passing a party resolution granting primary election suffrage only to whites. Minority leaders objected and took the state and party to court. The U.S. Supreme Court rejected their argument in *Grovey* v. *Townsend*.

The Court sided with the Democratic Party, which maintained that as a private organization, it could include or exclude people at its discretion. This argument ignored the party's domination of Texas government. The party and the government were, for all practical purposes, the same.

By 1944, the character of the U.S. Supreme Court had changed. President Franklin Roosevelt's appointees had made the Court more liberal. In **Smith v. Allwright**, the Court overturned *Townsend*. Because primary elections are conducted under state authority and because state courts can review conflicts arising from primary elections, the Court ruled that political parties are "an agency of the state." As such, they must abide by federal law regarding political participation and suffrage.[2]

Although African American voter registration numbers increased rapidly, the last vestiges of the white primary continued in some parts of Texas. With the state Democratic resolution struck down by the court, some county Democratic organizations passed their own white primary resolutions. It took a few additional years before federal courts struck down these provisions as well.[3]

☐ Poll Tax

Another device that worked to hold down voter turnout was the **poll tax**, passed into law in 1902. A citizen had to pay this tax in order to register to vote. While this tax worked to reduce minority turnout, it also negatively affected all economically disadvantaged and politically unaware people. The greatest impact was, as intended, on the minority community, where poverty was concentrated. This tax was part of the same "progressive" reforms that brought about the primary. The progressives wanted to formalize the election registration process to help root out corruption. Also, by reducing the number of poor voters, they could increase their chances of bringing about a prohibition on the sales of alcoholic beverages. By limiting alcohol sales and voting rights, progressives believed that they were "saving" the poor from their own excesses.

Faced with having to pay the tax to register, many poor people decided their votes were not important enough to sacrifice limited financial resources. Prior to *Smith* v. *Allwright*, this was particularly true for African Americans. Barred from the Democratic primary, where the actual election occurred, they had no compelling reason to pay the tax. Another problem with the poll tax stemmed from the requirement that it be paid before the end of January in each election year. No reminder notices were sent into minority and poor communities to urge on-time registration. If people missed this deadline, they lost their right to vote.

In 1964, the Twenty-fourth Amendment was added to the U.S. Constitution to ban poll taxes in federal elections, specifically for president, vice president, and the U.S. Senate and U.S. House of Representatives. Texas tried to get around the ban. It created a dual-ballot system. Everyone received a federal ballot, but only those who paid their poll taxes received state ballots. Even though the Twenty-fourth Amendment referred specifically to federal elections, not state offices, the U.S. Supreme Court struck down the Texas law in *Texas* v. *United States*[4] in 1966.

Smith v. *Allwright*
U.S. Supreme Court case that overturned the white primary.

poll tax
A tax paid for registering to vote (this tax no longer exists).

Voting Rights Act of 1965
National act protecting minorities from discrimination in the voting or the registration process.

☐ Federal Court Intervention

After the poll tax decision, federal courts became more active in regulating state voting requirements. In a series of rulings, these courts struck down provisions requiring annual registration and a year of residence in Texas before a person could vote. As the Texas Mosaic on Barbara Jordan shows, the impact was almost immediate. Federal courts also rejected a provision of the Texas constitution allowing only property owners to vote on bond issues.

☐ The Voting Rights Act

The **Voting Rights Act (VRA) of 1965** had a significant impact on minority voter turnout. Although not fully extended to Texas until its renewal in 1975, the act protects minorities from discrimination in the registration or voting process. Additionally, it requires all affected states and municipalities to submit redistricting plans to either the U.S. Justice Department or a federal court for approval. This provision of the VRA weakened the ability of the state to engage in racial gerrymandering—the process of drawing district lines to dilute minority voting strength. As a result, the number of minority officeholders in Texas has increased dramatically. Minority political power has increased as well.

Three African American Republicans held statewide positions after the 2012 elections, but that number dropped to one in 2013 after Railroad Commissioner

---

Texas ★ Mosaic

Increasing Diversity in Elective Politics:
Barbara Jordan

One thing is clear to me: We, as human beings, must be willing to accept people who are different from ourselves.
—Barbara Jordan

"**F**irst" might not have been Barbara Jordan's last name, but it could have been. The adjective followed her surname in so many instances that the words tended to appear in tandem.

Born in 1936 to a working-class family in Houston's Fifth Ward, Jordan refused to settle for a "second-class" life. After attending segregated public schools and a segregated state university—Texas Southern—she obtained her law degree from Boston University. She returned to Houston in 1960, opening a law office and working in Lyndon Johnson's presidential campaign. Among her duties in the Johnson campaign was helping register African American voters. She would continue with these efforts after that campaign was finished. In 1962, and again in 1964, she ran unsuccessfully for the Texas Senate, as the odds were stacked too heavily against her. Black voter registration was still low, and Texas House and Senate districts were gerrymandered in such a way as to splinter and dilute the minority vote. By 1966, however, federal court intervention, as well as voter registration efforts by Jordan and others like her, had sufficiently leveled the playing field. Jordan became the first African American elected to the

Texas senate since 1883. Reelected in 1968, she would become president pro tempore of the state senate and served as "governor-for-the-day," an honor that accompanies the office.

In 1972, Jordan became the first African American woman from the South elected to the U.S. Congress. Two years later, she came to national prominence for her eloquent, hard-hitting questioning during the Watergate hearings, which helped end the Nixon administration. Coupled with her distinctive voice, Jordan became a political star and was chosen to deliver the keynote speech at the 1976 Democratic National Convention. She was the first woman to deliver the keynote address.

After three terms in Congress, Jordan returned to her home state and took a professorship at the LBJ School of Public Affairs at the University of Texas. She would later serve as an ethics adviser to Governor Ann Richards. She delivered a second Democratic National Convention keynote address in 1992; the Democrats were 2–0 in presidential elections following keynote speeches by Jordan. She passed away in 1996.

1. **How have expanded minority voting rights affected Texas?**

2. **Why was federal intervention integral to expanding voting rights in Texas?**

Michael Williams ran unsuccessfully for Congress and state Supreme Court Justice Dale Wainwright resigned to go into private practice. With the election of Ted Cruz to the U.S. Senate in 2012, Texas had three Latino statewide officials. Furthermore, it was minority Democrats who helped tip the balance toward Republican Tom Craddick in the race for Speaker of the house in both 2003 and 2007, and, to a lesser extent, Joe Straus in 2009 and 2011.

Voting in Texas: Qualifications and Registration

3.2 Explain voter registration requirements in Texas.

In order to vote in Texas today, a person must be at least 18 years old by Election Day, a U.S. citizen, and a Texas resident, as indicated in the Texas Constitution box. (A person can apply at age 17, 10 months.) The prospective voter must be a resident of his county 30 days prior to the election and must register to vote 30 days in advance as well. Convicted felons are not allowed to vote until after their sentences, including probation and parole, are completed.

Registration

Registering to vote in Texas is simple. You only need to fill out a postcard-size form. Additionally, a voter can register a spouse, parent, or child, provided that the second person meets voting qualifications. In Texas, registration is permanent. As long as a person maintains the same address, registration will be automatically renewed. If you move, you need to reregister. Furthermore, it is not necessary to have your registration card in order to vote. If you have misplaced your card, simply produce another form of identification, such as a driver's license. If you never received a card, you may be asked to sign a sworn affidavit confirming that you did properly register.

The Texas Constitution

A Closer Look

The Texas constitution grants its citizens near universal suffrage:

Article VI. Suffrage

Sec. 1. Classes of Persons Not Allowed to Vote.

a. The following classes of persons shall not be allowed to vote in this State:
   1. persons under 18 years of age;
   2. persons who have been determined mentally incompetent by a court, subject to such exceptions as the Legislature may make; and
   3. persons convicted of any felony, subject to such exceptions as the Legislature may make.
b. The legislature shall enact laws to exclude from the right of suffrage persons who have been convicted of bribery, perjury, forgery, or other high crimes.

1. Are the restrictions on voting rights reasonable?

2. How have liberalized election laws impacted Texas politics?

turnout
Percentage of registered voters who cast ballots.

Under the "motor voter" law passed by the U.S. Congress, a person can also register to vote when applying for a driver's license without even filling out a form. The law requires that a person be allowed to register to vote when he or she applies for a driver's licenses, public assistance, or other public services. By simply affirming they wish to register, citizens are added to the registration rolls. In the first month the process was in effect, Texas added 80,000 new potential voters.[5] One criticism of the law was that legally unqualified voters, such as noncitizens, may be registered in error simply by answering yes to the registration question. In response, Texas became one of the first states to require agencies that register voters to determine their eligibility using records at their disposal.

Turnout in Texas

3.3 Analyze causes of low voter turnout in Texas.

T he irony of **turnout** in the United States is that, despite the long fight for the right, relatively few people vote, especially in comparison to other Western democracies. Descendants of the groups that fought the hardest and longest to secure the right to vote are among the least likely to turn out. Additionally, many eligible citizens do not register. Because these people are not counted in traditional turnout percentages, actual voter participation is even lower than it appears.

The greatest single factor in determining turnout is level of education. In fact, if education and income levels are controlled, minorities and whites vote at roughly the same rate. The more educated a person is, the more likely he or she is to vote. Nonetheless, there is a correlation between race and turnout. Anglos are more likely to vote than minorities. In the 1998 Texas governor's race, 72 percent of the voters were white. African Americans comprised 10 percent of the voters, slightly less than their percentage of the state's population. Hispanics accounted for just 16 percent of voters. In 2002, the percentage of Hispanic voters increased to 17 percent. In contrast, African American voters dropped to 7 percent and white voters to 71 percent. In 2010, as noted in Figure 3.1, non-Hispanic whites accounted for 67 percent of voters, Hispanics 18 percent, Africans Americans 13 percent, and Asian Americans 2 percent. (Because no comprehensive exit polling was done in Texas in 2012, we don't have accurate demographic turnout numbers for 2012.)

A huge factor, second only to level of education, is family tradition. Citizens from families that support the idea that voting is a civic duty are much more likely to turn out than those from a nonvoting family. If your parents vote, you will probably turn into a voter, even if you aren't one now. Voters are also likely to be older and wealthier than nonvoters.

Another component of turnout is the type of election. Presidential elections, the most prominent, draw the most media attention and the highest turnout. State elections, such as the governor's race, are next. Local elections attract low turnout, usually bringing out less than 10 percent of registered voters. School board races routinely draw even fewer voters.

Voter turnout numbers in Texas have varied in recent years. In 1986, only 47.2 percent of registered voters cast a ballot in the governor's race. By 1990, turnout increased to 50.5 percent. In 1994, it edged up to 50.8 percent. The number of ballots cast increased from 3,441,460 in 1986 to 3,892,746 in 1990 and 4,392,580 in 1994. In 2010, 38 percent of voters turned out, which translated to 4,979,890 ballots.[6]

Texas had about 9 million registered voters in 1994 and has a little over 13.7 million today. These numbers show not only that not only the percentage of registered voters has increased, but also the number of registered voters. Prior to 1994,

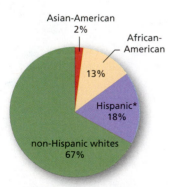

*Hispanic turnout was well below its share of the population.

FIGURE 3.1 Texas Voter Turnout, 2010.

A slow primary election day at precinct 97 in Corpus. Election Judge Carlos Valdez looks on as Pompeyo Valdez casts his ballot. Late in the afternoon, this voter was only the thirteenth to cast his ballot at this location.

less than two-thirds of voting-age Texans were registered to vote. From the mid-1990s forward, registration has hovered close to 80 percent of the voting-age population. At least part of this increase was due to relaxed registration laws and an intense effort by the last several secretaries of state to enlarge voting rolls. The motor voter law also had an effect, although many of those registered under the act never intended to vote. When comparing turnout before and after the act, raw numbers provide a better comparison than percentages.

The last two elections of the 1990s reversed that trend, however, as numbers dropped, both in terms of total number of voters and percentage of registered voters turning out. In the 1996 general election for president, only 5,611,644 voters cast ballots. This equals 53.2 percent of registered voters. In the 1998 governor's race, turnout was 3,738,078, or 32.4 percent. Much of the downtrend might be attributable to the fact that the 1996 and 1998 races were seen as noncompetitive. Although Bob Dole carried Texas in 1996, it was widely believed that Bill Clinton would win reelection. George W. Bush was so clearly ahead in the 1998 governor's race that the contest was considered over by early summer. Only 52 percent of those registered voted in 2000. Again, the presidential race wasn't competitive because Bush was heavily favored in his home state. In the 2002 governor's race, only 36 percent of voters showed up at the polls. Like good football games, highly competitive races draw more interest than dull blowouts. In 2004, turnout was back up to 57 percent. Just over one-third of registered voters participated in 2006. In 2008, 59.5 percent of eligible voters cast ballots.[7] In the 2010 midterm election, just under 5 million voters produced a 37.5 percent turnout. In 2012, almost 8 million Texans, or 58.4 percent of those registered, voted.

disenfranchised
Persons who cannot vote, or who
believe their votes don't count.

☐ Who Turns Out

Who turns out has a huge impact on who is elected. In 1994, 88 percent of African
Americans and 71 percent of Hispanics who turned out voted for Ann Richards for
governor, yet together these ethnic groups made up only 22 percent of voters. If Hispanics and African Americans had voted in a percentage equal to their share of the
population, and if their margins of support for Richards had held, she would have been
reelected by about eight percentage points. This is almost identical to the margin by
which she lost.

Lower turnout in minority communities is a product of several factors. First, persons from disadvantaged socioeconomic groups often have had fewer positive interac-
tions with government than middle- or upper-class voters. This can lead to distrust
of government in general, causing citizens to question why they should bother voting.
Such people often feel **disenfranchised**, believing their votes either do not matter,
since there is little concrete connection to their day-to-day lives, or do not count, due
to perceived "corruption" within the system.

Second, family tradition has an impact on voter participation. A person who
grows up in an environment in which voting is important is more likely to participate.
In Texas, there has been a history of barriers placed between minorities and the voting booth. In addition to governmental blocks, minorities faced barriers from society
at large. Violence and intimidation were used to discourage minority voting. In south
Texas, many Hispanic voters faced the loss of a job if they cast a ballot. If past generations were prohibited from participating, it is more difficult to establish a family
tradition that views voting as a civic duty.

Third, especially within the Hispanic community, language can be a barrier to
participation. Even though ballots and registration cards are bilingual—trilingual in
Harris County, which now prints ballots in Vietnamese as well—it is more difficult
for non-English-speaking citizens to obtain information on registration, voting, issues, and candidates. Nonetheless, the efforts of the Southwest Voters Education and
Registration Project to encourage Hispanics to participate have resulted in significant
increases in registration and voting within the Latino community. More Hispanics
now serve in elected office than at any time in the state's history.

Turnout among young people is historically low. Many consider government issues too far removed from their everyday existence to be important. More register
and vote as they become older and more aware of the issues. However, government
policies—from setting college tuition rates to speed limits, and from the drinking age
to student loan programs—have a profound impact on young people. If anyone wants
to influence the future, there is no better way to start than by registering, paying attention to the political world, and voting.

States with a traditionalistic political culture tend to have lower-than-average
turnout. In addition, one-party states tend to have lower turnout because many believe their votes won't matter. While Texas no longer falls under the one-party state
classification, years of Democratic domination still negatively affect turnout because
voting is a learned trait and parents who don't value the political process tend to
produce children who don't vote. Besides, Republicans now dominate statewide politics much as the Democrats dominated a generation ago. Finally, low voter turnout
can point to general voter satisfaction. When citizens are angry about something,
they tend to let their voices be heard. But when things are going well, some citizens
become apathetic about exercising their political rights. This may partially account
for low turnout in the late 1990s and 2000, and, conversely, higher turnout in 2008
and 2010.

☐ Texas Factors in Registration and Turnout

A major factor that affects turnout is the large number of elections in Texas. During
a single year, a citizen may be asked to vote in a party primary, a party primary runoff, a city election, a city election runoff, a local bond election, a local recall election,

a tax rollback election, a special election, a special election runoff, and a general election. Even when cities, school boards, and junior college districts hold their elections on the same day, a voter might be asked to visit three different polling places in order to participate in all three elections. Texas voters can develop **election burnout**, and only the most dedicated citizens vote every time they have the opportunity to cast a ballot.

The **long ballot** that confronts Texas voters also has a detrimental effect on turnout. In large urban counties, a voter might be asked to select the best person for 30 or more different judicial positions, from the Texas supreme court to justice of the peace. It is unlikely that the average Texan is familiar with more than one or two of the judicial candidates. In addition, voters are asked to fill several positions whose responsibilities are misunderstood. For instance, the Texas Railroad Commission has little to do with railroads. Few Texans can identify the duties of the comptroller or land commissioner, yet these offices appear on the ballot. Selecting the best person to fill the positions becomes a near impossibility under the circumstances. Instead of picking the wrong candidate, some choose not to vote at all. Many voters don't know that they are not required to vote for every office in order to have a valid ballot. They can vote for only one candidate, or just those candidates with whom they are familiar.

Another aspect of Texas law that discouraged voter registration was that, prior to 1992, jury duty summons lists were compiled from voter registration rolls. Many people chose not to register because they did not want to be called for jury duty. Although jury selection lists now comprise virtually all adult citizens, many people still believe that registering to vote is, in essence, registering for jury duty. Even those aware of the change have not necessarily registered.

Some reforms would make participation easier. Several states allow Election Day registration. A person may decide to participate at the last minute, instead of having to register 30 days prior to the election. Other states have experimented with expanded voting by mail. In Texas and most other states, a person who is out of the state or disabled can vote by mail. Primary and general elections in Oregon and Washington are carried out exclusively through the mail. Many other states have liberalized their voting rules, allowing voters to cast ballots by mail merely by asking.

Turnout would be higher, it is argued, if all a voter had to do was pick up a ballot from the mailbox, fill it out at his or her convenience, and return it through the mail. Likewise, the prevalence of the Internet offers an opportunity to create easier access to the ballot.

Both Election Day registration and alternative ballots have their critics. In each case, opportunity for fraud exists. A 30-day registration window allows election officials to check records for fraud. States that use same-day registration, however, have not reported significant problems. With a mail-in or Internet ballot, it would be easy for "helpful" campaign workers to give illegal voting assistance. This has already occurred in nursing homes in this state, where some overenthusiastic campaign workers have "saved" elderly Texans trouble by filling out the ballots for them. In fact, the elimination of such fraud is another suggested reform. Giving significant prison time to those who engage in such activity, it is argued, would increase the perception that the vote is a sacred, protected right that is not easily manipulated. In 2011, the legislature passed the voter ID bill, which required photo identification to cast a ballot. Implementation of the law was blocked by the U.S. Department of Justice under the Voting Rights Act, and the law was subsequently struck down by the U.S. Court of Appeals for the District of Columbia. Texas promised to appeal to the U.S. Supreme Court.

Opponents of lenient registration and voting laws believe there is a cost to making it too easy to vote: Uninformed citizens might be more likely to cast ballots. As long as registration and voting require some affirmative act, the process tends to weed out the least prepared voters. This makes a difference if you believe that an informed public makes better choices than an uninformed one.

election burnout
Occurs when citizens believe there are too many elections, and thus, fail to vote.

long ballot
A system under which many officials are up for election at the same time.

primary election
The process through which major parties choose their nominees for the general election.

EARLY VOTING One reform enacted in Texas that has increased turnout is the state's no excuse early voting policy. In many states, voters can only vote absentee—or early—if they are going to be out of town on Election Day. In Texas, however, voters can vote early without such a restriction. For primary and general elections, the period for early voting begins 15 to 17 days—and ends 4 days—prior to the election. The county clerk or elections administrator determines starting dates.

Voters can go to any of a number of designated locations across the county and cast their ballots. Early voting is popular in Texas. In 2008, early voters comprised 42 percent of total voters. In 2010, an astounding 53 percent of those who cast a vote for governor in Texas voted early. By 2012, early voting accounted for 63 percent of the total vote.[8] Such numbers influence campaigns because consultants realize the importance of getting the candidate's message out early. It doesn't help to connect with voters after they have cast their ballots.[9] This has added to the expense of running an election, both for the state and the campaign, as instead of one Election Day, there are a whole string of them. It may be an incremental cost for the state, but it carries a significant and strategic cost for the campaign. Most election contests are decided before Election Day, something that savvy campaign managers understand. A candidate needs to build momentum ahead of the opening of early voting and maintain it through the entire period. This costs money for mailings, phone banks, robo-calls, and canvassing. Since early voting records are public record (just the fact that you voted, not who you voted for), more sophisticated campaigns can be expected to track individual voting trends and focus increasingly on dependable voters who have not yet cast ballots as the traditional Election Day nears.

Several other states have followed Texas's lead and enacted more lenient early voting laws. Although turnout has generally increased in states with looser rules, some critics have questioned whether there is a social cost to extended voting. They ponder whether Election Day as a civic institution loses some of its meaning when we, as a nation, don't actually cast our ballots on the same day.

Types of Elections

3.4 Differentiate among primary, general, and special elections.

☐ Primary Election

Texas holds partisan elections for all state offices from governor to constable. Before the Democrat and Republican can run against each other in a general election, the parties must determine their nominees for each office. These nominees are chosen through the **primary election**. The direct primary allows all registered voters to help select the nominees for the party of their choice.

In Texas voters do not register as Democrats or Republicans. Rather, official party affiliation is not determined until the day of the primary election. In this sense, the Texas system is open. A person can be standing in line to vote in the Democratic primary, change his or her mind, and go to the Republican primary. A citizen voting in one primary may not, however, vote in the other party's primary—it's against the law. Furthermore, a person who votes in one party's primary cannot cross over and vote in the other party's runoff, if one is necessary. In this very limited way, from the primary election date until the runoff several weeks later, a voter is bound by party affiliation. A quirk in state election law, however, allows a citizen who did not vote in either primary to cast a ballot in the runoff of his or her choice.

In Texas, primary elections are held on the first Tuesday of March. (The 2012 primary was an aberration, as it was delayed until late May amidst legal challenges to the state's redistricting map.) This was intended to coincide with the Super

Tuesday primary on which several predominantly Southern states held their presidential primaries, but Texas kept the date even as several other states moved theirs up. Some states separate the presidential vote from their other elections, holding the primary for state offices closer to the general election in November. Texas, however, in order to avoid expenses incurred by scheduling two elections, holds all primary elections in March, even in nonpresidential years. To win a primary election, a person must receive the majority of the votes cast. If no one receives more than 50 percent, a runoff election is held between the top two vote-getters for that particular office. The party's nominee will be the person who wins the runoff. With two active, strong political parties, some runoffs are inevitable. So many candidates file for some offices in the primaries that it is unlikely that any person will receive a majority.

Historically, runoffs were held five weeks after the primary. Today, because of the federal 2010 Military and Oversees Voters and Empowerment Act, ballots have to be provided to Americans abroad at least 45 days prior to the election. If one figured in time for potential recounts, election validation, and ballot printing, the minimum separation between the primary and the runoff would be about nine weeks, the gap between the delayed 2012 primary and its runoff. That gap had a profound impact on the outcome of the Republican race for U. S, Senate, allowing Ted Cruz to gain name recognition and overcome the better funded campaign of establishment candidate David Dewhurst. The Cruz campaign might provide a blueprint for future insurgent campaigns.

Ted Cruz thanks his wife, Heidi, as he wins the Republican nomination for U.S. Senate in the 2012 primary. The candidate ran an impressive campaign, taking advantage of the extended period between the primary election and the runoffs to make up his primary day deficit and pummel his better known opponent. Cruz would cruise to general election victory in November.

3.1

general election
The process through which office-holders are elected from among party nominees.

3.2

plurality
Exists when a candidate has more votes than any other candidate, even if the total is less than 50 percent.

3.3

3.4

gubernatorial election
The election for governor and other executive offices.

3.5

Straight ticket
selection at the top of the ballot that allows a voter to pick every candidate of a chosen party.

This extended period between the primary and runoff may well help underfunded candidates who can manage to force a runoff. With many races and other candidates out of the picture, underdog candidates may draw more media attention and obtain financial support that was not available until they made it into the final round. A nine-week gap would not only give the unknown candidate more time to make a name, but would also give the established candidates' supporters longer to forget. Primary turnout, in general, is relatively low; runoff turnout is even lower. The Cruz runoff numbers may not be our best predictor here, as voters—because of Republican domination—knew they were choosing the next U.S. senator. In low-profile campaigns, lower-level office-holders may find it difficult to get their supporters to return. Elections could turn on the basis of enthusiasm for a candidate from among his or her supporters.

Not all parties in Texas are required to hold primaries. Minor parties, such as the Libertarian Party, have not proven strong enough to warrant the expense of statewide elections. Unless its candidate received at least 20 percent of the vote in the last governor's race, a party is entitled to select its candidates through its county, district, and state convention.

☐ General Election

General elections determine who will hold office. The winners of the primaries, as well as the nominees of minor parties, have their names placed on the general election ballot. It is very difficult for a third party to qualify for ballot access in Texas, particularly in statewide elections. Unless one of your candidates received at least 5 percent of the vote in the last general election, you need the signature of almost 50,000 citizens (1 percent of the last general election total for that office) who did not vote in either the Republican or Democrat primary. And you have only 30 days after the primary to collect your signatures. For all practical purposes, this means that in Texas, only the Republicans, the Democrats, and the Libertarians have a permanent spot on the ballot. The Green Party used the petition method to qualify for the 2010 ballot, where they earned a spot for 2012.

General elections require a **plurality** of the votes, not necessarily a majority, to win. Plurality simply means more votes than any other candidate. In the 2006 governor's race, for example, Rick Perry received only 39 percent of the vote, while Democrat Chris Bell received 30 percent. In an unusual year by any measure, two popular figures, one political and one cultural, managed the difficult task of getting on the ballot as independents. Cultural icon "Kinky" Friedman received over 12 percent, while former Republican Comptroller Carole Keeton Strayhorn garnered 18 percent. Despite receiving less than 40 percent of the vote, Perry held onto office without a runoff.

Gubernatorial elections, in which the governor and other executive officials are picked, are held during even-numbered years between presidential elections. The off-year elections mean that voters pay more attention to these statewide executive races. If they were to be held during presidential years, they would receive less media coverage due to the intense focus on national politics. Also, turnout tends to be lower in nonpresidential years, meaning that more dedicated voters show up for gubernatorial elections. This makes a party's ability to turn out its voters a key factor in winning. Parties tend to concentrate on those voters who participated in their primary as they attempt to get out the vote. They reason that primary voters are both loyal to the party and more likely to turn out than the average citizen.

The winning party in the governor's race is listed first on the ballot in elections for the following four years. While this might not be significant at the top of the ballot, it can have an influence on lower-level races. When voters don't recognize either name, they are more likely to vote for the first one on the list.

In Texas, the general election ballot allows voters to choose a **straight ticket** option, selecting a party designation at the top that fills in the remainder of the ticket with their party's nominees. A surprisingly—some would say alarmingly—large number of Texans chose that option in 2012. In Harris County, the state's largest, fully 68 percent of voters cast straight-ticket ballots. In a county that had a virtual dead heat in each of the top of the ticket races, the split among straight-ticket voters was almost even as well. In Tarrant County, the most solidly Republican of the state's large counties, 64 percent cast straight-party ballots, again almost perfectly mirroring the total votes in the top of the ticket races. In more Democratic Bexar County, 64 percent voted a straight ticket, with these voters skewing slightly more Democratic than county voters as a whole. In Travis County, the most Democratic large county in the state, only 55 percent of voters chose the straight-ticket option, Travis County straight-ticket voters were slightly more Democratic than county voters as a whole.

A voter can pick "Democratic Party" at the top of the ticket and then choose Republicans in individual races, overriding their original choices in those races only. We have no way of knowing with certainty how many voters pick straight party at the top, then stray from that in their final selection, but an examination of down-ballot races, those lower on the ballot that the high profile races at the top, gives us little reason to believe that cross voting is common among initial straight-ticket selectors. Conversely, we don't know how many people fail to mark the straight-ballot designation, yet go on to vote for candidates of only one party.

This variable has different impacts depending on which political division we are considering. Certainly, in statewide races, it is an advantage to Republicans. But in Bexar and Travis counties, it is an advantage to Democrats in countywide races. In Tarrant, it is an advantage to Republicans. Harris County is so evenly divided that it didn't have a significant impact in 2012, while straight ticket voting provides a sizable advantage to Democrats in Dallas County.

☐ Special Election

Special elections are held to fill vacancies, ratify state constitutional amendments, or approve local bond issues. Special elections to fill vacancies are "nonpartisan," require a majority to win, and usually occur outside of the traditional March and November dates.

The best-known special election over the last 30 years was held to fill the U.S. Senate seat vacated when former Senator Lloyd Bentsen resigned to become President Bill Clinton's treasury secretary in 1993. Former Governor Ann Richards appointed fellow Democrat Bob Krueger to fill the position until a special election could be held. Krueger joined a field of 23 other candidates that included prominent Texas politicians such as Congressmen Jack Fields and Joe Barton, business leader (and future Dallas Federal Reserve President) Richard Fisher, and state Treasurer Kay Bailey Hutchison. A number of political unknowns were on the ballot as well. With so many candidates, it was not a surprise that no one received a majority of the votes during the initial round of balloting. Hutchison and Krueger emerged from the pack and made it into the runoff. Hutchison easily won the runoff, garnering two-thirds of the votes.

Referring to special elections as nonpartisan is somewhat misleading. In 1993, everyone interested in the political process knew that Hutchison, Fields, and Barton were Republicans and that former state Attorney General Jim Mattox, Fisher, and Krueger were Democrats. All appealed to their traditional party bases as they ran for election. The race was nonpartisan in the sense that candidates did not have to go through the primary process in order to appear on the ballot.

Campaigning

3.5   Explain the obstacles to running a campaign in Texas.

ampaigning for office in Texas can be a daunting undertaking. While many races for local offices, such as city council or school board, still allow for a great deal of person-to-person contact, especially in small towns and cities, the process of seeking elective office in the state's large metropolitan

special election
An election held to fill a vacancy, ratify a state constitutional amendment, or approve a local bond issue.

3.1

3.2

3.3

3.4

3.5

areas is becoming increasingly distant from the people and is taking a significant commitment of time and resources.

This problem of distance between candidates and voters is even more acute when the political race is regional or statewide. Many state senate districts, especially in west Texas, sprawl over huge areas encompassing many counties. Two examples will suffice to make our point. Under the court-ordered interim redistricting plan approved for the 2012 elections, Senate District 19 extends from the southern and eastern edges of Bexar County (San Antonio) to Eagle Pass on the Rio Grande River and westward to the Big Bend and a quartet of counties lying west of the Pecos River. The total linear distance across the district is roughly 350 miles. Similarly, Senate District 31 encompasses almost the entire Texas Panhandle, runs along the entire length of Texas's north-to-south border with New Mexico, and includes both Midland and Odessa. From north to south, the district stretches over 300 miles and includes 37 of the 254 counties in Texas within its boundaries.

While urban Senate districts are not as geographically far-flung as those in the rural areas of Texas, campaigning in them can be as expensive, if not more so. It is not unusual for a closely contested race for the Texas Senate to require a candidate to spend between a million and two million dollars (and even such astronomical sums do not necessarily guarantee victory). Even a race for a seat in the Texas house (which usually involves an even more circumscribed geographic area) can be startlingly expensive. Candidates for such seats in Houston, Dallas–Fort Worth, or San Antonio can easily spend $500,000 or more, and even incumbents without opponents may spend as much as $250,000 in an election. In a state with virtually no limits on campaign contributions, raising money is imperative. Take a look at the differences between U.S. and Texas campaign laws in the Inside the Federalist System box.

After the 2012 general election, a *Texas Tribune* reporter performed an interesting analysis of campaign spending, He tracked the cost per general election vote by comparing a campaign's total disbursement of funds to votes received in the general election. The *Tribune*'s numbers were less than the actual expenditure per vote, because they did not include spending during the last eight days before the general election. Some of the expenditures per vote were misleading as well, because many of the heavy spenders had dropped most of their money into highly competitive primary races, facing only token opposition in the general election. Still, the numbers provide an interesting frame of reference.

At the top of the disbursement per vote list was Speaker of the House Joe Straus, who spent just under $64 per vote—a total of over $3 million[10]—despite having only token opposition in both the primary and the general election. How do you spend that much money without real opponents? A significant amount was contributed to Republican causes, but most of it was spent on the expenses of being Speaker. There is significant travel—to bolster Republican candidates—and entertainment expenses, because the office hosts a bunch of meetings and conferences. All of these expenses can be covered through campaign funding, but very little of that money was spent on retail campaigning.

Much more instructive are the numbers on Senate District 10, where Democratic incumbent Wendy Davis narrowly retained her seat against Republican challenger Mark Shelton, even though the district had slight Republican leanings. It was the only competitive senate race in the state. Davis spent over $24 per vote, or a total of $3.6 million. Shelton spent just under $8 per vote, a total of $1.1 million,[11] which included some primary spending in a race where Shelton was an overwhelming favorite.

In House District 43, Republican Jose Lozano spent over $31 a vote, or almost three-quarters of a million dollars, which is more than what most successful senate candidates spent, although senate seats have roughly five times as many voters. His opponent, Democrat Yvonne Toureilles Gonzales, spent less than $5 per vote, or about $110,000. Lozano eked out a narrow victory. In House District 144, an open seat, Republican David Pineda spent $20 a vote, or about $220,000, in a losing effort against Democrat Mary Anne Perez, who spent a little over $11 a vote, or about $140,000.[12]

In two of the closest house races, spending made a big difference, In District 105, Republican incumbent Linda Harper-Brown spent over $19 per vote—more than $420,000—to win by less than 2 percent over Democrat Rosemary Robbins,

A phone bank worker reacts after securing another vote for Barack Obama during the 2008 primary. Campaign work comes in many forms, from phone calls to emails to walking a precinct to drum up support.

who spent just over $3 per vote, or about $65,000. In District 107, Republican incumbent Kenneth Sheets spent almost $17 per vote to defeat Robert Miklos, who spent over $6 per vote. Sheets was able to build a sizable lead in early voting with his $430,000, while Miklos, who spent a bit over $150,000,[13] won a slim majority of Election Day ballots.

Getting the least bang for her buck was Republican House District 34 incumbent Connie Scott, who spent $19 per vote—a total of more than $360,000—yet received less than 43 percent of the vote. Her opponent, Abel Herrero, spent over $8 per vote, a total of over $210,000.[14]

Of note were expenditures by successful Republican Railroad Commission candidates Christi Craddick and Barry Smitherman. They spent about $2.5 million and $3 million, respectively, on races that did not draw a Democratic candidate, but each had to make it through both a Republican primary and runoff before the general election.

Republican judges on the statewide Court of Criminal Appeals and justices on the state supreme court spent virtually nothing on their races. Judge Elsa Alcala, who drew only third-party opposition, spent only a penny per vote. Judge Barbara Hervey spent less than that. Presiding Judge Sharon Keller also spent less than a penny a vote even though she drew a Democratic opponent, but that opponent only put $85,000 into the statewide race.

Races for statewide offices, such as U.S. senator, governor, and other executive positions, or the state's highest appellate courts require candidates to roam the length and breadth of the state, often traveling farther in a single day than the distance from Texarkana to Chicago or from El Paso to San Diego. In light of these geographically imposed constraints, campaigning in Texas has become increasingly based on the electronic media, targeted mass mailings, and, more recently, the Internet. Television and radio have become the major avenues for candidates to reach voters. But the price for gaining access to the airwaves is steep, especially in the major metropolitan areas and especially if you want to ensure that your ad makes it onto the airwaves. Media outlets are required to offer advertising time to political candidates at what is referred to as the lowest unit rate (LUR). This is, as the name implies, a relatively economical rate. However, time purchased at this rate is subject to preemption. So, to ensure that their ads do appear at the most desirable times, most candidates purchase time at a higher, nonpreemptable rate, especially during the final weeks of a campaign. For example, the cost of a half-minute prime-time political advertising spot on KTVT Channel 11, the CBS affiliate in the Fort Worth–Dallas metropolitan area, ranges from $4,000 to $15,000, depending on the ratings of the program during which the ad appears. But there's more involved than the cost of a single ad.

Political consultants know that in a world where voters are increasingly inundated with a veritable avalanche of electronic blandishments (such as the very real possibility of potential voters having hundreds of cable or satellite TV channels from which to choose), a candidate's message must be repeated many times in order to penetrate the mind of those voters. Running *one* 30-second political ad four times daily Monday through Friday on *one* major TV affiliate in *one* major media market in Texas could cost a candidate anywhere from $300,000 to $500,000. Multiply that, then, by the number of other major market buys necessary to mount a statewide campaign and it's no surprise that media expenses are the largest item in the campaign budgets of most high-profile candidates.

As media costs have risen, many candidates have begun to rely more on targeted mass mailings. Of course, campaign "junk mail" has been a part of American politics almost as long as there has been a postal service, and you've probably used such material to line the birdcage or train the puppy. Today, though, mass mailing has become incredibly sophisticated, targeting specific voting blocs with messages designed to energize and mobilize.

Instead of mailing one generic campaign flier to all voters, candidates produce numerous tracts focusing on specialized topics or issues and send them to specific groups. They usually make use of computer-generated mailing lists compiled and marketed for just such purposes.

Thus, a member of the National Rifle Association will receive a pamphlet that extols the candidate's stalwart support of gun ownership (complete with a photograph of said candidate blasting away at some sort of winged game fowl), while a member of the Sierra Club will open a mail-out that proclaims that same candidate's undying devotion to sound ecological principles (complete with a photograph of said candidate petting a spotted owl).

Of course, the more groups a candidate tries to reach, the greater the costs of a campaign. Well-financed campaign phone banks have begun using the aforementioned tactics developed for mass mail-outs. For example, you might receive a call telling how Representative Righteous shares your concerns about the need to reintroduce public prayer in our schools. These and other cost-intensive strategies have greatly increased the price of getting elected and have served to narrow the field of candidates who can realistically undertake such high-dollar campaigns. A perfect example of such electoral costs can be seen in the race for Texas governor in 2002, which broke all previous spending records for statewide races in Texas. Fueled by a massive infusion of his own money, Democrat Tony Sanchez exceeded Republican Rick Perry in spending, and both candidates combined to lay out about $100 million. Many students of Texas politics had scoffed at the idea of a $60 million gubernatorial campaign in Texas, but

Inside the Federalist System

State and Federal Campaign Contribution Limits

A stark difference between the federal and state law is demonstrated through the different approaches to campaign finance law. This chart shows limits on contributions to people running for U.S. Congress:

Contribution Limits 2011–2012

	Contribution Limits for 2011–2012 To each candidate or candidate committee per election	To national party committee per calendar year	To state, district & local party committee per calendar year	To any other political committee per calendar year[1]	Special Limits
Individual may give	$2,500*	$30,800*	$10,000 (combined limit)	$5,000	$117,000* overall biennial limit: $46,200* to all candidates $70,800* to all PACs and parties[2]
National Party Committee may give	$5,000	No limit	No limit	$5,000	$43,100* to Senate candidate per campaign[3]
State, District & Local Party Committee may give	$5,000 (combined limit)	No limit	No limit	$5,000 (combined limit)	No limit
PAC (multicandidate)[4] may give	$5,000	$15,000	$5,000 (combined limit)	$5,000	No limit
PAC (not multicandidate) may give	$2,500*	$30,800*	$10,000 (combined limit)	$5,000	No limit
Authorized Campaign Committee may give	$2,0005	No limit	No limit	$5,000	No limit

(Source: http://www.fec.gov.)

Texas, on the other hand, has no practical limits. Corporations and labor unions may not contribute directly to candidates, but their political action committees can. The only contribution limits are in judicial races. Other candidates can accept unlimited contributions as long as they properly disclose their source.

Although the initial reaction of many is that Texas should have contribution limits similar to those at the national level and in other states, there are factors that favor the Texas model. Meaningful limits on campaign spending are difficult to enact without running afoul of the First Amendment to the U.S. Constitution. Moreover, it often seems that new federal campaign finance law becomes little more than full employment laws for lawyers and accountants. In other words, even as members of Congress pass laws aimed at closing campaign loopholes, their campaign teams are figuring out ways to get around the laws. As such, at the federal level, with all of the Super PACs and other outside campaign organizations, it is difficult to tell exactly who is contributing what money to which candidate. In Texas, because there is no need limit on contributions, there is no reason to hide the source of funding. You can find where all of a candidate's money came from through a simple search at the Texas Ethics Commission website.

Do unlimited contributions matter from a policy perspective? If we try to give a simple answer, it will almost certainly be wrong, or, at best, incomplete. Certainly, contributors give money to candidates who share their basic views. But that doesn't mean that a contributor can be assured of an elected officials support on a certain issue, especially when many officials receive money from contributors on both sides of many specific issues. You can't please everyone, and it is doubtful that many officials "add up" their contributions before deciding how to vote on a particular bill. To the extent that money influences policy, it probably kills more laws than it passes, but more bills are killed than passed anyway.

1. Should Texas adopt campaign contribution limits similar to the federal government? Why or why not?

2. Is contribution disclosure important? Why or why not?

clearly Sanchez and Perry have taken the race to places where candidates for that office have never been before.

However, hope for those who don't own the Hope Diamond (or a modestly productive gold mine) may lie in the Internet, which many candidates are using as a relatively cost-effective way to get their message(s) to the public. In 2006, virtually every candidate for statewide office maintained slick, user-friendly Web pages loaded with information about the candidates and their campaigns. By 2012, many Texas candidates were using targeted Web advertisements that popped up if you read relevant news articles, with the Cruz U.S. Senate campaign using this most effectively. Of course, such an approach will not reach low- to moderate-income voters who often don't have ready access to computers. But it may help generate voter turnout among younger people who have not been receptive to more traditional campaign strategies, and as more members of our society gain access to the information superhighway, such electronic campaigning will only become more commonplace.

As more people become more comfortable with the Web as a source of political information, the very real possibility exists that candidates who don't necessarily have Ross Perot's billions (or David Dewhurst's millions) may be able to compete and even win in today's electoral arena. Cruz proved that ability.

Along with the increase in the monetary costs of campaigning has come a concomitant rise in the emotional costs of seeking office. A particularly troublesome manifestation of this whole matter has been the tendency of campaign advertising to portray opponents in a negative light, often focusing more on personal traits and alleged character flaws than on a person's ability to govern or legislate. Although nothing is new in American (and especially Texas) politics, this trend seems to have become almost standard operating procedure for many candidates. The reason for this is relatively simple, though rather cynical. It's easier to malign a candidate in 30 seconds or a minute than it is to delve into the intricacies of most of the issues with which a candidate must deal while seeking office. And because many voters cannot or will not take the time to familiarize themselves with these issues, they tend to respond to the candidate who hurls the most eye- and ear-catching accusations against an opponent. Most of us as voters say we deplore the use of such negative tactics, but because history as well as survey research shows us responding to them, most candidates either choose to or are forced to resort to them at one time or another.

Many analysts believe that one reason George W. Bush was able to defeat popular incumbent Ann Richards in 1994 was his use of an essentially positive campaign style as opposed to her more combative approach, which voters may have perceived as negative. In the 1998 elections, the brothers Bush (George W. and Jeb) both ran positive, inclusive types of campaigns and were able to win significant victories, while other candidates with similar resources and similar groups of core supporters ran negative, divisive campaigns and lost. Still, the 2002 election seems to have produced a return to a more attack-oriented style of campaigning, at least in the Lone Star State, and by the 2006 gubernatorial race, mud and an almost eager willingness to sling it had become the order of the day for most of the candidates. Candidates for statewide office didn't hesitate to resort to negative ads in an attempt to paint their opponents as everything from accidental officeholders to big-spending liberals. In 2012, the Dewhurst–Cruz primary battle started out in the gutter and never got out of it. Much the same could be said for the Davis–Shelton state senate race.

Another factor that has an impact on Texas political campaigns is the rather lax campaign contribution laws that adhere in the Lone Star State. As one would expect in a state where the individualistic political culture is such a dominant force, these laws for the most part are predicated on the notion that requiring candidates to publish the contributions that they receive is all the "regulation" that is needed in this part of the political arena. Yet these data are often cursory in the extreme and are characterized by a vagueness as to actual source and specific amount. This makes it quite difficult for a layperson to gain a practical understanding of just how much a particular candidate has received and from whom the candidate has received it.

In the final analysis, money is the engine that sits under the hood of most political campaigns. As campaign costs have risen, candidates must devote more and more time and energy, both before and after an election, to fund-raising. It is not unusual to see a losing candidate spend months seeking funds to pay off a huge campaign debt. Little wonder that more and more citizens who might consider public service are choosing not to enter the political arena or are doing so only reluctantly. Win or lose, it takes a lot of money to play politics in Texas.

Review the Chapter

Listen to Chapter 3

A History of Voting Rights

3.1 Identify past restrictions on voting rights in Texas.

Women didn't receive the right to vote in Texas until 1920. Although African American males obtained constitutional voting rights shortly after the Civil War, most were ineligible to vote by 1900. In the early 20th century, the white primary furthered suppressed meaningful African American participation until the 1940s. The poll tax suppressed turnout among the poor and served as another procedural roadblock to those less educated in registration procedures.

Voting in Texas: Qualifications and Registration

3.2 Explain voter registration requirements in Texas.

To vote in Texas, a person must be at least 18 years of age by Election Day, a U.S. citizen, registered to vote 30 days prior to the election, and a resident of the county in which they registered. Felons are barred from voting until two years after their sentence.

Turnout in Texas

3.3 Analyze causes of low voter turnout in Texas.

Voter turnout is low in Texas for a number of reasons. Historically, Texas suppressed minority turnout, which still impacts voting today. Family tradition is a key factor in turnout.

The state's high dropout rate is a partial answer because turnout rises with level of education. The relative noncompetitiveness of statewide races causes some to wonder "why bother?" The length of the Texas ballot can be intimidating and discourages some from voting.

Types of Elections

3.4 Differentiate among primary, general, and special elections.

The Democratic and Republican parties choose their nominees for office through primary elections. The party nominees meet each other in the general election.

Special elections are used to fill vacancies or to vote on constitutional amendments. Both primary and special elections require a majority to win; general elections require only a plurality.

Campaigning

3.5 Explain the obstacles to running a campaign in Texas.

Campaigns in Texas are expensive. Television, radio, and mass mailings can quickly add up. Targeted ads seek to reach specific segments of the voting population. Many candidates have become proficient at reaching potential voters through the Internet, through ads, e-mail, and social media.

Learn the Terms

Study and **Review** the **Flashcards**

disenfranchised, p. 66
election burnout, p. 67
general election, p. 70
gubernatorial election, p. 70
long ballot, p. 67

plurality, p. 70
poll tax, p. 61
primary election, p. 68
Smith v. *Allwright*, p. 61
special election, p. 71

straight ticket, p. 70
turnout, p. 64
universal suffrage, p. 60
white primary, p. 60
Voting Rights Act of 1965, p. 62

Test Yourself

3.1 Identify past restrictions on voting rights in Texas.

The practice of keeping African Americans from voting in Democratic primaries was called the

 a. grandfather clause.
 b. poll tax.
 c. primary process.
 d. white primary.
 e. literacy test.

3.2 Explain voter registration requirements in Texas.

Prerequisites to voting in Texas include all EXCEPT being

 a. a resident.
 b. at least 18 years old.
 c. born in the United States.
 d. out of prison.
 e. a citizen.

3.3 Analyze causes of low voter turnout in Texas.

Factors in low voter turnout in Texas include all EXCEPT

 a. language barriers.
 b. the emergence of a second major party.
 c. the state's traditionalistic culture.
 d. past discrimination.
 e. the long ballot.

3.4 Differentiate among primary, general, and special elections.

Winning a general election requires

 a. a majority of the vote.
 b. a minority of the vote.
 c. a plurality of the vote.
 d. first winning a special election.
 e. winning a contested primary.

3.5 Explain the obstacles to running a campaign in Texas.

The most important asset in a political campaign is

 a. money.
 b. television ads.
 c. radio spots.
 d. free media.
 e. newspaper endorsements.

Explore Further

Cheek, Kyle, and Anthony Champagne. *Judicial Politics in Texas: Partisanship, Money, and Politics in State Courts*. New York: P. Lang, 2005.

"Money in PoliTex: A Guide to Money in the 2010 Texas Elections." *Texans for Public Justice.* http://info.tpj.org/reports/politex2010/Introduction.html

Ryan Murphy, "Interactive: Cost Per Vote for Texas Candidates for State Office." *The Texas Tribune*, http://www.texastribune.org/library/data/state-general-cost-per-vote/

The Texas Elections Division http://www.sos.state.tx.us/elections/

The Texas Ethics Commission http://www.ethics.state.tx.us/

4

Political Parties in Texas

Within the next six to eight years, I believe that Texas will at least be a purple state, if not a blue state.

—Julian Castro, Democratic Mayor of San Antonio

It will all go out the window if there is not a continued effort on Hispanic outreach.

—Steve Munisteri, State Chair of the Republican Party of Texas
Both speaking immediately after the 2012 election

In a state where incumbents almost always win, especially in state legislative races, the 2013 session brought an unusual number of new faces to Austin. An astounding 44 of 150 house members were new to the legislature. The senate didn't experience nearly that rate of turnover, as most of the handful of new members replaced former senators who had voluntarily retired. Although Democrats did pick up a few more house seats than they held prior to the election, that accounted for

4.1	4.2	4.3	4.4	4.5	4.6	4.7
Explain why political parties exist.	Differentiate between ideological and coalitional parties.	Describe the levels of political party organization in Texas.	Explain the long and successful history of the Democratic Party in Texas.	Explain the Republican Party's recent success in Texas.	Analyze the challenges facing each major party in the 21st century.	Explain the role of partisanship in Texas governance.

Wayne Christian was one of an unusually high number of incumbents to be defeated in 2012. Some Republican members lost to Tea Party affiliated challengers from the right. Christian lost in the Republican primary to a more moderate opponent, who was backed by the party's establishment.

4.1	**political party** A group of people who share common goals and attempt to control government by winning elections.
4.2	
4.3	
4.4	
4.5	
4.6	
4.7	

only a small number of the new house members. Instead, most of the turnover was due to battles in the party primaries, where many incumbents lost to well-organized opposition, or, reading the writing on the wall, voluntarily retired before primary voters had the chance to turn them aside. Some members were sufficiently frustrated by their legislative experience that they chose to retire from public life, while others were so invigorated that they chose to run for the state senate.

How will the turnover affect the operation of government? Such a question is not easy to answer. While a superficial analysis might lead to the conclusion that Tea Party forces had succeeded in purging moderate Republicans, it ignores the races where very conservative Republicans were ousted in the primary by voters who thought 2011 education cuts had been too deep. Conservatives who believed they could stop the reelection of house Speaker Joe Straus were quickly disappointed when, on the first day of the 2013 session, his only opposition withdrew from the field. What is clear after the 2012 election is that there are few swing seats—those that regularly switch back and forth from one party to the other—in either the house or the senate.

Political Parties

| 4.1 | Explain why political parties exist. |

T he two major parties in Texas politics, the Democrats and Republicans, have more in common than you might think. In fact, the main goal of each of these organizations is the same thing: Win elections. You can't govern if you can't win. In order to win, you have to put together a coalition of voters large enough to give you at least a plurality of the vote. That does not mean that you have to like, or even always agree with, your fellow party members. It simply means that your disdain for your allies has to be less than your distaste for the other party.

For more than a century, Texas was dominated by the Democrats, and Republicans had little chance of winning an election. But times have changed. Republicans have won every statewide seat since 1994, a streak that no party in any other state can match. Since 2003, Republicans have controlled a majority in both the Texas house and senate. Democrats retained strength along the border and in many urban areas, but the party's longtime dominance, at least for now, has been ended.

Everyone would probably agree that voting is the easiest way for citizens in a democracy to voice their opinions and express their choices; but it is certainly not the only way. Political parties provide another medium through which we can act. And although in recent years parties have fallen into some disfavor with many people, they still represent an important avenue of access within the political system. If you've never thought of a political party as a way to get involved, think again. And pay attention— this chapter will show you how.

A **political party** is a group of people who share a common body of principles or goals and who attempt to control government by gaining and controlling public offices. A political party differs from an interest group in that it is usually larger, it addresses a broader array of issues, and it nominates and formally runs candidates for office. Parties were not part of the original scheme of government and politics envisioned by the nation's founders and are not mentioned in the U.S. Constitution. James Madison realized that parties were inevitable and believed that the constitutional system of checks and balances could help alleviate their worst aspects. He wrote to a friend, "There is nevertheless sufficient scope for combating the spirit of party, as far as it may not be necessary to fan the flame of liberty, in efforts to divert it from the more noxious channels; to moderate its violence, especially in the ascendant party; to elucidate the policy which harmonizes jealous interests; and particularly to give to the Constitution that just construction, which, with the aid of time and habit, may put an end to the more dangerous schisms otherwise growing out of it."[1]

Party Structure

Differentiate between ideological and coalitional parties.

coalitional
Alliances consisting of a variety of individuals and groups in support of a particular candidate for elected office.

ideological
Characterizing a group or party built around a unifying set of principles.

platform
The statement of principles passed by a political party's convention.

4.1

4.2

4.3

4.4

4.5

4.6

4.7

The basic structure of the two major political parties in the United States (and in Texas as well) can best be described as **coalitional**. This means that each party comprises a number of different subgroups that band together for the main purpose of winning elections. Today, political scientists refer to such subgroups as factions. These groups usually agree on some sort of basic, often vaguely defined set of ideas, but there is also a fair amount of tension and rivalry. Sometimes with this kind of political party, the discord is so great that there is little beyond the decision to form a coalition holding it together. But winning matters more than ideology, so unpopular ideas can be left in the dust if expedience dictates. Note how the national Republican Party was so quick to back away from its entrenched stance on illegal immigration once it admitted that the 2012 elections underscored its declining share of the Latino vote.

Parties in other countries—as well as many minor (or so-called third) parties in this country—frequently exhibit a structure that can be labeled **ideological**. An ideological party is united by a single principle or a narrowly defined set of principles to which all members are expected (and often required) to adhere. Factionalism tends to be rare, and fidelity to principle is often deemed more important than winning an election. These people would rather be "right" (as *they* define it) than president, or governor, or state representative, or county tax assessor-collector. As we've already implied, ideological parties have a pretty hard time in United States—as well as Texas—politics. The chief reason lies in the heterogeneous nature of our population. We've already noted that Texas is made up of many different cultural, economic, and political groups. No one single group is likely to control what happens. In order to be successful, political parties have to appeal to a broad array of groups. This also tends to force the resolution of most issues to the middle of the political road. The "true believers" in each party find such pragmatism distasteful. Former Texas Agriculture Commissioner Jim Hightower, a noted ideologue, once scornfully remarked, "The only things in the middle of the road are yellow stripes and dead armadillos!" However, the pragmatism which he mocked is the key to victory in most contests, including the one in which he was defeated for reelection.

It is these very factors—a broadly based model of political party structure as well as a general political climate that encourages centrist solutions—that often lead one or the other (and sometimes both) major parties to literally steal the core idea or ideas that underpin many ideological parties. In doing so, the major parties hope to woo the smaller group's supporters into their respective folds. The net effect is to broaden the base of the major party while rendering the ideological party politically superfluous. Examples of such action can be seen in the Democrats' appropriation of most of the Populist Party platform (and even William Jennings Bryan, their presidential candidate!) in 1896; in the eventual incorporation of many elements from the Progressive Party's **platform** into the New Deal agenda; and in the adoption by both Democrats and Republicans of a sizable portion of the issue base of George Wallace's American Independent Party in the early 1970s.

Texas has had its fair share of ideological political parties—the Libertarian Party, which stands for significantly smaller government and individual liberty, is the most prominent contemporary example. Prior to 2010, the Libertarian Party was the only third party to regularly appear on the Texas ballot. Libertarians are likely to remain on the ballot because—given recent Republican domination in statewide elections—Democrats don't run candidates for every office. Texas voters are contrarian enough that at least 5 percent of them are going to vote against *any* incumbent, given a choice. Contesting every race and thereby knocking the Libertarians from future ballots would not be in the Democrats' best interest, as

4.1

4.2

4.3

4.4

4.5

4.6

4.7

most Libertarian voters would cast Republican ballots if not given a third choice. Sometime in the future, if Castro is correct about Texas turning purple, that could make a difference.

Conversely, by securing a place on the 2010 ballot, the left-leaning Green Party, with its emphasis on environmental and social justice issues, should marginally aid Republican candidates, as it would logically draw votes from the Democratic Party. The Greens won a place on the 2010 ballot through the state's difficult petition process. An intriguing aspect of the Green Party's petition success in 2010 is that much of the effort's funding seems to have come from contributors normally associated with Republican candidates. It is easy to see why they might want a Green candidate on the ballot. In both 2010 and 2012, the Green Party exceeded the 5 percent threshold in a couple of statewide races, securing a place on the ballot at least through 2014.

The Libertarian and Green Parties: Movement, Protest or 'Against?'

Ideological parties, like the Libertarians and Greens, draw a certain percentage of their support from true believers—those who think that their party is so correct on the issues that Texans will eventually follow them on their righteous path, or that the correctness of their position outweighs more practical positions, like whether their candidates can actually win an election. For the Libertarians, and even more so for the Greens, those numbers are very low. One need look no further than the top of the Texas ticket races in 2012. For president, the Libertarian candidate garnered only 1.1 percent of the vote, the Green candidate 0.3 percent. For the U.S. Senate seat, the Libertarian received 2.05 percent of ballots cast, while the Green nominee polled 0.86 percent. Though difficult to quantify, some of those third-party ballots were more of a protest against both parties than support for any particular third party. It is also conceivable that some dedicated Libertarian and Green voters may abandon their party at the top of the ticket—the races they see as having the biggest impact—and return to ideological purity for the remainder of the ballot. Taking all of these factors into consideration, we can create a crude estimate that true Libertarian believers account for something less than 1.5 percent of Texas voters while their Green counterparts comprise something less than 0.5 percent. Those are your movement voters.

Libertarians and Greens did better in some other fully contested statewide races, with Libertarians garnering over 3 percent in a Supreme Court race and Greens hitting almost 2 percent in a Railroad Commission seat. Of course, these third parties did best in races where one of the major parties opted out. In a couple of court of criminal appeal races that did not draw Democratic candidates, Libertarians drew just over, and just under, 22 percent. A Green candidate eclipsed 8 percent in a Supreme Court race without a Democratic foe. (Remember, however, that Republican strategists were partially responsible for getting the Green Party on the Texas ballot in the first place, so some of these voters were almost certainly Republicans "helping" the Greens maintain their ballot status.) For the most part, though, these Green and Libertarian ballots are "protest" votes, voicing general displeasure with the established parties in a race that doesn't matter because everyone knows the establishment party will win, or "against" votes, where, in this particular example, Democratic voters have another chance to vote against a Republican candidate. This works both ways. A number of legislative and congressional districts are drawn so decidedly Democratic that Republicans opt out of contesting them; third-party candidates give Republicans in these districts a way to vote against Democrats.

The closest a Libertarian came to "winning" in 2012 was in the state House of Representatives District 52 race, where Lillian Martinez Simmons racked up 29.7 percent of the vote against Republican Larry Gonzales' 70.3 percent, a margin that didn't exactly have the Republican sweating. In District 113, Green Party candidate Angela Sarlay picked up 19 percent against Democrat Cindy Burkett, the high-water mark for the Greens. Libertarians routinely picked up between 15 and 20 percent in races where only one major party fielded a candidate; Green candidates scored between 10 and 15 percent in similar circumstances.

Without question, most of these are protest or "against" votes. If they were true movement votes, we would see these parties receive a larger percentage in races with both Republican and Democratic opponents. It also indicates some level of frustration with politics in general that may manifest itself as something significant down the road. And the fact that Libertarians are routinely receiving between 3 and 6 percent of the vote in down-ballot races where both major parties field candidates has to mean something. Add in the fact that third-party candidates seldom have access to advertising funds—Simmons hit almost 30 percent of the vote without raising or spending a dime.

Is there a perfect storm in which a third-party candidate could actually win? Perhaps. If such a candidate could raise a reasonable amount of contributions, or self-fund, and if the major party candidate ran into some type of trouble, like a scandal, after the filing deadline has passed, and if the public is sufficiently disgruntled. Well, that's a bunch of "ifs" and "ands, "but once upon a time, experts thought that it would take such a set of circumstances for a Republican to win a race in Texas.

conventions
Formal party meetings to select leadership, delegates, and create a platform.

precinct
A political subdivision through which elections are carried out.

4.1
4.2
4.3
4.4
4.5
4.6
4.7

The Organization of Political Parties in Texas

4.3 Describe the levels of political party organization in Texas.

☐ Conventions

Third parties may on occasion tip the results of an election to one or the other major party, and, in our perfect storm scenario, may someday capture a seat. However, the chances of their winning across the board are about as remote as those of a snowball lasting through an August day in McAllen. We, therefore, will concentrate on explaining the structure of the two major parties in Texas because that's where the vast majority of Texans who are inclined to get involved with a political party will find themselves. The internal structure of the Republican and Democratic parties in Texas is similar enough to allow for a single description that will generally apply to both parties.

Both parties have internal structural elements that allow for short-term as well as long-term participation by citizens. The short-term elements are essentially a series of **conventions** in which party supporters participate; the long-term elements comprise a series of elected offices within the parties that party supporters try to win. These conventions and elected party offices exist at several levels within the party structure.

☐ The Precinct Level

The voting **precinct** is a small geographic area created to facilitate the conduct of elections. Every county in Texas is divided into such precincts, so the political parties have made this the basic entry level into their organizations. The easiest way for most people to get involved within a political party is by attending a precinct convention. This meeting is held (in most cases) on the evening of the party's primary election, and the only thing you have to do in order to participate is vote in the party primary. Those who attend the precinct convention will be helping to direct the activities of

4.1

4.2

4.3

4.4

4.5

4.6

4.7

precinct convention
The basic or grassroots level at which delegates are selected to the county party convention.

resolutions
Proposed planks in the party platform; formed and submitted through the convention system.

their party and will also have an opportunity to help identify and develop the party's stance on major issues.

A typical **precinct convention** will begin with the election of a convention chair and secretary, after which participants move on to selecting delegates. Delegates are voters attending the convention who will go on to the next level within the convention process and who in essence will represent and speak for their precinct there. Each precinct convention is allocated delegates based on how much support the precinct gave to the party's last candidate for governor. For the more mathematically inclined, this is determined by a ratio: 1 delegate for every 25 votes cast in the precinct at the last general election for the party's nominee for governor. It sounds complicated, but it really boils down to this idea: The more people in the precinct who voted for your party's candidate for governor, the more delegates your precinct convention will be allowed to select. (It should be noted that, in an effort to bolster participation in these conventions, the Democrats have instituted a revised ratio of 1:15.)

After the delegates are chosen, anyone participating in the convention may offer **resolutions**. These are statements that express the party's stance on an issue, and they are a way for you to try to get the party to see things your way. If, for example, you would like to see more state (or federal) funds be made available for college loans and grants, you could introduce a resolution to that effect at your precinct convention. Resolutions are approved by majority vote of those attending the convention and become a kind of platform for that precinct. They are sent—along with the precinct's delegates—to the next convention.

Precinct conventions are one of the best-kept secrets in Texas politics. They're close at hand, take up very little time (usually), and are remarkably accessible. In fact, the odds are that if you were to go to your next precinct convention, you'd probably wind up a delegate! It's not unusual for there to be fewer people at a precinct convention than there are delegates to be chosen. So if you've ever said to yourself, "I wish the Democrats (or the Republicans) would talk about *my* issues," here's your chance.

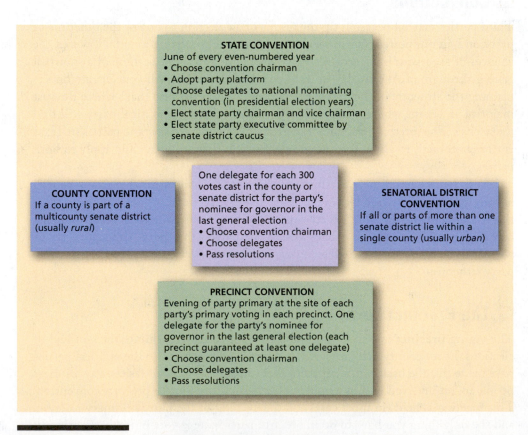

STATE CONVENTION
June of every even-numbered year
• Choose convention chairman
• Adopt party platform
• Choose delegates to national nominating convention (in presidential election years)
• Elect state party chairman and vice chairman
• Elect state party executive committee by senate district caucus

One delegate for each 300 votes cast in the county or senate district for the party's nominee for governor in the last general election

COUNTY CONVENTION
If a county is part of a multicounty senate district (usually *rural*)
• Choose convention chairman
• Choose delegates
• Pass resolutions

SENATORIAL DISTRICT CONVENTION
If all or parts of more than one senate district lie within a single county (usually *urban*)

PRECINCT CONVENTION
Evening of party primary at the site of each party's primary voting in each precinct. One delegate for the party's nominee for governor in the last general election (each precinct guaranteed at least one delegate)
• Choose convention chairman
• Choose delegates
• Pass resolutions

FIGURE 4.1 The Conventions of Texas Political Parties.

The County (or District) Level

Delegates selected at the precinct conventions go on to either a county convention or a **state senatorial district convention**. How do you determine which one? Essentially, it's a function of where you live: Generally speaking, rural counties hold county conventions and urban counties hold district conventions. To be more specific, counties that lie completely within a state senate district hold county conventions. Counties that contain more than one or parts of more than one state senate district hold a district convention in each district or part of a district within that county.

At these county or district conventions, essentially the same agenda and rules apply as did at the precinct convention. First, a convention chair and a secretary are elected. Then delegates are selected, much as they were at the precinct convention. The only difference is that the ratio for determining the number of delegates chosen is changed. Each county or district convention is granted one delegate for every 300 votes cast in the county or part of a district with the county at the last general election for the party's nominee for governor. (As was the case with the precinct conventions, in an effort to bolster participation in these conventions, the Democrats have instituted a revised ratio of 1:180.) After this, attendees debate and vote on resolutions brought from the precinct conventions and approved by the convention's resolutions committee, as well as new ones offered from the floor. Those approved are sent—along with the delegates selected—to the party's state convention.

As we said earlier, being chosen a delegate at a precinct convention is relatively easy. Being chosen a delegate at a county or district convention is a bit tougher. There are fewer chosen per capita, and the competition is more intense. But it is certainly possible, and if you can convince enough people (especially those on the convention's nominating committee) that you're part of that "new blood" every party needs from time to time, it is likely to happen, especially in a nonpresidential year.

The State Level

The highest level of the parties' conventions, and the place to be for most party activists, is the state convention, held in June of even-numbered years. The sites for these conventions are usually the state's major cities, with Dallas, Houston, Fort Worth, Austin, and San Antonio frequently being chosen. Delegates selected in the county or district conventions attend the state convention, which usually lasts from two to three days.

Those who participate in this convention begin by choosing a chair and a secretary. At this level, a fair amount of time may be devoted to discussing changes in the party's rules and other administrative responsibilities. One of the most important actions taken here will be to finalize the state party platform—the list of ideas and issues that the party deems important. Voters may use the platform as a mechanism for assessing the party's candidates for office. The elements that make up this platform (the "planks") are usually those resolutions that rank-and-file party supporters got passed at the precinct conventions and then at the county or district conventions. Ideas born at the precinct convention in March may very well become a part of the platform by June. An example of this process at work can be seen in recent Republican state party platforms, which have reflected many of the issues embodied in resolutions that evangelical Christians within the party passed at their precinct conventions. For Democrats, it can be seen in recent platform resolutions urging protection of gay rights.

A couple of other state convention chores have to be taken care of in presidential election years. They include electing delegates to the party's national nominating convention and selecting a list of potential presidential electors. These people become the official electors of the state only if the party's candidate for president carries Texas in the November general election. Finally, the state convention delegates must elect the state chair, other state party officials, and state executive committee members before adjourning. We'll cover this in more detail when we turn to a discussion of the elected offices within the party.

state senatorial district convention
Midlevel party meeting between precinct and state; same level as county convention.

4.1

4.2

4.3

4.4

4.5

4.6

4.7

4.1

4.2

4.3

4.4

4.5

4.6

4.7

STATE CHAIRMAN/VICE CHAIRMAN
Elected by party's delegates at the state convention. No salary. Same basic duties as county chair, but on a statewide scale. If one is male, the other must be female.

COUNTY CHAIRMAN
Elected by party's voters county-wide in the primary. Two-year term with no limits. No salary. Oversees primary election in county. Often serves as liaison with state party official candidates. Often engages in fund-raising.

STATE EXECUTIVE COMMITTEE
Composed of one man and one woman from each of Texas's 31 state senatorial districts. Election is by state senatorial districts caucuses at party's state convention. No salary. Assists and advises state chairman.

PRECINCT CHAIRMAN
Basic elected official of the party. Chosen by party voters in each precinct in the party primary. Two-year term with no limits. No salary. Will conduct party primary election in his precinct. May do other things to enhance support for the party.

COUNTY EXECUTIVE COMMITTEE
An official body composed of all the party's precinct chairman from the county. Assists the county chairman in carrying out his duties and serves in an advisory capacity. No salary.

FIGURE 4.2 Elected Offices within Texas Political Parties.

A NOTE ON LIBERTARIANS AND GREENS Both the Libertarian and Green parties hold precinct conventions, although few precincts have delegates show up. You don't have to attend the precinct convention in order to be a county delegate. County conventions are the true first real step for these parties. At the county convention and the district conventions that follow, the Green and Libertarian Party delegates don't simply write a platform and choose whom to send to the state convention; they actually nominate candidates, depending on the geographic jurisdiction of the office in question, In some counties, the entire convention may be comprised of less than a dozen people, so a small group can have a real impact on who gets on the ballot. Similarly, these parties use their state conventions to nominate their statewide candidates.

☐ Elected Party Offices

THE PRECINCT LEVEL The jumping-off point for involvement with the elected offices within the party organization, as shown in Figure 4.2, also can be found at the precinct level, in the office of precinct chair. This person is the basic point of contact between the party and the people who support it. The precinct chair is elected by the party's voters in the primary election and serves a two-year term. There is no limit on the number of terms you may serve, and many precinct chairs are routinely reelected, often without opposition. This is an unpaid position, so those who seek it tend to be political junkies.

Precisely what does a precinct chair do? The Texas Election Code lists a number of responsibilities for this party official, but essentially, a chair does as much or as little as he or she wants to. Because the position provides no compensation for its holder, activity levels vary greatly from precinct to precinct. If nothing else, the precinct chair will usually be responsible for holding the party's primary election in his precinct. This includes overseeing the polls on primary election day, lining up workers to help, and reporting results to the party's county office. Beyond this rather rudimentary task, some precinct chairs actually promote the party by registering people to vote, mailing out newsletters, soliciting campaign contributions, and arranging for transportation on election day. In this office, the personalities of the people involved and their

4.1
4.2
4.3
4.4
4.5
4.6
4.7

Rising Democratic star Julian Castro, the mayor of San Antonio, speaks at the state Democratic convention. He is part of a movement determined to turn Texas from Republican red to Democratic blue over the next several years; or, at the very least, to a blue-tinged purple.

commitment to the party's principles are crucial in determining how much and what will get done.

Should you become a precinct chair? There's no filing fee to get on the ballot and it involves a relatively small number of voters, so it's not a terribly difficult office to attain. And if you'd like to have a little more say in the political world, it might be a good place to start. The job of the precinct chair is often a thankless one, yet the person who holds it can have a significant effect on the political process. In a precinct where the two major parties are roughly equal in strength, the difference in a given election may very well be the efforts put forth by the precinct chair. If going to a precinct convention has whetted your appetite for things political, a logical next step might be to run for precinct chair.

THE COUNTY LEVEL At this level, you'll find a couple of offices within the party's structure. The first of these, the county chair, oversees the party's activities across the county. The person who holds this office, like the precinct chair, is elected by the voters of the party in the primary election. The term of office is two years, with no limits on reelection, and again, no regular salary accompanies this office. The county chair's job is considerably broader than that of the precinct chair.

Here the responsibility for conducting the primary election is countywide, and the chair must make sure every precinct has someone to oversee the election. The county chair plays a much larger role in fund-raising than does the average precinct chair. Also, those who direct the campaigns of state or area office-seekers often single out the county chair as a point of contact. So if the party's candidate for governor

4.1

4.2

4.3

4.4

4.5

4.6

4.7

wants to visit Tyler, the county chair of Smith County often arranges for a meeting hall, coordinates transportation, and makes sure an enthusiastic throng of supporters greets the candidate.

The county executive committee helps the county chair carry out these tasks. Who are the members of this committee? They're all the party's precinct chairs in that county. Every precinct chair is automatically an ex officio member of the county executive committee. They meet regularly with the county chair and perform whatever tasks may be delegated to them. This group is especially important in urban counties where the demands on the county chair can at times be overwhelming. There, you often see subcommittees formed within this body to provide for a more effective division of labor. You may also see in such urban counties the formation of senatorial district committees for the same reason. The office of county chair requires a significant commitment of time and effort. There is no pay, and the hours can be long, especially in highly urbanized areas where the position is, for all practical purposes, a full-time job. Not many people can afford to invest that much of themselves in what is essentially a voluntary act. Nevertheless, those willing to do so have a proportionally greater voice in their party's affairs.

THE STATE LEVEL Selection of the party's highest elected officials takes place at the party's state convention. All delegates to that convention vote for the state chair and, in separate ballots, various other state party offices. These officials serve two-year terms, with no limit to the number of terms they may serve. Like the other party offices we've discussed, these do not come with a salary. Yet their duties can be time consuming, and, in the case of the state chair, the position can be a full-time job and more. All of the things done by the county chair will be done by the state chair, but on a much larger scale. This is especially the case with regard to raising money for the party, something that in itself could easily occupy the time and energy of the chair to the exclusion of all other tasks. When current Republican state chair Steve Munisteri took the reins in 2010, he found a party $500,000 in debt. He spent the better part of the summer and fall working to get the party back on firm financial footing. Additionally, the state chair must often serve as a liaison with the national party and its presidential campaign.

The state chair presides over the state executive committee, which includes one man and one woman from each of the state's 31 senatorial districts. Chosen by state convention delegates who divide into senatorial district caucuses (meetings) for this purpose, state executive committee members serve two-year terms, may be reelected without limit, and (you guessed it!) receive no salary. This body assists the state chair in carrying out his or her many duties, one of the most important of which is planning and holding the next state convention.

The executive committee convenes several times a year, and though the job is not as demanding as that of the state chair, members invest a good bit of their own time and money in meeting their responsibilities. Realistically, holding any state office within the party is going to lie beyond the realm of possibility for many Texans. But those who can serve will have much to say about the direction and goals of their party.

The Democratic Party

> **4.4** Explain the long and successful history of the Democratic Party in Texas.

☐ Foundations

The Democrats were one of the first political parties to organize in Texas, establishing themselves formally in 1854. They tended to dominate the political scene, although they occasionally saw challenges from the dying Whig Party and the secretive Know-Nothing Party during the 1850s. Although the issue of secession divided Texas Democrats, it did not tear them apart as was the case with the national party organization.

When Texas did secede in February 1861, most officeholders who took the new oath to the Confederacy were Democrats, and this pattern continued throughout the course of the Civil War.

During Reconstruction, virtually all people who had held office in Confederate or state government were barred from holding further office, and most were disenfranchised. Republicans (and occasionally, Independents) therefore held the majority of elected offices during the period. Only in the early 1870s were former officeholders' rights to vote and hold office restored, but once this happened, they reemerged with a vengeance. By 1873, as a reaction to the perceived excesses of Reconstruction (and the identification of those "excesses" with the Republican Party), most Republicans had been routed from office, and for the next 100 years, the Democrats, for all practical purposes, would be the only game in town.

□ Dominance

The fact that there was only one viable political party in Texas after Reconstruction did not mean that there was no political competition. Simply put, Democrats fought other Democrats for political dominance. The key players in this drama would be **factions**—identifiable subgroups within a political party. These groups are united by a commonly held belief, issue, or personality, although they generally are not tightly organized and may vary greatly in size and influence. The first factions to emerge among Democrats after Reconstruction were primarily economic in their orientation. The Redeemers, so-called because they wanted to "redeem" the South from the Republicans, slashed government spending, cut back on state support for education, and rewrote the state's constitution. They hoped these actions would create a climate favorable to business and industry. To this end, they enacted laws that allowed public land to be given to various railroad companies as an inducement to extend their tracks across Texas. This practice, along with the increasingly pro-business attitude of the Redeemers, gave rise to an opposing faction among Texas Democrats.

Growing discontent among farmers had led to a number of protest movements in Texas during the 1870s and 1880s, including the Grange and the Farmers' Alliance. These various movements began to coalesce as an identifiable "Agrarian" wing. With James Stephen Hogg as their standard-bearer, these Agrarians gained control of the party in 1890 and inaugurated a period of reform that would last more than 20 years. They sought to regulate business, protect the farmer, and enact reforms that would make things easier on the "little guy." Under their leadership, Texas passed its first child labor law and made extensive changes in the way elections were conducted.

By the second decade of the 20th century, the lines between these early economic factions had begun to blur. The election of Jim Ferguson in 1914 gave rise to a new intraparty matchup. For the next 20 years, politics in the Democratic Party would revolve around "Farmer Jim" and his wife Miriam. The factions that emerged were personality-based, with one group strongly supporting Ferguson and others opposing him. Of course, these skirmishes continued during his wife's several campaigns for office, but after her second term as governor (1933–1935), Ferguson and his politics of personality began to recede.

By the mid-1930s, two reformulated groups began a decades-long struggle for control of the Democratic Party. Liberals and conservatives emerged as relatively ideological factions that initially revolved around support of or opposition to the policies of Franklin Roosevelt and the New Deal. Liberals supported Roosevelt and enthusiastically endorsed the more activist role for government that the New Deal programs set up. Texas politicians like Lyndon Johnson, Ralph Yarborough, and James Allred were among this group. They were opposed by the conservatives, whose dislike of Roosevelt and his New Deal was pronounced and whose supporters included John Nance Garner and Coke Stevenson.

During the 1930s, the liberals controlled the Texas political agenda. This can best be seen in the programs advocated by Governor Allred during his two terms (1935–1939). These programs complemented the work of various federal agencies that were created

factions
Divisions within a political party.

4.1

4.2

4.3

4.4

4.5

4.6

4.7

4.1

4.2

4.3

4.4

4.5

4.6

4.7

Texas Regulars
A conservative faction of the Democratic Party during the 1940s.

Democrats of Texas
A liberal faction of Democrats formed in the 1950s.

during that period. However, by the early 1940s, the factional winds were shifting. Texas conservatives found a rallying point by opposing a third-term nomination for Roosevelt, and when he won nomination to a fourth term in 1944, they briefly deserted the party and organized themselves as the **Texas Regulars**. These dissidents returned to the party fold and by the late 1940s had gained almost complete control of the party machinery. The death of Roosevelt in 1945—combined with the increasingly conservative mood of the country following World War II—played a large part in this power shift.

Liberals made several attempts to mount a comeback over the next several decades. In the mid-1950s they formed the **Democrats of Texas** to back Ralph Yarborough in his race for Texas governor. Yarborough lost in the primary, but with help from liberals he won a special election for a U.S. Senate seat in 1957, a seat he would hold until 1971. That was about the extent of the good news for this group. The 1950s weren't exactly the best of times to be a liberal in Texas, and though liberals enjoyed a brief resurgence in the 1960s (at least nationally), the generally conservative nature of the average Texan has made it difficult for this faction to enjoy much success. In recent years, only Jim Hightower's election as agriculture commissioner in 1982 could be construed as a statewide victory for an out-and-out liberal.

☐ Retrenchment

The victory of Republican Bill Clements in the 1978 governor's race ended 105 years of Democratic control of that office. It was also a slap in the face to Texas Democrats, who began to realize that they no longer could enjoy the luxury of fighting among themselves. In the years since, intraparty divisions have been somewhat muted, particularly as many more overtly conservative Democrats have left to join the Republican Party. Although the party did recapture the governor's office in 1982 and again in 1990, the ascendancy of the Republicans since the early 1990s means that Texas's days as a one-party Democratic state are gone for the foreseeable future.

In this new millennium, Texas Democrats face a daunting task. The party must hold on to its traditional supporters while broadening its appeal statewide. Traditionally supporters have included minorities, members of labor unions, blue-collar workers, and rural conservatives (the so-called yellow dog Democrats). In recent elections, Republicans have made some potentially significant inroads into these core constituencies. For example, then-Governor Bush's landslide reelection in 1998 saw him rack up a larger percentage of Hispanic votes than any Grand Old Party (GOP) candidate ever. Union support also wavered, at least as measured in the 1998, 2002, and 2006 gubernatorial elections. It remains to be seen whether this shift is temporary or fundamental. In races for the Texas Legislature, Democrats still do well among both African Americans and Hispanics. In fact, many of the seats in the legislature in south and southwest Texas remain in the Democratic column. The nomination of Tony Sanchez for governor and Ron Kirk for U.S. Senate in 2002 was a significant effort for the Democrats as they tried to retain their bases of support in the Hispanic and African American communities of Texas. While it failed to achieve the desired results in that election (and while the 2006 and 2010 general election saw no similar attempt by the Democrats to nominate minority candidates to major statewide office), such a strategy is sure to be an important part of future party efforts, especially in light of the demographic trends discussed earlier. Democrats have managed to hold on to some of their union supporters in areas such as Beaumont–Port Arthur and the petrochemical suburbs of the Houston-Galveston area. But the fastest-growing areas of Texas—the booming suburbs—represent a challenge to the party that it has only begun to address. Calling for stronger families, better public education, and economic "fairness" are the way Democrats have chosen to go after this crucial bloc of voters. This, of course, represents an attempt to recapture the middle ground of the Texas political landscape, which, as we have already seen, you must control if you are going to win. Unfortunately for Democrats, election results seem to indicate that they have not been able to get these issues and

4.1
4.2
4.3
4.4
4.5
4.6
4.7

Inside the Federalist System

A Look at the State Democratic and Republican Party Platforms

In Texas, as within the United States in general, there is a distinctive difference in the major political parties' interpretation of federalism. In general, Republicans believe that decision making should be closest to the people, with significant powers dispersed to state and local governments. Democrats believe in a strong national government that protects the interest of individuals while promoting a stronger union. These excerpts from the 2012 state party platforms, although not exactly parallel, help illustrate the different philosophies. The Democratic platform calls for increased national government spending; the Republican alternative calls for downsizing the federal government. Don't forget that platforms are less of an instruction book for how to run government and more of a cheerleader's notes for whipping the party faithful into a frenzy,

Democratic Platform

To rebuild our American infrastructure, Texas Democrats support a requirement that public funds and contracts be awarded to American companies that use American workers who have a vested interest in the security and prosperity of our nation. For a generation, America has neglected its public infrastructure: roads, bridges, railroads, ports, water and sewer systems, schools, parks and libraries. We support a federal initiative to foster a sustained increase in public capital investment. We must not only increase funding to maintain aging infrastructure, but also to build new and more reliable public works.

Source: 2012 Texas Democratic Platform, p. 10.

Republican Platform

Fiscal Responsibility—We urge state and federal legislators to reduce spending. We also support a "cap" on government spending at all levels, with adjustments limited to the effects of inflation and population change.

Unfunded Mandates—We oppose all unfunded mandates by the federal and state governments.

Downsizing the Federal Government—We support abolishing all federal agencies whose activities are not specifically enumerated in the Constitution; including the Departments of Education and Energy. We support a sunset provision law at the federal level. All non-military spending should be returned to at least pre-2008 levels.

Source: 2012 Republican State Platform, p. 16.

The preceding passages demonstrate dramatically different philosophies regarding the scope of what government should do, but different approaches to the specifics as well. In reality, in order to remain economically competitive in the coming decades, Texas has to make improvements to its infrastructure, particularly with regard to transportation and water. Most Republican leaders admitted as much when the legislature convened in January 2013. Likewise, the prospects of a major infusion of federal dollars into infrastructure will remain nothing more than a pipe dream until Washington gets its fiscal house in order. Dismal is too optimistic a description of the chances for a new major federal stimulus plan. Ideas such as jettisoning the U.S. Department of Education may have an impact if implemented, but even many Republicans outside of Texas would stop such an effort. And while Republicans like to rail against federal interference, the vast majority of education policy is still formulated at the state and local level.

1. Why do platforms matter?

2. How do the differences in these planks reveal a difference between the parties in their attitude on governance?

ideas across to suburban voters: In the last several elections, the party has lost every statewide office on the ballot.

Although 21st-century Texas Democrats might be inclined to agree with Thomas Paine that "These are the times that try men's souls," developments at the national level of politics in 2008 may have had the effect of reinvigorating and renewing the Democratic Party and its supporters. The unprecedented candidacies of Hillary Clinton and Barack Obama seemingly galvanized Texas Democrats in a way not seen in many years. Participation in the Democratic Party primary election in March of 2008 broke all records for voter turnout. But perhaps of more significance were the heretofore unheard of rates of participation in the party's precinct conventions as both Clinton and Obama enthusiasts sought to gain an edge for their respective candidates in the all-important drive to acquire delegates to the national nominating convention. However, that enthusiasm was not sustained through the 2010 and 2012 elections, as Republicans continued to control all statewide races and maintained large majorities in the Texas house and senate.

4.1

4.2

4.3

4.4

4.5

4.6

4.7

The Republican Party

4.5 Explain the Republican Party's recent success in Texas.

☐ Post–Reconstruction

Before 2003, the last time the Republican Party controlled Texas was during the reign of E. J. Davis. After Reconstruction ended, the Democrats quickly consolidated their grip on state government. Republicans survived primarily as a radical and African American party. Legislative representation, albeit in relatively low numbers, continued until the beginning of the 1900s, when African Americans were successfully purged from the voting rolls through a variety of methods.

The party's resurgence did not begin until the advent of presidential Republicanism in 1952. Despite Democratic domination of all state offices, the state began turning to Republican presidential candidates. Two factors helped create this trend. First was the disparity between the national and state Democratic organizations. The national party was becoming more liberal, but the state party continued its conservative tradition. Texans still elected conservative Democrats within the state, but balked at the prospect of electing a liberal Democrat to national office.

A second factor was the differences between the Republican and Democratic presidential candidates in 1952. Republican Dwight D. Eisenhower was a war hero. Popular and grandfatherly, he was moderately conservative. Importantly, Eisenhower backed Texans on the "Tidelands" controversy. Texas and California claimed the right to issue oil and gas leases for the areas immediately off their coasts. Democratic nominee Adlai Stevenson, a liberal, disagreed. He backed a 1947 U.S. Supreme Court ruling that granted these rights to the national government.[2] This issue not only meant a lot of money to the state of Texas, but it was also important for state sovereignty. In 1956, the Stevenson–Eisenhower confrontation repeated itself. Texas again backed Eisenhower. Between 1952 and 2012, Democratic presidential candidates would carry Texas only four times. Factor out the 1960s and only one Democratic presidential nominee has carried the state since Harry Truman.

Despite successes on the presidential level, Republicans failed to pose any serious threat to the Democrats throughout the 1950s. The Grand Old Party managed to elect one U.S. congressman, Bruce Alger from Dallas, in 1954, but retaining that seat was essentially the limit of Republican success.

☐ John Tower, Lyndon Johnson, and a U.S. Senate Seat

In 1960, U.S. Senator Lyndon Baines Johnson (LBJ), a Democrat who may have been the most powerful figure in the history of Texas politics, wanted to run for president. LBJ faced a problem, however: 1960 was the year in which his Senate seat was up for reelection. State law prohibited a person from running for two offices at the same time, and Johnson was not sure he could win the presidency. As majority leader of the U.S. Senate, LBJ was neither ready nor willing to give up sure power in return for an opportunity to hold higher office.

Johnson confronted the problem in a way only he could—he pressured the Texas legislature into changing the law. It now prohibits a person from running for two offices at the same time unless one is U.S. senator and the other is president or vice president of the United States. As it turned out, LBJ lost the Democratic presidential nomination to John F. Kennedy and settled for the second spot on the ticket, vice president.

In the 1960 Senate race, the GOP chose as its standard-bearer John Tower, a political science professor at Midwestern State University in Wichita Falls. LBJ won easily, but Tower still managed to garner more than 40 percent of the vote, an unexpectedly high percentage against the popular Johnson.

4.1
4.2
4.3
4.4
4.5
4.6
4.7

Texas ★ Mosaic   John Tower

John Tower was the father of the modern Republican Party in Texas. He created the foundation on which the party was built. A political science professor at Midwestern State University in Wichita Falls before entering the political arena, Tower was the son and grandson of Methodist ministers. From the time of his 1961 special election victory, he was instrumental in the emergence of the party. As a high-profile, successful officeholder, he helped recruit candidates and raise money for the party. For almost 20 years, Tower was *the* face and *the* voice of the Texas GOP.

Tower made it easier for other Republicans to raise funds and win elections. During his time in office, the Republican Party was transformed from a minor irritant to the Democrats into a viable entity that had elected a governor and a significant number of legislators. Tower helped guide the party through its formative years.

A longtime member of the Senate Armed Services Committee and its chair after Republicans took control of the Senate in 1981, Tower was a "hawk" when it came to foreign policy. He favored a strong military; a large, viable defense industry; and a proactive role for the United States in foreign affairs. He was an ardent anti-Communist. These views, shared by many Texans, helped him win reelection three times.

The conservative Tower believed that with the exception of the Department of Defense, government should be small. He feared government power and opposed unnecessary government interference in both business and personal endeavors. This view would cause him problems with some Texas Republicans late in his career. Tower supported abortion rights, at one time even voting for federal funding of abortions for poor women. As a result, some GOP extremists in Texas tried to deny the former senator a seat at the Republican National Convention in 1988. The incident drips with irony. First, without Tower, the Republican Party in Texas might never have left the ground. Second, most of the people involved in the movement to oust Tower had roots in the Democratic Party, leaving only after their issues were continually ignored.

Therefore, they were not involved with Republican politics during the time when Tower was building the GOP. Yet in 1988 they argued that Tower was not a true Republican. Ultimately, their effort would fail, and Tower would be present when his old friend George H. W. Bush—George W.'s father—was nominated to the presidency of the United States.

It is another irony that the election of Bush would bring a bitter end to Tower's political career. Upon his election, Bush appointed Tower to be his secretary of defense. Because of his long tenure on the Armed Services Committee, most political observers believed that his nomination would fly through the Senate. Despite some Democratic grumbling over the high income Tower had made as a defense consultant after leaving the Senate in 1985, it appeared he had enough votes to win confirmation.

It has been said that politics makes strange bedfellows. Never was this truer than during the 1989 confirmation hearings. Some radical Republican activists were

U. S. Senator John Tower was the first Republican elected statewide since E. J. Davis. With his win, the diminutive political science professor laid the ground work for the party that would become dominant some forty years later.

angered enough by Tower's stand on abortion rights that they were determined to derail his nomination. They began to leak stories about Tower to both the media and select Democrats. Some Democrats had legitimate reservations about Tower, others disliked him, and still others were anxious to get back at Republicans after their rough handling of presidential Democratic nominee Michael Dukakis during the 1988 presidential campaign.

Tower was an easy target. While many of his tastes were simple, he liked to dress in expensive clothes. Twice divorced, he had a reputation as a ladies' man. He was known to throw back a drink or two. (Every Texas Independence Day, Tower would gather his staff in his office at noon, close the door, and break the seal on a good bottle of bourbon. Tower would then read William B. Travis's moving "I will never surrender" letter from the Alamo. There was seldom a dry eye in the room as the staff would drink a toast to Texas heroes long since gone.)

Some of the charges were ridiculous, particularly the one alleging that he and a Russian ballerina had disrobed on a grand piano at a posh River Oaks party. Others may have had some substance. Tower played into his enemies' hands when he agreed to give up liquor during his tenure in office. This implied, in the eyes of many, that he did indeed have a problem with alcohol. The allegations, coupled with the Senate's increasing partisanship, doomed the nomination. Tower refused to step back from the nomination, though, forcing a Senate vote. He lost and returned to a defense consulting job and teaching position at Southern Methodist University in Dallas.

Tower, along with a daughter, was killed in a plane crash on April 5, 1991.

Source: John G. Tower, *Consequences* (Boston, MA: Little, Brown,).

1. What was ironic about Tower's role in the Texas Republican Party?

2. How was Tower able to become the first Republican elected statewide since Reconstruction?

4.1

4.2

4.3

4.4

4.5

4.6

4.7

Kennedy and Johnson captured the White House. Johnson had the ability to manipulate Texas law, but even he was unable to overcome the U.S. Constitution's prohibition against serving in both the executive and legislative branches. As a result, a U.S. Senate seat opened in Texas, and a special election was called to fill the vacancy. Concurrently, many conservative Democrats formally broke ties with their old party after the 1960 elections.

Tower was the only serious Republican candidate to opt into the race for the Senate seat now left vacant by Johnson's move to the vice presidency in 1961. Several well-known Democrats threw their hats into the ring, including liberal stalwart Henry B. Gonzales and future U.S. Speaker of the House Jim Wright, but the front-runner was William Blakely. Governor Price Daniel Jr. had appointed the ultraconservative Blakely to fill the now open seat until the election could be held. A total of 71 candidates appeared on the ballot. No one received a majority of the vote in the initial round of balloting.

Tower led with 31.5 percent. Blakely joined him in the runoff with 18.3 percent, edging Wright, who received 16.4 percent.[3] The conventional wisdom was that the Democrats would put aside their differences and back Blakely, allowing the Democrats to retain the Senate seat. Liberal Democrats had other ideas. By withholding support for Blakely, they hoped to defeat him and, as a result, force conservatives out of the party. Many liberals voted for Tower, while others opted not to vote at all.

Tower was also aided by the Bay of Pigs fiasco in 1961. Many Texans blamed the recently elected president for the failure of the abortive invasion of Cuba. Kennedy had called off U.S. air support of the anti-Communist Cuban nationalists' invasion. The nationalists were routed by Fidel Castro's superior forces. Some Texans believed that Kennedy was soft on communism: a serious charge in Texas. Since they could not vote against the president, many voted against the nearest Democrat, who happened to be Blakely. Tower won by about 10,000 votes out of almost 900,000 cast.[4] Suddenly, a party that had no representation in the state legislature and only one representative in the congressional delegation had one of two U.S. senators from Texas.

☐ Slow Growth

Senator Tower's victory in 1961 laid the foundation for the growth of the Republican Party. He was reelected in 1966, but Republicans held only 3 of 150 seats in the Texas House.[5] In 1972, Tower won again. With a popular President Richard Nixon heading the ticket, Republicans managed their best showing yet. Tower won by the largest margin of his career. The Sharpstown Bank scandal also hurt the Democrats as Republican membership in the Texas house grew to 17, including future Speaker of the house Tom Craddick.[6]

What happened in 1978 was a total surprise. Not only was Tower reelected, but Texas also chose a Republican governor for the first time since Reconstruction. Tower's campaign against Democrat Bob Krueger was one of the dirtiest in the history of Texas—a state not exactly known for clean campaigns. Both candidates found their personal lives the subject of attack and innuendo. Tower survived his final election bid by a margin of a little more than 12,000 votes.

The election of Bill Clements as governor was a huge upset. Polls showed Democrat John Hill leading by as much as 11 percentage points. On Election Day, the conservative Clements edged the liberal Hill by almost 17,000 votes. Even Republicans were surprised. Democrats, however, still controlled the legislature, holding 27 of 31 senate seats and 128 of 150 house seats.

☐ The Reagan Revolution

Ronald Reagan's conservatism resonated with Texans in 1980, as he rode a landslide victory into the White House. On his coattails, and as the national party took on a decidedly more conservative bent, Republicans made substantial inroads into the state house and senate, electing 35 representatives and 8 senators, both post–Reconstruction highs.

In 1982, Republicans took a step backward as they lost the governor's office. In 1984, they rebounded quickly. Reagan and Bush again led the ticket. Tower surprised everyone by opting out of the U.S. Senate race, but Democrat-turned-Republican Phil Gramm was overwhelmingly elected to the open seat. GOP gains were most pronounced in the Texas house, where Republican representation leaped to 52 seats. By exceeding one-third of the House's membership, Republicans gained the ability to block constitutional amendments.

The year 1986 marked the political resurrection of Bill Clements. Playing to his advantage were the political misfortunes of Mark White, the Democrat who had the unfortunate distinction of being governor when oil prices collapsed. White bore the brunt of the blame for the economic decline in Texas. Worse, he had earned the wrath of the state's high school football coaches, having been an integral part of the school reforms that had included the "no pass–no play" rule. The provision prohibited students who failed a course from participating in extracurricular activities for six weeks. When this rule began to affect Texas high school football, many were outraged. Meddling with high school football was definitely "messing with Texas." The Bubba faction joined with the football coaches and displaced oil workers to oust White from office. The Republicans held their strength in the senate and gained four seats in the house, bringing their total to 56. For the first time since Reconstruction, Republicans had both the governorship and more than a third of the seats in the house. In effect, this insulated the governor's veto from override.

Texas, however, could not be considered a two-party state in 1986. Republicans showed an absolute inability to win statewide down-ballot races. **Down-ballot races** are contests below the level of president, governor, or U.S. senator. The designation includes such offices as lieutenant governor, attorney general, supreme court justice, railroad commissioner, and comptroller. In 1986, Texas was still a Democrat-dominated state with a Republican governor and a significant number of Republicans in the house. That year, the GOP did not even run a serious candidate for lieutenant governor—widely considered to be the most powerful office in the state—in part because no one wanted to run against Bill Hobby. Gubernatorial candidate Clements refused to share the podium with the man who was the Republican nominee for that office, viewing him as a far-right extremist.

☐ A Two-Party State

Texas became a two-party state on Election Day 1988. The top of the ballot told part of the story: Texans overwhelmingly voted for Republican George Bush for president over Democrat Michael Dukakis, despite the fact that Dukakis's running mate was Texas Senator Lloyd Bentsen. On the next line of the ballot, many of the same voters chose Bentsen over his Republican rival for the Senate by about the same large margin. (Bentsen had taken advantage of the "LBJ law" in order to run for both offices.) The bigger story, though, was in the down-ballot races. Republicans won three supreme court seats, including the chief justice's position. Additionally, a Republican captured a railroad commission seat.

Students of politics still view the 1990 Texas gubernatorial race as a case study in how to lose an election. Republican Clayton Williams's political gaffes cost him an early lead of 20 points.[7] The GOP did manage to elect two rising stars: Kay Bailey Hutchison as treasurer and Rick Perry as agriculture commissioner. Republicans also won two supreme court races.

☐ Republican Gains

The biggest victory for the Republican Party in 1992 was not at the ballot box, but in the courtroom. Three Republican-appointed federal judges ruled that the Democrat-controlled state senate had illegally gerrymandered its 1991 redistricting plan. The judges created their own new districts and ordered that the 1992 elections be held under a plan much more favorable to the Republicans. GOP Senate strength soared from 8 to 13.

down-ballot races
Statewide races below the level of president, U.S. senator, or governor.

4.1

4.2

4.3

4.4

4.5

4.6

4.7

4.1

4.2

4.3

4.4

4.5

4.6

4.7

In 1993, Hutchison won her U.S. Senate seat in the June special election run-off. As a result, Republicans now hold both U.S. Senate seats from Texas, with John Cornyn elected in 2002 to succeed Phil Gramm in the Tower seat. In 2012, Ted Cruz scored a spectacular upset in the race to succeed Hutchison by defeating the much better funded—and better known—Lieutenant Governor David Dewhurst in the Republican Primary. Cruz easily defeated Democrat Paul Sadler in the general election to become the highest profile Latino elected official in Texas history.

In 1994, Republican George W. Bush, son of the former President George H. W. Bush, was elected governor. While Democratic incumbents retained all five statewide executive offices, Republican incumbent Rick Perry held on to his office as well. Significantly, the GOP took control of the state supreme court for the first time since Reconstruction. Republicans also won an additional railroad commissioner's seat. In fact, Republicans captured all down-ballot races in which the Democrats didn't have an incumbent.

Of major interest to Texas political observers was the outcome of the state senate races. After the 1992 elections, Democrats had successfully appealed their redistricting case to a higher federal court. As a result, the 1994 senate elections were run under the original Democrat-drawn districts. Most experts expected the GOP to lose at least some of their 1992 gains. Surprisingly, Republicans picked up a seat, increasing their representation to 14, two short of senate control. Republican success can be attributed to two factors. First, the incumbency factor held. The GOP was able to hold onto seats it won in 1992, even though the districts were not drawn as favorably in 1994. Second, President Clinton's lack of popularity in Texas hurt all Democrats. In 1996, Republicans did what would have been unthinkable a decade before: They carved out a 17–14 advantage in the Texas senate. In the house, Republicans held 64 seats after the 1994 elections, a 1995 special election, and defections by former Democratic representatives.

From 1996 through the 2012 elections, Republicans won all statewide races on the ballot. This trend marks a fundamental shift in Texas politics. Twenty years ago, when average Texans reached the point on the ballot where they were no longer familiar with the candidates, they automatically voted Democratic. Today, faced with the same proposition, they vote Republican. In statewide elections, that spells trouble for Democrats, who now must overcome obstacles of both incumbency and partisan preference. Republicans hold every statewide office, including all seats on the state supreme court and court of criminal appeals.

The 2002 election saw Republicans post remarkable gains in the legislature as well. They extended the barest of majorities in the senate to a 19–12 advantage. More importantly, they went from minority status in the house to a huge 88–62 advantage, giving Republicans the Speaker's position for the first time since Reconstruction (see Figure 4.3). Democrats kept their advantage in the Texas delegation to the U.S. Congress, holding a 17–15 edge. Republicans picked up the two new seats dictated by

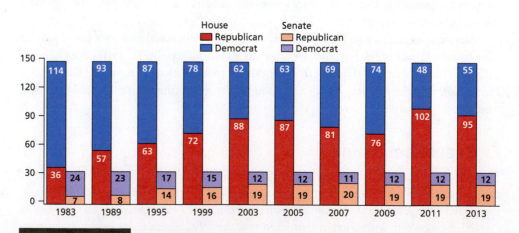

FIGURE 4.3 Growth of the GOP, 1983–2008.

congressional reapportionment. The biggest factor here was incumbency; every member of Congress from Texas who ran again was reelected.

That Democratic edge would evaporate in 2004 as a result of one of the most controversial partisan actions in recent Texas history: a mid-decade redistricting scheme that left Republicans with a 21–11 advantage in the congressional delegation. By 2012, when Texas garnered four new congressional seats, Republicans had extended their majority to 24–12. Democrats came out of the 2004 elections with at least one small reason to celebrate. Although Republicans maintained their 19–12 advantage in the senate, the Democrats picked up a seat in the house, cutting the Republican advantage to 87–63. It was the first time Democrats had gained a seat in a generation. In 2006, Democrats made up more ground, as the Republican edge shrank to 81–69. And in 2008, the Democrats almost recaptured the house, leaving Republicans with a bare two-seat majority. Republicans responded by capturing a two-thirds advantage, 101 seats, in 2010, a year in which Texas Democrats faced tough sledding as a result of widespread opposition to the policies of President Obama. Democrats rebounded a bit in 2012, but Republicans still held a 95–55 advantage upon entering the 2013 legislative session. Interestingly, except for a single session in which Republicans managed a twentieth senator, that chamber has maintained its 19–12 split since 2003.

Party Politics in the New Millennium

4.6   Analyze the challenges facing each major party in the 21st century.

 quick look at the 2012 election returns might lead a casual observer to conclude that Texas is a solid Republican state, with Democrats relegated to a minor role. That may be true for the next couple of election cycles, but after that, all bets are off. As we look at Texas political parties in the 21st century, we will consider the challenges facing each of the major parties and the changes within Texas itself that will prompt significant shifts in political power. Let's start with examining how the state's shifting demographic makeup will impact politics.

☐ Demographics Is Destiny (Perhaps)

In 1830, Mexican government officials realized that their liberal immigration policies had allowed the Texas territory to amass a 90 percent Anglo population. Non-Latino whites would maintain an absolute majority in Texas until 2004, when Texas became a majority–minority state. By 2015, Latinos will outnumber Anglos. By 2040, only one in four Texans will be Anglo.

That does not mean that most voters are minorities, or will be in the near future. A large percentage of today's minority population is under the age of 18. A smaller but significant percentage are not citizens. Non-Hispanic whites will be a majority of the

The Texas Constitution

A Closer Look

For a document as verbose as the Texas constitution, it may seem odd that there is but one passing reference to parties in the entire text. Article III, Section 24 requires that each party be represented on the Texas Ethics Commission.

1. Why are parties barely mentioned in the state constitution?

4.1
4.2
4.3
4.4
4.5
4.6
4.7

4.1

4.2

4.3

4.4

4.5

4.6

4.7

Texas electorate into the next decade. But at some point beyond that, it will no longer be the case.

This matters because there are partisan patterns associated with demographic characteristics. Black voters in Texas have delivered more than 90 percent of their ballots to Democrats in most races over the last several decades. White voters have given a majority of their votes to Republicans since the late 1980s, a majority that has grown larger over the years. Latino voters are more likely to vote Democratic, but some Republicans—like George W. Bush, Rick Perry, and Kay Bailey Hutchison—have done very well with Latino voters. However, the harsh anti-illegal immigration stand taken by the national Republican Party, and echoed in the state party's platform, has chased away some Latino voters. One great question for the Republican Party in Texas is whether it can make significant inroads into the emerging Latino and Asian voting blocs. Republicans don't necessarily need a majority, but they must capture a significant percentage of these voters. If not, Democrats can simply wait until demographics make them, once again and well into the foreseeable future, the majority party in Texas.

☐ The Parties' Constituents

Let's create a short roster of the members of the two major party's teams. Republicans depend on the support of business, Bubba, and conservatives in general. Evangelical Christians tend to vote Republican. So do business owners, both large and

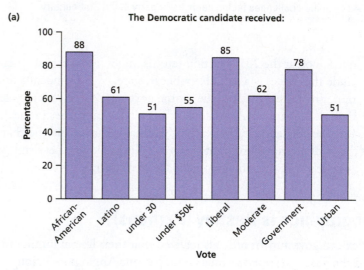

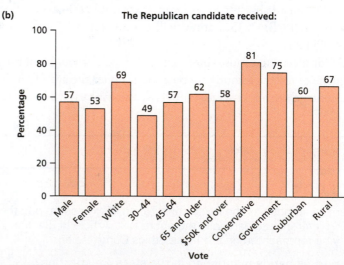

FIGURE 4.4 Party Constituents and the 2010 Governor's Race in Texas

small, as well as those who believe that government plays too big a role in our daily lives. Whites in Texas are more likely to vote Republican than Democrat. So are married couples. Upper middle-class and higher-income brackets are more likely to be Republican.

Democrats depend on the support of liberals, although in some parts of the United States, liberal Republicans are not completely extinct. Democrats receive significant support from minorities, as mentioned above. African Americans vote almost exclusively for Democrats, while—at least until the second decade of the 21st century—Latinos were more up for grabs, with a majority usually voting Democratic—but the size of that majority varies from year to year and from contest to contest. The party has relied on "yellow-dog" Democrats as well, the one portion of the demographic picture that does not work to the party's long term advantage. Yellow dogs are white, conservative voters who vote Democratic because everyone in their family always has. These voters, with ties to the old Texas and its confederate heritage, have all but timed out from the voting pool. Democrats also do better than Republicans among those who have been to graduate school in fields other than those leading to the medical or legal professions.

REPUBLICAN CHALLENGES Earlier in this chapter, we considered how factions once plagued the Democratic Party, as conservative, liberal, and progressive wings each vied for power. Although Republican majorities pale in comparison to the absolute dominance that the Democrats once enjoyed, the party is divided among a number of factions that, while all falling under the conservative banner, have very different opinions as to how policy should be implemented.

Traditionally, we have divided Republicans among economic conservative, social conservative, and libertarian conservative factions. Although admittedly overly simplistic, we will start there, as it reveals some of the basic tensions in the party's foundation. Economic conservatives—sometimes derisively called country club Republicans—are most concerned with economic issues. They favor low taxes and limited business regulation. Many are ambivalent on illegal immigration, as some businesses profit from the cheap labor. Many don't have strong opinions on social issues; others are quietly progressive. Social conservatives, on the other hand, believe that moral decay is the basis of the state's and nation's problems. They are often referred to as the Religious Right. They oppose abortion, gay marriage, and pornography while firmly espousing the Judeo-Christian heritage. They agree with economic conservatives on tax matters, but not necessarily on regulatory ones. Libertarian conservatives want smaller government and less regulation, but they oppose the social agenda of the religious conservatives. In fact, they want to be left alone in their business and personal lives, free from governmental constraint. They agree with economic conservatives on taxes, although they would prefer even less government spending. If they agree with social conservatives on any issue, it is generally a viewpoint accidentally reached from opposite perspectives. Libertarian Republicans share many of the same views as the Libertarian Party, but they are willing to compromise on some of their principles in order to win elections.

When Republicans were on the outside looking in at Texas politics, the divergent groups could put aside their differences to unite against the Democrats. As Republicans have become more powerful and more entrenched, each faction wants to see its policies enacted. So far, the fissure has yet to reach critical mass, held together at various times by opposition to Democratic action in Washington—as it was during the Clinton and Obama administrations—or a loyalty, sometimes grudgingly, to Bush during the interceding Republican administration. At some point, though, at least one group is apt to envision itself as receiving the short end of the stick and will either demand more power or threaten to leave the coalition. As far as Republican primary voters go, economic conservatives seem to hold a slim plurality. Social conservatives have done a better job controlling the state and county executive committees. Libertarian conservatives are the smallest of the factions, but they are too large to completely ignore.

If those divisions were not enough, there is the cross-cutting specter of the Tea Party movement, with its dream of a radical restructuring of the government,

4.1
4.2
4.3
4.4
4.5
4.6
4.7

4.1

4.2

4.3

4.4

4.5

4.6

4.7

returning it to its historic roots. The Tea Party is not a party, but rather a political movement, working primarily within the Republican Party. At first glance, because of their insistence on a return to tradition, many voters, and some members of the media, confuse them with social conservatives. Although some Tea Party advocates may share some social views with religious conservatives, the movement as a whole is much less tied to social issues and it wasn't social issues that started the movement. Tea Party members were vehemently opposed to the financial bailouts of Wall Street, the banks, and the auto industry, actions that were backed by many economic conservatives. The catalyst for the movement was the Troubled Asset Relief Program (TARP), a plan launched by President George W. Bush during the 2008 financial meltdown. Bush was an economic conservative with strong ties to social conservatives.

Although many are quick to dismiss the long-term consequences of the movement, the Tea Party was instrumental in Ted Cruz's successful U.S. Senate race in 2012. As this movement has gained substance, its strong ties to economic issues have been tempered with a greater concern for social issues. If the state Republican Party follows the national lead and tries to moderate its rhetoric on immigration policy, it is likely to receive significant pushback from the Tea Party movement.

DEMOCRATIC CHALLENGES For Democrats, the challenge is simple: Get more voters to the polls. Years of being uncompetitive at the state level may have dampened the enthusiasm of some core voters. In Texas, minority voters still turn out at a lower rate than white voters. With minorities as their key constituency, Democrats need to change that. Simply ramping up the turnout of these groups, coupled with the shifting demographics of the state, could create a new Democratic majority. Texas Democrats would do well to emulate the ground game deployed by President Barack Obama in his 2008 and 2012 presidential campaigns. Obama invested significant resources to identify friendly voters and to coax them to the polls. A strong get-out-the-vote effort could pay quick dividends in Texas.

Democrats must parry any pivot to the Latino population if Texas Republicans take such a step. Many Latino voters are more conservative on religious, social, and fiscal issues than the typical Democratic elected official, so the party must reinforce its long-standing pro-immigration and pro-education credentials. Furthermore, Democrats can expand their efforts to register Latino voters, whose registration rates still lag behind those of other demographic groups. And Democrats need to ensure that the Latino and African American factions of the party don't start to see public policy in terms of a zero-sum game, where one group has to suffer for another to prosper. They must convince all minority groups that Democrats can grow the pie, not just each faction's share.

If the Democratic Party wants to win now, it has to concentrate on picking off parcels of suburban white voters. Part of this effort entails framing the party as moderate, engaged, and fair, and framing the Republican Party as extreme. In particular, Democrats can appeal to suburban voters on the issue of education. Recent state cuts have forced local districts to both cut spending and raise property taxes to nearly their limit. Democrats can argue that an adequate state funding mechanism can both ensure quality education and allow local property taxes to be cut. Since these taxes are the single largest state or local tax liability for most suburban voters, such a stance can have significant appeal.

Of course, Democrats must continue to safeguard its liberal and progressive bases. Although neither faction has a place waiting for it in the Republican Party, the Green Party offers an alternative. Most liberals would not "waste" their vote on a third party; some, if their interests were ignored in the Democratic Party, might take a "Why not, we are going to lose anyway" approach, or simply stay home. Of course, Democrats show no sign of abandoning their liberal roots.

More importantly, Democrats must reestablish their ties to blue-collar whites and union members. Over the past couple of decades, Texas Republicans have made inroads into both of these groups. Democrats need to shepherd these groups back into the fold. These traditional supports need to be coaxed back so that they become part of the new Democratic coalition.

Partisanship in Texas Governance

4.1

4.2

4.3

4.4

4.5

4.6

4.7

4.7 Explain the role of partisanship in Texas governance.

Campaigns—particularly party primaries—are often about partisanship. Candidates play to the base of their party. With the prevalence of straight-ticket voting in Texas, it is evident that, at least in most cases, this holds true for the general elections as well. Parties are not about compromise; they are about drawing sharp distinctions. Most dedicated party members—and we will define these as regular primary voters and campaign workers—want their party's views to prevail on most of the issues. If they win a majority, they expect to control the agenda.

In the U.S. Congress, the House and the Senate are structured along strict party lines. After the 2012 election, Democrats controlled the Senate and Republicans controlled the House. What that means from a power perspective is that every chair of every Senate committee is a Democrat and every chair of every House committee is a Republican. Experience and expertise don't matter: Chairs go to the party in power, And since chairs exercise tremendous control over the legislative process, the choice has consequences. A chair might not be able to ensure passage of legislation, but he or she can almost certainly kill a bill.

Let's imagine that the Democrats take the U.S. House in 2014 and the Republicans take the U.S. Senate. (We know this is not a likely scenario, but stay with us: We are making a larger point.) With the Congress taking office in 2015, every chair would shift from one party to the other. Leadership and experience would be cast aside. New chairs would get bigger offices, and former chairs would see their offices downsized as majority members would receive better parking. Congress would be destabilized.

We don't do things like that in Texas. Throughout the 1970s and 1980s, as Republicans grew to a significant minority in both the state house and senate, Democratic speakers and lieutenant governors began appointing a small number of Republicans as committee chairs. As early as 1975, for instance, future Republican Speaker Tom Craddick was chair of the House Natural Resources Committee and chaired a subcommittee as early as 1973. Once he became Speaker, Craddick continued the tradition by appointing a significant number of Democratic committee chairs, a practice that has been followed by Speaker Straus.

The senate was a little less progressive on the issue of bipartisan appointment. The lieutenant governor did not appoint a Republican to a major senate committee chair until 1981, when Ike Harris was appointed to head the Senate Economic Development Committee. From that point forward, Democratic lieutenant governors would appoint an increasing number of Republican chairs. When Republicans Rick Perry and David Dewhurst followed into that office, they continued bipartisanship by appointing a number of Democratic chairs.

None of this is to imply that partisanship does not exist in the Texas Legislature. In fact, the Texas Legislature has become increasingly partisan during the last few sessions, In particular, the voter identification bill and recent redistricting map votes have been along party lines. The last few appropriation bills have passed with mostly Republican support and Democrats have mostly opposed them. Even redistricting has not reached the ugliness it did in 2003, when first house Democrats, then senate Democrats, left the state in an effort to stop passage of a Republican-created mid-decade congressional redistricting plan. Overall, however, the vast majority of bills that reach the floor of the house and senate do so with broad bipartisan support. A large majority of bills that pass in the Texas house do so with little or no opposition. In the Senate, bills that draw a handful of "no" votes are most likely to do so from a small cadre of Republican senators, even as most Republicans vote for the specific pieces of legislation. If you see that a bill passed the senate by a vote of 28–3, it is likely that either Republican Dan Patrick or Jane Nelson or Steve Ogden or some combination

4.1

4.2

4.3

4.4

4.5

4.6

4.7

of the three were among the dissenters. In fact, Nelson has been part of the senate for so long that she was often the "1" vote in 30–1 divisions back when the Democrats controlled the Senate. Nonetheless, more bills pass their final vote in the senate 31–0 than are contested.

And this is also meant to imply that chairs are divided equally. With Republicans in control, a majority of the chairs are going to Republicans. In the 2013 senate, for instance, the percentage of Republican chairs essentially mirrored the percentage of Republicans in the senate. It should surprise no one that the plum appointments went to Republicans. But Democrats still found themselves chairing important committees, as John Whitmire was reappointed chair of the Senate Committee on Criminal Justice and Royce West was appointed chair of the Senate Committee on Jurisprudence. Chairs don't always go to the most experienced or knowledgeable member, but those are factors that are weighed alongside partisanship. House appointments were similar in nature.

Furthermore, recent house and senate leaders appointed more opposition party chairs than most rank-and-file party members would like. Dewhurst, Craddick, and Straus all received intense criticism for appointing too many Democrats as chairs. Many Texas Republicans, especially those with Tea Party ties, would like to transition to a Washington-style system where the majority party appoints all of the chairs. At least to this point, expertise, experience, and the ability to get along still trump absolute partisanship in the Texas Legislature. In fact, it was a 2013 freshman house member who initiated a bipartisan effort by which all fellow newcomers wore purple, to signify they were neither Republican red nor Democratic blue, but united.

Although Republicans control all statewide offices today, executive positions were split between the two parties as recently as 1998. The state weathered a decade of split leadership with little ill effect. At times during this period, there was more party infighting than interparty conflict. Lieutenant Governor Bob Bullock, a Democrat, had a much better relationship with Republican Governor George W. Bush than he did with his Democratic predecessor, Ann Richards. Republican Governor Rick Perry fought a legendary and very public battle with former Republican Comptroller Carole Keeton Strayhorn. And lest you think that partisan sniping is reserved for the executive branch, things have not always been rosy sunsets and daisies between Perry and legislative Republicans.

Review the Chapter

(((**Listen** to Chapter 4

Political Parties

4.1 Explain why political parties exist.

The two major parties exist for the purpose of winning elections. In the United States in general and Texas in particular, these parties are dedicated to bringing enough voters together to win offices, with the ultimate goal of controlling the executive branch, the legislative process, and the judiciary. Within limits, political expediency is more important than pure ideology.

Party Structure

4.2 Differentiate between ideological and coalitional parties.

The Republican and Democratic parties are coalitional. Their members sometimes hold vastly contrasting views on important issues, yet they put their differences aside in order to gain power. Ideological parties, like the Green Party and the Libertarian Party, are formed by members who adhere to a rather narrow set of goals. Ideas are more important to them than winning. Not surprisingly, they seldom win.

The Organization of Political Parties in Texas

4.3 Describe the levels of political party organization in Texas.

The organization of the two major political parties is almost identical. Both have temporary and permanent elements. The temporary elements include a series of conventions that select delegates to higher-level conventions and write platforms that depict where each party stands on the issues. The permanent elements include a number of standing positions, including precinct and county chairs—who are elected in primary elections—and state chairs and executive committees—who are chosen through state conventions. The Libertarian and Green parties have many of the same elements, but they don't have primaries, precinct convention attendance is sporadic at best, and the county, district, and state conventions—not primary voters—choose the parties' nominees for office.

The Democratic Party

4.4 Explain the long and successful history of the Democratic Party in Texas.

From the end of Reconstruction until the end of the 1970s, Democrats exercised almost absolute control over the Texas political system. Despite constant Democratic domination, various factions vied for power, creating de facto parties within the party. Although conservatives held power for much of the time, progressives and liberals each had periods of ascendency.

The Republican Party

4.5 Explain the Republican Party's recent success in Texas.

Although John Tower's election to the U.S. Senate in 1961 was a catalyst for the birth of the modern Republican Party in Texas, it would be years before more than a handful of fellow party members joined him in office. It wasn't until 1978 that a Republican was elected governor, and it took another decade before the party captured a single down-ballot statewide race. Yet, by 1996, all statewide seats had turned Republican and, by the early 21st century, the party controlled both houses of the legislature as well.

Party Politics in the New Millennium

4.6 Analyze the challenges facing each major party in the 21st century.

Republicans came out of the 2012 elections looking good. They controlled the house and senate and held every statewide office in both the executive and legislative branches. But interparty fighting and demographic shifts threaten the party's majority status. Adding the Tea Party movement into the already volatile mix of conservative factions makes the battle for control of the party agenda all the more interesting. Long-term demographics favor the Democrats unless the Republicans can make inroads into the emerging Latino and Asian voting blocs. More immediately, the Democrats need to cut into the Republicans' strong advantage with suburban voters.

Partisanship in Texas Governance

4.7 Explain the role of partisanship in Texas governance.

The party that controls the house and senate controls the appointment of committee chairs. Unlike Washington, though, not all committee chairs are members of the majority party. In the Republican-controlled house and senate, many significant committees are chaired by Democrats. Although some issues are extremely partisan, most bills that pass the Texas Legislature enjoy wide bipartisan support.

Learn the Terms

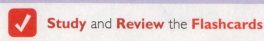 **Study** and **Review** the **Flashcards**

Test Yourself

 Study and **Review** the **Practice Tests**

4.1 Explain why political parties exist.

The most important goal of a major political party is to

  a. win elections.
  b. influence policy.
  c. run the government.
  d. frame important issues.
  e. raise money.

4.2 Differentiate between ideological and coalitional parties.

Which of the following is a coalitional party?

  a. Republican
  b. Green
  c. Libertarian
  d. Socialist
  e. Right to Life

4.3 Describe the levels of political party organization in Texas.

A senatorial district convention is on the same level as a

  a. precinct convention.
  b. county convention.
  c. state convention.
  d. national convention.
  e. elector convention.

4.4 Explain the long and successful history of the Democratic Party in Texas.

Liberals controlled the Texas Democrats' political agenda

  a. from Reconstruction to today.
  b. from 1940 until today.
  c. during the 1930s.
  d. during the 1950s.
  e. during the 1960s.

4.5 Explain the Republican Party's recent success in Texas.

Today in Texas

  a. Republicans dominate statewide offices.
  b. Democrats carry Texas in most presidential elections.
  c. Democrats control the house and senate.
  d. the state is moving toward a three-party structure.
  e. Democrats have regained control of the house.

4.6 Analyze the challenges facing each major party in the 21st century.

The biggest challenge for the Democrats today is

  a. converting conservative voters.
  b. attracting the Bubba vote.
  c. gaining liberal support.
  d. attracting the religious right.
  e. increasing minority turnout.

4.7 Explain the role of partisanship in Texas governance.

Which is true of partisanship in Texas?

  a. Democrats control all senate chair seats.
  b. Committee chairs are evenly divided among Republicans and Democrats.
  c. Most committee chairs are Republican.
  d. Most bills pass along strict party lines.
  e. Experience always trumps partisanship.

Explore Further

Texas Democratic Party: http://www.txdemocrats.org

Texas Republican Party: http://www.texasgop.org

Texas Libertarian Party: http://www.lptexas.org

Texas Green Party: http://www.txgreens.org

Texas League of Women Voters: http://www.lwvtexas.org

Anders, Evan. *Boss Rule in South Texas: The Progressive Era.* Austin: University of Texas Press, 1982.

Black, Earl, and Merle Black. *The Rise of Southern Republicanism.* Cambridge, MA: Belknap Press, 2002.

Davidson, Chandler. *Race and Class in Texas Politics.* Princeton, NJ: Princeton University Press, 1990.

Dyer, James A., Jan E. Leighley, and Arnold Vedlitz. "Party Identification and Public Opinion in Texas, 1984–1994: Establishing a Competitive Two-Party System," in *Texas Politics,* ed. Anthony Champagne and Edward J. Harpham. New York: Norton, 1997.

Elliott, Charles P. "The Texas Trial Lawyers Association: Interest Group under Siege," in *Texas Politics,* ed. Anthony Champagne and Edward J. Harpham. New York: Norton, 1997.

Garcia, Ignacio. *United We Win: The Rise and Fall of La Raza Unida Party.* Tucson: Mexican American Studies and Research Center, University of Arizona, 1989.

Green, George Norris. *The Establishment in Texas Politics, 1938–1957.* Westport, CT: Greenwood Press, 1979.

Hrebenar, Robert J., and Clive S. Thomas, eds. *Interest Group Politics in Southern States.* University: University of Alabama Press, 1992.

Key, V. O. *Southern Politics.* New York: Vintage Books, 1949.

Knaggs, John R. *Two-Party Texas: The John Tower Era, 1961–1984.* Austin, TX: Eakin Press, 1986.

Lenchner, Paul. "The Party System in Texas," in *Texas Politics,* ed. Anthony Champagne and Edward J. Harpham. New York: Norton, 1997.

Navarro, Armando. *La Raza Unida Party: A Chicano Challenge to the U.S. Two-Party Dictatorship.* Philadelphia: Temple University Press, 2000.

San Miguel, Guadalupe, Jr. *Let Them Take Heed: Mexican Americans and the Campaign for Educational Equality in Texas, 1910–1981.* Austin: University of Texas Press, 1987.

5

Interest Groups in Texas Politics

You can't sling a cat around your head without hitting a lobbyist!

—*Veteran House Member During a Session of the Texas Legislature*

A t times, interest groups and the people who represent them seem to be crawling all over the political landscape. While this appears to be especially true during a session of the Texas Legislature, interest groups are full-time participants in this state's politics, and many of these groups work year-round to advance their causes. In the 82nd regular session of the Texas Legislature, topics such as regulating payday lenders, requiring women to view a sonogram before an abortion, and allowing concealed handguns to be carried on campus (see discussion of this issue below) brought about clashes among and between numerous interest group that reflected the pivotal role such groups play in the formulation of Texas public policy. In the 83rd legislature that convened on January 8, 2013, such interest group confrontation was perhaps best symbolized by the different stances enunciated by educators on the one hand and gun rights advocates on the other over the emotionally charged issue of allowing guns in public schools in the wake of the Newtown,

5.1	5.2	5.3	5.4	5.5	5.6
Identify and explain the roles of interest groups in politics.	Compare and contrast the different types of interest groups in Texas.	Analyze the methods used by interest groups to influence policy makers.	Explain the relationship between money and interest groups in the political process.	Show the links between interest groups and other participants in the Texas political environment.	Identify practical ways that you can become involved in the activities of interest groups.

The National Rifle Association, a powerful national interest group, has a significant impact in, and draws considerable support from, Texas. Here, NRA Vice President Sandra Froman addresses a national convention held in Houston.

5.1

5.2

5.3

5.4

5.5

5.6

interest group
A collection of individuals who share a common set of ideas or principles and who attempt to advance those ideas or principles by influencing public-policy makers.

Connecticut, elementary school massacre. Interest groups are among the most powerful forces in Texas politics. They also generate strong opinions about what they do and how they do it. Some people endorse interest groups as a vital and even necessary element in our political equation, but others deride them as divisive and self-seeking "special interests," placing private gain before public good. Tell people you serve as legislative liaison for a state trade association and they might be impressed. Confess that you're a lobbyist for an interest group and they may treat you as a bird flu carrier!

The Roles of Interest Groups

5.1 Identify and explain the roles of interest groups in politics.

☐ Interest Groups Defined

In order to explain the role of interest groups in Texas politics, we should begin by defining this entity. An **interest group** is composed of people who share a common set of ideas or principles and who attempt to advance those ideas or principles by influencing public-policy makers. This definition shares some of the same components as that of a political party in that both entities are united (albeit sometimes rather loosely) around a core of ideas or principles and both are organized (again, to widely varying degrees). However, interest groups differ significantly from political parties in at least two ways.

First, interest groups do not run candidates for office. At first glance, this may seem to be an artificial distinction. After all, haven't we heard elected officials proudly proclaim that they are life members of the NRA, the PTA, or some other such group? Obviously, members of interest groups can run for and win political office. But when they seek public office, they are identified on the ballot as the candidate of a political party, not of the interest group to which they happen to belong. Their path to the general election leads through the party primary, and their campaign benefits from the support of the party that has nominated them. Moreover, in those elections where party designations on the ballot are forbidden (including races for school board, city council, community college board of trustees, and others at local levels of government), no group label whatsoever will appear by the candidate's name.

Rather than formally trying to capture elected office by running candidates, an interest group focuses on attempting to persuade those who already hold office, as well as those occupying positions of executive or administrative responsibility, to see things their way. They also may mobilize their members to work on behalf of particular candidates who are friendly toward the group and its goals. They may even help raise money for a candidate's campaign. But they don't nominate their members for political office, so you aren't going to see a candidate from the National Rifle Association Party on the ballot.

A second difference between interest groups and political parties can be found in their focus. Parties both in the United States and Texas usually tend to address a broad array of issues in their attempt to build a winning coalition among voters. They may take positions on such topics as abortion, free trade, gun control, environmental action, business regulation, crime prevention, and many other political subjects. The party's position on these topics sometimes appears to be superficial because the breadth of their appeal limits the depth to which they can develop their stances. Simply put, parties try to say a little about a lot.

Interest groups, on the other hand, focus on a single issue or a narrowly related group of issues. Because they are not preoccupied with coalition building, they can afford to expend most of their efforts on the subject that is of prime concern to their members. They don't have to (and usually aren't inclined to) take a position on nonrelated issues. Thus, the National Rifle Association probably won't take a public stance

The Texas Constitution

A Closer Look

The U.S. Constitution seems to allude to something that could be described as interest group activity in the First Amendment when it states, in part, that "Congress shall make no law . . . abridging . . . the right of the people peaceably to assemble, and to petition the Government for a redress of grievances."[1] Those who supported adoption of this proposed new Constitution saw benefit in the actions of what we would today call interest groups. In *Federalist No. 10,* James Madison made the point that competition among such groups (whom he referred to as "factions") would likely prevent one single group from cornering the market on political and governmental power. In like manner, the Texas constitution specifically guarantees that "citizens shall have the right, in a peaceable manner, to assemble together for their common good and apply to those invested with the powers of government for redress of grievance or other purposes, by petition, address or remonstrance."[2] At the very least, this means that you and your friends or fellow believers can get together and, as long as you do not participate in violent behavior, can try to make some senator or representative see your point of view and help you get what you want.

In light of the growing influence of money in American and Texas politics, is Madison's assertion that competition among "factions" would keep a single group from gaining political and governmental power still valid today?

1. What are specific examples of interest groups (Madison's "factions") seeking to have their grievances redressed?

5.1

5.2

5.3

5.4

5.5

5.6

on the issue of abortion. Likewise, the Texas State Teachers Association does not express a group position on the issue of emissions testing for automobiles in metropolitan areas. By focusing on a narrow range of topics, interest groups can develop more in-depth levels of information than can a political party. Simply put, interest groups try to say a lot about a little.

☐ Interest Groups: Okay

While it may not be popular to say so publicly, an argument can be made for the notion that interest groups are a vital part of our political process. For one thing, they probably have a kind of backhanded blessing from both the U.S. and Texas constitutions (see the rationale for such an assertion in The Texas Constitution: A Closer Look).

Constitutional considerations aside, interest groups are useful for a couple of reasons: They magnify voices, and they multiply choices. By magnifying voices, these groups make it more likely that your opinions and your ideas will be heard. One person walking back and forth in front of the capitol in Austin carrying a sign that says "Save the Paluxy" might get a curious glance and a fleeting reflection from a passing legislator on just what kind of endangered species a "Paluxy" is. An organized group of a thousand people e-mailing, tweeting, writing, and calling that same legislator urging her to enact legislation to protect the Paluxy River from development will likely get more of her attention, especially if they include her constituents. They may even be able to enlist her support. Each of those thousand people has a personal belief in that group's goal, but collective action through an interest group allows each person to voice that belief more effectively and more pervasively.

Interest groups also multiply choices. To illustrate this idea, let's look at the two-party system in this state. If you don't like the Republican Party position on an issue, you can always turn to the Democrats. But what if you don't like what the Democrats have to say on that issue? If neither of the two parties takes a position with which you agree, you can end up extremely frustrated. You may in fact conclude, as did early-20th-century humorist Will Rogers, that choosing between Democrats and Republicans is an exercise in futility. As Rogers wryly stated, "The more you read and observe about this Politics thing, you got to admit that each party is worse than the other."[3] To someone in this situation, interest

5.1

5.2

5.3

5.4

5.5

5.6

Occupy Austin, an offshoot of Occupy Wall Street, is a diverse, grassroots movement with room for numerous anti-establishment messages. Movement politics provide both a way to be heard and an outlet for frustration.

groups may provide just the avenue along which to advance a heartfelt cause. Also, interest groups can (and usually do) address questions that parties often ignore as being too trivial. For example, neither major party may be overly concerned with saving the Paluxy River, but an interest group could easily make that issue one of its paramount concerns. If that's the issue that most concerns you, then that interest group becomes a more likely choice for realizing your political aims. However, interest groups not only multiply choices for citizens, they also multiply choices for policy makers. As interest groups ply their "wares" (information) among legislators, regulators, and other decision makers, the competing viewpoints thus presented afford a broader array of possible policy options.

☐ Interest Groups: Not Okay

Of course, some will argue that interest groups have a negative side as well. It is often pointed out that the proliferation of special interest groups in the political arena seems to have contributed to the much publicized fracturing of American culture. This school of thought holds that the division and redivision of our society into groups that are often hostile toward other competing groups helps to create a politics of confrontation and somehow heightens the struggle for what often are perceived as scarce public services and resources. Those who are leery of interest groups suggest that in a society such as ours, which is already ethnically and culturally diverse (and all too often divided along these lines), these added internal divisions only make it more difficult for people to come together and to find consensus. When the social fabric seems always to be badly frayed, if not outright shredded, such divisiveness is seen as something without which we would be better off.

Another possible problem that interest group politics may pose is the disparity that often occurs among such groups in terms of their actual ability to organize, inform, and influence policy makers. Not all interest groups are created equal, and differences in the size and wealth of various groups often create a political playing field that is anything but level. Moreover, the added dimension of representation afforded citizens by interest groups may be largely mitigated if the citizen in question is not aware (or does not particularly care) that he or she is a member of such a group. Most Americans (and most Texans) belong to, are affiliated with, or have some connection to more than one interest group, but those Americans (or those Texans) need to be aware of that link and its potential benefits in order to take *full* advantage of what the group has to offer. Of course, one of the good things we've already pointed out about pluralism is that, with so many groups out there, most people's views are represented whether or not they choose to participate (or are even aware of their group ties). But lack of membership awareness can mean that some potentially powerful or influential groups may not be successful in achieving their ends, especially if such success is predicated on mobilizing large numbers of group members in support of policy goals (see the Membership Mobilization section later in this chapter).

centralized interest group
One with decision making concentrated near the top among a relatively small leadership group.

decentralized interest group
One with decision making widely dispersed among the membership.

The Types of Interest Groups

5.2   Compare and contrast the different types of interest groups in Texas.

T here are literally thousands of actual (not to mention potential) interest groups in Texas. This is partly because there are a lot of people in Texas. However, a large population alone does not guarantee a bumper crop of interest groups. That large population has to be sufficiently diverse in its composition to produce identifiable subgroupings of people who may share common ideas. These groups then have the potential to organize themselves as true interest groups. Obviously, Texas has such diversity within its large population, and this helps account for the many interest groups there.

This plethora of groups also exhibits an interesting variety of organizational forms. Some of these groups are highly **centralized** in their organization. They concentrate decision making at or near the top of the group's structure and exercise leadership through a small group at that level. An example of such a group is the Texas Community College Teachers Association. Although this group has approximately 6,000 members, a legislative committee of 15 members proposes its public-policy agenda, which is then ratified by a six-member executive committee. Its president and its professional staff make most of the group's political contacts, although in recent years the association has hired a professional lobbyist to serve as a point of contact with policy makers. While rank-and-file members are occasionally called on to engage in large group activities, the association tends to avoid demonstrative or confrontational politics, focusing instead on providing timely information to key decision makers in the legislature and in certain executive agencies.

Other groups have a more **decentralized** internal structure. In these groups, decision making and leadership are often widely dispersed among the membership, and the members focus on a good bit of regional and local political activity in addition to dealing with issues before the state legislature. The Chamber of Commerce in Texas is a good example of this type of organizational structure. Although there is a state-level chamber, there are also numerous regional and local bodies that pursue their own political agendas in addition to working with the state office. These local organizations are often very active in contacting legislators and other policy makers in support not only of their general group goals, but also of their own more local agendas as well.

5.1
5.2
5.3
5.4
5.5
5.6

5.1

5.2

5.3

5.4

5.5

5.6

amorphous interest group
One with tenuously connected membership and often unclear interest focus.

Some groups in Texas even lack the most rudimentary of organizational structures. The people who make up these groups may have only a tenuous connection to the group and may only occasionally act as a group. We could best describe the structure of such groups as **amorphous**. The homeless and welfare recipients might well fit into this category. Communication among the "membership" of such groups is difficult and sporadic, and they rarely are able to orchestrate action in support of specific policy goals. Political activities by such groups are usually spontaneous and in response to some immediate perceived threat to the group.

A classic example of this kind of spontaneous group activity was seen in the activities of the various "Occupy" groups ("Occupy Wall Street," "Occupy Houston," "Occupy Austin," and the like) who objected to the bailout of large banks and other such public policies that seemed to favor the "One Percent" enacted in the wake of the financial crisis of 2008–2009. These groups erected tent cities, proclaimed manifestos, sang protest songs, and otherwise tried to focus the attention of policy makers on what the groups considered to be egregiously unfair actions on the part of government. Some would argue that such loose collections of people really shouldn't be called interest groups. However, like more formally structured interest groups, amorphous groups do exhibit collective activity on occasion and, in this particular instance, did attempt to influence public policy. When they do, they are functioning as if they were an interest group. A major problem, of course, lies in the lack of knowledge and experience regarding the policy-making process that characterizes many such groups. And in interest group politics, as in playing baseball or the guitar, practice makes perfect.

Business Interests

Groups that represent the business community in Texas consistently prove to be the most powerful and influential in the state. Texas's political climate is quite friendly toward its large business community, as you would expect in a state where the individualistic political culture is so prevalent. These groups, often called trade associations, can consistently gain the ears of policy makers because of their numerical (and financial) strength and because most have access to a vast amount of information that legislators can use (see the Methods of Interest Groups section later in this chapter). Armed with that information, most of these groups try to maintain a friendly regulatory climate, promote a tax structure that is favorable to the business community, and lend their support to legislation that can benefit their own particular enterprises.

One perennial power among business interest groups is the Texas Good Roads and Transportation Association. With a membership drawn primarily from construction contractors, this group works hard to promote the extension and renovation of the state's highway system, which is one of the largest in the nation. This of course results in more state contracts, which in turn helps keep the association's members busy.[4]

Another group in this category is the Texas Taxpayers and Research Association (TTARA). This innocuous-sounding organization began operating more than 70 years ago as the Texas Research League. Later, it merged with the Texas Taxpayers Association, and its membership includes a veritable who's who among the Texas business community. The TTARA specializes in generating data related to the state's tax structure and is particularly interested in helping to develop the state's overall fiscal policies. The legislature and many state agencies make routine use of this powerful group's information, enabling its members to enjoy an advantage in shaping policy from the very beginning of the process.[5]

Labor Interests

Interest groups that act on behalf of organized labor have not fared well in Texas politics. The same political climate that favors groups from the business community often generates an attitude of antipathy toward labor groups. When you look at the issues that labor emphasizes, they often conflict with those that might help produce a "healthy business climate." Labor groups, usually organized as unions, tend to push for enhanced workplace safety, preservation of rights under worker's compensation laws, and, in the case of farm laborers, limitations on the use of pesticides. Such views on these issues are not the sort to set a businessman's heart singing. The AFL-CIO and the Oil, Chemical and Atomic Workers of Texas are among the more effective labor organizations in the state. The latter group has had some impact on the political agenda in southeast Texas, especially in the Galveston Bay–Beaumont area. Because of the many oil refineries and petrochemical plants located there, the union workers in those plants have, on occasion, been able to flex some political muscle. However, in most cases, unions and other labor interest groups wind up fighting a kind of rearguard action, hoping to minimize losses but rarely ever enjoying a clear-cut victory.[6]

☐ Professional Interests

Most professions—doctors, teachers, lawyers, accountants, and others—form and maintain interest groups. These groups also are some of the most powerful forces in Texas politics and often rival the more broadly based business groups in their influence on public-policy formulation. Most of these groups focus on issues that relate directly to their fields of expertise, such as determining the criteria for admission to the profession or setting the operational boundaries of that profession.

Some of the more influential of these groups include the Texas Medical Association, the Texas Trial Lawyers Association, and, on a somewhat lower power plane, the Texas State Teachers Association.[7] Much of their power, especially in the policy areas of medicine and the law, flows from the fact that those topics often involve issues that are complex and esoteric. The specialized knowledge that members of those two professions can bring to bear on such issues gives them a decided advantage in most cases. As a matter of practical reality, most legislators who are neither doctors nor lawyers either have to take the word of one or the other of these groups on such issues or reject their information out of hand.

When groups like these clash with each other or with groups from the business community, sparks fly, political tensions increase dramatically, and money flows like a Hill Country river after a thunderstorm. Some of the fiercest interest group battles in the legislature have been waged over issues such as medical malpractice, which can pit lawyers, doctors, and insurance companies against one another. And in the now-classic Pennzoil-Texaco battle over antitrust legislation, millions of dollars were spent in a period of days, and both sides hired so many lobbyists that a scorecard was needed just to keep track of who was working for whom. More recent examples of these kinds of titanic interest group struggles can be seen in legislative battles over deregulation of the telecommunications and public utilities industries. Because almost all of us buy gas, use phones, turn on lights, and go to the doctor, such confrontations among and between business and professional groups can have long-lasting impact on all the citizens of Texas.

☐ Ethnic Interests

A number of interest groups have formed to represent ethnic groups in the political process, but most have not fared well in their attempts to influence public policy. Although Texas presents a mosaic of ethnic and cultural communities, this diversity is not reflected among the major purveyors of influence in Austin.

African American Texans have for many years had their concerns voiced by the National Association for the Advancement of Colored People (NAACP). This group's legislative successes have been rare, but its willingness to use the courts has resulted in significant gains for the African American community, notably in the areas of public access and accommodation as well as voting rights.[8]

In like manner, groups such as the League of United Latin American Citizens (LULAC) and the Mexican American Legal Defense and Educational Fund (MAL-DEF) have sought to protect and advance the interests of Hispanic Texans over the years. As with the NAACP, these Latino interest groups have often sought to influence policy through court action rather than through legislative activity. Recently,

5.1

5.2

5.3

5.4

5.5

5.6

5.1

5.2

5.3

5.4

5.5

5.6

single-issue groups
Interest groups, such as the NRA and MADD, that devote their energies to pursuing a single, narrowly defined policy goal.

MALDEF has become heavily involved in court cases arising out of the passage of local anti-immigrant ordinances in such cities as Farmers Branch, and the group has won several preliminary legal battles to enjoin the enforcement of such local laws.[9]

In reality, such ethnic interest groups are often frustrated, not only by the vestiges of racism and cultural bias that still mark our political system, but also by a sometimes stubborn unwillingness to work together on issues of common concern, such as equal pay for equal work and equal access to higher education opportunities. Intergroup jealousies frequently have led to a squandering of political influence and opportunity. By the time these groups finish fighting each other, they often have nothing left to expend on other opponents, many of whom had them outmanned and outgunned (monetarily) from the beginning.

☐ Other Interests

Many other kinds of interest groups abound in Texas. Some of the most zealous in pursuit of their aims are what can be called **single-issue groups**. Business, labor, and professional groups may address issues in several areas related to their primary field of concern, but these single-issue interest groups—as their name suggests—focus on one issue only. One of the most consistently influential of these groups is the National Rifle Association (NRA). The NRA wields national influence, but it has been especially successful in pursuing its goals in Texas. The group advocated for the passage of a concealed handgun law in this state for years, and in the 1995 legislative session they saw this goal realized. The last two sessions of the legislature saw this group supporting a measure that would have allowed possessors of concealed handgun licenses (CHLs) to carry their weapons onto public college and university campuses. As this scenario played out, the power and influence of the NRA was augmented by the support of a veritable grab bag of other interest groups, including survivalists, conservative student groups, and even some women's groups (normally, not the most energetic supporters of enhanced gun rights). Some of these groups were, like the NRA, highly organized, while others tended to form as the issue gained the attention of both the public and policy makers and were thus more amorphous in structure. The bill died in both sessions, but not for lack of intense pressure by the groups supporting it or, for that matter, sponsors in both the house and senate. In 2013, the NRA announced plans to once again push for the adoption of this policy and to expand its application to public school teachers in the wake of the Sandy Hook Elementary School shootings in December of 2012.[10]

Another single-issue group that has gained a fair amount of attention over the years is Mothers Against Drunk Drivers (MADD). A true grassroots organization, MADD worked for years to toughen DWI laws in Texas, often with little success. For example, the group failed in its attempt to ban all open containers of alcoholic beverages in vehicles during the 1995 session of the legislature. But groups like MADD lie outside the Texas power zone of business and the professions and therefore rarely get what they want the first time around. The primary lesson such groups must learn is that you've got to "suit up and show up" at every legislative session. MADD's dogged persistence in pursuit of its legislative agenda was rewarded during the 1999 session when the house and senate agreed to lower the blood-alcohol limit for determining legal intoxication from .10 to .08. Two years later, MADD returned, once more seeking to ban all open alcohol containers in vehicles. This time they won.[11]

Environmental organizations are another example of single-issue interest groups. For many years, they've been a voice crying in the wilderness of the Texas political landscape. Traditional Texans, who tend to view nature as something to be conquered and subdued, have little regard for those they often derisively refer to as "tree huggers." However, the continued population growth in the state has generated new concerns over such issues as air and water quality, gridlock, open space, and urban sprawl. Many environmental groups have attempted to address these concerns from a lifestyle, rather than a purely environmental, perspective. This shift in strategy has opened up discussions with many who formerly disdained them (e.g., alliances

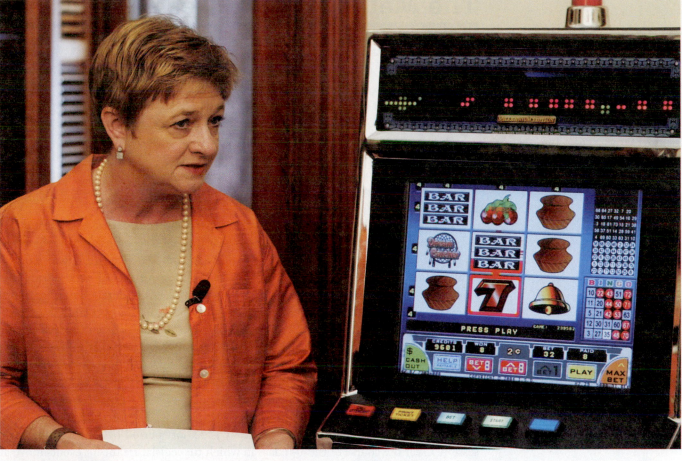

Lobbyist Suzi Paynter of the Christian Life Commission speaks against the expansion of legalized gaming in Texas. Pro-gaming interests are working hard to legalize casino gambling in Texas.

between environmentalists and hunting and fishing enthusiasts are becoming more common). The Nature Conservancy, for one, has proved innovative in avoiding the more confrontational strategies often favored by such groups. They have pioneered the building of partnerships among disparate communities of interest—particularly businesspeople, sportsmen, and environmentalists—that have led to creative programs of public-private land acquisition and management. These programs have, in turn, saved some of the most fragile and unique natural areas in the state of Texas.[12]

Some interest groups form out of a desire to provide public service to the general citizenry. The League of Women Voters works to advance political awareness and informed decision making on the part of voters (and by the way, you don't have to be a woman to join the league). The league routinely publishes information about candidates (usually in the candidates' own words) prior to most elections. The LWV doesn't endorse candidates and doesn't contribute to the election campaigns of any candidates. In this way they have maintained their objectivity and earned the trust of parties and groups that span the political spectrum.[13]

Finally, there are groups promoting particular points of view with regard to morality and lifestyle. The Christian Life Commission of the Baptist General Convention of Texas, a staunch and consistent opponent of legalized gambling, also frequently speaks out on family issues. Groups like the Parent Teacher Association (PTA) focus on children's issues, and numerous pro-life (Texas Right to Life) and pro-choice (Pro Choice Texas) organizations regularly confront each other and lawmakers on the issue of abortion. Finally, a growing number of groups representing the gay and lesbian communities of Texas (such as Equality Texas) are speaking up and working to advance their goals.[14] If you haven't found a group somewhere out there to represent your interests, chances are you just haven't looked hard enough.

5.1 5.2 5.3 5.4 5.5 5.6

5.1

5.2

5.3

5.4

5.5

5.6

The Methods of Interest Groups

5.3 Analyze the methods used by interest groups to influence policy makers.

information dissemination
The process whereby an interest group representative makes information about issues available to policy makers.

Interest groups attempt to gain their ends in a number of different ways. Many of their methods focus on the Texas Legislature because that body is the primary policy-making agent in Texas politics. The nature and structure of the legislature itself help to shape the methods used by interest groups and enhance the role of these groups as some of the most powerful forces in Texas politics. Let's look more closely at how the legislature's methods of operation make interest groups so effective.

The Texas Legislature meets in regular session for a maximum of 140 days beginning in January of every odd-numbered year. In that five-month period, between 6,000 and 7,000 pieces of legislation likely will be introduced. The entire two-year (biennial) budget for the state of Texas must be hammered out and adopted during this time span. Complex issues such as tort reform, electric utility deregulation (or, more recently, reregulation), casino gambling, toll road construction, and equitable funding for public education often are the focus of the legislature's attention. All of this legislating is to be done by so-called citizen-legislators who are paid $600 per month before taxes and who have extremely limited in-house research and staff resources available. Merely reading all the bills that are introduced in a legislative session is virtually impossible; being able to understand the subtleties of every piece of legislation simply cannot be done without help.

This volume of work is compounded by the short period of time allotted for a session. Over the course of the 140 days in which the legislature meets, events move at an accelerated pace, reaching a frenetic climax during the last month. Although many have described Texas as having a "part-time legislature," a more accurate description would be to call it a "full-time legislature part of the time." That's not merely a semantic difference. For these five months, lawmakers tend to be consumed by the tasks confronting them. Workdays often begin at dawn or before and end at midnight or beyond. It is this combination of too much to do and too little time in which to do it that enhances the power of interest groups.

In this pressure-cooker environment, the most important commodity available to legislators isn't gold, silver, oil futures, or pork bellies; it's information. Legislators with information usually get to call the shots. Legislators with information usually get what they want. Those without information usually get left out and left behind. Given this reality, what kind of entity is in a position to generate the sort of specialized information crucial to the legislative process? If you said a legislator's own staff, sorry, you lose. If you said an interest group, then you get to play in the championship round.

Interest groups exert the kind of influence they do in Texas politics in large part because they give legislators the one thing they need the most and have the least: information. Successful interest groups spend a great amount of time in **information dissemination**. This process will likely begin months before a legislative session actually convenes. Once a particular issue is identified as being on the front burner politically, groups on all sides of that issue will delve into the topic, research its pros and cons, and look for compelling evidence that reinforces their stance. Please note that we said all aspects of the issue will be explored by the groups concerned. Not only do you need to know the facts that will help your group; you also need to know what will hurt it. And you need to know the legitimate points that are likely to be made by opposition groups.

Harvesting information is probably the least glamorous and most burdensome aspect of interest group activity. It involves slogging through various and sundry legal codes, compilations of state law, administrative rules and regulations, as well as the hundreds of other sources relevant merely to one issue. Yet it is this kind of persistent digging that can provide a group with its best ammunition. Of course, the continuing evolution of the Internet as a source of broadly accessible information has meant that interest groups no longer may exert almost exclusive control over facts and figures. Yet, despite this apparent "democratization" of information access, most legislative staffers have such large workloads that they find it impossible to compete with large, well-financed interest groups in generating in-depth information of a specialized nature. Therefore, it is not an exaggeration to say that most groups' successes (or failures) on a given issue will be determined in large part by the kind of research they do and the resultant information they are able to generate.

ESTABLISHING A LINK Once a group has researched a particular topic and staked out a position on a particular issue, it has to be able to deliver the information to policy makers. The best information in the world is worthless if you don't have **access** to those who can help your cause. Gaining this access is one of the most important things a group can do to ensure its success.

Most interest groups try to gain access through the activities of a lobbyist. A **lobbyist** is a person who works on behalf of an interest group and serves as the point of contact between the group and policy makers. It is the responsibility of the lobbyist to take the information gathered by (or for) the group and use it to persuade legislators and other public officials to the group's point of view. While some lobbyists volunteer their services (usually to the groups of which they are a member), more and more groups are hiring lobbyists today than ever before, as noted in the Inside the Federalist System box. These lobbyists are paid (and often paid extremely well) for their professional services. Not surprisingly, the number of lobbyists in Austin and elsewhere throughout Texas has increased sharply over recent years.

Who are these people? Where do lobbyists come from, and how do they operate? Anybody can rent office space in Austin and hang out a sign announcing that they are a "legislative advocate," but the most successful lobbyists come from several readily identifiable groups. Some of the busiest lobbyists are former members of the Texas Legislature. That stands to reason: A man or woman who has actually served in the house or the senate is likely to know not only how the legislative process is *supposed* to work but also how it *actually* works. In most cases, knowledge of the latter is much more important. For example, knowing that a certain senator is chair of a key

5.1

5.2

5.3

5.4

5.5

5.6

access
The ability of an interest group to contact policy makers in an attempt to enlist their help. Access is crucial, for without it an interest group's information is largely useless.

lobbyist
A person who works on behalf of an interest group and who serves as a point of contact between the group and policy makers.

Inside the Federalist System

Interest Groups in Texas

Because our government operates at both the state and national level, interest groups work in both Austin and Washington. When most people think about lobbyists, they think of K Street in Washington and of their interaction with the national government. In Texas, though, interest groups might hold even more power, as legislators have less access to unbiased information than members of the U.S. Congress do. Although there are more lobbyists in the District of Columbia, Texas has more per dollar of government expenditure. According to the Texas Ethics Commission, there were 1,474 registered lobbyists in Texas in 2012. The Center for Responsive Politics lists 12,051 federal lobbyists in 2012. However, it should be noted that these two interest group sectors do not necessarily operate independently of one another. While the federal government and state governments often focus on different problems (states, for example, don't concern themselves with foreign policy), they do from time to time address the same policy issues. When this happens, interest groups at both the

federal and state levels will often coordinate their activities in order to maximize their influence on the formulation of public policy. For example, as the U.S. Congress and the Texas Legislature convened in January of 2013, both the American Medical Association and the Texas Medical Association announced their respective legislative advocacy agendas. Both groups sought to promote an adequate health care workforce, provide appropriate funding for physician services, and reduce red tape and regulations on health care providers.[15] By coordinating their efforts at both the federal and state level, these two groups hope to maximize their influence on the formulation of public health care policy.

1. Why are interest groups especially effective in influencing the formulation of public policy in Texas?

2. How does the schedule of regular legislative sessions in Texas enhance the influence of interest groups?

5.1

5.2

5.3

5.4

5.5

5.6

Lobbyists for Partners in Mobility, a business-oriented group which favors greater roadway spending, gather outside the Texas Highway Department prior to a formal meeting. Encounters with elected and agency officials can impact legislation and regulations. Coalitions formed with like minded lobbyists can provide benefits as well.

hired gun

A professional, outside lobbyist employed by an interest group to represent its interests on a particular issue. The relationship lasts until the issue is settled.

committee is well and good. However, knowing that the senator has not one clue as to what goes on in the committee, and that the really knowledgeable person you need to talk to about a bill is the clerk of the committee, can be crucial. This kind of insider's knowledge, along with a generally well-developed network of friends within the legislature, makes the retired house or senate member an excellent lobbyist. Examples of such lobbyists include Gib Lewis (a former Texas house Speaker), former state senator Kent Caperton (who in 2005 joined the Ben Barnes Group, an influential lobbying firm headed by former Texas lieutenant governor Ben Barnes), and former state representative Mike Toomey, featured in this chapter's Texas Mosaic.

Of course, not all lobbyists are ex-legislators. Many entered the field after being involved in politics as a staff member of an elected official. This kind of background allows for building a network almost as good as that of a former legislator. Examples of such advocates include the late George Christian, and his son and partner, George Scott Christian. The elder Christian, a fixture in Texas politics for three decades, was a former press secretary to President Lyndon Johnson with a vast network of contacts across the Texas political landscape. George the younger also served a staff apprenticeship as a legislative aide to former State Senator Ray Farabee. Another example of a staff member-turned-lobbyist is Russell "Rusty" Kelley, who was chief aide to the late Billy Clayton during Clayton's tenure as Speaker of the house. These lobbyists, as well as many who are former legislators, are sometimes referred to as **hired guns**. This simply means that anyone can engage their services (if they can afford to). The client pays a fee to have the lobbyist represent the group on an issue. When the issue is settled, the job is done, and lobbyist and client may part company until another issue brings them together. However, these lobbyists work hard to retain their most lucrative clients on a continuing basis, and consistent success in representing these clients is usually the best guarantee of such retention.

Then there are lobbyists who are lawyers and who use their legal training to represent their clients. Of course, it's not unusual for a hired-gun lobbyist to be a lawyer, but the fact is that more and more law firms across the state are using attorneys from their staffs for the sole or primary responsibility of lobbying for the firm's clientele. For many years, one of the most successful such lobbyists in Austin has been Gaylord Armstrong. His firm, McGinnis, Lochridge, and Kilgore, employs numerous staff attorneys to serve the legislative interests of a number of important corporate clients. Over the years, Armstrong has represented such clients as American Express, Exxon Mobil Corporation, Texas Cable and Telecommunications Association, and Texas Instruments before the legislature. Other giant law firms from around the state, like Baker Botts in Houston and Hughes and Luce in Dallas, maintain scores of lawyers on staff to do this sort of lobbying exclusively, and some firms try to maximize their efforts by hiring lawyers who are also former legislators.

Some interest groups still use the services of their own members as lobbyists, but this practice is not as widespread as it once was. The rising costs of lobbying and the fact that such advocacy has in many cases become a year-round activity has made it much more difficult to use amateurs. For example, the Texas Community College Teachers Association (TCCTA) will usually offer testimony on issues of concern to the group through its elected president and occasionally through various committee chairs, all of whom are members of the organization. But it can be very difficult (and sometimes impossible) for someone who must be in the classroom every day also to be available, often at a moment's notice, to run to Austin and speak on the group's behalf. Therefore, so in recent years, TCCTA has employed the services of a professional lobbyist, Beaman Floyd. Many groups who use their own members as lobbyists are constrained by their small membership or lack of sufficient operating funds. Obviously, a group's size and relative affluence can be crucial factors in its overall influence.

FORMAL CONTACTS Most interest groups will attempt to make some kind of formal contact with legislators in order to win their support. Usually, this will mean that the lobbyist for the group will sit down and talk directly to the legislator, outlining the issue as the group sees it, and answering any questions the legislator may have. In these meetings, the lobbyist will try to be as brief as possible and still get his or her point across. Timing can be very important in this process. If contact is made too far in advance of debate on an issue, any information given tends to be forgotten. Wait too long and you may not have time to explain your position fully. Often, when you share the information is as important as what you share.

It has been our experience that many students assume lobbyists will routinely misrepresent the truth to legislators in order to get them to go along with their group's ideas. In fact, that rarely happens, not because all lobbyists are as pure as the driven snow with regard to their ethics, but because most fear the consequences of this behavior. If a senator or representative discovers that a lobbyist has deliberately lied, what are the chances that legislator will ever believe that lobbyist again? Those lobbyists who have been the most successful over the years know that their success rests in large part on their credibility and that one lie can destroy that credibility. Now this doesn't mean that a lobbyist won't present the facts in a way that is most favorable to the group represented. That, after all, is the nature of the job. But deliberate lies are not part of the arsenal of reputable lobbyists. In fact, many lobbyists will also allude to the arguments that might be offered up against their position by opposing groups, if only to be able to deal with those arguments in a preemptive manner and thus neutralize their effect.

Beyond individual meetings with legislators, interest groups may try to influence policy formation during the meeting of legislative committees. Committees are the heart of the legislative process, and the fate of most legislation is decided there. In many instances, the best opportunity for a group to get a bill passed (or killed) will be here. Lobbyists routinely testify before committees and subcommittees and often try to work with committee members and staff to alter wording, add amendments, or delete offensive clauses in proposed legislation. This can be a very time-consuming

5.1

5.2

5.3

5.4

5.5

5.6

5.1

5.2

5.3

5.4

5.5

5.6

Texas ★ Mosaic

A Lobbyist's Tale

Had Chaucer included a lobbyist among his pilgrims, Mike Toomey could have spun a most interesting tale for his fellow travelers. One of the most active and successful lobbyists in Austin today, Toomey took a typical road to his current occupation. After representing the Houston area for several terms in the house, he then served as chief of staff for Governors Bill Clements and Rick Perry before going into the lobbying business. He is a prototypical lobbyist who has parlayed his legislative experiences and expertise into an extremely lucrative postgovernment career. Toomey numbers among his clientele a wide array of powerful business and professional entities in Texas. The following list highlights a dozen of his 2012 clients as well as the range of the fee each contracted to pay Toomey over the course of the year.

Associated Builders and Contractors of Texas
$25,000–$49,999.00

AT&T
$50,000–$99,999.99

Cigna
$50,000–$99,999.99

Corrections Corporation of America
$50,000–$99,999.99

Green Mountain Energy
$50,000–$99,999.99

Liberty Mutual Insurance Co.
$50,000–$99,999.99

Merck Sharp & Dohme Corp.
$50,000–$99,999.99
01/28/09–12/31/09

Plough Pharmaceuticals
$50,000–$99,999.99

Sam Houston Race Park Ltd.
$100,000–$149, 999.99
01/28/09–12/31/09

Texans for Lawsuit Reform
$25,000–$49,999.00

Texas Hotel and Lodging Association
$25,000–$49,999.99

Xerox Business Services LLC
$25,000–$49,999.00

Texas Ethics Commission, 2012 List of Registered Lobbyists with Employers/ Clients. http://www.ethics.state.tx.us/tedd/lobcon2012e.htm.

1. Can you identify some reasons Mr. Toomey's clients might have wanted to retain his services during 2012, which was not a year in which the legislature met?

2. Based on the identities of the groups represented by Mr. Toomey, could you draw any conclusions about his own political beliefs?

(not to mention frustrating) ritual. Lobbyists may spend hours waiting to offer testimony only to have a hearing canceled at the last minute. Often the committee's work has to be monitored daily (and sometimes hourly) to make sure nothing contrary to the group's interests has been added to a bill. Factor in having to monitor several (or several score) bills at the same time and you can see what a formidable task effective lobbying can be.

INFORMAL CONTACTS You can see how overwhelming the frantic pace of a legislative session can be for both lobbyist and legislator. Days filled with floor sessions, committee meetings, visits from constituents, and the myriad other chores of a regular session can leave little time for extended communication between interest groups and policy makers. At this juncture, many groups seek to provide such opportunities through what can be called informal contacts. These allow for the cultivation of relationships in a more leisurely and personable way than do formal meetings and committee hearings.

Most groups who develop such contacts use social occasions to do so. Interest groups will often host various kinds of parties and get-togethers on a regular basis during a legislative session. At these parties, group members and lobbyists can mix and mingle with legislators, committee staffers, even secretaries in a relaxed, depressurized atmosphere. Issues can be discussed in detail, and subtle nuances of policy can be explored. Perhaps most important, lobbyists can get to know legislators as people and can begin to cultivate personal relationships with them. As most people know, talking to a friend is much easier than talking to a stranger.

The importance of these contacts is underscored by the number of groups who engage in such activities and the amount of money they spend on them. In the course of trying to shape legislation, interest groups spend hundreds of thousands of dollars for wining and dining legislators during (as well as before and after) a regular session. Although new ethics legislation has helped to curb some of the more egregious examples of such spending (see the Regulating Interest Groups section), the words of Charles Deaton still ring true. Deaton, the founding editor of the *Texas Government Newsletter*, was speaking to a group of college students who were in Austin for a field trip. He suggested that if a legislator went to every breakfast, brunch, lunch buffet, cocktail party, and sit-down banquet hosted by scores of interest groups during a regular session, at the end of the 140 days, that legislator ran the very real risk of becoming a 700-pound alcoholic!

So how are we to regard such efforts by interest groups? Are they blatant attempts to buy a member's vote with fun, food, and frivolity? Or are they merely gatherings where people with common interests get together to relax and have no material influence on policy? As is usually the case in politics, the truth probably lies somewhere between these two extremes. No one who has watched Texas politics over the years can deny that such contacts often prove beneficial to the group that initiates them. Yet to say that such events "buy" votes for that group is an oversimplification. The vast majority of legislators don't have their votes on the market. Even if one did, it's doubtful that a steak dinner or a plate of barbeque could affect such a purchase. No, these events don't buy votes. But they may help a lobbyist gain access, and that can be crucial. In an atmosphere where both time and information are in short supply, having the time to make your point is often the difference between success and failure. The best information in the world is useless if you don't have access to those who can use that information to help you and your group. They may not agree with what you tell them. They may even wind up voting against you. But it won't be because they never knew what you had to say on the issue.

This question of access brings up another point for consideration. Although all kinds of groups are free to organize as interest groups and attempt to influence public policy, not all are able to compete equally in the social arena. Many groups simply can't afford to wine and dine legislators to the same extent as others. And legislators, if they aren't very careful, may find themselves paying more attention to the suggestions of their friends across the dinner table than to those (meritorious though they may be) who can't afford to throw a party. Once again, it becomes obvious that the resources available to an interest group have a direct bearing on the group's success.

☐ Membership Mobilization

Much of the attention we've given to interest groups has focused on the activities of their lobbyists in Austin, but there are times when groups orchestrate activities around the state in an attempt to exert influence on policy makers. Such attempts to mobilize a broad outpouring of unified opinion on an issue can sometimes move a legislator who has resisted other appeals made by the group.

Typically, such an effort would begin with the group's lobbyist communicating with group members about the need to contact certain policy makers. This usually happens when a committee is considering a bill of particular interest or before a bill is to come up for a vote on the floor. Group supporters will be urged to express their thoughts on the bill by writing, phoning, faxing, or e-mailing messages to committee members, especially if these members are their own representatives. Legislators do tend to listen to their constituents, and a well-organized campaign, such as we've described, can often help in the overall attempt to persuade members to the group's point of view.

However, such **membership mobilization** needs to be carefully crafted. Effective grassroots efforts take a lot of work and oversight, and the better organized a group is, the more likely such actions will succeed. Obviously, groups with small memberships

membership mobilization
The act of enlisting the rank-and-file members of an interest group in attempting to sway policy makers; often includes massive letter-writing and e-mail efforts and may also include marches and demonstrations.

5.1

5.2

5.3

5.4

5.5

5.6

5.1

5.2

5.3

5.4

5.5

5.6

may find themselves at a disadvantage here, and those where decision making is concentrated at the top with little membership input may also have trouble enlisting enthusiastic support from those members.

Even the means of membership communication need to be carefully monitored. Nothing will so quickly guarantee that a legislator will ignore a group's plea as the receipt of 500 or so e-mails or photocopied letters, all saying exactly the same thing. Most legislators will rightly conclude that a troop of reasonably bright chimpanzees could be trained to produce such letters and will discount completely any such effort. Groups that hope to be successful in mobilizing large numbers of people have to be able to convince their members to sit down and write a personal letter expressing each individual's feelings. Guidelines may give the members ideas about what to say, but how that is said should be left up to each member. Legislators tend to pay more attention to these kinds of communication.

Other more dramatic methods of membership mobilization can include marches and demonstrations, often on the steps of the state capitol and usually during a legislative session. Rank-and-file group members often like such activities because they can draw the media's attention to the group's cause and may expand public awareness of the group's issues. Moreover, many ex-hippie baby boomers, who now belong to perfectly respectable interest groups, never have quite gotten that urge to protest out of their systems! A striking example of such a demonstration was seen when motorcyclists from all over Texas descended on the Capitol several years ago to urge the legislature to repeal the state's "helmet law." Such efforts may get you on the six o'clock news, but they rarely have a lasting impact on legislators (although in the instance just cited, lawmakers did make some changes for which the group had lobbied). In truth, most legislators simply don't have time for such exercises. Even efforts to blanket the

Tea Party activists rally in Austin against Democrats in general and President Obama in particular. On most issues, they share little in common with the Occupy movement, although both oppose bank bailouts and subsidies to Big Business. As with Occupy, frustration plays a part in such public rallies.

legislature and blitz members with flyers and position papers on a group's "day" at the Capitol usually are only marginally successful. Again, the hectic schedule maintained by most senators and representatives makes it difficult to gain their time and attention through such grandstanding tactics.

☐ Interim Oversight

interim oversight
Various actions by an interest group aimed at protecting its gains and promoting its goals between sessions of the legislature.

5.1

5.2

5.3

5.4

5.5

5.6

Just because the legislature adjourns and goes home after a regular session does not mean that an interest group's work is done for another 19 months. In the past, this interim may have brought a measurable slowdown in group efforts, but most veteran lobbyists will tell you that today the work goes on, in session or out. For many groups, the job may only be starting once your bill has passed.

State agencies and departments will be responsible for implementing the provisions of most bills. (For more on the executive branch, see Chapters 8 and 9.) Many groups will seek to monitor the actions of these agencies, verifying that they are indeed doing what the law requires. This is especially true of those interest groups representing professions that are licensed, regulated, or funded by the state. For example, teachers' organizations will constantly monitor the actions of the Texas Education Agency and of local school boards to make sure those bodies are doing what they're supposed to with regard to teacher rights and responsibilities.

Another **interim oversight** strategy draws from the idea of membership mobilization mentioned above. Although mass meetings and group demonstrations during the legislative session are rarely effective, encouraging a group's members to contact legislators during the interim can be useful in building support for the group's agenda. When the legislature is out of session, members have time to sit down with the public and discuss issues of concern. They can look at what was done as well as at what might be on the political horizon, and interest group members can get to know their representatives on a personal level. Such personal relationships can be extremely helpful once the legislative circus is back in town.

For the same reasons, interest groups may continue to host legislators at various outings during the interim. These activities have been restricted by new ethics legislation, but they remain a useful tool for cultivating legislators' goodwill. Likewise, lobbyists may find themselves doing research and even offering testimony before committees during this "down" time. Even though the legislature may be adjourned, numerous interim committees, appointed to explore various issues prior to the next sessions, remain at work. Lobbyists frequently use these meetings to stake out their group's position early. One of this book's authors, David Clinkscale, did that very thing on several occasions while serving as president of the Texas Community College Teachers Association, offering testimony on funding recommendations for higher education and opposing the offering of freshman and sophomore courses by junior- and senior-level institutions. As you can see, interest groups in Texas have to work year-round in order to be effective.

☐ Regulating Interest Groups

For years, interest groups and the lobbyists who represented them were virtually free of any kind of meaningful regulation. Following the Sharpstown scandal in the early 1970s, however, the Texas Legislature did enact the Lobbyist Registration Act. This law, one of public interest group Common Cause's first legislative successes in Texas, sought to identify those who were attempting to influence legislation on behalf of a client group. Until recently, the basic thrust of interest group regulation in Texas has tended to focus primarily on such registration as a means of controlling interest group actions. However, since the mid-1990s, tighter restrictions have been placed on certain kinds of expenditures by interest groups and their representatives, and the responsibility for monitoring their activities and expenditures has been vested with the Texas Ethics Commission, to whom all interest groups and their lobbyists must report periodically.

5.1

5.2

5.3

5.4

5.5

5.6

Under current law, a person must register with the Ethics Commission as a lobbyist if he or she receives more than $1,000 in a calendar quarter as compensation for engaging in communications with legislative or executive branch members that are intended to influence the passage of laws or the formulation of administrative rules. A person also must register if he or she expends more than $500 in a calendar quarter on such communications aimed at such influence.[16] "Communications" here refers to a rather broad array of activities, including the provision of food and beverages, entertainment expenses, gifts, awards and mementos, mass media advertising, and fundraisers. The reporting of these activities, generally on a monthly basis, must specify the recipient of the "communication."

In addition to these rather detailed reporting requirements, certain activities are specifically prohibited, such as providing loans, transportation and lodging (with certain exceptions), and expenditures for entertainment, awards, and/or gifts that exceed $500 per person in a calendar year.[17] These regulations certainly have helped to reduce the kind of freewheeling lobby spending that characterized Texas politics during most of the 20th century. However, experienced advocates representing a wide array of influential businesses and associations can still drop a lot of money in a short period of time in the pursuit of successful legislation.

Money and Interest Groups

5.4 Explain the relationship between money and interest groups in the political process.

Money may not be the only thing in Texas politics, but as political consultant Bill Emory once remarked, "It's way ahead of whatever's in second place." Indeed, money is often referred to as the "mother's milk" of politics. This is obviously the case with interest group activity because much of what such groups accomplish depends on funding, both internal and external.

☐ Internal Funding

Internal funding refers to the processes by which a group raises money for its ongoing political operations. All interest groups must raise some money for such activities, but the amount the group can raise in most cases depends on the size and composition of the group. Obviously, larger groups have a greater capacity to raise money for operations than do smaller ones. Still, small groups made up of more affluent members can often compete on an equal financial footing with larger, but less affluent, groups.

Most groups raise money for internal operations by levying membership dues. Not every dollar raised in this manner will be earmarked for political activity, but many will be used to promote the group's interests in the political arena. Here again, organizational structure may be decisive in determining how much money a group can raise. Those groups with high levels of membership commitment to group goals (such as the NRA) usually have no trouble raising the money they need. The less cohesive the group, the more difficult it will be to raise such funds. Groups with memberships that wax and wane may have better luck holding garage sales and car washes rather than attempting to collect annual dues from a tenuously allied membership.

When you recall all the possible activities in which an interest group may engage, you can see how important money is to that group and its success. The differences in money-raising capabilities among groups translate into significant differences in the kinds of activities in which groups may be able to participate. Not all groups can afford to hire a George Christian or a Mike Toomey to lobby on their behalf. Not all groups can afford to offer a daily (or even weekly or monthly) lunch buffet for legislators. Not all groups can afford to underwrite the costs of mass mailings on behalf of the group's members. The Texas constitution says all citizens have an equal right to join together and pursue group goals before policy makers. The reality of Texas politics says such efforts are rarely equal when it comes to money.

□ External Funding: PACs

Interest groups raise money not only to fund their own operations but also, increasingly, to contribute to election campaigns. To anyone seeking elected office, money talks. That being the case, it can be safely said that in Texas interest groups often monopolize the conversation. The relationship between interest groups and campaign contributions is tricky in this state. Texas law specifically forbids labor unions and corporations (or groups composed of such entities, often referred to as trade associations) from contributing money directly to individual political campaigns. That would seem to bar any interest groups representing such entities from giving money to a person running for office. However, there is a huge loophole through which interest groups of all sorts have poured hundreds of thousands of dollars. That loophole is the **political action committee, or PAC**.

A PAC is a voluntary association of individuals who band together for the purpose of raising and distributing money for political campaigns. The key word here seems to be "voluntary." For example, under state law, Compass Bancshares, Inc., one of the largest banking companies in Texas, could not set aside corporate money to be contributed to Rick Perry's campaign for lieutenant governor. However, employees of Compass Bancshares could contribute their own money to a political action committee that they had voluntarily joined, and this money could then be disbursed to the Perry campaign or others.

Such groups are perfectly legitimate. However, to many people they give the appearance of being a very obvious way around legal restrictions on giving to campaigns. Questions are often raised, for example, regarding just how "voluntary" membership is in such organizations. Even if nothing specific is said to an employee or union member, a sense of coercion may be present if "everyone" at work is joining the PAC and you haven't. Such pressures may lead some people to go along in order to get along.

As they proliferate, political action committees are playing a larger and larger role in electoral politics in Texas. In recent election cycles, PACs have collected millions of dollars to invest in Texas political races, and that trend will likely continue in the future (see Table 5.1). Adding impetus to this trend has been the U.S. Supreme Court

political action committee (PAC)
A voluntary association of individuals who band together for the purpose of raising and distributing money for political campaigns.

5.1

5.2

5.3

5.4

5.5

5.6

TABLE 5.1 EXPENDITURES BY SELECTED PACs, JAN. 1, 2010 THROUGH OCTOBER 23, 2010

Political Action Committee	Amount Expended
Back to Basics PAC	$4,141,466.43
Texans for Lawsuit Reform PAC	$3,469,367.63
Annie's List	$931,983.41
ActBlue Texas	$657,544.93
Texas Oil and Gas PAC	$243,247.74
Beer Alliance of Texas	$139,350.00
Texas Credit Union League PAC	$128,050.00
Associated General Contractors of Texas PAC	$111,850.00
Texas Deer Association PAC	$83,318.98
Texas and Southwestern Cattle Raisers Association State PAC	$58,884.55
Texas Motor Transportation Association PAC	$41,100.00
Texas Our Texas	$20,950.00
Alief Federation of Teachers Committee on Political Education	$4,000.00

Source: Texas Ethics Commission, *Campaign Finance Report Totals,* 2010.
http://www.ethics.state.tx.us/dfs/c_elists.htm

5.1

5.2

5.3

5.4

5.5

5.6

decision in *Citizens United*.[18] In that case, the Court ruled that groups representing companies, unions, and trade associations (through their political action committees) cannot be restricted in the amount of money they spend in support of candidates independent of those candidates' formal campaign organizations. In the opinion of the Court, to attempt to do so would be to breach these groups' rights of free speech under the First Amendment. This decision has had the effect of opening a veritable floodgate of contributions at the presidential campaign level, and indicators from the 2012 primary elections in Texas seem to point to similar huge increases in such contributions in support of candidates for state office. As PACs pour more and more money into state elections, they contribute to the upward spiral in the cost of getting elected. That trend may send candidates for public office scurrying in search of more PAC contributions, which, in turn, may further drive up the costs of running for office. Such a vicious circle may make it difficult for a person without ties to PACs to have a realistic chance to run for office. It also means that interest groups without the financial base to play PAC politics may increasingly find themselves outside the policy-making process.

PAC money may also contribute to a subtle but very real erosion of access to elected representatives by the citizenry. Let's say you decide to run for a seat in the Texas house. At today's rates, that race will cost about $500,000, if you can catch one on sale. Unless your family is filthy rich or you just won the lottery, you won't have that kind of discretionary money floating around, so you'll have to try and solicit contributions to your campaign. Well, let's suppose that PACs representing 25 different interest groups each give you $5,000. That will account for 25 percent of your campaign budget. If you get elected, and a representative of one of those interest groups then wants to talk to you, will you take the call? Of course you will. By giving you a substantial portion of what you needed to get elected, those groups have gained the kind of access that Judy Doe from Lampasas, Texas, can't come close to matching. How ironic, then, that a device originally conceived to expand participation in and access to the political process may be restricting these more and more with each passing year.

The Iron Triangle

5.5 Show the links between interest groups and other participants in the Texas political environment.

The so-called iron triangle is a coalition formed among interest groups, the legislature, and government departments that accounts for the creation of much public policy in Texas. The triangle, as illustrated in Figure 5.1, operates because each point on the model has something that it can give to each of the others. In return, each expects to receive something from the others.

As we have said, interest groups have two primary means at their disposal for use in obtaining favorable policies. One is campaign contributions. Legislators need money in order to run for office, and an interest group's PAC can help the legislator meet these needs. The other is information. Because the legislature is understaffed, lobbyists for interest groups can provide information, formulate position papers, and even draft bills. Anything that makes a legislator's job easier makes him or her more likely to support an interest group's viewpoint, especially if that legislator has no strong opinions in that area.

In return for this help, the interest group expects favorable consideration by legislators. In its interaction with government departments, legislators expect to receive staff services. The staff of a department will help members of the legislature gather information about that agency. Again, a factor in the success of this process is the understaffing of the legislature: It makes information a valuable commodity. In return for this assistance, the department expects funding from the legislature.

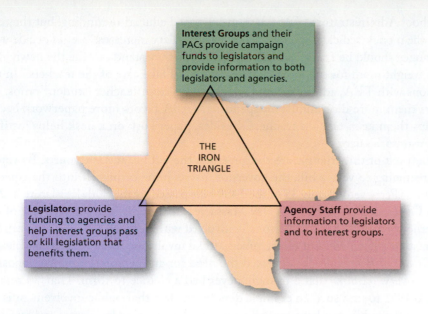

FIGURE 5.1 The Iron Triangle.

5.1

5.2

5.3

5.4

5.5

5.6

Legislative appropriations are the lifeblood of government. Without them, an agency cannot exist.

It is the department's job to implement policy passed by the legislature. They turn policy into programs. Interest groups hope that programs are shaped to their benefit. To ensure that this occurs, interest groups can arrange expert testimony at legislative committee hearings that involve a particular agency. Because these hearings help determine an agency's funding, favorable testimony can be helpful. Agencies realize this and work to keep interest groups on their side as they implement legislation. In a sense, many agencies see interest groups as their clients.

In order to have a better understanding of how this works, let's plug in some real entities. The legislative point will be filled by the House Public Education Committee because most legislation is shaped in committee. The interest group will be the Texas State Teachers Association (TSTA), which represents elementary and secondary teachers in the state. The logical government department would be the Texas Education Agency (TEA). First and foremost, TSTA wants the legislature to provide higher salaries for teachers. Through its PAC, it will deliver campaign contributions to committee members. Additionally, it will provide committee members with information that supports its arguments. For example, the group might provide information that compares Texas with other states, showing that states with higher teacher salaries have higher standardized test scores.

The legislature provides funding to TEA. In return, TEA provides information on its activities to the understaffed legislature. If TEA has an ally on the Public Education Committee, a representative from TEA and that member might even script out questions and answers prior to committee hearings on the agency's budget. This would make both the legislator and the agency look good during the hearings because the member would know what to ask and the agency would know how to answer.

Beyond salary concerns, two chief complaints of teachers are classroom overcrowding and excessive paperwork. TEA can provide relief by enforcing teacher–student ratios and restricting state-mandated paperwork. In return, TSTA can find an expert from a university with a highly regarded education department, like the University of North Texas, and send a Ph.D. to tell the legislature, "TEA is doing a wonderful job. They would do even better if they had more funding."

Why, then, does TSTA not always get its way? Because dozens of interest groups compete in the area of education policy alone. Some want lower taxes. Businesses want graduates who can read, write, and do math. Others, like the Texas Association

5.1

5.2

5.3

5.4

5.5

5.6

of School Administrators (TASA), want increased education funding, but they don't want the money dedicated exclusively to teacher salary increases. "Let *us* decide where the money should be spent," administrators say as they stand outside the newly renovated weight room for the football team, "and we'll take care of the teachers." In their relations with TEA, administrators want waivers from teacher–student ratios. This allows them more discretion over spending. TASA favors more paperwork because it helps them keep tabs on teachers. Besides, paperwork on a desk helps justify an administrator's salary.

Left out of this triangle are the governor, the public, and the courts. By vetoing or threatening to veto a bill, the governor inserts him- or herself into the equation. Governor Perry vetoed only 35 of the 1459 bills passed by the 80th legislature in 2009. Even Governor Perry's Father's Day Massacre killed only a small percentage of bills. Governors generally become personally involved with perhaps a couple of dozen bills. The rest are passed without direct gubernatorial involvement. In 1991, when Lieutenant Governor Bob Bullock suggested the need for an income tax, public opposition was so overwhelming that a triangle never had a chance to form. That we must go back to 1991 to find such an example denotes the fact that public involvement is rare, although the public can have some involvement by choosing legislators and by joining interest groups. Of course, the courts can become involved when they declare a law to be unconstitutional. Although such occurrences are often dramatic, they are usually quite rare.

Interest Groups and You

5.6 Identify practical ways that you can become involved in the activities of interest groups.

What are you going to do with your newfound knowledge about interest groups? You could use it as another avenue of participation in the political system here in Texas. Yes, you're "just" a student. But you might have more than a passing interest in things like tuition costs, residence requirements, and curriculum mandates. Changes in any of these areas could have an enormous impact on your life. So it might be to your advantage, when such issues are being discussed, to work through an interest group in order to make sure you get in your two cents' worth.

Moreover, by participating in interest group activities now, you'll be ready to take an expanded role in such activities when you're out of school and have entered a business or profession that is represented by such groups. If you're going to be an accountant, you can be sure that you'll need to interact with the government regarding your profession at some time during your career. If you go into business, the same is true. Decisions by government will directly affect your livelihood, and you'll want to have some input into those decisions. Health care professionals will face ever-increasing interaction with government in the coming years. Even when you retire, you and all your friends will still need to keep an eye on what the government does with things like state retirement accounts and tax breaks for senior citizens. So get used to it, and get involved. The interest you protect will probably be your own.

Review the Chapter

((•   **Listen** to Chapter 5

The Roles of Interest Groups

5.1 Identify and explain the roles of interest groups in politics.

An interest group is composed of people who share a common set of ideas or principles and who attempt to advance those ideas or principles by influencing public-policy makers. Interest groups differ from political parties in that they do not run candidates for office and that they have a narrower issue focus. They facilitate the exercise of our constitutional right to petition the government, and interest groups magnify our voices and multiply our choices as citizens. However, the proliferation of interest groups may contribute to the fracturing of American and Texas politics, and not all interest groups are created equal.

The Types of Interest Groups

5.2 Compare and contrast the different types of interest groups in Texas.

Some interest groups concentrate decision making near the top among a relatively small leadership group. Others disperse decision making more widely among the group's membership. Still others have tenuously connected membership and a strategy focus that sometimes lacks clarity. The most influential interests groups in Texas represent members of the business community. Professional interest groups are also important players in Texas politics, while groups representing labor unions and ethnic communities are less influential.

The Methods of Interest Groups

5.3 Analyze the methods used by interest groups to influence policy makers.

Interest groups use a variety of methods to get their message across to policy makers. One is to disseminate the information directly, usually through a lobbyist. Informal contacts such as social gatherings can also enhance a group's ability to gain access to policy makers. Occasionally, an interest group will attempt to mobilize its members in support of a particular policy goal by encouraging them to contact legislators directly. And even when the legislature is not in session, interest groups often continue to monitor the implementation of relevant policies by state agencies and their personnel.

Money and Interest Groups

5.4 Explain the relationship between money and interest groups in the political process.

Money is the mother's milk of politics. Interest groups must raise money from their members in order to be able to pursue their public-policy agendas. And while Texas law does not allow corporations, labor unions, or trade associations to contribute money directly to the campaigns of candidates, such groups may form political action committees (PACs) and these organizations may make contributions to such campaigns. Moreover, the U.S. Supreme Court, in its *Citizens United* decision, has opened the door for PACs to give unlimited amounts of money in support of candidates as long as the contributions are not made to the candidates' formal campaign organizations.

The Iron Triangle

5.5 Show the links between interest groups and other participants in the Texas political environment.

The "iron triangle" is a coalition formed among interest groups, the legislature, and government departments that accounts for the creation of much public policy in Texas. The triangle operates because each element in the coalition has something that it can give to each of the others. In return, each expects to receive something from the others.

Interest Groups and You

5.6 Identify practical ways that you can become involved in the activities of interest groups.

To the extent that you are willing to involve yourself in the activities of an interest group, you enhance your potential influence in the political system. During your working life, your involvement with interest groups can positively benefit you and others who share your profession, and even in retirement, your continued participation in interest group activities can enable you to address lifestyle issues that often become increasingly important.

Learn the Terms

Test Yourself

 Study and **Review** the **Practice Tests**

5.1 Identify and explain the roles of interest groups in politics.

An interest group is best defined as an organized entity sharing common ideas that
- **a.** tries to get its members elected to public office.
- **b.** tries to influence public-policy makers to adopt the group's ideas.
- **c.** tries to achieve the violent overthrow of the government.
- **d.** tries to do both a and b.
- **e.** tries to do neither a nor b.

5.2 Compare and contrast the different types of interest groups in Texas.

The most powerful interest community in Texas is that of
- **a.** labor groups.
- **b.** ethnic groups.
- **c.** single-issue groups.
- **d.** business groups.
- **e.** public watchdog groups.

5.3 Analyze the methods used by interest groups to influence policy makers.

A person who works on behalf of an interest group and serves as the point of contact between the group and policy makers is a
- **a.** staff member.
- **b.** client.
- **c.** lobbyist
- **d.** gubernatorial aide.
- **e.** legislative assistant.

5.4 Explain the relationship between money and interest groups in the political process.

A voluntary association of individuals who band together for the purpose of raising and distributing money for political campaigns is called a
- **a.** special interest.
- **b.** lobby guild.
- **c.** political action committee.
- **d.** political party.
- **e.** campaign organization.

5.5 Show the links between interest groups and other participants in the Texas political environment.

Of the following elements, which is not part of the so-called Iron Triangle?
- **a.** district judges
- **b.** legislators
- **c.** government agencies
- **d.** interest groups
- **e.** bureaucrats

5.6 Identify practical ways that you can become involved in the activities of interest groups.

Involving oneself in the activities of an interest group allows a person to
- **a.** exercise a constitutional right to petition the government.
- **b.** multiply the choices available for political participation.
- **c.** magnify one's voice within the political arena.
- **d.** all of the above.
- **e.** none of the above.

Explore Further

Citizens United v. Federal Election Commission, 558 U.S. 50 (2010).

Deaton, Charles. *The Year They Threw the Rascals Out.* Austin, TX: Shoal Creek Publishers, 1973.

Jillson, Calvin C. *Lone Star Tarnished: A Critical Look at Texas Politics and Public Policy.* New York: Routledge, 2012.

Politifeist. *Interest Groups in Texas.* http://www.politifeist.com/Interest_Groups_in_Texas

Project Vote Smart. http://votesmart.org/interest-groups/TX/

Texas Ethics Commission. *Promoting Public Confidence in Government.* http://www.ethics.state.tx.us/

Wilson, Robert H. (ed.) *Public Policy and Community: Activism and Governance in Texas.* Austin: University of Texas Press, 1997.

6

The Media and Public Opinion in Texas

*"If this [radio] is going to be a menace to newspapers
we had better own the menace."*

—*Amon Carter to Harold Hough, 1922*

Long before there were communication and journalism majors, there was news. On June 19, 1865, General Gordon Granger arrived on Galveston Island with news that the slaves had been emancipated. Although African Americans living in Texas had reason to rejoice, if news had traveled faster, they would have celebrated a full two and one-half years sooner, on the day that President Lincoln signed the Emancipation Proclamation. Of course, Confederate officials had reason for not sharing the news, and freedom of the press did not extend to slaves. What

6.1	6.2	6.3	6.4	6.5
Trace the evolution of the print media in Texas.	Describe how radio emerged as a component of the Texas media.	Evaluate how television changed the way Texans consume news.	Evaluate how the media covers Texas politics.	Evaluate the importance of polling and public opinion in Texas politics.

ON TO THE RUNOFF!

JUL 3

REPUBLICAN *for* US SENATE

TED★CRUZ

PROVEN CONSERVATIVE

This campaign sign notes Ted Cruz's web site, which is only the tip of the iceberg in his well managed internet campaign. Web saturation is a big part of modern politics. In 2012, Cruz effectively used an internet-centered campaign, using web-embedded advertisements, to target like minded voters and fuel his successful insurgent effort against his better funded and better known opponent. Cruz's success may influence how Texas campaigns are run well into the future.

TEDCRUZ.ORG

PAID FOR BY TED CRUZ FOR SENATE

6.1

6.2

6.3

6.4

6.5

Fairness Doctrine
A federal law that required radio and broadcast television stations to devote equal time to opposing viewpoints. It was repealed in 1987.

we observe as "Juneteenth" the actual emancipation of slaves in Texas, would not exist as a holiday in today's day and age. Indeed, news that happened yesterday is, well, yesterday's news. Today, we see news as it happens, and we can see and read about it from a variety of sources. The proliferation of the Internet has had a profound impact not only on how we get our news, but also on how candidates and elected officials communicate with voters.

Over the last 30 years, newspaper readership has declined significantly, and network news ratings have plummeted. Of course, this should not imply that Texans are less informed than they were as the 1980s began. Cable News Network (CNN) was in its infancy and available in very few homes, and analysts doubted that a 24-hour news station could sustain itself over the long haul. The Internet was available only to the Department of Defense, NASA, and a handful of research universities. Radio news programming was already in decline, and talk radio was unknown. Many radio stations had shied away from extensive news broadcasts because of the **Fairness Doctrine**, a 1954 law that required stations to air both sides of controversial issues. That law was repealed late during President Reagan's second term, and soon talk radio proliferated.

For those of us who observe the media as part of our job, we live in interesting times. Indeed, no corner of the political landscape has changed more than delivery of information. A casual observer may see the evolution of journalism as a rise and fall, but in this chapter we'll see the reality that each time one medium fell, another rose to take its place. The story, so-to-speak, is hardly over. There's no telling where technology will take us, but wherever it goes, it will surely be carrying the latest, breaking news with it. The traditional media may not exist in recognizable form 40 years from now.

Today, Texans have more sources than ever through which they can receive news. Communication has evolved to the point that there is disagreement on exactly who comprises the media today. Almost all newspapers, broadcast stations, and cable stations have their own websites. However you choose to define media, some 65 percent of Americans' primary news sources are online sources.[1] Most people who are interested in an event have read about it hours before it hits the newsstands or your front porch. Add in bloggers, political websites, Twitter, and Facebook, plus the ever expanding number of cable and satellite television news networks, and there is something to meet almost anyone's needs. More information than ever before is available unfiltered, over the World Wide Web, directly from government sources, politicians, and watchdog groups. You can find out who gave what money to which politician on your own. You don't have to depend on the *Houston Chronicle's* explanation of a Supreme Court decision when you can read it directly on the Court's website. You may even have your own political blog, or you may contribute to one on a regular basis.

There is no formal requirement, in either the United States or Texas constitution, that the media cover governmental or political news or act as "watchdogs" over the actions of government. Nonetheless, most consumers of media expect that these functions will be carried out. Most journalists believe that these functions are an important part of their jobs. But the resources deployed in both pursuits have been reduced over the years. Political scandals may sell papers or bring in viewers, but not on a regular basis. However, even as the traditional media has cut back on such coverage, bloggers and interest group researchers have stepped in to occupy the void. It is important to understand that individuals or groups who take the time to run a political website or blog almost certainly have an agenda. That does not make their reporting inaccurate; it simply means that, as a consumer, you should consider whatever biases may be implicit, just as you should with the mainstream media.

Texas Newspapers

6.1   Trace the evolution of the print media in Texas.

Until the advent of radio, newspapers were the primary source of news for virtually all of America, and this is especially true of Texas, since many homes in the state did not even have electricity until well into the Great Depression. As late as 1935, fewer than 3 percent of Texas homes had electricity.[2] As recently as the 1980s, the news media consisted primarily of one or two daily newspapers in most urban areas, and three network affiliates that broadcast both national and local news programs. Most Americans, including most Texans, watched one of the evening national news broadcasts, and most read a daily newspaper. By 2012, only NBC Nightly News drew as much as 2 percent of American viewers. Newspaper readership was down dramatically, and three major Texas dailies, the *Houston Post*, the *San Antonio Light*, and the *Dallas Times Herald*, had gone out of business.

The first Texas newspaper, the *Gaceta de Tejas*, was published in Nacogdoches in May 1813.[3] Although written and typeset in Texas, the publication was actually printed in Louisiana. Even though this Spanish-language paper dealt with Texas issues, it is uncertain whether anyone living in Texas ever had access to it, and it seems likely that only a single issue was ever released. The first English-language paper published in Texas also traced its roots to Nacogdoches. Called the *Texas Republican*, it was the official account of the Long Expedition and its effort to establish an independent Texas. The revolution failed, as did the newspaper. Texas's first daily newspaper, the Houston *Morning Star*, made its debut in 1839.[4] Another new paper, the Austin *City Gazettee*, published its first edition that same year, in the newly relocated capital.[5] The Galveston *Zeitung*, probably the first German-language newspaper in Texas, was founded in 1847. The first religion-affiliated papers appeared in Houston about the same time.

After American expatriates became more common in Mexican Texas, more newspapers appeared, although publication was irregular. The *Texas Republican*, in Brazoria, published an issue on the same day that Texas declared its independence.

Early Texas newspapers, like early Texas political parties, tended to coalesce around the colossal personality of Sam Houston. The *Texas State Gazette* was decidedly anti-Houston, whereas the *Nacogdoches Chronicle* and the *Campaign Chronicle* in Houston were strong Houston backers.[6] This highly partisan tone permeated papers throughout the 19th century in Texas and the United States. No one even pretended to be fair and balanced.

The *Galveston News*, the oldest surviving newspaper in Texas, began continuous publication in 1843.[7] During the period prior to the Civil War, it joined the faction of papers opposed to Houston's actions. Although many papers thrived during the late era of the Republic and early statehood, almost all ceased publication during the war. The *Galveston News* was one of the few that continued to publish throughout the conflict, although it moved its presses to Houston to protect against Union occupation. In 1885, the paper expanded into north Texas, initiating the publication of the *Dallas Morning News*. Innovatively, and foreshadowing the electronic media by over a century, the *Galveston News* used telegraph lines to send the bulk of their work to Dallas, with local news supplementing the telegraphed work.[8] The *Galveston News* performed one of the greatest journalistic feats ever in the wake of the 1900 Galveston hurricane, a storm that killed more than 15 percent of the island's residents and permanently reduced the city's status as a center of population and trade. Scarcely 24 hours after the storm passed, the *News* published a one-page special edition. Two days later, the paper was back to publishing regular editions. The paper's reporters spread the story of almost indescribable destruction to readers throughout the world, as the stories were

Partisan Press
Newspapers and other media that reported a single viewpoint in an effort
to persuade readers.

6.1

6.2

6.3

6.4

6.5

This copy of *The Texas Republican* is dated March 2, 1836: The day that Texas declared its independence from Mexico. The lead story is about the independence convention as Washington on the Brazos, but sovereignty had not been formally asserted as this paper went to press. If you look closely, you will see that the front page includes advertisements as well as news.

picked up by other newspapers. The storm and its fallout, however, marked the beginning of the end of the *Galveston News* as a major force in Texas politics.

The Civil War halted publication of most Texas papers for a variety of reasons, almost all tied in some way to the economy. Texans didn't have money to buy papers. Companies couldn't afford advertisements. Printing supplies, especially paper, were expensive and in short supply. Even those papers that did somehow publish were shorter and less frequent in distribution. Because the war devastated the state's economy, newspapers were slow in their return, publishing less often and with smaller editions.

◻ Partisanship and Early Newspapers

As newspapers reemerged during the Reconstruction era, the **partisan press** was still the norm. As papers divided over Sam Houston before the war, they divided over E. J. Davis during Reconstruction.

The bias was obvious from the time the press labeled those aligned with Davis as Radical Republicans, although there was little about their positions that could be called radical. *Flake's Bulletin*, despite its Unionist roots, had turned against the Davis wing of the Republican Party before the 1869 election, characterizing its followers as "political invalid—they suffer from torpid livers—they see everything through a vision clouded with bile."[9] Likewise, the *Austin Republican* trashed the Davis wing in both its editorial and news pages. *Flake's Bulletin* declared open warfare on Davis in the 1870 pre-Fourth of July edition, publishing a "Declaration of Wrongs" against the governor. The *Bulletin* declared Davis "to be a tyrant and his government to be oppressive, and we ask the Federal government to relieve us of the same."[10] And that diatribe was from a Republican paper which simply backed a different faction of the party. The Democratic press was even harsher. They advocated a return to Democratic rule and the reassertion of states' rights. Davis had his papers as well, chief among them the *State Journal*. The *Houston Union* was generally sympathetic to the Davis faction, as was the *Sherman Patriot*. Even before Reconstruction, the venerable *Galveston News* was distancing itself from its peers by becoming less partisan and more even-handed in its coverage of the news.

By the end of the 19th century, the most overt partisanship of newspapers was on the wane. Part of this change came about because papers had become more reliant on advertising revenue. Papers could not afford to alienate subscribers because ad rates were based on circulation. As important a factor, however, was the development of large, far-flung news organizations like the Associated Press (AP), whose members shared stories, sources, and coverage. Often, the AP would send one reporter to cover a story of regional or national significance, and that reporter's work would appear in applicable papers. Because such stories would be published in a wide variety of newspapers, there was an emphasis on reporting straight news, without a bias, so that readers could draw their own conclusions. Newspapers could editorialize as they wished, but reporting became more even-handed. It was only then that the notion that reporting should be unbiased crept into the public perception.

☐ Ethnic and Bilingual Newspapers

It would be the middle of the 20th century before mainstream Texas newspapers took interest in the issues most important to African Americans. After the Civil War, even newspapers with Unionist roots, like *Flake's Bulletin*, were less than sympathetic, and at times hostile, to the newly freed slaves. The *Galveston Spectator* was among the first African American-owned-and-operated Texas newspapers, debuting in 1873. The *Houston Informer and Texas Freeman* first published in 1893. It would survive for more than 100 years. The *Dallas Express* and the *San Antonio Register* were the primary African American papers in those cities. The *Houston Defender*, still in publication, started in 1930. These papers not only provided information for black audiences and led the battle for civil rights, but they also nurtured the career of African American reporters who would be ready to work for mainstream news organizations once the doors creaked open for minority reporters.

As we've pointed out, many early Texas newspapers were published in Spanish, and this practice was no doubt driven by the audience. Today, there are at least eight Spanish-language newspapers published in Texas, as well as several Vietnamese dailies in circulation. A look into Texas's newspaper history provides insight into the state's rich diversity. Texas's first (and perhaps only) trilingual newspaper appeared in 1899 and was called The Giddings *Deutsches*.[11] Although most articles were in German, the paper often included stories in English and occasionally in Wendish (Sorbian). Subscriptions peaked at 1,200 in the 1920s but fell to 400 in 1949. It was the only shop in the United States able to print in Wendish, a unique Slavic language that requires the use of special characters in combination with the German Fraktur type.[12] The paper published local and international news and helped maintain the use of both the Wendish and the German languages. Not surprisingly, Texas has had a number of Czech newspapers, as well.

☐ Big-City Dailies

The emergence of major big-city newspapers coincided with a rising increase in literacy and more reliable, efficient methods of production and distribution. This era of journalism, which is often referred to as the era of the **penny press**, started at about the time of the Civil War and continued through the Depression. Advertisements

Penny Press
Inexpensive newspapers characterized by sensational stories to attract public readership.

6.1

6.2

6.3

6.4

6.5

offset much of the production costs, and these papers sold for as little as a penny. Newspapers of this era often contained exaggerated or sensationalized accounts of major events, and they survive today as tabloids housed in the supermarket checkout lines. Publishers such as William Randolph Hearst and Joseph Pulitzer made their names—and their fortunes—by means of the penny press.

Like the *Dallas Morning News*, many of the big-city dailies, several of which still wield some influence today, began in the era between the end of Reconstruction and the opening year of the 20th century. The *Houston Post* began publication in 1885. It looked different from the standard paper of today, with advertisements taking up a significant portion of the front page. The *Post* would become heavily involved in political issues. One of its early business and political reporters was William B. Hobby, who, after leaving the paper, would become lieutenant governor of Texas, ascending to the governor's office when Jim Ferguson was impeached. He was subsequently elected as governor. After that term, Hobby returned to the *Post* to serve as its president before acquiring the paper outright in 1939, to go along with two Beaumont papers that he had owned for some time. His wife, Oveta Culp Hobby, would serve as the first secretary of Health, Education, and Welfare in President Dwight Eisenhower's cabinet, while his son, Bill would hold the powerful lieutenant governor's office for 18 years.

The *Houston Chronicle* began publication in 1901. Unlike most dailies, its front page carried only news and editorials, with no advertisements.[13] The *Chronicle* was overtly political from the beginning, campaigning for or against elected city officials and leading a fight to close bars on Sunday afternoons.[14] Later, the *Chronicle* would be instrumental in the successful fight for creation of the Houston Ship Channel and the Port of Houston.

The *Dallas Times Herald* debuted in 1888, after the merger of two existing papers. As did most of the other prominent Texas dailies of the time, it promoted a pro-business agenda. Like the *Morning News*, the *Times Herald* believed that public infrastructure investment would spur economic growth. The *Morning News* would become the first Texas paper with a permanent Washington correspondent. The *News*, which had once been boycotted by church groups for accepting advertisements for beer and liquor, became one of the first prominent Texas dailies to support Prohibition. It stopped accepting alcohol advertisements in 1907.[15]

The *San Antonio Express News* traces its roots to 1865. Its main competition, the *San Antonio Light*, would begin publication in 1881. Although the *Express* was a Republican paper during Reconstruction, the *Light* was the only major Republican daily in post–Reconstruction Texas, a status it would maintain into the 20th century. Like their counterparts in other cities, San Antonio papers backed a pro-business agenda. The *Light* was bought and folded by the Hearst Corporation in 1992; Hearst already owned the *Express* by that time.

The *Austin American Statesman* began as the *Democratic Statesman* in 1871. It was a partisan paper at its inception, standing against the Republican Reconstruction government. After merging with another city daily, it published as the *Austin Statesman and Review*. In 1973, the afternoon *Statesman* merged with the morning *Austin American*, becoming the *Austin American Statesman*.

The *Fort Worth Telegram* began publication in 1879. The *Fort Worth Star* began in 1906 and bought out the *Telegram* in 1908, and the merged *Fort Worth Star Telegram* began publication in 1909. The *Star Telegram's* publisher was Amon G. Carter, who was both the city's biggest booster and a smart newspaperman. Carter realized that there was a vast part of Texas west of Fort Worth without access to a major daily, so he aimed to make that his territory. Through aggressive pursuit of subscribers and the ingenious use of the railroads to reach towns to the west, by the 1920s the *Star Telegram* had more subscribers than any daily in Texas. In 1923, it added the motto "Where the West Begins" to its masthead.[16]

The major Texas papers would play an important and influential role from their inception through the 1930s. Local ownership by men personally invested in their communities played a part in the development of Houston, San Antonio, Dallas, and Fort Worth. For the most part, the Texas publishers fended off the efforts of the large Hearst and Pulitzer syndicates from gaining a lasting foothold in Texas. As a result, Texas papers were not as drawn to sensationalism and yellow journalism as their counterparts on either coast. Both Edwin Kiest at the *Times Herald* and George Dealey at the *Morning News* were important city advocates. Dealey was instrumental in the construction of the Trinity River viaduct, which greatly reduced the devastating floods to which Dallas was periodically prone. Carter, famous as a booster of Fort Worth, used his paper to attract business to the city. Since he saw all of west Texas as part of his distribution area, he used his considerable influence to push the legislature to establish the college that would become Texas Tech University in Lubbock. Carter was not above burying stories that might put his city or its businesses in a bad light.[17]

By the second decade of the 20th century, all major Texas newspapers exclusively backed Democratic candidates for state and local offices; even the *San Antonio Light* had come around by then. So while the papers had political stances and backed certain causes, they were not really partisan as such, since the Democrats were the only game in town. During the first three decades of the 1900s, two of the major issues that dominated the political statewide storyline were women's suffrage and the reemergence of the Ku Klux Klan as a political force in the state.

The editorial policies of the major dailies varied on the issue of suffrage. The *Chronicle* was the most supportive, backing the cause in a 1915 editorial, and in many to follow. The *Morning News* had a female columnist, Isadore Callaway, as early as 1899; she continually advocated for suffrage and a variety of other issues that were of concern to women.[18] Importantly, newspaper coverage of the suffrage movement, even from papers that didn't publicly back the cause, helped keep it at the forefront of the public agenda until the Nineteenth Amendment established women's right to vote.

Opposition to the Klan garnered support from the *Chronicle* and the *Dallas* and *Galveston News*. It wasn't that the papers espoused especially progressive racial views, but the Klan was seen as bad for business. As it was with suffrage, the *Chronicle* was among the first to come out strongly in opposition to the Klan. The *Post* was less outspoken in its opposition and at times was even sympathetic to Klan members, if not Klan goals. It wasn't until the Klan turned violent in south Texas that the *Post* began to oppose it more vigorously. In Dallas, the *Morning News* took on the Klan as soon as it became a visible force. It cost the Dallas paper a good deal of its readership and eventually led the Belo Corporation to sell the *Galveston News* in order to firm up its balance sheet.

☐ Newspapers in Decline

How far have newspapers declined? Let's look at the question from a national perspective. Daily newspaper circulation today is only three-quarters of what it was in 1940. Think about that for a minute. U. S. population was about 132 million in 1940, and it was 315 million in late 2012. Yet daily newspaper sales had declined from more than 40 million a day at the beginning of the period to less than 30 million at the end.

It is true that television news, radio, and magazines have all seen a decline in audience share in recent years, but none of the media have waned in significance as markedly as the newspaper. Texas has three fewer major newspapers than it had 30 years ago. Influence in the community has dropped as well, at least partially because of the dearth of local ownership. It is hard to imagine that a newspaper today would have the clout to almost singlehandedly force civic reform or a public works project.

While newspaper circulation has declined, most papers have enjoyed significant increases in unique visitors to their online websites, as noted in Table 6.1. But

TABLE 6.1 MANY READ LEADING NEWSPAPERS DIGITALLY

		Read mostly in		
	Print	Computer/ Mobile	Other/ DK	N
Based on regular readers of	%	%	%	
New Yorker, Atlantic, Harpers	72	23	4=100	103
Economist, Bloomberg Busweek	55	37	8=100	111
Wall Street Journal	54	44	2=100	142
USA Today	48	48	4=100	127
New York Times	41	55	5=100	174

PEW REASEARCH CENTER 2012 News Consumption Survey. Q90. Based on regular readers. Figures may not add to 100% because of rounding.

From: Pew Research Center, January 4, 2011 Internet Gains on Television as Public's Main News

Source: More Young People Cite Internet than TV.

that's not enough to offset print declines. Since most newspapers started with free websites (see the relationship between newspapers and early radio in Texas later in the chapter), many have had a hard time convincing readers to pay for online content.

The decline of the newspaper has little to do with the product itself. Simply put, there are so many other sources of information and of entertainment that readership decline was inevitable. Stories that once were available only in print, and only the following day, are now accessible by radio, network television, cable news, and the Internet. A laptop or a smartphone allows almost instant access to information that was once only available once a day, in printed format. Papers may survive as a niche in the communication market, but the traditionally daily newspaper has faded in significance and may soon disappear into the electronic pages of history.

Radio

6.2 Describe how radio emerged as a component of the Texas media.

There is a difference between radio and licensed radio. Radio was possible by the beginning of the 20th century, but it wasn't financially viable. Few people owned radio receivers, and fewer still had access to transmission equipment. Until the United States entered World War I, radio was a hobby indulged in by a few individuals with which the government had limited concern. By the time the war began, however, there were thousands of stations and hundreds of thousands of enthusiasts. The first efforts at regulation were aimed at limiting transmissions to a certain frequency, so as not to interfere with military and emergency broadcasting. When the United States entered the war, the president and the navy effectively forbade private broadcasting for the duration of the conflict. As early as 1915, the University of Texas had an operating noncommercial station. It primarily broadcast weather and crop reports. Unlike most amateur stations, it was allowed to operate during the war. After the war, with the commercial implications of radio becoming clear, the U.S. Department of Commerce began issuing licenses for broadcasters to ensure that stations broadcast at an assigned frequency. Certain frequencies were reserved for government and military use.

☐ First Licensed Stations

Radio was as important a source of news as it was a source of entertainment. To promote this new form of media, Congress created an oversight committee that eventually became known as the **Federal Communications Commission (FCC)**. The FCC operates as an independent U.S. government agency, oversees the public airways, and provides guidelines for appropriate use.

Walter Dealey was, by far, the most influential individual in making radio a major force in Texas. He tried to convince his father that the *Dallas Morning News* should operate the state's first radio station, as he was convinced that the future lay over the air. His father disagreed. Undaunted, and with his fascination with radio unsated, the younger Dealey worked with the city of Dallas to create WRR radio, the first licensed radio station in the state and only the second in the United States. The first city-owned radio station anywhere was initially intended to facilitate communication among the city's police and firemen, but during downtime, the air was filled with music, jokes, or whatever else Dallas firefighters dreamed up. Residents started to listen, and, not long after, the station began selling advertising.

The WRR's quick popularity helped Walter convince his father that the *Morning News* needed its own radio station. WFAA went on the air in June 1922, becoming the second licensed station in Texas. WFAA carried news, sports scores, dramas, and music. Importantly for Texas, in the fall of that first year, the station broadcast the state's high school football championship game, where Waco defeated Abilene 13–10. (The term *broadcast* is used loosely here. The announcers were in a studio, not in a

FCC
A federal agency that regulates publicly broadcasted radio stations.

WRR was the first licensed radio station operating in Texas. Here, we see the studio in its early days. The station, owned by the city of Dallas, has an all Classical music format and generates a small profit for the city, which is dispersed into a city Arts Endowment.

Inside the Federalist System

Journalistic shield laws protect reporters from having to divulge their sources; this is an important factor when writing about potentially illegal activity. One might imagine that the ability to protect one's sources is implied by the First Amendment, but the U.S. Supreme Court, in *Branzburg v .Hayes* (1972), held that no explicit protection exists, leaving the decisions to the state and federal governments, respectively. Most states have passed some sort of shield law, but neither the state of Texas nor the national government has enacted such a law. Not all state laws offer absolute protection, but they do prevent the routine prosecution of reporters for contempt of court if they do not reveal their sources to prosecutors. Michigan's shield law, for example, protects reporters in all cases except those where the suspect's ultimate sentence could be life in prison and where the information is not available from any other source.

Both Texas and U.S. prosecutors, however, can charge reporters with contempt for failing to provide criminal information. Although most prosecutors are reluctant to do so, such charges do occur. For example, in Texas, writer Vanessa Leggett refused to share the interview notes that she had collected for a true crime book with a Harris County grand jury investigating the murder of a Texas millionaire's wife. She served five months in jail in late 2001 and early 2002. (Since this was a capital murder case, the Michigan shield law would not have protected her from a persistent prosecutor.) Nationally, reporters have been jailed in a couple of prominent cases during the past decade. In the Barry Bonds steroids case, reporters Lance Williams and Mark Fainaru-Wada were sentenced to 18 months in federal prison for failing to divulge the source of the illegally obtained grand jury testimony that provided the basis for part of their book, *Game of Shadows*. After they were sentenced, but before they began to serve, the attorney who provided the leak pleaded guilty to obstruction and disobeying court orders, rendering their contempt sentence moot. In 2005, former *New York Times* reporter Judith Miller spent 12 weeks in jail for refusing to out her source for a story she was researching, but had not written, on an exposed CIA operative. After 12 weeks in jail, her source released her from her confidentiality pledge and she was subsequently freed.

In Texas, there is no great push for a shield law. In a conservative state, a law that may be perceived as aiding criminals, or even journalists, is unlikely to find its way to the top of the agenda, as neither criminals nor journalists elicit great sympathy from most Texans. It may take a high-profile case involving a popular figure to get the legislature to act, or a judicial reinterpretation of what freedom of the press means in Texas, for such protection to be extended to Texas journalists.

1. Should Texas adopt a shield law?

2. How does confidentiality affect a writer's ability to report a story?

Golden Age of Radio
The era in which radio reached its peak in popularity, generally in the 1930s–1940s.

stadium, and they re-created games on the basis of ticker-tape accounts.) At its inception, the radio station wasn't considered to be a money-making asset; instead, it was viewed as a public service provided by the paper.[19]

Other Texas newspapers followed the lead of the *News*. The *Star Telegram* opened Fort Worth's first radio station, WBAP; the *Post* started KPRC in Houston; Jesse Jones, owner of the *Chronicle*, established KTRH; and WOAI in San Antonio was formed by the owner of the *Express News*.

☐ The Golden Age of Radio

By the 1930s, radio was entering its **Golden Age**. Americans listened to music, sports, the news, and soap operas.

Although radio didn't penetrate Texas and the rest of the South to the degree that it did the nation as a whole, the number of Texans who listened to radio continued to grow as newspaper readership slipped. Even as the Depression deepened, listenership increased. After the initial purchase of the radio, use was essentially free, except for the small cost of electricity or batteries. As radio stations proliferated, many began to carve out a market niche, like WBAP did with its country music format. Coupled with its clear channel frequency, the station was popular with nighttime truck drivers across the country. Radio would become even more entrenched in the American culture during World War II, when it brought news from the front and at the same time provided a distraction from the war.

Although radio is a relatively old technology, it is clear that it is not following in the path of newspapers. The proliferation of Satellite radio has fostered a growth in channels dedicated to providing news. The channels that are currently available from Sirius Satellite Service are listed in Table 6.2.

TABLE 6.2 NEWS CHANNELS AVAILABLE FROM SATELLITE SERVICES

Service	Channel	Category	Channel Name	Description
Sirius	90	News	MSNBC	MSNBC: The Place for Politics
Sirius	92	News	CNN En Espanol	All-News Spanish Language
Sirius	94	News	Premiere Plus	Current Affairs French Language
Sirius	95	News	RCI Plus	International Talk French Language
Sirius	129	News	CNBC	First in Business Worldwide
Sirius	130	News	Bloomberg Radio	The World Leader in Business News
Sirius	131	News	Fox News Channel	We Report. You Decide.
Sirius	132	News	CNN	The Worldwide Leader in News
Sirius	133	News	CNN HLN	News and Views
Sirius	137	News	CBC Radio One	News Canadian News
Sirius	140	News	World Radio Network	News Around the World
Sirius	141	News	BBC World Service	BBC World Service
Sirius	145	News	Fox News Talk	Talk Radio from Fox News
XM Radio	96	News	Canada 360	A New Canadian Perspective on News
XM Radio	120	News	MSNBC	MSNBC: The Place for Politics
XM Radio	121	News	Fox News Channel	We Report. You Decide.
XM Radio	122	News	CNN	The Worldwide Leader in News
XM Radio	123	News	CNN HLN	News and Views
XM Radio	125	News	Quoi De Neuf	French-Language Arts & Entertainment
XM Radio	126	News	CNN En Espanol	All-News Spanish Language
XM Radio	127	News	CNBC	First in Business Worldwide
XM Radio	129	News	Bloomberg Radio	The World Leader in Business News
XM Radio	131	News	BBC World Service	BBC World Service
XM Radio	132	News	C-SPAN Radio	C-SPAN
XM Radio	135	News	World Radio Network	News Around the World
XM Radio	152	News	Extreme Talk	Entertaining, Informative, & Extreme
XM Radio	166	News	SIRIUS XM Patriot	Conservative Talk
XM Radio	168	News	Fox News Talk	Talk Radio from Fox News
XM Radio	172	News	Radio Parallèle	French-Language Canadian News & Talk

Television

6.3 Evaluate how television changed the way Texans consume news.

Television was developed over several decades and was significantly intertwined with the invention of the radio. Although still images had been transmitted earlier, the first live images were broadcast in 1925. The Federal Radio Commission issued the first television license in the United States three years later, but few Americans owned TVs. Development would have occurred more rapidly had it not been for World War II, but all electronic component production was diverted to the war effort. Texas did not have commercial television until the war ended.

As had been the case with radio, Amon Carter was an early adapter. He obtained the first commercial television license in the state in 1948, using the call letters WBAP, just as he did for radio. WBAP was the first television station in the southern United States. By 1950, six stations were in operation, half of those in the

Texas ★ Mosaic

The Power of a Politician

Lyndon Baines Johnson exercised political power in a manner we may never see again. His life doesn't fit in a book: It is a five-volume megabiography. In 1943, Lyndon's wife, Lady Bird Johnson, inherited some money. Lyndon, already in Congress, had friends in the FCC. Lady Bird used her inheritance to purchase Austin radio station KTBC, with the FCC granting quick approval to her application for ownership. In short order, the station was moved to a less crowded frequency on the radio spectrum and allowed to both expand to a 24-hour format and increase its broadcast power by five-fold, its signal reaching all of central Texas. That meant more advertising revenue for Lady Bird's station. A lot more. After Congressman Johnson met with the president of CBS, the Austin station was suddenly a CBS affiliate. KTBC changed its call letters to KLBJ in 1973, after the former president's death.

And when the FCC opened the bidding for Austin's first television station, only the Johnsons put in an application. From 1952 to 1965, it was the only television station in Austin, primarily carrying CBS programming. The media empire put Johnson in a unique position. He carried enormous clout, and the broadcast company's aggressive advertising wing was difficult for business to ignore, especially after he was elected to the U.S. Senate in 1948. Only five years later, his fellow Democrats chose him as the Minority Leader. In 1955, Johnson ascended to Majority Leader when the Democrats retook control of the Senate. After John F. Kennedy's assassination in 1963, he became president of the United States. Advertising revenues continued to rise. Of course, it wasn't just the advertising revenue that made the media outlets worthwhile. LBJ indirectly oversaw the content of the largest radio and television outlets in the region, which also provided feeds to national networks.

Lyndon Johnson never backed away from his story that Lady Bird was the brains, money, and driving force behind the radio station. Robert Caro's biography proved, however, that Lyndon was involved every step of the way.

Source: Caro, Robert A., *The Years of Lyndon Johnson: The Path to Power.* New York: Alfred A. Knopf, 1982.

1. How would owning a media empire help an aspiring politician?

2. Could you limit media ownership of broadcast entities by politicians without violating the First Amendment? Why or why not?

Dallas–Fort Worth area, and the newly christened Federal Communications Commission, noting the rapid proliferation of television broadcasters across the nation, issued a two-year moratorium on granting new licenses until it had the opportunity to more closely evaluate the need for regulation. WOAI debuted in San Antonio in 1949. KRLD in Dallas, owned by the *Times Herald*, started in 1949. WFAA, owned by Belo, was on the air a year later. Houston's first television station struggled in its first year before being bought out by the *Houston Post* and becoming KPRC in 1950. KEYL signed on in San Antonio in 1950, but was bought by the *Express News* four years later.

In the early 1950s, Texas became one of the nation's largest markets for television sets, accounting for almost as many sales as the rest of the South combined. Television was quick to spread after the war partially because of the increased productive capacity in the country and partially because of pent-up demand that resulted from rationing during the war. Americans had more money to spend and more things to spend it on. Television changed the way we saw the world around us. Prior to the 1950s, most Americans had never seen a Major League Baseball game. They had read about one in the paper, listened to one on the radio, and seen film clips of one at the movie theater, but most had never had the opportunity to see a game live. For Americans with television sets, the World Series came to them.

The advent of television changed the way we looked at politics, too. Texas and Texans were at the forefront of the era. Speaker Sam Rayburn presided over the U. S. House for twice the time of any other individual. During his time in the House, he presided over three Democratic National Conventions; the first, in 1948, was televised mainly on the East Coast. The next two conventions received national coverage, and Rayburn became not only a name, but an image. Texas and television would play an important role in the election of the telegenic and charismatic John F. Kennedy and his Texas running mate, Lyndon Johnson, in the 1960 presidential race. Rayburn and Johnson would play a more somber role in the coverage of the aftermath of Kennedy's assassination in Dallas in 1963. Part of Kennedy's legacy, with a big push from Johnson, was mandating that the National Aeronautics and Space Administration land a man on the moon by the end of the decade. As a result, the first word spoken from the lunar surface and broadcast across the world in July 1969 was "Houston."

In the 1970s, the Watergate hearings brought a couple of Texans to television prominence. U. S. House Representative Barbara Jordan was a key member of the Judiciary Committee that voted to recommend the impeachment of President Richard Nixon. Leon Jaworski served as the special prosecutor for the case, which ended with Nixon's resignation.

Texans made an impact in the television anchor chair as well. Perhaps the most famous, and best loved, news anchor of all time was University of Texas graduate Walter Cronkite. Controversial and folksy Dan Rather, from Wharton, followed Cronkite. Bob Schieffer of Fort Worth spent time in the anchor chair as well. Texan Scott Pelley holds the CBS anchor chair now, and that is just the lineage at one network. Other Texans who built a solid national career include Sam Donaldson at ABC and former CNN anchor Lou Dobbs.

Today, Texas has over 150 broadcast television stations. California, the largest state by population, has 11 NBC affiliates, while Texas has 23. Part of the reason for the disparity is that Texas's physical size requires a large number of stations to reach the dispersed population.

Veteran newscaster Walter Cronkite, along with former Houston-based astronaut Wally Schirra, holding up the July 20, 1969 edition *New York Daily News* during CBS coverage of the moon landing. The University of Texas-educated Cronkite was one of America's most trusted news anchors, back in a time when most people watched the evening news.

The Texas Constitution

A Closer Look

Article 1. Bill of Rights

Sec. 8. FREEDOM OF SPEECH AND PRESS; LIBEL. Every person shall be at liberty to speak, write or publish his opinions on any subject, being responsible for the abuse of that privilege; and no law shall ever be passed curtailing the liberty of speech or of the press. In prosecutions for the publication of papers, investigating the conduct of officers, or men in public capacity, or when the matter published is proper for public information, the truth thereof may be given in evidence. And in all indictments for libels, the jury shall have the right to determine the law and the facts, under the direction of the court, as in other cases.

1. Why does the Texas constitution emphasize truth in regard to publication?

2. Do we put too much or too little emphasis on freedom of speech and the press?

The Mainstream Media and Political Coverage in Texas

6.4 Evaluate how the media covers Texas politics.

With a few notable exceptions, the mainstream media's coverage of local and state politics has been superficial at best. Take the typical 30-minute 10 P.M. news broadcast on a local network affiliate. On average, eight minutes is consumed by commercials. Another five or six minutes is devoted to sports; five more is set aside for weather. Already, the 30-minute broadcast is down to 12 minutes. The lead story is almost always about murder, child abduction, a five alarm fire, or an automotive crash big enough to close a freeway. That takes out another four minutes. Everything else covered by the local broadcast has to fit into the remaining eight minutes. That includes human interest stories, upcoming festivals, routine crime coverage, and investigation into consumer fraud. If any time is left for political coverage, it is more likely to focus on national stories rather than local or state. When state and local politics does get air time, it tends to be "horse race" coverage of elections instead of in-depth coverage of policy issues. And with these leftover minutes, even if it all were devoted to politics, there is simply not enough time for much depth. The only times that state political issues are likely to receive airtime on Texas television affiliates are in the days before or after an election, or at the beginning or end of a legislative session. Short of a scandal, Texas politics otherwise receives scant television coverage. Many Texas television stations have dramatically cut back, or completely done away with, their Austin bureaus, so they don't have reporters in place to ferret out important stories or to recognize the importance of issues as they emerge.

Again, with few exceptions, Texas daily newspapers do little better. Newspapers want to sell copies. On a day-to-day basis, editors believe that customers don't want to read about state or local politics. In a way, this becomes a self fulfilling legacy. Because readers aren't fed political and governmental news on a regular basis, they have a hard time understanding the intricacies of such stories when they do make the front page. Furthermore, a decline in subscriptions, as noted in Figure 6.1, and related advertising revenue, means that the surviving papers have to cut expenditures to stay in business. Here, the effect is twofold. Again, Austin bureaus are among the first to feel the budget cuts. Outside of the Austin bureau, however, newsroom cuts tend to target the

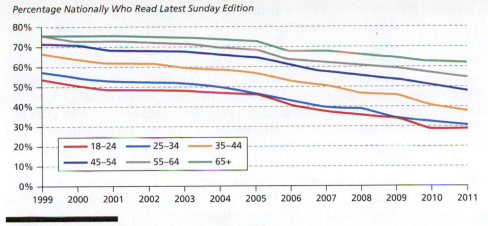

Percentage Nationally Who Read Latest Sunday Edition

FIGURE 6.1 Falling Readership Over the Last Decade.
Source: 2012 State of the Media. Pew Research Center for Excellence in Journalism.

best paid, and most experienced, reporters. If you are going to cut costs, you save more money by removing those who are paid the most. Inevitably, it means you lose writers with the deepest understanding of the political system. For example, when the owners of the venerable *Austin American Statesman* were considering selling the paper in 2009, they began offering buyout packages to senior staff. Among those who took them up on the offer was Laylan Copeland, an investigative reporter who had covered city and state politics for 35 years. His investigations were part of what led to charges against former Texas House Speaker Gib Lewis, and former U.S. House Speaker Tom DeLay, among others. Although Copeland returned to the paper's business desk a year later, political coverage has suffered a blow. Similar buyouts have occurred at dailies around the state, most notably at the *Fort Worth Star Telegram*. In March 2012, the paper announced the closing of its Austin bureau.

A big change in Texas media coverage that has occurred over the last few decades has been the demise of local ownership of newspapers. Only the *Dallas Morning News* is still owned by the A. H. Belo Corporation. The company also owns the *Denton Record Chronicle* and a couple of out-of-state papers. The company spun off its television side as the separate Belo Corporation. In addition to WFAA in Dallas, the company operates KHOU in Houston, KVUE in Austin, KENS in San Antonio, and a number of out-of-state stations from Seattle to Charlotte to New Orleans. Carter's *Star Telegram* is now owned by the McClatchy Company. The *Chronicle* is owned by Hearst, as is the *San Antonio Express*. The *American Statesman* is owned by Cox Enterprises. The dearth of local ownership has impacted the resources allocated to cover local and state politics.

When the Media Did Matter: Texas Monthly, CBS and the Texas Supreme Court

Every rule has its exceptions. In several instances, media coverage impacted Texas government and helped force change. No example is as dramatic as that of the transformation of the Texas supreme court in the late 1980s. Among the first newspapers to pick up on the story were the *San Antonio Express* and the *San Antonio Light*, which reported that appellate cases were being shifted from one appellate court to another, without sufficient cause, by the order of state supreme court justices. That led to a more detailed investigation by *Texas Monthly* and culminated with the *60 Minutes* expose "Is Justice for Sale" in December 1987. Eventually, three members of the court would be forced into early retirement.

Although the *60 Minutes* broadcast brought the most publicity, *Texas Monthly* helped focus the attention of both the state and national media on the Texas court. The 40-year-old news magazine doesn't fit neatly into our newspaper category, but it comes close enough. It is as politically influential as any printed publication in the state. No one relishes being the recipient of one of its "Bum Steer" awards or being named one of the state's 10 worst legislators (although some do wear the label as a badge of honor).

By the mid-1980s, the Texas supreme court had evolved into a strange animal. In a state that is and has been pro-business, the Texas supreme court consistently staked out an antibusiness position. From a practical position, this meant that the top civil court in Texas made it relatively easy to sue and to collect significant damages, a position that is not conducive to a healthy business environment. In a day when all Texas supreme court justices were Democrats, the entire electoral ball game was in the Democratic primary. Republicans didn't even field candidates for most races until 1988. Plaintiffs' lawyers, the ones who are doing the suing, carefully recruited and financed sympathetic judicial candidates and picked winnable primary races.

The problem was that some of the justices that the plaintiffs' coalition had managed to collect believed they owed special consideration to their biggest campaign donors. What first drew the attention of the media was the abnormal movement of the appellate cases. Part of what brought that to light was another unique feature of the Texas judiciary. Unlike almost every other state and the national Supreme Court, law clerks sat in on the deliberation conferences of the Texas supreme court. They took notes, as that was part of their job, and several quickly became uncomfortable with what they were witnessing.

The controversy started when a Texas supreme court administrator asked the clerk for the fourth district court of appeals to move several cases from that appellate court to another. That was not unusual. The supreme court often transfers cases to close a backlog. What was unusual was that this request included the two specific cases that should be included in the transfer. Neither had been on the docket very long. The clerk went to his boss, fourth circuit Chief Justice Carlos Cadena, who wanted to know why. According to *Texas Monthly*, after a conversation with the justice who ordered the transfer, C. L. Ray, "Cadena concluded that the cases were being transferred because Pat Maloney, Sr., a San Antonio attorney who was a friend and political supporter of C. L. Ray, wanted them in another court."[20] Such preferential treatment allows a lawyer to walk away from a court predisposed toward rendering a negative ruling and to move the case to a friendlier venue. Soon, several newspapers were questioning the docket moves, and the chair of the House Committee on Judicial Affairs called a series of public hearings to look into the matter. Chair Frank Tejeda began calling law clerks to testify.

Some did. And what they had to say was unflattering, including allegations that Ray had discussed a pending case with a state legislator, action that constitutes a gross violation of confidentiality.[21] More disturbing was the manner in which Ray tried to maneuver a decision toward one of his biggest contributors, oilman Clinton Manges, who had a sizable judgment awarded against him. Manges hired Maloney as his appellate attorney. Ray wanted the Supreme Court to overturn the verdict. It took a long time for Ray to craft a decision that both favored Manges and gained support of the Court. At the end, it seemed as if Ray would fail on a technicality. One justice recused himself because of a prior lawsuit against Manges. Another, Ted Robertson, considered recusal because Manges and Maloney had funded a huge portion of his successful primary campaign. When it came time for the final vote, Robertson opted for recusal. Although that left four justices siding with overturning the case and three with letting it stand, the chief justice said, "As I read the Texas Constitution, you have to have five votes to reverse, so I guess this means we affirm the Court of Appeals."[22] In that moment, Robertson withdrew his recusal, voted for the Ray decision, and reversed the appellate court. This incident called national attention to the way Texas elects judges and to what lengths some judges are willing to go to appease their benefactors.

Tejeda subpoenaed Kilgarlin and Ray. Both refused to testify, citing the need to maintain a constitutional separation of power. A district court judge agreed. When Tejeda persisted in questioning more briefing clerks, the justices filed a lawsuit against one who had already testified. The threat was implicit. If any other clerk testified, they faced the real prospect of being sued.[23] And since testifying meant divulging information that, by its nature, was supposed to be confidential, no one was sure whether they were protected, especially under the plaintiff-tilted playing field that the court had created.

The victory of the justices was pyrrhic. Although they would effectively stave off further house investigation, as Tejeda did not want to endanger the livelihood of potential witnesses, none would win another election. The Texas Commission on Judicial Conduct offered a rare public rebuke of both Ray and Kilgarlin. Once their practices were divulged and dispersed by the media, each was unelectable. It proves that, in the rare instance where the press locks in on a story, it can have a significant impact.

Local Access

From the early days of cable television through the 1990s, local access television was popular, if not with the larger public, then at least with those who broadcast on local access channels provided as a "public service" by cable stations. These channels might have yoga classes, high school sports reports, or programs devoted to gardening or other hobbies. A substantial amount of this content was political in nature, giving a venue to viewpoints that might be unconventional from the mainstream media's perspective. One participant said, "Local cable access shows were usually low budget affairs, a marriage of a teenager's poorly executed video blog and the Sean Hannity show."[24] Low budget as they may have been, they gave rise to a forum for broadcasting alternative information.

Narrowcasting

As cable and satellite television expanded their offerings to hundreds of channels, the industry transitioned from broadcasting programs that appealed to the largest possible audience to include narrowcasting within their offerings. With so many channels, shows with relatively low appeal had the opportunity to air. From a political standpoint, this allowed the proliferation of news channels, each with a different audience and spin.

Internet

The Internet has had important implications for all media platforms. Although both newspaper readership and television news viewership are down, it is important to remember that every newspaper and television station in Texas has a website, where viewers can retrieve information at their convenience. Unfortunately, none of the major Texas daily newspapers has a website that is close to the quality of those run by the *New York Times*, *Washington Post*, or *Los Angeles Times*. Much of the *Morning News* and *Star-Telegram* content is behind a pay wall, for subscribers only, and it is possible that more Texas newspaper websites will move toward that model.

One bright spot among Texas news websites is the *Texas Tribune*, an online-only newspaper overseen by former *Texas Monthly* editor Evan Smith. The *Tribune* covers only government and politics, but it does so well, evenhandedly, and is easily navigable. It has quickly established a solid stable of writers since its founding in 2009.

Internet penetration is significant. By early 2012, more than 75 percent of Americans owned a desktop or laptop computer, with 44 percent owning a smartphone and more than 18 percent a tablet.[25] As the Figure 6.2 shows, Americans who own Internet-accessible devices are prone to using them to access news, which coincides with the viewpoint that Texans have greater access to information than ever before.

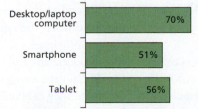

Percent of device owners who get news from...

Desktop/laptop computer — 70%

Smartphone — 51%

Tablet — 56%

N's: Desktop/laptop = 2,342; smartphone = 1,180; tablet = 511

FIGURE 6.2 Where People with Internet Access Get Their News.

Source: 2012 State of the News Media: Pew Research Center's Project for Excellence in Journalism.

6.1

new media
Forms of delivering instant communications in a digitized or electronic format.

6.2

6.3

6.4

6.5

The lessons learned from local access and narrowcasting have reached fruition with the Internet. Sites such as YouTube and the increasing use of vlogs have allowed anyone with a webcam to venture into the world of journalism and political commentary.

☐ Texas Political Websites

In addition to news websites and those maintained by political parties, a number of other Texas political blogs provide insight. The *Quorum Report* does an excellent job of collecting breaking Texas political stories. Although most of its information is behind the pay wall, it is a quick way to keep up with the latest news. The *Burnt Orange Report* is probably the best known liberal website in Texas. It has been in operation for a decade and, as the name implies, is based in Austin. *Texas Insider* is a conservative-leaning website. In general, liberals have been more successful in establishing blogs and websites than conservatives, although conservatives have made an effort to catch up over the last several years. Judging by the number of sites, though, liberal bloggers and websites still enjoy a significant advantage in Texas. For good, balanced, and insightful coverage of Texas politics on the Web, it is hard to do better than *Texas Monthly* senior editor Paul Burka's *BurkaBlog*.

Candidates, interest groups, political parties, and virtually all things political have embraced social media as a prime outlet for making unfiltered information available to a mass audience. Even government agencies and most Texas colleges and universities optimize their use of Facebook, YouTube, Twitter, Flickr, and other resources—some to a great extent. These technologies are called **new media** and are ever expanding. As a matter of fact, you may be reading this by some form of new media.

☐ Bias in the Media

We have dismissed the idea that once, in our ancient past, the media was pure and unbiased. In fact, we have put forth the argument that in its news coverage, the media is less biased than it was during the first half-century of the state's existence. Nonetheless, most media outlets have an editorial bias. In their opinion pieces and editorials, they take sides. One of the clearest examples of this at the national level is the stark contrast between the editorial programming on Fox News and MSNBC. Fox has a conservative slant, MSNBC a liberal one. While you may well receive similar straight news from both stations, the majority of their airtime is devoted to editorial content. Viewers of MSNBC tend to be liberal; those of Fox tend to be conservative. This is a natural process we'll call selective exposure. When you watch a television news network or read a newspaper columnist, you are likely to spend your time with those who share your views. Certainly, some will watch or read their polar opposites for the pure pleasure of becoming angry, but most avoid the cognitive dissonance created by contrary information. From that perspective, media may matter less than many suppose. If we watch or read only those who share our views to begin with, the effect of the media is likely to simply reinforce what we already think.

In Texas, selective exposure affects which columnists you may read rather than which newspapers you choose for the simple reason that there is no real competition among dailies. In almost all of the state, there is only one daily in town. In fact, eastern Tarrant County is the only place in the state where two major dailies have squared off, with the *Star Telegram* and *Morning News* both serving the area. Even there, in terms of editorial policy, the difference is essentially between the center-left *Telegram* and the center-right *News*.

Despite the waning influence of newspapers, politicians still seek their endorsement. At the top of the ticket, it doesn't really matter. If you were a supporter of Barack Obama before the *Dallas Morning News* endorsed Mitt Romney, it is unlikely that you changed your vote as a result. However, with Texas's long ballot, endorsements do mean something for the down-ballot races. For comparison sake, and because presidential endorsements give some insight into a paper's editorial philosophy, the *Dallas Morning News* endorsed Romney in 2012, John McCain in 2008, and George W. Bush in 2004. The *Houston Chronicle* endorsed Romney, Obama, and Bush. The *San Antonio Express* backed Obama,

McCain, and Bush, while the *Star Telegram* picked Romney, Obama, and Bush. The *American Statesman* endorsed Obama in 2008 and Bush in 2004. In 2012, in what may be a precedent-setting move, the *Statesman* chose not to endorse in the presidential race.

6.1

6.2

6.3

6.4

6.5

polling
A measure of the public's opinion, intensity, and direction about government and politics.

☐ The Texas Government, Transparency, and the Media

It may surprise many that Texas has a greater degree of transparency than most of its counterparts. Decades ago, the state adopted Open Meeting and Open Records laws that unlock the door to myriad information about government operations, if you know where to look. The media does know where to look and regularly files open record requests when it believes that a government agency or subdivision is withholding information. Interest groups and individuals file requests as well. The process is fairly straightforward. Most public documents are subject to an open records request, with some common-sense exceptions such as employee social security numbers and home addresses. If a government agency believes that information is exempt from disclosure, it must report to the state's attorney general why they believe it is exempt. Failure to respond to a request waives exemption claims. The government entity can charge reasonable costs for copying and retrieving information provided in a records request.

The Open Meetings Act is vigorously enforced, to the point that if, for instance, several members of a city council meet informally, say at a high school football game, and discuss business that is on the city council's agenda, they are subject to prosecution. The idea is that government affairs should be discussed out in the open, in the light of day. It prevents elected officials from making deals outside of the scrutiny of the public and the press. There are exceptions to the rule, such as when a body is dealing with personnel or real estate matters, but even those conversations can occur only after the body reconvenes into executive session and posts the general topics of their discussions.

Public Opinion and Polling

6.5 Evaluate the importance of polling and public opinion in Texas politics.

 ublic opinion and polling matter to both politicians and the media because they help gauge where the public stands on various issues. Therefore, we need to understand both in order to evaluate their impact on public policy in Texas. **Polling**, if it is done correctly, can tell us what public opinion is.

☐ Public Opinion

In essence, public opinion comprises the beliefs of Texans on a variety of issues. Public opinion is related to political culture, but the two are not exactly the same. Much of public opinion does derive from political culture, but culture is a broader perspective than opinion, which deals with specific issues.

Public opinion deals with salient issues, those that resonate with the public. We care about issues like gay marriage, abortion, and taxes. Fifty years ago, segregation was salient in Texas; fortunately, that is no longer the case. Though most Texans agree on the basic concept of equality, specific issues such as affirmative action in college admission remain controversial.

If there is one constant in the arena of media, from infancy right on to the present, it is that it has served as a tool in shaping public opinion. Sometimes the influence is patent, as we've seen in our discussion about the partisan and the penny press. Other times it is more subtle, as evidenced by bias, both intentional and coincidental. But the most fascinating form of media influence on public opinion can best be examined by its public policy-making implications. Issues do not become issues until and unless they appear on the public agenda, and there is no greater source of agenda-creating than media. That's how we find out about the things that are happening around us.

tracking polls
Polls that trace public opinion over time.

Media coverage of events, trends, and observations get the public talking, and discussion is the womb from which all public policy is born.

It's no secret that public opinion polling is used by persons seeking public office, because it is important for candidates to know and focus on issues that are important to the public—particularly the voting public. Political parties rely heavily on the ability to gauge public sentiment, and they temper their messages accordingly. We learned that the interest groups' primary mission is public dissemination, and we know that the media is the best—if not the only—way to accomplish that mission.

☐ Polling

Polling, whether done by the media, interest groups, or politicians, is aimed at capturing public opinion. Most media use professional polling organizations, such as Gallup, Rasmussen, or Pew Research. These organizations specialize in writing poll questions and are generally reliable pollsters. Polling done by interest groups may be less reliable, as they deliberately word questions in a manner designed to evoke a certain response. That's why both sides of an issue can claim to have broad public support; responders are simply not answering the same questions. The same is true of internal polling done by campaigns, which has several purposes; one of these purposes is to have results that can be leaked to the media which shows that a candidate is leading or at least viable.

It is important to understand that polling offers a snapshot of a race or an issue. What it shows is the beliefs of the sample polled at the moment they were questioned. Events may have overtaken the poll and made it virtually worthless by the time it comes out. **Tracking polls** can show how opinions evolve, but only if you are tracking the same polling organization asking the same questions. You can't track results from one poll to another, though, as differences in results may be due to differences in the way a question is asked, rather than an actual shift in opinion. Both media and campaigns make use of tracking polls because it gives insight into both movement among voters and how specific issues affect voter opinion.

Campaigns can further hone their issues through the use of focus groups. By bringing randomly selected likely voters in for interviews, they can gauge which issues resonate and which damage their candidate. Focus groups are essentially more intense polling with a smaller sample size. A campaign may, for instance, show the select groups several versions of television commercials in order to judge which are most effective across various voting demographics.

☐ The Science of Polling

For a poll to be valid, it has to be a sample of universal population. If you were conducting a poll on the Texas governor's race, for instance, you would poll a random sample of all of the likely voters in the state. It does no good to poll nonvoters or noncitizens, and most pollsters will choose likely voters over registered voters. If, on the other hand, you were polling on which professional football team is most popular in the state, your universe would be all Texans.

The reliability of a poll is determined by its confidence rate and margin of error. You may learn in your statistics course the mathematics behind polling, but for our purposes, it is important to understand the terms, not how they are derived. Margin of error denotes the accuracy of a poll. For most national polls, expect to see a margin of error of ±3 percent. If, given that margin, the president had a 52 percent approval rating in the poll, this means that, had the entire universe of registered voters been polled, the president's actual approval rating could be as high as 55 percent or as low as 49 percent. The confidence rate tells us how likely it is that the poll, given its margin of error, represents the entire universe. The standard confidence rate is 95 percent. In our example, that means that our poll, 19 out of 20 times, would be valid if we actually contacted every American registered voter. One time it would not be.

The margin of error and confidence rate might not be as narrow in a state poll. The simple reason is that state polls often interview fewer participants than national polls, making their results less accurate. This is certainly true when the state numbers are derived from a national poll; the state portion is inherently less accurate. State-specific polls are more likely to mirror the accuracy of national polls.

It is important to remember that, no matter how accurate the poll, it is only measuring the question asked. A badly worded question may yield misleading results. Something as simple as which candidate is listed first in a preference poll can influence outcome. For that reason, most legitimate pollsters will alternate the candidate listed first as they move from one respondent to another.

Polls that you read in the newspaper or see on television and the Internet are rarely random samples. Instead, most are weighted so that their results mirror demographic data. If a poll samples fewer Latinos than would naturally occur in the population, most services will weight the results from the Latinos polled more heavily to account for the discrepancy. Among the major pollsters, only Rasmussen weights its polls according to party identification, a practice that is much more difficult to actually gauge, but, if done right, can offer a much more accurate projection for elective offices. Or it can fail miserably like it did in 2012. These different rating techniques often account for a large portion of the discrepancy among the various polls.

☐ Exit polls

Exit polling is valuable to political scientists and analysts because it gives insight into what helped voters make their decisions. Exit polls also help media make quicker calls on races on Election Night. Their greatest value, though, is in helping us determine who voted for whom and why. Respondents are broken down by gender, age, income, race, religion, education, wealth, and practically any other demographic you can imagine.

One particular issue with exit polls, particularly in Texas, is that they fail to account for early voters. In many states, the issue may be of minor consequence. In Texas, that is not the case, as more than half of the voters in the 2010 gubernatorial election took advantage of the state's liberal early voting laws and voted prior to Election Day. Those early voters in Texas tend to be more conservative and more likely to vote for Republican candidates than the Election Day voters. With that caveat in mind, let's take a look at what the exit polls told us about the Texas electorate in 2010. Exit polls are collected through pooled resources, where the networks and newspapers share both the cost of and information from the data collection. In 2012, and as yet another example of cost cutting, the media conglomerates opted out of conducting exit polling in Texas and other states where the results of the contest were in little doubt.

The 2010 exit polls showed that 69 percent of Texas voters came from households making more than $50,000 a year. Seventy-nine percent of voters had at least some college. Twenty-eight percent considered themselves Democrats, 39 percent Republicans, and 33 percent identified themselves as independents. Only 14 percent called themselves liberals, while 51 percent identified as conservative and 35 percent as moderate. Thirty-five percent classified themselves as white Evangelicals.[26]

Sixty percent of Texas voters believed that the government should do more, compared to 36 percent who believed it should do less. Forty-eight percent supported the Tea Party movement, 25 percent opposed it, while 23 percent had neutral feelings. Forty-nine percent believed illegal immigrants should be granted a path to citizenship. Forty-two percent believed they should be deported.[27] Remember that this exit poll was simply a snapshot of what voting Texans believed on Election Day 2010.

☐ Push Polling

Push polling is not really polling at all, but a technique of political attack disguised as a legitimate poll. Typically, an alleged pollster will call, ask whom you support in a race, and, if you give the wrong answer, ask "Would you still support Mr. Smith if you knew he supported amnesty for illegal aliens on welfare?" The great distortion here is that Mr. Smith may have never supported anything of the sort, but the voter may now associate the candidate with the policy. Many polls are legitimate, but it is important to realize when you may be the target of an illegitimate effort.

push polling
A tactic intended to persuade respondents, disguised as a poll.

6.1

6.2

6.3

6.4

6.5

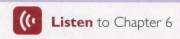
Texas Newspapers

6.1 Trace the evolution of the print media in Texas.

After an inauspicious beginning, newspapers gained significance during the Republic era. Up until the Civil War, papers tended to editorialize for or against Sam Houston. During the war, publication all but ceased in Texas due to economic constraints. After the war, papers divided along allegiance to E. J. Davis. By the turn of the 20th century, however, big-city dailies became an important force in the Texas media, often engaging in local boosterism and advocating for pro-business causes. Declining circulation and out-of-state ownership each contributed to the decline in newspaper influence.

Radio

6.2 Describe how radio emerged as a component of the Texas media.

Many of the first licensed radio stations in Texas were affiliated with newspapers. Especially during the Depression, radio listenership increased as newspaper circulation declined. During World War II, radio became even more prominent as a source of both news and entertainment.

Television

6.3 Evaluate how television changed the way Texans consume news.

Like radio, most early Texas television stations were associated with newspapers. Sales of televisions in Texas were brisk in the early 1950s, and viewers were able to see things they had only read about or heard before. Several Texans came to national political prominence because of television exposure. Likewise, Texans played an oversized role in national anchor booths.

The Mainstream Media and Political Coverage in Texas

6.4 Evaluate how the media covers Texas politics.

Media coverage of state and local politics is limited. Political stories, especially policy stories, don't tend to draw in viewers or readers, both of which are important for the advertising revenue they generate. Local television news time is limited, and both newspapers and television stations have cut back on their Austin bureaus during austere times. Although all major Texas newspapers have websites, they lag in style and substance when compared to those of prominent big-city dailies outside of the state. The *Texas Tribune*, a Web-only news offering, is an exception. Even if traditional media provides limited resources to Texas politics, political blogs have added a new dimension to coverage in the state. Candidates and interest groups have also created both Internet and social media presences.

Public Opinion and Polling

6.5 Evaluate the importance of polling and public opinion in Texas politics.

Public opinion reflects the collective views of Texans on issues both political and nonpolitical. From our perspective, polling gives us insight into specific political issues and voters' ever-changing stance regarding candidates for office. Polling, when done correctly, can help us track shifting opinions and voter sentiment. Polling offers a snapshot of an issue or race and is only as good as the question asked and the population sampled. Exit polls not only allow the media to call elections more quickly after the polls close, but also give us insight into why voters chose the candidates they voted for.

Learn the Terms

 Study and **Review** the **Flashcards**

Fairness Doctrine, p. 136
FCC, p. 143
Golden Age of Radio, p. 144

New media, p. 152
Partisan Press, p. 138
Penny Press, p. 139

Polling, p. 153
Push polling, p. 155
Tracking polls, p. 154

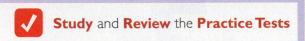
6.1 Trace the evolution of the print media in Texas.

At the beginning of the 20th century, most Texas newspapers

a. were supporters of business-friendly initiatives.
b. engaged in rumor mongering to sell papers.
c. were owned by out-of-state corporations.
d. had their own radio stations.
e. were owned by the Belo Corporation.

6.2 Describe how radio emerged as a component of the Texas media.

Most early Texas radio stations were

a. network affiliates.
b. operated by city governments.
c. affiliated with newspapers.
d. owned by the Belo Corporation.
e. antibusiness.

6.3 Evaluate how television changed the way Texans consume news.

Which is true of television news today?

a. Most Texans watch a local daily news show.
b. Most Texans watch a national daily news show.
c. Texas television stations have increased their resources for political coverage.
d. Television has helped make politicians more recognizable.
e. Television has reduced the avenues of access that Texans have to news.

6.4 Evaluate how the media covers Texas politics.

Which of the following is most accurate when describing media coverage of Texas politics?

a. Most daily newspapers have a large presence in Austin.
b. Political stories often lead local news broadcasts.
c. Newspapers value experienced political reporters over all others
d. Newspaper readership continues to rise in Texas.
e. *Texas Monthly* picked up the supreme court scandal before *60 Minutes* did.

6.5 Evaluate the importance of polling and public opinion in Texas politics.

The most important part of exit polling it that it

a. attempts to push voters in a certain direction.
b. is weighted for partisan identification.
c. helps the media determine the winner more quickly.
d. helps explain why voters voted the way they did.
e. helps confirm the margin of error.

Explore Further

Acheson, Sam Hanna. *35,000 Days in Texas: A History of the Dallas News and Its Forbears.* Westport, CT: Greenwood Press, 1973.

The Austin American Statesman http://www.statesman.com/

Cash, Wanda G., and Ed Sterling. *The News in Texas: Essays in Honor of the 125th Anniversary of the Texas Press Association.* Austin, TX: Center for American History, 2005.

Cox, Patrick L. *The First Texas News Barons.* Austin: University of Texas Press, 2005.

The Dallas Morning News www.dallasnews.com

The El Paso Times http://www.elpasotimes.com/

The Fort Worth Star Telegram http://www.star-telegram.com/

The Galveston Daily News http://galvestondailynews.com/

The Houston Chronicle www.chron.com

Huffaker, Robert. *When the News Went Live: Dallas 1963.* Lanham, MD: Taylor Trade Pub, 2004.

Quorum Report http://www.quorumreport.com/

The San Antonio Express http://www.mysanantonio.com/

Texas Monthly http://www.texasmonthly.com/

The Texas Tribune www.texastribune.org

The Portal to Texas History http://texashistory.unt.edu/

7

The Legislative Process in Texas Politics

They really meant two days every 140 years!

—*Plaque on the Wall of a Member of the Texas
House of Representatives*

A rancher in Andrews, Texas, finds out that a low-level radioactive waste dump is being built a mere three miles from where his cattle graze. How did that happen? A high school junior, as a prank, sends a sexually suggestive photo of his girlfriend to a buddy via text message. Shortly thereafter, he's charged with a class C misdemeanor, made to pay a hefty fine, and required to attend a class designed to prevent such "sexting." Who knew? A young mother finds that her third grader's class contains 33 students, whereas his second grade class had numbered 22. What's going on? What's going on is the process of lawmaking in

7.1	**7.2**	**7.3**	**7.4**	**7.5**	**7.6**
Explain, analyze, and compare the structure and composition of the Texas Legislature.	Explain redistricting and gerrymandering and analyze their impact on the Texas Legislature.	Analyze the roles of the presiding officers and "The Team" in the legislative process.	Identify the different types of committees in the Texas Legislature and discuss the importance of the committee system.	Trace the process of how a bill becomes a law and identify ways in which a bill may be killed.	Analyze the forces outside the legislature that can impact lawmaking.

House Speaker Joe Straus gavels a special session of the Texas legislature to order. The legislature operates under extreme pressure, meeting only every other year to governor the second largest state in the nation. Often, that is not enough time, and the legislature is forced into special session to finish their business. Strong leadership from the Speaker and Lieutenant Governor can help keep the legislature on track, but often there is nothing the leaders can do to avoid going into overtime.

regular session
The constitutionally scheduled, biennial session of the legislature limited to 140 days.

special sessions
Extralegislative sessions called by the governor and limited to 30 days.

Texas. The Texas Legislature is the lawmaking branch of Texas government, and as such it assumes primacy in the state's political scheme. After all, before the courts can interpret the laws and before the executive branch can put the laws into effect, someone has to create the laws. As can be seen by the aforementioned examples (which reflect laws passed in the most recent session of the Texas Legislature), actions by this body touch virtually every aspect of our lives from health and safety regulations to educational policy and curricula, from crime prevention and criminal justice to environmental protection. Moreover, the legislature in essence oversees a multibillion dollar "corporation" by virtue of the fact that it approves the state's biennial budget.

Anyone trying to figure out politics in the Lone Star State has to come to an understanding of the role and scope of this monumentally important institution. To find out virtually anything you want to know about this body, take a look at one of the best websites available for delving into Texas government. Log on to and check out Texas Legislature Online (http://www.capitol.state.tx.us). When everything is said and done, this deliberative body is the biggest dog in the Texas political kennel.

Visitors who observe the legislature in action are either appalled by the apparent chaos that seems to reign on the floor of the house or puzzled by the apparent lack of any meaningful activity on the floor of the senate. Members who may have spent hundreds of thousands (and more recently, millions) of dollars to win an office that pays $600 a month before taxes may find themselves mentally and emotionally overwrought by the hectic end of a regular session.

Furthermore, these legislators must also endure the jibes of a public that little understands what they do or how they do it. One frequently sees displayed on vehicles in and around Austin a bumper sticker that warns, "Lock Up the Women and Children and Bury Your Money! The Legislature's Back in Town!" As the late House Speaker Billy Clayton, who spent 20 years on the west (house) side of the Capitol building, was fond of saying, "There are two things you should never watch being made: sausage and laws. Doing so can easily cause you to lose your taste for both." Yet what happens on the second floor of that domed building in the middle of Austin remains the essential expression of the concept of representative democracy in Texas. So despite the warnings of tacky bumper stickers and former presiding officers, we're going to take a close look at the structure and dynamics of this intriguing institution.

The Legislature in Texas

7.1 Explain, analyze, and compare the structure and composition of the Texas Legislature.

☐ Structure

The Texas constitution specifies that the Texas Legislature is to be a bicameral body. This means that legislative power is vested in a two-house assembly. The senate, which some people (mostly its own members) call the upper house, is composed of 31 people. The House of Representatives numbers 150 members. Both of these figures represent the maximum for each chamber allowed by the constitution. The legislature meets in **regular session** for not more than 140 days every two years, beginning in January of odd-numbered years. Other meetings of this assembly for lawmaking purposes—referred to as **special sessions**—may only be called by the governor, are limited to an agenda determined by the governor, and can last no longer than 30 days (although there is no limit on the number of special sessions a governor may call).[1]

The structure of the Texas Legislature clearly reveals the suspicion with which the authors of the constitution viewed government in general and lawmaking bodies in particular. Created to handle the political business of a sparsely populated, largely rural state in the late 19th century, this body was designed to do its job and then get out of town. Although Texas has become one of the largest, most complex urban states in the nation, that same attitude prevails today. Remember that plaque in the house member's office? It reflects a common sentiment found among members of the legislature that the less frequent and the shorter the durations of that body's meetings, the better. So while overseeing the operation of anything the size of Texas by all rights ought to be a full-time job, serving in the Texas Legislature is a full-time job only part of the time. For 19 months out of every two years, legislators pursue their careers and live somewhat more normal lives, although there is still a good bit of intrusion from the legislature. Then for five months, they come together in a gigantic political and governmental pressure cooker and attempt to govern a $90 billion-a-year monster. It is this constant constraint of time more than anything else that shapes the people of the legislature and what they do.

☐ Membership

The citizens of the state elect members of the Texas Legislature in partisan elections.

Members of the House of Representatives serve two-year terms, and there is no limit on the number of terms one may serve. To serve in the house, a person must:

- be a U.S. citizen and a registered voter;
- reside in Texas two years prior to election;
- reside in the district one year prior to election; and
- be at least 21 years old.

House members receive a salary of $600 per month as well as a per diem (living expense) during the most recent legislative session of $150 daily.[2]

Senators are elected to four-year terms, and they too are not limited regarding how many terms they may serve. In order to ensure some degree of membership continuity from session to session, one-half of the senate is elected every two years. The exception to this rule occurs after each decennial (ten-year) reapportionment, when all senate seats are contested. Following such an election, lots are drawn to determine which 15 senators will serve a single two-year term before reverting back to the normal term of four years. In order to serve in the senate, you must:

- be a U.S. citizen and a registered voter;
- reside in Texas five years prior to election;
- reside in your district one year prior to election; and
- be at least 26 years old.

Senators receive the same salary and the same per diem as house members.[3]

Legislators enjoy a number of privileges as elected representatives of the people, including constitutional guarantees that they may not "be questioned in any other place for words spoken in debate in either house." This is to ensure free and unfettered discussion in the process of conducting public business. Another interesting privilege accorded legislators is freedom from arrest (except for treason, felony, or breach of the peace) during a legislative session and while going to or coming from a regular or special session. This is intended to protect members from intimidation or retaliation because of their legislative activities.[4]

7.1

7.2

7.3

7.4

7.5

7.6

7.1

7.2

7.3

7.4

7.5

7.6

We can look at the demographic makeup of the legislature in order to gain a better understanding of its aggregate membership. One obvious measure of its internal composition is party affiliation. In 2009, the House of Representatives contained 76 Republicans and 74 Democrats. This represented a significant increase in seats for Democrats over the party's nadir in 2003. Also in 2009, the senate numbered 19 Republicans and 12 Democrats, an increase of one Democrat over the previous session.[5] In 2010, however, Republicans dramatically reversed the gains that Democrats made in 2008. Although senate composition remained the same, Republicans—in many cases energized by Tea Party activists—eventually captured 101 seats in the Texas House of Representatives, leaving the Democrats with only 49 seats. That was an all-time high for Republicans in the house (as well as a new low point for Democrats). The 2012 election left the senate unchanged at 19 Republicans and 12 Democrats, one of whom, Senator Mario Gallegos Jr. of Houston, died just weeks before the election![6] In the house, the Republicans' majority shrank slightly, leaving them with 95 members while the Democrats increased to 55.[7]

The diversity in the Texas population is not as readily apparent in the legislature. The membership tends to overrepresent middle- and upper-income groups, and relatively few of what might be called "working Texans" (people with "8-to-5" jobs or who punch a time clock every day) will be found among the legislative ranks. The largest single professional group among legislators has always been lawyers. Business is also well represented in the legislature. The popular (though largely unfounded) notion that only lawyers can create laws may account for the former, and a desire to protect the climate in which their businesses operate can explain the latter. Yet the predominance of these two occupation groups may be due to that key element we mentioned before—time. Lawyers and businesspeople who can more closely control their own schedules, especially if they're in some kind of partnership, are more likely to be able to adapt to the "full-time part of the time" nature of the legislature. Those who must be at work on a regular basis likely will not be able to consider legislative service seriously.

Over the past several decades, the Texas Legislature has begun to inch to a closer approximation of the state's ethnic mosaic. The 83rd legislature that convened in January of 2013 included 31 Hispanic, 18 African American, and 3 Asian American members in the house.[8] This represented a slight gain in African American members (up from 17 in the 82nd legislature) and for but a slight loss in Hispanic representatives (down from 32 in the 82nd). The membership of the senate included seven Hispanics (one more than in the previous session) and two African Americans (the same as in the previous session).[9] Gains in minority legislative seats are attributable in part to the use of single-member districts since the 1970s (for a discussion of legislative redistricting, see Apportionment in the next section). Though encouraging, these numbers still lag behind the overall percentages of each group in the general population. Moreover, federal court rulings questioning the constitutionality of race-based apportionment schemes, coupled with persistent Republican electoral strength up and down the ballot, may not be good news for those who seek to increase minority representation in the legislature.

More startling is the discrepancy between the legislature and the general population with regard to gender. Currently, there are 31 female house members (one fewer than in the previous session) and seven female senators.[10] Although these numbers reflect gains in recent years for women, they indicate that women are still underrepresented in the legislature. However, it should be pointed out that the rising tide of Republican fortunes resulted in a significant number of female Republican candidates winning election up and down the ballot in recent elections, and this trend may continue in the future. Yet the state's conservative political culture, which responds slowly and reluctantly to change, may cause this development to lag behind other states.

Apportionment

7.1

7.2

7.3

7.4

7.5

7.6

7.2 Explain redistricting and gerrymandering and analyze their impact on the Texas Legislature.

Apportionment refers to dividing the population into districts for purposes of election and representation. The Texas constitution stipulates that the house and the senate, respectively, are responsible for dividing the state into such districts.[11] These districts must be contiguous, which means you can't have part of a senate district in Brownsville and the other part of it in Amarillo. And they are to be redrawn (or redistricted) every 10 years following publication of the federal census.

The process of **redistricting** is one of the most troublesome issues to confront the legislature. Redrawing district lines is necessary because as people move from place to place, each district's population ebbs and flows. Some districts gain population and become quite crowded; others lose people and become underpopulated. Neither situation is fair. People who live in a district with only one-half or one-third the population of another district wield more political influence than their more crowded neighbors. Think about it: Would you rather be one out of 50,000 or one out of 250,000? If you're part of the less populous district, your voice has a better chance of being heard. Your vote is five times more powerful than that of those in the larger district. In this way, people in an overpopulated district wind up casting a diluted vote.

apportionment
Dividing the population into districts for purposes of election and representation.

redistricting
The process of redrawing district lines to maintain the concept of "one person, one vote."

As is usual, the last day of the 2009 session found many bills still pending. This byproduct of biennial sessions had legislators scrambling to reach compromises. One reason that last minute deal-making is common is that one stalled bill can kill everything behind it. There is an incentive, provided by all the other members, to settle differences and move on.

7.1

7.2

7.3

7.4

7.5

7.6

"one person, one vote"
A principle of representation that means the vote of one citizen should be worth no more or no less than the vote of another citizen; districts with equal population ensure this.

The remedy for such inequities would seem to be simple—just move a few lines on a map, and instant fairness results. It's never that easy in Texas politics.

The very people who are charged with the responsibility of redrawing these lines are usually the most reluctant to do so. Senators and representatives become such by winning in their own districts. So regardless of whether that district is over- or under-populated, they usually want to keep it just like it is. This reluctance caused redistricting to become undone in many states for many years. However, in the early 1960s, the federal courts began ordering redistricting at a number of levels of government, and Texas soon came under the reapportionment gun.

The 1964 U.S. Supreme Court case of *Reynolds* v. *Sims*[12] ruled that in a bicameral state legislature, both houses had to be apportioned on the basis of equal population among districts. This principle has best been expressed in the phrase **"one person, one vote."** Very simply, this means that the vote of one citizen should be worth no more or no less than the vote of another citizen. Districts with equal population assure this principle is upheld. Texas was not involved in the *Reynolds* case, which had challenged apportionment in the Alabama Legislature, but the precedent it set was soon applied to this state and its district-drawing practices.

THE SENATE The 1876 constitution of Texas has always required that both house and senate districts reflect an equal division of the population, but it also stipulated that "no single county shall be entitled to more than one Senator." By the mid-20th century, these two constitutional mandates became increasingly at odds with each other. As urban growth progressed, several counties—such as Harris (Houston), Dallas, Bexar (San Antonio), and Tarrant (Fort Worth)—experienced booming population growth but remained limited to one senator each, and thus increasingly underrepresented. Mindful of the *Reynolds* case, a Houston attorney—Bill Kilgarlin (who later served on the Texas supreme court)—filed suit in a Houston federal district court seeking to overturn the "one senator per county" limit. The court, citing *Reynolds*, found that particular constitutional restriction to be in violation of the "one person, one vote" principle and struck it down.

The implications of this case, *Kilgarlin* v. *Martin*,[13] were enormous. Because the most populous urban counties had been restricted to one senator, power in the Texas senate had remained largely in the hands of rural senators, even though their population base had steadily eroded. Once new senate districts were ordered, a significant shift in power began. Urban counties gained more senate seats and acquired more influence over the agenda and actions of the senate. Today's senate districts may vary greatly in geographic size (District 26 in San Antonio is one of the smallest; District 19—see Figure 7.1—in west Texas is one of the largest), but regardless of geographic size, each must adhere to the principle of one person, one vote. And when

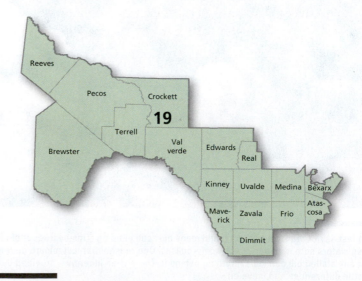

FIGURE 7.1 Texas Senate District 19

new senate districts based on the 2010 Census data are finally approved by the courts, each district, reflecting Texas's dynamic population growth over the past decade, will contain an average population of 811,147. Of course, it would be practically impossible to create 31 districts, each of which would contain the exact number of constituents in an "ideal" district. Therefore, the courts have allowed the legislature some leeway in this process, and in general, districts may deviate above or below the "ideal" district size by about 5 percent.

THE HOUSE The Texas house suffered its share of headaches on the redistricting front. Senate districts had always been **single-member districts**; that is, each specific geographic area contained the same number of people and elected one person (a "single member") to represent that area in the Senate. The House, however, in response to court pressures to redistrict, had created several multimember districts in the largest urban counties. Such districts seemed to adhere to the letter of the "one person, one vote" pronouncement, but they actually subverted its spirit. Here's how they worked: Instead of taking a large urban county and dividing it into individual districts with each electing one representative, the house declared these counties to be giant districts in and of themselves, and every voter in that county could choose a number of representatives, all of whom would, in theory, represent them in the legislature. Consider this example: Assume that a fair calculation of the "one person, one vote" rule would produce a ratio of one elected representative for every 50,000 citizens. Then say that a particular county has 300,000 citizens. That county would thus be entitled to six representatives under "one person, one vote." The simplest and the fairest way to do that would be to count out 50,000 people, draw a line around them, and let each group elect their own representative. However, if the county were a multimember district, then all the citizens in the county could vote in six different races to choose six different representatives, all of whom would supposedly represent all of the county's citizens.

Such an arrangement might seem like a good idea, but it presents serious problems. Under these multimember schemes, nothing would prevent all the district's representatives from living in one area, one neighborhood, or even on one street. This could make it difficult for other areas of the county to have their concerns voiced. Moreover, this system makes it difficult for those outside the power structure to gain a foothold. Because they had to appeal to voters countywide, minority candidates like Hispanics and African Americans (and in the 1960s, liberals and Republicans) stood little chance of being elected, even though they might have enjoyed overwhelming support in their own communities. In truth, these multimember districts were simply a kind of rearguard action to help the ruling rural conservative Democrats preserve their power in the house for as long as possible, in the face of changing demographic and political forces. Such action is, of course, entirely consistent with the traditionalistic political culture that is so prevalent in Texas.

These multimember districts began to disappear in the early 1970s. First the Legislative Redistricting Board—charged with redrawing district lines when the legislature fails to do so (this group is described in more detail below)—ordered the replacement of a 23-seat multimember district encompassing all of Harris County with 23 single-member districts. Court cases challenging multimember districts in Bexar and Dallas counties, then Tarrant, Nueces (Corpus Christi), and Jefferson (Beaumont) counties soon followed. In each case, single-member districts were ordered and subsequent elections saw more minorities and Republicans winning House seats than ever before. As had been the case in the senate, the rural power bloc in the house was thus forced to share power with a more diverse group within the legislature. Today, all 150 house districts in Texas are single-member districts and, based on the 2010 Census data, each now must contain an average of 167,637 constituents (See Figure 7.2). Again, deviations of 5 percent above or below this norm are allowed in creating these districts.

single-member district
A specific geographic area with a population equal to that of other districts that elects one person (a single member) to represent that area.

7.1

7.2

7.3

7.4

7.5

7.6

7.1

7.2

7.3

7.4

7.5

7.6

gerrymandering
The act of drawing representative districts in order to help or hinder a person, or a political party, to win an election.

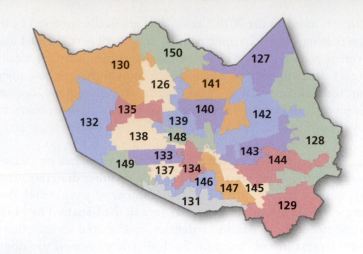

FIGURE 7.2 Texas House Districts in Harris County

GERRYMANDERING: ROUND ONE By the early 1980s, single-member districts were used across the entire state for choosing legislators. By then, another aspect of apportionment was coming under closer scrutiny, the phenomenon of **gerrymandering**. This involves drawing districts so as to either help or hurt a person's or a party's chances of winning election. For example, if you know you can do well among labor unions, you will try to have your district drawn to include as many union members as possible. Conversely, if you want to minimize a group's political influence, you will try to split its members up among several districts, thus denying them sufficient numbers to win any one seat.

Gerrymandering is about as old a practice as electing representatives. However, in recent years it has become a more complex political problem because of both the sophistication of political data available and the heightened political awareness of more groups in society. Whereas formerly arguments involved whether one county should or should not be in a particular district, those arguments now center on whether one census tract or even one side of a block should be included or excluded. Combine this with more widely available data on the Internet, and it's no wonder that charges of gerrymandering are routinely tossed about after every redistricting plan is revealed.

Such charges were exaggerated by the growing partisanship of Texas elections and by the willingness of Republicans to challenge the legality of districts drawn primarily by Democrats in the 1990s. Because many recent reapportionment plans created by the legislature have been challenged in the courts (and often overturned), many people have found themselves in a different senate or house district in almost every election. The redistricting plan enacted following the 2000 Census exemplifies this trend. The Legislative Redistricting Board—made up of the attorney general, lieutenant governor, Speaker of the house, comptroller of public accounts, and land commissioner—stepped in to redraw district lines when the house and the senate failed to do so in the 2001 session of the legislature. Four of the five members of this body were Republicans; hence the resultant legislative districts took on a decidedly Republican tone in their makeup. As a direct result of this redrawing, the Republicans gained control of both houses of the legislature. Obviously, who draws the districts is as important as how they are drawn.

GERRYMANDERING: ROUND TWO The most controversial issue before the legislature in 2003 was the proposed redistricting of the state's delegation to the U.S. Congress. The year 2003 was not supposed to be a redistricting year. Under normal circumstances, redistricting is a once-a-decade phenomenon, concluded the year after the U.S. Census and, thankfully, not revisited for 10 years.

In 2001, the Texas house and senate failed to create a redistricting map, and, eventually, responsibility for congressional redistricting fell to a panel of federal judges.

Republicans were not happy with the results. After the 2002 elections, Democrats held 17 of the 32 Texas congressional seats, despite the fact that Republican candidates captured 60 percent of the congressional vote statewide. The short version of how this came to pass is that the judges drew lines that protected incumbent members, reiterating in many ways the pro-Democratic lines drawn by the Democratic-dominated legislature in 1991. But because Texas had two more congressional seats after reapportionment, thus leading to the creation of two new districts, Republicans were able to gain those new seats.

In the 2002 legislative elections, Republicans made great strides. By controlling the legislative redistricting process in 2001, Republicans had been able to carve maps that gave them large majorities in both the Texas house and senate. Since nothing in Texas law or the state constitution *prohibits* redistricting at any time, Republican leaders decided to push forward with the effort. Most of the impetus for this unprecedented maneuver came from the majority leader of the U.S. House at that time, Representative Tom DeLay of Sugarland. DeLay was committed to enlarging the Republican majority in the U.S. House and saw Texas as a fertile ground for such an endeavor. It was at his urging that the controversial redistricting process was begun. As was to be expected, the Democrats were outraged.

In the 2003 regular session, redistricting never got legs, largely due to two main obstacles. First and foremost, the senate in general and Lieutenant Governor Dewhurst in particular seemed less than committed to visiting the issue. A huge factor was the senate's long-standing "two-thirds rule," an internal mechanism that requires the support of two-thirds of the members in order for a bill to reach the floor (see the discussion of this odd rule below). With Democrats comprising more than a third of the senate and with no push from Dewhurst, redistricting was dead on arrival in the senate.

Not taking any chances, House Democrats ensured that the issue would die when 55 of them walked out of the chamber and headed to Oklahoma, thereby preventing a quorum. Without two-thirds of its members present—100 representatives—the house could not do business. They didn't return to Austin until after the deadline for all bills to be out of **committee**, thereby killing the redistricting plan and, along with it, dozens of other bills. The entire controversy left ruffled feathers all around, with Democrats believing that Republicans had destroyed the bipartisan atmosphere that had historically prevailed in the legislature (most recently under former Republican Governor George W. Bush) and Republicans believing that Democrats had thwarted the will of the people of Texas by running to Oklahoma (an act some Texans compared to 1960s-era "draft dodgers" fleeing to Canada).

Undeterred, Governor Perry called a special session for late June, extending into July. Again, the two-thirds rule prevented redistricting from reaching the floor, but by the end of the first special session, Dewhurst was perturbed at house and senate Democrats and was feeling pressure from his fellow Republican leaders. He believed that senate Republicans had offered a reasonable redistricting plan and wondered why Democrats wouldn't accept a plan that would protect most of their incumbents. He began sounding ominous warnings about the two-thirds rule, reminding senators that it was an internal senate regulation that could be rescinded by the majority—meaning Republicans—at any time. It was clear, the Democrats thought, that the first order of business in a second special session would be to suspend the rule and allow legislation to reach the floor by a majority vote. This time, senate Democrats considered leaving.

Republicans anticipated their move. Governor Perry devised a plan to end the first session a day early, immediately convene a second session, and catch the Democrats still in Austin. Democrats were quicker, though. Eleven immediately left for the Marriott in Albuquerque, New Mexico—perhaps demonstrating better judgment than their house cohorts, who earlier had fled to the Holiday Inn in Ardmore, Oklahoma. (Why flee out of state? Legislative rules require senators and representatives to be on the job during session. If they are absent within the state—see the Texas Mosaic on the "Killer Bees" in this chapter—the Texas Rangers can compel

committee
Division of a legislative body charged with initial deliberations on legislative proposals.

7.1

7.2

7.3

7.4

7.5

7.6

7.1

7.2

7.3

7.4

7.5

7.6

them to return. Once they cross state lines, though, they are beyond the Rangers' jurisdiction.)

With Democrat Ken Armbrister remaining in Austin, the 11 had the bare majority they needed to block a quorum. But the defection of just one would be enough to get the senate up and running again. Through the second special session, the boycott held. As the session ended, however, Houston Senator John Whitmire returned to Austin, saying that he believed Governor Perry would continue calling sessions until redistricting passed. The boycott crumbled, and the remaining Democrats returned as well.

Even then, redistricting was not a sure thing. Republicans began fighting among themselves as house members favored one plan and senators favored another. The house version won out—it included a separate congressional district for Midland and another in DFW tailor-made for Speaker Tom Craddick's ally Kenny Marchant—and that plan resulted in a huge gain in congressional seats for Republicans in the 2004 general election. Thus, the precedent was set for the legislature to undertake redistricting just about any time it chose to do so and for just about any reason.

To no one's surprise, the house, senate, and congressional districts created by the overwhelmingly Republican house and the senate following the 2010 Census sought to expand the number of "safe" districts for the GOP. And to no one's surprise, these plans were almost immediately challenged in numerous courts by Democrats, minorities, and other groups who felt they had been disenfranchised by these new maps. The confusion wrought by this plethora of court cases resulted in the extension of the filing deadline for candidates—many of whom were clueless as to which district they would actually wind up in—and the postponement of the party primaries from March to May. As you can see, such actions and their impact on representation in Texas in the coming years will result in more, rather than less, partisan wrangling over the always divisive issue of redistricting.

The Presiding Officers

7.3 Analyze the roles of the presiding officers and "The Team" in the legislative process.

Many people have observed that the candidates who run for elective office tend to have extremely—how shall we put this?—*healthy* egos. This is nowhere more evident than in the Texas Legislature. When you bring together 150 such egos in the house and then stir in 31 more in the senate, the potential for chaos and confrontation is enormous. In order to get anything accomplished in the legislative arena, someone has to organize these people and get them moving in the same direction. That responsibility falls to the presiding officers in each house, two of the most important and powerful figures in Texas politics.

Most Texans are shocked to find out that their governor isn't all that powerful in the great cosmic scheme of Texas politics. Many Texas political observers will argue that the most powerful officeholder in the state is in fact the lieutenant governor, who presides over the senate. Only slightly less powerful is the presiding officer of the House of Representatives, the Speaker. Their power derives in part from the 1876 Texas constitution, which, in stripping away many of the governor's prerogatives, tended to bolster these two positions. It also derives in part from the rules under which the two bodies operate. Perhaps most importantly, however, their power grows out of custom and tradition, out of a time-honored realization by individual legislators that they each must yield some of their individual power in order to be able to work together collectively. The beneficiaries of this arrangement are the presiding officers, who thus become a combination head coach and referee for their respective houses. In this role they can exert more influence over legislation than anyone in Texas. Let's take a closer look at each of these officers and how they function.

The Lieutenant Governor

Although nominally a member of the executive branch of Texas government, the lieutenant governor is charged by the constitution with presiding over the senate. It is in this capacity that he fills his most important role. The occupant of this office is chosen in a statewide election and serves a four-year term with no limit on reelection (former Lieutenant Governor Bill Hobby set a longevity record by holding the office from 1973 to 1991). Although elected at the same time as the governor, these two officials don't run as a team and don't constitute a "ticket" as do the president and vice president at the national level. Indeed, it is entirely possible for the governor to be from one party while the lieutenant governor is from another. The lieutenant governor receives a salary of $7,200 per year, the same as all other members of the legislature. The powers given the lieutenant governor are quite significant. To begin with, he may recognize individual members who wish to speak from the floor of the senate. Now at first glance, this may not seem significant. After all, how much political savvy does it take to point at someone and say, "The chair recognizes the senator from Harris [County]"? But if you think about it, you'll realize that the lieutenant governor could easily use this power to mold the direction and tone of debate on an issue. Even the order of business in the senate can be affected by whom the lieutenant governor chooses to recognize. If a senator who is "carrying" a bill in the senate on behalf of a colleague in the house cannot gain the floor, there's little chance the bill will survive. Without being recognized, a senator may not formally participate in senate debate and thus may not be able to make a point she deems vital to that debate or to express the views of her constituents. Most recent holders of this office have made a good faith effort to give everyone who wishes to speak the opportunity to do so, but the fact that they do *not* have to do so can be a potentially powerful factor in shaping legislation.

The lieutenant governor also appoints the members of all senate committees as well as their chairs and vice chairs. As will be discussed in more detail later in this chapter, committees form the backbone of the legislature. They have the power to make or break legislation. By determining *who* serves on each committee, the lieutenant governor can go a long way toward shaping *how* each committee deals with legislation. This is especially true when it comes to naming committee chairs. These appointees are usually close friends of the lieutenant governor, senators with whom he has worked and whom he can trust. The personal dimension of such appointments allows the lieutenant governor to contribute to a committee's deliberations routinely. Occasionally this is done directly. More often, it happens through the expression and implementation of political views shared among the committee's chair, its key members, and the presiding officer. Because of this, it's safe to say that most legislation opposed by the lieutenant governor never makes it out of committee.

Not only does the lieutenant governor appoint members of senate committees, he also appoints the senate members of all conference committees. These groups must resolve the differences between the senate and house versions of a bill, and their ability to do so often depends on the personalities of the five senators and five representatives who make up each committee. The lieutenant governor chooses people on whom he can depend to safeguard the interests of the senate in any deliberations leading to a compromise. As mentioned earlier, no one held the office of lieutenant governor of Texas longer than Bill Hobby, who presided over the senate from 1973 to 1991. A quiet, scholarly man, Hobby often surprised people with his quick, dry wit. Once, when addressing a group of college students that was visiting Austin during a legislative session, he was asked if it were true (as their professor had told them) that the lieutenant governor was the most powerful elected official in Texas. Without missing a beat, Hobby replied that that honor belonged to the district attorney of Travis County. When the student looked puzzled, Hobby pointed out, with a twinkle in his eye, that the Travis County DA was the official responsible for bringing charges against elected state officials—including, of course, the lieutenant governor! The DA aside, even the lieutenant governor doesn't always get his way, as illustrated in the Texas Mosaic on the "Killer Bees."

7.1
7.2
7.3
7.4
7.5
7.6

7.1
7.2
7.3
7.4
7.5
7.6

Texas ★ Mosaic

The Killer Bees: Rattling the Texas Political Cage

Rarely can an individual legislator challenge the power of a presiding officer and get away with it. In 2003, disgruntled Democrats in both the house and the senate tried but ultimately failed to prevent Republicans from gerrymandering Texas's congressional districts. But this was not the first time such tactics were used in Texas politics. A group of senate mavericks did clash with then-Lieutenant Governor Bill Hobby in May 1979, and, to the surprise of many veteran political observers, prevailed. This incident, known as "the attack of the Killer Bees," has assumed the status of legend in Texas politics. It all began late in the legislative session when Hobby tried to push through the senate a bill that would establish separate-day presidential and state primary elections. He hoped this would enable conservative Democrats to vote for former Texas governor and Republican presidential hopeful John Connally in a Republican presidential primary before returning to the regular state Democratic primary to choose candidates for state offices. However, Hobby could not bring the bill up for consideration because 12 senators refused to vote to suspend the rules to do so. In a rare fit of pique on the part of the lieutenant governor, he announced that he was going to supersede the rules and bring the bill up anyway. The 12 senators who had opposed him on the dual-primary bill then turned the rules against their own presiding officer.

Knowing that a *quorum* (the minimum number of members required to be present on the floor of the senate in order to conduct business) was 21, they realized that if they didn't show up on the floor, the senate could not meet and transact business. Because the end of the session loomed, such a halt would throw that body into a panic that could in turn pressure Hobby into relenting. So, these guys went "over the wall" (so to speak). They disappeared and, sure enough, the senate ground to a standstill for lack of a quorum. Furious, Hobby invoked his power as lieutenant governor, ordering the Department of Public Safety and the Texas Rangers to begin an all-out search for the missing dozen senators. Of course, word quickly spread, and soon the media joined in the hunt for the wayward 12, fueling rumors of "sightings" all over the state.

While the media circus expanded and Hobby grew more frustrated, the missing senators were hiding out in a garage apartment in Austin, playing cards, and generally beginning to get on one another's nerves. One of the fugitives, Gene Jones, decided that he'd had enough of his colleagues. He sneaked back to his Houston district, but word leaked out that he had been spotted in that city. Hobby sent a Texas Ranger, Charlie Cook, in a Department of Public Safety helicopter to snag the wayward senator and "escort" him back to the senate. When Gene Jones spotted the Texas Ranger approaching his door, he asked his brother, Clayton, to go out and pick up the morning paper. Ranger Cook, armed with a photo of Senator Jones, confronted the senator's brother and told him he had orders to return him to Austin. Clayton Jones would only say that the Ranger was making a mistake, to which Cook replied that Jones would have to come with him.

When they got to Austin and Clayton Jones was brought into the senate, the sergeant-at-arms, Kelly Arnold, immediately pointed out that this man was *not* Senator Gene Jones. When questioned as to why he had not clarified his identity, the senator's brother responded that he'd never ridden in a helicopter before and it sounded like a really fun thing to do!

Needless to say, the Texas Rangers found themselves with considerable egg on their faces, and Lieutenant Governor Hobby still lacked the necessary quorum to conduct business. Under increasing pressure from other senators, Hobby finally relented and announced that the dual-primary bill was dead for the session. The 12 wayward senators, given assurances that they would not face retaliation for their actions, shortly thereafter returned in triumph to the senate chamber and the session ended without further incident.

The name "Killer Bees"? It was given the missing senators by one of Hobby's aides who said they reminded him of the characters who dressed up in bumblebee outfits in a *Saturday Night Live* skit starring John Belushi. Hobby, more familiar with the classics than with pop culture, later admitted sheepishly that he'd never seen or heard of the show.

1. **What lessons does this episode teach us about the importance of knowing the rules of the legislature?**

2. **In what ways does this incident reveal the limits on the powers of the presiding officers?**

The lieutenant governor determines the jurisdiction of all committees and then refers all bills to those committees. A committee's jurisdiction simply refers to the kinds of bills it can consider. Most of the time, these boundaries are rather broadly drawn. In fact, most bills could go to any number of committees, depending on how one interprets the bill's intent and on each committee's "turf." As you can see, this enhances the lieutenant governor's control over the fate of bills. With a good bit of discretion in this matter, he can send a bill to a "friendly" committee or to a "hostile" committee that will likely kill it. If this happens (and it does with some regularity), a bill opposed by the lieutenant governor will for all practical purposes be "dead on arrival" when it gets to a committee.

Finally, the lieutenant governor holds several *ex officio* positions that further strengthen his role in Texas politics. These are offices he holds automatically because he occupies another office (in this case, that of lieutenant governor). One of the most important of these *ex officio* positions is chair of the **Legislative Budget Board (LBB)**. This body oversees a staff whose recommendations become a kind of working document for the state's biennial budget. And since its members are all appointed either directly or indirectly by the presiding officers, you can be sure that the final budget will bear a striking resemblance to the one proposed by the LBB. As its chair, the lieutenant governor thus becomes *the* major player in the budgetary process. He or she also serves on the Texas Legislative Council, which directs the research services of the legislature. In addition, the lieutenant governor appoints members to numerous boards, including the Sunset Advisory Commission, which recommends the re-creation or abolition of most administrative agencies of the state.

Because the real power of the lieutenant governor lies in his role as president of the senate, not much thought is usually given to his role as successor to the governor should that office become vacant. However, it was not business as usual in Texas politics in the late 1990s. Governor George W. Bush's overwhelming reelection victory in 1998 served as the launch pad for his 2000 presidential campaign, and it set off an interesting chain reaction within the corridors of Texas government. The Texas constitution as it was then written provided that the lieutenant governor (at that time, Rick Perry) would assume the governor's office upon the swearing-in of President Bush. However, the constitution was unclear as to whether or not the lieutenant governor was required to give up that office on assuming the duties and responsibilities of the governorship, and here's where things really got interesting. The Texas constitution states that the president pro tempore of the senate, elected from among the senate's members at the beginning of a session, is to perform the duties of the lieutenant governor in the latter's absence. A constitutional amendment adopted in 1999 requires that the lieutenant governor resign his office on succession to the governor's office. If the lieutenant governor's office thus becomes vacant, then the president pro tempore must convene the senate within 30 days of the vacancy. The senate is then charged with electing a sitting senator to perform the duties of the lieutenant governor *in addition to his duties as senator* until the next general election.[14]

This is exactly what transpired following the 2000 presidential election. Prior to his swearing in as president, George W. Bush resigned the governorship of Texas. Lieutenant Governor Rick Perry succeeded to the office of governor and, in keeping with the 1999 constitutional amendment, resigned his position as lieutenant governor. The Texas senate then elected one of its own, Senator Bill Ratliff from Mount Pleasant, as the new lieutenant governor. This election could have positioned Ratliff to make a run for that office in 2002 when he technically would have been the incumbent. But Ratliff declined to run, and the lieutenant governor's race pitted former state comptroller John Sharp against incumbent land commissioner David Dewhurst. Dewhurst won handily and assumed control of the senate in January of 2003, a position he continues to hold today.

☐ The Speaker of the House

The presiding officer of the House of Representatives is the Speaker. His powers are similar to those of the lieutenant governor, with some important differences. For example, the Speaker is chosen from among the house members by the house members themselves. So if you want to be the Speaker, you have to win two elections: one in your district and one in which you persuade a majority of your colleagues in the house that they can't possibly live another session without you as their leader. Until the 1940s, most Speakers served a single two-year term and did not seek reelection. From the 1950s to the 1970s, two terms became the norm. Then, in 1975, Billy Clayton, a veteran legislator from west Texas, was elected to the first of four

7.1
7.2
7.3
7.4
7.5
7.6

Legislative Budget Board
A body made up of members of the house and senate, including the two presiding officers, which oversees a staff responsible for preparing the basic working budget for the legislature's consideration.

A somewhat pensive David Dewhurst, addressing supporters on the night of the 2012 Republican primary for the U. S. Senate seat. After failing to win the outright majority he and many others expected, Dewhurst would lose the runoff nine weeks later, returning him to Austin as Lieutenant Governor. Many wondered whether he would be politically weakened, but he continued to take an active and prominent role during the 83rd session of the legislature.

7.1

7.2

7.3

7.4

7.5

7.6

The Texas Constitution

A Closer Look

It is tempting to look at the Texas constitution and make comparisons between this document and the United States Constitution. After all, both documents create a government in three parts. Both establish checks and balances that regulate the relationships among the three branches of government. And each provides a framework for structuring the basic operation of each branch created. But significant differences emerge in the practical applications of these two collections of fundamental law. Nowhere is this difference more obvious than when one begins to compare the role laid out for the lieutenant governor under the Texas constitution and that prescribed for the vice president by the U.S Constitution. At first glance, one might assume that they occupy roughly equivalent places in their respective legislative assemblies.

After all, the U.S. Constitution, in Article I, Section 3, Clause 4, has this to say about the vice president: "The Vice President of the United States shall be President of the Senate, but shall have no Vote, unless they be equally divided."

Similarly, the Texas constitution, in Article 4, Section 16, Clause (b) says: "The Lieutenant Governor shall by virtue of his office be President of the Senate, and shall have, when in Committee of the Whole, a right to debate and vote on all questions; and when the Senate is equally divided to give the casting vote."

These two passages sound remarkably similar, don't they? Yet when one looks closely at the role each plays in their respective assemblies, some rather profound differences become apparent. The vice president is essentially a caretaker in the U.S. Senate. He assumes no major leadership role in that body's governance. The creation of a legislative agenda and the imposition of discipline upon members fall primarily on the respective party leaders (the majority leader and the minority leader as well as their respective leadership teams). On the other hand, the lieutenant governor exerts enormous control over the activities and outcomes in the Texas senate. For example, as the Texas Legislature convened in January of 2013, the state comptroller issued her projection of revenue available for the new biennium that was significantly higher than previously. This raised the hope among some legislators that draconian cuts to public education made by the previous legislature might be restored. However, Lieutenant Governor Dewhurst quickly shot down that idea, making it known in no uncertain terms that any potential increase in education funding would await the outcome of a court case challenging Texas's method of funding public schools. History clearly shows that if the lieutenant governor says something isn't going to happen, it almost never happens.

The difference would seem to lie in the internal rules under which each body operates. The rules of the Texas senate give the lieutenant governor rather extraordinary power to control events in that chamber. In the U.S. Senate, its rules give very little real power to the vice president. Little wonder then, that as vice president, John Nance Garner—himself a Texan and a former Speaker of the U.S. House of Representatives—once famously put it, "Being vice president isn't worth a bucket of warm spit!" To our knowledge, no one has ever used such a metaphor to describe the office of lieutenant governor.

1. What historical factors could account for the difference in real power between the offices of vice-president and lieutenant governor?

2. What role do you think political parties (or the lack thereof) may have played in shaping the roles of these very different presiding officers?

terms in the office. Gib Lewis of Fort Worth succeeded Clayton and went him one better by serving five terms as Speaker. As the average tenure has increased, so has the competition for the office. Candidates seek early pledges of support from their colleagues, even to the extent of having them sign pledge cards expressing their loyalty. They raise and spend thousands of dollars and crisscross the state in search of votes. An example of such a campaign that produced some surprising results came in 1991–1992 and pitted two veteran west Texas representatives against each other. The initial favorite appeared to be Jim Rudd, chair of the powerful House Appropriations Committee. However, his close ties with outgoing Speaker Gib Lewis, who at the time was beset with charges of ethics violations, may have proved costly.

In a somewhat surprising development, Representative Pete Laney, who promised a more "open" speakership, won the office.

Elected in the 1993 legislative session, Speaker Laney hoped to be elected to an unprecedented sixth term in the 2003 session. Even the possibility of Republican control of the house after the 2002 election did not prevent his gathering much support from members of both parties. However, Laney's district was one of those substantially redrawn by the Republican-dominated Legislative Redistricting Board, and his reelection was by no means a sure thing. Although he did manage to hold on to his own seat, the magnitude of the Republican victory in the house led him to release those members who had pledged their support to him. This cleared the way for the election of Tom Craddick of Midland, then the senior Republican in the house, as that party's first Speaker since Reconstruction.

In the past, a sitting Speaker was usually guaranteed reelection if he sought it. This process was aided enormously by the fact that, well in advance of the election, the Speaker would hand out the aforementioned pledge cards, on which members were encouraged to express their support for him and "join the team" (see the following section for a fuller explanation of this concept). Take the power inherent in the office, add to it the enormous pressure brought to bear by the pledge card system, stir in the fact that this is an open ballot election for all to see (including the sitting Speaker), and you have a recipe that makes it difficult for a house member to oppose an incumbent Speaker and have any kind of meaningful legislative career thereafter.[15] Craddick's election did not deviate substantially from this time-honored formula.

Once elected, the Speaker shares many powers and prerogatives with the lieutenant governor. Like the lieutenant governor, the Speaker determines the jurisdiction of committees, refers all bills, and designates committee chairs. However, in naming committee members, the Speaker is more restricted than his counterpart in the Senate. This came about in response to some rather heavy-handed tactics used by Speaker Gus Mutscher during the Sharpstown scandal of the early 1970s. After Mutscher left office in disgrace, the House instituted a **limited seniority system** for choosing committee members. Under this plan, with the very important exception of the Appropriations Committee, one-half the membership of standing substantive committees in the house (excluding the committee chairs and vice chairs) must be appointed on the basis of seniority. Take the example of the Natural Resources Committee, which has 11 members. The Speaker appoints the chair and vice chair, leaving 9 members to be named. Five are appointed based on their seniority (i.e., how long they have served in the house), and the remaining members are named at the Speaker's discretion. This means that someone who's been around for a long time may be able to get a desired committee assignment even if he or she happens to be a political enemy of the Speaker. This system doesn't place severe limitations on the Speaker, but it does diminish his or her power slightly in comparison with that of the lieutenant governor. In fact, many consider the Speaker to be second only to the lieutenant governor in terms of the power he wields in Texas politics.

The Speaker also holds a number of *ex officio* positions in state government. Like the lieutenant governor, he is a member of the Legislative Budget Board and the Texas Legislative Council, on both of which he serves as vice chair, and he can also appoint members to various other boards, including the Sunset Advisory Commission. As is the case with the lieutenant governor, the Speaker may use these *ex officio* positions to enhance his already considerable legislative powers.

☐ The Team

Those who hang around the legislature long enough will hear repeated references to **"The Team."** This term refers to those legislators who are supporters and allies of the presiding officers. The Speaker's team in the house and the lieutenant governor's team in the senate help these two presiding officers run their respective shows. Team members have developed a good working relationship with the presiding officer; having earned their trust, they often are called on to help with implementation of his or her legislative strategy.

The relationship between team members and presiding officers is a complex one. To begin with, it is not a completely servile one on the part of the members. As

7.1

7.2

7.3

7.4

7.5

7.6

limited seniority system
A method of committee selection used in the house that limits the Speaker to appointing half the members of most standing committees (plus the chairs); the other members gain their seats by seniority.

"The Team"
Unofficial term for those legislators who are supporters and allies of presiding officers and who form the leadership core of the legislature.

7.1

7.2

7.3

7.4

7.5

7.6

powerful as they are, presiding officers can't routinely operate in a dictatorial manner (though they may get away with doing so on occasion). If one does, his or her colleagues may very well not reelect the Speaker, or a lieutenant governor may see that the senate changes its rules to strip him or her of powers. Prior to the 1998 and 2002 elections, there was speculation that such rule changes might be effected for purely partisan reasons if voters gave control of the senate to Republicans but elected Democrat John Sharp as lieutenant governor. Rick Perry's victory in 1998 and David Dewhurst's wins in 2002 and 2006 have stilled such speculation for now. On the other hand, most observers credit the heavy-handed tactics of Speaker Craddick—particularly toward the end of the 2007 legislative session—with helping to foment a rebellion that led to the election of Joe Straus as Speaker at the beginning of the 2009 session. A complicated system of rewards and punishments, rather than pure partisanship, enables these officers to exercise their powers and helps build and nurture the legislature's "teams."

Legislators know better than most the fundamental rule of Texas politics: You never get something for nothing. Therefore, if you want the presiding officer's help in trying to pass a bill or achieve some other legislative goal, you have to be willing to help him or her when called on to do so. This system has been described in many ways—quid pro quo, "You scratch my back and I'll scratch yours," and "Go along to get along." It simply boils down to this reality: The people who consistently help the presiding officers are usually named as committee chairs, appointed to the committees they desire, and wind up with close-in parking and the best office space at the Capitol. Their bills get good committee referrals and favorable calendar placement. Those who don't do these things wind up in committee "twilight zones," never quite seeming to be able to get their bills processed, and have to park a long way off!

One last thing that needs to be said about "The Team" is that, until the 21st century, traditionally it has not operated on a partisan basis. Political party affiliation has rarely been

Tom Craddick spent three decades amassing a Republican majority in the Texas house and was rewarded with the speakership. After three terms, though, his seemingly abrasive manner wore on some members and he was ousted from power, as a group of moderate Republicans aligned with Democrats to replace him with fellow Republican Joe Straus.

a factor in determining team membership, and the presiding officers have been remarkably nonpartisan in how they have run their respective houses. Even during the 1970s and 1980s, when Republicans still constituted a minority in both houses, they regularly were appointed to chair committees and consulted by both presiding officers. One reason for this was the fact that the presiding officers during that era were conservative Democrats who found it easy to work with Republicans. For example, during his tenure as lieutenant governor, Bob Bullock (himself a conservative Democrat) actively sought Republican input in developing the senate's legislative agenda and, during his last term, appointed GOP senators to chair five of the senate's 13 standing committees, including the powerful Education and Jurisprudence Committees.[16] In like manner, Lieutenant Governor Perry resisted calls for increased partisanship in the Senate and named Democrats to chair five such committees. His successor, Bill Ratliff, divided 12 committee chairs evenly between Republicans and Democrats in the 2001 legislative session. On the house side of the Capitol, increasing partisan rhetoric (and, in particular, partisan attacks on former Speaker Laney by some Republican members) contributed to more tension than had usually been the case. Nevertheless, Laney named 12 Republicans to chair committees in the Democrat-controlled house. However, upon his accession to the office of Speaker, Tom Craddick promoted a decidedly more partisan (some would say confrontational) style of leadership in the house.

Evidence of a resultant breakdown of the team concept in the house can be seen in the events that transpired in the closing days of the 2007 regular session of the legislature. At that time, the already strained atmosphere in the house threatened to explode in a revolt against Speaker Craddick. A group of frustrated lawmakers, Democrats and Republicans alike, reacted to what they saw as the heavy-handed tactics of the Speaker by offering a motion to remove Craddick from his office. This led to a parliamentary storm that saw: (1) the Speaker refuse to recognize the members who sought to make the motion, (2) the house parliamentarian overruling of the Speaker's action, (3) the refusal of Craddick to abide by the parliamentarian's ruling and, finally, (4) the resignation of the parliamentarian in protest over what the Speaker asserted to be his "absolute right of recognition." The entire affair left bad feelings all around on the part of many house members (both Republican and Democrat) This animosity carried over to the beginning of the 2009 session of the legislature, when a coalition of moderate Republicans and Democrats succeeded in forcing Craddick's resignation as Speaker and replacing him with Joe Straus, a moderate Republican from San Antonio. Straus reverted to a much more collegial method of running the house, but he still appointed a disproportionate number of Republican chairs, especially to key committees. And following the election of a number of "Tea Party" Republicans in 2010 and 2012, Straus has come under increasing fire to imprint an even more partisan, even ideological stamp on the house leadership. This pressure manifested itself in the days leading up to the opening of the 2013 session of the legislature when a conservative representative from east Texas, David Simpson, announced that he would challenge Straus for the speakership in the 83rd legislature. However, the rebellion died aborning as Simpson withdrew his candidacy on the opening day of the session and Straus was reelected without opposition.

Speaker of the House Joe Straus, in his office in the Capitol Building. As Speaker, Straus exercises vast powers in the chamber. He appoints all committee chairs, most committee members and assigns bills to committees. The Speaker's support doesn't ensure passage of a piece of legislation, but his disapproval means all but certain death.

The Committee System

7.4 Identify the different types of committees in the Texas Legislature and discuss the importance of the committee system.

Committees function as little legislatures. Because of the immense volume of legislation routinely introduced each session, some sort of system for dividing labor and making an efficient use of limited time is needed. The committee system has evolved to meet these needs. Every piece of legislation introduced is referred to a committee and no legislation will be debated on the floor of either house unless a committee has first considered it. Moreover, the house and senate almost always follow their recommendations, so committees exercise what amounts to life or death control over legislation.

7.1

7.2

7.3

7.4

7.5

7.6

standing committee
A deliberative body formed each time a legislature meets that deals with topics of recurring interest.

Committees have attained this power in part because they allow the legislature to make better use of its time. As we have already noted, time limitations are *the* decisive factor in the legislative process. By dividing the membership into multiple smaller bodies, the committee system allows the legislature to consider more bills and to deliberate more fully on those bills that are introduced. In effect, the committee system acts as a screening mechanism, allowing the legislature to differentiate the good, the bad, and the ugly among bills and to do so more efficiently and effectively than would be the case if every bill had to be considered by the entire membership of each house.

Committees also provide a way for a somewhat transitory body like the legislature to develop institutional expertise and memory. Remember, the legislature is not a *continuously* full-time institution. It's in business for five months every two years; then, barring special sessions, it disappears. (However, we should point out that even when the legislature is out of session, many of its committees continue to work.) Add to this the high rate of turnover (sometimes 25 percent or more) from session to session, and you have a potential problem. Not only does a new session open more than a year and a half after the last one adjourned, but also many of the faces in this latest legislative crowd will be brand new, and a newly elected member is usually as lost as a goose when it comes to the intricacies of the legislative process. The committee system helps prevent the legislature from having to reinvent the wheel each session. Even though there may be many newcomers, there are always a number of veteran legislators around. These veterans typically are assigned to the same committee each session; thus they develop a depth of knowledge on specific topics that can be invaluable in wading through the legislative swamp. Each committee therefore builds a core of experts on whom other members, both inside and outside that committee, can depend for reliable guidance. The fact that some of these veterans come back session after session gives the legislature a kind of topical memory it might not otherwise have.

A good example of this expertise can be seen in the career of former State Senator Bill Ratliff. Senator Ratliff served in the senate for many years before retiring from public life, and for most of that time he was a member of the Senate Education Committee. The knowledge he developed regarding colleges, universities, and professional schools in Texas was so extensive that he was routinely consulted regarding all aspects of this topic. His presence on the Education Committee served to give that body credibility among senate members who might not have known the difference between a contact hour and a happy hour, but knew they could find answers to pertinent questions by asking Ratliff. Ironically, one of the unintended consequences of the movement to limit legislators' terms in office would be the eventual loss of such valuable expertise.

□ Standing Committees

The most important committees in the legislature are **standing committees**. Formed each time the legislature meets, these bodies deal with topics of recurring interest. It is through service on these standing committees that members develop that expertise just discussed. All members are appointed to these committees, with most serving on two or three of them each session. In 2013, the house formed 38 such committees and the senate formed 18, as noted in Table 7.1. These numbers may vary slightly from session to session as the issues that come before the legislature change. But, by and large, these bodies will be around every time the house and the senate convene.

SUBSTANTIVE COMMITTEES The more numerous of the standing committees are the substantive committees, which deal with specific public-policy topics. These include the House Appropriations and the Senate Finance Committees, which handle state spending and budgetary matters and are the most powerful committees of this type in the legislature. Other important substantive committees include the House Public Education and Higher Education Committees, the Senate Education and Higher Education Committees, the House Criminal Jurisprudence Committee, the Senate Jurisprudence Committee, and the State Affairs Committees in both houses. These bodies hammer out the specifics of legislation that can affect the lives of every

7.1

7.2

7.3

7.4

7.5

7.6

TABLE 7.1 STANDING COMMITTEES OF THE SENATE AND HOUSE, 83RD TEXAS LEGISLATURE

Senate Committees[17]	
Administration	Higher Education
Agriculture, Rural Affairs & Homeland Security	Intergovernmental Relations
Business and Commerce	Jurisprudence
Criminal Justice	Natural Resources
Economic Development	Nominations
Education	Open Government
Finance	State Affairs
Government Organization	Transportation
Health & Human Services	Veteran Affairs and Military Installations

House Committees[18]	
Agriculture and Livestock	Insurance
Appropriations	International Trade and Intergovernmental Affairs
Business and Industry	Investment and Financial Services
Calendars	Judiciary and Civil Jurisprudence
Corrections	Land and Resource Management
County Affairs	Licensing and Administrative Procedures
Criminal Jurisprudence	Local and Consent Calendars
Culture, Recreation, and Tourism	Natural Resources
Defense and Veterans' Affairs	Pensions
Economic & Small Business Development	Public Education
Elections	Public Health
Energy Resources	Redistricting
Environmental Regulation	Rules and Resolutions
General Investigating and Ethics	Special Purpose Districts
Government Efficiency & Reform	State Affairs
Higher Education	Technology
Homeland Security and Public Safety	Transportation
House Administration	Urban Affairs
Human Services	Ways and Means

Texan, from the amount of money it takes to run state government to the curriculum in the schools to the amount of time people will spend in prison for the crimes they commit. These committees address the complex issues that face Texas time and again.

PROCEDURAL COMMITTEES Procedural committees seem at first glance to be less important than their higher-profile siblings, the substantive committees. Yet these bodies, which deal with the internal operations of the two houses, can play a vital role in the legislature. Keeping the house and the senate going is a difficult task, and procedural committees help to do that. They may coordinate the distribution of office space among the members, a job carried out by the administration committees of the two houses. They may establish the parameters of debate when bills are considered, a task that falls to the Rules and Resolutions Committee in the house. They may determine the order in which bills will be taken up for discussion and debate, a role undertaken by the House Calendars Committee. And lest you think that such committees are a kind of legislative swamp into which powerless senators and representatives disappear, never to be heard from again, think again. If you were one of a handful of house members who could decide the fate of a bill merely by its placement on a list of pending legislation, you could exert tremendous influence over the kinds of laws that are

7.1

7.2

7.3

7.4

7.5

7.6

special committee
A temporary committee formed by the legislature for limited or nonroutine purposes.

conference committee
Joint committee of house and senate members whose purpose is to iron out the differences between house and senate versions of a bill.

interim committee
A special committee formed to study a topic or problem between sessions of the legislature.

ultimately passed. Members of the House Calendars Committee, the most powerful procedural committee in the legislature, can do just that. Not surprisingly, these committees tend to be well stocked with team members loyal to the presiding officers.

☐ Special Committees

From time to time, the legislature has to create temporary committees to deal with special situations. The most common of these **special committees** are the conference committees. The presiding officers appoint five representatives and five senators to the **conference committee**. These committees attempt to iron out differences between house and senate versions of a bill. It is rare for any bill to pass one house in the exact form as in the other, so these bodies are a routine part of legislative business. On occasion, one house's conferees may convince their counterparts to accept their version of a bill, but the more common scenario has both sides giving and taking in order to reach a compromise acceptable to all. Most conference committee work tends to concentrate near the end of legislative sessions, so service on such a body can be nerve wracking.

Another kind of special committee frequently seen in the legislature is the **interim committee**. An interim committee is given a particular assignment to be carried out between sessions of the legislature. This can be done either by appointing existing standing committees to act as interim bodies or by creating new committees for specific purposes (these are sometimes referred to as select committees). Meeting while the legislature is out of session, such committees are usually asked to study a specific problem and make recommendations at the next legislative session. In carrying out these duties, committees frequently hold hearings in various parts of the state and allow public testimony on their assigned topics. In recent years, such bodies have studied the TASP program (a testing program to determine the need for remediation among college freshmen), juvenile justice, payment of health care providers, state employee compensation and benefits, and public school funding. Prior to the 2009 regular session, such committees were charged with examining the impact of changes in the state tax system on businesses as well as the effect of reforms to the Texas Youth Commission enacted during the 2007 session. Committees charged with studying flooding and evacuations, human trafficking, Alzheimer's disease, and open government prepared reports to submit to the 2013 session of the legislature. Interim committees give the legislature a head start on upcoming issues, but depending on the topic, serving on these bodies can create an additional burden of time and expense for legislators.

☐ How Committees Work

The fate of every piece of legislation introduced is in the hands of committees. They can change, rearrange, pass, or kill bills as they see fit. Legislators spend more time in committee meetings than in any other facet of the legislative process. Visit the legislature and observe a daily session of the full house or senate and you'll wonder *if* they ever get anything done. Visit a committee during testimony or "mark-up" and you'll see *how* they get things done. The legislature in committee is the legislature at work.

COMMITTEE CHAIRS The chair of each committee exerts enormous influence over the actions of that body. This person, usually a close friend or political ally of the presiding officer, is responsible for organizing the committee, overseeing its general operation, and presiding over its meetings. The chair recognizes members to speak, determines the order in which bills referred to the committee will be considered, and, in general, acts as a kind of "minor league" presiding officer. It is no exaggeration to say that if a committee chair opposes a bill, that bill's outlook will be very bleak. There have been instances when a chair took exception to the way a committee member voted on a favorite bill and thereafter refused even to bring up that member's bills for consideration at any time during the remainder of the session. Such behavior may not be the norm, but it happens often enough to make members wary of crossing swords with the chair.

SUBCOMMITTEES If committees represent an attempt by the legislature to create an efficient division of labor, then subcommittees represent a furtherance of that aim. Some committees formally divide themselves into smaller groups, with each such group having its own formal structure. For example, in the 81st legislature, the Senate Intergovernmental Relations Committee created a Subcommittee on Flooding and Evacuations. This was in response to the confusion and displacement that followed the battering of the Texas Gulf coast by several recent hurricanes. In the 82nd legislature, the Senate Finance Committee created several subcommittees, among which were those on Medicaid, Public Education Funding, and Higher Education Funding. As the topics of these subcommittees clearly show, such bodies are usually formed to deal with issues of immediate importance to the legislature. Such subcommittees study the bills given them, then recommend action to the full committee, which in turn can accept or reject the recommendation. In most cases, they go along with the subcommittee. Even those committees that don't adopt such a formal structure may nevertheless divide into informal working groups during "mark-up" (see the Committee Action section for an explanation of this process) in order to consider their bills more effectively. Subcommittees simply enable the committees to get more work done.

COMMITTEE STAFFS Most standing committees are provided with a minimal staff to facilitate their work, although the size and importance of a committee may have some bearing on the size of its staff. In most cases, this staff will include a committee clerk and perhaps one or two assistants. These people often are the unsung heroes of the legislative process. Usually underpaid and consistently overworked, they conduct research; help clarify legislation; keep track of where the committee is in its agenda; make coffee; and provide all kinds of other support services to committee members, all of whom seem to want to call on staff members at the same time. Of crucial importance among these

7.1
7.2
7.3
7.4
7.5
7.6

Ursula Parks, then a member of the Legislative Budget Board's Public Educations Team, testified before a meeting of the House Public Education Committee. Often, state agency staff appear at legislative committee meetings. These staff members, especially from the LBB, provide much of the expert opinion that legislators depend on to make decisions.

7.1

7.2

7.3

7.4

7.5

7.6

staffers is the clerk of the committee. These clerks often are the most knowledgeable people regarding a committee's business, and some of them are bona fide experts in the matters that come before their committee. Along with the members themselves, most successful lobbyists will be quick to tell you that they regularly depend on the information and expertise of these people in tracking legislation important to their cause. Although these staff members are rarely recognized for their work, they are the difference between a smoothly running committee and one in which the wheels come off on a regular basis.

How a Bill Becomes a Law

| 7.5 | Trace the process of how a bill becomes a law and identify ways in which a bill may be killed. |

T he path taken by a bill as it becomes a law is long and torturous, and although many are called, few are chosen. The percentage of those that never become law is extremely high—usually in the 80 percent range—and the vast majority of bills never make it much beyond their introduction. In the 2009 regular session of the legislature, a total of 5,796 bills were filed, but only 1,379 bills eventually reached the governor's desk for his action, an attrition rate of almost 80 percent.[19] Passing a bill into law requires a shifting combination of skill, perseverance, nerve, flexibility, and plain old-fashioned luck. Yet this act lies at the heart of the legislative process, and watching it unfold can provide a fascinating glimpse into the dynamics of Texas politics. Figure 7.3 provides a visual rendering of the process.

☐ Introduction of a Bill

Any member of the legislature (but only members) may introduce a bill, although the real author may be anyone from a constituent to a lobbyist to a staff assistant to an actual member. Bills may be introduced in both houses, but the constitution stipulates that all revenue bills must originate in the House of Representatives. Since 1989, the legislature's rules have allowed for the prefiling of bills. This simply means that members may begin filing bills for an upcoming regular session as soon as the November general election is concluded. This can be advantageous because bills filed early generally have a better chance of passage.

Multiple copies of each bill introduced are filed with the appropriate clerks in each house. Bills are designated "HB" (House Bill) or "SB" (Senate Bill) and then assigned a number in the general order in which they are filed. Of late it has become fashionable for the leadership in both houses to "reserve" numbers, usually single digits, for the more important bills. For instance, in the two most recent legislative sessions, the general appropriations bill was designated as HB 1. After filing, the clerks see that every bill is reproduced and distributed to all members. This begins a paper barrage. *Every* time changes are made in a bill, those changes are noted and new copies distributed. The ability to access bills online would seem to have mitigated this problem somewhat, but members still complain that they are drowning in paper. After filing and numbering, a bill moves to first reading and referral. All bills must be read three times on separate days, a practice dating to medieval England when most members of Parliament were illiterate. This is probably not the case in today's Texas Legislature, so the "readings" usually consist only of stating the number, author, and title of the bill. And many bills routinely contain an emergency clause suspending this three-day rule. The presiding officer then refers the bill to the committee of his choice.

☐ Committee Action

The way committees work has already been discussed in general terms; now let's look at some specifics of what goes on when bills get to committee. The chair of each committee is largely responsible for deciding the order in which bills are considered.

7.1

7.2

7.3

7.4

7.5

7.6

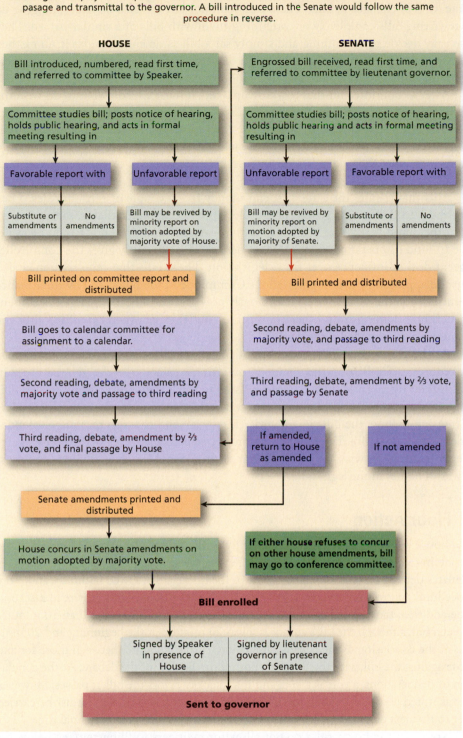

This diagram displays the sequential flow of a bill from the time it is introduced in the House to final pasage and transmittal to the governor. A bill introduced in the Senate would follow the same procedure in reverse.

FIGURE 7.3 How a Bill Becomes a Law.

Once that order is determined, the Texas Open Meetings Law requires that advanced public notice of committee hearings on a bill must be posted. Anyone may appear at these hearings and offer testimony on a particular bill or on a number of bills. Those who wish to do so simply fill out a witness affidavit card that calls for some basic personal information, and then wait their turn. Witnesses may testify for a bill, against a bill, or on a bill, and committee members may in turn question witnesses. Depending on the bill, such hearings may last a few minutes or stretch over several days.

Once testimony has been taken, the committee moves into "mark-up." In this intensive work session, committee members roll up their sleeves and go through the bill with a fine-tooth comb. Although it is technically possible for a bill to emerge

7.1

7.2

7.3

7.4

7.5

7.6

pigeonholing
The act of a setting aside a bill in committee and refusing to consider it, thereby "killing" it.

from mark-up in its exact original form, this rarely happens. Committees usually make some kind of changes in bills. These can be minor but can also be major, ranging up to rewriting bills completely or combining them with bills of a similar nature. They also may decide to do nothing and simply set a bill aside and consider it no further. Such a practice, known as **pigeonholing** a bill, effectively kills the bill and is the most common committee action taken.

After a committee finishes marking up a bill, it must vote on what to do with the bill. Committee votes are by majority, and if the bill meets with the group's approval, it will be referred to the entire house with a recommendation that it be enacted. This committee recommendation is crucial because the house and senate almost always go along with what their committees suggest. Getting your bill out of committee puts you a long way down the road to passage.

Bills that require the state to spend money face a couple of extra hurdles. They must be "certified" by the state's comptroller of public accounts; that is, the comptroller's office must verify that if the bill were to pass, sufficient revenue would be available to fund its operation for the budget period. This obviously gives the comptroller a great deal of influence over fiscal legislation. Then, bills that require money also must be approved by the Appropriations Committee in the house and by the Finance Committee in the senate. These enormously powerful bodies can't change the content of such bills coming from other committees, but they can (and often do) alter the amount of money called for in a bill.

At the point where bills come out of final committee action, senate and house procedures differ. Bills in the senate go on a single calendar in the general order in which they are received. In the house, bills go to the Calendars Committee, which is responsible for placing them on one of several calendars used by the house. This committee can arrange the bills in any order they wish and can also rearrange calendar orders if they so desire. The Calendars Committee basically serves as the house's gatekeeper by deciding what bills will make it to the floor. As such, it is one of the most powerful bodies in the legislature.

☐ Floor Action

The house and the senate differ significantly in their floor action procedures. Because it contains almost five times as many members as the senate, the house more rigorously regulates debates on bills. Calendar orders in the house are followed faithfully, and more procedural controls are imposed. When a bill hits the house floor, it is read a second time and then the debate begins. House members may speak no more than 10 minutes on each bill, although the bill's author is given 20 minutes at the beginning and 20 minutes at the conclusion of the debate. Discussion usually alternates between those for and those against the bill, with the Speaker controlling the flow of the debate. At the conclusion of deliberations, a vote is taken, and if a majority favors the bill, it passes. However, as was noted above, if the bill doesn't contain an emergency clause, it must be carried over to the next day, read a third time (with no debate), then voted on a final time.

Note that the house rules do not allow for members to filibuster (see below for a fuller discussion of this senate tactic). However, a kind of multimember, "tag team" quasi-filibuster is used on rare occasions, especially during divisive house debates. This procedure, known as chubbing, involves a large number of members, each of whom uses his or her full-time period allotted for debate and many of whom stall the proceedings with obscure parliamentary inquiries and motions. Chubbing can drastically slow down debate and can be especially effective at the end of a legislative session when certain deadlines for considering and adopting legislation come into play. An example of this tactic can be seen in the action of some Democrats in the house at the end of the 2009 regular session. The house was debating a voter identification bill, one of the most volatile and divisive issues to confront the 81st legislature and one to which most Democrats were adamantly opposed. By chubbing the bill, they succeeded in delaying its consideration past the deadline for adoption specified in the house rules. But in killing that bill, they ignited a firestorm of anger among other house members, many of whose bills died as a result of this parliamentary delaying tactic. And in keeping with the old Texas adage that "it's okay to get mad but it's better to get even," supporters of the voter ID bill, buoyed by the "supermajority" produced in the 2010 Republican electoral landslide, handily enacted the law during the 2011 session.

The senate does things differently. For one thing, its debate is more relaxed. Discussions on the senate floor seem more personal, and senators often speak to an issue several times. Moreover, the senate places no limits on debate, so senators may engage in **filibustering**. This amounts to talking endlessly on a particular bill in the hope of delaying a vote. A senator may not be interrupted as long as he or she stands at his or her desk and makes remarks that pertain to the bill. Such action can be a crucial element in legislative tactics, especially near the end of a session. This tactic came into play at the end of the 2011 regular session of the legislature when Fort Worth Senator Wendy Davis used the last hours of the session to filibuster the appropriations bill that cut some $4 billion from public education funding for the upcoming biennium. Davis's action forced the governor to call a special session immediately following the expiration of the regular one, and even though it did not result ultimately in any significant reductions in the funding cuts, it helped to focus public attention on the impact of such cuts across the entire state. And while her actions made Davis something of a rising star in Democratic Party circles, they wound up costing her later. Lieutenant Governor Dewhurst, in announcing senate committee appointments for the 2013 legislative session, chose not to reappoint Senator Davis to the Education Committee, thus sending her an unmistakably clear message about the consequences of crossing swords with the lieutenant governor.

The senate also differs in the way it goes about calling up bills for debate. Like the house, the senate for many years had a rule that required bills to be taken up in calendar order. Unlike the house, however, the senate would routinely suspend that rule in order to conduct its business. To force such a suspension, a bill that no one wished to consider would be placed at the top of the senate calendar. In a number of sessions of the legislature, this "blocking" bill was one that dealt with county compost! Custom and tradition dictated that this piece of legislation never be considered. Thus, every other bill taken up by the senate was technically out of order—even if they followed each other on the calendar—because this first one had been skipped. The senate eventually simplified its procedures by adopting a rule that required an absolute two-thirds majority vote—21 of 31—to bring a bill to the floor (this is the rule that became a source of contention during the gerrymandering brouhaha discussed previously). Once a bill is brought up and debated, then a simple majority—16 of 31—is all that is required to pass it. Historically, then, the senate has required more people to agree to talk about a bill than it has required to pass that bill.

This may seem puzzling, but there really is a reason for this practice. Over the years, the senate decided it should use precious debate time on those bills that have the greatest likelihood of passage. After all, nothing is more frustrating to a legislator than to spend hours or even days debating a bill only to reach some impasse that prevents passage. Requiring a two-thirds vote to call up a bill forces its author and supporters to seek consensus before the bill gets to the floor. Compromises made to get the bill up for discussion make it more likely that the bill will pass once it is brought up. Conversely, issues that create sharp, often irreconcilable differences among senators usually don't even make it to the floor. Seen in this light, the senate's peculiar way of doing business makes a bit more sense. However, critics of this process charge that the "two-thirds" rule precludes many important issues from senate deliberation simply because they are controversial and not readily amenable to the kinds of compromises needed to secure the necessary number of votes to allow debate. This in turn may allow problems to grow and thus may place the legislature in more of a crucial policy quandary at a later date. Moreover, the increased spirit of partisanship manifested in both regular and special sessions in recent years have led some in the senate to at least consider abolishing this time-honored means of regulating the agenda.

As in the house, the senate votes on a bill at the conclusion of debate and a majority vote passes the bill. But remember: Once a bill passes one house, it must be sent to the other and undergo the rites of passage once again. Some legislators attempt a

filibustering
The practice of delaying or killing a bill by talking at great length; grows out of the senate's rule allowing unlimited debate.

7.1

7.2

7.3

7.4

7.5

7.6

7.1

7.2

7.3

7.4

7.5

7.6

shortcut here by lining up a member of the other house to introduce an identical bill in that chamber. With both bills working their way through the house and senate at the same time, final passage sometimes can be hastened.

If the versions of a bill passed by the two houses differ, then a conference committee must be appointed to work out those differences. Composed of five representatives and five senators, this body tries to reach a compromise agreeable to both houses. Any such compromise must be arrived at by majority vote of both groups of conferees. The agreed-on compromise is then sent back to the respective houses for their reactions. They may

Texas ★ **Mosaic**   **There Oughta Be a Law . . .**

And Now There Is! The 82nd Texas legislature adjourned its regular session *sine die* on May 31, 2011. By that time, legislators had sent 1,379 bills to the governor, of which he eventually vetoed 25. These new laws dealt with a multitude of issues both old and new, including the following.[20]

Money. The biennial state budget enacted by the legislature called for spending $172.3 billion. This amount was less than that provided in the previous budget and reflected the significant revenue shortfalls with which the members had to wrestle during the session. The austerity in the budget can plainly be seen in the difference in spending levels between the first year of the biennium ($93.9 billion) and the second year ($78.4 billion).

Public Education. The state's public education budget was reduced by some $5 billion over previous levels of funding. This led many districts across the state to lay off teachers, increase class sizes, and frantically scramble to be able to provide educational services as mandated by both the Constitution and statute. Also, the funding formula for public schools was altered, and schools are now required to implement policies to combat bullying.

Higher Education. Funding for public higher education suffered an overall reduction as the state struggled to deal with the ongoing fiscal crisis. New standards for awarding TEXAS (Toward Excellence, Access, and Success) grants to first-time entering college students were implemented, and the Higher Education Coordinating Board was directed to consider so-called performance-based funding in devising its overall funding formula.

Health. The legislature enacted legislation requiring any woman seeking an abortion to view a sonogram and listen to an ultrasound of the fetus before the procedure can be done. Reimbursement to hospitals that provide care to illegal immigrants was restricted, as was funding to family planning providers with links to providers of abortion services.

Criminal Law. The legislature prohibited policies that would facilitate the establishment of so-called sanctuary cities in the state. They also provided for deferred adjudication for those charged with a first offense of intoxication, revised the state's human trafficking laws, and made "sexting" a criminal offense.

Voter Identification. After failing in the previous session to secure passage of a measure that would require all voters to present a valid form of photo identification in order to cast a ballot, House conservatives pushed the measure through in the 82nd legislature. Almost immediately, opponents—including groups representing minorities, the elderly, and the poor—filed lawsuits challenging the law's constitutionality. Because of these suits, the law was barred from being implemented during the 2012 elections.

Radioactive Waste Disposal. Members enacted legislation to allow for the creation of a low-level radioactive waste-disposal facility in Andrews County in west Texas. The facility will receive and store nuclear waste transported to Texas from Vermont.

Highway Speed Limits. The legislature authorized the raising of highway speed limits to 75 miles per hour and, on some roads, to 85 miles per hour. It also abolished the distinction between daytime and nighttime speed limits as well as those between cars and trucks.

And Now There Isn't! Several pieces of legislation did not make it through the meat grinder that is the Texas legislature during the most recent session, and these included bills on the following topics:

Payday Lenders. A bill requiring such companies to clearly post their interest rates and to secure a state license to operate died in the house. Industry lobbyists worked furiously to kill this bill.

Railroad Commission. An attempt was made to abolish the Railroad Commission—arguably the most powerful regulatory agency in state government—and replace it with an Oil and Gas Commission. This would have more accurately reflected the primary responsibilities of the Commission, which hasn't regulated railroads in Texas since the 1980s. It died in conference committee.

Texting and Driving. A bill to make texting while driving a misdemeanor was vetoed by Governor Rick Perry, who claimed it was an unwarranted restriction on the personal liberty of Texans.

Concealed Handguns. Once again, bills to allow holders of concealed handgun licenses to bring their weapons onto public college and university campuses were defeated.

1. In what ways do the laws highlighted above reveal the priorities of the current Texas Legislature?

2. What may the funding reductions embodied in the current state budget portend for the future in critical public service areas?

accept or reject the committee's recommendation, but they may not amend it. If accepted by both houses, the bill goes to the governor for his or her action. If he doesn't veto it, the bill becomes a law, and the bill's author can relax for the first time in months.

☐ Ways to Kill a Bill

Of course, the process we've just described seems rather orderly when viewed on paper as part of a nice, neat flowchart. Remember, however, that hundreds of bills are at various points on that chart at any given time. Committees may be juggling scores of bills in various stages of study. Members rush from floor session to committee meeting and back numerous times in a day.

In the midst of such frantic activity, it becomes very difficult to keep track of one bill, much less several. It also becomes very easy to kill a bill in all the confusion. In fact, if bills were birds, they'd be on the endangered species list. The reason is fairly simple: to pass a bill you have to do several hundred things right, but to kill one you only have to mess up one of those several hundred things. Let's look at only a few of the ways a bill can be killed. The presiding officer can effectively kill a bill by referring it to a hostile committee. So, if the Speaker or the lieutenant governor doesn't like you or your bill, you lose even before you've had a chance to play. If you make it by the presiding officer, you've got to deal with a committee. If a committee chair doesn't like you, your bill will get pigeonholed and never see the light of legislative day. Or the committee could amend your bill to death, incorporating so many changes that it no longer does what you wanted it to do the way you wanted it to be done. In such a situation, the author usually withdraws the bill from consideration, effectively killing it.

If your bill makes it out of committee, it may run afoul of the House Appropriations or Senate Finance Committees, which could decide to gut the funding for it. In that case, even if your bill passed, it couldn't be implemented and you'd still lose. Then there's the Calendars Committee in the house. If one of its members recalls the time you embarrassed her at a cocktail party, she may even the score by placing your bill so far down on the calendar that it will never reach the floor. During floor action, your bill may be saddled with crippling amendments. And the senate provides some added opportunities for legislative homicide at this point. Remember the "two-thirds" rule? Make 11 senators mad and they'll vote not to call your bill up. No debate, no vote, no bill. Or let one senator get bent out of shape and he's likely to start talking. Such a filibuster in the waning days of a session can prove fatal. Then there's **"tagging."** Under this rule, any senator may request in writing a 48-hour delay in considering a bill in order to allow for adequate public notification. Although a bill may only be "tagged" once, when this happens at the end of a session, it also can deal a deathblow to a bill.

Finally, your bill may not find a sponsor in the opposite house. Or a conference committee might not be able to find a compromise both houses can live with. Or the governor could veto it. So the wonder of the legislative process is not that a bill is ever killed; the wonder is that some do occasionally make it through this labyrinth and actually become laws. In the nearby Texas Mosaic, you will find a listing of some of the bills that passed, or failed, in the 2011 session.

"tagging"
A senate rule that allows a senator to postpone committee consideration of a bill for 48 hours in hopes of killing it.

7.1

7.2

7.3

7.4

7.5

7.6

The Legislature in the Political Arena

7.6   Analyze the forces outside the legislature that can impact lawmaking.

 he internal complexities of the legislative process are enough to drive a reasonably sane person to the point of distraction. But legislation does not occur in a vacuum. Numerous elements from the larger political arena also affect the making of laws, and these factors can prove to be crucial at times.

7.1

7.2

7.3

7.4

7.5

7.6

☐ Legislative Support

Information is the most valuable commodity in the legislature. During the hectic pace of a regular session, members need as much information as they can get. For this, they often rely on a number of governmental support groups.

Aside from their own staff members, legislators can also call on the resources of the **Texas Legislative Council**. This body was created to provide research and bill-drafting services to members. Overseen by a group of legislators, including the two presiding officers, the staff of the council can help legislators with legal and other kinds of research and with the actual writing of bills. Legislators also have access to the Legislative Reference Library, an extensive collection of materials including up-to-date compilations of Texas and U.S. legal codes. Each session the Legislative Budget Board provides members with a working budgetary document, and the Legislative Clipping Service furnishes them with a daily anthology of political news items taken from newspapers around the state. You can see what's happening at the Legislative Council, the Reference Library, and the LBB by logging on to the previously mentioned Texas Legislature Online website at http://www.capitol.state.tx.us and navigating to their respective home pages.

Another source of support for legislators is information received from state agencies. These agencies depend on the legislature for their very existence, so they manage to develop a kind of mutually beneficial relationship with members over time. This is especially true of agency heads and the committees with which they regularly interact. For example, Commissioner of Higher Education Dr. Raymund Paredes regularly represents the interests of the agency he heads, the Higher Education Coordinating Board, before house and senate committees. These committees and their chairs have frequently called on Paredes as well as the Coordinating Board staff for timely information, or have asked them to study and make recommendations with regard to higher education policies and practices. Such relationships can give legislators the information they need and provide the agencies involved with familiar (and friendly) faces at budget time.

Last, but certainly not least, are interest groups. As we've discussed previously, interest groups can often generate far more accurate and detailed information than the various in-house groups on which legislators frequently depend. And, as is the case with veteran agency heads, members often ask experienced lobbyists to provide data from the interest group's information storehouse. In fact, veteran observers of the legislature note that sometimes it's difficult, if not impossible, to tell the lobbyists from the legislators without name tags. Over the years, as legislators, lobbyists, and agency heads find themselves spending hours together hammering out public policy, certain bonds of respect and dependence develop. Such relationships are important for the information they can provide members, but they also can create problems when the narrow, parochial interests of agencies and interest groups are promoted over the broader interests of the general public.

☐ Other Players

The final group of players in the legislative game comes from many areas. One of the more important is the governor. Although the office of governor in Texas is constitutionally weak, a governor with the right kind of personality can have a significant impact on the legislative process. A governor who shows a willingness to work with the legislature usually stands a good chance of seeing some of his or her own programs adopted. Successful governors carefully choose issues with which the legislature is already sympathetic, quietly cultivate personal relationships with house and senate members, and avoid confrontations with the presiding officers.

In this regard, Governor George W. Bush gave a clinic in gubernatorial-legislative relations during his tenure in office. For example, as he prepared to assume the office for the first time in 1995, he noted which issues—tort, welfare, and education reforms, along with revising juvenile justice—had been the focus of legislative attention prior to the regular session. Realizing that these issues would probably be around for some time, he endorsed them as his own. During the course of that session, he managed to invite every senate and house member to the mansion for informal visits. And early on, he made clear his willingness to work with Lieutenant Governor Bullock and Speaker Laney in achieving mutually agreed-on goals. This strategy resulted in a clean sweep for Bush and his legislative allies in those areas.

His successor, Rick Perry, has not been as successful in his dealings with the legislature. His perceived aloofness from the legislative process has produced a distinctly cool relationship with members of the house and senate, and he is viewed by a number of legislators as being unwilling to get involved in the hammering out of tough policy solutions. His ill-fated attempt to mandate human papillomavirus (HPV) immunizations for young girls in 2007 gave members an excuse to "put him in his place" by rebuffing his proposed policy.

Two statewide elected officials can also have an impact on legislation, one of whom is the comptroller of public accounts. The constitution requires that the state maintain a balanced budget, and to ensure that this happens, the legislature is prohibited from spending more money than the comptroller certifies as being available during a biennium. This gives her some powerful leverage in the budgetary process. The legislature states how the money will be spent, but the comptroller says how much will be spent. The attorney general can also affect the course of lawmaking by issuing advisory opinions. These are analyses of prospective legislation as to their potential constitutionality or lack thereof. Obviously, if a proposed bill is likely to be declared unconstitutional, a senator or representative will likely think twice before investing the time, resources, and political capital necessary to secure its passage.

Within the house and senate, the various legislative caucuses occasionally have an impact on the formulation of public policy. In this context, a caucus is simply a group of legislators who share a common bond or interest and who come together to promote or protect that interest. Examples in the Texas Legislature include the House Republican and House Democratic Caucuses, which are obviously partisan-based; the Texas Conservative Coalition, uniting conservative Democrats and Republicans alike; and groups like the Mexican American Legislative Caucus and the Legislative Black Caucus, whose organizational basis is the ethnicity of their members. Such groups try to build coalitions and rally support for issues of particular concern to their members.

An often overlooked factor in the lawmaking process in Texas is the courts, especially those in the federal judiciary. Very often, court rulings will establish the constitutional parameters for what can and cannot be done by state legislative assemblies. This is often the case regarding the Texas Legislature, which sometimes runs afoul of these parameters. In recent years, the courts have been asked to rule on any number of laws enacted by the legislature, and often these rulings have contravened the wishes of that body. Such legislative enactments as the state's plan for redistricting, its new voter identification law, and its pre-abortion sonogram law have been or are being challenged. Court rulings against previous acts by the legislature can become checks on future legislative enactments.

Another force to which legislators occasionally respond is constituents, who provide input from time to time. Unfortunately, this is not always as important a source of information and ideas as it should be. In an ideal world, an informed, interested electorate would regularly communicate its wishes to elected representatives. If experience is any indicator, Texas is no ideal world in this respect. House and senate members rarely hear from their constituents at all, and often the messages they do receive are indecipherable. An additional source of distortion for legislators is the tendency of the most vocal of their constituents to come from the ideological edges. Activists of both liberal and conservative stripe tend to overwhelm their respective representatives with a blizzard of communication. Yet these groups often do not accurately reflect the ideas and wishes of a majority of a representative's or senator's district. The simple fact is this: A legislative session usually is not a good time to try contacting a senator or representative to express your concerns. Things are just too hectic during that time, and your representative probably won't be able to give you the attention you deserve.

7.1
7.2
7.3
7.4
7.5
7.6

7.1
7.2
7.3
7.4
7.5
7.6

Inside the Federalist System

The 2009 Stimulus Act

That the relationship between the national government and the state governments is constantly changing is almost a given. This can readily be seen in both the economic recession that began in 2008 and the resultant policy initiatives that have come from the federal government to assist financially strapped state governments. The 2009 economic stimulus package passed by Congress provided hundreds of millions of dollars to state governments to enable them to meet their current obligations and/or expand their services in response to the human needs engendered by the downturn. While some state officials, including Governor Rick Perry, quickly sought to make political hay with conservative supporters by threatening to refuse such federal funds, it became apparent early in the 2009 legislative session that members of the Texas house and senate would not be so quick to reject such stimulus money. Several members of the legislature publicly called the governor out on such threats, and the house even went so far as to create a select (temporary) committee—the Federal Economic Stabilization Funding Committee—to direct the use of the federal largesse that was due the Lone Star State. Despite the governor's much publicized animosity to such federal "interference" in a state's business, the legislature that session was only able to balance the state's budget (as required by the Texas constitution) by accepting a rather large slice of stimulus money. Most of this money went to support Texas's share of the Medicaid program as well as other state-federal partnerships, and the same strategy was used by the legislature in the 2011 legislative session as well.

1. In what ways do the differences between Governor Perry and the legislature regarding the use of federal stimulus money by Texas highlight the principle of checks and balances built into our constitution?

2. If Texas were to refuse all federal funds, what would be the best strategies to adopt in order to provide the basic services Texans have come to expect from their government?

□ The Legislature and You

So how are you supposed to relate to these men and women elected to act on your behalf? We've already seen that they are impossibly busy during a legislative session. And the demographic reality of modern Texas is such that you're not likely to run into them in the express checkout lane at H-E-B or Wal-Mart. As we have seen, each Texas senator represents more than three-quarters of a million people, and each representative counts more than 167,000 people as constituents. Making yourself heard in such a crowd might seem to be difficult, but it's not impossible. Make contact. Communicate with your legislators and express your concerns, then maintain this contact. One communication from a constituent may be easy to ignore; regular correspondence from that constituent isn't. All legislators have e-mail addresses, and you can find these at the website for the legislature, Texas Legislature Online. Additionally, many members have discovered Facebook and Twitter, and can be contacted via those social media channels. *Regular* communication with your elected representatives is as close and convenient as a personal computer.

Finally, a communication strategy that may set you apart from other constituents is to tell your representative what you like about his or her actions. Most legislators get both ears full when they do something people don't like, but they rarely hear from folks when they get it right. Make an effort to meet your senator or representative in person, preferably between sessions of the legislature when his or her schedule is less hectic. And after you've had your say, listen to them. You might learn something. Most importantly, hold them accountable. Monitor what happens during the session and see if they do what they promised. If they don't, call their hand. Remember, they work for you. Will this sort of citizen response (and responsibility) take place? We hope so, but it will take a concerted effort on your part because democracy is neither quick nor easy. In any event, you can't claim ignorance of the process. The next move is up to you.

Review the Chapter

The Legislature in Texas

7.1 Explain, analyze, and compare the structure and composition of the Texas Legislature.

The legislature is the primary branch of government in Texas. A bicameral (two-house) body, it is composed of the 31-member senate and the 150-member house. It meets in regular session in odd-numbered years for no more than 140 days. Senators are elected to four-year terms, and representatives serve two-year terms. Members' terms are not limited. Salaries for senators and representatives are $7,200 annually, plus a per diem allowance paid during sessions. The legislature does not reflect the demographic profile of Texas, as women, minorities, and nonprofessionals are underrepresented in both the house and the senate.

Apportionment

7.2 Explain redistricting and gerrymandering and analyze their impact on the Texas Legislature.

Through the process of redistricting and the practice of gerrymandering, legislators draw their own district lines. Redistricting must be done every 10 years following the decennial federal census in order to reflect changes in population distribution, but in recent years, the legislature has engaged in redistricting on a more frequent basis. Federal court rulings have required states to adhere to the "one person, one vote" principle to assure equity among the electorate. Gerrymandering is the drawing of district lines so as to favor or harm an individual member's or a political party's chance of winning election. In certain circumstances, gerrymandering is illegal, but it is often difficult to prove in a court of law.

The Presiding Officers

7.3 Analyze the roles of the presiding officers and "The Team" in the legislative process.

The lieutenant governor presides over the senate, and the Speaker presides over the house. The lieutenant governor is elected in a statewide election and serves a four-year term. The Speaker is elected from among the members of the house to serve a two year term. Both have the power to recognize members to speak, to assign members to committees, to choose the chairs of committees, and to serve on a number of ancillary bodies within the legislature. "The Team," a group of friends and political allies among each house's membership, aids them. Becoming a member of the team can enhance a legislator's ability to get things done. Being outside the team can leave a member wandering in the legislative wilderness.

The Committee System

7.4 Identify the different types of committees in the Texas Legislature and discuss the importance of the committee system.

The main work of the legislature is done by committees, which allow the two houses to divide their labor efficiently and thus get more work done. The most important of these bodies are the standing committees, which are formed each time the legislature meets. These bodies act as miniature versions of the legislature and are usually where the fate of most legislation is decided. Procedural committees, like the Calendars Committee in the house, deal with the internal operations of the legislature. Conference committees—which reconcile differences between house and senate versions of bills—and interim committees, which study topics of interest to the legislature between sessions, are temporary committees.

How a Bill Becomes a Law

7.5 Trace the process of how a bill becomes a law and identify ways in which a bill may be killed.

All bills introduced will be referred by the presiding officer to a standing committee. The committees will take action on the bills by recommending passage, usually after amending them, or by refusing to consider them. Bills reported out go on the calendar, then to the floor for debate and vote. Bills in the house are considered in their calendar order; bills in the senate must secure a two-thirds majority vote to be considered. Passage in both houses is by a simple majority. If a bill passes in one house, it is then sent to the other house for consideration. If the house and senate pass different versions of a bill, a conference committee tries to reach a compromise. Bills agreed to by both the house and the senate then go to the governor for his action.

The Legislature in the Political Arena

7.6 Analyze the forces outside the legislature that can impact lawmaking.

Members of the legislature may avail themselves of several internal resources such as the Texas Legislative Council and the Legislative Budget Board. These entities can play critical roles in shaping legislation. Other elected officials—such as the comptroller of public accounts and the attorney general—can also influence the course of legislation. Citizens can also be a factor if they are patient and persistent. Legislators must deal with agency heads, lobbyists, the governor, and sometimes the courts while engaged in the legislative process.

Learn the Terms

 Study and **Review** the **Flashcards**

apportionment, p. 163
committees, p. 167
conference committee, p. 178
filibustering, p. 183
gerrymandering, p. 166
interim committee, p. 178
Legislative Budget Board (LBB), p. 171

limited seniority system, p. 173
"one person, one vote", p. 164
pigeonholing, p. 182
redistricting, p. 163
regular session, p. 160
single-member districts, p. 165
special committee, p. 178

special sessions, p. 160
standing committees, p. 176
"tagging", p. 185
Texas Legislative Council, p. 186
"The Team", p. 173

Test Yourself

 Study and **Review** the **Practice Tests**

7.1   Explain, analyze, and compare the structure and composition of the Texas Legislature.

Members of the Texas senate must reside in the state for _____ years prior to election.

　a. three
　b. four
　c. five
　d. six
　e. ten

7.2   Explain redistricting and gerrymandering and analyze their impact on the Texas Legislature.

The process of drawing legislative districts so as to either help or hurt a person's or a party's chances of winning election is known as

　a. chubbing.
　b. gerrymandering.
　c. filibustering.
　d. cheating.
　e. purging.

7.3   Analyze the roles of the presiding officers and "The Team" in the legislative process.

As presiding officers, the lieutenant governor and the Speaker have all of the following powers except one. The exception is:

　a. They both serve a four-year term in office.
　b. They both recognize members to speak from the floor.
　c. They both serve on the Legislative Budget Board.
　d. They both appoint the chairs of committees.
　e. They both refer bills to committees.

7.4   Identify the different types of committees in the Texas Legislature and discuss the importance of the committee system.

The type of committee in the legislature that deals with specific topics or subjects is a(n)

　a. procedural committee.
　b. interim committee.
　c. conference committee.
　d. substantive committee.
　e. topical committee.

7.5   Trace the process of how a bill becomes a law and identify ways in which a bill may be killed.

In order to bring a bill before the senate for consideration and vote, a senator must secure

　a. a three-fourths majority vote.
　b. a majority vote.
　c. a unanimous vote.
　d. a three-fifths majority vote.
　e. a two-thirds majority vote.

7.6   Analyze the forces outside the legislature that can impact lawmaking.

Which of the following is often the least likely factor in influencing legislators?

　a. other members
　b. constituents
　c. the courts
　d. the governor
　e. the presiding officers

Explore Further

Brammer, Billy Lee. *The Gay Place*. Austin: University of Texas Press, 1995. [This edition is a reissue of a classic fictional treatment of Texas politics first published in 1978.]

Deaton, Charles. *The Year They Threw the Rascals Out.* Austin, TX: Shoal Creek Publishers, 1973.

Jillson, Calvin C. *Lone Star Tarnished: A Critical Look at Texas Politics and Public Policy.* New York: Routledge, 2012.

McNeely, Dave, and Jim Henderson. *Bob Bullock: God Bless Texas.* Austin: University of Texas Press, 2008).

Research Division of the Texas Legislative Council. *Presiding Officers of the Texas Legislature, 1846–2002.* Austin, TX, 2002.

Texas Legislature. *Legislative Budget Board.* http://www.lbb.state.tx.us.

Texas Legislature. *Legislative Reference Library of Texas.* http://www.lrl.state.tx.us/index.cfm.

Texas Legislature. *Texas Legislative Council.* http://www.tlc.state.tx.us.

Texas Legislature. *Texas Legislature Online.* http://www.capitol.state.tx.us/Home.aspx.

Texas State Historical Association. *The Handbook of Texas Online.* Denton: University of North Texas. http://www.tshaonline.org/handbook/online.

8

The Governor in Texas

I'm not afraid to shake up the system, and government needs more shaking up than any other system I know.

—*The Late Governor Ann Richards*

Traditionally and constitutionally, the **governor** of Texas has limited powers. That is as the authors of the 1876 constitution intended. What they did not count on was one person occupying the governor's mansion for over a dozen years. Rick Perry ascended to the office when former governor George W. Bush resigned in December 2000 as Bush prepared to take the office of the president. Perry has been there ever since,

The governor's powers are constitutionally limited by the plural executive, whereby major department leaders are elected independent of the governor. The legislature has further restricted the office by establishing a system of boards and commissions that, while members are appointed by the governor, their six-year overlapping terms make it difficult for a governor to control the boards and commission—that is, unless he serves for more than six years, which no one had done prior to Perry.

Because Perry has served for over a dozen years, he has appointed every member of every board and commission. He has also been more active in other areas than most Texas governors. He has issued more vetoes than any of his cohorts, both within a single session and over the course of his career. He has issued executive orders more frequently than his predecessors, although some of the most controversial have been overturned by legislative action. And he has coordinated his actions with the lieutenant governor and Speaker of the house in order to affect out-of-session reform.

8.1	8.2	8.3	8.4	8.5	8.6	8.7
Outline the qualifications to hold the office of governor.	Describe the most significant powers possessed by the governor while acting as chief executive.	Characterize the governor's integral role in the legislative process.	Explain the judicial and clemency powers of the governor.	Describe the governor's informal powers.	Illustrate the impact of the governor's staff.	Determine how reform might impact the governor's office.

Governor Rick Perry shares a private moment with Lieutenant Governor David Dewhurst prior to a speech to a business group. Because of the relative weakness of the office, a governor has work with legislative leaders, like Dewhurst, in order to advance his agenda. In turn, these leaders understand that because vetoes are so hard to overturn in Texas, they must have a working relationship with the governor as well.

8.1

8.2

8.3

8.4

8.5

8.6

8.7

governor
The state's highest elected executive official.

Twenty years from now, the Perry administration may be viewed as an aberration, a time when an unusual set of circumstances led to a uniquely empowered governor. Or it may lead future governors to seek ways in which to utilize similar authority.

Qualifications, Term, and Salary

8.1 Outline the qualifications to hold the office of governor.

A person must be at least 30 years old, a resident of Texas for five years, a U.S. citizen, and a registered voter in order to be elected to any executive office in Texas. In reality, successful candidates for governor tend to be financially well off and have spent years building credibility and name recognition within their party. Running for governor is an expensive endeavor, and even wealthy candidates need financial assistance from PACs and interested individuals. Once in office, the governor's salary is $115,345. This makes him or her one of the highest-paid governors in the nation.

In 2002, in a race that will likely prove to be an aberration, the top two candidates combined spent almost $100 million on their election efforts. The independently wealthy Democrat, Tony Sanchez, ponied up more than $60 million of his own money in his losing effort. Incumbent governor Rick Perry, spending less than half of his opponent's total, still won by about 18 percentage points. Even under normal circumstances, however, it cost $20 million for a candidate to fund a serious race. In 2010, Perry's campaign spent over $41 million, while his Democratic challenger spent almost $25 million. Historically, governors in Texas have been white men. Ann Richards is the most recent exception.

Governor Bush was unique in that he had never held elective or appointive public office before winning the governorship in 1995. Most Texas governors are married, Protestant, and between their late 40s and early 60s when first elected to office. The term of office is four years. Attempts to limit terms have repeatedly failed. This lack of term limits gives the Texas governor an advantage over colleagues in other states. Term limits make governors instant lame ducks, allowing the legislature to discount their significance because of their upcoming departure. Likewise, some governors have two-year terms, forcing them to run for reelection on an almost continuous basis.

Prior to Governor Bush's reelection in 1998, no Texas governor had ever been elected to consecutive four-year terms. In a state where incumbents generally fare well in statewide races, this office was the exception. The primary factor in the governor's inability to retain office has been the divergence between the public's expectations and the governor's actual power. Voters expect much from the governor and hold him accountable when things go wrong. The Texas constitution, meanwhile, limits his ability to act in an effective manner. Governors can seldom live up to their promises or to the people's expectations. Nonetheless, Perry was reelected in 2002, 2006, and 2010.

Executive Powers

8.2 Describe the most significant powers possessed by the governor while acting as chief executive.

ost experts consider the powers of the Texas governor to be limited. Keith Mueller's classic study attempted to compare the power of governors by ranking them according to four criteria (see Table 8.1). He concluded that only two states, South Carolina and Mississippi, have less powerful governors than Texas. Texas falls well below the mean score of state chief executives.

TABLE 8.1 RANKING OF SELECTED GOVERNORS USING MUELLER'S SCALE

formal powers
Powers granted by the constitution or statutes.

8.1

8.2

8.3

8.4

8.5

8.6

8.7

State	Tenure	Appointive	Budget	Veto	Total
Massachusetts	5	5	5	5	20
New York	5	4	5	5	19
California	5	3	5	5	18
Ohio	4	4	5	5	18
Michigan	5	2	5	5	17
Alabama	4	3	5	4	16
Oklahoma	4	2	5	5	16
Arkansas	2	4	5	4	15
Texas	5	1	3	3	12
Mississippi	3	1	1	5	10
Mean: 16.18					

Source: Keith J. Mueller, "Explaining Variation and Change in Gubernatorial Powers, 1960–1982," *Western Political Quarterly* 38 (1985). Reprinted by permission of the University of Utah, copyright holder.

Such studies may be interesting from a comparative perspective, but they nonetheless contain serious shortcomings. For instance, in determining total power ranking, the index weights all four factors equally. In reality, some powers are more important than others. Furthermore, the study only considers constitutional or statutory powers without examining the way in which the powers are used within the political environment in each specific state (see the Veto Power section below).

It is clear, however, that compared to the situation in many states, the **formal powers** of the Texas governor are limited. For instance, the governor has little budgetary authority. In 41 other states, the governor has the primary responsibility for creating the budget.

Although the governor has thousands of opportunities to make appointments to various boards and commissions in a single four-year term, two factors limit this power. First, overlapping terms ensure that the former governor continues to affect Texas politics after leaving office. Second, the most important executive offices in the state are elected by voters, not appointed. Still, the governor has several notable formal powers that he can use to influence government operations. More importantly, the governor must use his or her informal powers pragmatically in order to govern effectively.

☐ Executive Powers

The primary purpose of the executive branch is to carry out laws. In this capacity, the governor can appoint executive boards and commissions, as well as exercise law enforcement and military responsibilities. The governor has little control over the day-to-day operations of the executive branch, however, as most government employees are picked through a merit selection process that precludes their removal for political reasons. From a positive perspective, this process ensures that competent workers cannot be removed because of political differences. From a negative point of view, it prevents a governor from dismissing public employees who work to thwart his or her agenda.

☐ Appointment Powers

The governor of Texas has significant power to appoint board and commission members. It is common practice in Texas for governors to appoint major campaign contributors to these positions. For example, when openings occurred on the Parks and Wildlife Commission, Governor George W. Bush appointed Richard Heath, who had

8.1

8.2

8.3

8.4

8.5

8.6

8.7

senatorial courtesy
A discretion allowing senators to derail a governor's nomination from within their home district.

overlapping terms
Terms of appointed board members that are staggered to ensure continuity of experience.

contributed $114,849 to his campaign, and Lee Bass, who gave $47,500. Likewise, many of Perry's appointees had contributed to his campaign; Texans for Public Justice found that during his first decade in office, Perry received over $17 million from more than 900 appointees. One of Perry's biggest contributors, James Dannenbaum, received an appointment to the University of Texas Board of Regents after he and his wife donated some $320,000 to Perry campaigns. About 17 percent of Perry appointees had contributed to the governor.[1]

Governors' appointments often receive close scrutiny as to the segments of the population represented. Hispanics made up only 11 percent of Bush's first-term appointments, and African Americans, 7 percent. In each case, this represented substantially less than the representation given to the respective minority groups through Richards's appointments.[2] Richards tried to mirror the racial and ethnic diversity of Texas in her appointments, and she came close to doing so. In fairness to Bush, his appointments more nearly reflected the election returns. During his initial run for governor, his deepest support came from, and most of his early appointments went to, white males. Likewise, Perry's appointments have mirrored his supporters. Several years into his service, 16 percent of his appointments had been Hispanic; 11 percent black; and 3 percent from other minority groups. During this period, 36 percent of Perry's appointees were female.

One legislative restraint on the governor's appointment power is the practice of **senatorial courtesy**. Under this informal practice, state senators can derail appointees from their home district. If the senator disapproves of the choice, tradition dictates that the appointment be defeated. Another constraint is that all appointments must be approved by two-thirds of the senate. The importance of this is heightened by the evolution of Texas into a two-party state. Because neither party will control a two-thirds majority in the foreseeable future, no governor can ignore the opposition during the appointment process. Realistically, though, few appointees are rejected, as many have been serving for months before the legislature comes into session. Rejecting them after the fact would create chaos for the board or commission on which they served. The year 2009 was something of an exception, as two high-profile appointees, one to chair the State Board of Education and one to serve on Pardons and Paroles, were rejected by the senate.[3] The rejected parole board nominee, Shanda Perkins, was best known for her part in the prosecution of a Burleson woman who sold sex toys at Tupperware parties, a charge that would eventually lead the U.S. Court of Appeals for the Fifth Circuit to overturn the state's sex toy law.

The major restraint on the governor's power in the appointment process is the six-year **overlapping terms** of board members. For at least the first two years of a term, a new governor interacts with agency boards dominated by appointees of the previous governor. Texas law makes no provision for the chief executive to remove seated board members who were appointed by his predecessor. Essentially, this means that when Governor Bush entered office, he had to deal with a bureaucratic structure dominated by board members appointed by Governor Richards, the person he defeated in the previous gubernatorial election. Governor Perry has been the only chief executive to appoint every board and commission member in the state.

The governor is restricted even in efforts to remove his own appointees—he can do so only with two-thirds approval of the senate. This limits the governor's control over state agencies. Once appointed, board members are all but free to ignore the governor's wishes. These restrictions are intentional. Conservative policy makers wanted to ensure that no governor would have absolute control over boards and commissions. One hundred and forty years after E. J. Davis left the governor's office, his legacy lives on in a system designed to limit power.

Unlike many states, Texas has a plural executive, a concept that will be more fully explored in the following chapter. Key executive department heads, such as the attorney general and the comptroller, are elected independent of the governor. As a result, the governor has no formal control over their actions or their agencies. All of these officials have the primary responsibility for implementing policy within their respective agencies. Although they may listen to the governor's advice, they are under no obligation to follow it. The governor has no formal or constitutional power that would allow him or her to override the decisions of other elected executives. This significantly weakens the governor, who is thereby reduced to a figurehead in respect to bureaucratic oversight, being unable to review and control the actions of these agencies.

From 1991 to 1999, governors had to deal with major department heads who were from the opposition party. During his first term, Bush, a Republican, worked with a Democratic lieutenant governor, comptroller, attorney general, and land commissioner. In his second term, however, all department heads were Republican. When Rick Perry took office in 2000, and after he was reelected governor in 2002, 2006, and 2010, Republicans continued to hold all statewide executive offices. Perry's third straight four-year term is unprecedented in Texas gubernatorial history.

martial law
The power to impose military rule during a crisis.

☐ Military Power

The Texas constitution gives the governor specific military powers. He can declare **martial law**. In the case of rioting or looting, the governor has extensive power to enact and enforce curfews and take other unconventional actions, although these powers are rarely used. He can also call out the Texas Guard in an emergency. Most often, the National Guard is deployed when there is a natural disaster, such as the flooding that often accompanies hurricanes on the Gulf coast. These powers are limited because significant military power resides with the national government.

Members of the Texas National Guard at a deployment ceremony at Baylor University. The guard is under the command of the Texas governor, unless called in to service by the president, as was the case here. In Texas, the Guard is often the first line of relief during hurricanes and flooding.

8.1
8.2
8.3
8.4
8.5
8.6
8.7

8.1

8.2

8.3

8.4

8.5

8.6

8.7

☐ Law Enforcement Powers

The governor has limited law enforcement powers. He appoints the public safety commissioner. He or she may also take control of the Texas Rangers (not the baseball team) in certain situations. Additionally, the governor can introduce legislation aimed at combating crime.

Legislative Powers

| 8.3 | Characterize the governor's integral role in the legislative process. |

☐ Session-Calling Power

One of the governor's most significant powers is the ability to call special sessions. Not only does he have the sole authority to call these special legislative sessions, he also sets the agenda. This allows the governor to put the legislature in the spotlight and pressure it into action. If it fails to perform in a special session, where performance often translates into endorsing the governor's proposals, the legislature runs the risk of incurring the wrath of voters.

In most states, the legislature can call itself into session, but not in Texas. Reserving this power for the governor not only strengthens the executive, it also limits the legislature. The Grange gave the governor this power exclusively in order to create a roadblock for overzealous legislators.

The governor has sole power to set the agenda for such a session. The legislature cannot bring any issue to a vote in special session without the governor's approval. An astute governor can use this power to increase his or her influence, especially when the legislature has an issue it wishes to pass. Because the governor can add issues to the agenda, he or she can insist that the legislators pass the governor's program first. In 1984, for example, Governor Mark White knew that the legislature was not particularly interested in passing his controversial and expensive education reform bill in an election year. He also knew that highway construction programs are always popular with campaigning politicians. Therefore, he promised to open the session to highway construction if education reform was passed first. His plan worked.

The governor can keep the legislature in session indefinitely, providing another incentive for it to cooperate. Although each special session can last no more than 30 days, the governor may call an unlimited number of sessions. The threat of a special session can likewise be used to encourage the legislature to enact the governor's agenda during the regular session. With pay of only $600 per month, legislators don't want to spend more time in Austin than is absolutely necessary. In 1995, when his education reform package seemed to be foundering, Bush encouraged the legislature to pass a bill by issuing such a threat. As a result, the package passed in regular session. Throughout the 1990s, special sessions, common in the 1980s, became less frequent as legislators learned the value of finishing their business on time.

The early 21st century would be a different story. After having no special sessions from 1991 to 2001 (comprising the entire Bush administration), Governor Perry called three sessions in 2003, one in 2004, two in 2005, one in 2009, and one in 2011. The three sessions of 2003 dealt primarily with redistricting. The 2004 session—a spectacular failure—tried to restructure the state's education financing system. When the 2005 regular session likewise failed in its reform efforts, Governor Perry called the house and senate back into special session twice, producing no significant results. The legislature's repeated refusal underscores an important point: In Texas, the governor can't *make* anyone do anything. However, in 2006, facing a Texas supreme court order to reform funding or face a school system shutdown, the legislature did enact reform; significantly cutting local property taxes while expanding business taxes. In 2009, a special session was required after the legislature failed to complete legislation renewing several major agencies, including the departments of Transportation and Insurance. In 2011, a special session was necessary because of unresolved budget matters.

☐ Message Power

The state constitution requires the governor to address the legislature on the condition of Texas. This "State of the State" address occurs at the beginning of each legislative session. It gives the governor the opportunity to address the entire legislature directly and to make suggestions, presenting his or her legislative agenda. The significance of this power is directly related to the governor's persuasive ability (see the Informal Powers section below).

☐ Veto Power

Studies of gubernatorial powers routinely rank the Texas governor among the lowest. As noted earlier, the mid-1980s study by Mueller placed the Texas chief executive 48th out of the 50 state governorships. The low scores for appointive and budget powers are essentially correct, and only seven governors ranked below Texas in **veto power**.[4] Yet, in the past 60 years, the legislature overrode only one veto by a Texas governor (see the Inside the Federalist System box). Few other states' governors can make such a claim. In fact, the one override came under unique circumstances.

In 1979, during the first legislative session under Republican Bill Clements, Democrats still controlled both the house and senate with more than a two-thirds majority. When the governor vetoed a relatively minor local bill, the Democratic legislature used the opportunity to send two messages. First, despite the change at the governor's mansion, the Democrats were still firmly in control of the legislature. Second, a rookie governor should not interfere with a legislative tradition: local bills, which affect only a limited area, generally do not garner opposition.

Under normal circumstances, obtaining a two-thirds majority to override a veto is a daunting task. Many bills pass the house and senate with overwhelming margins, yet still fall victim to the governor's veto pen. A major difficulty in overriding the governor's veto lies in the structure of the legislative session. Meeting for only 140 days every two years means that a great deal of legislation must be created in a short time-span.

Because of legislative rules, most bills that pass do so toward the end of the session. The Texas constitution gives the governor10 days, excluding Sundays, to decide whether to veto a bill, sign it, or let it become law without his or her signature. If that time frame extends beyond the end of the session, the governor may hold the bill for an additional 20 days. Unlike the Louisiana Legislature, which can call itself into session for the sole purpose of overriding a veto, the Texas Legislature cannot override a **post-adjournment veto**. Such vetoes are absolute. The great majority of bills are passed within the last two weeks of the session, so this enables the governor to kill most legislation with which he or she disagrees.

In 2011, Governor Perry used the post-adjournment veto to kill HB 1768, a measure that would have allowed county regulation of roadside vendors in unincorporated areas. He vetoed the bill despite the fact that it passed overwhelmingly—141:1 in the house and 30:1 in the senate. Nonetheless, Perry was able to stop the legislation by holding his veto until after the legislature had left Austin.

The governor can often accomplish more with the threat of the veto than with the actual use of it. The fact is that, under normal circumstances, few bills are vetoed. In 1999, for instance, fewer than 2 percent of the bills that passed the

veto power
The ability of the governor to strike down legislation, subject to override.

post-adjournment veto
A veto administered after the legislature has adjourned; in Texas, it cannot be overridden.

8.1

8.2

8.3

8.4

8.5

8.6

8.7

8.1

8.2

8.3

8.4

8.5

8.6

8.7

legislature were vetoed. The rest became law. Nonetheless, legislators know that the governor has almost absolute power to kill a bill. They also realize that because of biennial sessions, a dead bill stays dead for two years. (The governor will not allow a bill that he or she opposes to be considered in special session.) Therefore, if the governor expresses opposition to provisions of a bill, the sponsors of that bill are likely to attempt a compromise. Because of this, and because the governor wants to maintain cordial relations with the legislature so that his or her agenda will be given proper consideration, the overwhelming majority of bills that pass are signed into law.

The year 2001 was an entirely different story. In his first year in office, Rick Perry vetoed 82 of the 1,600 bills passed by the legislature in what became known as the Father's Day Massacre. Eighty of the 82 were applied on the third Sunday in June, after the legislature had adjourned. More than 5 percent of the legislature's bills were killed by the governor's pen. It was not, however, the *number* of vetoes that was remarkable; that percentage isn't that much higher than the historical norm (1999 was unusual for the low percentage of vetoes issued). It was the *manner* in which Perry went about killing the legislation.

Normally, Texas governors indicate what they are going to veto. Perry, however, killed numerous bills that legislators thought he was going to sign, infuriating many, including several within his own party. Major fence-mending was needed as the former rancher entered his first full-term in office. Perry vetoed 48 of 1,384 bills passed in 2003, only 19 of 1,389 in 2005, 51 of 1,481 in 2007, 34 of 1,459 in 2009, and 25 of 1,379 in 2011.[5]

In 1995, Governor Bush showed that he knew how to use gubernatorial power despite the fact that he was new to political office. One of the cornerstones of his legislative program was welfare reform. Among the items that Bush considered vital were limits on the time a person could spend on welfare and a freeze-out period that would keep applicants from reapplying for a specified period of time. The bill that entered the conference committee did not meet his standards regarding a freeze-out, so he let it be known that he would veto it unless the three-year exclusionary period was lengthened. He would either call the legislature into special session in order to pass an acceptable welfare reform bill or use his executive power to petition the federal government to grant Texas a waiver, so that it could impose stricter rules on a trial basis. One opponent of the freeze-out ended up supporting it in conference committee, pointing out that welfare reform might become even more restrictive in a special session or under a federal government waiver. He acknowledged that Bush had managed a victory on the issue by threatening to veto the bill.[6]

In 1991, Ann Richards wielded power in a unique way when she decided not to veto a controversial bill. The legislature had passed a redistricting bill favored by Democrats in the Texas senate. In most cases, a Democratic governor would be happy to sign such a measure, but representatives of many minority interest groups believed the bill was unfair to minority voters, who had been a big part of Richards's 1990 electoral victory. They pressured her to veto. Senate Democrats let it be known that a veto would derail the advancement of her future legislative initiatives. Richards's solution was to let the bill become law without her signature—if a Texas governor does nothing with a bill, it becomes law. As a result, she could tell minority groups that she sympathized with their argument and therefore refused to sign the bill, yet still give Senate Democrats the redistricting plan they wanted.

In 2007, there was a notable increase in filing statements attached to bills that passed without Governor Perry's signature. All 20 bills that passed without the governor's affirmation included his specific objections or constitutional concerns. Because of the governor's lack of executive power, it would be difficult for him to use these statements as a basis for thwarting implementation of policy. In 2011, Perry attached such statements to only 4 of the 27 bills that became law in this manner. Perry was much more likely than his predecessors to allow a bill to become law without taking action.

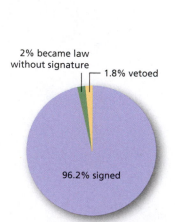

2% became law
without signature

1.8% vetoed

96.2% signed

Note: the overwhelming number of bills passed by the legislature become law without interference from the governor.

FIGURE 8.1 The Governor's Vetoes, 2011.

8.1
8.2
8.3
8.4
8.5
8.6
8.7

Inside the Federalist System

Comparative Power of the Veto

Although the Texas governor is generally regarded as a weak executive, one area where he or she has more power than almost any other chief executive—especially the president—is veto power. Because of the biennial structure of Texas legislative sessions and the post-adjournment veto, the governor's negative is almost impossible to override. Since the Spring of 1945, only 1 out of 1,173 vetoes have been overridden by the Texas Legislature. During that same period, 51 out of 482 presidential vetoes have been overridden.

From a policy perspective, this has important consequences. The legislature understands that the governor can singlehandedly kill a bill. They cannot cut the governor out of the process and they have to take his perspective into consideration. Granted, the governor doesn't have a strong opinion about the majority of bills that come before the legislature, but on those bills where he does have a stake, he is an important player. In fact, in those situations, the governor has equal power with the house and senate as to whether a bill passes, and constant communication with the governor on these issues has a significant impact on the policy that emerges from the process.

Over the last few sessions, some legislators have considered amending the constitution to allow post-adjournment bills to be overridden. This would dramatically change the balance of power and significantly weaken the governor in the legislative process. Given that most bills pass both houses with more than a two-thirds majority, overriding would not be difficult in most situations. Although a majority of experts on Texas politics, including the authors of this text, believe that the ability to override post-adjournment vetoes would require amendment, some members of the legislature believe the override could be implemented through a reinterpretation of house and senate rules. Constitutional change, even though it begins with the legislature, would be difficult to achieve, as such a fundamental shift in procedure would garner resistance in a conservative body.

1. How can the governor effectively use the knowledge that the veto is almost impossible to override?

2. Should the legislature be granted the power to override post-adjournment vetoes?

☐ Line Item Veto Power

In addition to a standard veto, the governor has a **line item veto**. This allows him or her to veto one or more items in the appropriations bill while signing the rest into law. Although it technically has the authority, the legislature has not overridden a line item veto in state history. Appropriations bills are always passed at the end of the session, allowing the governor to hold the bill past the legislature's adjournment and issue a post-adjournment veto, which cannot be overridden. This gives the governor an extraordinary amount of negotiating power on spending bills. The Texas governor does not, however, have a reduction veto, which would allow him or her to reduce an appropriations item without eliminating it. In those states that allow the governor to reduce a spending item without vetoing it, the legislature usually has the opportunity to override the reduction and reinstate the original spending figure.

Generally, the line item veto is used as incremental budget management—that is, the governor cuts a small percentage of overall state spending. In 2005, however, Perry vetoed the entire $33.6 billion public education budget, forcing the legislature into special session with orders to reform education finance so that schools could open in the fall. Under attack in some quarters for a perceived lack of leadership, Perry took a bold step to put himself at the center of the political storm. In fact, the action ended up being more show than substance as the governor signed a reintroduced version of the $33.6 billion budget when significant education reform failed to materialize. Perry did, however, make legitimate cuts of about a half a billion dollars to the $139 billion document. In 2007, Perry line-item-vetoed $647 million, including $153 million for community college worker health insurance—funding that was later restored through a compromise with the Legislative Budget Board. Prior use of the line item veto has been more typical. In 2003, Perry vetoed about $79 million from the final budget; in 2001, he used the line item veto for a little more than half a billion dollars from the $113.8 billion biennium budget. Most of the axed items were appropriations for bills that either failed to pass or were vetoed. They had to be included in the budget because their fate was unclear when the final appropriations bill was put

line item veto
The governor's ability to delete individual items in the appropriations bill.

clemency power

Power to pardon, commute, or parole.

8.1

8.2

8.3

8.4

8.5

8.6

8.7

together. Over the past several sessions, most such vetoes have been of items that were dead anyway, so the action is usually more of a housekeeping measure than a substantive political action. In 2009 and 2011, none of Perry's legislative vetoes were substantive, as all were either of bills that failed to pass or bills that the governor vetoed.

☐ Budget Creation Power

In 42 states, the governor has full responsibility for drafting the budget. Texas is one of only eight states in which the governor shares this power with the legislature. In practice, not much sharing occurs. The Legislative Budget Board controls the budget process in Texas. In fact, the legislature pays no attention to the governor's budget at all. In 2003, Governor Perry submitted a budget containing nothing but zeros. Although he caught significant flak from the media, his broader point was that the legislature should start with a blank slate while preparing the state's appropriations bill. The house and senate paid no attention.

This lack of budgetary power contributes significantly to the governor's weakness, at least in comparison to his counterparts in other states. The governor can transfer or withhold funds from an agency only on approval by the LBB. Legislation in 1991 further weakened the executive's budgetary authority by allowing the LBB to initiate such changes, then seek approval from the governor. This allowed legislators to ignore the governor during initial deliberations on such transfers or withholding. Remember, however, that the line item veto helps the governor retain a significant role in spending decisions.

Judicial Powers

8.4 Explain the judicial and clemency powers of the governor.

☐ Appointment Power

Although the Texas constitution requires the popular election of state judges, the governor nonetheless has a significant role in shaping the judiciary. Because the governor appoints judges to fill vacancies at the district level or above, almost half of Texas judges were originally appointed. Like all other appointments, the senate must approve the governor's nominee by at least a two-thirds concurrence.

☐ Clemency Power

The **clemency powers** of the Texas governor are quite restricted. Unlike the chief executive in many states, the governor of Texas has no independent power to pardon or parole.

The governor can make recommendations to the Board of Pardons and Paroles and can approve or reject their recommendations of pardon or sentence reduction. A 1934 constitutional amendment, which we discuss in the Constitution box, stripped the governor of independent power. This amendment came in the wake of a scandal. During Miriam Ferguson's term as governor, the easiest way to win a loved one's freedom was to visit Ferguson's husband, Jim, with cash in hand (see Texas Mosaic: James E. Ferguson). Removing pardoning powers from the governor lessened the chance that the chief executive would be directly involved in graft or corruption.

The only independent clemency power that the governor possesses is the ability to grant a 30-day reprieve in a death penalty case. In today's law-and-order society, the reprieve is seldom granted. Politicians cannot afford to appear soft on crime if they wish to win reelection. One notable case of a granted reprieve took place in 1979 when Governor Clements issued a stay for Randall Dale Adams. Adams, who sat for years on death row, was later released from prison when further evidence exonerated him. The governor can issue only one such reprieve per prisoner. In 1993, after Ann Richards issued a stay in the Leonel Herrera case, Herrera was rescheduled for execution. With no further reprieves possible, the prisoner was put to death.

Informal Powers

8.1

8.2

8.3

8.4

8.5

8.6

8.7

8.5 Describe the governor's informal powers.

Because of limited formal powers granted by the constitution or state law, the governor often relies on **informal powers** to affect government operations. These powers lie outside the constitutional mandate of the office. Nonetheless, they are an important part of the total arsenal of weapons that the governor has at his or her disposal.

informal powers
Powers not specifically granted in the constitution or statutes.

Governor Rick Perry fires a six-shooter during the opening ceremonies for the Texas 500 NASCAR event. The event gave Perry an opportunity to reinforce his image as a Texan with the boots, gun and stock car setting, thus strengthening the informal powers associated with the office. In 2013, the race was renamed "The NRA 500."

8.1

8.2

8.3

8.4

8.5

8.6

8.7

The Texas Constitution

A Closer Look

Compared to the president, who has unlimited power to pardon those accused of federal offenses, the governor's clemency powers are rather limited. The primary reason for the limits, of course, was the perceived abuses that occurred during the tenures of James E. and Miriam Ferguson. The governor is encumbered with a Board of Pardons and Paroles, as provided for below.

Article IV

Sec. 11. Board of Pardons and Paroles; Parole Laws; Reprieves, Commutations, and Pardons; Remission of Fines and Forfeitures.

(a) The Legislature shall by law establish a Board of Pardons and Paroles and shall require it to keep record of its actions and the reasons for its actions. The Legislature shall have authority to enact parole laws and laws that require or permit courts to inform juries about the effect of good conduct time and eligibility for parole or mandatory supervision on the period of incarceration served by a defendant convicted of a criminal offense.

(b) In all criminal cases, except treason and impeachment, the Governor shall have power, after conviction, on the written signed recommendation and advice of the Board of Pardons and Paroles, or a majority thereof, to grant reprieves and commutations of punishment and pardons; and under such rules as the Legislature may prescribe, and upon the written recommendation and advice of a majority of the Board of Pardons and Paroles, he shall have the power to remit fines and forfeitures. The Governor shall have the power to grant one reprieve in any capital case for a period not to exceed thirty (30) days; and he shall have power to revoke conditional pardons. With the advice and consent of the Legislature, he may grant reprieves, commutations of punishment and pardons in cases of treason.

1. Should the governor have independent clemency powers?

2. Does clemency undermine the judicial process?

☐ Partisan Leader

The governor is the leader of his or her political party. It is the governor's responsibility, as the party's most visible member, to articulate political positions. In effect, and with apologies to the state chairs, the governor speaks for the party. The governor can introduce a legislative package that reflects the values of his or her party. He or she must be able to convince members to vote the party line on key votes. Concurrently, the governor must be able to work with members of the opposition party and not appear to be so partisan as to alienate the public. While some Republicans criticized Bush for not being partisan enough, the governor managed to forge an effective relationship with Democratic leaders. Governors do not always take the partisan role as seriously as do other party members. When asked about the controversial Republican state platform during the 1994 campaign, Bush claimed he had not even read it. Perry's election in 2002 marked the first time since Reconstruction that the Republicans won both the governorship and control of both houses of the legislature.

☐ Persuasive Power

Most people, both in and out of Texas, see the governor as the state's leader. This perception allows the governor to achieve goals in areas that may be beyond the office's constitutional or statutory reach. As a representative of Texas, the governor strives to project a positive image for the state. Former Governor Richards effectively used the platform of her office to induce businesses to move to Texas, as we discuss in the nearby Texas Mosaic on her tenure. In a weak governor system, acting as an advocate for the state is one of the most valuable roles the governor can assume.

8.1

8.2

8.3

8.4

8.5

8.6

8.7

Texas ★ Mosaic

Two for the Price of One:
James E. Ferguson

James E. "Pa" Ferguson rose from humble beginnings to be twice elected governor of Texas. Despite his sparse formal education, Ferguson was both a lawyer and a bank president before entering politics in 1914. A political unknown, he vaulted to the governor's office through his astute handling of the hot topic of Prohibition: He refused to take a side. He argued that Texans had been hung up on the wet/dry issue long enough and were tired of it, and that there were other, more important issues that the state needed to address.

Pa was something of a populist, advocating and signing into law a provision that limited the rent landowners could charge tenant farmers. The law made him popular with poor Texans, although it would ultimately be overturned by the Texas supreme court. Ferguson also worked to improve the education system and oversaw the creation of the state highway department. His first term was a legislative success.

Ferguson's second term was not as smooth. In June 1917, after serious quarrels with the faculty and administration of the University of Texas at Austin, Ferguson line-item-vetoed the entire appropriation for the school. Although a technicality created by the attorney general kept the university open, Ferguson had committed a political blunder. Antagonizing the University of Texas alumni association is not exactly a swift political move. Repercussions followed quickly.

Texas Speaker of the house Franklin Fuller called a special session of the Texas Legislature in order to consider the impeachment of Ferguson. This, of course, was not a legal action, as only the governor can call a special session. Having just been indicted on criminal charges for the misappropriation of state funds, Ferguson took the bizarre step of endorsing the session,

making it legal. Had he not given his approval, he could not have been impeached.

The house impeached Ferguson on 21 charges. The senate found him guilty on 10, removed him from the governorship, and barred him from holding office again. The day before he was removed, Pa resigned, claiming this action enabled him to run again. He did attempt to run in 1918, but was handily defeated by William Hobby in the Democratic primary.

The Hobby defeat did not mark the end of Pa Ferguson in Texas politics. Although initially an opponent of women's suffrage, Ferguson took advantage of the newly enfranchised gender by running his wife, Miriam "Ma" Ferguson, for governor in 1924. Working as a team, the Fergusons campaigned against the Ku Klux Klan, which controlled Texas politics at the time. Miriam won, becoming the first woman governor of Texas, and Jim set up office in the Capitol. Clearly the power behind the throne, Pa established policy and made a bit of money on the side as he did his best to ease prison overcrowding.

Ma Ferguson was defeated in her 1926 reelection bid. In 1932, however, as the Great Depression spread through the state, Miriam was elected again. When she—or he—chose not to seek reelection in 1934, the Ferguson era finally came to an end.

Sources: Rupert N. Richardson, Adrian Anderson, and Ernest Wallace, *Texas: The Lone Star State* (Englewood Cliffs, NJ: Prentice Hall, 1993). *Seymour v. Conner, Texas: A History* (Arlington Heights, IL: Harlan Davidson, 1971).

1. **What do you think was the legacy of the Fergusons?**

2. **Was Ma Ferguson as significant a figure as Ann Richards?**

More than any other state official, the governor can influence public opinion. The governor's speeches are more likely to receive media coverage. The governor has access to a statewide network of newspapers and television stations. Through effective manipulation of the media, a governor can bring pressure on both the legislature and other members of the executive branch. Television and the Internet give contemporary Texas governors an advantage that their predecessors did not have: the ability to go into the living room of virtually every home in the state. Texas governors have failed to exploit this power to its full advantage, however. They have seldom made effective use of the media in order to prod the legislature into action. Rather, most seem to prefer a hands-on approach to legislative influence. Governor Perry, more media savvy than most, was the first Texas governor to have a blog, Twitter, and Facebook presence.

Governor Bush used his personality to inject himself into the governmental process. Through frequent meetings with legislators, he tried to maintain a presence within the system. By the end of his first legislative session, almost all members of the Texas house and senate had visited the governor's mansion for lunch. Even the state Supreme Court justices had dined with the governor. Bush displayed a willingness to listen to those with more governmental experience. As a result, he integrated himself into the legislative process and earned favorable reviews from state leaders, even those within the opposing party.

8.1

8.2

8.3

8.4

8.5

8.6

8.7

Interacting with a cross section of legislative members helps ensure that the governor does not become isolated. All too often, chief executives at both the state and national level surround themselves with like-minded individuals—this happened with Bush during his presidency. If all the governor's closest advisers share common views, he or she can become isolated from dissenting opinion. This can lead to a policy mistake that would have appeared obvious to outsiders.

As governor, Bush avoided such problems by maintaining connections that transcend both political ties and branches of government. His successor, Rick Perry, has had problems getting along even with members of his own party. He did not maintain the close legislative ties that Bush had created, and actions like the Father's Day Massacre further strained legislative relations. Despite this tension, he is the longest serving governor in state history.

Perry has benefited from being a good campaigner, from maintaining ground game and networking strategies that are quite similar to those deployed by President Obama, and, at least until his abortive run for the White House in 2012, a certain amount of political luck. His network effectively delivers votes. In 2002, it allowed him to retain the office despite being outspent 3 to 1. In 2006, with his popularity flagging a bit, Perry drew not only Democratic and Libertarian opposition, but two well-known Texans, Carole Keeton Strayhorn and Kinky Friedman, gained access to the ballot as well. The divided opposition allowed Perry to capture the office with less than 40 percent of the vote. In 2010, Perry's real challenge was in the Republican primary. There was a decidedly anti-Washington sentiment in Texas—even more so than usual—and Perry used that to effectively run against Washington, as his opponent was long-time U.S. Senator Kay Bailey Hutchison.

☐ Congressional Liaison

Governors Richards and Bush actively lobbied Congress for programs that benefited Texas. Richards worked to ensure that the state would receive proper reimbursement after the cancellation of the Super Collider project, which would have been the world's most powerful particle accelerator had Congress not cancelled funding. Often, she worked with Republican Senator Kay Bailey Hutchison in lobbying for fairness in federal funding for Texas. Likewise, Bush used the power of the governor's office to plead with Congress for a just allocation of Medicaid money. Both governors realized that the visibility of their office entitled them to speak on Texas's behalf regarding state interests. Governors have a unique opportunity to influence members of the U.S. House and Senate, especially those from their home state. Perry, with his ideological opposition to big government, has been more hostile toward Washington. On more than one occasion, such as when he refused over half a billion dollars in expanded unemployment benefits, he declined participation in programs that would have brought significant federal matching funds because he feared long-term state commitment.

☐ International Relations

With the growing importance of international trade to the Texas economy, the governor also plays an important role in international relations, especially with Latin America in general and Mexico in particular. Governors Bush and Perry have both worked to improve the relationship with our neighbor to the south. Implementation of the North American Free Trade Agreement (NAFTA) has pushed trade to the forefront of relations between Texas and Mexico, but the state and nation have also worked closely on water resource questions and other border issues. Although the relationship is much friendlier than it was a decade ago, points of tension remain. In late summer 2002, for example, President Vicente Fox canceled a trip to meet with Bush at the "Texas White House" to protest Perry's refusal to stop the execution of a Mexican citizen convicted of capital murder. No permanent damage occurred, however, as Fox almost immediately scheduled a meeting with Perry shortly thereafter. Perry also stood in opposition to those in his party who wanted to build a wall along the entire border between Texas and Mexico, believing that the proposal was impractical and unworkable. It is important to

8.1
8.2
8.3
8.4
8.5
8.6
8.7

Texas ★ Mosaic

Increasing Gender Diversity:
Ann Richards

For years, the executive branch of Texas government was a males-only club. Although Miriam "Ma" Ferguson held the office, she did not hold the power. Ann Richards helped bring down the ceiling that blocked women from holding some of the highest offices in the state.

After six years as a Travis County commissioner, Richards ran for state treasurer. During her two terms she did much to modernize the office. She shortened the time between the receipt of funds and their deposit in interest-bearing accounts, began the process of tax flow analysis for the state, and ensured that more state funds were deposited in interest-bearing accounts. Richards also introduced computerization, a big step in allowing for the treasury's eventual merger into the comptroller's office.

In 1990, Richards ran for governor. Her steady, enthusiastic campaign, although underfunded in relation to Republican opponent Clayton Williams, managed to capture a close race. Richards won because, unlike Williams, she made few mistakes along the way. An experienced campaigner, she took advantage of the Republican's political naïveté. Williams had a practice of saying the wrong things to the press at the wrong time. His statements made great headlines, but they helped Richards look like the more savvy and stable candidate.

As governor, Richards worked to bring businesses to Texas. She was so successful that the state of California began to run anti-Texas ads in nationwide business magazines. Although less successful in helping the state preserve the federally funded Super Collider project, she did manage a financial settlement on terms favorable to Texas.

Richards's legislative efforts were less productive. She successfully blocked both limitations on abortion rights and a bill allowing Texans to carry concealed weapons, but the former schoolteacher was unable to pass comprehensive education reform. She did manage to ram through a funding equalization bill that passed state supreme court scrutiny, but it won her few friends among voters who had defeated a similar proposal in a statewide vote less than three months before.

Richards, who lost her reelection bid in 1994, appointed more minorities and women to state boards and commissions than any other governor. While her

Governor Ann Richards, like Perry, knew how to take advantage of a photo opportunity. Such a stunt might seem frivolous, but anything that helps the governor connect with voters or seem like a 'real' person can translate into political power, which makes such events a necessity of the position, especially given the office's limited formal powers.

rhetoric often sounded liberal, she would become the first governor in years to sign a budget without a tax increase. She believed that the Texas government could be responsive, efficient, and inclusive. Richards passed away in September 2006.

1. What do you believe was the most significant aspect of Richards's service as governor?

2. How do Richards's accomplishments underscore the relative weakness of the office?

realize that because of Texas's special relationship with Mexico, the job of the governor has evolved to include informal ambassador as well.

☐ Leadership Style

In Texas, a governor's approach to his job has a significant impact on how much power he wields. In the past, some governors have approached the office in a manner consistent with the wishes of the creators of the Texas constitution. They chose not to

staff
The governor's aides; not subject to legislative approval.

involve themselves heavily in day-to-day operations. As a result, their impact on government was minimal. During Bill Clements's second term, for example, the governor failed to fill hundreds of vacancies on boards and commissions. Dolph Briscoe ran the governor's office like it was a part-time job he did not really need. He seemed more interested in playing the role of gentleman rancher.

In contrast, governors Richards and Bush threw themselves into the political fray. Richards played the part of the political veteran, an insider who had all the answers. She was an expert on Texas government and let those around her know it. She was not afraid to rub political opponents, or allies, the wrong way. Bush, on the other hand, first played on the perception that he was a newcomer to Austin, soliciting advice and opinions. More congenial in the role than Richards, he took care not to criticize members of the opposition party openly, and he attempted to build consensus. It was a quality Bush maintained through his second term and into his run for the White House. His bipartisan approach was not as easy to maintain once he arrived in Washington.

Another difference between Richards and Bush is that Richards involved herself in more policy decisions. Bush, during his first legislative session, concentrated on four key issues: welfare reform, juvenile justice reform, education reform, and tort reform. The legislature passed measures acceptable to Bush on each of these issues, but Bush realized that he would expend too much political capital fighting every fight. Instead, he concentrated on battles he either knew he could win or believed were of fundamental importance. On other issues he let his opinion be known. Rather than creating political showdowns over relatively minor bills, he knew he could issue a post-adjournment veto to stop those that he opposed. The important common denominator between the leadership styles of these two successful governors is that each created a distinct, comfortable working environment and stuck to it.

Perry ascended to the office after Bush became president. Although he had been elected as lieutenant governor in 1998, Perry had neither the benefits nor the limitations of having established an agenda while running for governor. This is part of what led to tensions with the legislature; no one was sure where the new governor stood on issues, and Perry wasn't quick to stake out his stands. The Father's Day Massacre strained relations even more. However, when running for the office on his own, Perry put forth an agenda that would set the course for the 2003 term, giving himself a set of goals and his opponents a set of targets. Hit by a huge budgetary shortfall that was not of his making but rather was a result of a nationwide recession and economic downturn, the new Republican leadership experienced a very tough 2003 session. Perry's endorsement of Speaker of the house Tom Craddick's and U.S. Congressman Tom DeLay's efforts for a midcensus redistricting of Texas congressional seats damaged the office's bipartisan perception. In both the 2004 and 2005 sessions, which were respectively called and regular sessions, Perry failed to shepherd through an education finance reform package, leading to the 2005 special sessions, which failed just as miserably. However, as we discussed earlier in this chapter, education finance reform finally passed in 2006. Perry's successful 2010 election bid focused on his "antigovernment" leanings, which he parlayed into his abortive run for the presidency in 2012.

The Governor's Staff

8.6 Illustrate the impact of the governor's staff.

 competent **staff** is critical to effective governing. In the early 1990s, the governor's staff in Texas grew to be among the largest in the nation. In 1994, and again in the early days of the Bush administration, the office was downsized. Some functions were transferred from the governor's office to executive departments and agencies and others were eliminated. Examples of

8.1

8.2

8.3

8.4

8.5

8.6

8.7

transferred programs include Headstart, which was moved to the Health and Human Services Commission; and the governor's energy office, which now resides in the General Services Commission. Nonetheless, the staff of about 270 remains large enough to serve the governor's needs effectively, giving him or her a substantial advantage over counterparts in other states. About half of this staff works directly for the governor; the other half works for trusteed offices such as the Texas Film Commission and the Texas Enterprise Fund.[7] Many governors' offices are significantly understaffed.

The governor's office is divided into several separate entities, such as the Administrative Office, the Criminal Justice Division, and the Policy Office. Staff members are chosen by the governor and serve at the governor's discretion. Unlike other gubernatorial appointments, no legislative approval is necessary. The staff is accountable to the governor alone and must look after his or her best interests as they give advice.

In addition to carrying out the governor's policies, staff members are often involved in intergovernmental relations. They work with national or local levels

TABLE 8.2 TEXAS GOVERNORS SINCE 1899

Joseph D. Sayers	Jan. 1899–Jan. 1903
S. W. T. Lanham	Jan. 1903–Jan. 1907
Thomas Mitchell Campbell	Jan. 1907–Jan. 1911
Oscar Branch Colquitt	Jan. 1911–Jan. 1915
James E. Ferguson[a]	Jan. 1915–Aug. 1917
William Pettus Hobby	Aug. 1917–Jan. 1921
Pat Morris Neff	Jan. 1921–Jan. 1925
Miriam A. Ferguson	Jan. 1925–Jan. 1927
Dan Moody	Jan. 1927–Jan. 1931
Ross S. Sterling	Jan. 1931–Jan. 1933
Miriam A. Ferguson	Jan. 1933–Jan. 1935
James V. Allred	Jan. 1935–Jan. 1939
W. Lee O'Daniel[b]	Jan. 1939–Aug. 1941
Coke R. Stevenson	Aug. 1941–Jan. 1947
Beauford H. Jester[c]	Jan. 1947–July 1949
Allan Shivers	July 1949–Jan. 1957
Price Daniel	Jan. 1957–Jan. 1963
John Connally	Jan. 1963–Jan. 1969
Preston Smith	Jan. 1969–Jan. 1973
Dolph Briscoe	Jan. 1973–Jan. 1979
William P. Clements	Jan. 1979–Jan. 1983
Mark White	Jan. 1983–Jan. 1987
William P. Clements	Jan. 1987–Jan. 1991
Ann W. Richards	Jan. 1991–Jan. 1995
George W. Bush[d]	Jan. 1995–Dec. 2000
Rick Perry	Dec. 2000–

Source: Texas Almanac, 2006–07 (Dallas, TX: Dallas Morning News, 2006), pp. 423–424.
[a]Impeached and resigned.
[b]Resigned from office to join U.S. Senate.
[c]Died in office.
[d]Resigned from office to become president of the United States.

8.1

8.2

8.3

8.4

8.5

8.6

8.7

of government to aid in the implementation of laws and policies. One of the most important offices within the governor's staff is the Legislative Office. These staff members are, in effect, the governor's lobbyists. They present the governor's views and advocate his or her positions to the legislature. They help develop policy initiatives.

The governor has little time to take broad ideas, such as reforming welfare policy, and turn them into concrete programs. Staff help decide what specific measures the proposals should contain. In addition, the staff advises the governor on how to get the most out of the legislative process, helping to bring proposals forward when they are most likely to pass.

Over the course of a four-year term, the governor will make about 3,000 appointments to various boards, commissions, and judicial vacancies. No individual can know the best potential appointee for each position, so an able staff is invaluable. Two sections of the governor's staff, the Office of Governmental Appointments and the Policy Office, share primary responsibility for assisting with appointments. The Office of Governmental Appointments also works as a liaison between the governor and the agencies, boards, and commissions. Members of the Policy Office bear the responsibility of ensuring that the governor's policies are implemented.[8]

Options for Reform

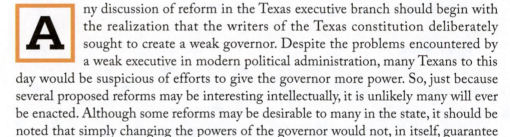

8.7 Determine how reform might impact the governor's office.

Any discussion of reform in the Texas executive branch should begin with the realization that the writers of the Texas constitution deliberately sought to create a weak governor. Despite the problems encountered by a weak executive in modern political administration, many Texans to this day would be suspicious of efforts to give the governor more power. So, just because several proposed reforms may be interesting intellectually, it is unlikely many will ever be enacted. Although some reforms may be desirable to many in the state, it should be noted that simply changing the powers of the governor would not, in itself, guarantee better government.

One way to increase the governor's power would be to give him or her removal power over executive department appointees. Likewise, board terms should conform to the governor's term, allowing former appointees to remain on the job only until the new governor appoints new people. In this way, board members are directly accountable to the governor, and the voters can justifiably hold the governor responsible when board members prove either incompetent or at odds with public opinion.

The plural executive could be changed to a cabinet form of government. The governor could appoint the attorney general, comptroller, and other executive offices with policy-making powers. With these offices serving at the governor's pleasure, a team concept would develop in the executive branch. Infighting would be reduced (though not eliminated). The endless squabbles occurring within any presidential administration in Washington, as an example, mean that Politics, among other things, Happens.

Another option to increase the governor's power would be to return budget preparation authority to the governor. This is the norm in most states. In Texas, however, the Legislative Budget Board's handling of the budget during the past several years has been so astute that such a change makes little sense simply in order to give the governor more power.

The reforms suggested here, no doubt, would strengthen the governor. More importantly, they would increase accountability while simultaneously giving the governor power to make government operate more effectively. It would give the governor the tools to meet the expectations placed on the chief executive by the voters.

8.1
8.2
8.3
8.4
8.5
8.6
8.7

Review the Chapter

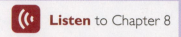

Listen to Chapter 8

Qualifications, Term, and Salary

8.1 Outline the qualifications to hold the office of governor.

In order to be governor of Texas, a person must be a Texas resident for at least five years, a registered voter, and at least 30 years of age.

Executive Powers

8.2 Describe the most significant powers possessed by the governor while acting as chief executive.

The governor appoints thousands of members to boards and commission during a single term in office. He exercises limited military and law enforcement powers.

Legislative Powers

8.3 Characterize the governor's integral role in the legislative process.

The governor's veto power is significant because it is so difficult to override. Since the legislature understands that the veto is all but absolute, the legislature has a vested interest in negotiating with the governor. Often the threat to veto is more important than the actual use of the veto. The governor's line item veto may be even more significant, as it has never been overridden. The governor has sole power to call the legislature into special session.

Judicial Powers

8.4 Explain the judicial and clemency powers of the governor.

The governor appoints judges to fill vacancies at the district court level and above. Unlike most governors, the Texas chief executive does not possess the independent power to pardon; he shares it with the Board of Pardons and Paroles. The governor can independently grant a 30-day stay of execution.

Informal Powers

8.5 Describe the governor's informal powers.

The governor is the de facto leader of his or her political party. In order to be successful, a governor must effectively use the power of persuasion. An ability to interact with Congress and the administration in Washington is also helpful. Because of our border with Mexico, the governor also engages in international relations.

The Governor's Staff

8.6 Illustrate the impact of the governor's staff.

The governor's staff facilitates relations between the governor and the legislature. They also work with both national and local government officials on policy implementation. It would be impossible for the governor to effectively fill board, commission, and judicial vacancies without staff expertise.

Options for Reform

8.7 Determine how reform might impact the governor's office.

Several reforms could increase the power of the governor. If board terms were concurrent with the governor's term, or if the governor could appoint a cabinet, the office would exercise more control over the executive branch. Given Texas's traditional fear of concentrated power, such reforms are unlikely to occur.

Learn the Terms

Study and **Review** the **Flashcards**

clemency power, p. 202
formal powers, p. 195
governor, p. 194
informal powers, p. 203

line item veto, p. 201
martial law, p. 197
overlapping terms, p. 196
post-adjournment veto, p. 199

senatorial courtesy, p. 196
staff, p. 208
veto power, p. 199

Test Yourself

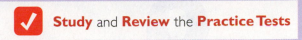

8.1 Outline the qualifications to hold the office of governor.

Which is not a requirement to be governor of Texas?

a. be at least 30
b. be born in the state
c. be a resident
d. be registered to vote
e. be a citizen

8.2 Describe the most significant powers possessed by the governor while acting as chief executive.

Regarding boards and commission appointments, the governor can

a. appoint members independently.
b. remove his or her own appointees with two-thirds senate approval.
c. remove a previous governor's appointees with two-thirds senate approval.
d. independently appoint board members, but must have senate approval for commissioners.
e. independently appoint commissioners but must have senate approval for board members.

8.3 Characterize the governor's integral role in the legislative process.

The most significant aspect of veto power is that

a. the threat of a veto can influence legislation.
b. the veto is absolute.
c. the governor can veto portions of nonappropriations bills.
d. it is automatically applied to any bill the governor does not sign.
e. no veto has ever been overridden.

8.4 Explain the judicial and clemency powers of the governor.

In Texas, the governor appoints

a. all judges.
b. all appellate judges.
c. Supreme Court justices only.
d. district court and higher judges in the case of a vacancy.
e. all courts above justice of the peace in the case of a vacancy.

8.5 Describe the governor's informal powers.

Which is an informal power of the governor?

a. veto
b. session calling
c. stay of execution
d. pardon
e. persuasion

8.6 Characterize the impact of the governor's staff.

The governor's staff

a. must be approved by the senate.
b. must be approved by the house and senate.
c. is appointed by the Office of Civil Servants.
d. helps the governor interact with the legislature.
e. deals exclusively with board and commission appointments.

8.7 Determine how reform might impact the governor's office.

The reforms for the governor's office suggested in this chapter

a. have been approved by the legislature.
b. have been approved by the voters.
c. are unlikely to be incorporated.
d. were rejected by the voters in 2011.
e. have been endorsed by legislative leaders.

Explore Further

The governor's home page: http://www.governor.state.tx.us

Barta, Carolyn. *Bill Clements: Texan to His Toenails.* Austin, TX: Eakin Press, 1996.

Beyle, Thad. "Governors: The Middlemen and Women in Our Political System." In *Politics in the American States: A Comparative Analysis* (6th ed.), ed. Virginia Gray and Herbert Jacob. Washington, DC: CQ Press, 1996.

Gantt, Fred, Jr. *The Chief Executive in Texas: A Study in Gubernatorial Leadership.* Austin: University of Texas Press, 1964.

Hendrickson, Kenneth E. *Chief Executives of Texas: From Stephen F. Austin to John B. Connally Jr.* College Station: Texas A & M University Press, 1995.

Morris, Celia. *Storming the Statehouse: Running for Governor with Ann Richards and Dianne Feinstein.* New York: Scribner, 1992.

Tolleson-Rinehart, Sue. *Claytie and the Lady: Ann Richards, Gender, and Politics in Texas.* Austin: University of Texas Press, 1994.

9

The Plural Executive and the Bureaucracy in Texas

Everyone says the state's population is going to double by 2060. And I guess you could say there's enough water. But it's not in the right place.

—*Land Commissioner Jerry Patterson, on the State's Impending Water Crisis*

The governor made it clear that the state's water problems would require a long-term solution. There was no doubt, he said, that conservation and water management were keys to solving the water shortage and that any serious efforts would involve both federal and state agencies working together. "A permanent solution must be found," said Governor Allan Shivers,[1] some 60 years ago. After

9.1	9.2	9.3	9.4	9.5
Differentiate between cabinet and plural executive forms of government.	Explain the roles of the lieutenant governor, attorney general, comptroller, land commissioner and commissioner of agriculture.	Determine how the bureaucracy impacts the operation of state government.	Differentiate among the functions of various types of boards and commissions.	Describe the purpose and process of the Sunset Advisory Commission.

Water is one of the state's biggest challenges in the 21st Century. During the height of the 2011 drought, Texas Parks and Wildlife biologist Jeff Bonner looks out at the drying bed of what should have been the Canadian River, in Amarillo. Reliable water resources are a necessity for continued economic progress.

cabinet
A form of government whereby the chief executive appoints other major executive department heads.

plural executive
A political system whereby major executive officers are elected independent of the governor.

decades of planning, building, legislating, and governing, water may well be the most important issue facing the state in the coming years. As we explore the plural executive and the state's bureaucracy, we will keep our focus on how these agencies approach water policy against the larger backdrop of managing the government.

A Deliberate Division of Power

9.1 Differentiate between cabinet and plural executive forms of government.

U nlike the national government's cabinet form of government, where the president appoints the heads of various government departments, Texas has a plural executive, whereby major department heads are independently elected. While this system leads to a certain amount of discord, it adds the benefit of multiple sources of thought as to how to handle the challenges faced by the state. As we consider the plural executive specifically, and the boards and commission that help execute policy in Texas, we will focus on one looming issue in Texas politics: the ability of the state to secure an adequate supply of water over the next 30 years. With the possible exception of Medicaid funding, water supply is the biggest problem facing Texas. While it may be obvious that growth and drought have created a water crisis in the state when it comes to watering lawns, it is important to understand the vital role of water in the production of electricity and the sustainability of Texas economic growth, which has far outstripped that of the nation as a whole. By the beginning of the 2013 legislative session, it was obvious that a broad coalition of Texas leaders had reached at least one consensus: If the "Texas Miracle" is to continue, a reliable and expanding source of water is an integral part of the equation for success. As we explore the plural executive, we will do so from the unifying theme of how to address this monumental challenge.

As the chief executive of the United States, the president selects his or her top department officers—or **cabinet**—in order to help run the nation. (See the Inside the Federalist System box.) At the state level, the cabinet system is also the normal structure. Thirty-nine states have such a form of government.

Texas, however, does not have a cabinet system. Instead, the state has a **plural executive**, whereby the governor, lieutenant governor, attorney general, comptroller, land commissioner, and agriculture commissioner are elected independently, as we illustrate in Figure 9.1. This reflects the state's conservative tradition, which feared the concentration of power in too few hands.

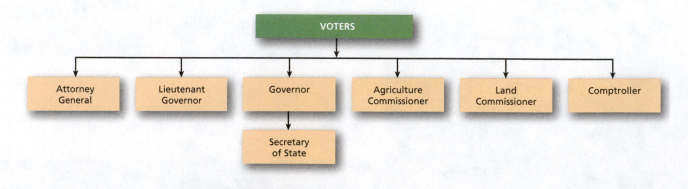

FIGURE 9.1 The Executive Branch Offices.

Inside the Federalist System

United States

One of the most important structural differences between the Texas and U.S. governmental systems is the limited executive power of the Texas governor. Most notably, the president appoints his or her cabinet, while the governor is encumbered with a plural executive. The table on the right shows the disparity of power.

We often think of policy as being made by the legislature or Congress, but executive agencies make rules that have the power of laws. For instance, the Departments of Agriculture at both the state and the national level set agricultural policy in their jurisdictions. Rules concerning worker safety and the use of fertilizer and pesticides are set by the agencies, and these rules have the force of law unless Congress or the legislature overrules them. In Washington, agency and department heads report to the president, which gives the president ultimate responsibility over policy, although he often defers to his appointed officials.

In Texas, since many of the major department heads are elected independently by the voters, the governor has little control over policies set by these agencies. These elected officials are directly involved in creating policy and deciding how much rule-making authority to give the professional staff that works under them. Instead of owing loyalty to the governor, the Texas agriculture commissioner owes loyalty to the constituency who elected him and the contributors who helped finance his campaign. (We are not saying that contributors own the office, but, as we indicated in our earlier discussion of interest groups, contributors garner greater access.) That's not necessarily bad; stakeholders have greater access to policy makers. For instance, both stakeholders and the Texas Department of Agriculture have a vested interest in opening broader markets for the products of Texas farms and ranches. But it also means that the chief executive has little control over the process. Unlike the president, the governor can't fire his agriculture commissioner. Only the voters can fire the Texas agriculture commissioner, and they only get that shot once every four years.

1. Should Texans vote for the offices of the plural executive? Why or why not?

2. How does the plural executive affect the manner in which policy is carried out?

THE U.S. PRESIDENT APPOINTS:

Secretary of Agriculture

Secretary of Commerce

Secretary of Defense

Secretary of Education

Secretary of Energy

Secretary of Health and Human Services

Secretary of Homeland Security

Secretary of Housing and Urban Development

Secretary of Interior

Secretary of Labor

Secretary of State

Secretary of Transportation

Secretary of Treasury

Secretary of Veterans Affairs

The Attorney General

EPA Administrator

U.S. Trade Representative

U.S. Ambassador to the United Nations

NATIONAL OFFICIALS INDEPENDENTLY ELECTED:

None

THE TEXAS GOVERNOR APPOINTS:

Secretary of State

Insurance Commissioner

Adjutant General

TEXAS OFFICIALS INDEPENDENTLY ELECTED:

Attorney General

Agriculture Commissioner

Commissioner of the General Land Office

Comptroller

Lieutenant Governor

Railroad Commission

As a result, power is dispersed. One decidedly negative consequence is that most citizens are not aware of the identity of a comptroller or land commissioner: neither do they realize the talents needed to perform these jobs well. Yet, citizens are still responsible for choosing the best person through the elective process. It is a safe bet that a majority of voters can neither name the executive officers they voted into office nor define the responsibilities of these leaders. A consequence of the plural executive is that consistency and teamwork are sacrificed.

Elected and Appointed Officials

Explain the roles of the lieutenant governor, attorney general, comptroller, land commissioner, and commissioner of agriculture.

☐ The Lieutenant Governor

Many political scientists believe that the office of lieutenant governor is the most powerful position in the state. Ironically, the greatest powers are in the legislative arena because of the office's role in the Texas senate and the Legislative Budget Board. From an executive perspective, the lieutenant governor's role is to succeed the governor in the case of death, removal, or resignation. The lieutenant governor also serves in the governor's capacity when the governor is out of the state. In Texas, as is the case in about half of the states, the governor and lieutenant governor run for office independently. This creates the possibility that these executive officers will be from different parties, as was the case following the 1994 elections, but that has not been an issue over the last decade, as Republicans have won all statewide races.

In 1998, Rick Perry became the first Republican elected to hold the office, succeeding, the colorful Bob Bullock, profiled in the nearby Mosaic. Perry ascended to the governor's office when George W. Bush became president. For two years, the office was technically vacant, although Senator Bill Ratliff served as acting lieutenant governor after being selected from among his peers. In 2002, Republican David Dewhurst was elected to the post. Dewhurst, the former land commissioner, a self-made millionaire who made his fortune in real estate and investments after serving as a CIA agent, defeated Democratic stalwart John Sharp by five percentage points, the closest of the statewide elections that year. His 2006 and 2010 reelections were by landslides. He lost his bid for the Republican nomination to the U.S. Senate in 2012, returning to Austin instead for the 2013 legislative session.

The office has been active in water planning since the mid-1990s, when Bullock helped pass Senate Bills 1 and 2, the first efforts at creating workable solution to long-term water problems. Bullock also led the effort that consolidated several environmental boards into one. Senate Bill 1 specifically decentralized the water planning question, pushing much of the decision making to local and regional authorities. At the same time, it sought to create a statewide perspective for water planning. This multifaceted approach necessitated the involvement of a variety of agencies and stakeholders. Senate Bill 2, passed in 2001, provided incentives for innovation and created new groundwater districts and the Water Infrastructure Fund.

Dewhurst maintained that "if we don't have enough water, it is going to dramatically slow down the growth of this state."[2] In order to pass Senate Bill 3 in 2007, Dewhurst held seven house bills hostage until the house passed the latest water bill, mandating the creation of 19 new water reservoirs throughout the state. Dewhurst emphasized that the state must work with both the federal and local governments in order to deploy an effective plan. Still, with the financial difficulties of the last several years, the legislature has failed to fully fund the 2007 water plan.

Among the charges that Dewhurst gave to the interim Natural Resources Committee prior to the 2013 session were to find ways, working with local government, to fund the plan, work on conservation initiatives, and examine the feasibility of using nonpotable water for electric generation and mineral extraction. Early in the 2013 session, Dewhurst endorsed tapping the state's Rainy Day fund to help pay for the infrastructure to address long-term water development.

The lieutenant governor's race, once an Election Day obscurity, despite being perhaps the state's most powerful office, has certainly entered the big leagues of Texas politics. The Dewhurst campaign spent close to $30 million on the 2002 election—at least $10 million from the candidate's own pocket—and started running television ads 18 months before the election. Sharp spent less, but still was in the eight-digit neighborhood, which is an enormous amount for a position that pays $7,200 a year.

☐ The Attorney General

The **attorney general** (AG) is the state's lawyer. The office defends the state and its constitution in court and represents Texas in any litigation that the office initiates. As is the case in most states, the attorney general is elected. In Texas, he or she serves a four-year term.

The attorney general's position, while among the most prominent in the state, is one of the least understood. In the past, most candidates for AG ran on a platform promising to be tough on crime, although the state's chief litigant has little to do with criminal prosecution. In Texas, prosecution is routinely handled by the county or district attorney's office. In most states, the attorney general can initiate criminal proceedings. Here, the chief legal officer has no such power. The Texas attorney general is one of the few who cannot, of his or her own initiative, intervene in local prosecutions. Campaigning as a tough-on-crime candidate, then, is quite cynical. It panders to the public's fear of crime and insinuates that the average voter doesn't know enough to see through this approach. In the last three elections, however, candidates have run on issues actually related to the office.

The Office of the Attorney General (OAG) has about 4,200 employees. It employs some 400 attorneys and has 70 regional offices. One of the most important and active of the departments is the Consumer Protection Division. This office seeks to protect consumers from deceptive trade practices and citizens from unsafe conditions.[3] In the past decade, attorneys general from several states, including Texas, have joined together to sue companies such as Quaker Oats for making unsubstantiated health claims regarding their products. The Consumer Protection Division also investigates unfair and anticompetitive

attorney general
The state's lawyer; elected.

Texas ★ Mosaic   Old-Style Texas Politics: Bob Bullock

"This morning, God got the first of many performance reviews from Bob Bullock. I'm sure heaven will become a much more efficient place, now that he is there," said Senator David Sibley on the day Bullock died.

Bob Bullock was by no means a warm and cuddly politician. But he knew more about Texas government than anyone else. And he got things done—sometimes through fear and intimidation, other times through doggedly finding the right answer and stubbornly sticking with it until others fell into line. During his 16 years as comptroller, he singlehandedly modernized the office, giving it computers and professional financial analysis. He created the Texas Performance Review, which enabled the comptroller to save the state billions of dollars by recommending cost-saving measures at various state agencies. He parlayed that position into an eight-year stint as lieutenant governor, running the state with an iron fist. He was at the forefront of efforts to revamp the state's education funding system. He helped reform welfare and criminal justice and won passage of legislation that limited lawsuits.

To call Bob Bullock a Texas legend is an understatement. Although there were many significant political leaders in Texas during the 20th century, none wielded power in quite the same way as the former lieutenant governor. Controversial, stubborn, and outspoken, Bullock gave "colorful" a whole new meaning in Texas politics. Bullock wouldn't have agreed with that particular adjective; he said, "I just had a propensity for getting into trouble." A reformed alcoholic, he battled a lifelong addiction to cigarettes, had numerous health problems, was treated for depression

and anxiety, endured a heart attack and a bypass operation, and married numerous times. His temper was quick and legendary. And you didn't ever want to end up on his bad side because he had a tendency to remember. He worked impossibly long hours and expected the same devotion from his staff.

A lifelong Democrat, Bullock once circulated a photo of former governor John Connally's head on the body of a turkey when the latter switched parties. Nonetheless, Bullock was one of the first political leaders to discern the national appeal of Republican George W. Bush. As early as 1997, he was touting Bush as a future president. He endorsed the governor's reelection bid in 1998, despite the fact that Bush's opponent was a former employee and the father of Bullock's goddaughter.

Bullock's signature expression was "God Bless Texas," a sentiment he felt so strongly about that, coming from him, it was part prayer, part demand.

Lieutenant Governor Bob Bullock was an icon in Texas Politics. He Wielded the Gavel like it was a Sledgehammer.

1. What makes the lieutenant governor's office so powerful?

2. What qualities made Bullock effective?

practices of businesses within the state. This enforces a state constitutional mandate to ban monopolies and protect consumers. In the late 1990s, attorneys general successfully pursued cases against tobacco companies for damages incurred by citizens who end up receiving state-financed medical care. These cases resulted in significant revenue for the state.

Through such lawsuits, the attorney general can significantly increase his name recognition. In 1994, as his reelection bid approached, former Attorney General Dan Morales filed a lawsuit against several fast-food chains operating in the state. He claimed that their smoking sections created unreasonable health dangers to children, whose business they were attempting to solicit. Morales not only reached an out-of-court settlement, whereby the franchises agreed to ban smoking, but he also saw his name splashed across newspaper headlines throughout the state.

The primary purpose of the highly visible Child Support Enforcement Division is collecting child support. It works to establish paternity and locate absent parents. Funding for the office comes from a mixture of federal and state funds because child care enforcement is mandated under federal law. As a result, the office is somewhat limited as to how it operates because case priority is set by federal regulation. Former AG John Cornyn made a highly visible effort to publicize parents delinquent in their child support payments. His "Top Ten Evaders" posters were popular with the media.

As is the case in most states, the Texas attorney general has a significant role in tax collection and antitrust law. The Collections Division works to recover delinquent taxes. If a business is behind in its tax payments, the OAG can intervene. The OAG also has the responsibility of providing legal counsel to all state agencies, centralizing a service that was earlier provided by the individual agencies.

One of the most important branches of the OAG is the Opinion Committee, which provides interpretations of laws and regulations, or of the U.S. or Texas constitutions, for government agencies and the legislature. The opinions may either attempt to clarify existing laws or rules, or they may assess the constitutionality of proposed laws or rules. In 2003, for example, Attorney General Greg Abbott issued an opinion in regard to whether Texas could operate video lottery terminals under the state's constitution. In effect, "video lottery" machines can be set up to mimic slot machines. Abbott ruled that, short of a constitutional amendment, the Texas constitution bars such devices. These opinions can be overturned by Texas courts, but they carry significant weight with the Texas court system. The Texas supreme court and court of criminal appeals have shown a willingness to follow the attorney general's opinions in most situations. The opinions carry the force of law unless overturned by the courts.

Traditionally, Texas attorneys general used the office as a stepping-stone to a higher position. Former Governor Mark White, elected in 1982, had previously served as the state's attorney general. Likewise, former attorney general Jim Mattox ran for governor in 1990 and Dan Morales ran in 2002. Both were defeated in the Democratic primary. Of the last nine governors, only White had previously served as attorney general.

In 1998, John Cornyn became the first Republican elected to the office. He had served on the state's supreme court prior to becoming the state's top lawyer. During his term in the office, Cornyn concentrated his efforts on lessening federal controls on the prison system, modernizing the state's child support collection efforts, and strengthening Texas's Open Meeting Laws, which keep the government from operating without public scrutiny.

The role of attorney general does not include active participation in water policy, but he has an important influence nonetheless through the office's aforementioned opinions. For instance, in May 2012, Abbott issued his 923rd opinion since taking office in response to a query from the Brazos County criminal district attorney who had prosecutorial responsibility in a water code violation case. Abbott answered that if the complaint was filed in a justice court, it was the district attorney's responsibility, while it was the city attorney's responsibility if it was filed in municipal court.

Greg Abbott was first elected to the office in 2002. Also a Republican, he had served on the state supreme court. He pledged that he wouldn't carry a political agenda into office, saying that the attorney general's job is to enforce the law regardless of whether he agrees with it. Abbott was elected to the office for a third time in 2010 and is considered a likely candidate for governor in 2014.

☐ Comptroller of Public Accounts

Texas is one of only 13 states to elect the **comptroller** of public accounts. The comptroller is the state's accountant and chief tax collector. Significantly, the comptroller estimates state revenue and certifies that the legislature's appropriations bill falls within the revenue estimate. This is a by-product of the balanced budget provision of the state's constitution.

The comptroller's office exercises important powers. The position of state accountant may not sound like an enticing job and in most states, it's not, but in Texas, the office carries power for three primary purposes: (1) the comptroller tells the legislature how much money it has to spend, (2) the comptroller finds ways to save the state money and to spend funds more efficiently, and (3) the comptroller fills out federal grant paperwork. If the forms are filled out correctly, the state, with little or no additional effort, can end up with considerably more federal money. The office employs about 2,850 workers.[4]

Susan Combs, a former state representative and the previous agriculture commissioner, was elected comptroller in 2006. She defeated her Democratic opponent with 60 percent of the vote and did not draw a Democratic challenger in 2010. Combs worked to make the comptroller's office more transparent by giving the office a more navigable and inclusive online presence.

Prior to 2003, the comptroller had significant performance review power, allowing her to investigate state agencies and public schools, looking for inefficient practices, and searching for ways to save public money. It proved a successful endeavor, saving the state more than $10 billion during its dozen-year life span. Most of those review powers were stripped, however, when the previous comptroller, former Republican Carole Strayhorn, got into a political dust-up with Governor Perry, whom she would unsuccessfully challenge in an independent bid for his office in 2006. Performance review was transferred to the Legislative Budget Board.

comptroller
The state's chief accountant and financial officer.

9.1

9.2

9.3

9.4

9.5

Comptroller Susan Combs releases the Biennial Revenue Estimate. The BRE is one of the most important documents issued by a public official in Texas, as it sets the cap for state spending unless additional revenue is raised. The January BRE sets the parameters for the budget process. The May BRE is binding and usually offers a little relief from the initial estimate.

land commissioner
State official responsible for overseeing the leases and uses of state-owned land; elected.

One of the most interesting revolutions in Texas politics occurred in the 1995 session, when the legislature opted to abolish the treasurer's office. In 1994, Democrat Martha Whitehead was elected treasurer, when she made the unusual promise to abolish her office. Whitehead was able to shepherd her proposal through the legislature, even though it required two-thirds approval, because abolishing the office required a constitutional amendment. In November 1995, the voters approved the amendment, and the treasurer's functions were folded into the comptroller's office. Although the monetary savings have been minimal, actually closing a state agency is an important symbolic step in a politically conservative state.

With the addition of the treasury functions, the comptroller's office now receives and manages all state money from the time of collection until the state's bills came due. Former state treasurer Ann Richards ensured that all state monies were deposited in interest-bearing accounts. Prior to that, some state funds essentially served as welfare for bankers, who were the major contributors to candidates running for the treasurer's office.

The Unclaimed Properties Division of the comptroller's office is the depository for unclaimed property. In addition to providing a public service, the comptroller uses this function to gain political recognition. The office annually publishes a list of people with property, such as valuables left in safe deposit boxes or a dormant bank account, which is unclaimed. Not coincidentally, the annual Sunday newspaper supplement is published in late October, just prior to the November elections. People finding that they have money coming are happy with the comptroller as a result. The comptroller also benefits from reinforced name recognition among those who merely skim the publication but do not find their names.

The comptroller has taken an active role in water policy. In her special report on water policy, she noted that agricultural losses alone exceeded $5 billion as a result of the 2011 drought. Most electricity-generating facilities in Texas, as she pointed out, use water for cooling. Since electric demands are highest when it is hot and dry, another prolonged drought could endanger large parts of the state's utility grid. Combs points to Albuquerque, New Mexico, as a model that Texas may be forced to adopt. New Mexico's restrictions include limits on landscaping option, bonuses for xeriscaping, enhanced public education, and heavy fines for wasting water. Tucson, Arizona, now requires that all new homes and commercial establishments use xeriscaping.[5]

Fiscal Notes is one of the numerous publications produced by the comptroller's office. In the 2012 article "Water for Power," the office explained the vast need for water in order to produce electricity. Ian Duncan, a scientist at the University of Texas said, "It is possible that, with ongoing drought, Texas could face power shortages triggered by plant closures due to lack of cooling water,"[6] The hotter it gets—and summer droughts tend to be hot—the greater the demand on the electricity grid, and the greater the need for water. It takes 0.39 gallons of water for each kilowatt hour of energy produced in Texas.[7] For comparison purposes, that is about what a medium-sized window air conditioner uses in an hour, or what a small refrigerator uses in a day. Conserving electricity helps save on water; conserving water helps ensure that enough is available for generating electricity.

☐ The Commissioner of the General Land Office

The commissioner of the General Land Office has the responsibility for leasing and use of the state's public land. Like the other positions we have discussed, the **land commissioner** serves a four-year term. Much of the state's public land is dedicated to the Permanent School Fund (PSF), which receives income from leases as well as from oil and mineral production. The PSF has a market value of about $25.5 billion.[8] The land commissioner also serves as the chair of the Veterans Land Board, which provides low-interest loans to veterans wishing to buy land.

Republican Jerry Patterson won the 2002 land commissioner's race by about a dozen percentage points. He was reelected in 2006 and 2010. The conservative former state senator, who won with a strong grassroots effort, vows to increase oil and gas production in the state, which would bring more money to Texas schools.

Patterson has been a vocal advocate for desalinization of the brackish water that lays hundreds of feet below the state's fresh-water aquifer. While desalinating water in the Gulf is cost prohibitive, the brackish water has significantly less salt content, though still too much to either drink or irrigate agriculture. That decreased salinity makes the process much less costly, but not cheap. Patterson says that it is twice as expensive as traditional water development, but new technologies could change that. He has hired private engineers to analyze extraction and is considering setting up a plant on land owned by the Permanent School Fund, which is overseen by the land commissioner.[9]

☐ The Commissioner of Agriculture

The agriculture commissioner is the one statewide elected executive office that is not constitutionally mandated, as noted in the following Texas constitution feature. It was created by statute in 1907. The commissioner's job requires the candidate to be a practicing farmer. This simply means that when filing for election, the candidate must claim to be an experienced farmer. Texas is one of only 11 states to elect this position.

The commissioner oversees the 700-employee Texas Department of Agriculture (TDA), which is responsible for regulating the use of pesticides and providing information, training, and licenses for their use. Along with being a regulatory agency, the office also promotes the consumption of Texas-grown food, wine, fiber, and nursery plants through its Marketing and Agribusiness Development Division. TDA has helped Texas farmers sell products throughout the world, involving itself in projects as diverse as kicking off ceremonial cattle drives and promoting the sale of long-stem bluebonnets.[10]

An interesting function of the office is its responsibility for establishing the accuracy of weights and measures. Under this mandate, the agriculture commissioner certifies that gasoline pumps work properly. Commissioners have had the political savvy to put their names on the gas pump inspection stickers so that motorists see it every time they fill up their vehicles.

In 2012, Commissioner Staples created the Texas Water Smart Coalition, a cooperative group comprised of public and private entities dedicated to conservation. Members include a diverse mix ranging from Home Depot to Municipal Utility Districts to the Texas Retail Institute and from Kroger to the Royse City to the Texas Water Development Board, all stakeholders in the continued availability of water. Staples said, "Simple changes in our water use habits can make a big difference."[11] The

The Texas Constitution

A Closer Look

The Texas constitution mandates the creation of the major offices of the executive branch, requiring the election of all but the secretary of state. The Agriculture Commission is created by state law.

Article IV. Executive Department
Sec. 1. OFFICERS CONSTITUTING THE EXECUTIVE DEPARTMENT. The Executive Department of the State shall consist of a Governor, who shall be the Chief Executive Officer of the State, a Lieutenant Governor, Secretary of State, Comptroller of Public Accounts, Commissioner of the General Land Office, and Attorney General. (Amended November 7, 1995)

Sec. 2. ELECTION OF OFFICERS OF EXECUTIVE DEPARTMENT. All the above officers of the Executive Department (except Secretary of State) shall be elected by the qualified voters of the State at the time and places of election for members of the Legislature.

1. How would Texas government be impacted if the governor had the power to appoint these executive officials?

2. Should the governor have the power to appoint these officials? Why or why not?

Texas ★ Mosaic

Increasing Diversity in the Executive Branch: The Secretaries of State

Like most of the executive branch in Texas, the secretary of state's office was long a bastion of white, male Democrats. In recent years, that profile has been altered drastically.

With the advent of Republican governors in 1979, the party barrier fell. The racial barrier was first cracked in 1968, when Governor John Connally appointed Roy Barrera Sr., a Hispanic, to the office. In 1983, Governor Mark White named Myra McDaniel to the post, making her the third woman and the first African American to hold the office. (Interestingly, the two other women served long ago, in the 1920s, shortly after women were given the right to vote.)

Recent secretaries of state such as Democrat Ron Kirk and Republicans Tony Garza and Alberto Gonzales reflect the more inclusive nature of contemporary Texas politics. Governors realize that reaching out to the minority community in making high-profile appointments can bring political gains. The almost universal respect afforded to these men helps open doors for other minority aspirants in jobs both in and out of government.

Kirk, an African American, replaced Governor Ann Richards's initial secretary of state, who resigned to become a federal judge. Kirk, a lawyer, had served as the chair of the state's General Services Commission. Popular before becoming secretary of state, Kirk used the additional exposure gained in the office to propel himself into the Dallas mayor's seat in 1995. He brought together a group of supporters that included liberals, conservatives, Republicans, and Democrats, and he scored an easy victory over a field of opponents. As mayor, Kirk tried to be a mediator among the various factions within the fractured Dallas city council. He was reelected in 1999 and staged a high-profile but unsuccessful race for the U.S. Senate in 2002.

Garza, a Hispanic, already had a career in Republican politics before accepting the secretary of state appointment. A tough conservative, he had served seven years as county judge in Cameron County. Garza served two and a half years as secretary of state, before Governor Bush appointed him to a vacant seat on the Texas Railroad Commission, a position to which he was subsequently reelected. He later became the U.S. ambassador to Mexico. His replacement in the secretary of state post was Alberto Gonzales, whom Bush appointed to the Texas supreme court in 1999. When Bush became president, Gonzales resigned to become White House legal counsel. In 2005, Gonzales became attorney general for the United States, resigning after a controversial two years of service.

Rick Perry's first secretary of state was Henry Cuellar. The new governor reached across party lines to appoint the Democrat, the fourth Hispanic to hold the office. Gwen Shea, a Republican who had served a decade in the legislature, became the fourth woman to hold the office, replacing Cuellar in January 2002. She served for 18 months before resigning to go to work for the Harrah's casino conglomerate. She was replaced by Geoffrey Conner in 2003, who served 15 months before entering the private sector. Dallas–Fort Worth car dealer and major Republican contributor Roger Williams followed him in 2005. Williams is now a member of Congress. Phil Wilson took office in 2007, leaving after a year to join the energy industry. In 2008, Perry appointed Hope Andrade, the first Latina to hold the office. Andrade resigned after the 2012 election to return to private life. Her successor is John Steen, a San Antonio lawyer and businessman who has made significant financial contributions to Governor Perry and the Republican Party.

1. **What is the political advantage of mining a diverse pool for secretary of state appointments?**

2. **Should the secretary of state be appointed or elected? Why?**

---

coalition's purpose is to encourage businesses and individuals to think carefully about their water consumption.

Current agriculture commissioner Todd Staples was elected in 2006 and reelected in 2010. A Republican, he previously served in both the Texas house and senate. He has followed in the footsteps of former commissioner Susan Combs, continuing an emphasis on providing schoolchildren with healthy food choices. He has tried to help farmers and ranchers improve their profit margins and has been an advocate of property rights.

☐ Appointed Offices

Although the most important department heads are independently elected, the governor appoints the secretary of state, the insurance commissioner, and the adjutant general. Additionally, the governor selects the education commissioner, as well as the health and human services commissioners, positions that are discussed in more detail later in this chapter.

Secretary of State

For a state obsessed with electing every possible official, Texas is ironically one of the few states that does not elect the **secretary of state**. The governor's appointment is subject to senate confirmation. The chief election officer for Texas, the secretary of state interprets the election code. The office provides training for election clerks and maintains a master roll of all registered voters in the state. The office also issues charters for businesses incorporated in the state. The office has been a state-level entry point for many Texas political figures, as discussed in the Texas Mosaic. The *Texas Register*, which reports administration agency rules, attorney general opinions, and other government information, is published by the secretary of state's office.

Insurance Commissioner

With skyrocketing home insurance rates, the insurance commissioner's office became a political lightning rod in the early 21st century. The department, with about 1,700 employees, regulates insurance company practices and helps ensure that these companies have financial resources to cover potential claims.[12] The insurance department was initially overseen by a three-member board, but it was replaced by a single commissioner, appointed by the governor, in 1994. It's easier to target one person than a group, so the department's head has come under intense scrutiny as rates have increased.

Although the department is supposed to cap insurance rates, recent deregulatory efforts left most homeowners policies, as well as auto insurance rates, outside of the state's regulatory reach. Through a constitutional amendment, Texans have capped medical malpractice liability, and it has become progressively harder to collect damages in the state.

Adjutant General

The governor appoints the adjutant general for a two-year term. The appointment is subject to senate approval. With the exception of the governor, the adjutant general is the highest-ranking state military leader. Along with two assistants, the general oversees the Army National Guard, the Air National Guard, and the Texas National Guard.

The Bureaucracy

9.3 Determine how the bureaucracy impacts the operation of state government.

When the legislature passes a law, government policy does not magically change. Laws must be carried out—that is, executed—by the executive branch. That's where the **bureaucracy** comes into the picture. To most people, "bureaucracy" is a bad word. Citizens tend to believe that faceless bureaucrats are lazy or power hungry, or both. They associate bureaucracy with "red tape" and inefficiency. Almost everyone has had a bad experience with a government agency. There are rumors that even state colleges are imperfect. (Registration procedures may be inefficient, bookstores may run out of textbooks, financial aid departments might mess up your grants, and professors may be detached and arrogant. Finding no research that bolsters these claims, we dismiss them.)

For the most part, the sinister reputation attributed to government departments is too harsh. Generally, Texans take government services for granted. When the traffic on a state-built and state-financed road flows smoothly, when state-financed traffic lights work, when government regulations keep chemical plants from blowing up, and when professors show up for class, we don't stop and think, "Wow, the government did a great job today." But these desirable occurrences are not automatic. Without myriad

secretary of state
The state's chief election officer; appointed by the governor.

bureaucracy
Executive branch departments that carry out the law.

9.1
hierarchy
Chain of command.

9.2

9.3

9.4

9.5

government agencies working in cooperation with each other, no public policy goal would ever be accomplished. But when things go wrong, we notice immediately and blame the government and its workers. These employees, constrained by rules and regulations intended to ensure efficiency and fairness, are often doing the best job possible.

□ Size

About 150,000 employees (not counting education workers) labor for the state's bureaucracy.[13] Although that may seem like an extraordinarily large number, it pales in comparison to the almost 3 million employees in the civilian federal workforce. Local governments in Texas employ a million additional workers, with 70 percent of those in education-related jobs. In comparison to other states, the employee level of the state government is reasonable. Texas has the second-largest number of state employees, but one must bear in mind that Texas also has the second-largest state population. Table 9.1 shows Texas's rank among selected states in the number of state employees per 10,000 people in its population. Almost 90 percent have a higher rate of full-time state employees.[14] Realize, however, that states with large populations tend to have fewer state employees per capita. There are efficiencies associated with having a large population.

□ Hierarchy and Expertise

One characteristic of a bureaucracy is its hierarchical nature. In a **hierarchy**, there is a definite chain of command. A person at the lower level of the pyramid-shaped structure does not report directly to the agency head, but rather to his or her boss, who is at the next highest level. Likewise, this person reports to a boss at the next highest level. Each boss has a span of control—the number of people who work under him or her—established at a level intended to make the organization operate efficiently. In most cases, the span of control will number between 5 and 12 workers.

TABLE 9.1 NUMBER OF FULL-TIME EQUIVALENT STATE EMPLOYEES PER 10,000 POPULATION FOR SELECTED STATES

State	Employees
Alaska	376
Delaware	290
Alabama	188
Utah	186
New Jersey*	173
Oregon	171
Virginia*	156
Michigan*	147
Massachusetts*	146
50-State Average	142
Idaho	140
Pennsylvania*	132
Tennessee	131
New York*	130
Georgia*	128
Texas*	126
Ohio*	121
California*	110
Florida*	98

*15 most populous states

The bureaucracy is intended to create experts and therefore instill efficiency in government. Each person, whether a typist, an accountant, or an engineer, should be an expert in his or her field. With each person paired with the job for which he or she is best prepared, there should be no waste of effort. Of course, this is an idealized version of how government operates. In reality, waste and mismanagement occur in government just as in every other aspect of life. In government, however, this waste is more controversial because "our money" (i.e., tax dollars) is involved.

In the past, a person needed "connections" to get a government job. The "spoils system" all but ensured that jobs went to workers within the winning political party. While this patronage system still exists for appointed board and commission positions, the trend in government is toward a merit system of hiring for most government employees. This means selecting the best person for a job, based on skills and qualifications. Such a system also allows for affirmative action—the practice of giving preferential treatment to members of groups discriminated against in the past. The goal of this highly controversial practice is to make the workforce more closely mirror the demographic makeup of the state.

☐ Accountability

In Texas, most of the bureaucracy is decentralized. The governor does not exercise direct control over agencies, and most state boards and commissions are directly accountable to no one. Elected executive heads provide some measure of accountability for certain agencies. For example, employees of the Agriculture Department are, in at least some small way, accountable to the agriculture commissioner, who is accountable to the voters. The 3,400 employees of the Texas Workforce Commission, however, are removed from direct accountability. The governor appoints the commission members, but, as discussed earlier, has limited power over any board, because he or she cannot remove prior appointees from office and because board members' terms overlap. As a result, the average citizen can do little to direct displeasure toward a particular agency. These agencies are, however, more accountable to interest groups. The agency's "clients" have an important impact on its ability to receive adequate funding from the legislature.

Despite being part of the executive branch, agencies are much more accountable to the legislature than to the governor. First, funding is the lifeblood of these agencies, so they depend on the legislature for appropriations. Without money, no agency can survive. Without funding increases, no agency can grow. Second, agencies are subject to the sunset review process, which ultimately allows the legislature to close an agency. The governor can, of course, use line item veto power to punish agencies that fail to cooperate with his or her agenda, as Pa Ferguson did in 1917, when he vetoed the entire appropriation for the University of Texas. Most governors have not been willing to use such heavy-handed tactics.

Texas Boards and Commissions

9.4 Differentiate among the functions of various types of boards and commissions.

TEXAS RAILROAD COMMISSION "One of the enduring truths of the nation's capital is that bureaucrats survive. Agencies don't fold their tents and quietly fade away after their work is done. They find something new to do. Invariably, that something new involves more people with more power and more paperwork—all involving more expenditures."[15]

When former president Gerald Ford wrote these words, he was talking about national government agencies. No organization in the country, however, fits this description better than the **Texas Railroad Commission (TRC)**. Most Texas voters are not aware of what the commissioners really do. Established by an 1890 amendment to the Texas constitution, the original intent of the agency was to regulate rail rates within Texas. However, the national government's Interstate Commerce Commission (ICC)

Texas Railroad Commission (TRC)

State commission that oversees oil and gas production; elected.

State Board of Education (SBE)
Elected board that oversees the Texas Education Agency.

so greatly controls railroads that the Railroad Commission has had very few railroad-related responsibilities for years.

But the agency has found other things to do. Over the years, the Railroad Commission gained control over pipelines, oil and gas production, and trucking. Federal legislation took away the commission's power to set intrastate trucking rates in the mid-1990s and gave control to the ICC. In response to the federal changes, remaining transportation regulation has been transferred to the state departments of transportation and public safety.

The most important aspect of the TRC is its control over oil and natural gas. Production levels are set by the agency. The Railroad Commission sets the rates for gas utility companies. Liquid petroleum gas and compressed natural gas are also regulated by the TRC.

Hydraulic fracturing, the highly controversial process used to remove natural gas from areas that were once unextractable, uses significant amounts of water, as the name implies. Since the TRC oversees gas extraction, it has primary responsibility for regulating fracking. In the Barnett Shale and the Eagle Ford Shale, the commission has been proactive in encouraging and approving permits that allow companies to recycle fracture fluids, requiring the use of less ground and aquifer water.

The Railroad Commission has three members, elected in a partisan manner to overlapping six-year terms. Current members, who are all Republican, are Barry Smithernan, who was appointed to the commission in 2011 and elected in 2012; David Porter, who was elected in 2010; and Christi Craddick, who was elected in 2012. The chair of the commission is the member next up for election, an honor that significantly helps with campaign fund-raising. As this text went to print, the 2013 house had based a bill changing the name to the more descriptive Texas Energy Resources Commission. A counterpart bill had passed out of senate committee and was pending before the bull senate.

STATE BOARD OF EDUCATION Texans also elect the **State Board of Education (SBE)**, which has limited oversight of the Texas Education Agency. The 15 board members serve overlapping four-year terms and are elected by district, not statewide. In selecting the education commissioner, the SBE forwards three suggestions to the governor. The governor chooses from among the nominees, and with the senate's consent, the commissioner serves a four-year term.

The SBE has seen its authority reduced in recent years as a group of far-right conservatives ran a series of "stealth" candidates for the board. Their strategy was to run well-financed campaigns in the Republican primary elections for these low-profile positions, then take advantage of the ascendancy of the party to win the general elections. Although they never comprised an outright majority on the board, the group's members make up a sizable faction. In 1995, the legislature and Governor Bush moved to strip the board of much of its power before the group could enact its anti-public education agenda. However, the SBE reasserted itself in 2002, with a strict reading of its charge to ensure against errors in textbooks. In essence, anything that the SBE disagreed with became an "error." The board used this provision to exert significant pressure on publishers of social, political, economic, and science texts. Additionally, the board has restructured the public high school curriculum in a decidedly conservative direction. In the 2010 elections, however, the right wing of the board lost control of a couple of seats, which has had a moderating impact.

The legislature has tried to decentralize school administration. Local schools can petition for campus charters under the reforms, allowing for easier creation of magnet schools and for escape from many state requirements. Additionally, independent charter schools can apply for and receive state funds with SBE approval. The results of the charter school law have been somewhat mixed. Hundreds of applications for charter schools were filed, but by the end of 2012 just under 200 schools were in operation. The SBE revoked, rescinded, or failed to renew the charters of several schools, and more were on questionable financial footing or had gone bankrupt; these schools garnered more media attention than the charter schools that were apparently succeeding.[16] Although most charter schools underperform when compared with traditional public schools, one must keep in mind that many charters cater to at-risk students. Further, on average, charter schools spend less per student than their traditional counterparts. On the other hand, several charter schools were ranked exemplary or were recognized in the top rankings awarded by the Texas Education Agency.

As boards that are elected rather than appointed, the SBE and the Railroad Commission are exceptions. This denotes their importance, as Texans want to retain direct control over the key components of government in order to ensure accountability.

□ Administrative Boards

Some of the more significant appointed boards are discussed in the following sections.

TEXAS WATER DEVELOPMENT BOARD One type of board oversees administrative agencies, such as the Parks and Wildlife Department, the Department of Health, and the Department of Human Services. Not surprisingly, the Texas Water Development Board (TWDB) is the state body most directly involved with water policy. The TWDB is a six-member board, appointed by the governor through overlapping six-year terms. Day-to-day operations are overseen by an executive administrator. Since 1957, the board has had primary responsibility for overseeing conservation and planning development of the state's water resources. Every five years, the TWDB issues the State Water Plan. The board helps finance water projects throughout the state. The TWDB administers state bonds money for water projects, specific state appropriations, and federal water grants. The TWDB also administers the federally funded National Flood Insurance Program in the state.

In the cover letter of the 2012 State Water Plan, board chair Edward Vaughan summed up the issue succinctly: "In serious drought conditions, Texas does not and will not have enough water to meet the needs of its people, its businesses, and its agricultural enterprises."[17] The plans are forward-looking reports, assessing the state's needs over the ensuing 50 years. In order to meet those goals, the board recommends building more water reservoirs, acquiring sites for additional reservoirs, and requiring public utilities to monitor their water loss more closely.

PARKS AND WILDLIFE DEPARTMENT The Parks and Wildlife Department is overseen by a nine-member board appointed by the governor and is headed by an executive director, who is appointed by the board. The purpose of the department is to protect wildlife, maintain parks, and provide for recreational opportunities. The department publishes *Texas Parks and Wildlife* magazine. Game wardens enforce hunting and fishing laws, as well as water safety provisions. The department also manages the state's historic sites and public parks.

The department's magazine devotes one issue a year to water concerns. The department is involved with a wide range of water resource concerns, from fishing to controlling invasive aquatic species to ensuring an adequate supply. Their 2011 water issue denoted the problem of sediment in the state's reservoirs, which displace water storage capacity.

HEALTH AND HUMAN SERVICES COMMISSION Health and Human Services (HHSC) underwent a major overhaul and consolidation in 2004. Eleven agencies were merged into four, with each reporting to the HHSC. The departments include Aging and Disability, Assistive and Rehabilitative Services, Family and Protective Services, and State Health Services. Consolidation should make it easier for Texans to find where to turn for services. An executive commissioner oversees the commission with the assistance of a nine-member council, appointed by the governor.

In the normal course of governing, you may not think of water as a health and human services issue. However, water policy is such a ubiquitous concern that even HHSC generates a quarterly report on agency water conservation.

DEPARTMENT OF TRANSPORTATION The Texas Department of Transportation (TxDOT) is one of the largest agencies in the state and employs about 12,000

Public Utility Commission (PUC)
Agency that regulates utility companies; appointed.

full-time workers.[18] TxDOT's executive director, who is appointed by the three-member board, must be an engineer. The department was created in 1917, as the State Highway Department. Over the years, it has evolved so that it covers land, water, and air transportation. It is responsible for developing a statewide transportation plan. A second appointed board within the TxDOT structure, the six-member Motor Vehicle Board, regulates motor vehicle registration.

University Boards and the Coordinating Board

Texas has a dual system of oversight for public universities. Each system has its own board, each with members appointed by the governor. For systems like the University of Texas, all individual universities are governed by a single board. These boards are responsible for setting policy and hiring top administrators. Many universities, such as Stephen F. Austin University, have their own boards. Community colleges have locally elected boards, much like public schools.

The Texas Higher Education Coordinating Board oversees all higher education in the state. The nine-member board administers the Texas Higher Education Assessment (THEA) program. It also sets standards for course transferability both among universities and from community colleges to universities. The board is influential in determining the allocation of higher education funding. The Legislative Budget Board (LBB) gives significant weight to the coordinating board's funding priorities, if not its funding levels, when the LBB puts together the budget.

The overlapping functions of these boards provide insight into how government operates. In any given policy area, many bureaucratic entities and boards may have some responsibility. Coordination becomes imperative for government to function efficiently. All too often, however, the involved organizations do not work well together and policy bogs down.

Occupational Licensing Boards

A significant number of boards in Texas set standards for occupational licensing. Examples include the Texas State Board of Plumbing Examiners and the Board of Nurse Examiners for the state of Texas. Most boards are comprised of both workers in that field and members of the public, with the workers in the field having the majority of the seats. Licensing is regulated in areas as diverse as cosmetology, dentistry, occupational therapy, psychology, polygraphy, and audiology.

Regulatory Boards

Many commissions in the state are involved in business regulation. Among the most significant are the **Public Utility Commission (PUC)** and the Texas Alcoholic Beverage Commission (TABC).

The main function of the PUC is setting utility rates. Utility companies make rate hike requests based on their expenses. The commission holds public hearings on the proposed increases before setting rates. The PUC has authority over privately owned utility companies, but not those operated by city governments. The PUC regulates electric and phone companies. It became most controversial in the late 1980s when an appointee of Democratic Governor Mark White and an appointee of Republican Governor Bill Clements publicly clashed over their philosophical and personal differences. The *CBS Evening News* televised a tape of one of the more contentious shouting sessions, embarrassing many state government officials. Although meetings are often still volatile, most discussions are now limited to policy matters. As a result, the commission has not attracted as much attention in recent years. Nonetheless, because of its regulatory power over the utility industry, it remains one of the most significant boards in the state.

The TABC oversees alcohol-related commerce in Texas. Day-to-day operations are carried out by administrators hired by the commission. The TABC regulates both liquor stores and establishments that serve alcoholic beverages. Liquor licenses and "happy hours" fall under their jurisdiction. Over a decade ago, happy hours became a point of controversy. Mothers Against Drunk Driving (MADD) has lobbied to ban such promotional practices, arguing that they lead to increased inebriation resulting in traffic accidents. Restaurant and bar owners, along with alcohol manufacturers, lined up in opposition. TABC banned two-for-one drink promotions as a result of pressure from MADD, but happy hours were not eliminated. Neither side was able to win complete victory.

The TABC inspects alcohol manufacturers, including the state's expanding beer and wine production industry. One division of the commission monitors the collection of alcohol-related taxes.

Sunset Advisory Commission
Appointed joint commission that reviews state agencies.

9.1

9.2

9.3

9.4

9.5

The Sunset Advisory Commission

9.5   Describe the purpose and process of the Sunset Advisory Commission.

In recognition of the enormous growth in the number and scope of state agencies, the **Sunset Advisory Commission** was created in 1977 to help determine whether agencies had outlived their usefulness. The commission is composed of five senators appointed by the lieutenant governor, five representatives appointed by the Speaker, and two members of the public, one appointed by the Speaker and the other by the lieutenant governor. The commission has a full-time staff that aids in the research and review processes. Additionally, the commission can make recommendations to agencies, including those not currently under review, in order to increase efficiency and save the state money. It also has the authority to bring an agency up for review out of order. As a result, these recommendations are taken seriously and are usually implemented.

Under the review process, all nonconstitutionally mandated agencies must be renewed by the legislature every 12 years. The Sunset Commission plays a vital role in this process. When an agency is up for review, it must first complete a self-evaluation. Next, public hearings take place. Finally, the commission will make its recommendations to continue, abolish, or merge the agency. The recommendation is not binding; the legislature has the final say as to the fate of an agency.

In most cases, the legislature must reauthorize an agency under review in order for it to continue. Constitutionally mandated agencies are not subject to this automatic abolishment. Most agencies survive the review process: Only about one in seven are eliminated. As a result of sunset recommendations, 37 have been completely abolished and 41 more have been abolished, with their functions transferred to different agencies. Additionally, several committees and boards have been abolished or restructured.[19]

Review the Chapter

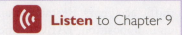 **Listen** to Chapter 9

A Deliberate Division of Power

9.1 Differentiate between cabinet and plural executive forms of government.

In Texas, the executive department is fragmented, fractured, and weakened. Due to influences from the state's past, including the Texas Grange and the state's traditionalistic political structure, the Texas constitution limits the power of the governor. It seeks to keep any one person from exercising too much power.

Instead of a cabinet system of government, under which the chief executive would have the power to appoint most department heads, Texas has a plural executive. The lieutenant governor, attorney general, comptroller, treasurer, land commissioner, and agriculture commissioner are all independently elected. As a result, these officers are not directly accountable to the governor.

Elected and Appointed Officials

9.2 Explain the roles of the lieutenant governor, attorney general, comptroller, land commissioner, and commissioner of agriculture.

The lieutenant governor runs separately from the governor. Although formally a member of the executive branch, the office's powers are primarily legislative. The attorney general is the state's lawyer, representing Texas in civil matters and issuing opinion on the constitutionality and legality of state actions. The comptroller is the state's accountant. The office certifies projected revenues and determines whether the budget will balance. The land commissioner oversees sales and leases of state-owned land. The agriculture commissioner implements agriculture policy and promotes the state's farming and ranching industries.

The Bureaucracy

9.3 Determine how the bureaucracy impacts the operation of state government.

The state bureaucracy performs most day-to-day functions of the state government. Some 150,000 workers are employed by the state. Texas employs fewer workers per capita than most large states. The bureaucracy allows for chain of command and merit hiring, where civil service workers are hired for their skills, not their political loyalties.

Texas Boards and Commissions

9.4 Differentiate among the functions of various types of boards and commissions.

Although most board and commission members are appointed by the governor, subject to senate approval, members of the Railroad Commission and the State Board of Education are elected by the voters. The Railroad Commission, despite its name, regulates oil and gas production. Many of the appointed boards, like the Texas Water Development Board, are administrative. Other boards set occupational licensing standards or perform regulatory functions, like the Public Utility Commission.

The Sunset Advisory Commission

9.5 Describe the purpose and process of the Sunset Advisory Commission.

The Sunset Advisory Commission gives Texas a structured way to determine whether state agencies have outlived their purpose. Members of the legislature and public review agencies on an ongoing basis and recommend their continuation or abolition. The commission recommendation follows an agency's self-evaluation and a series of public hearings. In addition to the question of agency survival, the commission also offers recommendations that allow surviving agencies to operate more efficiently.

Learn the Terms

 Study and **Review** the **Flashcards**

Test Yourself

✓ **Study** and **Review** the **Practice Tests**

9.1 Differentiate between cabinet and plural executive forms of government.

What is not typical of the cabinet form of government?

- **a.** concentrated power
- **b.** independently elected officials
- **c.** the governor is more accountable
- **d.** the governor appoints most executives
- **e.** a team mentality

9.2 Explain the roles of the lieutenant governor, attorney general, comptroller, land commissioner, and commissioner of agriculture.

Duties of the attorney general include all the following EXCEPT

- **a.** enforcing child support.
- **b.** enforcing antitrust legislation.
- **c.** appointing county attorneys.
- **d.** giving counsel to state agencies.
- **e.** giving an official opinion on the constitutionality of a proposed law.

9.3 Determine how the bureaucracy impacts the operation of state government.

About how many noneducation workers does Texas employ?

- **a.** 10,000
- **b.** 21,000
- **c.** 150,000
- **d.** 230,000
- **e.** 260,000

9.4 Differentiate among the functions of various types of boards and commissions.

The state agency that regulates oil and gas production is the

- **a.** Railroad Commission.
- **b.** Public Utilities Commission.
- **c.** Parks and Wildlife Board.
- **d.** Fracking Board.
- **e.** Land Commissioner

9.5 Describe the purpose and process of the Sunset Advisory Commission.

What is the first step in the sunset review process?

- **a.** the governor's report
- **b.** a self-evaluation
- **c.** the sunset staff recommendation
- **d.** a public hearing
- **e.** the comptroller's fiscal evaluation

Explore Further

Fiscal Size Up: 2012–13. The Legislative Budget Board. Austin, TX, 2012.

Frederick, Douglas W. "Reexamining the Texas Railroad Commission." In *Texas Politics: A Reader,* eds. Anthony Champagne and Edward J. Harpham. New York: Norton, 1997.

McNeely, Dave, and Jim Henderson. *Bob Bullock: God Bless Texas.* Austin: University of Texas Press, 2008.

Prindle, David. *Petroleum Politics and the Texas Railroad Commission.* Austin: University of Texas Press, 1981.

Texas General Land Office. *The Land Commissioners of Texas.* Austin: Texas General Land Office, 1986.

The Attorney General's website is https://www.oag.state.tx.us.

The Comptroller's website is http://www.window.state.tx.us.

The agriculture commissioner's website is http://www.agr.state.tx.us.

The Secretary of State's website is http://www.sos.state.tx.us.

The *Texas Register* website is http://www.sos.state.tx.us/texreg/index.shtml.

The Railroad Commission's website is http://www.rrc.state.tx.us.

The Texas Water Development Board website is http://www.twdb.state.tx.us.

The Sunset Advisory Commission website is http://www.sunset.state.tx.us.

10

The Texas Courts System

The question is, how much justice can you afford?

—*Frequent Criticism of the Judicial System*

I n many ways, the judicial branch is the branch of government that is closest to the average person. Although we may not regularly think about what's going on with the governor or what the legislature is doing, we think about the courts every day. High-profile court cases are often the lead story on local and national news, we are bombarded with billboards and other advertisements for attorney services, and we refrain from speeding up when late for work because we consider the consequences. Moreover, the court system plays a dominant role in entertainment and popular culture today. It seems that the highest form of drama is the courtroom scene.

While it may be true that the courts were not created to keep us entertained, there can be little argument about their impact on our daily lives. The courts were created to resolve conflict, which is not only inevitable, but necessary, to our republic and to our state. Conflict may stem from contracts, disputes over property ownership, or personal injury; or they might originate from police action or from the interpretation of a statute, a law, or a phrase contained in a legislative act.

10.1	10.2	10.3	10.4	10.5
Differentiate between civil and criminal law.	Outline the structure of the Texas court system.	Analyze how the Texas judiciary plays an important role in shaping public policy.	Explain why the method for selecting Texas judges is under constant criticism.	Evaluate the merits of suggested judicial reforms.

Municipal Judge David Fraga presides over a hearing for teens and their parents regarding juvenile community service in Houston. There are many levels in the Texas court system, but most individuals interact primarily at the municipal court level.

At first glance it may seem the structure of the state's judicial system is overwhelmingly complicated. After all, there are over 3,400[1] courtrooms and 51,000[2] licensed attorneys in Texas, and it seems they all specialize in one area or another. In reality, the system is fairly simple, and it is certainly not an oversimplification to state that the entire system contains only four levels of courts.

The courts perform a remarkable array of functions. They are looked up on to resolve conflict, interpret statutes, guide the criminal justice system, enforce our property rights, and sanction the predatory practices of dishonest entities, among others. And the courts are expected to accomplish all this in the most fair, equitable, and consistent manner. If it were a perfect system, the services of the court would be open to all and justice would be truly blind to all prejudices. On some occasions, the courts bring opposing sides in agreement, such as when a compromise that is regarded as fair to both parties is reached. More often, though, there are winners and losers, and one or both sides make the claim that justice was not served. You don't have to look far to find examples of dissatisfaction with the judicial system, but when you look at the big picture it becomes more apparent that the court system continues to make strides toward true accessibility and equality.

The Texas court system was established by a 1891 constitutional amendment.[3] That amendment established a dual supreme court system (discussed later in this chapter) and inferior courts to be authorized by legislative action. Jurisdiction of the various levels of courts is established by constitutional provision and by statute. Statutory jurisdiction is established by general statutes providing jurisdiction for all courts on a particular level, as well as by the statutes setting up individual courts. Thus, to determine the jurisdiction of a particular court, first we must turn to the constitution, second to the general statutes establishing jurisdiction for that level of court, and third to the specific statute authorizing the establishment of the particular court in question.[4]

The Texas Court System

10.1 Differentiate between civil and criminal law.

☐ Determining Jurisdiction

The term **jurisdiction** means the court's authority to hear a particular case, and it is the first and last step in determining what each of the courts do. A court must have jurisdiction over the matter before it can hear it. For example, a criminal case cannot be filed in a court that has only civil jurisdiction. By the same standard, a civil case in which a billion dollars is in dispute cannot be heard by your neighborhood small claims court, which has jurisdiction only up to $10,000. Cases are assigned to specific courts based on the type of law and on the type of court.

Texas's 3,400 courts settle more than 10 million disputes per year.[5] As daunting as it sounds, determining which court will hear a particular case is a relatively simple task because each court is set up to hear specific types of cases. By understanding a few basic concepts about the jurisdiction, you'll be able to determine which court will hear a particular case. The fact that the Texas judicial system consists of five levels of courts makes it especially simple.

The first step in determining which court will hear a case is to know whether the case is civil or criminal. If the case is civil in nature, and if you know what or how much is being disputed, you'll be able to name the court that will hear the case. If the case is criminal, all you'll have to know is what level of crime is under consideration.

☐ Two Types of Law

Most simply stated, civil cases are cases that involve disputes between two or more *parties* (usually persons or businesses) and that are not criminal in nature, such as divorce cases and suits to collect debts. More specifically, civil cases usually involve private parties where one party (the *plaintiff*) brings suit against another (the *defendant*) and asks the court to enforce a private right or to require the defendant to pay.[6] **Civil law** exists to protect rights and property and to hold individuals accountable for their actions. Civil lawsuits usually involve two private entities, at least one of which is attempting to recover damages or to correct a situation that the party perceives as unfair. All civil cases, regardless of which court hears them, have two sides, namely, a plaintiff and a defendant. The **plaintiff** is the person or party that initiates the lawsuit and is always listed first. For example, in the case of *Smith* v. *Jones*, we know that Smith is the plaintiff because her name appears first. Ms. Smith is suing the defendant, Mr. Jones. The **defendant** is the person or party that is being sued. Among the more frequently heard civil cases are contract disputes. For example, a dissatisfied homeowner may sue a remodeler for monetary damages in civil court. Other civil cases may involve inheritances, divorces, and product liability. With few exceptions, anyone may file a civil lawsuit if the plaintiff believes that the defendant has caused some type of monetary, emotional, or physical harm. You may have heard the expression: "Anyone can sue anyone for anything." This is for the most part true, as evidenced by the civil lawsuit filed against the drive-through restaurant by a woman who claimed that she was harmed by coffee that was served much hotter than industry standards of reasonableness. In winning her case, she introduced evidence that management knew the coffee was being served hotter than necessary and failed to take corrective action.

Criminal law, as illustrated in Table 10.1, focuses on regulating people's conduct and protecting society from the unlawful actions of individuals. If you are a criminal justice major, you know this to be "prohibitive law." All criminal law is prohibitive in nature. There are no laws that allow conduct, but there are plenty of laws that ban certain acts. For example, there is no law that says it is legal to proceed through a green light at an intersection, but there are laws that prohibit running a red light. We sometimes hear of people who want the government to "legalize marijuana," but in reality, they're asking for a repeal of the law that makes marijuana illegal. Other criminal acts include theft, robbery, assault, and identity theft. Criminal law is further distinguished from civil law by the fact that it is structured and codified, meaning that the criminal laws are contained in various "codes," such as the Penal Code, Education Code, Elections Code, Transportation Code, and about a dozen others. These codes clearly define what conduct is criminal, and they provide for specific penalties.

Criminal cases are those in which someone is charged in court with having violated certain laws called *criminal* or *penal statutes*. A person who violates one of these statutes is said to have committed a *crime*. In Texas, an act is not a crime unless, before the act occurred, the legislature has passed a statute making the act unlawful.[7]

Because criminal law reflects societal values, it is subject to change and revision. In recent years, the laws against driving while intoxicated were modified in order to prosecute persons whose blood-alcohol content is .08, down from the previous level of .10. This revision was made to further discourage drinking and driving and was largely the result of lobbying by Mothers Against Drunk Driving and other groups committed to fighting Driving While Intoxicated (DWI). A society's criminal laws also reflect the changing social climate. In 2009 Texas DWI laws were further strengthened, making it a felony to drive drunk with a child in the car and requiring defendants to submit to blood tests when they drive drunk with a child passenger.[8]

10.1
10.2
10.3
10.4
10.5

civil law
Law that deals with private rights and seeks damages rather than punishment.

plaintiff
The person or entity that initiates a civil lawsuit.

defendant
The person charged with a crime or the subject of a civil suit.

criminal law
Laws that regulate individual conduct and seek to protect society by punishing criminal acts.

TABLE 10.1 TYPES OF LAW

	Civil	Criminal
Purpose	Protect property	Regulate conduct
Plaintiff	Aggrieved	Government
Source of Law	Unrestricted	Criminal codes
Burden of Proof	Preponderance	Beyond reasonable doubt
Final Remedy	Usually monetary	Fine or incarceration

☐ Other Distinctions Between Civil and Criminal Law

A critical distinction between civil and criminal law is the burden of proof. Civil cases are decided on a preponderance of the evidence. The plaintiff must convince the jury that his or her argument is more reasonable than the defendant's, in order to prevail in a civil lawsuit. This practice of "weighing" the evidence and testimony is known as **preponderance**. If the plaintiff proves, in the minds of the jurors, that the defendant is mostly at fault, the plaintiff wins. By contrast, a person prosecuting a criminal case must convince all the jurors that the defendant is guilty beyond a reasonable doubt. This is a fairly lofty standard; if even one juror does not vote "guilty," the defendant cannot be convicted. The term "**beyond a reasonable doubt**" does not mean absolute certainty, but it does suggest that, under the circumstances, any reasonable person would conclude that the defendant did commit the crime.

Civil cases can be initiated by an individual, group, or corporation. In contrast, criminal cases are initiated by a **prosecutor** who is employed by the state. It is the prosecutor's job to prove the case in court. In a criminal case, the victim does not need to retain an attorney, as the prosecutor fills this role. In contrast, most of the litigants in a civil case are represented by attorneys they personally hire.

☐ Can an Act Be Both Civil and Criminal?

In a word, yes. Sometimes an event, such as a crime of violence, can be the cause for both civil and criminal actions. For example, a person who injures another may be prosecuted for assault because there is a specific law prohibiting this conduct. The victim would also be entitled to sue the assailant in civil court to recover medical expenses, lost wages, and monetary damages for pain and suffering.

☐ Other Types of Cases

There are some types of cases that fall between civil and criminal. *Juvenile* cases, involving children between the ages of 10 and 17, may resemble criminal cases in many ways, but are normally considered to be civil in nature.[9] When a juvenile commits an act that is criminal in nature, it is classified as either *delinquent conduct* or *conduct indicating a need for supervision*. Generally, delinquent conduct is defined as conduct by a child that, if committed by an adult, would be a serious criminal offense. Conduct indicating a need for supervision is a status crime (it is a crime only because of the defendant's status as a juvenile) and includes truancy, running away, and activity, which would be considered a minor criminal violation if committed by an adult.[10] Under certain circumstances and after a hearing, the juvenile court judge may certify a juvenile for trial as an adult if the juvenile was at least 14 years of age at the time of the offense.

Two Types of Courts

10.2 Outline the Structure of the Texas court system.

☐ The Trial Courts

Trial courts, or courts of **original jurisdiction**, hear a case for the first time. The trial court's function is twofold: (1) it determines the facts of the case, and based on those facts, (2) it applies the existing law to reach a verdict. The trial court is where witnesses testify, evidence is introduced, objections are raised, and juries determine whether there is liability or guilt. There are four levels of trial courts in Texas: municipal, justice, county court-at-law, and district. We will visit each of these courts later in this chapter.

The Appellate Courts

If the verdict of a trial court is appealed, an **appellate court** reviews the case. Appellate courts exist to determine whether the trial courts have correctly applied the law. These courts review both the manner in which the law was applied and whether established legal procedures were followed. A party appealing a trial court verdict cannot introduce new or additional evidence at the appellate level. The party can only question whether the evidence introduced at trial was sufficient to support the trial court's findings of fact.

After an appellate court reviews a case, it can come to one of three conclusions. The most common finding of the appellate court is to **uphold**. This means the appellate court did not find cause to change the verdict of the trial court and thus the trial court's verdict stands. The opposite happens when the appellate court's decision is to **reverse and render**. This means the verdict of the trial court is overturned (reversed) and the verdict now favors the other party (the decision is rendered in favor of the appealing party). The third possible outcome of an appeal is **reverse and remand**. This means the appellate court has found that errors were made in the trial, but it does not want to render its own verdict. In this case, the appellate court remands (sends back) the case so that another trial can be held. The new trial, obviously, will use a new jury. There are two levels of appellate courts in Texas: the courts of appeal and the supreme courts. Each of these will be examined later in this chapter.

Structure of the Texas Courts System

By now, you should understand the basics of the court system. You know that some cases are civil and some are criminal; and you know that some are trials and some are appeals. Armed with this knowledge, we can outline the structure of the Texas court system. Determining which courts hear which cases is a relatively simple task. We will examine each of Texas's six levels of courts as illustrated in Figure 10.1; namely, four trial and two appellate levels, starting with the lowest court and working our way up to the Texas supreme court.

Trial-Level Courts

THE MUNICIPAL COURT Under its constitutional authority to create "such other courts as may be provided by law," the Texas Legislature has created municipal courts in each incorporated city. Presently, there are 923 municipal courts.[11] They have jurisdiction over all Class C misdemeanors occurring within the city's geographic limits. Violations of this type include speeding, making illegal turns, failing to stop at a stop sign or at a red light, parking illegally, driving with an expired driver's license, and most other traffic and parking violations. Municipal courts do not have the authority to hear more severe traffic offenses, such as those involving injuries or intoxication. The maximum punishment the court can order for any traffic-related offense is $500, plus court costs.

Municipal courts are further empowered to hear Class C state law violations that are punishable by fine only. These include simple assault (those that do not result in bodily injury), petty theft (under $50), and public intoxication and disorderly conduct. Like the traffic offenses, these crimes carry fines that may not exceed $500.[12]

Other cases heard by the municipal court include city ordinance violations, including noise disturbances, fireworks-related offenses, curfew violations, and violations of the city or town building codes. A city **ordinance** is a law that is passed by the city council and is enforceable only within that particular city. Cities are free to enact and enforce ordinances, and many Texas cities have recently enacted ordinances prohibiting cell phone communications in school zones. Because municipal courts have exclusive original jurisdiction to hear these cases, a defendant's only recourse is to plead his or her case in this court. Although municipal courts can assess a maximum fine of $500 for all other Class C offenses, violations of city ordinances are punishable by fines of up to $2,000.

appellate court
Courts that hear appeals from lower courts.

uphold
Higher court leaves ruling intact.

reverse and render
The high court overturns the lower court and enacts a final verdict.

reverse and remand
The high court overturns the lower court and orders a new trial.

ordinances
Laws enacted by incorporated cities and towns; violations punishable by fine only and heard in municipal court.

10.1

10.2

10.3

10.4

10.5

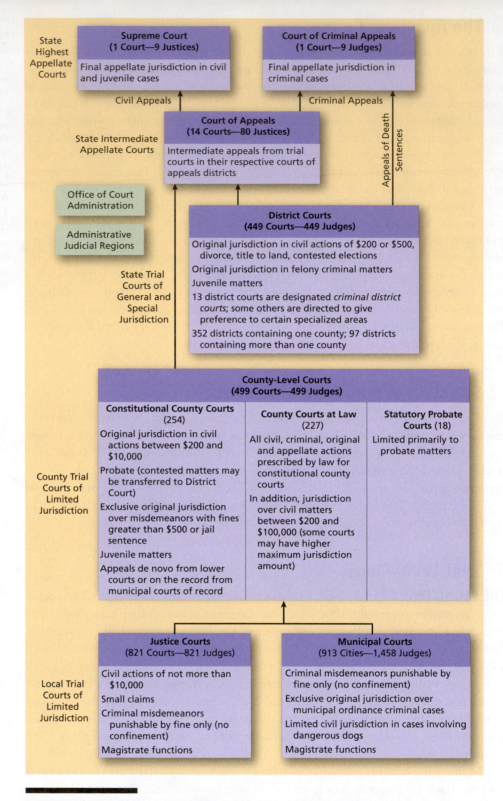

FIGURE 10.1 The Texas Court System. The courts and their jurisdictions.

State law allows a city to determine qualifications for its municipal judges. Most are appointed by the city council, and most cities require the judge to live within the city. Although state law does not require municipal judges to have law degrees, most larger cities and towns that retain full-time municipal judges require them to be attorneys or have extensive legal training. Statewide, about 50 percent of municipal court judges have graduated from law school.

Most small-town municipal courts are courts of nonrecord, meaning there is no official recording or transcript of the cases heard before the court. Courts of record maintain tape recordings or transcripts of court proceedings so that appellate courts can determine whether any errors were made during the original trial. Where there is no official record, there can be no appeal. In the event that a defendant is not satisfied with the verdict from a court of nonrecord, the defendant may request a **trial de novo**, which, literally translated from Latin means "new trial." These trials are held at the county court at law level, which is a court of record.[13] Until recently, many defendants paid lawyers to file their traffic tickets at the higher-level courts. This caused the county courts at law to become bogged down with cases and forced them to dismiss many of the tickets. To counter this, many municipal courts have become courts of record, thereby eliminating the defendant's option of requesting a trial de novo.

There are two ways in which a municipal court may become a court of record. One method requires the city to conduct a special election. The other, more common method requires legislative action. Under this approach, city administrators ask a member of the state legislature to sponsor a bill making its municipal court a court of record. If the bill is passed by both the Texas house and senate, the city can create the new court without holding a local election. Cities seeking to establish a court of record are allowed to determine for themselves which approach to take.

THE JUSTICE COURT This court goes by many names, including "small claims" and "the people's court." Each of the state's 819[14] justice courts is presided over by a justice of the peace (JP), a locally elected judicial official. These courts are highly versatile because they are empowered to hear both criminal and civil cases. The Texas constitution specifies that each of Texas's 254 counties has a justice of the peace and—depending on the county's population—can have as many as eight.[15]

The criminal cases heard by these courts are of the same level as the municipal court: Class C misdemeanors. The answer to the question "How do I know whether the municipal court or the justice court will hear my ticket?" depends on the agency that gave you the ticket. If you are charged with running that stop sign in the city by a city police officer, the local municipal court will have jurisdiction. On the other hand, if a county sheriff's deputy or a state trooper presents with a citation, the case will be heard in justice court by the local JP.[16]

The justice court's jurisdiction in civil matters is extensive, since it is the lowest court in the state having civil jurisdiction. These courts hear most of the civil cases in which the amount in dispute is under $10,000. If a plaintiff wishes to sue someone for more than that amount, he must file the case in a higher court. A person who wants to file a civil case valued at less than $10,000 may file in justice court or in a higher court. What's the difference? Since the justice court is somewhat informal, plaintiffs and defendants are not required to hire attorneys to state their cases. For this reason, the court is often referred to as "small claims court" or "the people's court." Filing a case in justice court is less costly and usually gets on the docket much sooner than do cases in the higher courts.

The Texas constitution empowers JPs to perform a variety of other judicial duties, including arraignments of prisoners and issuance of criminal arrest warrants at the request of law enforcement officers. Justice courts possess exclusive jurisdiction for issuing peace bonds against people whom the judge believes may become hostile or violent toward another individual. A **peace bond** is a court order designed to keep the peace by protecting someone who has been threatened, but not harmed. When a justice of the peace issues a peace bond he or she is ordering the person who made the threats to deposit money with the court. If the person who made the threats commits the threatened criminal action, then the deposited money will be given to the state.

The justice of the peace also serves in the capacity of a committing magistrate, with the authority to issue arrest warrants for the apprehension and arrest of persons charged with committing criminal acts.[17] In addition, the justice of the peace serves as the coroner in those counties where there is no provision for a medical examiner, serves as an *ex officio* notary public, and may perform marriage ceremonies for additional compensation.[18]

trial de novo
Cases that are retried by the county court after being heard in lower courts of nonrecord.

peace bond
A court order providing a jail sentence issued by a justice of the peace against a person who had threatened another person.

Texas ★ Mosaic

Judge Roy Bean

Perhaps he had never heard of the Texas Bar, but that's exactly where Judge Roy Bean held court. From his saloon called the Jersey Lilly in the town of Langtry, Texas, Judge Bean meted out more than justice—he was the Law of the West. That saloon/courtroom in the small town on the banks of the Rio Grande is now a Texas shrine. For 19 years, Judge Bean presided over a territory so wild and vast that it hadn't even been named. Langtry hasn't grown much since the days when the legendary judge would operate his saloon and hold court in the same building. Today, the town has about 25 inhabitants.

Many myths have been written about the "hanging judge" who sentenced many to death by lynching, but in reality Judge Bean was quite lenient. He never sentenced anyone to death by hanging or otherwise. On one occasion, the sheriff brought a man charged with carrying a concealed weapon to the Jersey Lilly. Judge Bean told the sheriff that the charges wouldn't stick. He reasoned that if the man was just standing, he wasn't "carrying" anything. And if the accused was walking, well then, "he was a travelin', and travelin' men have the right to possess a weapon." Although he was relatively merciful in the punishment he administered, there was something about Bean's brand of justice that was unattractive to the criminal element. Perhaps it was the sign that hung in the courtroom that read, "Argumentum Adjudicum." Judge Bean told anyone who asked what it meant, "Don't argue with the judge." Legend has it that Bean was about as tolerant of the state government as he was of criminals; which is to say, he wasn't. On receiving a letter from then-Governor Jim Hogg that Judge Bean's court had failed to transfer money from fines to Austin, Judge Bean responded with his own letter: "Dear Governor, Why don't you run things in Austin and let

Judge Roy Bean in front of his courthouse, the Jersey Lilly
Archives Division.

me run them down here?" Austin neither received any money from or appropriated any for Judge Bean's court. Evidently, the arrangement suited both parties just fine.

From the many stories one hears about Judge Bean, one may presume that the stages of arrest as outlined in this chapter were not followed to the letter, if at all. We do know that he was regarded as fair, swift, and impartial, and for that very reason the criminals feared him.

How many modern-day judges can make that same claim?

1. Judge Bean enjoyed a great amount of autonomy and had wide discretion. Should today's judges be allowed so much discretion, or should sentencing guidelines be strict to ensure consistency?

One does not need a law degree to become a justice of the peace; neither does one need any previous legal training or experience. The law requires JPs who are not licensed attorneys to complete extensive civil and criminal training programs. Justices of the peace may be removed from office if they do not complete the required training successfully. Some critics (most of them unemployed or underemployed attorneys) have argued that JPs should be required to earn law degrees and be practicing attorneys. Although it is true that some justices of the peace, especially in rural areas, may not be as qualified as some attorneys in the legal education arena, the fact remains that most are highly competent in performing their duties. In addition to issuing search and arrest warrants and peace bonds, JPs also perform marriages and, in counties without a medical examiner's office, serve as coroner. Most modern JPs don't have quite as colorful a resume as that of the legendary Roy Bean, featured in the Mosaic.

THE COUNTY COURTS In Texas, there are county courts at law and there are county commissioner's courts. Although similar in name, there is a world of difference between the two. The county courts discussed in this chapter are judicial courts, meaning they are part of the Texas judicial system. By contrast, the county commissioner's courts are legislative bodies and are not judicial in scope.

There are three categories of county-level courts: the county court-at-law, the constitutional county court, and the probate court. The first two are the only courts in the state to have both original and appellate jurisdiction. The courts' appellate jurisdiction is limited and stems from cases that are appealed from municipal courts and justice courts. Cases that have been decided by lower courts of nonrecord are retried de novo at this level. This is not an appeal, but rather a brand-new trial heard at this (the county court) level.

The Texas constitution provides for one constitutional county court in each of the state's 254 counties. As some of Texas's counties grew more urbanized, it became clear that these courts could not handle the volume of cases generated by an ever-increasing population. In response, the Texas Legislature created county courts-at-law, which serve as county-level courts authorized to hear cases of both criminal and civil nature. To date, the legislature has authorized about 200 of these county courts-at-law. In creating these courts, the legislature established more stringent qualifications for the judges. For example, county court-at-law judges are required to be licensed attorneys, whereas judges presiding over constitutional county courts are required only to be "well informed in the law." As in the justice court, criminal cases typically dominate the docket, accounting for nearly three-quarters of the county court-at-law's activity. The court's original jurisdiction in criminal cases includes driving while intoxicated, assault resulting in bodily injury, possession of marijuana (under 4 ounces), and other Class A and B misdemeanors.

The types of civil cases heard in the county court-at-law and in the constitutional county court include personal injury lawsuits and tax disputes. The legislature authorizes some county courts-at-law to hear cases involving up to $200,000, but the constitutional county courts are generally limited to cases in which the plaintiff seeks considerably less. In criminal cases, defendants have the option of choosing either a bench trial or a jury trial. A **bench trial** is a trial without a jury in which the judge determines issues of fact. If the defendant elects to have a bench trial, no jury is selected and the judge alone renders a verdict. In recent years, fewer than 5 percent of the defendants in criminal trials conducted in the state's county courts-at-law have opted for jury trials.

Also at the county level are the probate courts, which hear matters involving wills and estates. There are 16 of these courts, all of them located in the more populous counties. Like justices of the peace, all county-level judges are chosen in countywide partisan elections and serve four-year terms. All candidates for these courts must possess a law degree and be licensed to practice law in Texas.

THE DISTRICT COURTS The district courts are the state's highest-level trial courts. They have both criminal and civil jurisdiction, although many of them are set up to hear exclusively one or the other. There are about 450 of these courts, most of them located in the state's more populous areas. A "district" can be as small as a county, and some counties have eight or more district courts. In the less densely populated areas, a district may encompass many counties. Since this is the highest trial court in the state, it hears the most serious of cases—felonies. Statewide, a majority of the court's criminal cases are disposed of by **plea bargaining**, a process in which the lawyer for the accused negotiates a relatively lighter sentence in return for a guilty plea. Plea bargaining is controversial but necessary, especially in the urban areas where the dockets are stacked with thousands of cases. The practice saves taxpayers millions of dollars each year—money that would otherwise be spent prosecuting the accused.[19]

bench trial
A criminal trial that is held without jury, as requested by the person charged.

plea bargaining
A process in which the accused receives a lighter sentence than could be expected from a trial verdict in exchange for a guilty plea.

10.1

10.2

10.3

10.4

10.5

In the civil arena, there is no limit as to the monetary damages a plaintiff may seek in the district court. Each year we see more cases in which the amount in dispute is in the billions of dollars. The most common types of civil cases heard in district court are divorce, child custody, and family law matters. Other civil cases include state tax disputes, personal injury lawsuits, workers' compensation claims, and contract disputes. District court judges are elected to four-year terms and run in partisan elections. Candidates must be at least 25 years of age and must either be a licensed attorney or have served as a judge in another court for at least four continuous years.

☐ Appellate Courts

The state's appellate court system is comprised of two levels: intermediate and supreme. These courts' jurisdiction extends only to cases that have already been tried in the courts of original jurisdiction. Appellate justices hear cases in odd-numbered panels. In other words, three, five, up to nine justices preside over every appellate case and they vote on the outcome. In most instances, a panel of three judges will hear a particular case, allowing the courts to hear several cases simultaneously and thus resolve many cases at the same time. About two-thirds of the cases heard by the intermediate courts are criminal in nature, and these courts generally make dispositions in all cases in fewer than two years. All Texas justices are elected to six-year terms in partisan elections, a practice that has come under fire and is discussed in greater detail later in this chapter.

INTERMEDIATE COURTS OF APPEAL The intermediate courts hear all appeals from the state's county and district courts, except capital murder cases in which the defendant is sentenced to death. Death penalty cases bypass the intermediate courts and get an automatic review to the court of criminal appeals, but in all other cases, one of the litigants must request an appeal. Candidates for these courts are required to be at least 35 years of age and must have practiced law for 10 or more years or have served as a judge in a court of record for 10 or more years. There are 14 courts of appeals, arranged by geographic region (see Figure 10.2).

The appellate courts review the transcripts of the lower courts and briefs of the lawyers to determine if the trial court followed the law or violated any rules during the trial. At times, these appellate courts find themselves the target of public criticism, especially when they overturn a trial court's conviction on what the public perceives as a "technicality." This was the case in Amarillo, where an appellate court reversed a 62-year prison sentence given to a woman convicted of suffocating her young daughter. The appellate court ruled that the trial court erred on several important points, namely, allowing inadmissible evidence to be introduced. Most appeals are based on the allegation that the judge made a mistake during the trial stage. The judge, for instance, may have disallowed admissible evidence or misinterpreted a law. The facts of the case are not subject to appeal, only the application of the law. In other words, one cannot appeal a case merely on the grounds that there is a disagreement on the outcome. In order to have a successful appeal, the party must demonstrate that the judge may have made an error during the trial.

DUAL SUPREME COURTS Texas is one of only two states that has a "dual" supreme court system (Oklahoma is the other). The supreme court actually consists of two separate and distinctive entities: the Texas supreme court, which hears civil cases, and the Texas court of criminal appeals, which hears criminal cases, with such exceptions as are spelled out in the accompanying Constitution box. All other states use the federal model, in which a single supreme court hears both criminal and civil cases. Neither the Texas court of criminal appeals nor the Texas supreme court is "superior" to the other. These courts are the highest appellate courts in the state; thus any appeals beyond these courts must be heard in the federal appellate court system.

FIGURE 10.2 Texas Courts of Appeals.

244

The Texas Constitution

en banc
When an appellate court convenes all of its members to hear an appeal.

10.1

10.2

10.3

10.4

10.5

A Closer Look

An Exception to the Rule

This chapter points out that Texas has a dual supreme court system: The supreme court hears cases that are civil in nature, and the court of criminal Appeals, as its name implies, hears cases that are criminal in nature. There is an exception, however. From a legal standpoint, crimes committed by juveniles (individuals age 16 and under) are civil actions and are tried in civil courts. Technically, juveniles are not arrested but rather are "taken into custody"; and they are not jailed but "detained." Consequently, the state's highest appellate court for hearing criminal cases involving juvenile defendants is the Texas supreme court, and not the court of criminal appeals.

A chief justice and eight associate justices preside over each court, although they are referred to as judges in the criminal court. Supreme Court Chief Justice Wallace Jefferson is profiled in the accompanying Mosaic. Most of the time, cases at this level are heard **en banc**, meaning that all nine members of the court sit in on the case. In death penalty cases, all nine members of the court of criminal appeals must be present. Justices of the supreme court and court of criminal appeals are selected in partisan statewide elections and serve six-year terms. Terms are staggered to ensure that a majority have appellate court experience.

Criminal cases heard in any of the state's 14 courts of appeals may be appealed to the court of criminal appeals by the defendant, in limited circumstances by the state, or by both. The Texas constitution requires cases in which the defendant is given the death penalty to be reviewed by the Texas court of criminal appeals. This is often referred to as an "automatic appeal," but that term is erroneous because the court is *required* to review the case even if the defendant does not wish to appeal his or her death sentence.

The Texas supreme court has the exclusive authority to issue licenses to practice law and has established a Board of Law Examiners to administer this function. The Texas constitution granted the Texas supreme court the responsibility for establishing civil procedural rules and for overseeing the efficient administration of the state's entire judicial system. The supreme court's administrative responsibilities include overseeing the administration of all criminal courts as well, even though the court itself does not hear criminal cases.

1. Should Texas abolish the dual supreme court system and replace it with a single supreme court?

2. Should the practice of automatic review of death penalty cases be rescinded?

The Court's Role in Public Policy Making

10.3 Analyze how the Texas judiciary plays an important role in shaping public policy.

Most Americans are taught to view the major government institutions (the executive, the legislative, and the judiciary) as three distinct entities with separate and narrow powers.

We might have learned in high school that the U.S. government has "three branches" and that the legislative branch makes the laws and the courts interpret the laws. This view is somewhat oversimplified. The fact is that the courts often modify and even create laws, although that is not their prescribed function. Sometimes, the courts are asked to weigh in on current controversies, and the courts' decisions have the effect of law—at least temporarily. In 2012 the Kountze,

judicial activism
A philosophical approach dictating that the purpose of the courts is to take an active role in public policy making.

Texas, high school cheerleaders were banned by the district's superintendent from displaying bible verses at football games. Parents filed a lawsuit and asked Hardin County District Judge Steven Thomas for an order to temporarily allow the cheerleaders to display the banners. Judge Thomas, a Perry appointee, agreed, and the cheerleaders were allowed to display the verses at home games. Several high-profile groups, including the Anti-Defamation League, have called the banners state-sponsored religion, but others, including Texas Attorney General Greg Abbott, disagree, calling it private speech that is protected by the U.S. and Texas constitutions. And since there are constitutional implications, the case is likely headed for the federal courts.

For decades, legal experts have discussed the merits of **judicial activism**, a philosophy that promotes court intervention in policy making. The debate continues today, as fierce as ever and fueled by federal and state court decisions that often contradict—and thus overrule—the expressed desires of the legislative branch and popular opinion. This has certainly been the case in the controversial Texas homosexual conduct law. In 1973 the Texas Legislature amended the Texas Penal Code (Section 21.06) to make homosexual conduct unlawful. The law was seldom, if ever, enforced because it was thought impossible for a police officer to see the law being broken in a private place, such as a house. But in 1998 two men were arrested after Houston police entered an apartment while investigating a disturbance and observed two men engaging in homosexual conduct. They were convicted in the trial court. The appellate court at first overturned the conviction but later reaffirmed it, finding the Texas law constitutional. The Texas court of criminal appeals refused to hear the case, so the defendants challenged the law on constitutional grounds to the U.S. Supreme Court, and in 2003, the law was struck down as unconstitutional. So contentious is this issue that the law remains on the books even though the words "Section 21.06 was declared unconstitutional by *Lawrence v. Texas*" appears in the statute.

Over the years, both the Texas supreme court and the Texas court of criminal appeals have rendered decisions that have in practice had the same effect as legislation. The Texas high courts have declared unconstitutional much legislation, including that relating to the financing of public schools. In these cases, the courts have taken it upon themselves to establish guidelines that have had the effect of law. The Texas supreme court ruled in 1989 that the school finance system was unconstitutional because the disparities among the "property-rich" and "property-poor" districts were causing an ever-increasing gap among the dollars per student these districts had available. The legislature changed the way funding was disbursed several times since then, and each time the Texas supreme court again found the system unconstitutional. The court ruled the changes were too incremental and did not address the inequities. Then, in 2006, the legislature made a comprehensive change in the way schools are funded by lowering the burden on local property owners and raising the state's contribution. The money came from increased state taxes. It was not over, however, because the 2011 legislature, in an effort to balance the state's budget, made significant funding adjustments that left the schools with fewer dollars while facing the burden of increasing enrollments and tighter regulations. Hundreds of school districts filed lawsuits in Texas district courts in 2012, and no one doubts that no matter how these courts rule, the Texas supreme court will ultimately determine—or at the least remain a major player in—school finance policy.

Critics of judicial activism claim that policies created by the courts are in themselves unconstitutional because the policies were not made by the process of representative democracy. Actually, this claim is only partially valid because the members of the court are elected, albeit not for the express purpose of making laws. The argument goes that when the courts create legislation, they deprive citizens of the right to participatory democracy. On the other hand, proponents of judicial activism claim that the courts have the responsibility to protect the interests of all sides, even if one side happens to be in the minority in terms of public opinion.

Selection of Judges

10.4 Explain why the method for selecting Texas judges is under constant criticism.

The process used by Texans for selecting judges is highly politicized and thus a source of criticism. Although municipal court judges can be appointed by city councils or by other city officials, the judges presiding in every other level of the Texas court system—from justice of the peace to chief justice of the supreme court—are selected through popular election.

Texas is one of only seven states requiring its judges to run in partisan elections. Most other states follow the federal model of executive appointment with legislative confirmation, eliminating some of the politics that are inherent in any partisan election. Texas's system makes it necessary for judicial candidates to identify with a political party and to hit the campaign trail, much as if they were running for a legislative seat.

There are two reasons why Texas elects, rather than appoints, most of its judges. The first, and probably the most influential, reason stems from Texas's own traditionalistic and individualistic political culture. This culture is still prevalent today, as evidenced by the resistance to judicial reform. So strong is the resistance that reformists have experienced remarkable difficulty in getting the legislature even to discuss, much less adopt, some of the proposals. The second reason stems from the first. Even before the current Texas constitution was drafted, Texans held a basic distrust of government in general and politicians in particular. The framers of the Texas constitution, as we note in the Inside the Federalist System box, reasoned that a popularly elected judiciary would be more responsive to the people than to the full-time politicians and special interests. This is truly one of the greatest ironies in Texas politics because modern-day voter apathy has caused judicial candidates to recognize (some would say "and to serve") the special interests—from whom they get the majority of campaign contributions—more than most voters. The fact is that most judges raise most of their campaign money from attorneys who do business before their court, creating at least the perception of impropriety. The people who wrote the Texas constitution were relying on an informed and active electorate to choose their judges.

The framers of the Texas constitution established a system of electing judges in large part to curtail the governor's appointment powers. There is a great irony here, too, because the same system allows the governor to make judicial appointments in the event that a vacancy occurs between elections. Table 10.2 indicates that six of the nine Texas supreme court justices first assumed office by means of gubernatorial appointment. Given the framers' distrust of government generally and their disdain for governors specifically, it is doubtful that they anticipated such a high rate of appointments to the state's highest courts. Being appointed to fill a term of office provides a huge advantage to the appointee, because it allows the justice to run as an incumbent in the next election.

☐ First Assumed Office

The positive consequence of judicial appointment has been a striking increase in the number of women and minorities sitting on the bench. Governor Ann Richards kept her campaign promise to appoint persons who better reflect the actual demographics of the state. Governors Bush and Perry embraced that policy too, and the effect is a

Finding an effective way to solicit votes is always difficult for judicial candidates. Judge Leticia Hinojosa used this billboard in an effective re-election campaign.

TABLE 10.2 METHOD OF INITIAL JUDICIAL SELECTION

Supreme Court	Court Crim Appls	Cts Appl	Dist Cts	County Cts	Justice Cts	Muni Cts
Appointed: 6	2	45	175	103	207	1520
Elected: 3	7	34	281	404	607	20

Inside the Federalist System

Federalism allows each state to determine how its supreme court justices are to be chosen. You learned in this chapter that the method of selecting Texas supreme court justices is through regularly scheduled partisan elections. Some states, as indicated in Figure 10.3, follow the federal model, which is appointment through a process of executive selection and legislative confirmation. Some states use hybrid systems that combine appointments and regular elections. While the system used in Texas is highly controversial, we can take comfort in the fact that federalism allows us to change it through proper channels, and federal approval is not required.

1. Should Texas supreme court justices continue to be elected, or should they be appointed for life terms, as are federal judges?

2. In the event of a vacancy, the governor is empowered to make judicial appointments. Should this power be turned over to a special committee? If so, how should the committee be constituted?

The Texas Supreme Court listens to the Governor's State of the State address. Often, public office requires actions that are not directly connected to its formal duties. These symbolic appearances help reinforce the concept of a vibrant democracy, although critics question whether the justices appearing at a chief executive's political address undercuts separation of powers.

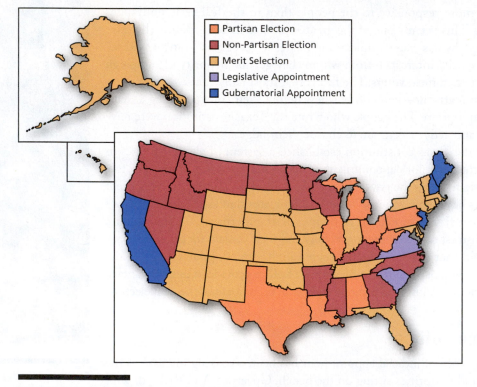

- Partisan Election
- Non-Partisan Election
- Merit Selection
- Legislative Appointment
- Gubernatorial Appointment

FIGURE 10.3 Judicial selection methods among the states.

more diverse judicial system. In 2004 Perry appointed Wallace B. Jefferson, the state's first African American Texas supreme court chief justice. The former chief justice, Tom Phillips, resigned his post after serving for 17 years.

Justices running in statewide elections must raise hundreds of thousands of dollars in order to pay for campaign advertisements, and because they have even less name recognition, challengers often must raise even more. Some supreme court candidates have raised more than $1 million, most of which came from political action committees.

Texas ★ Mosaic

Chief Justice Wallace B. Jefferson

In 2004, Governor Perry appointed Wallace B. Jefferson to be chief justice of the Texas supreme court. Justice Jefferson grew up in San Antonio and earned his law degree at the University of Texas. Besides being one of the youngest chief justices, he is the first African American to serve in that capacity. Justice Jefferson was no stranger to high courts, having argued and won two cases in the U.S. Supreme Court while practicing in his San Antonio law firm.

Justice Jefferson was named the Outstanding Young Lawyer by the San Antonio Young Lawyers Association in 1997. In 1998, he served as president of the San Antonio Bar Association which, during his tenure, hired personnel whose sole mission was to coordinate the provision of legal services to the poor. He was named a "40 Under 40 Rising Star" in 1996 by the *San Antonio Business Journal* and in 2001 by the *Texas Lawyer*. Justice Jefferson was recognized as a "Pillar" of the Northside Independent School District in 1999 and received the Distinguished Alumni Award from James Madison College at Michigan State University in 2002. His professional activities have included serving on the Supreme Court of Texas Advisory Committee, the Texas State Commission on Judicial Conduct, and chairing the host committee for the 2000 Fifth Circuit Judicial Conference. He is past president of the William S. Sessions American Inns of Court. Justice Jefferson has lectured across the country on appellate advocacy and received national recognition from the American Bar Association. He previously served as a director of the San Antonio Public Library Foundation, the San

Wallace Jefferson is the first African American to serve as Chief Justice of the Texas Supreme Court. His great, great, great grandfather was a slave, who, upon emancipation, was elected to the Waco city council. Jefferson is the president of Conference of Chief Justices, which represents all fifty states.

Antonio Bar Foundation, and the Alamo Area Big Brothers/Big Sisters organization.

1. Should the Texas governor retain the power to appoint judges in the event of vacancies, or should special elections be held?

2. Should governors be required to appoint a certain number of women and minority judges to reflect the diversity of the population?

Judicial candidates are prohibited from discussing pending cases while on the campaign trail, but that prohibition hasn't stopped some judges from violating it. Law clerks, attorneys, and even former supreme court justices have testified that the rules are routinely broken.

In the late 1980s, allegations of power abuses made against Texas supreme court justices brought an array of investigative reporters to Austin. The Texas high courts received nationwide publicity and were even featured in a *60 Minutes* segment. Justices were accused of trading votes for campaign contributions and for changing liability law in favor of the plaintiffs' attorneys in return for large campaign contributions. The implicated justices were all voted out of office or left the bench.

The Call for Judicial Reform

10.5 Evaluate the merits of suggested judicial reforms.

The fact that candidates for Texas's highest courts are elected on an at-large basis has also created controversy, particularly among minority groups. The 18 justices comprising the two most powerful courts hardly mirror the racial and ethnic makeup of the state. There is widespread agreement that were it not for the fact that recent governors have appointed minorities to fill judicial vacancies, there would be much less diversity in the Texas judicial system. Reformists have suggested a process that uses single-member districts in order to provide Hispanics and African Americans equal opportunity to select and to serve as members of the state courts. These reformists even include former and current judges serving on Texas's highest courts. Former Texas Supreme Court Chief Justice Tom Phillips has said that Texas has "the most expensive judicial races in the world and the most politicized judicial races in the world." Former Lieutenant Governor Bob Bullock's plan, which was ultimately rejected, called for district judges to be elected in nonpartisan elections in county commissioner districts. The plan would have meant fewer costly elections and would have ensured more minority representation.

A reform measure called the Missouri Plan would once and for all alleviate the rising costs of campaigning, depoliticize the judicial system, and provide opportunities for qualified minority representation on the courts. Versions of the plan have been successfully adopted by a majority of the states. It combines the features of appointment while preserving the right of the voters to remove judges. A typical Missouri Plan system begins with a list of qualified candidates submitted to the governor by a panel consisting of legislators, judges, and citizens. The governor then appoints judges from the list to serve a term, which is usually four years. At the end of the term, the voters are given the opportunity to vote on whether to keep the judge in office. If the majority of the votes are to retain the judge, he or she serves an additional term of seven years. If the voters choose to remove the judge, the governor selects another candidate from the panel's list. Under this system, judicial candidates are required neither to identify with a political party nor to raise campaign contributions. Many of Texas's presiding judges favor implementation of the Missouri Plan. The greatest opposition has been from certain special interest groups that have been effective in promoting their own candidates.

Additional reforms have been proposed in recent years by various groups, elected officials, and judges:

- *Court Structure.* Proposed reforms include abolishing the Texas court of criminal appeals, making the Texas supreme court the highest court for all civil and criminal cases.
- *Judicial Selection.* Reformists argue that justice would be better served if judges presiding in courts of original jurisdiction were appointed by the appropriate legislative bodies, such as the city council and county commissioners. Others argue that a system of appointing judges would make the selection process even more political than it already is and would take control away from the voters.
- *Nonpartisan Judicial Elections.* The most persuasive argument posed by reformists favoring this measure is that judicial candidates will no longer need to "conform" to a single political ideology and can thereby exercise a greater degree of judicial freedom. Many reformists also argue that nonpartisan elections would cost much less and would allow women and minority candidates to compete on a more equitable plane.
- *No Straight-Ticket Voting.* This proposal would virtually eliminate the "coattail effect" that takes place in major elections. Over the past 10 years, many sitting judges (and other locally elected officials) have switched parties not for ideological reasons, but for the purpose of capturing the votes of straight-ticket voters in state and national elections.

Most Texans cannot name more than two or three justices on the supreme court or court of criminal appeals. (And we are probably being optimistic when we say two or three.) Nonetheless, voters are more likely to recognize the name of a sitting justice than the name of a political newcomer. Name recognition is an important advantage for an incumbent seeking judicial office in Texas. This advantage, combined with the fact that most citizens pay little or no attention to the politics of the judiciary, virtually ensures reelection. Occasionally, however, judges do make the news. In Houston, for example, a county court-at-law judge was publicly reprimanded after he allegedly consumed alcoholic beverages and fondled female prosecutors while on the bench. In a DWI case being heard in his court, the judge allegedly drank the evidence and later commented to prosecutors, "I am sure glad you lost so that I don't have to preserve this evidence."

Review the Chapter

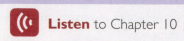

The Texas Court System

10.1 Differentiate between civil and criminal law.

Civil lawsuits are filed when the plaintiff makes a claim that the defendant failed to do the responsible thing or take appropriate action. Usually, the plaintiff seeks justice in the form of compensation or other property. Examples of civil law include contract disputes and personal injury. Criminal law always involves the government as the plaintiff and seeks justice in the form of punishment against the defendant. Criminal law deals with statutes that specifically describe prohibitive conduct, and in order to convict, the government must prove its case beyond a reasonable doubt that the defendant is guilty.

Two Types of Courts

10.2 Outline the Structure of the Texas court system.

The term *jurisdiction* means the authority to hear a case. Therefore, every type of case is matched to the appropriate court by means of jurisdiction. Courts of original jurisdiction—also called trial courts—are where a case is heard for the first time. When the losing party seeks review, it files an appeal in the appropriate appellate court. Appellate courts do not determine the facts of the case. Instead, they review the actions of the trial court and determine if errors are made. Appellate courts have the power to uphold or reverse the trial court's verdicts.

The Court's Role in Public Policy Making

10.3 Analyze how the Texas judiciary plays an important role in shaping public policy.

Although public policy is primarily a legislative function, the court system plays an important role through the practice of judicial review. Sometimes, appellate courts create public policy when they overturn an existing policy, such as declaring a particular statute unconstitutional. This action is referred to as judicial activism.

Selection of Judges

10.4 Explain why the method for selecting Texas judges is under constant criticism.

With the exception of municipal court judges, all judges and justices in Texas are elected. This system has caused controversy primarily because elections, especially partisan ones, politicize the judicial branch. Judicial candidates must act a lot like politicians in that they are required to identify with a political party and are required to campaign. Most Texans would rather see judges and justices separated from the political party scene.

The Call for Judicial Reform

10.5 Evaluate the merits of suggested judicial reforms.

The most prominent reform measure, already adopted by many other states, is called the Missouri Plan. The Plan requires judicial appointment, rather than election. After a specified period of time—typically four to six years—the judges appear in retention elections, whereby the people get to determine whether or not the judge should serve another term. Other measures of reform include the elimination of partisan judges (identified by a political party affiliation), the elimination of straight-ticket voting, and merging the two Texas supreme courts into a single court.

Learn the Terms

 Study and **Review** the **Flashcards**

Test Yourself

10.1 Differentiate between civil and criminal law.

Court cases of a civil nature differ from criminal cases in that civil cases

  a. are determined by a preponderance of evidence.
  b. usually result in judgments that involve money.
  c. do not always feature the government as the plaintiff.
  d. are not tied to established codes and statutes.
  e. all of the above.

10.2 Outline the structure of the Texas court system.

Which of the following is not a trial court?

  a. the supreme court
  b. the district court
  c. the justice court
  d. the municipal court
  e. the county court

10.3 Analyze how the Texas judiciary plays an important role in shaping public policy.

A philosophy that promotes court intervention in policy making is

  a. judicial noncompliance.
  b. judicial activism.
  c. judicial restraint.
  d. judicial review.
  e. judicial reform

10.4 Explain why the method for selecting Texas judges is under constant criticism.

What stands most in the way of implementation of the Missouri Plan?

  a. the state legislature
  b. the Texas Attorney General's Office
  c. the political parties
  d. the judges that currently hold office
  e. interest groups

10.5 Evaluate the merits of suggested judicial reforms.

One way to resolve the controversial nature of the Texas judicial system would be to

  a. require justices of the peace to have law degrees.
  b. allow municipal judges to hear civil cases.
  c. prohibit straight-ticket voting in judicial elections.
  d. televise all district court proceedings.
  e. require partisan judicial elections.

Explore Further

Champagne, Anthony. "Campaign Contributions in Texas Supreme Court Races." *Crime, Law, and Social Change* 17 (1992), 91-106.

Hill, John. "Taking Texas Judges out of Politics: An Argument for Merit Election." *Baylor Law Review* 40 (1988), 340–365.

Horton, David M., and Ryan Kellus Turner. *Lone Star Justice: A Comprehensive Overview of the Texas Criminal Justice System.* Austin, TX: Eakin, 1999.

Texas Bar Association www.texasbar.com

Texas Courts Online www.courts.state.tx.us

11

Local and County Governments and Special Districts in Texas

All politics is local.

—Former U.S. Speaker of The House Thomas "Tip" O'Neill

It's a typical morning. The lead story on the TV morning news is the bank robber who is on trial at the district court. You take out the trash and pet your dog, which you recently adopted from the local animal shelter. During your drive to the nearby community college, traveling through a school zone, you see a police officer approaching from the opposite direction and you instinctively check

11.1	**11.2**	**11.3**	**11.4**	**11.5**
Compare and contrast the two types of cities and several forms of city government.	Evaluate the various structures of municipal government, including elections and forms of government.	Identify the major sources of revenue and expenditures of local governments.	Explain why counties were established and how they have evolved.	Summarize the importance of special districts in Texas.

Second grade teacher Omar Garcia greets his students as they arrive to start a new day. Local governments perform many functions, from building roads to enforcing laws to providing education. Public school teachers often perform functions, like this, that are not purely educational in nature.

your speed. People are jogging on trails at the city park, and street department personnel are clearing the debris from last night's thunderstorms. You chuckle as you imagine if the storms knocked the red light cameras out of commission. Later, perhaps on a toll road, you observe a work crew re-striping the roadway. You pull over for an ambulance racing to the county hospital. You arrive, barely on time for your first class, Texas Government, and think to yourself that you must now focus on the topic at hand.

If you caught the dozen or so references to local government in the preceding paragraph, you'll probably do really well on your next exam. If not, you're not alone. When most people think of government and politics, they think about state or national issues. The fact is that local government plays a large part in how we live, work, and play. Welcome to the dynamic arena of local government.

Local government is defined as any level of government below the state level. Specifically, it includes three levels: municipal (or city), county, and special district. Although local government is the essence of American democracy, most people cannot identify the type of local government in their own hometowns, much less name their county commissioners or city council members. The profound irony of American democracy is that although participation in local government affords citizens the most control over their own lives, voter turnout is lower for local elections than for any other level. Texas citizens insist on local control, yet a turnout of 10 percent of the qualified voters for a municipal election is common and a turnout of 20 percent is celebrated.

Texas ★ Mosaic

Increasing Texas Diversity:
Julian Castro

Julian Castro personifies several key points of this chapter. At 37 years of age, he is the youngest mayor of a Top 50 American city.

After graduating from Stanford University with honors and distinction and earning a law degree from Harvard Law School, he became engaged in local politics and became the youngest elected city councilman at that time in San Antonio history.

His commitment to education is as genuine as it is noteworthy. His wife, Erica Lira Castro, is an elementary school teacher, and Castro himself has taught courses at the University of Texas at San Antonio, Trinity University, and St. Mary's University. Under his leadership, the city in 2010 opened Café College, a one-stop counseling center offering advice on financial aid, college admissions, and standardized test preparation to any student in the San Antonio area. In its first year, Café College served more than 5,000 area students, spurring an expansion of the facility in 2011.

In 2010, Mayor Castro, along with young executives from Google and Twitter, were named to the World Economic Forum's list of Young Global Leaders. Later that year, *Time* Magazine placed him on its "40 under 40" list of rising stars in American politics. Mayor Castro also serves on the board of directors of the National League of Cities, where he has earned a reputation as a hard-working and industrious leader.

He was chosen by President Obama to give the keynote address at the 2012 Democratic National Convention, and that exposure vaulted him into the national spotlight. It was only eight years earlier that Obama, then a virtual unknown Illinois state legislator, was asked to give the keynote address.

San Antonio Mayor Julian Castro delivers the keynote address at the 2012 Democratic National Convention. As mayor, Castro has used his personal clout to make for the relatively weak official powers. He even convinced voters to raise taxes that would be used to a fund pre-school program.

There is no doubt that Castro was influenced by his mother, Rosie Castro, a prominent activist with La Raza Unida, a 1970s political movement aimed at increasing Mexican American political power in the Southwest. His twin brother, Joaquin, serves in the Texas state House of Representatives.

1. **How does Julian Castro represent a new generation of American political leaders?**

2. **How will Castro's experience as a city councilman and mayor of a major Texas city influence him in the national political arena?**

Local government is where many of the state's top public figures launched their political careers. There, they put their ideas and ideals to the test and acquire political skills. Former governor Ann Richards started her highly successful political journey as a Travis County commissioner. Before long, she ran for and won the statewide offices of treasurer and then governor. Former San Antonio city councilman Henry Cisneros also served as the city's mayor and was later chosen by President Clinton to serve as the secretary of housing and urban development. Had Cisneros not established a track record as both an able politician and an effective administrator at the local level, he would likely not have been considered for a cabinet position. The lesson here is that local, or "grassroots," politics is the fountainhead of state and national politics. Our system of federalism depends on the dynamics of both intra- and intergovernmental relationships at all levels.

Today, local governments perform a wide range of services, from building roads and keeping them clean and safe to collecting garbage and providing health care for the homeless. Many students are astounded to learn how much local government costs. For example, in 2010 the city of Houston spent about $1.5 billion on the police, fire, and city courts alone.[1]

In an era of ever-increasing demands and limited resources, many of today's successful local government leaders are managing and operating more like businesspeople than politicians. The field of public administration has grown as tomorrow's leaders seek professional training in order to deliver expected services more effectively. Colleges and universities across the country offer advanced degrees in public administration and related fields to prepare our leaders for challenges ranging from long-term waste disposal, education, and infrastructure improvement to water management and homeland security. No matter where in Texas you live, you are soon likely to be logging more miles on toll roads. Although the planning, funding, and construction of these roads remain primarily a state and national issue, supervision and enforcement will always be a responsibility of local government.

Three very broad levels of local government exist: municipal, county, and special district. The cities, towns, and villages throughout the state operate as municipalities. Four of five Texans live within the boundaries of a municipality,[2] but every Texan lives in—and is therefore affected by—one of the state's 254 counties. Special districts, including the approximately 1,100 independent school districts, are specially created units of government that may encompass only part of a city or several counties.

Although Ann Richards would later serve as state treasurer and governor, she started her career in grassroots politics. Her first elective office was as a Travis County commissioner, which is an administrative office with primarily executive power.

Municipal Government

11.1 Compare and contrast the two types of cities and several forms of city government.

Among the local governments, there can be little doubt that cities perform the greatest array of functions. As noted in Figure 11.1, more than 80 percent of Texans live within the boundaries of some 1,200 municipalities. Municipal governments, performing a variety of services, uniquely reflect the citizens who reside within them. The term *municipal government* applies to cities, towns, and villages that are recognized by the legislature as being a governmental entity. Although a municipality can be classified in one of two ways, general law or home rule, countless variations in the form of government operate in these cities.

Throughout the Republic of Texas era and continuing until 1845 (when Texas became a state), cities were chartered by special acts of the Republic of Texas. Nacogdoches has the distinction of becoming Texas's first "incorporated" city on June 5, 1837. Later that year, the Republic granted charters to San Augustine, Richmond, Columbus, San Antonio, Houston, and 12 others.[3]

257

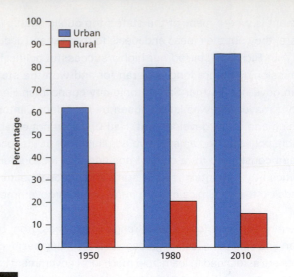

FIGURE 11.1 Texas Historical Rural and Urban Populations, 1950–2005.
Source: U.S. Census Bureau

general law
A highly restrictive, and the most fundamental type of, legal status for municipal government.

☐ Types of Municipalities

There are in essence two types of cities: general law and home rule. Both types of government are of great importance to Texans because although a majority of the cities operate under general law, a majority of Texans reside in cities with a home rule charter.

GENERAL LAW Three-fourths, or approximately 900, of Texas's municipalities are classified as general law cities. General law cities can be any size, but almost all cities under 5,000 in population are general law cities. **General law** cities have limited autonomy. These cities are closely regulated and monitored by the state and may do only those functions that are permitted by state or federal law. In other words, these cities are characterized by having lower taxes, smaller populations, fewer employees, and providing only the most basic services.

General law cities are not heavily populated and do not usually provide "big-city" services such as libraries, public recreation facilities, and public housing. These cities are limited by the generic laws pertaining to local governments in the Texas constitution, as noted in the accompanying box on the state's constitution. General law cities are less autonomous than home rule cities because the Texas constitution limits their local tax rates and compels them to a limited form of government. In other words, general law cities are governed more by state regulation than by the local population.

The Texas constitution authorizes several subtypes of general law cities; namely, Types A, B, and C. Most new cities begin as Type B general law cities under a state law that permits the incorporation of any area containing more than 201 persons. There are six elected city leaders, and they are called aldermen. One of the six aldermen serves as mayor. Once a city reaches a population of 600, it can request reclassification to Type A general law. The state still regulates these cities heavily, as compared to home rule cities, but an example of the greater autonomy can be found in the governing body, which in the case of Class A cities is called the city council. In addition to the city council, the citizens may determine whether or not it requires additional employees, such as a finance director, city secretary, city attorney, or engineer. A Type C General Law city is one governed by a board of commissioners, which is much different from the aldermanic or city council types of governing body. The board of commissioners always consists of any number of elected commissioners, one of whom is designated as the mayor. Each commissioner is responsible for a specific city function. For example, these cities may have a police commissioner, parks commissioner, and so on. No other elective officers are required; however, the board of commissioners must appoint a city clerk and may require the election or appointment of other officials. There are only a few commission forms of municipal government, or Class C general law cities, in Texas today, but it did enjoy some popularity in the early

20th century, when nearly 500 cities used this form of government. It came about in 1900, when a major hurricane devastated the city of Galveston. The city's business leaders, eager to establish a quick and an effective government to get the city back on its feet, convinced the governor to appoint a commission to govern the city during its reconstruction. Today, most of the cities that adopted the commission form of government (including Galveston) have reestablished themselves as home rule cities.[8]

HOME RULE For the most part, **home rule** cities have the opposite characteristics of general law cities. The major difference is the degree of autonomy, or local control. A home rule city may do anything that its own charter authorizes and does not conflict with any existing state or federal law. This degree of autonomy enables home rule cities to provide a greater array of services, including transportation, health care services, and public housing. These services, of course, come at the cost of higher local taxes. When you consider the fact that some 80 percent of Texans live in home rule cities, you may conclude that these people don't mind paying higher tax rates in return for services such as water and sewage, parks, libraries, and senior citizens centers. Many Texans regard these and other city-funded projects, like convention centers, municipal pools, golf courses, youth centers, and museums, as enhancements to the quality of life. It's a trade-off, and it gives Texans a choice. The Texas Municipal League sums up the essence of home rule: "Home rule is the right of citizens at the grassroots level to manage their own affairs with minimum interference from the state. Home rule assumes that governmental problems should be solved at the lowest possible level closest to the people."[9]

Home rule cities, though less restricted by the state, do not enjoy complete autonomy. In order to obtain home rule status, the city must adopt a charter as noted in Table 11.1, which must be approved by the Texas Legislature. Much like the federal government has the ability to create subgovernments (i.e., the states), the state has the power to create and have some degree of control over local governments. Home rule city charters require transparency, and perhaps more importantly, professional management. The functions of the city manager will be discussed later in this chapter.

☐ Forms of Municipal Government

Essentially three forms of municipal government exist in Texas: mayor-council, council-manager, and commission. Each home rule city can create and modify its form of government based on the desires or needs of the community. General law cities may make some modifications to suit the needs of the citizens, but to a much lesser extent.

MAYOR-COUNCIL This type of arrangement is widely used in most of Texas's less populated and rural cities.

It is a simple form of government in which most of the day-to-day executive operations are carried out by either the mayor or by a city council. Most mayor-council municipalities have only a few departments; therefore, the salary of a full-time, professional administrator or manager is not justified.

TABLE 11.1 TYPICAL CITY CHARTER PROVISIONS

- Description of the city's governmental and propriety powers.
- Provisions establishing the city's form of government (mayor-council or council-manager) and its legislative and judiciary machinery.
- Organizational provisions establishing the administrative structure of the city government and the means of financing its operations.
- Provisions governing the procedures of the city council and advisory boards and commissions, and procedures for granting franchises, assessing and collecting taxes, and conducting annexations.
- Popular controls over the city government, such as elections, referenda, initiative, and recall.
- Provisions relating to procedures for amending the charter.

Source: "Local Governments in Texas," Texas Town and City, January 2009 (http://www.tml.org/HCW/LocalGovernmentsinTexas.pdf).

home rule
A legal status that gives municipalities more autonomy in establishing tax rates and providing services; must be approved by a majority of the voters in municipalities consisting of 5,000 or more persons.

11.1

11.2

11.3

11.4

11.5

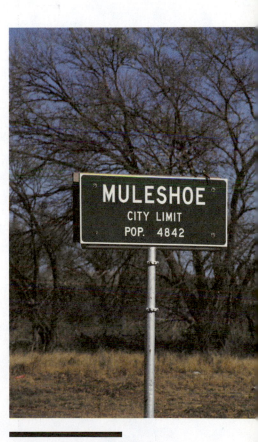

Muleshoe is a general law city in the state's panhandle. General law cities have much less autonomy than home rule cities, which greatly restrict their policy options. Most of their powers are limited by the state.

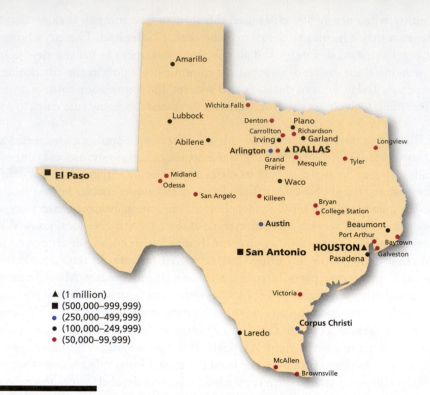

FIGURE 11.2 Texas Cities with More Than 50,000 People.

These smaller cities often do not have police or fire departments; the county sheriff's department and volunteer firefighters usually see to these public safety needs. Public utilities are frequently provided by cooperatives or special districts, not the local government. Two main variations of the mayor-council form of government can be found in Texas: weak mayor and strong mayor. In a weak mayor system, the mayor has limited policy implementation and no veto powers. Mayors working within this system cannot, for example, establish policies without the consent of the city council; neither can they appoint or remove department heads such as the police chief or fire marshal.

The Texas Constitution

A Closer Look

The Texas constitution sets limitations on the amount of taxes a city can levy. Article xi, Section 4 prohibits cities with fewer than 5,000 residents from becoming home rule cities, and it places strict limitations on the amount of taxes that can be levied. Section 5 allows cities with home rule charters to levy significantly higher local taxes, but sets a cap and sets further restrictions.[10] One of the most notable restrictions is a prohibition against adopting local laws inconsistent with state law.

In order to obtain home rule status, a municipality must have a population of at least 5,000 citizens, and the eligible voters must approve a city charter in a popular election.[11] The charter specifies the name of the municipality and the form of government to be implemented.

A home rule charter allows a municipal government greater independence in devising a tax rate structure and in determining the form of government best suited for its citizenry. A charter is essentially a constitution for the city: a contract setting out the powers and the limitations of municipal government. Home rule cities have a greater degree of flexibility in setting local tax rates, deciding which services to provide, and determining the form of government to be used.

1. Should general law cities be granted the autonomy to enact city ordinances?

2. What are the advantages of living in a general law/home rule city?

In the strong mayor cities, the mayor is often empowered to veto policies and ordinances passed by the council and to hire and fire city personnel as he or she deems appropriate. This form of local government is neither common nor popular in Texas, a state that traditionally avoids giving much power to any single person. In addition to these powers, mayors of strong mayor municipalities also have more extensive budgetary powers than do their counterparts in weak mayor systems.

The mayor-council form of municipal government is used primarily by the smaller cities of Texas, with one significant exception. Houston, the largest city in Texas and fourth-largest American city, operates under this form of government with great efficiency. Houston's strong mayor sets the city council agenda and presides over council meetings. He or she also has veto power that in practice is often final. Former Dallas mayor Laura Miller attempted to have her city's government changed from council-manager to the mayor-council form. She failed in this attempt.[12]

COUNCIL-MANAGER The council-manager form of government is used by most medium- and larger-sized cities in Texas, as noted in Table 11.2, and throughout the United States. The qualified voters who reside in the city elect a city council and a mayor, which in turn hire a **city manager** to carry out the council's policies. This system allows for both professional management and local political control. City managers usually are formally trained in urban studies or public administration and have extensive knowledge of budgeting, finance, and personnel laws. Typically, the highest-paid city employees earn salaries comparable to CEOs of midsized corporations. Dallas's city manager earns $261,000, Fort Worth's earns $253,000, Lubbock's $225,000, and Laredo's earns $180,000.[13] Mayors under this system have limited powers and, somewhat like the governor, must rely on the force of their personality to have an impact. Some, like San Antonio mayor Julian Castro, profiled in the Mosaic, have made their presence known on the state or national stage.

The city manager hires other qualified professionals to oversee the various departments, although in most cities, the council must approve the hiring and removal of department heads. Because the city manager, whose typical duties are listed in Table 11.3, is appointed based on his or her training, ability, and merit, the position is apolitical (at least in theory). This means that the manager is allowed to make policy decisions based on need and in the best interest of the community as a whole. For this very reason, the council-manager form of municipal government has its advocates and critics.[14]

The strongest argument in favor of this system is that there is very little waste. The professional qualifications of the city administrators and their staffs allow them to carry out the council's—and the people's—desires in a cost-effective, efficient manner without considering the political implications. Proponents point out that professional municipal administration results in lower tax rates and an optimum level of service because the administrators are trained to research policy decisions thoroughly prior to implementation.

The commission system is often criticized for being too fragmented, as there is usually no single individual who has overall responsibility of the local government.

city manager
Professional political appointee who oversees city operations on a day-to-day basis

11.1

11.2

11.3

11.4

11.5

TABLE 11.2 TYPICAL DUTIES OF A CITY MANAGER

- Enforce all city ordinances, rules, and regulations.
- Supervise all municipal employees and programs.
- Prepare and execute the city's annual budget pursuant to the revenue and expenditure plans adopted by the council.
- Manage the city's funds and prepare periodic reports that advise the council and the general public of the city's fiscal condition.
- Provide information to the council to facilitate its ability to make informed decisions in the best interests of the city.
- Prepare council meeting agendas and attend all such meetings to serve as a resource to the council and the public.
- Draw the council's attention to city needs and recommend alternatives by which the council can respond to those needs.

Source: "Local Governments in Texas," Texas Town and City, January 2009 (http://www.tml.org/HCW/LocalGovernmentsinTexas.pdf).

TABLE 11.3 FORM OF MUNICIPAL GOVERNMENT IN SELECTED TEXAS CITIES

City	Form of Government	Year Adopted
Abilene	Council-Manager	1981
Amarillo	Commission	1913
Arlington	Council-Manager	1990
Austin	Council-Manager	1991
Benbrook	Council-Manager	1990
College Station	Council-Manager	1992
Commerce	Commission	1954
Conroe	Mayor-Council	1992
Corpus Christi	Council-Manager	1993
Corsicana	Commission	1956
Dallas	Council-Manager	1907
Denton	Council-Manager	1959
Dumas	Commission	1991
Fort Worth	Council-Manager	1986
Friendswood	Council-Manager	1971
Galveston	Council-Manager	1991
Hillsboro	Council-Manager	1981
Houston	Mayor-Council	1946
Huntsville	Council-Manager	1992
Keller	Council-Manager	1982
Kingsville	Council-Manager	1986
Laredo	Council-Manager	1982
McAllen	Commission	1980
Pasadena	Mayor-Council	1992
Richardson	Council-Manager	1989
San Angelo	Council-Manager	1915
San Antonio	Council-Manager	1951
Texarkana	Council-Manager	1969
Texas City	Mayor-Council	1946
Tyler	Council-Manager	1937
Waco	Council-Manager	1958

Source: Dallas Morning News; Texas Almanac.

This system most closely resembles the plural executive system found at the state level. It was first implemented in Galveston shortly after the devastating hurricane of 1900 that claimed an estimated 8,000 lives and effectively wiped out the local government.[15] The city has since abandoned the commission system in favor of a council-manager form of municipal government.

Municipal Elections

11.2 Evaluate the various structures of municipal government, including elections and forms of government.

 ll municipal elections in Texas are nonpartisan, meaning that the political party affiliation of the candidates is not identified during the campaign or on the ballot. The mayor and council members of your city do not run as Republicans, Democrats, or by any other party label.

Membership on a city council is one way of getting involved in local politics at the grassroots level. Because political parties generally play little or no role in council elections, the cost of running a successful campaign is relatively low. The candidates do not receive support or funding from "the party." In the larger cities, successful candidates attempt to form **coalitions**; that is, they try to garner the support of members associated with various civic and professional groups such as parent–teacher associations, neighborhood associations, and chambers of commerce. In most cases, individuals who seek elected office at the grassroots level do so because they wish to fulfill a sense of civic duty. To be sure, it is not the money that attracts city council candidates. In most cases, members are paid $10 to $50 per council session. The type of election system adopted by the local government determines the composition of the city council. The three types of city council elections are the at-large system, the place system, and the single-member district system.

☐ Types of Municipal Elections

AT-LARGE SYSTEM The **at-large system** is the most common type of local election because it works best for small towns, and the majority of Texas's 1,200 towns have populations of less than 5,000.[16] The term *at-large* means citywide. Since there are no precincts or districts, voters are free to choose whomever they wish to represent them. The candidates essentially all run against one another, and the top vote-getters sit on the city council.

PLACE SYSTEM The **place system** is most often used in the medium-sized, more homogeneous cities of Texas. In this variation of the at-large system, the seats on the city council are distinguished by numbers, such as "places" one, two, three, and so on. Candidates filing for office are required to run for a particular place, and only one council member is selected per place by way of popular vote. The place system most benefits political newcomers because it does not force them to compete against established, popular incumbents. Rather, candidates may choose the seat for which they would like to run.

SINGLE-MEMBER DISTRICTS The state's larger cities tend to be more diverse and thus prefer to have diversity on the city councils. The way to achieve diversity is through **single-member districts** (sometimes called wards). Under this system, the city is divided into districts, and voters within these districts only may vote for candidates who reside within them. The system is the best way of ensuring that ethnic or political minorities receive representation on the city council. Usually, the mayoral candidate runs at large, because the mayor represents the city as a whole. Lately there has been a divide along this issue. Those in favor of creating single-member districts point out the importance of having greater ethnic and geographic diversity on the city council. Opponents point out the complexities and the cost. In 2006, the issue was raised on the Amarillo ballots, and it was defeated by the narrowest of margins (1,003 votes). Further evidence of the potential divisiveness is evidenced by the fact that voters in Potter County voted for and voters in Randall County voted against single-member districts.[17]

☐ The Effects of Group Participation on Municipal Government

The impact of special interest groups in politics and public policy at the state and national levels is well known, but it is a relatively new field of study that gained widespread legitimacy in the 1970s. The effect of locally based groups on public policy at the local level can be equally as profound. Former U.S. Speaker of the House Thomas "Tip" O'Neill once declared, "All politics is local." This saying has endured, perhaps because the people who study government understand that the decisions that most

coalitions
Alliances consisting of a variety of individuals and groups in support of a particular candidate for elected office.

at-large system
A method of electing representatives where there are no districts or wards drawn, and the candidate may draw votes from the entire area to be governed.

place system
A system of electing local government leaders whereby the candidates must campaign for a particular seat on the city council.

single-member district
A specific geographic area with a population equal to that of other districts that elects one person (a single member) to represent that area.

11.1

11.2

11.3

11.4

11.5

ad valorem
A system of taxation that is assessed "according to value," whereby the more a property is worth, the higher the tax to be paid on it.

affect the lives of citizens are made by the local school board, in the city hall, and in the county courthouses. Government at the local or "grassroots" level is the fountainhead of state, national, and global politics. Locally based groups have made great strides in determining the course of local government by affecting some of the most important decisions made by city leaders. Ethnic groups, neighborhood associations, and municipal employee associations continue to play a major role in formulating local government policy.[18]

ETHNIC GROUPS When compared with the struggles faced in addressing discriminatory practices at other levels of government, ethnic and race-based groups have found that local government is relatively more accessible. Many larger cities are seeing greater equality in the hiring and promotion of minorities, in part due to the implementation of single-member district elections and the resulting election of minority representatives. This more-inclusive representation in elected and appointed positions has fostered ordinances and other mandates to award minority-owned businesses more opportunities to participate in bidding on government work contracts, such as the construction and maintenance of roads, buildings, parks, and other public facilities.

NEIGHBORHOOD ASSOCIATIONS Homeowners and neighborhood associations, chambers of commerce, civic organizations, and coalitions formed by these groups have discovered that the key to change is political involvement. Through their numbers, resources, and activities (including endorsements of candidates willing to voice the groups' interests), these groups have gained for themselves an array of benefits that otherwise may not have come their way. Throughout Texas, active and well-organized neighborhood associations have lobbied the city council for road improvements, parks, lighting, and even the placement of additional fire department substations.

Often, these groups take advantage of low voter turnout by ensuring that their own members and their families and friends vote. The general voter apathy often enables groups to control virtually all aspects of local governments. Members of these groups are more prone to vote and to entice others to vote in the same manner. In addition, members often attend the council meetings and stay informed of decisions that might affect them.

MUNICIPAL EMPLOYEE GROUPS Employee groups have realized incredible gains from political participation at the local level. In San Antonio, for example, the local police officer's association campaigns hard for city council candidates who promise to support better pay and better working conditions. The association enlisted literally hundreds of volunteers to promote their interests, resulting in the redirection of millions of dollars to fund these benefits. The Association PAC currently has more than $237,000 in reserves.[19] As a direct result of this grassroots participation in Texas, more than 100 local police associations have banded together and hired lobbyists to support the passage of bills favorable to them.

Municipal Finance

11.3 Identify the major sources of revenue and expenditures of local governments.

T he majority of Texas municipalities rely heavily on property taxes to fund the services they provide. The tax rates are determined by each of the cities' governing bodies, using guidelines established by the Texas constitution, city policy, and the needs of the community. Property taxes are assessed using an **ad valorem** structure, meaning that each property is taxed "according to value." Values are determined by the county property assessment office. Most Texas home rule cities have established an ad valorem rate of between $0.50 and $0.75 per $100 of assessed value. Home rule cities may tax at a rate of up to $2.50 under state law, but such a move would be detrimental to attracting businesses and housing developments. A homeowner whose property is valued at $100,000 and who lives in a municipality with a $0.50 tax rate would pay $500 per year in property tax. By law, the ad valorem tax rate cannot exceed $1.50 per $100 of assessed value in general law cities.

In Texas, everyone who pays for housing is affected by the local property tax rates, whether they own a home or pay rent on a house or apartment. Landlords and apartment management companies figure taxes into tenants' lease agreements. Many renters hold the mistaken notion that since they do not own property, they are not affected by the property tax rates.

Other revenue generated by Texas municipalities includes a sales tax rebate from the state. Businesses and services operating within the municipalities collect state sales tax and forward the proceeds to the state's comptroller of public accounts. After the funds are certified, the comptroller's office sends each city a rebate check that amounts to the taxable product collected by the city's merchants. Cities also collect franchise taxes from utility companies that place lines or wires along and under city streets.

Like the sales tax rebate, the **franchise tax** is collected on a percentage of the total sales collected. In addition to the state sales tax rebates, cities are allowed to collect their own sales tax of 1 percent. Like the half-cent rebate, these funds are collected by the merchants and sent to Austin, where the state comptroller certifies the taxes and

franchise tax
A specific tax paid by businesses operating in Texas.

11.1

11.2

11.3

11.4

11.5

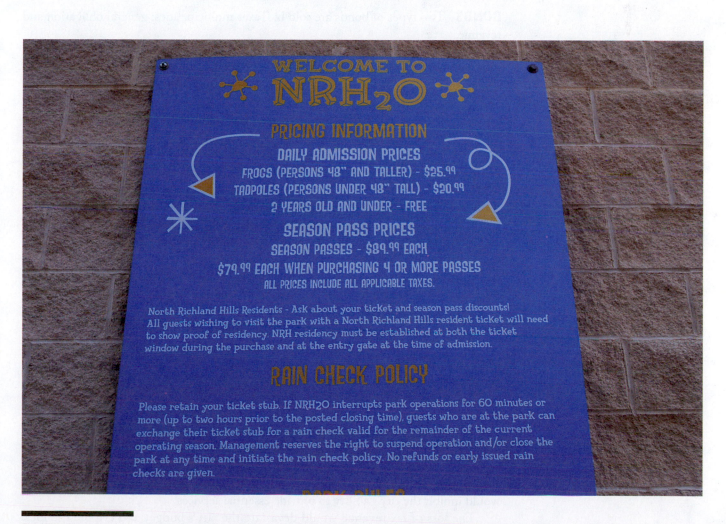

The NRH2O water park in North Richland Hills was financed through the issuance of revenue bonds, which would be repaid as the facility attracted paying customers. The park, in operation since 1995, has been producing revenue for the city since 2005.

11.1

11.2

11.3

11.4

11.5

user fees
Monies paid to local governments by citizens who utilize a particular government service (e.g., tuition at a state school or fees at a public boat ramp).

capital improvements
Long-term infrastructure improvements, such as roads, that are often built with bond money

general obligation bond
A bond issued by a local government for the purpose of making capital improvements and, like a mortgage, are paid off in small, yearly payments.

revenue bond
Issued by local governments for the purpose of capital improvements and repaid by revenue generated by the improvement; examples include sports arenas and public facilities for which there is an admission charge.

sends the city a rebate check. Almost every municipality in the state takes full advantage of this opportunity.

User fees, such as admittance charges to public golf courses, amusement parks, boat ramps, and other government-owned facilities, may comprise 30 percent or more of the revenue of some of Texas's municipalities. Court fees and fines collected by municipal courts and permit fees collected by city hall are also sources of revenue for the cities.

In addition to the general sales taxes, some cities implement special taxes to fund or supplement specific projects or services. Examples include Fort Worth's crime district tax, a half-cent levy that pays for crime prevention and after-school programs. Other examples include library taxes and stadium taxes. Growing cities may implement an economic development tax, which is an add-on sales tax used to offer business economic incentives in return for locating stores or offices in the city, thereby creating jobs and sales tax revenues. Before implementing these special taxes, the city must call an election and voters must approve them.

Cities are bound by law to fund their day-to-day operations, like paying employees and purchasing fuel, with money collected from taxes and fees. In most circumstances, the cities must borrow money for major expenditures, such as flood control systems, buildings, street construction and repair, or major equipment. Large expenses that are not part of the day-to-day operations of the city are known as **capital improvements**. In order to raise the money necessary for these and other capital projects, the city may sell municipal bonds. Individuals purchase these bonds as investments through private brokers. Like paying a mortgage, the city pays off the bonds in small increments that include interest payments.

BONDS Two types of bonds are sold by Texas municipalities: general obligation and revenue.

General obligation bonds are sold when the city needs to raise money to build or improve city-owned facilities. They are paid back gradually from the usual sources of revenue available to the city. **Revenue bonds** are sold for the construction or improvement of a city-owned property that is expected to generate revenue, such as a sports arena or public water park. These bonds are paid back from the revenue generated by the capital improvement.

EMINENT DOMAIN: CAN IT BE USED IN THE NAME OF ECONOMIC DEVELOPMENT? The Texas Constitution allows municipalities the right to reclaim private property in the name of the government if the property is needed for the greater public good. This power, called eminent domain, has been used to displace landowners in the interest of constructing highways, airports, shopping malls, and military installations. The laws governing eminent domain require the government to compensate the landowner for "fair market value." The city of Hurst, Texas, made national headlines when it chose to use eminent domain for the purpose of expanding a shopping center. In 1997, the city made plans to allow developers to expand North East Mall into an existing residential neighborhood. With proceeds generated from a special half-cent sales tax, the city sought to purchase 127 homes. The owners of 117 of these homes agreed to the city's offer, which in some cases was nearly twice the current market value.

The remaining 10 homeowners fought the city to the end, but lost. The holdouts claimed that the city should compensate the homeowners at a much higher commercial, rather than residential, property rate. They filed an unsuccessful lawsuit against the city. Meanwhile, the homeowners in Hurst have been forced out by city officials, who condemned their homes. The city claims that the mall must be expanded because major tenants, such as department stores, will move elsewhere and the revenue lost would inhibit the city's ability to provide essential services.

The loss of tax revenue would devastate the city's budget and cripple the local economy, according to city officials. Area residents are divided over the matter. Those who side with the city want convenient shopping and the economic benefits that come from the sales tax revenue, which will be in the millions. Those opposed say the city has overstepped its bounds and has selectively interpreted the Texas constitution in an unfair manner.[20] They argue that the purpose of the constitution is to protect private property, and that the city of Hurst has stolen it.

As ugly as the Hurst case became, it is attractive when compared to the turmoil and alleged scandal that occurred a few years later in El Paso. The city's central business district is bordered by, well, the border. The Rio Grande made it impossible to further develop the business district, so a group of businesspeople started a campaign to buy up and rebuild it. Central to the issue was Senate Bill 7, an act relating to limits on the use of power on eminent domain passed in 2005. This bill, passed after the Hurst debacle, allows local governments to take land for nonpublic projects only when the land is deemed "blighted." The bill also contained a provision that the captured, blighted land could be developed only if "economic development is a secondary purpose." Some alleged that the people behind the project were skirting the letter and intent of the law for economic gain, while the developers and city officials contended that the development would enhance the tax base—and thus the quality of life—for the citizens of El Paso.[21]

In 2007 the Texas Legislature passed a bill that prevents local governments from using eminent domain solely for the purpose of generating a larger tax base. As a result of the Hurst and El Paso cases, a constitutional amendment limited eminent domain takings for private use and dramatically curtailed instances in which property could be condemned as a public nuisance. Since then, at least 32 other states have passed or considered similar bills.

BUDGETING The budgeting process for municipal governments requires extensive research and planning, as cities strive to maintain the lowest tax rates possible while maintaining the highest level of service. Most Texas cities put their yearly budgets into effect on the first day of October, and planning for the next year starts on the second day of the same month, if not earlier. Providing municipal services to residents is just one of many challenges facing Texas's cities. City officials must create a favorable climate for business because businesses provide important benefits to the community.

A large shopping center can create hundreds of jobs in the community and generate thousands of dollars in local sales tax rebates, so it is often considered to be in the city's best interest to attract retailers to the area. In smaller cities that have many businesses, homeowners often enjoy lower ad valorem rates because the businesses generate enough revenue to provide basic services. Of course, increased commerce also fosters the need for additional services such as road repair and public safety, all of which require additional funding. In order to attract business and commerce, many municipalities offer financial incentives, called **abatements**. Abatements come

abatement
A financial incentive offered by governments to business and commercial concerns as a means of luring them to set up operations within the borders of a particular city.

Inside the Federalist System

In Step

Although public safety is primarily a function of state and local government, it is hardly exclusive of federal government intervention. The federal Strategic Traffic Enforcement Program (STEP) provides us with an example of how federal funds assist cities across Texas. Under the program, local governments may seek federal dollars to fund special enforcement efforts, such as regarding seat belt violators and speeders. Many cities have shown an increasing reliance on these grants to assist them in their efforts to keep us safe.

1. Should federal tax revenues be used to enforce local traffic laws?

2. Do such federal subsidies interfere with the concept of home rule and local control?

in the form of lower taxes for a specified time and are often instrumental in a corporation's decision to locate an office or a plant within the limits of a particular city. Abatements are hardly new to Texas; in fact, the state was a pioneer in offering incentives. In the 1820s, Stephen F. Austin, in his effort to populate Texas, offered an exemption from all general taxes for the first 10 years to people moving from the United States.

Today, two trends are apparent in financial incentives: First, abatements offered by municipalities have escalated in both frequency and monetary amounts, and second, more businesses are seeking these tax incentives in order to reduce their costs. The practice of offering incentives to business concerns has become widespread as citizens have come to appreciate the positive economic benefits and conveniences that industry and retail establishments bring. In 1989, the Texas Legislature authorized cities to enact a half-cent sales tax for the purpose of creating "economic development corporations." Revenue from this special tax is used for advertising, purchasing land, and developing infrastructure intended to attract commerce.

County Government

11.4 Explain why counties were established and how they have evolved.

The Texas constitution calls counties "administrative arms of state government"; we find this to be a most brilliant definition. Everything the counties do is on behalf of the state. For example, your Texas license plates are distributed by the county tax office, state law violators are prosecuted in the county courts, and state health services are administered through county-run facilities.

☐ Structure of County Government

Although counties act as branch offices of state government, they are considered "local governments" because county officials are elected locally from within the county they serve. This system allows the community to determine how best to deliver state resources to the local area. While each of Texas's 254 counties serves the same purpose, the system allows for some individuality.

Compared to cities, counties are relatively weak in terms of autonomy. That's because unlike home rule cities, counties do not have home rule charters and cannot adopt ordinances. County government is much like the plural executive model of government that exists at the state level in that no single executive or officer controls or is accountable for the county's policy-making personnel.

Texas's 254 counties are as diverse as the people who inhabit them. Unlike cities, which regularly see geographical expansion, the counties' boundaries are permanent. In fact, many Texas cities extend into as many as four counties. County populations range from fewer than 70 (Loving County in far west Texas) to more than 3 million (Harris County, which is where Houston is located). Some counties are smaller than large cattle ranches, and others are larger than some small states. Obviously, each county has specific needs according to its size, location, population density, and other factors. And these needs obviously grow as the populations increase. But the reverse is also true in nearly 50 Texas counties, where the population is actually decreasing. These counties, as well as the independent school districts contained within them, have been consolidating services.

Despite the stunning geographical and population diversity among the counties, the Texas constitution mandates that all 254 counties, as shown in Figure 11.3, be governed in essentially the same manner. Each county is governed by a commissioners court, and all elected county officials serve four-year terms of office.

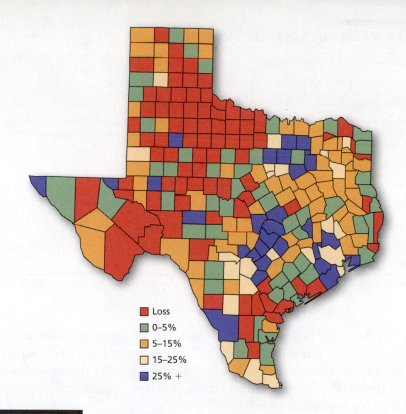

Loss
0–5%
5–15%
15–25%
25% +

FIGURE 11.3 Population Change by County: 2000–2010.

COMMISSIONERS COURT Each county, regardless of size and demographic composition, is governed by a five-member county commissioners court composed of four commissioners and presided over by a county judge. The county is divided into four precincts of equal population, with each precinct electing its own commissioner.[22] The county judge is elected at large, meaning countywide. Although it is called a "court," the function of this body is strictly administrative. That is, no trials are held in the commissioners court, and its members serve no judicial functions. The commissioners court acts as a city manager more than it does a court.

The commissioners court appoints key administrators and other personnel; sets the county tax rates; adopts the county budget; awards contracts for construction, repair, and maintenance of county buildings and roads; provides medical care for the indigent; and performs other related administrative tasks as required by the Texas constitution and legislature.

Harmony among the various elected county officials is especially vital because of the fragmented nature of county government. For example, the commissioners court provides the sheriff with the funds to purchase equipment and provide public safety services. Yet, the commissioners enjoy little, if any, oversight on how these funds are used. Since the sheriff is elected independently, he or she might choose to implement policies that are not approved by the commissioners. Fortunately, such conflicts are rare and last only a few years—until the next elections.

☐ Other Elected Officials

SHERIFF Although the law enforcement duties of the sheriff are countywide, each of Texas's 254 counties has an elected sheriff, whose primary responsibilities are to provide law enforcement services to areas of the county that are not served by a police department and to oversee the county jail. By law, the sheriff is a Texas peace officer and a conservator of the peace; enforces the criminal laws of the state; and is responsible for bail bonds, civil process, and security of the courts. In some small counties the sheriff is also the tax collector.[23] Most Texans live in incorporated cities and towns that

TABLE 11.4 MAJOR DUTIES OF THE COMMISSIONERS COURT

1. Set tax rate and adopt county budget.

2. Appoint county officials authorized under statutory law and hire personnel.

3. Fill county elective offices and appointive vacancies

4. Administer elections, including establishment of voting precincts, the appointment of an election administrator, the appointment of precinct judges, the calling of county bond elections, and the certification of election returns.

5. Let contracts and authorize payment of all county bills.

6. Build and maintain county roads and bridges.

7. Build, maintain, and improve county facilities, including jails.

8. Provide for libraries, hospitals, and medical care for the indigent.

9. Provide for emergency relief and civil disaster assistance.

10. Provide for fire protection and sanitation.

Source: Texas Commission on intergovernmental relations, An Introduction to County Government (Austin, TX: 1985), p. 9.

are served by municipal police departments and thus are seemingly unaffected by the sheriff. Most sheriff's offices have small staffs because they serve small populations. Indeed, most Texas counties do not even have a county jail. For the approximately 20 percent of Texans who live in the rural areas of the state, the sheriff's department is the only local law enforcement agency available.[24]

Although vested with law enforcement powers, there is no provision that requires a sheriff to be a licensed peace officer when seeking office. This lack has been the cause of some concern. Essentially, any person eligible to vote in a given county may run for and be elected sheriff. This is an additional reason to pay attention to the qualifications of persons running for local office.

CONSTABLE Constables are Texas peace officers and require the same training as any sheriff deputy, municipal police officer, or state trooper. Their primary duties are to work with the justice of the peace courts, serving subpoenas and notices, carrying out evictions, and performing other civil and criminal tasks. Each county elects one constable for each justice of the peace, and depending on the county's population, there can be as many as eight justices of the peace and constable precincts. In many areas, the Commissioners Court provides additional funding for constables to carry out more traditional law enforcement duties, such as monitoring traffic and serving warrants.

DISTRICT OR COUNTY ATTORNEY The district or county attorney is the county's legal officer and adviser. Not every county has its own elected attorney, and those without one contract these services from neighboring counties. The office provides legal services for county agencies and officials acting in a public service capacity, and it also provides representation when a lawsuit is brought against the county. On the recommendation of the commissioners court, the district or county attorney may initiate a lawsuit against another governmental agency or private concern.

The office of the district attorney presents a vivid example of the degree of discretion given to our locally elected officials. As the criminal prosecutor, the district or county attorney has sole discretion in determining whether an individual will be held accountable for committing a crime. Although all prosecutors enforce the same state laws, they have tremendous discretionary powers, and these powers are often driven by the wants of the community. For example, the decision on whether to seek the death penalty in a capital murder trial is made by the elected district or county attorney. The district attorney's stand on the death penalty is often a key issue in counties where the local population supports it.

The district attorney, though not officially a law enforcement official, can have a direct impact on the safety and quality of life. In Tarrant County, for example, the

District Attorney's Office has proven its determination to combat the issue of drunk driving by providing programs such as "no refusal weekends." When suspected drunk drivers are arrested during no refusal weekends, they are required to provide blood specimens, which hold up in court better than breath test results.

DISTRICT CLERK The district clerk is the official custodian of county records, including all filings and proceedings for the district courts and county courts at law they serve. The clerk is registrar, recorder, and custodian of all documents that are part of criminal, juvenile, family court, and civil actions. Since most court proceedings are public record, the office must store, manage, and disseminate court-related data efficiently. For many Texans, the first encounter with the district clerk is a jury duty notice. The district clerk's staff manages these notices and assigns prospective jurors to the various courts. In the larger counties, the office collects filing fees and other funds on behalf of the courts.

COUNTY CLERK The functions of the county clerk vary greatly, depending on the county. The office is responsible for maintaining the county's legal records and vital statistics, such as birth and death certificates, marriage licenses, and real estate transactions. Unless the commissioners court has appointed other individuals to perform these specific tasks, the county clerk records the court's minutes and certifies all candidates running for countywide office. Many county officials agree that the county clerk is the busiest person on the county payroll.

TAX ASSESSOR–COLLECTOR In the past, tax assessors were burdened with tremendous pressure from property owners seeking lower property values. The reason was clear: the lower the property value, the lower the taxes due. Due to changes in the method used to determine the value of property, the title of this office no longer reflects the officeholder's primary duties. Although the tax assessor–collector no longer "assesses" property value, he or she does have the important responsibility of identifying taxable property and collecting taxes that are due to the state and county.

Prior to 1992, each assessor–collector was free to develop his or her own criteria for determining the value of taxable property. Needless to say, this led to inconsistency throughout the state. As a result of state constitutional amendments passed in recent years, the assessment of property is now more structured and provides greater uniformity (and thus, fairness) within the state.

Most Texans are familiar with their county tax assessor–collectors because that office collects registration renewal fees and issues titles for motor vehicles. The office also registers voters in some counties. In the most rural counties of Texas, the office of tax assessor–collector is not filled, and the sheriff carries out the duties.

TREASURER The county treasurer, or the person who performs the treasurer's duties, has been referred to as the county's official bookkeeper. He or she is responsible for tracking all collections and expenditures and has considerable input in formulating the county's budget.

Many urban counties have eliminated this elected office (a process that requires a constitutional amendment) and have allowed the commissioners court to appoint a county auditor to perform these tasks. Obviously, the appointed auditors generally have greater qualifications than do the elected treasurers, and this has worked well in counties having budgets that run into the tens of millions of dollars. People looking to reform county government cite the appointed auditors as positive proof that appointed officials can be held to higher standards than can elected officials.

County Government Finance

Compared to municipalities and special districts, counties are subject to stringent restrictions when it comes to raising revenue. Because ad valorem taxes are the counties' largest single source of revenue, the constitutionally imposed maximum tax rate of

Firework stands are often located just outside of city limits, escaping the reach of municipal law. County governments, without ordinance making power, have little ability to regulate these businesses.

$0.80 per $100 valuation is a significant restriction. In order for the counties to raise the tax rate beyond $0.80, the commissioners court must first obtain legislative approval by both the house and senate. After obtaining approval, the proposed tax rate increase must be approved by the qualified voters in the county. Many municipalities, particularly in urban areas, are allowed to assess much higher property tax rates without such legislative approval.

County ad valorem tax rates typically fall between $0.25 and $0.30 per $100 of valuation. This means that a homeowner with a property valued at $100,000 in a county where the tax rate was $0.25 per $100 would pay $250 yearly in county property tax.

Counties may, under certain circumstances, issue bonds just like the municipalities. Here again, they must comply with constitutional requirements that are more stringent than those for the cities. The county cannot, for example, issue bonds for an amount that exceeds 35 percent of the total countywide assessed valuation.

In addition to selling bonds to generate revenue, many counties are eligible for federal grants-in-aid for the construction of hospitals, airports, flood control projects, and other capital improvements. Much of this grant money is used by the counties for optional services (those not required by law but that provide services to residents), such as parks, libraries, airports, and sports complexes.

All Texas counties operate on a yearly budget cycle, which is usually prepared by the county auditor or budget officer with input from all department heads and interested residents. Much like the case of municipal budgeting, the public hearings are sparsely attended. The final draft of the budget is then forwarded to the commissioners court for review and acceptance before it is put into effect.

☐ Criticism of County Government and Proposed Reform

Texans have been critical of the constitutional limitations imposed on counties ever since the counties were created. They have been suggesting ways of making county government more effective and more responsive to local needs. The major stumbling block on the path to reform is, of course, the Texas constitution. The constitutional prohibition against the counties establishing home rule charters, ordinances, and the constitutionally mandated plural executive system severely limits any reform measures by citizens. The following section lists the most common complaints about county government.

THE LONG BALLOT One of the reasons voters are apathetic about county government is that they are required to elect as many as six individuals to perform executive and administrative functions, yet no single person can be held accountable for the efficiency of the overall operation. Reformists have suggested implementing a system modeled after the council-manager form of municipal government. Such a system would allow the elected commissioners to appoint a professional county manager, who in turn would hire a professional staff. Accountability would be placed in the office of the county manager, and there would be a greater likelihood that the people in executive and administrative positions would be well qualified and properly trained.

INABILITY TO ESTABLISH HOME RULE Unlike the cities and special districts, counties are constitutionally prohibited from tailoring their system to the needs and desires of local residents. Ironically, a provision in the Texas constitution would have allowed counties to enact home rule charters. That provision was eliminated in 1969, and because it was so complex, not a single county had been able to establish a charter before it was taken off the books.

INABILITY TO PASS ORDINANCES The commissioners court is not empowered to create countywide ordinances to serve the safety, convenience, and moral expectations of the citizens. For example, nearly every incorporated city in the state has ordinances banning the sale and possession of fireworks and regulating the operation of sexually oriented businesses. For this reason, people traveling through the state often see these types of businesses in clusters within a few feet of the city limits. Some reform has occurred in this area. By an act of the Texas Legislature in 1995, Harris County was granted permission to establish a teen curfew. Although such acts clearly demonstrate reform, they are difficult to attain because they require action by the state legislature.

SPOILS SYSTEM Although it does not exist to the extent that it did a few decades ago, the **spoils system** is still a fact of life in many counties. This system awards government jobs and contracts to individuals and firms who have helped in the elected person's political campaign. Many elected officeholders are permitted to hire personnel to assist them in their duties. These jobs often go to individuals who were friendly and loyal to the elected official, without regard to the person's qualifications, skills, or abilities.

In order to alleviate the effects of the spoils system and to attract the most qualified persons, many counties have established a **civil service** system. Under this system, individuals seeking a job with the county government must meet specified job-related requirements and are hired and promoted based on merit. Most of the larger counties require applicants to take written exams and to compete for entry-level positions and promotions. Another advantage of the civil service system is that county employees are not subject to losing their positions if the person who hired them is defeated in an election. This ensures continuity not only in the employees' careers but also in government operations.

spoils system
A system in which elected officials provide jobs and promotions to personal affiliates; see civil service.

civil service
Merit-based system of selecting government employees.

11.1

11.2

11.3

11.4

11.5

273

Special Districts

special district
A type of local government established for a specific geographic area and for a specific purpose such as education, flood control, or public utility service.

independent school district
Local-level limited-purpose government that determines public school policy.

 special district is the third classification under the broad title of "local government." A special district is a local government established to deliver a specific service to a limited geographic area. These districts vary tremendously in terms of size, function, and scope, but all of them share three unique features. First, they are substantially independent from other governments. In other words, they provide a product or service that no other government does. For example, the Dallas Independent School District (DISD) is totally independent from Dallas's city government. It has separate boundaries, budgets, and governing bodies. A second common feature among special districts is that they have "governmental character," which is another way of saying they have a source of funding. Some special districts, such as ISDs, are funded primarily by property taxes, as noted in Figure 11.4. Others, such as regional transportation districts, are funded by local sales taxes and tolls. A third shared feature is a "recognized existence." The special district must be chartered by the state or otherwise approved by the state legislature. Recognition includes the requirement that business is conducted openly as it is in all other governments.

◻ The Nature of Special Districts

Only California and Illinois have more special districts than does Texas. Special districts comprise the fastest growing form of government in the nation today, and this is especially true for Texas, where the number of special districts has increased by 45 percent since 1992.[25] There are more than 4,000 special districts in Texas—more governments than the number of cities and counties combined. Although some special districts are bounded by city limits or by county lines, most transcend these political boundaries and serve larger regions of the state.

◻ Types of Special Districts

EDUCATION DISTRICTS The most common form of special district in Texas is the **independent school district** (ISD). During the Davis administration, the state controlled the entire public education system, and all discretionary power was in the hands of the governor. As a reaction to this centralization, the framers of the current constitution allowed for the creation of ISDs to ensure more local control of Texas's public schools.

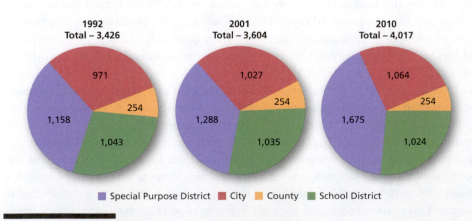

FIGURE 11.4 Growth in Texas Special Districts: 1992–2010.
From the Texas Comptroller of Public Accounts: "Your Money and the Taxing Facts."

Rush hour in Austin, only partially alleviated by a city bus. How does the individualistic nature of most Texans ingrain resistance toward mass transit?

Texas public school expenditures are astonishing and growing by the year. The Dallas ISD's 2010 budget is more than $2 billion. This includes money raised in local districts and contributions from the state's Foundation School Program, as well as other state and federal grants. Because some districts have much greater property wealth than others, wealthier districts have been ordered by both the state courts and the legislature to share some of their property tax revenue with the poorer districts. For many Texans, school districts come to mind first when the topic of local government is raised; many families even choose their residences based on the school district in which it falls, rather than the city or county.

Each of Texas's approximately 1,000 ISDs is governed by a school board—often called the board of trustees—consisting of between four and nine members chosen in local nonpartisan elections. Their diversity is not unlike the state's cities and counties. About 800 of the state's ISDs have fewer than 1,000 students, while others serve 100,000 or more. School board members are not paid for their service, and there is no requirement that members have children attending public schools in their district. The school board's most important function is to hire a professional manager, usually called a **superintendent**, to oversee the day-to-day operations of the school system. Other duties of the school board members include establishing a school calendar, setting teacher salaries, establishing teacher qualifications and standards, constructing and maintaining school buildings, vehicles, and other equipment, establishing the property tax rate, and selecting textbooks.

Most public school education funding comes from the property taxes levied by the ISDs' school boards, but virtually all Texas ISDs also receive funding from state and federal sources. In most instances, the school tax is 50 to 100 percent higher than the municipal taxes. Since most of the funding comes from local property taxes, there is a wide disparity among ISDs when it comes to resources. The terms *property rich* and *property poor* districts refer to the amount of property taxes collected by

superintendent
The appointed manager of a public school system.

ISDs. Obviously, the property rich districts are located in areas where land is developed and therefore the property tax revenues are much higher. ISDs that collect more revenue than what the state says is required to operate the local schools are required to send the "excess" money to the state. The Glen Rose ISD has sent over $520 million to the state in such a manner, including a payment of $14.7 million required in 2010–2011. Table 11.5 compares Texas school rankings in a variety of areas to other states.

Texas has approximately 50 community college districts that offer academic and vocational programs. Until recently, state grants were the primary source of operating revenue for the community colleges, but today, a majority of the funding comes from property taxes and tuition. Virtually all community colleges throughout the state have been forced to raise tuition and tax rates to offset the reduction in state dollars. A typical community college district's tax rate is between 10 and 20 cents per $100 valuation. Using the hypothetical $100,000 home in a district with a tax rate of 10 cents, the homeowner would pay a yearly community college tax of $100.

NONEDUCATION DISTRICTS Throughout the state, hundreds of special districts have been established for delivering services ranging from water and utilities, public housing, and hospitals, to public transportation and flood control. Some areas of Texas have even established "noxious weed control" and "wind erosion" districts to provide these specific services to those areas in need.

As is the case in school districts, most of the funding for noneducational special districts comes in the form of property taxes. Other sources of revenue include user fees (fares, licensing, etc.), special sales taxes, and grants from the state and federal governments.

TABLE 11.5 TEXAS RANKINGS IN THE 2009–10 SCHOOL YEAR

Benchmark	Texas Rank	Texas	High (#1)	Low (#50)	US Avg.
Number of Districts*	1	1,280	1.280 (TX)	1(HI)	n/a
Enrollment	2	4,850,210	6,263.449 (CA)	88,155 (WY)	n/a
% Change in Enrollment - 2003–2008	3	9.7%	12.9% (UT)	− 8.8% (RJ)	1.5%
Number of Teachers	1	333,164	333,164 (TX)	7,166 (WY)	n/a
Student to Teacher Ratio	25	14.6 to 1	10.6 to 1 (VT)	22.9 to 1 (UT)	15.4 to 1
Average Teacher Salary	34	$46,705	$70,785 (NY)	$34,799 (SD)	$54,819
Total Staff	1	662,369	662,369 (TX)	15,983 (ND)	n/a
Student to Staff Ratio	26	7.3 to 1	4.8 to 1 (VT)	12.7 to 1 (NV)	7.8 to 1
Total Expenditures per Pupil (no debt serv.)**	41	$8,562	$17.746 (NY)	$6,612 (UT)	$10,591
Instructional Expenditures per Pupil**	41	$5,138	$12,276 (NY)	$4,275 (UT)	S6,456
% Students Eligible for Free and Reduced Price Lunch Program	14	50.3%	70.7% (MS)	23.5% (NH)	46.9%
Avg Freshman Graduation Rate-Hispanic**	19	69.6%	89.4% (AK)	41.6% (NH)	n/a
Avg Freshman Graduation Rate-Black**	23	68.0%	100% (NH, ND)	56.3% (AK)	n/a
Avg Freshman Graduation Rate-White**	20	82.7%	95.0% (WT)	63.3% (MS)	n/a
2010 Percent of Graduating Seniors Taking SAT	22	53%	92% (ME)	3% (IA, MS, SD)	47%
2010 Mean SAT Math Score (out of 800)	40	505	613 (IA)	467 (ME)	516
2010 Mean SAT Reading Score (out of 800)	48	484	603 (IA)	468 (ME)	501
2010 Mean SAT Writing Score (out of 800)	46	473	582 (IA)	454 (ME)	492
2010 Mean SAT Total Score (out of 2,400)	45	1,462	1.793 (IA)	1.389 (ME)	1.509

*Includes charter schools which are considered school districts in Texas
**2008–09 school year
***2007–08 school year
Note: States with a low percentage of graduating seniors taking the SAT test tend to have higher scores

Sources: National Center for Educational Statistics

TABLE 11.6 FUNCTIONS OF COUNCILS OF GOVERNMENTS

Regional services offered by councils of governments are varied. Services are under taken in cooperation with member governments, the private sector, and state and federal partners, and include but are not limited to the following functions:

- planning and implementing regional homeland security strategies;
- operating law enforcement training academies;
- promoting regional municipal solid waste and environmental quality planning;
- providing cooperative purchasing options for governments;
- managing region wide services to the elderly;
- maintaining and improving regional 9-1-1 systems;
- promoting regional economic development;
- operating specialized transit systems; and
- providing management services for member governments.

Soruce: From the Texas Association of Regional Councils.

☐ Councils of Government

Although the needs of the local governments vary depending on a variety of factors, the basics of providing governmental services are the same for virtually all local governments. For this reason, nearly all municipal and county governments, as well as most special districts, participate in a **council of government** (COG). The 24 COGs in Texas, as shown in Figure 11.5, represent distinct regions. All local governments within their respective regions are eligible for membership. COGs have been created to allow cooperation and communication by local governments within a specific region. Because COGs are not governments, they have no taxing power and cannot pass laws, rules, or ordinances; nor can they impose sanctions against any government. The COGs provide training for city managers, council members, mayors, public safety officers, and other elected and appointed officials. They are also useful in assessing the future environmental, transportation, economic development, labor, and land-use issues, as well as other social needs of the region. In addition, they often prevent unnecessary duplication of research or work.

council of government (COG)

A regional voluntary cooperative with no regulatory or enforcement powers; consists of local governments and assesses the needs of the area as a whole.

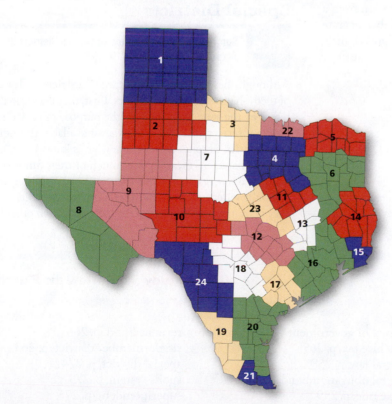

FIGURE 11.5 Boundaries of the 24 Texas Councils of Government (COGs).

Review the Chapter

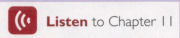
Municipal Government

11.1 Compare and contrast the two types of cities and several forms of city government.

There are two broad categories of cities in Texas: general law and home rule. Although general law cities greatly outnumber home rule cities, most Texans live in home rule cities. That is an indication of the first and most important distinction—general law cities are smaller in terms of population. Since they are smaller in size, they have smaller operating budgets and therefore have lower taxes. Continuing the contrast, general law cities provide fewer services to its citizens.

Municipal Elections

11.2 Evaluate the various structures of municipal government, including elections and forms of government.

The method of staffing city councils and the form of government the cities adopt depends largely on the type of city. All municipal elections have the common feature of being nonpartisan, meaning the candidates do not run under a party label. Since most Texas cities are comparatively small in size and lower in population, they operate under general law provisions and council members are elected at-large. Single-member districts have been implemented in the larger urban areas of the state, where the need for representation from a diversified population justifies the cost. Most cities operate under the more informal mayor-council form of government, which gives the mayor a good deal of control over the city's day-to-day operations.

Municipal Finance

11.3 Identify the major sources of revenue and expenditures of local governments.

For most cities, the greatest single source of revenue is the property tax, which is assessed on an *ad valorem* (according to value) basis. Other major sources of revenue include sales taxes, franchise fees, and permits. By a large margin, public safety is the most expensive function of the cities.

County Government

11.4 Explain why counties were established and how they have evolved.

Counties are best described as being the administrative arms of state government. Because providing certain state services from a single state office would prove to be inefficient, counties serve as a system of branch offices. Despite the incredible diversity among the 254 counties, all of them are structured in essentially the same way. Each county has a governing body, called the commissioners court, and each county has certain elected officials—such as a sheriff, constable, and clerks. These elected officials serve four-year terms of office and are chosen in partisan elections.

Special Districts

11.5 Summarize the importance of special districts in Texas.

Although there are over 2,000 special districts in Texas, each of them shares three characteristics. First, they are created (chartered) by the state legislature for the purpose of providing government services that are otherwise unavailable through cities and counties. Second, they all have what is known as a "governmental character," meaning that much of their funding comes from local sources, such as the property tax. Lastly, they are substantially independent from other local governments, meaning they do not overlap services or compete with each other.

Learn the Terms

abatement, p. 267
ad valorem, p. 264
at-large system, p. 263
capital improvements, p. 266
city manager, p. 261
civil service, p. 273
coalitions, p. 263

council of government (COG), p. 277
franchise tax, p. 265
general law, p. 258
general obligation bond, p. 266
home rule, p. 259
independent school district, p. 274
place system, p. 263

revenue bond, p. 266
single-member district, p. 263
special district, p. 274
spoils system, p. 273
superintendent, p. 275
user fees, p. 266

11.1 Compare and contrast the two types of cities and several forms of city government.

A government entity with a city charter and city manager is most likely a

a. special district.
b. council of government.
c. general law city.
d. home rule city.
e. government corporation.

11.2 Evaluate the various structures of municipal government, including elections and forms of government.

In Texas, all municipal elections are nonpartisan, meaning

a. elections are held in even-numbered years.
b. there is no political party affiliation.
c. citizens are not allowed to contribute funds to candidates.
d. these elections are nonbinding.
e. all candidates must run under a major party label.

11.3 Identify the major sources of revenue and expenditures of local governments

The largest source of revenue for most Texas cities

a. property tax
b. fines and penalties
c. building permits
d. sales tax
e. state and federal grants

11.4 Explain the necessity and functions of the counties.

Counties were established as a means of

a. fostering better relations between the state and national governments.
b. providing redundancy in an effort to eliminate waste and fraud.
c. enhancing the delivery of state-provided services at the local level.
d. educating municipal officials about the benefits of revenue sharing.
e. improving the efficiency of public education.

11.5 Summarize the importance of special districts in Texas.

A government entity established to deliver a specific service to a limited geographic area.

a. special district
b. home rule status
c. at-large system
d. home rule charter
e. nonpartisan councils.

Explore Further

Texas Comptroller of Public Accounts http://www.window.state.tx.us/
This site is a must-visit for both research and for public access. It contains in-depth analysis of the budgetary system as it pertains to local government as well as reports on school districts and cities across the state.

Texas Municipal League http://www.tml.org
A not-for-profit association of Texas cities, both general law and home rule. The site provides links to all its affiliates and access to various publications, rules, statutes, as well as in-depth data on issues affecting Texas cities presently and in the future.

Texas Association of School Boards http://www.tasb.org
An association whose membership includes the hundreds of ISDs across the state, it provides a portal for research, scholarship, and a guide to what the school districts do and how they function.

Texas Association of Counties http://www.county.org

The association's website serves as a citizen's portal into the various functions of county government and administration.

DeLeon, Arnoldo, Ethnicity in the Sunbelt: A History of Mexican-Americans in Houston. Houston, TX: University of Houston Press, 1989.

Hanson, Russell L., ed., Governing Partners: State and Local Relations in the United States. Boulder, CO: Westview, 1998.

Polsby, Nelson, Community Power and Political Theory, 2nd ed., New Haven CT, CT: Yale University Press, 1980.

Davidson, Chandler, and Luis Ricardo Fraga, "Slating Groups as Parties in a Non-partisan setting," Western Political Quarterly 41 (June 1998)

Thomas, Robert, "City Charters and their Political Implications," in Perspectives on American and Texas Politics, edited by Donald S. Lutz and Kent L. Tedin. Dubuqe, IA: Kendall/Hunt, 1987

12

Public Policy in Texas

There can never be anyone too poor to vote.

—*Lyndon Baines Johnson*

I always avoid prophesying beforehand, because it is a much better policy to prophesy after the event has already taken place.

—*Winston Churchill*

By definition, a government has no conscience. Sometimes it has a policy, but nothing more.

—*Albert Camus*

A number of states, as shown in Figure 12.1, have followed Texas's lead in passing what has come to be known as a "Castle Law." In general terms, these laws loosen restrictions on citizens' ability to lawfully carry concealed handguns on or about their persons and while in public places. The laws have been controversial, and newsworthy events serve to ensure that the controversy will continue. The 2012 shooting incidents in Sanford, Florida in which Andrew Zimmerman shot and killed Trayvon Martin, the movie theater incident in Aurora, Colorado, and the schoolhouse massacre in Newtown, Connecticut, are cases in point.

12.1	12.2	12.3	12.4
Explain why public policy is the cornerstone of politics.	Outline the stages of the public policy paradigm.	Analyze why some policy-making decisions have few or no fiscal implications.	Evaluate why the controversy over voter ID laws has remained at the forefront of the public policy debate.

The Texas Legislature has strongly supported the Castle Doctrine, or Castle Law, as it is referred to here. As the name implies, the law affirms the British common law doctrine that a person's home is that person's castle, with an inherent right to defend it from attack. In Texas, that doctrine extends to your person, automobile, and residence, which you can defend with deadly force if necessary, immune from both civil and criminal legal actions.

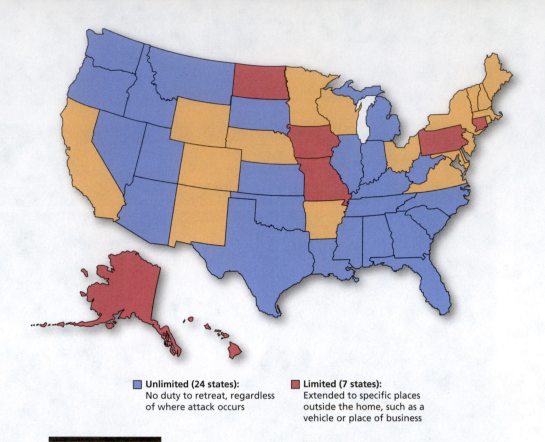

■ **Unlimited (24 states):**
No duty to retreat, regardless
of where attack occurs

■ **Limited (7 states):**
Extended to specific places
outside the home, such as a
vehicle or place of business

FIGURE 12.1 U.S. "Stand your ground" laws.   Thirty-one states have so-called "stand your ground" laws that allow for use of deadly force in self-defense with no duty to retreat either when outside the home or in specic locations outside the home.

public policy
Any act, law, legislation, or program enacted by a public entity.

Elected officials monitor these and other incidents as closely—and maybe even more closely—than anyone else, including the media. They view these occurrences through a public policy lens and are concerned about the implications, including constitutional interpretation, crime rates, gun violence, issues of self-defense, and even race. What will be the outcries and demands of various groups, segments, and communities? How and for how long will the media play a role? What will public opinion be after the dust settles? What have other states done in terms of legislation, public awareness, and community relations? What lessons were learned, and how will future events be monitored, evaluated, and interpreted? All these questions and many more represent the incredible universe political scientists have termed *public policy*. The implications in our example are constantly evolving and dynamic.

So then, what settled course of action will the government of Texas adopt or follow? We may not know the answer, but whatever it is, it will be known as public policy. In this chapter we consider why some problems reach the public agenda, why some solutions are adopted while others rejected, and why some policies appear to succeed while others appear to fail. We will primarily examine policy making at the state government level, but we will look at examples from the local level as well.

Public Policy

12.1   Explain why public policy is the cornerstone of politics.

ublic policy can be defined as any course of action taken by the government that affects any segment of the public. It takes its form in laws, statutes, regulations, rules, and legislation. Although the legislative branch is formally responsible for "making the laws," public policy is actually created by every branch of government. The executive branch, through executive orders and policy initiatives, produces public policy, often without the input—or the approval—of the legislative branch. The courts, through judicial review and precedent, establish public policies that affect all Texans.

It can be said that the very nature of government is to create public policy. Public policy is the very essence of government because it is made at all levels of government. The federal government, for example, regulates foreign trade and domestic spending. State governments create public policies such as speed limits and motorcycle helmet laws. Local governments, county commissioners' courts, city councils, and school districts affect public policy by determining how land should be used, what hours the public library should operate, and how many students should be allowed to enroll in a particular class.

The study of public policy represents an entire subfield of political science. Public policy analysts probe the interaction resulting from the dynamics among the institutions of government and the public. Like politics itself, public policy analysis is the study of power, distribution, and outcomes. Public policy takes into consideration the various choices available to solve a problem or issue. We often find that the final product—the resulting policy—represents a compromise among competing interests.

☐ Public Policy, as Distinguished from Company Policy

Before examining public policy, we should take a moment to point out the critical distinctions between public- and private-sector policy. Virtually all companies and private corporations have policies, practices, operating procedures, and other rules. Sometimes these policies are popular—"casual Fridays" comes to mind. Surely you've heard the term *company policy*, as in "the store's company policy requires a receipt for all returns." You may even have established some personal policies, such as "I always fill up my gas tank when the gauge reads ¼."

In the most basic form, policies are decisions about what to do or not to do in a given situation. In that context, there is no difference between a government-made policy (or, as we prefer to call it, "public policy") and a policy made by your company's CEO. Aside from the basics, however, there is a world of difference between the private and the public sector when it comes to making policy. The key difference is contained in the definition. Public policy, by definition, affects everyone.

In the broadest sense, all policies attempt to do the greatest good for the clients, company, or community. They also tend to clear up conflict and confusion by allowing us to follow a predesignated course of action when faced with a particular set of circumstances. Policies are almost always intended to improve the organization whether by increasing productivity, enhancing morale, or preventing loss or injury. Students with an eye toward running a private-sector corporation would be well-served to seek a degree in business, such as an MBA (Master of Business Administration). The coursework prepares them for the challenging responsibilities that come with running a corporation, and includes classes in management, finance, marketing, and leadership. By contrast (and perhaps by comparison), individuals seeking to administer government programs are advised to seek an MPA (Master of Public Administration) degree. The basic principles of these degree plans are consistent and there is some overlapping of coursework, but there is also one very notable exception: The private sector is grounded in money; whereas public-sector administration is grounded in law.

There are several lesser distinctions between public policy and private-sector policy. The first one is that public policy does not generally reflect personal values, because it involves so many inputs. It would be more accurate to say that in many instances public policy reflects societal values, or at least those values embraced by the stakeholders. A notable exception may be found in the event of an executive order, which is a unilateral action taken by a single individual. For example, in 2010 President Obama, in an effort to enhance the safety of personnel operating government-owned vehicles, signed an executive order banning the use of cellular phones by government employees operating vehicles.[1] The second distinction is that public policies can be

Types of Public Policy	Redistributive	Distributive	Regulatory
	Policies that shift resources from the "haves" to the "have nots."	Policies funded by all taxpayers that address the desires of particular groups.	Policies designed to restrict or monitor the actions of certain groups or individuals.

FIGURE 12.2 Types of Public Policy.

studied, compared, and analyzed using a long-standing model developed by political scientists. This model is aptly called the Stages of Public Policy Model.

Types of Policy

Political scientists have identified three broad categories of public policy: redistributive, distributive, and regulatory, as described in Figure 12.2. Redistributive polices are typically the most controversial because they often cause divisions among social classes. Examples of **redistributive policies** include most forms of welfare and subsidized school lunches. Recently, funding for the Children's Health Insurance Program (CHIP) has been a source of legislative debate, and with declining federal dollars for federal programs like Medicaid, more parents will be relying on state-funded programs like CHIP to cover their children's medical needs.[2]

By-and-large, when we think of redistributive policies we focus on national programs, such as unemployment benefits, Temporary Aid to Needy Families, and the Affordable Healthcare Act. Since Texas is not a "welfare-friendly" state, local governments—particularly cities—are looked upon to fill the void. Such attempts are often met with strong opposition. In Bexar County, where one in four children lives in poverty, advocates cite the continuing "tug-of-war" that policy makers must face in setting priorities.[3] Growing cities have turned to lobbying the national government for funding incentives designed to assist low-income and otherwise disadvantaged segments. In 2011, the housing authorities in nearly a dozen Texas Panhandle cities—including Borger, Memphis, Spearman, and McLean—received about $648,500 for public housing projects, according to U.S. Department of Urban Development statistics.[4] Unlike redistributive policies, where there is a perceived winner and loser, **distributive policies** are those that are intended to be neutral for taxpayers. Everyone pays, and everyone benefits. Gasoline taxes used to build and maintain highways are a classic example of distributive polices. One way of distinguishing among redistributive and distributive policy is by looking at the perceived winners and losers. Redistributive polices are often regarded as the haves contributing to the have-nots. Distributive policies are generally looked upon as having no winners or losers. Social Security is a distributive policy because those who contribute see a benefit. The GI Bill of Rights is another example of a distributive policy because beneficiaries have made a choice to serve in the armed forces.

While local governments occasionally provide redistributive policies, such as city-subsidized housing, these policies are more frequently put into place by state government. By and large, distributive policies are implemented by local governments in the form of providing public safety services, recreation opportunities, and public works projects. In the case of local governments, everyone pays for these services through a combination of property and other types of taxes, and all enjoy the results.

Regulatory policies are the most common and are enacted by state and local governments alike. As the name implies, they are created to regulate, and often to limit, specific activities. At the state level, policies that relate to environmental issues, legalized gambling, sales and distribution of alcoholic beverages, and motor-vehicle registration provide examples of the state's regulatory power. Castle laws provide us with an excellent example of a regulatory policy. Cities create zoning boards, inspection services, and ordinances restricting the operations of certain businesses, all in an effort to protect property values, enhance safety, or ensure a better quality of life.

Speed limits are one of the policy-making decisions that belong to state government. We hang 'em high here in Texas. The state has a new stretch of highway where the limit is 85 MPH. High speed limits show that policy-makers listen to the populous.

The Policy-Making Model

12.2 Outline the stages of the public policy paradigm.

P olitical scientists use the term **paradigm** to explain what we have come to understand using abstract ideas. A paradigm is a structural model that shows how things work. In physics and other "hard" sciences, they identify *laws*, such as the laws of gravity. Since the social sciences cannot realistically establish such concrete laws, political scientists have created paradigms.

Paradigms take what we know about a subject and place it into a simple conceptual model. The paradigm used to explain the stages of public policy illustrates the sequence brilliantly. In essence, the paradigm (or—if you prefer—model) involves five distinct stages: agenda setting, formulation, implementation, evaluation, and change. The section that follows explores each of these stages and, using the Castle Law example and other policy arenas, provides real-world examples of how public policy is born and evolves.

☐ Agenda Setting

On October 16, 1991, a man with a gun drove through the window of Luby's Cafeteria in Killeen, Texas, and opened fire, killing 24 people.[5] This event sparked debate over a handgun bill that was passed in 1996 and that we know as the "right to carry" law. This event—and the resulting government action—exemplify the birth of many public policies.

Before any government agency initiates action, the need for such action must be recognized. During the **agenda-setting** stage, the matter is brought to the attention of the government and a resolution is sought. Sometimes a single event can place an

paradigm
Models used by social scientists to explain and understand abstract concepts.

agenda setting
The first stage of the public policy-making model.

285

Amber Alert
A program enabling media and public safety agencies to immediately broadcast information in the event of a child abduction.

Castle Law
A policy establishing a person's home as his or her personal domain and allowing for reasonable force, up to and including deadly force, to defend it.

formulation
The second stage of the public policy-making model.

TABLE 12.1 STAGES OF THE POLICY PROCESS

Policy analysts use the following model.

Stage	Actions	Example
Agenda setting	Identifying a problem or an issue that requires attention. This can be a single event or a string of events that brings an issue to the public's attention.	High-profile incidents, such as shootings. A sudden rise in child abductions.
Formulation	Deciding a course of action and determining which agency will be responsible. Research is carried out and options are explored. Policy is finalized, formally announced, and (when necessary) funded.	Legislative action in the form of laws. Delegating authority to carry out, oversee, and enforce the policy. Final passage through the legislature.
Implementation	New or revised policy takes effect.	Public service announcements. Training for responsible agency employees.
Evaluation	Assessing the outcomes, ensuring there are no unintended consequences.	Sunset Advisory. Recommendations for modification made.
Change or termination	Adjusting or modifying the policy to enhance effectiveness, or to terminate the policy.	DWI laws enhanced. Repeal of the 55 MPH speed limit.

issue on the government's agenda. For example, in 1999, the Texas Legislature passed a bill that became known as the **Amber Alert**, which required law enforcement agencies to coordinate with local media outlets for the purpose of alerting citizens about child abductions. Prior to the Amber Alert's passage, several police departments and local media outlets established a voluntary program that was widely successful. The Texas Amber Alert made this a statewide network, and it was so successful that it was adopted by the U.S. Congress and extended nationwide.[6] The bill is named after Amber Haggerman, a young Texas girl whose abduction caused an outcry among citizens.

In other instances, pressure from ordinary citizens and interest groups like the National Rifle Association can put issues on the front burner. Such was the case with the **Castle Law** passed by the Texas Legislature in 2007. Major events are not exclusive to this stage, as evidenced by the Andrew Zimmerman case in 2012. That event renewed discussions in states that already had Castle Laws and generated a new agenda for states that were considering them.

The agenda-setting stage is important not only to those who wish to create new policies, but also to those who oppose governmental action. An individual, corporation, or group opposed to governmental intervention will often attempt to abort the policy process at this stage. Sometimes these groups are successful in the short term. In other words, some folks work very hard at keeping matters *off* the public agenda. For example, although public opinion polls identified the popularity of a law allowing Texans to carry concealed handguns in their cars, various groups—including law enforcement and educational groups—managed to keep the issue on the back burner, or "off the agenda."

Despite such organized opposition, or perhaps in response to the popularity of the legislation, Governor Perry promised to sign the bill into law if he was reelected in 2006. He did just that, and the Castle Law was one of the first bills passed in the new session.[7] The agenda-setting stage is also responsible for updating or modifying bills. For example, after some interest groups pointed out that the bill, as originally proposed, allowed persons convicted of family violence to carry concealed weapons, the legislature acted quickly and closed this and other loopholes.

☐ Formulation

Once a problem has been recognized, it has to be specifically framed. What should be done about it, and while we're at it, who should do it? In the **formulation** stage, the issue is defined and options are explored. Policy makers may decide that a new public policy is needed or that an existing one can be modified to address the concerns.

Citizens in Corpus Christi rally for a city ban on single-use plastic shopping bags, which are not only a source of litter, but a particular wildlife hazard in coastal communities. Corpus city officials decided to forgo a formal ban in favor of a consumer education campaign to encourage multi-use or canvas bags.

The level and degree of government involvement are also established during this stage. For example, after the legislature passed the Castle Law, the state's law enforcement officials and prosecutors were trained in the law's application. Texas lawmakers use this stage most effectively by learning from what other states have done. Such research prevents Texas from making the same mistakes others may have made. For example, Texas copied Maryland's "Give Them a Brake Laws" when in 2001 it implemented laws that doubled the traffic fines for certain moving violations committed where men and women are working on public roadways.[8] In 2003 Texas copied, nearly word for word, provisions for a "Move Over Law" that requires motorists to move one lane over for emergency vehicles parked on shoulders and roadsides.[9]

Often, a legislative body, such as Congress or a city council, determines the formulation of a public policy. Sometimes the courts make this determination, as has been the case in the areas of public school financing and prison overcrowding. In 2005, for example, three special sessions failed to produce education finance reform. The legislature resolved to let the Texas supreme court settle certain issues before meeting again to redraft an appropriations bill.

At other times, decisions are made by bureaucrats in government agencies, and all you have to do is examine recent efforts by the Texas Railroad Commission (TRC) to see examples of the policy formulation stage in action. In response to a rise in injuries and expensive repairs, the legislature passed a law that requires excavators and the public to call 811 to have underground pipelines located and marked before beginning any digging project.[10] Digging into even a small pipeline or utility line can cause injury, disrupt neighborhood services, and result in monetary penalties and repair costs. Not calling before digging or incorrectly marking pipelines can result in fines of up to $10,000 per day per violation. Additionally, the Commission may assess an enhanced violation of up to $25,000. The TRC launched "811 Day," as a public reminder. Incidentally, 811 Day falls on August 11 of each year.[11]

Of course, legislative bodies and government agencies are not the only stakeholders in public policies. This stage of the policy-making process is where many interest groups have made their reputations, or at the very least, have been highly visible. As we've seen, the cafeteria shooting served as a catalyst for Texas's right to carry law, but the law wasn't popular with everyone. Teachers groups, police groups, and medical professionals are only a few of the constituencies that opposed passage of a bill that would see citizens arming themselves. A look at the bill's finalized text reveals that some groups were effective at minimizing the impact on their respective turf. The final version of the bill, for example, does not allow handguns to be carried in public schools and colleges, regardless of whether a person has obtained a license; nor does it allow persons who have criminal records or who have been convicted of family violence to become licensed. Medical facilities may (and usually do) post signs on the entrances advising visitors to leave their guns elsewhere or risk breaking the law. The law even has a provision prohibiting handguns on premises where amusement rides are available for use by the public and are located in a county with a population of more than one million, encompasses at least 75 acres in surface area, is enclosed with access only through controlled entries, is open for operation more than 120 days in each calendar year, and has security guards on the premises at all times. You may ask, "where did that highly specific language come from?" Visit Six Flags Park in Arlington or Sea World in San Antonio for the answer, and enjoy yourself while conducting the research. The opposition from the teacher, medical, restaurant, and entertainment lobbies could not prevent this bill from passage, but they succeeded in formulating its final outcome.

According to the Texas Department of Transportation (TXDOT), there are nearly 15,000 crashes and more than 100 people killed in highway construction and maintenance zones in the state each year. The two leading causes of work zone crashes are excessive speed and the failure to remain alert while driving. As a result, one in three work zone crashes is a rear-end collision. In 2010, there were 3,073 distracted driver crashes in Texas work zones, involving 7,468 vehicles.[12] These distracted driver crashes resulted in 14 fatalities. Responding to TXDOT's request, the legislature looked at the polices and results that were in place in other states. They found that some of the others, namely, Michigan and Maryland's "Give 'em a Brake" campaign, were effective in slowing down motorists in work zones. TXDOT officials formulated policies at addressing this concern. As you would expect from these examples, state agencies and commissions are well suited in the policy formulation—as well as the adoption—stage of the process. Because the policies are critical to their missions, they formulate their policies with an eye toward public acceptance. Pennsylvania has taken the "Give them a Brake" program a step further. It recently started posting signs along construction zones that read: "Please slow down, my mommy works here."

Conflicts with existing policies are considered, as are costs and funding. Specific roles are defined for the government agency or agencies that will be responsible for carrying out the policy. Moreover, these agencies review past policy adoptions by Texas and other states. Chances are that other states have already adopted similar policies, and we can learn from their successes and failures.

☐ Implementation

At this stage, a government response to an issue is finalized and adopted. Policy is implemented when it is carried out. Timing, public education, and opinion regarding the policy have an impact on the success at this phase. Policy and perceived fairness are among the issues addressed here. It is important that the agencies responsible for **implementation** of public policy thoroughly understand and adhere to the letter and spirit of the law or inconsistencies will surely develop. The input into and acceptance by teachers of any education reform package will have a huge impact on its ultimate success.

The media are often involved here. When the state government implements a major new public policy, such as the sales tax holiday for school clothes and supplies, newspapers and television stations provide the public with a rundown of the rules and regulations. The state agencies often generate press releases and conduct interviews with members of the media to advertise and to clarify the new policy. When the Castle Law was implemented, the Texas Department of Public Safety and other agencies saw to it that the public had easy access to the terms and conditions of the new law. Legislatures often fund public awareness campaigns as part of the legislation, something you might have noticed when you see a billboard that reads "Click it or ticket."

Not all public policies are well received, and if those responsible for implementation of certain polices oppose them, this stage becomes every bit as contentious as the setting stage. This is especially true when the opposition wields considerable political and budgetary powers. It was no secret that Governor Perry and Lieutenant Governor Dewhurst were opposed to the Affordable Healthcare Act. As the Act neared the implementation stage, Perry, Dewhurst, and others announced that implementation in Texas may be delayed indefinitely because the national government's estimation of how much money is available was off base.[13] Dewhurst has said, "[the revised figures represent] an astounding number for us. Arguably, we have to crowd out public education or higher education to pay for this, or raise taxes. Those are unsustainable numbers." Proponents of national health care call these tactics "foot dragging," while opponents maintain that the federal government is forcing the state to be fiscally irresponsible.

☐ Evaluation

In theory, all public policies are evaluated periodically to determine whether they have had the desired effect. Problems arise here if the desired effect is not clear or the method for making these measurements is ill-conceived. Policy makers may discover during the **evaluation** process that the policy is in need of some change in order to be effective, and this may necessitate going back to the first or second stage of the process.

There is often disagreement on the effectiveness of public policies. For example, both opponents and proponents of affirmative action programs cite statistics to justify their position. One side calls for abolishing the programs; the other side indicates a need for their expansion.

More often than not, evaluation is carried out in a superficial manner. Government tends to evaluate what is easy to evaluate rather than those factors that show the effectiveness of a program. It is easier, for instance, to count the number of people or claims a government agency processes than it is to determine the effect of a policy. Texas does a better job than most states, thanks in part to the built-in evaluation process known as the Sunset Advisory Commission. Although the commission does not review the specific policies that are carried out by the agencies, it does conduct a comprehensive review of the agencies themselves.

An excellent example of how the evaluation stage works is found in the changes made to the Ashley Laws. In this case, the new law seems to be working well. The new public laws allowing local police to publish the names, addresses, and photographs of convicted child molesters is popular with everyone—except the offenders.

implementation
The third stage of the public policy-making model.

evaluation
The fourth stage of the public policy-making model.

12.1
12.2
12.3
12.4

change or termination
The final stage of the public policy-making model.

☐ Change or Termination

Sometimes public policies prove to be ineffective, very unpopular, or the times indicate that the **change or termination** must occur. An example of one or more of these reasons is the national speed limit mandate. During the 1970s, the U.S. government implemented a package of public policies aimed at conserving oil resources. A combination of factors, including unrest in the Middle East and environmentalists' concerns about air quality, turned the national spotlight on fuel conservation. Among the policies implemented was a federally mandated nationwide 55 MPH speed limit. This policy was repealed in the late 1980s as sources of oil became more reliable, cars became more efficient, and certain interest groups lobbied for higher speed limits.[14]

The Right to Carry (a concealed handgun) Law has been modified in every legislative session since it was introduced in 1995. Recent changes in the law empower municipal judges and justices of the peace to instantly revoke the licenses of those who commit, and in some cases even are accused of, family violence. The most recent change included the expansions provided by the Castle Law. The recent legislative history regarding laws against drunk driving further illustrate how public policies evolve—or change after they have been evaluated.

Texas joined most other states in passing mandatory seatbelt use in the 1990s, largely because of federal mandates. Prior to the passage of the first seatbelt laws, only

Texas ★ Mosaic

Michael Williams, Texas Commissioner of Education

The Texas Education Agency oversees the pre-kindergarten through high school education of nearly 5 million students. Governor Rick Perry named Michael Williams the agency's commissioner on September 1, 2012.

Williams's appointment as commissioner is the latest in what has been a lifetime of public service. After earning a Bachelor's, Master's, and law degree from the University of Southern California, Williams returned to his hometown of Midland where he served as an assistant district attorney. He went on to become a federal prosecutor in the Reagan Justice Department, earning the attorney general's Special Achievement Award for the conviction of six Ku Klux Klan members. Williams prosecuted the KKK cases under heavy armed guard after receiving death threats.

Prior to being named the Texas commissioner of education, Williams served as a Texas railroad commissioner for 10 years and was instrumental in administering relief efforts after Hurricanes Katrina and Rita.

Aside from serving the state in both elected and appointed capacities, Williams also served at the national level. In 1990, President Bush named Williams the assistant secretary of education for civil rights at the U.S. Department of Education. In that job, he acted as the principal advisor to the president and to Secretary of Education Lamar Alexander on civil rights matters.

Williams was involved with education well before he became a public official, and he has been an educator at all levels. Both of Williams's parents were public school teachers, and he has created his own summer camp, "Winnovators," that inspires sixth through

Michael Williams, a former elected Republican Railroad Commissioner, is the state's appointed Education Commissioner. As Railroad Commissioner, Williams was only the fourth African American elected statewide in Texas. He took control of an agency that had recently experienced significant budget cuts at a time where many Texans were questioning the state's approach to public education.

twelfth graders in areas of math and science. He taught courses at Texas Southern University, UT Permian Basin, and the Texas Wesleyan School of Law.

1. **What factors might motivate individuals like Michael Williams to serve in a public administration capacity?**

2. **Should appointed officials be required to have real-world experience relevant to the agencies they lead?**

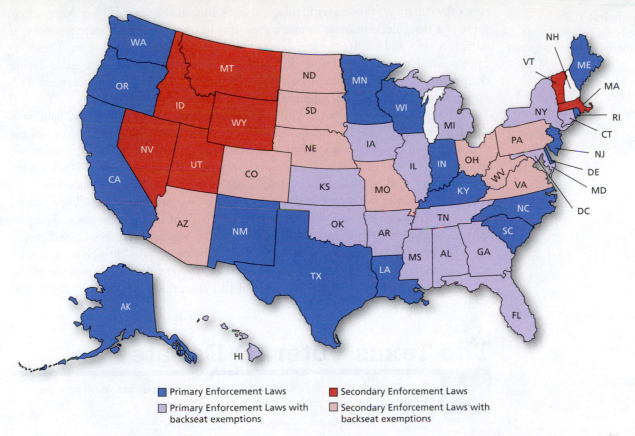

Primary Enforcement Laws

Primary Enforcement Laws with backseat exemptions

Secondary Enforcement Laws

Secondary Enforcement Laws with backseat exemptions

* Primary belt laws allow police to stop and ticket a motorist if the driver and passengers are not buckled up. Non-conforming primary laws allow exceptions for some vehicles, such as pick-up trucks. Secondary belt laws allow police to issue a citation only if the driver is first stopped for another infraction.

* Backseat exemption: Riders in the backseat do not have to wear seat belts after a certain age. Passengers can ride in the back seat without wearing seat belts ranging from age 7 to 18, depending on state law.

FIGURE 12.3 State Seat Belt Laws. Texas has among the most restrictive seat belt laws. Source: http://www.ncsl.org/issues-research/health/state-seat-belt-laws.aspx

76 percent of motorists and front seat passengers used seatbelts. After the first 10 years, that number increased to 94 percent, according to the Texas Transportation Institute. The National Highway Traffic Safety Administration reported that over the past 10 years, the Click It or Ticket campaign has saved more than 2,800 lives in Texas and has led to 48,000 fewer serious injuries while lowering related costs by $10 billion.[15] Evaluation of this law showed convincingly that seatbelt use saved lives and prevented injury, so in 2009 the legislature took it a step further by requiring all occupants of passenger vehicles to wear seatbelts. State law now requires that every person in a vehicle be secured by a seatbelt whether riding in the front or back seat. Fines and court costs for failing to fasten seatbelts can add up to $250 or more.[16] See Figure 12.3 for how Texas's seat belt laws compare to other states.

Nonfiscal Policy

12.3 Analyze why some policy-making decisions have few or no fiscal implications.

Some policy decisions do not have a direct impact on the state's fiscal plan. Recent examples include the Castle Law, abortion policy, and tort reform. Tort reform is aimed at reducing the cost of litigation by limiting the amount of damages a court may award a litigant. Sometimes, the policy process is fueled by ideological values, as is the case in the first two examples. Other

nonfiscal policies
Public policies that have little or no impact on the budget or budgetary process.

12.1

12.2

12.3

12.4

times the debate is framed over ideological lines, such as the voter ID law. More often, there is a tangible, economic interest, even if it has no bearing on state finances, as with tort reform. In 2007 the legislature passed the Castle Law, allowing Texans to carry concealed handguns almost anywhere. The issue was high on the agenda during the previous legislature, but apparently not high enough. Through negotiation with opponents and compromise, supporters of the bill carried the day.

For years, the business community in Texas complained about its potential liability in civil lawsuits. Tort reform makes it more difficult to win a lawsuit. Texas was one of the easiest states in which to win a lawsuit and collect damages. In 1995, their grievance was addressed by the legislature.[17] The legislature attempted further reform in 2003. Potentially, this has saved businesses millions of dollars annually, and consumers have been protected from some of the more outrageous increases in insurance premiums. The financial impact on the state's budget itself is limited. The impact on Texas businesses and on persons who believe they have been wronged by corporate negligence has been significant.

One thing that holds true about **nonfiscal policies** is that although compromise may be reached at a given time, the issues seem to stay at or near the top of the public agenda. There may be no better example of this than the voter ID law, which first went into effect in 2011.

The Texas Voter ID Debate

12.4 Evaluate the reasons why the controversy over voter ID laws has remained at the forefront of the public policy debate.

One of the most contentious policy issues of the decade relates to voter identification. Few policy arenas have been as explosive, and in recent years the debate has intensified to the point that the courts have become involved.

Voter ID laws require voters to show identification proving they are eligible to vote before they vote. The central question is whether voter ID laws interfere with free elections. Opponents charge that the laws discriminate against poor people because it costs money to obtain a state driver's license or identification card, and thus violates the constitutional safeguard against imposing any kind of tax on voting. Many citizens, as Figure 12.4 suggests, don't live close to a DPS office. They also

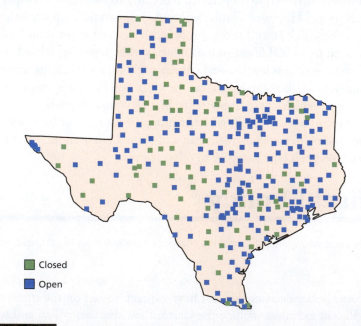

■ Closed

■ Open

FIGURE 12.4 Texas Department of Public Safety Offices. Green indicates that an office is closed. Blue means that the office is open.
Source: http://www.texastribune.org/library/data/texas-dps-office-locations/

Voting laws have received particular scrutiny in recent years, especially the voter ID controversy. This early voting location is at a south Austin grocery store. Although voter ID, if implemented, would almost certainly contract voting numbers, the state's early voting laws, among the most liberal in the nation, helped expand turnout.

claim that voter ID laws create an unreasonable burden on the elderly and on disabled individuals because many do not have government-issued identification papers.

In Texas, the controversy started in 2005, when the Texas house passed a bill that would require all voters to have a picture ID before casting a ballot. The bill was killed in the senate, but it underscored a concern with the potential for illegally cast ballots. From the outset, critics of the bill saw it as an attempt to suppress minority turnout. Similar bills were introduced in 2007 and again in 2009, but were killed. When the voter ID bill was reintroduced in 2011, it passed with much controversy, and in the years since, that controversy has not only intensified but has spread to a number of other states that passed similar legislation.

Opponents of lenient registration and voting laws believe there is a cost to making it too easy to vote: Uninformed citizens might be more likely to cast ballots. Even worse, they might be enticed or otherwise pressured into voting. As long as registration and voting require some affirmative act, the process tends to weed out those voters who are unprepared. Proponents of the law further argue that most states provide free voter identification certificates to qualifying individuals and that the requirement eliminates the chances of election fraud by keeping noncitizens from voting. Those opposed to the law cite statistical data indicating that low-income, particularly Hispanic Americans, are those most likely not to have identification cards. In 2012, Governor Rick Perry responded that the Texas law requires nothing more extensive than the type of photo identification necessary to receive a library card or board an airplane. The Texas law requires voters to present one of the following documents: a state-issued driver's license or identification card, a military photo ID, a passport, a U.S. citizenship certificate with a photo, or a concealed-carry handgun license.

The debate is framed among partisan lines. Since 2011, eight states, including Texas, have passed voter identification laws, and all but two of these states had

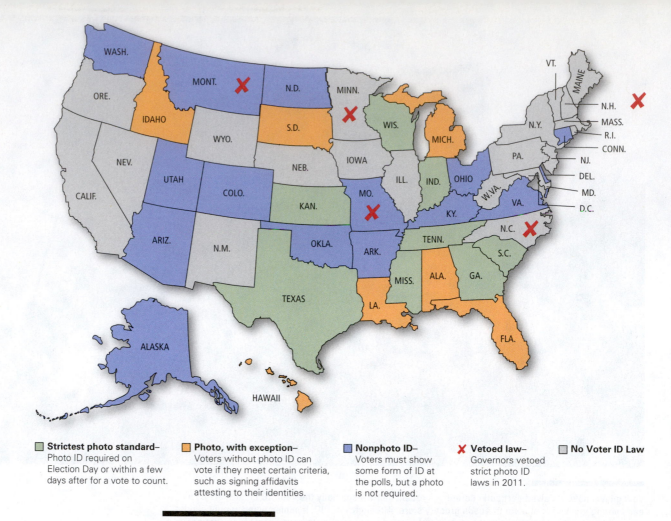

▇ **Strictest photo standard–** Photo ID required on Election Day or within a few days after for a vote to count.	▇ **Photo, with exception–** Voters without photo ID can vote if they meet certain criteria, such as signing affidavits attesting to their identities.	▇ **Nonphoto ID–** Voters must show some form of ID at the polls, but a photo is not required.	✗ **Vetoed law–** Governors vetoed strict photo ID laws in 2011. ▇ **No Voter ID Law**

FIGURE 12.5 Voter Identification Laws Across the United States.   Before 2011, only Georgia and Indiana required voters to show photo IDs. But in the past year, many more states considered or enacted laws to require more rigorous proof of identity. Most new laws will be in effect for the 2012 election, though some first require US Justice Department approval.

Republican legislators and Republican governors. Twenty-seven states already had some form of voter ID law on the books prior to 2011, as illustrated by Figure 12.5. Since there are constitutional implications, the federal government has stepped into the debate by challenging state voter ID laws. In 2012, U.S. Attorney General Eric Holder held that Texas, because of its history of voter discrimination, needed to get the voter ID law preapproved by the Justice Department. In response, Texas Republican Attorney General Greg Abbott filed a lawsuit in federal court to keep the law in place.

The voter ID issue brilliantly illustrates the dynamic nature of public policy making and, due to its divisiveness, shows how difficult it is to reach consensus, much less compromise.

Looking back at what we have learned about public policy making in this chapter, we can clearly identify the voter ID law as an issue that will not be resolved anytime soon. Most would agree that the sides are polarized particularly over party lines, which means this is an ideological issue. Because there are constitutional issues involved, namely, voting rights and due process, the national government has taken a deep interest. In terms of policy type, this one clearly falls into the category of regulatory public policy.

☐ Taking It Through The Stages

It would seem that since a public policy relating to voter ID was passed into law by the legislature, the issue would be well past the agenda-setting and formulation stages. But this is hardly the case, as this policy arena appears on all policy—and thus,

Inside the Federalist System

Texas-Style Welfare Reform

One of the last truly bipartisan actions taken at the federal level occurred in 1995, when, along with a Republican Congress, President Bill Clinton signed the federal Welfare Reform Bill into law. The law has been cited as the essence of devolution, as it returned much of the welfare system back to the states. Texas wasted no time and became one of the first to enact reforms in establishing its own welfare, workforce development, and subsidized child care systems.

The changes implemented by the Texas Legislature reflect three overriding philosophies in Texas government and political culture: (1) local control; (2) smaller, more efficient government; and (3) an emphasis on work and individual responsibility. To meet these goals, Texas devolved to the local level management of more programs than most other states—including Temporary Aid to Needy Families (TANF), employment training, workforce development programs, and child care.

As a result, TANF recipients are subject to time-limited benefits as short as one year, followed by a five-year "freeze-out." A strong Work First message and the Full Family Sanction of all TANF cash benefits for noncompliance with work requirements have motivated many TANF applicants and recipients to seek employment. Welfare reform in Texas enforces the importance of working, the temporary nature of public assistance, and the belief that parents are responsible for the care and well-being of their families. Caseloads in the state have dropped substantially since 1996, and as a result, Texas received more than $72.6 million in federal high-performance bonuses for effective welfare programs.

1. Should redistributive policies, such as welfare programs, be left entirely to the states to administer?

2. Should the amount of funds available for welfare be limited by a set percentage of the state's total funds?

political—stages. Stories of voter fraud and entire communities becoming disenfranchised fuel the agenda file. In other words, this is one arena that hasn't been laid to rest.

It is in the formulation stage that policy makers determine what agency will be accountable for the policy. In the case of the Texas voter ID law, we have not even determined what level of government (state or national) has the final say. The U.S. Department of Justice has deemed this a federal issue, and there are laws, such as the Voting Rights Act of 1965, that answer any questions. The federal government's claim that the Texas law usurps the constitution is refuted by the state attorney general's claim that this issue is to be left to the states. Unless and until the final arbiter is determined, the requirements for voting will always remain in the formulation stage.

Since the implementation stage centers on fairness and consistent application, we can be certain that the voter ID law will be, at best, difficult to implement. It doesn't help matters that the law can be interpreted differently, as this will almost certainly lead to allegations from both sides of selectivity, exclusion, and arbitrariness. Moreover, where most public policy is accepted at this stage, the voter ID issue remains unpopular with a vocal constituency.

Even before the law took effect, people on both sides predicted how the law would affect democracy. In other words, they took to evaluating the impact of the new law before the law went into effect. Predictably, proponents claim it will result in less voter fraud. Opponents fear that discrimination will become the accepted norm if the policy is not changed.

☐ Feral Hogs

One of the most unusual bills passed by the 2011 legislature was one that allows for hunting feral hogs from helicopters. The law, which some hunters call "The Pork-Chopper Bill," was passed in order to address an issue that was long on the agenda—the overpopulation of feral hogs. The Texas Parks and Wildlife Department estimates that the number of these hogs has increased to over 2 million. Feral hogs are among the most destructive invasive species in the United States today. Of the estimated 4 million wreaking havoc on 39 states, half are in Texas, where they do some $400 million in damages annually.

Feral hogs are a menace in Texas. State law allows them to be hunted from helicopters. Texas has more than two million of the hogs, and they do more than $400 million in damage each year. They destroy wildlife and crops and prey on animals as large as calves, in addition to spreading disease.

Feral hogs are domestic hogs that have escaped or been released into the wild. With each generation the animals' domestic characteristics diminish as they develop the traits necessary to survive in the wild. Moreover, they have no natural predators, and there are no legal poisonous substances to combat their increased numbers. They cause various kinds of agricultural and environmental damage, mostly by rooting, wallowing, and depredation. They also compete with wildlife and livestock for habitat and carry parasites harmful to domestic livestock and humans.

The new law providing for aerial hunting is a legal method of controlling feral hogs in Texas. Most of the aerial hunting is done with helicopters, which supporters claim have the advantage of being effective, especially in areas otherwise inaccessible by the more traditional methods.

By examining this issue through the public policy-making model introduced at the start of this chapter, we see a policy arena that is at the same time in several of the stages. The issue first came to the agenda in the 1980s, and laws pertaining to hunting these creatures were liberalized. Obviously, those policies were not effective enough to keep the issue off the public agenda—at least not during this decade. During the 2011 legislative season, the policies were modified to allow for hunting by air, which brought up a host of new policy issues. Businesses sprang up almost as soon as the law was introduced, and today one can rent a seat (and a gun) on a helicopter and partake in such hunts.

Feral hogs are distributed throughout much of Texas, generally inhabiting the white-tailed deer range, with the highest population densities occurring in east, south, and central Texas. North and west Texas have very low or no populations. However, reports indicate that populations are beginning to expand and increase in these areas. As noted earlier, there is currently an estimated population in excess of 2 million feral hogs in Texas.

The increase in population and distribution is due in part to intentional releases, improved habitat, increased wildlife management, and improved animal husbandry such as disease eradication, limited natural predators, and high reproductive potential. There seem to be very few inhibiting factors to curtail this population growth and distribution, although extreme arid conditions may impede it.

Review the Chapter

Listen to Chapter 12

Public Policy

12.1 Explain why public policy is the cornerstone of politics.

Public policy is created by all branches and at all levels of government. Everything the government does—or does not do—constitutes policy. It is the outcome of all government action, and it is a fluid and dynamic field of study that involves federalism, political group activity, judicial review, and enforcement.

The Policy-Making Model

12.2 Outline the stages of the policy-making paradigm.

Political scientists have created a paradigm containing five distinctive stages of the policy-making process. This model is beneficial because it simplifies the often very complex myriad of forces that are part of the process, and because it works to explain the process at all levels of government.

There can be no policy without identifying an issue or a problem. This "awareness" is part of the agenda-setting stage of the process. Many issues never make it past this stage, and indeed there often are forces working hard to keep certain topics off the public agenda. Agendas can be sparked by noteworthy events, by ideological differences, or by trends and patterns that become noticeable. The formulation stage is where discussion about what to do about the issue begins. What should we do? Who's going to do it? What have others done about it? These questions and more are addressed in the policy formulation stage.

The third stage, implementation, sees the policy go into effect. Agencies are funded, workers are trained, and the public, if it isn't already aware of the policy, is made aware. Evaluation is the fourth stage, and it is here where the effectiveness is measured. Naturally, political forces are at play in this stage, and often we see that a policy has created other areas of concern.

The fifth and final stage is change or termination. Public policies seem to evolve over time. Examples of DWI laws that are becoming increasingly stronger, and changes to the Castle Law are cited in the chapter.

Nonfiscal Policy

12.3 Analyze why some policy-making decisions have few or no fiscal implications.

Nonfiscal policy can be among the most contentious issues because it often involves ideological forces, which by their very nature can be difficult to overcome through compromise. Other examples cited include the Texas voter ID law and tort reform.

The Texas Voter ID Debate

12.4 Evaluate why the controversy over voter ID laws has remained at the forefront of the public policy debate.

The Texas voter ID law is a regulatory policy with severe ideological implications. This is not surprising, since at the heart of the matter is the issue of democracy, equality, and due process. The issue has become especially contentious because the federal government has become a stakeholder. The case for voter ID will likely be at the forefront for years to come.

Learn the Terms

 Study and **Review** the **Flashcards**

Test Yourself

12.1 Explain why public policy is the cornerstone of politics.

The term *public policy* is best defined as

a. the outcome of government action.
b. the process of judicial review.
c. the structure of regulatory agencies.
d. the measure of public trust.
e. the media's reaction to political debate.

12.2 Outline the stages of the public policy paradigm.

The first stage in the policy-making process is

a. implementation.
b. adoption.
c. evaluation.
d. agenda setting.
e. political action.

12.3 Analyze why some policy-making decisions have few or no fiscal implications.

Nonfiscal policies are characterized by

a. contested budget hearings.
b. a short cycle on the policy agenda.
c. their relationship with local tax issues.
d. the general agreement among all sides.
e. having no direct impact on the state's fiscal plan.

12.4 Evaluate why the controversy over voter ID laws has remained at the forefront of the public policy debate.

Opponents of voter identification cite all of the following except

a. It creates an unfair burden on the poor.
b. It creates an unfair burden on the elderly.
c. It allows unregistered voters to cast ballots.
d. It was passed with partisan intent.
e. It creates an unfair burden on those who live in rural areas.

Explore Further

Anton, Thomas J. *Federalism and Public Policy: How the System Works*. New York: Random House, 1989.

Cochran, Clarke E., Lawrence C. Mayer, T.R. Carr, and N. Joseph Cayer. *American Public Policy: An Introduction*, 8th ed. Belmont, CA: Thomson Wadsworth, 2006.

Dye, Thomas R. *Understanding Public Policy*, 12th ed. Upper Saddle River, NJ: Prentice Hall, 2008.

Harpham, Edward J., "Welfare Reform and the New Paternalism in Texas," in *Texas Politics: A Reader*, edited by Anthony

Champagne and Edward J. Harpham. New York: W. W. Norton, 1997.

Heclo, Hugh, "Issue Networks and Executive Establishment," in *The New American Political System*, edited by Anthony King. Washington, DC: American Enterprise Institute, 1978.

Walters, Jonathan. "Did Somebody Say Downsizing?" *Governing* 11 (February 1998), pp. 17–20.

13

Criminal Justice Policy in Texas

Texas is the poster boy state of judicial horrors.

—*Defense Attorney Alan Dershowitz*

Capital punishment. Those without the capital get the punishment.

—*Last Words of a Texas death row inmate*

ach year, millions of Texans anticipate the announcement of the *Dallas Morning News* "Texan of the Year." In 2012, the newspaper named co-recipients Christopher Scott and Michael Morton "Texans of the Year." Scott spent more than 12 years in prison for a murder he did not commit, and Morton spent twice that long (25 years) in prison after being wrongfully convicted of killing his wife.

Some critics claim that Scott and Morton were not recognized for what they did, but rather for what they didn't do—namely, commit horrific crimes. The newspaper's editorial board pointed out that these men deserved the distinction precisely for what they did. "Any man would need

13.1	13.2	13.3	13.4
Explain why crime rates are among the most important statistical data generated by government.	Discuss why the use of the death penalty has been on the decline and will continue to decrease.	Identify the major types of law enforcement agencies at the state and local level.	Explain how an individual's right to due process extends through all stages of the criminal justice system.

CRIMINAL D

Christopher Scott, waving to supporters, served 12 years in prison after being wrongly convicted of murder. He is one of many who have had their convictions overturned in Texas over the last decade. The state's alarming number of false convictions has drawn national attention, but it has led to a closer examination of some questionable sentences.

an ocean of inner strength to survive arrest, conviction and hard prison time for a crime he did not commit. It takes even more strength to cling to hope that someday, the system will make things right so he can clear his name and walk free."[1]

Wrongful convictions are only one in the myriad of issues involving crime, justice, and public policy. In recent years, Texans such as Dallas County District Attorney Craig Watkins have led the charge in enhancing the system's credibility.

Issues of crime and punishment pervade virtually all discussions of state and local government and dominate many political campaigns. It seems as if local news always leads with a story about a local, high-profile crime, criminal investigation, or some local trial. Being "tough on crime" is important to people seeking elected office, and candidates take advantage of the opportunity to have their photograph taken with law enforcement officials.

Although law enforcement at the federal level plays an important role, the fact is that public safety, crime prevention, and enforcement efforts are largely a state and local government concern. Indeed, spending on public safety by local governments often exceeds 50 percent of the budget. The fear of being victimized is real to anyone who has read about criminal street gangs, auto theft, carjackings, or drive-by shootings.

What to do about crime is always a political question, and the jury is split. Nearly everyone agrees on the importance of prevention, but few agree on how to go about it. Some say that a good education keeps people from committing street crimes out of necessity; others believe that crime prevention means educating potential victims about how to maintain their property and personal safety.

Do we have enough police officers to address the demand for service? Is the selection and training process for police officers, prosecutors, judges, and juries adequate, or is that part of the problem? Should the prison system administer punishment, reform, or a combination? Do defendants and criminals really "get all the rights," or are many disadvantaged defendants charged and convicted without the benefit of due process? As relevant as these questions are, Texas lawmakers are starting to look beyond these reactive issues, asking questions such as, "What can be done to diminish the need for more police, courts, and prisons?"

Measuring Crime

13.1 Explain why crime rates are among the most important statistical data generated by government.

Any conversation about the political, budgetary, and social implications of crime and punishment begins with data. After all, how can we know if the hiring of additional police officers has resulted in fewer burglaries; or if a special kind of probation program reduced recidivism; or if tougher murder laws lowered the incidence of capital murder? Crime statistics are meaningful because they measure, to a great extent, our quality of life. State and local governments track crime rates because of the budgetary implications. Department heads determine staffing and deployment needs. Crime statistics are equally important in the private sector. Insurance companies require crime data to justify rates, for example. Suppose your research assignment is to measure the effectiveness of a special motor vehicle theft task force that was launched in your county last year. Perhaps your first task might be to measure the number of auto thefts a few years ago against the most recent year. You must take into account the population increases and number of cars registered in the county, of course. Maybe your first task is to define "motor vehicle?" Will that include motor boats, airplanes, tractors, forklifts, and motorcycles? Then, of course, you must define "theft." For example, if an individual loans his car to an acquaintance for a few hours, but the car is not returned, does that constitute theft? What kind of activity, precisely, do you wish to track? You will have to answer these and many other questions before you even start collecting and analyzing data, so you'd better get started!

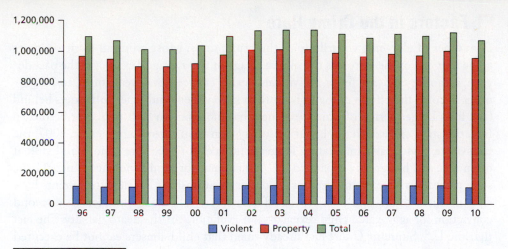

FIGURE 13.1 Index Crimes in Texas 1996–2010.
Texas Department of Public Safety.

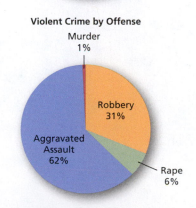

13.1

13.2

13.3

13.4

index crimes
Eight categories of crime used for statistical study by the federal and state governments.

There are three classical methods of measuring crime, and each shows a slightly different picture. Victimization surveys are effective and often used by academics and private-sector consulting firms. Incarceration rates presume that more arrests for a given crime reflect a greater number of those crimes being committed. Each of these has obvious deficiencies. Another measure, and the one that has become the official measure for governments at all levels, is the number of crimes recorded by (or, reported to) law enforcement agencies. It is not perfect because agencies often interpret the guidelines differently and not all crimes are reported, but such inconsistencies are, well, consistent throughout.

Crime data are collected by state agencies and then turned over to the FBI's Uniform Crime Reporting Division. The FBI publishes *Crime in the United States*, a comprehensive statistical breakdown of crime categorized by type, region, rates, and even time of day. The publication is prepared according to a standard called the Uniform Crime Reports (UCR). Measuring crime across America is a highly ambitious task. After all, each of the states has its own version of criminal laws and of which crimes should be included in the report. There are literally hundreds, maybe thousands, of different crimes on the books, and tracking all these would be a daunting task. To simplify things, the UCR devised a list of eight index crimes. The index works much like the Dow Jones stock market index, which tracks a handful of selected stocks representing the entire market. **Index crimes** are those eight offenses that the state and national governments use to perform statistical studies. They are murder, rape, robbery, aggravated assault, burglary, theft, auto theft, and arson. Index statistics are used to establish and compare crime rates among states and regions. During calendar year 2008, there was an estimated total of 1,093,428 index offenses in Texas. The crime volume decreased 1.2 percent when compared to 2007.[2] Nine of ten crimes committed in Texas, as indicated in Figure 13.2, are classified as property crimes, or those that do not involve violence toward any person.[3]

☐ Crime in Texas

Although the overall crime rate in Texas has been decreasing, each year more than 1 million people are arrested in Texas for the commission of major crimes. Despite significant decreases in murder, rape, and other assaultive offenses, the number of arrests continues to escalate, primarily due to the flourishing illicit drug trade. In the early 1990s, thousands of people connected to the manufacture of methamphetamine were jailed and given the maximum 20-year sentences. Now they're coming out of hibernation—so to speak—and the manufacturing of these homemade drugs is on the rise. So prevalent is this that in 2011 the legislature toughened laws requiring retailers to keep certain cold remedies (used to manufacture meth) behind their counters. Other legislation empowers police and social workers to physically remove children found in the presence of dope labs.[4]

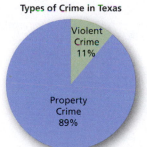

Types of Crime in Texas

Violent Crime 11%

Property Crime 89%

Violent Crime by Offense

Murder 1%

Robbery 31%

Aggravated Assault 62%

Rape 6%

FIGURE 13.2 Types of Crime in Texas, 2008.
Texas Department of Public Safety.

☐ Factors in the Crime Rate

A number of elements contribute to the crime rates. Most criminal justice experts agree that one of the factors is the increased age of the average Texan over the past decade, meaning there are fewer individuals in the "crime-prone" years of 17 to 24. Another factor is the efforts of the legislature to keep violent and repeat offenders behind bars for a longer period of time. Texas now has more prison beds than ever before. In fact, the state of Texas has a larger prison system than most countries. In 2007, the legislature passed laws mandating longer sentences for the more serious and violent offenders, and has greatly expanded the punishment for family violence.[5] In 2011 the state passed laws protecting persons in "dating relationships."[6] The punishments have also increased dramatically for repeat offenders. An individual who receives a second conviction for aggravated child sexual assault is eligible for the death penalty. The fact that the U.S. Supreme Court has already ruled that child abusers cannot be executed unless death results has not deterred Texas legislators from passing the law.[7]

Technology is one of the leading reasons for the reduction in crime. With knowledge that the overall incidence of crime is down and arrests are up, we can conclude that the justice system is getting more efficient. The use of computers has had a dramatic effect on crime-fighting efforts on the streets and in the courtrooms. Only a generation ago, identifying a suspect through fingerprints was an agonizing and tedious task. Clerks would have to ply through thousands of fingerprint cards. Today, all police have to do is scan a small portion of a print found at a crime scene and the computers will reveal the suspect's name, location, and photograph.

☐ Corrections

The corrections system is costly, largely due to the expense of housing individuals convicted of committing criminal acts. Other factors are contributing to the rising cost of corrections: the actual cost of housing the inmates and the increasing volume of the jail population. By a substantial margin, Texas leads the rest of the nation in the state inmate rate. How big is "the system"? It is astonishing. Texas leads the nation in the number of people under some form of supervision, with nearly 1 million people in jail, prison, probation, or parole. This means that 1 in nearly every 20 adults is on the bad side of the justice system, with as many as 5 percent of adult males in Texas currently incarcerated, on probation, or on parole. Both criminal justice agencies and lawmakers acknowledge that better education and employment opportunities would play an important part in reducing the number of incarcerated Texans. According to the Texas Department of Criminal Justice, almost 80 percent of Texas's prison inmates did not complete high school and half were not employed when they were arrested. Legislators, educators, and criminal justice officials are working cooperatively to address these and other problems. By the most conservative estimates, it costs more than $16,000 per year to keep an adult behind bars, compared to $354 for one year of adult education. The annual cost estimates of housing prisoners do not take into account the money spent investigating, arresting, trying, and convicting the individual offender.[8]

Capital Punishment

13.2	Discuss why the use of the death penalty has been on the decline and will continue to decrease.

T he use of capital punishment dates back to the beginnings of recorded history. During the colonial period, each of the 13 colonies used it to some extent, and some had dozens of capital offenses on the books.[9] In modern times, the states get to determine whether or not the death penalty is an option, but the parameters have been severely restricted. Where some colonies, and later

TABLE 13.1 CAPITAL CRIMES IN TEXAS

The following crimes constitute capital murder in Texas:

- murder of a peace officer or fireman who is acting in the lawful discharge of an official duty and who the person knows is a peace officer or fireman;

- murder during the commission or attempted commission of kidnapping, burglary, robbery, aggravated sexual assault, arson, obstruction or retaliation, or terroristic threat;

- murder for remuneration or promise of remuneration or employs another to commit murder for remuneration or promise of remuneration;

- murder during escape or attempted escape from a penal institution;

- murder, while incarcerated in a penal institution, of a correctional employee or with the intent to establish, maintain, or participate in a combination or in the profits of a combination;

- murder while incarcerated in a penal institution for a conviction of murder or capital murder;

- murder while incarcerated in a penal institution serving a life sentence or a 99-year sentence for a conviction of aggravated kidnapping, aggravated sexual assault, or aggravated robbery;

- murder of more than one person during the same criminal transaction or during different criminal transactions but the murders are committed pursuant to the same scheme or course of conduct;

- murder of an individual under ten years of age; or

- murder in retaliation for or on account of the service or status of the other person as a judge or justice of the supreme court, the court of criminal appeals, a court of appeals, a district court, a criminal district court, a constitutional county court, a statutory county court, a justice court, or a municipal court.

Source: Texas Penal Code, 2011–2013.

the states, prescribed death for crimes ranging from horse thievery to witchcraft, today the states are limited to just a few of the more heinous crimes, as noted in Table 13.1.

No state executes more prisoners than Texas. It is becoming increasingly difficult for Texas death row inmates to be granted clemency or stays of execution, even when evidence exists that may suggest their innocence. Well-known criminal defense attorney Alan Dershowitz has said that he could teach an entire course on abuse of justice using Texas as a case study. Every capital punishment case generates a degree of controversy, but few have ever been as contentious as that of Leonel Herrera, who was convicted in 1982 of killing a Texas state trooper near Brownsville, Texas. Eight years after his trial, Herrera's attorneys presented new evidence that suggested his brother actually committed the crime. His brother had died shortly before this new evidence came to light. The state denied the request for a new trial, citing a Texas law that required new evidence to be presented 30 days after the initial trial. The U.S. Supreme Court upheld the Texas law as constitutional,[10] over the objections of Herrera's attorneys who argued that executing an individual when there was still doubt about his guilt violates the provision against cruel and unusual punishment. Since Herrera's execution, the state has revised the law to allow the admission of new evidence even after the 30-day time period has passed.

Capital punishment is one of the most controversial contemporary issues. Much of this controversy stems from the myriad myths believed and often cited by individuals arguing for and against. For example, supporters of the death penalty claim that much-needed prison space would be available if the state expanded the list of capital crimes and executed more prisoners. This belief is invalid, as is the popular notion that putting the condemned to death would save the taxpayers money. At any given time, there are about 400 individuals on Texas's death row.[11] This comparatively small number of prisoners hardly would make a dent in the total inmate population even if all these individuals were executed tomorrow. Moreover, it costs taxpayers much more money—in some cases, several millions—to get a death penalty conviction. In almost all cases, the guilt of the accused is well established, and the appeals address the constitutionality of the death penalty.

The myths abound as to why nearly 40 percent of the executions performed in the United States occur in Texas. You may have heard some people say it is because Texas is such a large, populated state, or because Texas has a higher-than-average criminal element. Yet there is no correlation between a state's population and its execution rate. California has a much higher population, yet it performs very few executions. On the other hand, Oklahoma has a comparatively low population and yet ranks number two in the number of executions. Statistically speaking, Texans are a relatively law-abiding people. Violent crime rates statewide are the envy of many other states. Someone may tell you Texas executes more people because it has stricter laws. You might remind that person that Texas's laws are no stricter than those of other states. So why then does Texas have such a high execution rate? The answer to that question can be summed up in two words: political culture. The state's individualistic and traditionalistic aspects explain why prosecutors are more prone to seek the death penalty and why juries are more apt to give it.

"QUESTIONS OF LIFE AND DEATH" In Texas death penalty cases, jurors determine the punishment by following a specific formula set by the law. The judge asks the jury to answer the following three questions. Depending on the answers, the sentence is life or death.

1. Was the defendant's conduct that caused the death of the victim committed deliberately and with the reasonable expectation that the victim's death would ensue?
2. Is it probable that the defendant would commit additional criminal acts of violence that would constitute a continuing threat to society?
3. Is there anything in the circumstances of the offense and the defendant's character and background that would warrant a sentence of life imprisonment rather than the death sentence?

If the answers are yes/yes/no, the sentence is death. If the answers are anything but yes/yes/no, the sentence is life without the possibility of parole.

EXECUTIONS ON THE DECLINE As a result of recent U.S. Supreme Court rulings and changes to the Texas laws made in 2002 and 2007, criminal justice analysts predict a slow but steady decline in the number of executions carried out in Texas. Two of the three reasons for such a decrease in the use of the death penalty are U.S. Supreme Court decisions affecting juveniles and mentally retarded individuals. The third reason is the most significant: The legislature has empowered juries to sentence defendants to life without the possibility of parole.

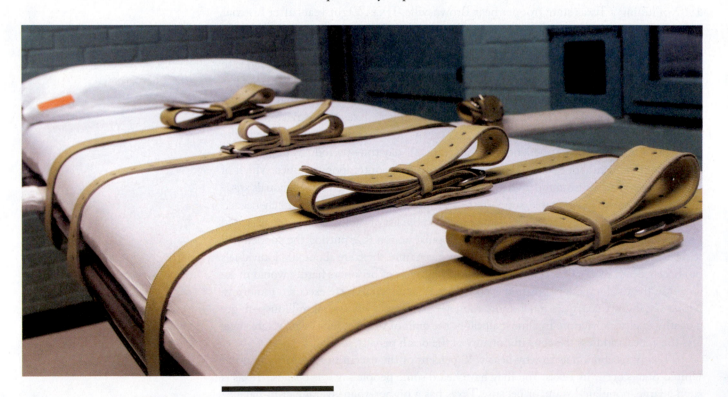

This is the death row gurney for the state of Texas. Although Texas leads the nation in executions, the numbers on death row have dropped significantly in recent years as prosecutors and juries have been less likely to ask for or assess capital punishment.

In *Roper v. Simmons* (2005), the U.S. Supreme Court held that persons who were 17 years old or younger at the time the capital crime was committed could not be executed.[12] Consequently, several death row inmates were transferred to the general prison population and are now serving life terms, meaning most will one day be eligible for parole. This was a highly controversial issue, largely because of differing interpretations of the term *juvenile*. In Texas, a juvenile means an individual who is 16 years of age or younger. Many other states define juvenile as a person younger than 18. Non-Texans were using the latter definition when they accused Texas of "executing juveniles." In modern times, Texas law has always prohibited the execution of any defendant who was under 17 when the offense was committed. But 17-year-olds, because they hold the status of "adult," were fair game, so to speak. In 1992 the U.S. Supreme Court came short of nationally defining "juvenile," but made clear that no one who was under 18 when the crime was committed could be executed. In another case, the U.S. Supreme Court ruled 6–3 that states could not execute persons found to be mentally retarded, on the basis that it violated the Eighth Amendment's protection against cruel and unusual punishment.[13] Consequently, Governor Perry commuted the sentences of 28 mentally retarded death row inmates to life.

An even more significant factor—in terms of sheer numbers—in explaining why there will be fewer executions in the future stems from changes made in how juries sentence convicted individuals. Prior to 2005, juries had but two choices in a capital case: the death penalty or life in prison. Over the years, many jurors who pronounced death were troubled by the fact that a sentence of life in prison meant a chance for parole after 40 years. The jurors said that they opted for the death penalty because it was the only

Jacob Ray Evans, far left, during a writ of habeas corpus hearing in Weatherford. Evans is accused of murdering his mother and sister. Charged with capital murder, he is not eligible for the death penalty because he was 17 at the time of the crime. This hearing is the first in a long process leading up to a trial, even though Evans admitted to the murders in his 911 call.

TABLE 13.2 EXECUTIONS

December 7, 1982 through November 15, 2012

Race	White		Black		Hispanic		Other		Total	
2012	4	27%	7	47%	4	27%	0	0%	15	100%
2011	6	46.00%	3	23.00%	4	31.00%	0	0%	13	100%
2010	7	41.20%	5	29.40%	5	29.40%	0	0.00%	17	100%
2009	4	16.70%	13	54.20%	7	29.20%	0	0%	24	100%
2008	6	33.30%	9	50.00%	3	16.70%	0	0%	18	100%
2007	12	46.20%	8	30.80%	6	23.10%	0	0%	26	100%
2006	5	20.90%	14	58.30%	5	20.90%	0	0%	24	100%
2005	11	57.90%	5	26.30%	3	15.80%	0	0%	19	100%
2004	8	34.60%	12	52.20%	3	13.00%	0	0%	23	100%
2003	14	58.30%	7	29.20%	3	12.50%	0	0%	24	100%
2002	17	51.50%	11	33.30%	5	15.20%	0	0%	33	100%
2001	10	58.80%	6	35.30%	1	5.90%	0	0%	17	100%
2000	19	47.50%	16	40.00%	5	12.50%	0	0%	40	100%
1999	17	46.60%	11	31.40%	7	20.00%	0	0%	35	100%
1998	13	65.00%	2	10.00%	5	25.00%	0	0%	20	100%
1997	21	56.80%	13	35.10%	2	5.40%	1	2.70%	37	100%
1996	1	33.30%	1	33.30%	1	33.30%	0	0%	3	100%
1995	8	42.10%	8	42.10%	2	10.50%	1	5.30%	19	100%
1994	9	64.30%	4	28.60%	1	7.10%	0	0%	14	100%
1993	6	35.30%	7	41.20%	4	23.50%	0	0%	17	100%
1992	5	41.70%	5	41.70%	2	16.70%	0	0%	12	100%

Source: http://www.tdcj.state.tx.us/stat/dr_executions_by_year.html, the official Texas government website.

way to ensure that the convict would never be free to commit crimes again. As a result of legislation, juries still have only two choices, but they are very different choices: the death penalty or life in prison *without the possibility of parole.* Criminal justice officials cite the fact that other states making similar moves have experienced a reduction in the number of death sentences. As Table 13.2 illustrates, the reduction in execution rates is apparent since the Supreme Court decisions and legislatively mandated sentencing options have taken hold. It will take a decade or more for this change to result in even lower execution rates, in light of the fact that the average tenure on death row is nearly 11 years.[14]

Law Enforcement

13.3 Identify the major types of law enforcement agencies at the state and local level.

☐ Various Levels of Law Enforcement

It has been argued that the most basic task of government is to provide protection for its citizens and their property. Although national law enforcement agencies such as the Federal Bureau of Investigation (FBI), Bureau of Alcohol, Tobacco, and Firearms (ATF), and the Drug Enforcement Administration (DEA) garner much publicity in their efforts to enforce the law, state and local governments provide by far the majority of police services.

In 1965, the Texas Legislature took steps to elevate the professionalism of its law enforcement ranks by creating the Texas Commission on Law Enforcement Officers Standards and Education. The commission mandated that all state, county, and local law enforcement officers complete basic training in order to be licensed. Today, the commission sets the criteria for licensing more than 80,000 police officers, reserves, jailers, and corrections officers throughout the state.[15] To be eligible for a peace officer license, candidates must complete an 800-hour basic police academy and must be physically and mentally fit. In addition, the commission requires licensed officers to attend regular in-service training on topics of current interest, which now include identity theft, family violence, racial profiling, crisis intervention, and other specialized investigative topics.[16]

STATE LEVEL The state law enforcement agency most visible to Texans is the Department of Public Safety (DPS) Highway Patrol. The DPS provides a wide array of police services, ranging from ensuring the safety of commercial vehicles (License and Weight) to tracking con artists who travel across the state (Bunco Division). A division of the DPS known even to non-Texans is the **Texas Rangers**, an elite group of 144 state troopers that investigates major crimes and allegations of police misconduct.[17] The subject of Texas folklore and even some movies, the Rangers were formed in 1837, when the Republic of Texas needed an inexpensive, yet effective, police force because Texas was an economically depressed and dangerous place to live.[2] "Captain Bill" McDonald remains a Ranger legend. In the 1870s, he was said to have come face to face with a mob of 20 angry men, all with shotguns leveled at him. Demonstrating great presence of mind, he told the mob, "I'm here to investigate a foul murder you scoundrels have committed—now, put up them guns."[18] After the men did as they were told, one witness observed, "Captain Bill would charge Hell with a bucket of water." Today, the Texas Rangers have evolved into a respected force of specially trained investigators who probe some of the state's most intricate crimes and are often called in to investigate allegations of police misconduct at the county and municipal level. The Texas Rangers Museum in Waco, Texas, houses thousands of artifacts and is well worth the trip.

More than a dozen other law enforcement agencies operate at the state level. The licensed peace officers assigned to these state agencies are empowered to enforce all state and local laws, but they serve in specialized fields. For example, the Texas Alcoholic Beverage Commission (TABC) regulates the manufacturing, transportation, distribution, and sale of alcoholic beverages throughout the state.[19]

COUNTY LEVEL Each of Texas's 254 counties has a **sheriff**, whose duty it is to maintain a county jail and to provide police service in the rural, nonincorporated areas of the county. Sheriffs are elected to four-year terms. In some rural areas, the sheriff and his appointed deputies must provide police services for the entire county because there are no cities or towns large enough to have police departments. In such cases, the state police may be called to assist the sheriff's office in the performance of these services. One of Texas's most famous sheriffs was Sul Ross, for whom the Alpine, Texas, university is named. In 1874 when Ross was sheriff of McLennan County, he called to order the first meeting of the Sheriff's Association of Texas and was thus one of the first in the law enforcement community to share intelligence.[20]

Like the sheriff, the **constable** is a county-level law enforcement official who is elected to four-year terms of office and empowered to provide police services. The constable's primary mission is to provide assistance and administrative support to the justices of the peace by serving subpoenas and other types of summons. The Texas constitution authorizes one constable for each precinct in each county.[21] The number of precincts in each county ranges from one to eight, depending on the county's population.[22]

Constables and their deputies generally carry out their duties in plain clothes, although in some precincts they wear distinctive uniforms much like other peace officers. Because they are licensed peace officers, they often assist the sheriff and local police by providing patrol services in high-crime areas.

SPECIAL DISTRICTS The Texas constitution authorizes the formation of law enforcement districts to provide specialized police services for specific areas. Most Texas colleges and universities have their own police departments, as do airports and public transportation systems. These specialized agencies are composed of licensed peace

Texas Rangers
An elite division of the Department of Public Safety that investigates major crimes and allegations of police misconduct.

sheriff
The county's chief law enforcement officer; elected to four-year term.

constable
County-level elected official who provides services to the justice of the peace.

Police conduct a murder investigation in College Station. With three people dead, officers are combing the area outside of the house where the killings took place, a manpower intensive operation that is an important part of crime investigation. Years of training are put into practice in situations like this.

community-based policing (CBP)
Department initiated programs that fosters more citizen involvement and better understanding.

officers who are responsible for preventing crime and ensuring the safety of the citizens within their district and the surrounding area. Contrary to popular belief (and to the consternation of many college students), the "campus cops" are empowered and obligated to take appropriate police action when the situation calls for it. They are not merely "rent-a-cops" or "the dream police." Nearly all areas of the state are served by narcotics task forces, which are made up of specially trained peace officers who gather information about the manufacturing, transportation, and sale of illegal drugs. These special districts often transcend city and county lines, and some are partially funded by state and federal grants. Some of these drug task forces are so effective that they fund themselves through the sale of the seized homes, vehicles, and other property previously owned by drug dealers. Indeed, these seizures have allowed law enforcement agencies to purchase high-tech equipment at no cost to the taxpayers.

LOCAL LEVEL Texas's urban and most populous counties may have as many as two dozen municipal police departments to provide citizens with law enforcement services. These police departments vary in size, from as few as one or two people to several thousand. The city of Houston's police department is the state's largest—and the fifth largest in the United States—with nearly 7,000 employees and a budget that exceeds $695 million.[23]

Salaries, training, and benefits for municipal police officers also vary greatly. Despite the efforts of the Texas Commission on Law Enforcement, some Texas peace officers receive little standardized professional training. Technology has already begun to remedy this dilemma, and much of the mandated continuing education and training is now available online.

A growing trend is the way municipal police departments deal with crime and the way they relate to members of the community. Often called **community-based policing (CBP)**, this innovative style of law enforcement empowers home and business owners, community leaders, and members of all segments of the community to participate actively in the day-to-day operations of their police departments. CBP programs, such as Citizen's Police Academies and Citizens on Patrol, have fostered a better understanding of the police role. Programs such as these thrive in cities and towns throughout Texas, contributing to positive and productive police–community relations. Community-based policing came about because of the unique challenges facing law enforcement policy makers. Since public safety is often the bulk of local government budgets, officials have sought ways to reach out for additional support by implementing policies that foster transparency and foster greater community involvement. In 2006 the Texas Police Chiefs Association developed an innovative program called the Best Practices Recognition. Texas's 2500 law enforcement agencies are challenged to meet or exceed 164 individual standards developed by the Association. If they do that, they become "Recognized" (see Table 13.3). This is no small task.

TABLE 13.3 TEXAS RECOGNIZED AGENCIES

1	Texas City	36	Benbrook
2	Longview	37	Belton
3	Canyon	38	Corinth
4	San Angelo	39	Kerrville
5	Texarkana	40	Sachse
6	Pampa	41	Rockwall
7	Austin ISD	43	Lakeway
8	Mount Pleasant	44	Angleton
9	UT at Houston	42	Hutchins
10	Decatur	45	Celina
11	Shenandoah	46	Richmond
12	Farmers Branch	47	Texas Comptroller
13	Woodway	48	Humble
14	Victoria	49	Cleveland ISD
15	Amarillo	50	North Richland Hills
16	Highland Village	51	Roanoke
17	Missouri City	52	Dickinson
18	Austin Com Colg	53	Alvin ISD
19	Irving	54	Alamo Heights
20	Allen	55	Baytown
21	Richardson	56	Royse City
22	La Porte	57	Bee Cave
23	Bridgeport	58	Abilene
24	Addison	59	Liberty
25	Carrollton	60	Bexar County Hospital district Police
26	Muleshoe	61	Farmersville
27	Lewisville	62	Bay City
28	Nacogdoches	63	Boerne
29	Webster	64	Paris
30	Cedar Hill	65	Kennedale
31	Hedwig Village	66	White Oak
32	McKinney	67	Harker Heights
33	Cedar Park	68	Brenham
34	Conroe	69	Wichita Falls
35	Fair Oaks Ranch	70	Waxahachie

As of 2013, fewer than 100 agencies have risen to the challenge.[24] "Recognized" agencies have proven to their communities that their policies and practices are among the most modern, efficient, and professional in the state.

Due Process

13.4 Explain how an individual's right to due process extends through all stages of the criminal justice system.

Most of the commonly cited state laws that regulate the conduct of individuals and groups can be found in the **Texas Penal Code**, which defines and categorizes crimes and provides for a range of punishments. The Penal Code classifies offenses as misdemeanors, which are relatively minor offenses punishable by a fine and up to one year in county jail, and felonies, more serious crimes in which a convicted person may serve time in the state penitentiary. Table 13.4 illustrates the categories of selected crimes and their scheduled punishments as contained in the Texas Penal Code.

Due process is the rights guaranteed to individuals accused of committing criminal acts. These rights include equal treatment and protection under the law, safeguards against cruel and unusual punishment, the right to trial by jury, the right to a court-appointed attorney if the defendant cannot afford to pay an attorney, and the right to face the persons who have made the accusation. Many of these rights are spelled out in the U.S. and Texas constitutions; others, such as the exclusionary rule, have evolved from past practice and court decisions.

The **exclusionary rule** demands that any items or evidence gathered during an illegal search of a person's private property be excluded as evidence against the

TABLE 13.4 CRIME CLASSIFICATIONS AND SELECTED OFFENSES

Misdemeanors			
Category	**Maximum Fine**	**Sentence**[1]	**Examples**[2]
Class C[3]	$500	none	Simple assault; theft under $50; most traffic violations; city ordinance violations; public intoxication; disorderly conduct
Class B	$2,000	180 days	DWI (first offense); prostitution; harassment; possession of marijuana (under 2 oz.)
Class A	$4,000	1 year	Assault causing injury; resisting arrest; some weapons violations

Felonies			
Category	**Maximum Fine**	**Sentence**[4]	**Examples**
State Jail	$10,000	180 days–2 yrs.	Unauthorized use of vehicle; vehicle burglary
3rd Degree	$10,000	2–10 years	Deadly conduct; kidnapping; escape; aggravated assault
2nd Degree	$10,000	2–20 years	sexual assault; robbery; intoxication manslaughter; burglary of a habitation
1st Degree	$10,000	5–99 years	Indecency with a child; murder; attempted capital murder; aggravated sexual assault
Capital	N/A	life/death[5]	Murder of a peace officer; serial or mass murder; murder for hire; murder of a child under 6

[1]Misdemeanor sentences are served in the county jails.
[2]Many classifications of crime span a wide range of punishment categories, depending on value and the defendant's prior record.
[3]City ordinance violations carry fines of up to $2,000.
[4]Felony sentences are served in the state jails or state penitentiaries.
[5]Punishment for a capital felony is either life in prison without parole or death by lethal injection.

Texas ★ Mosaic — Craig Watkins

Named "Texan of The Year" by the *Dallas Morning News* in 2008, Dallas County District Attorney Craig Watkins has brought a new standard of professionalism and integrity to the office. His personal motto, "Smart on Crime, Loyal to Victims," exemplifies his office's commitment to protect citizens while affording the highest degree of due process to the accused.

His office enjoys a conviction rate of over 99 percent, and at the same time is responsible for reviewing hundreds of cases that resulted in the freeing of at least 25 individuals who were wrongfully convicted. His efforts have garnered international attention and calls for a similar approach by chief prosecutors all over the country.

A product of the Dallas ISD, Watkins attended Texas A&M Prairie View and is a graduate of Texas Wesleyan University in Fort Worth. He is the first African American district attorney in Texas, and the first to establish a "Conviction Integrity Unit" as a means of assuring quality control. The results have led to unprecedented credibility and confidence among the citizens of Dallas County.

Dallas County District Attorney Craig Watkins has been a persistent critic of how death sentences are assessed in Texas. He has called for a systematic review of the process and has tried to slow executions as the legislature considers reform.

1. Watkins has come under criticism by those who claim the office should concentrate on convictions and not on investigating wrongful convictions. What role, if any, should the office play in reviewing allegedly wrongful convictions?

2. Should the Office of District Attorney be filled by appointment rather than by election in order to bring increased minority into the ranks?

---

defendant at the time of trial. Assume a police officer pulls a motorist over for speeding and demands to search the car for drugs. Although this officer lacks probable cause to believe the driver is carrying drugs, and the motorist objects to the search, the officer searches the car anyway and discovers 100 kilos of cocaine and a stolen copy of *Lone Star Politics* in the trunk. At the trial, the evidence against the defendant (the cocaine and the book) will be inadmissible if the officer cannot establish why he or she stopped and searched the motorist. For more on the exclusionary rule, see Inside the Federalist System.

That's why it is important that police follow the rules every step of the way and uphold due process, observing the constitutionally protected rights of persons accused of committing criminal acts. (And in case you're wondering: The motorist will get neither his drugs nor his stolen book back.) In recent years, the U.S. Supreme Court has reviewed the merits of the exclusionary rule and has retained it by a slim margin. Some citizens want to do away with it, citing case after case where defendants are caught "red-handed" only to be released because the police failed to observe their due process rights. They claim that it shouldn't matter *how* the evidence was seized, as long as the bad guys get punished.

Proponents of the rule point out that police already have a great deal of or perhaps too much discretionary power. They argue that doing away with the rule would result in police conducting arbitrary searches. The Court compromised by establishing what has come to be known as the "good faith" exception to the exclusionary rule, whereby incriminating evidence may be admissible if the police acted in good faith.

Inside the Federalist System

Search and Seizure

The 2009 U.S. Supreme Court case *Arizona* v. *Gant* provides a prime example of how judicial review can profoundly affect long-standing practices. Prior to this case, police in every state, including Texas, were authorized to search motor vehicles whenever a recent occupant had been arrested. It did not matter what the arrest was for. The police had blanket authority to search.

These searches "incident to arrest" often turned up evidence of other crimes, and the defendants were charged and convicted accordingly. For example, a motorist may have been arrested for an unpaid traffic ticket, and if during a search the police discovered drugs, or weapons, or any other items that offends the laws, that motorist was charged and convicted of the much higher crime.

Arizona v. *Gant* changed all that. Now the police can search a car only with the consent of the driver, unless they have reason to believe the car contains evidence that is directly connected to the crime for which the occupant was arrested.

While this is not the first time the federal courts have overturned Texas laws and practices, it certainly has changed the way local Texas police and sheriffs conduct their business. Opponents of the change claim that a lot more drugs will be left on the streets, while proponents are praising the high court's preservation of privacy rights.

1. In the interest of preventing crime, should law enforcement's power to perform blanket searches for contraband on vehicles that have been lawfully stopped be restored?

2. Should search and seizure issues such as the one raised in the *Gant* case be left for state legislatures?

---

probable cause
The total set of facts and circumstances that would lead a reasonable person to believe that an individual committed a specific criminal act.

bail
A cash deposit or other security given by the accused as a guarantee that he or she will return to court when summoned.

For example, an officer pulls up to a traffic accident where several victims are in critical condition. The officer opens a woman's purse in an effort to find the name of her doctor or next of kin and stumbles on a ski mask, handgun, robbery note, and marked currency connected to a recent bank robbery. This evidence would be admissible under the good faith exception.

Crime victims and law-abiding citizens often vent frustration when an individual who has been charged with a crime is provided with an attorney at no cost and that attorney manages to produce a successful defense. Frequently heard complaints about the system include "The criminal has all the rights," and "The courts let the criminal go because of a technicality." These "technicalities" are often actually gross violations of the accused's due process guarantees, and, if the concepts of equal protection and civil liberties are to be preserved, the courts have no choice but to let the defendant go.

☐ Stages of Due Process

ARREST, SEARCH, AND SEIZURE For the accused, the first formal stage of the criminal justice process is the arrest. Both the U.S. and Texas constitutions guarantee that no person shall be arrested unless **probable cause** has been established. The concept of probable cause is one of the most important in the entire legal system. Probable cause can be said to exist when it appears more likely than not that an individual has committed a criminal act. When it exists, the government is authorized to restrain an individual's freedom and liberties. Probable cause can be determined by a peace officer who makes the apprehension or by a judge who issues a warrant of arrest. Unless an individual is charged with the crime of capital murder, he or she is allowed the opportunity to post bail. **Bail** is a cash deposit posted by the accused as a guarantee that he or she will return to court when summoned. The amount of bail is determined by a judge, who must consider the nature of the crime, the accused's past record, and other factors.

Arrests are usually accompanied by one or more types of searches. The Fourth Amendment of the U.S. Constitution provides all citizens the right to be free from unreasonable searches and seizures of property by the government. The police and

A police officer and his drug-sniffing dog during a traffic stop in south San Antonio. This was part of an operation aimed at interdicting drug flow in the city. Such sweeps require a significant commitment of resources. Again, training and preparation for this kind of investigation take place behind the scenes.

prosecutors may not abridge this important safeguard while they are collecting evidence against a person accused of violating the law. Conditions under which police may lawfully conduct a search of an individual's property are highly regulated by law. Police can thoroughly search any person who has been arrested, provided the arrest was legal. Searches of homes, cars, and other private premises often require a search warrant, and the officers must show sufficient cause in order to obtain one. Many search warrant requests are denied because the officers fail to convince the judge that there are good reasons, or enough probable cause, to search.

Police officers may seize one or more categories of evidence during a lawful search. The first category, *fruits of a crime*, includes any items stolen or otherwise illegally obtained by the accused. The second category, *tools of a crime*, may be any item or instrument used during the commission of a criminal act. For example, a screwdriver used to steal a car would be considered a tool of a crime. Another category is called *contraband*. Mere possession of items considered contraband is illegal. Child pornography, some types of drugs, and gambling equipment fall under this category. The final category, *mere evidence*, pertains to items that tend to connect an individual with a crime. An example of mere evidence would be fingerprints or blood splatters found at the scene of a crime.

"I WAS ROBBED!" IS IT THEFT, BURGLARY, OR ROBBERY? Suppose you walk out to your car today only to discover that someone has broken in and stolen your favorite textbook. You might call the campus police and tell them you were robbed. You weren't robbed: You were burglarized.

Most Americans are somewhat familiar with the eight index crimes, but few among them are able to easily differentiate the subtleties among theft, burglary, and robbery. The common element is theft, which is the simple act of stealing. Shoplifting

grand jury
A panel composed of 12 citizens who determine whether enough evidence exists to charge a person with a felony and make him or her stand trial.

indictment
A finding by the grand jury that the case will proceed to the trial stage; also called a true bill.

The Texas Constitution

A Closer Look

Mention the "bill of rights" to people, and they will naturally think of the first 10 amendments to the U.S. Constitution. Many people do not know that all state constitutions also contain a bill of rights. You might be pleased to know that the Texas constitution affords us with even greater liberty than does the U.S. document. Here are two examples of constitutional protections provided by the state of Texas:

Sec. 18. IMPRISONMENT FOR DEBT. No person shall ever be imprisoned for debt.

Sec. 20. OUTLAWRY OR TRANSPORTATION FOR OFFENSE. This provision prohibits the state from requiring an individual to leave the state as part of his sentence or punishment.

1. Should the bill of rights contained in the Texas constitution be restricted to include only those rights addressed by the U.S. Constitution?

2. Should a Texas Constitutional Convention be convened from time to time to consider revising the bill of rights?

is a prime example of theft. Burglary and robbery amount to "theft plus." In the case of burglary, the offender commits a theft after breaking into or unlawfully entering a vehicle or structure. Burglary is defined as "theft plus" illegal entry.

Robbery is the most serious of the three because it is a crime against persons. You cannot be robbed unless you were present when the theft or attempted theft took place. In addition, a robbery requires the victim to be injured or placed in fear of imminent injury during the encounter. Robbery is "theft plus" a threatening or violent act.

So as bad as it would be to have your car burglarized, you may find comfort in the fact that you weren't the victim of a robbery. Don't let this happen to you—carry your textbook with you!

☐ Grand Jury and Indictment

For individuals accused of committing a felony, a critical component of due process is the right to have the facts of the case heard by a **grand jury**. The grand jury is comprised of 12 citizens who serve for three to six months and are chosen by judges of the district courts. The grand jury determines whether there is sufficient evidence for the accused to stand trial. After the facts and circumstances of a felony case are heard, the grand jury votes. If nine or more members find that the case should proceed to the trial stage, an **indictment** (also called a "true bill") is issued and a trial is scheduled. A nonindictment, or "no-bill," is declared if the grand jury determines that no crime was committed or the accused was justified in his actions. For example, the grand jury often concludes that homeowners who kill or seriously injure intruders were merely exercising their right to protect themselves. When an individual is no-billed by the grand jury, all criminal proceedings stop and the case is dropped.

The grand jury process has been controversial since its inception, not because of its role but because of the way the proceedings take place. Because grand jurors volunteer to serve for as long as six months, they are often not representative of the community as a whole. Most are financially secure. Another criticism is that grand juries operate in secrecy. Neither the person charged nor his attorneys are allowed to attend the proceedings, and it is illegal for jury members to discuss the cases with anyone. Because only the prosecutors and other government agents are allowed to present evidence, there is really no way of knowing what evidence was presented or withheld. For these reasons, the grand juries have been labeled as the "rubber stamp" of the police and prosecutor, meaning that they will conclude whatever the government wants them to conclude. Attempts have been made to reform the Texas grand jury system. Over two decades ago, then Texas Speaker of the House Gib Lewis introduced a bill that would have allowed an accused to have an attorney present during the grand jury proceedings. Not surprisingly, this occurred shortly after he was indicted by a Travis County grand jury.[25]

☐ Trial

After the indictment, the case is assigned to a prosecutor and prepared for trial. The **prosecutor** is an attorney representing the victim and the state against the accused. In felony cases, the accused has the right to an attorney who will represent his or her side. If the accused cannot afford one, the court appoints one for him or her. Most criminal cases are disposed of by way of **plea bargain**, the process of negotiating a settlement, usually for a lesser charge or less jail time. The plea bargain is another controversial issue in today's justice system. The fact is that there are not enough trial courts or prison beds in the state to handle all the cases, and plea bargaining has become a necessity. Due process rights at the trial stage include the right to a trial by jury, although the defendant often waives this right and elects to have a **bench trial,** wherein his or her case is heard by a judge and no jury. When a defendant opts for a bench trial, the judge hears the testimony and determines the verdict. Six jurors hear misdemeanor cases (those heard in municipal, justice, and

prosecutor
A government employee who initiates criminal cases against individuals.

plea bargaining
A process in which the accused receives a lighter sentence than could be expected from a trial verdict in exchange for a guilty plea.

bench trial
A criminal trial that is held without jury, as requested by the person charged.

13.1

13.2

13.3

13.4

Jury foreman Joe Collins speaks with the media after a capital murder trial. The media often want to know why a jury reached its decision. Jurors are under no obligation to talk, but often do. In high profile cases, jurors may want to explain how they reached a verdict to those who just saw snippets of the case on the news.

13.1

voir dire
Trial jury selection process conducted by attorneys for both sides.

13.2

double jeopardy
A criminal defendant's due process right to be protected from being tried a second time (after receiving a not-guilty verdict the first time).

13.3

13.4

hung jury
Term describing the failure to render a verdict in a criminal case.

county courts-at-law). Twelve jurors are required for felony jury cases, which are tried in the district courts.

Before 1992, jurors were selected exclusively from voter registration lists, and this practice tended to exclude many young, minority, and less affluent individuals. Today, in an effort to make juries reflect a true cross section of Texans, the courts select prospective jurors from the driver's license rolls. The courts may request lists of potential jurors from the secretary of state's office, which in turn provides randomly selected names from driver's licenses, state identification cards, and voter registration rolls. To be eligible for jury duty, an individual must be at least 18 years old, not convicted of or under indictment for a felony crime, mentally competent, and a U.S. citizen.[26] Potential jurors are entitled to automatic exemption if they are 65 years old or older, a full-time college or secondary school student, or the sole caretaker of a child 10 years of age or younger.[27]

Prior to the trial, a jury panel is interviewed by the defense and prosecution (or plaintiff and defense, in a civil case). This process is called **voir dire**, and its purpose is to ensure that none of the jurors is predisposed to making a decision until after all the evidence is heard. The term *voir dire* means, literally, to "tell the truth." In order to make this determination, lawyers on both sides often ask questions of a personal nature. In 1994, a Denton County woman, Dianna Brandborg, went to jail for refusing to answer a jury questionnaire sent to her by a district court. After writing "not applicable" to 12 of the 110 questions, the judge declared that Brandborg was in contempt of the court and sentenced her to three days in jail. The questions she refused to answer pertained to her income and political affiliation. She won an appeal in federal court in 1995. The federal judge ruled that the trial court did not balance the defendant's right to a fair trial with Brandborg's right to privacy and that questions asked of prospective jurors must be applicable to the case if a juror is required to answer.[28]

The trial begins with opening statements from both sides. Next, the prosecution presents its case. The defense then has the opportunity to present its own version of the incident and to introduce witnesses and evidence that might indicate the defendant's innocence. At no time does the defendant have to speak or testify before the jury. But, if the defendant wishes to address the court in self-defense, the prosecutor then has a right to cross-examine him or her. The fact that the accused does not have to answer any questions is an important example of due process rights under the Fifth Amendment to the U.S. Constitution. The Fifth Amendment prevents the government from compelling a person to testify against him- or herself (this is known as self-incrimination). The Fifth Amendment also provides for an attorney to represent the accused at no cost if certain conditions are met. Of course, the Texas constitution also contains a bill of rights, and many of these rights are the same as those found in the U.S. Constitution. One interesting amendment contained in the Texas constitution is a prohibition against outlawry. To be "outlawed" means to be banished from the state as part of one's punishment. Texans can rest assured that they can never be forced to leave the state, no matter what they do.

A conviction in a criminal jury trial requires that all members of the jury agree on a verdict of "guilty." Likewise, a unanimous vote is required for a finding of "not guilty." After the jury reaches a unanimous verdict of not guilty, the defendant cannot be tried again for the same crime. Doing so would violate the defendant's due process right against **double jeopardy**. The double jeopardy rule does not allow the government to prosecute an individual more than once for a specific charge. For this reason, the state must present its best possible case because, as some judges have observed, "The prosecution gets only one bite from the apple." If the final verdict is not unanimous, or if the jury fails to render a verdict at all, the judge declares a **hung jury** (a nonunanimous verdict) or mistrial, and the prosecutor has the option of requesting a second trial using another jury. Some of the factors the district or county attorney must consider when deciding whether to try a defendant again are cost and public sentiment.

Texas is one of a handful of states in which the jury decides the amount of time the accused will serve. When a jury trial results in a "guilty" verdict, a separate proceeding, with the same jury, is held to determine the sentence. No matter the outcome in a criminal trial, the defendant can still be sued in civil court by the victim or the victim's family. Because the civil trial is initiated by a private party and not the government, this practice does not violate the double jeopardy rule.

Review the Chapter

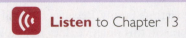 **Listen** to Chapter 13

Measuring Crime

13.1 Explain why crime rates are among the most important statistical data generated by government.

Crime rates have widespread implications. They allow us to identify and track trends, evaluate new programs, and compare quality of life issues among various communities. The crime rates are used by state and local governments to reflect budgetary priorities, and they are used by local government officials to determine staffing needs. Insurance companies and health care providers are among the public-sector entities that require accurate measures of crime.

Capital Punishment

13.2 Discuss why the use of the death penalty has been on the decline and will continue to decrease.

Although the number of capital crimes has remained steady, defendants are less likely to receive the death penalty. This is particularly true in Texas, and it is due to three factors. The first two factors are recent U.S. Supreme Court decisions that prohibit states from executing persons who were younger than 18 years of age when the crime was committed and from executing persons deemed mentally retarded. The third factor is a change in sentencing options. Now that "life imprisonment" means life without the possibility of parole, jurors seem to find it easier than sentencing the defendant to death.

Law Enforcement

13.3 Identify the major types of law enforcement agencies at the state and local level.

The Texas Department of Public Safety is the state's police force, and its various divisions include the famous Texas Rangers. Each of Texas's 254 counties has an elected sheriff, and each county precinct has one elected constable. There are special police forces for colleges, school districts, hospitals, and airports, as well as over 1,000 municipal police departments.

Due Process

13.4 Explain how an individual's right to due process extends through all stages of the criminal justice system.

The state's criminal justice process serves two important protective functions: preserving life and property, and preserving the due process rights of accused persons. A person's due process begins with arrest. The moment a person is restrained in liberty, the system guarantees certain safeguards, such as the right to a grand jury indictment, a right to a trial by jury, and a right to representation in court.

Learn the Terms

 Study and **Review** the **Flashcards**

Test Yourself

13.1 Explain why crime rates are among the most important statistical data generated by government.

Which of the following statements is true regarding crime statistics?

 a. The data are important to private-sector entities, such as insurance companies.
 b. The data should be largely ignored because it has been proven to be biased.
 c. The data is confidential and not released to the public.
 d. The data indicate a dramatic loss of confidence in the criminal justice system.
 e. All of the above are true.

13.2 Discuss why the use of the death penalty has been on the decline and will continue to decrease.

The use of capital punishment in Texas is expected to

 a. increase slightly.
 b. skyrocket due to the rising crime rate.
 c. remain constant over time.
 d. decrease in the next decade.
 e. stop immediately due to public opinion.

13.3 Identify the major types of law enforcement agencies at the state and local level.

The county official responsible for maintaining a county jail.

 a. constable
 b. police chief
 c. justice of the peace
 d. sheriff
 e. district attorney

13.4 Explain how an individual's right to due process extends through all stages of the criminal justice system.

An individual's due process rights begin when the individual is

 a. suspected of committing a crime.
 b. indicted for a felony offense.
 c. sworn in on the witness stand.
 d. taken into custody by law enforcement.
 e. convicted and sentenced.

Explore Further

Marion, Nancy E. and Oliver, W. (2012). *The Public Policy of Crime and Criminal Justice* (2nd edition). Upper Saddle River, NJ: Prentice Hall.

Anderson, Ken. *Crime in Texas*, rev. ed. Austin: University of Texas Press, 2005.

Horton, David M., and Ryan Kellis Turner. *Lone Star Justice: A Comprehensive Overview of the Texas Criminal Justice System*. Austin: Eakin, 1999

Marquart, James W., Sheldon Ekland-Olson, and Jonathan R. Sorenson. *The Rope, the Chair, and the Needle: Capital Punishment in Texas* 1923–1990. Austin: University of Texas Press, 1995.

Perkinson, Robert. *Texas Tough: The Rise of America's Prison Empire*. New York: Metroplitan Books/Henry Holt, 2008.

Texas Department of Criminal Justice http://www.tdcj.state.tx.us/ A source of information and statistics about Texas' corrections programs and administration.

Bureau of Justice Statistics http://www.ojp.usdoj.gov/ National and state statistics on crime, punishment, and death penalty information.

14

Finance and Budgeting in Texas

Government is 90 percent budget, the rest is poetry.

—*The Late Bob Bullock, Lieutenant Governor of Texas*

We live in a new era of finance and budgeting in the state of Texas. National economic conditions between 2008 and 2010 had a significant, negative impact on state-generated revenues. Because the Texas Legislature—unlike Congress—cannot spend more money than it has coming into its coffers, a major restructuring of the state's budget was required, in addition to the end of the state's near-constant, significant increases in spending that marked the better part of the last 35 years.

It is not as if Texas legislators were spending like drunken sailors (no insult to drunken sailors intended) prior to the 2012–2013 budget. Texas, for its population, has always spent less per capita on education and social programs than most of its counterparts. This new budget cycle meant a real reduction in dollars spent—a true downsizing of government—which will impact state spending and services well into the future. Governments often claim that they have cut their budgets even as they spend more dollars from one year to the next. They do this through a governmental accounting trick called the **current services budget**, which takes into account inflation and population increases. If a hypothetical government spent $100 billion one year, and budgeted $105 billion the next (to retain

14.1	14.2	14.3	14.4	14.5
Analyze the constraints on the budget process in Texas.	Explain the role of the Legislative Budget Board.	Differentiate among the major sources of tax revenue in Texas.	Explain how nontax revenue has surpassed tax revenue.	Describe the top three areas of expenditure in Texas.

Construction continues on Texas Highway 45 in fast-growing Williamson County, north of Austin. Providing for infrastructure is a major stress on the Texas budget, but adequate transportation is indisciplinable for economic growth to continue.

current services budget
Budget adjusted for increases in population and inflation.

the same services with price and population increases), but only spent $103 billion, most officials would call this a $2 billion cut. What Texas experienced, however, was not only a current services cut, but an actual reduction of $15 billion from the 2010–2011 to the 2012–2013 budgets. That's an 8 percent decrease over two years, even as prices and populations expand.

In 1978, the state's total budget was less than $8 billion, and that was a whopping 19 percent increase from the year before. More than half of all state money went to education. Less than a quarter of state revenue came from federal funds. Spending grew by double-digit percentages in almost as many years as not between 1978 and 1996, including an 18.7 percent increase in 1979 and 14.4 percent in 1992. When spending topped $20 billion in 1989, education still accounted for the lion's share, garnering 46.6 percent of expenditures. Federal funding was still less than a quarter of the total. The rate of spending increases slowed during the second half of the 1990s, and Texas spent more than $50 billion for the first time in 2001. Education spending had dropped to 38 percent of the budget, as health and human services grew to 34 percent. Federal funding comprised almost 30 percent of revenue. In 2011, the last year of the "old normal," expenditures topped out at $95.5 billion. Only 35 percent went to education, with 41 percent flowing to health and human services. As dollars from the Obama stimulus package flowed, 41 percent of state spending came from federal sources, down slightly from 42 percent the year before. Reduced to a sentence, Texas has experienced a huge increase in the scope of government, government spending, and federal funding over the last three and a half decades. New fiscal realities have changed the playing field for Texas budgeting.

This is not the first time Texas has faced a significant budgetary reallocation. State budgets are cyclical by their very nature, some more so than others. A challenge for states with a balanced budget provision is that revenues, whether based on income or sales taxes, tend to drop at the very time that the needs of the poor are on the rise.

For the better part of the second half of the 20th century, Texas's economy ran countercyclical to the national economy. Good times in Texas generally meant bad times for the nation as a whole, and vice versa. That is because higher oil prices made for a strong state economy and increased state revenue, but elevated energy costs tend to be a damper on the national economy. So when oil prices rose in the early 1980s, Texas coffers filled and the state increased spending. As late as 1982, oil and gas taxes alone funded 18 percent of the state's budget. With oil at $30 a barrel, analysts were forecasting that it would rise to $90. You could say they were correct, but it didn't happen until 2008, not 1988 like they were projecting. The legislature, banking on the inflow of revenue, was shocked that oil settled below $15 a barrel and stayed there for a decade. By the mid-1990s, with the oil boom a fading memory, the Texas economy fell into the same general cycle as the national economy. By 1996, oil and gas taxes produced less than 2 percent of state income. Oil's place in the Texas economy was not over, but it surely seemed like it at the time.

With extraction revenue falling in the 1980s, even as spending expanded, revenue had to come from somewhere else. The general sales tax bore the brunt of the increase, but taxes on cigarettes, beer, and gasoline were increased significantly as well. Texas didn't even have a general sales tax until 1961. There were taxes on cigarettes, gasoline, and motor vehicles before then, but not a general tax on most nonfood items. Prior to then, state revenues were limited and generated primarily from mineral extraction taxes, franchise taxes on business inventory, and relatively small taxes on beer, cigarettes, and gasoline. The 1956 and 1957 budgets were both around three-quarters of a billion dollars, and that was after cigarette taxes were increased from four to five cents per pack, beer tax doubled to 1.3 cents per bottle and gasoline taxes skyrocketed from 4 to 5 cents per gallon. The initial sales tax was 2 percent, increasing to 3 percent in 1968, 4 percent in 1971, 5.25 percent in 1986, 6 percent in 1987, and the current 6.25 percent in 1990. For reasons we will discuss later in the chapter, the sales tax rate is at or near its limit.

The last major restructuring of the Texas tax system occurred in 2006, when the legislature significantly changed the nature of the franchise tax on businesses. Faced with a state supreme court order to revise the funding mechanism for public education, the legislature devised a new business tax code unlike anything the state had ever used. Almost immediately, the state fell into recession and the new tax failed to generate the level of revenue its proponents had anticipated. Whether the tax has a fatal structural problem or a temporary economic one has not yet been completely determined.

Constraints on Budgeting

14.1   Analyze the constraints on the budget process in Texas.

reating the budget is the most difficult thing that any legislative body does. Competing interests have to be balanced in such a way that no one is ever completely happy with the finished product. The nature of budgeting all but guarantees that some good programs are underfunded. Those factors constrain budget makers almost anywhere. In Texas, though, there are additional cultural, legal, and constitutional obstacles that not every state faces. We will discuss both types of limits in the pages that follow.

balanced budget

A means to keep the government from spending more than it receives in revenues.

The Balanced Budget Provision and Other Constitutional Roadblocks

One of the greatest limits that can be placed on a government is requiring it to balance its budget. The **balanced budget** provision of the Texas constitution was intended to restrain the legislature. Just because the budget is 10 times larger than it was in the late 1970s doesn't mean that the provision has not been an effective restraint. We need look no further than the 2011 legislative session and its $15 billion budget cut brought about by recession and weakness in the economy.

The provision does not allow for flexibility. An argument can be made that running a deficit during a recession allows for the protection of vital programs, but that is not an option for Texas budget writers. The legislature could have raised taxes to spare spending cuts, but such increases in a shaky or recessionary economy can worsen the business climate, adversely affecting both jobs and revenue. The provision is also politically popular. Texans might not care for spending cuts, but any attempt to remove this measure from the constitution would meet a swift backlash.

The balanced budget requirement creates an integral role in the budget-making process for the comptroller of public accounts. The comptroller has the responsibility for both estimating and certifying revenue. Estimating revenue is an almost impossible task, given the many variables that factor into future economic activity. Nonetheless, that estimate is the outward limit of what the state can spend, short of an 80 percent vote by both the house and senate to override the comptroller's projection. In the real world of Texas politics, that is never going to happen. In a majority of districts, such a vote would earn the legislator a one-way ticket back to his home after the next election, never to be invited to Austin again. Even if there were a consensus that the comptroller had badly underestimated revenues, more than 20 percent of the house and senate would vote to uphold the estimate as a way to further reduce the size of government.

The balanced budget provision is not the only constitutional limit on the appropriations process. A 1978 amendment limits the growth of nondedicated tax revenue to no more than the overall growth of the Texas economy. That provision generally does not have a significant impact on the current budget, but it did come into play in 2013. Legislators can suspend that provision with a simple majority vote, but there may be a significant political cost for doing so.

Another provision limits state appropriations for welfare to less than 1 percent of the total budget. As current appropriations are less than 10 percent of that limit, that amendment is not a potential hindrance to state appropriations. A final provision prohibits the state from issuing additional bonds if total debt exceeds 5 percent of unrestricted general revenue, a level that the state is comfortably below.

The Biennial Budget System

A second great constraint on budgeting is the fact that the legislature meets in regular session every other year. The appropriations bill must, then, cover a two-year cycle.

The Texas Constitution

A Closer Look

The best way to limit government power is to limit the government's power to spend. With the balanced budget provision, the writers of the Texas constitution did just that. This provision's impact is more pronounced in Texas than in many of the other states that have similar restrictions, because of the state's strong antitaxation sentiment. It reads as follows:

Sec. 49. STATE DEBTS.

a. No debt shall be created by or on behalf of the State, except:
  (1) to supply casual deficiencies of revenue, not to exceed in the aggregate at any one time two hundred thousand dollars;
  (2) to repel invasion, suppress insurrection, or defend the State in war;
  (3) as otherwise authorized by this constitution; or
  (4) as authorized by Subsections (b) through (f) of this section.

Sections b–f are somewhat wordy, but in a nutshell they require the same process as a constitutional amendment before the state takes on bonded indebtedness. Bonds can be issued only for specifically stated purposes and only with the approval of two-thirds of the house, two-thirds of the senate, and the majority of voters who participate in the election called to consider constitutional amendments.

1. Is the balanced budget provision good public policy? Why or why not?

2. How does the balanced budget provision limit government power?

This makes the comptroller's job of estimating revenue much more difficult. In order to accurately project state revenue, a person would have to know oil prices, inflation rates, unemployment rates, personal income, gross state product, and a host of other economic numbers in each month from the beginning of the two-year economic cycle until the end. What makes it even more difficult is that the budget has to be passed six months before it goes into effect, so the actual projection period extends to 30 months. In addition, the national budget is passed annually, so there is no certainty to what federal funding will be in the second year of the cycle. With federal debt levels, states can no longer presume year-to-year increases in federal money. In fact, the biggest single factor in Texas' 2012–13 budget contraction was a reduction in money from Washington.

As a result of such uncertainties, Texas comptrollers tend to be conservative with their estimates. Because of this, the state usually ends the fiscal year with a surplus. That's not always the case, as evidenced by the massive shortfall entering the 2011 session, but it is impossible to account for every bad economic scenario. Because revenues generally exceed projections, the legislature will often pass a second appropriations bill, contingent upon the comptroller certifying additional funds.

Another issue with biennial budgets is that they make spending decisions more difficult. The legislature faces challenges in mapping out priorities over a 30-month period. Changing social, political, economic, and technological conditions can quickly make policy inadequate or obsolete. Unless called into special session, there is little the legislature can do to reformulate policy during the 19 months between legislative sessions. Like the comptroller, they must anticipate economic conditions and decide how appropriations are best deployed.

☐ Public Sentiment

Most people don't like paying taxes. In Texas, the anti-tax sentiment is more ingrained. Texans expect good roads, quality education, and strong prisons, but they don't want to pay more than the minimum for any of it. The individualistic nature of Texas political culture makes the populous somewhat suspicious of social spending programs. Even programs that might save money in the long term, like prenatal care and the Children's Health Insurance Program, are subject to intense scrutiny. Under such constraints, tax increases are an unpopular way to enhance revenue. Politicians recognize this. In the 2010 and 2012 elections, it was rare to find a candidate from either party and for any office who strayed from the "no new taxes" philosophy. Most Republican state house members have signed anti-tax advocate Grover Norquist's "I will never raise taxes under any circumstance" pledge.

dedicated funds
Revenues set aside for specific expense categories.

14.1

federal mandates
Regulations set by Congress that state and local government must meet.

14.2

14.3

14.4

14.5

☐ Dedicated Funds

A significant constraint on Texas budgeting is self-imposed. A sizable portion of state revenues are **dedicated funds**, monies that are earmarked for a certain purpose from the moment they are collected. A portion of the gasoline tax, for example, can only be used for highway construction and maintenance. A portion of the sales tax on sporting goods goes to the parks and wildlife account. All told, Texas has about 200 dedicated funds totaling about $41 billion over the two-year budget cycle.[1] Setting certain monies aside to ensure that some funds are available for specific expenditures is not an inherently bad idea. It stops the legislature from raiding a revenue stream for unintended purposes. Funds can be dedicated either constitutionally—which is more difficult to un-dedicate—or statutorily.

A problem, as demonstrated in Figure 14.1, for the Texas legislature is that such a high percentage of state revenue is restricted. Dedicated funds and state spending influenced by federal mandates, which will be discussed in the next section, account for over 82%[2] of the state's general revenue. The legislature therefore has limited flexibility in deciding how to budget. In 1995, legislation that removed more than $3.3 billion per biennium from dedicated sources took effect. Revenues not dedicated within the state constitution or rededicated by the legislature were freed for discretionary spending.[3] Two years later, however, the state fell back into the same trap as the move to dedicate funds began anew. Almost all lottery revenue was dedicated to education, although most of it was flowing to that purpose anyway. The legislature ties the hands of future lawmakers with such action.

☐ Congressional and Court Mandates

The federal government requires that states meet minimum standards in a number of areas, from health care to the environment and to access for the disabled. Growing **federal mandates** put a financial burden on state governments, especially since many of these are unfunded or underfunded. A total of $21 billion in the 2012–13 budget is required spending under either congressional or federal court mandates. Over the years, federal courts have ordered reform of the state's prisons and mental health systems and a reallocation of spending at public universities. State courts have repeatedly intervened in order to achieve equalization in public education spending. Every dollar spent as a result of congressional mandate or court-ordered reform is a dollar that cannot be spent elsewhere.

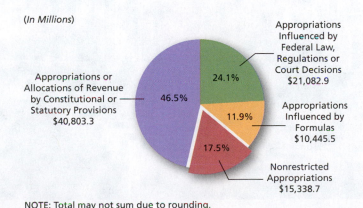

(In Millions)

- Appropriations Influenced by Federal Law, Regulations or Court Decisions $21,082.9 — 24.1%
- Appropriations or Allocations of Revenue by Constitutional or Statutory Provisions $40,803.3 — 46.5%
- Appropriations Influenced by Formulas $10,445.5 — 11.9%
- Nonrestricted Appropriations $15,338.7 — 17.5%

NOTE: Total may not sum due to rounding.

FIGURE 14.1 Restricted Appropriations from General Revenue Funds and General Revenue Dedicated Funds: 2012–13.

The Budget-Making Process

14.2 Explain the role of the Legislative Budget Board.

Legislative Budget Board (LBB)
A body made up of members of the house and senate, including the two presiding officers, which oversees a staff responsible for preparing the basic working budget for the legislature's consideration.

T he most important entity in the budget making process in Texas is the **Legislative Budget Board (LBB)**. The LBB is a joint House and Senate committee that is co-chaired by the lieutenant governor and the Speaker of the House. Other members include the chairs of the Senate Committee on Finance, Senate Committee on State Affairs, House Committee on Appropriations, and House Committee on Ways and Means. The lieutenant governor and speaker each appoint two additional committee members. Inasmuch as the lieutenant governor appoints all of the committee chairs in the Senate and the Speaker does likewise in the House, these legislative leaders have tremendous power over the purse. The LBB also has a sizable, professional, and permanent staff that aids in the budget-making process. The staff does much of the day-to-day work of crafting the budget and monitoring state agencies.

Technically, Texas has a dual budget system, as the governor is required to submit a budget document as well. The Governor's Office of Budget, Planning, and Policy does prepare a document, but it carries no weight with the legislature.

Budget creation begins at the agency level. Each agency makes a Legislative Appropriation Request (LAR) based on past expenditures and anticipated needs. Every agency has a long term strategic plan, setting goals over a five-year period, with a new plan established every other year. The LBB usually provides guidance to agencies in regard to their requests, telling them how much more—or less—they should expect to spend in the coming biennia. Sometimes, the LBB request an to agency present

The Neural Molecular Science Building, more popularly known as the 'Wet Lab,' is one of many buildings on the University of Texas campus constructed with Permanent University Fund money. A main function of this fund it to provide capital improvements on the campuses of UT and Texas A&M system schools.

Texas ★ Mosaic

The Dedicated Budget Funds

If you delve into even the shallow end of Texas budget discussions, you will soon encounter myriad individual state funds with specific purposes. Texas has more than 400 of these. Some have been around so long they have taken on lives of their own. Others are relatively new, created to tackle contemporary problems. We won't discuss all 400, but let's take a look at a few of the most significant.

The Granddaddy of them All—The Permanent School Fund

The Permanent School Fund (PSF) dates all the way back to 1854, when the legislature set aside $2 million for public schools. In 1876, half of the state's public lands were constitutionally dedicated to the benefit of the public school system, with sales and earnings from leases forming a public account, the earnings of which flow to the Available School Fund according to a complicated formula, which generally yields around 4–4.5% of the fund's total value. Assets are invested in a variety of vehicles, including the stock market and bonds. At the end of 2011, the fund had a total value $26.9 billion, making it the second largest public education endowment in the United States. The available school fund additionally receives some three-quarters of a billion dollars a year from a nickel's share of the motor fuels tax.

The Permanent University Fund

The Permanent University Fund (PUF) actually predates statehood, although initially it was more concept than concrete. The Congress of Texas set aside some 200,000 acres of land to endow higher education in 1839. When the legislature authorized the University of Texas in 1858, it added to the endowment. The Civil War got in the way of higher education, and UT didn't actually open until 1883. By then, the legislature had shifted parcels of land, added in some more, and the higher education endowment was up to a little more two million acres. The problem was that the land was in West Texas and virtually worthless. PUF generated a limited amount of revenue by leasing to ranchers who needed grazing land for cattle. Then oil was discovered on the land and everything changed.

Like the PSF, the PUF invests its assets in stock, bonds, and other financial holdings. With investment assets valued at over $13 billion, it is the largest public university endowment in the world. PUF money flows only to schools within the University of Texas and Texas A&M systems. The first obligation of PUF money is paying off bond interest and principal. Remaining money goes to scholarships, equipment, and libraries. With two-thirds of the distribution going to UT schools and the remainder to the A&M system, PUF contributed about $400 million to the schools in 2012.

Property Tax Relief Fund

Established by the Legislature in 2006 after a state supreme court ruling held that the previous tax structure had devolved into an unconstitutional statewide property tax, the property tax relief fund provides more than $2 billion a year to public education. The primary source of revenue is due to a restructuring of the franchise tax, which is the state's main tax on businesses. The portion of revenue above what the old formula would have generated is dedicated to the fund. The second largest source is the increased cigarette tax. Again, the "new revenue" from the increase is dedicated. Finally, a slight reworking of the motor vehicle sales tax aimed at assessing the "real value" of used cars, added its assessment-related increase into the fund.

Economic Stabilization Fund

More commonly known as the "Rainy Day Fund," this constitutionally-mandated fund was approved by voters in 1988. It dedicates 75% of both oil and natural gas collections above the 1987 standard to the stabilization fund, to be tapped during recession or for other economic necessity. In 2011, the legislature took $3.2 billion from the fund to help close the budget shortfall. It was, by far, the most ever taken in one year. Still, by the end of 2012 the fund held more than $8 billion, socking away almost $2 billion in that year alone. If growth continues at that rate, the fund will soon reach its cap of just over $13 billion, another number determined through a complicated formula.

The Rainy Day Fund has safeguards to ensure that it isn't raided on a sunny afternoon. It takes separate 60% votes in both the house and senate to tap the fund even if a deficit develops during a cycle—as it did in 2011—or if actual revenue drops from one biennium to another. Outside of those instances, it takes a two-thirds vote in each house to appropriate fund money.

Other Notable Funds

The Teacher Retirement System Trust Fund is financed through both state and employee contribution. The body of funds, worth over $110 billion, is invested, like the PSF and the PUF. Retirees are paid a defined benefit. Three separate parks and wildlife accounts are funded through a portion of the sales tax collected on sporting goods. Both the State Highway Fund and Texas Mobility Fund are concerned with transportation issues and are funded from a variety of sources, like fuel taxes and highway fines.

1. Under what circumstances should the legislature tap into the Rainy Day Fund?

2. Are dedicated funds outdated? Why or why not?

two budget requests: one, for instance, with no funding increase; another with a two percent increase. Using these LARs, the LBB begins to construct the budget.

Through the budget process, legislative leaders have much power. The Speaker and lieutenant governor are, in essence, the co-chairs of the committee that decides where the

tax revenue
Funds generated through the tax system.

state's revenue will be spent. The House and Senate will alter the LBB blueprint, but the basic priorities usually remain intact. True political power is defined by a person's ability to control the flow of government spending. As co-chairs of the LBB, the lieutenant governor and Speaker have greater control over the process than any other players.

At the beginning of the legislative session, the comptroller's Biennial Revenue Estimate is delivered to the legislature. The LBB plan is then introduced in both the House and Senate. Working from this blueprint, the Appropriations Committee in the House and the Finance Committee in the Senate craft spending bills. Individual lawmakers have the opportunity to affect spending both through these committees and through floor debate. The Senate and House will inevitably have some different spending priorities, so the final appropriations bill will emerge from conference committee. Even after the legislature approves the conference bill, the governor can veto individual line items from the budget.

Once the budget has passed, the LBB and the governor can alter spending without having to call a special session, which saves both time and money. They cannot increase spending, but they can either impound or transfer funds, as long as both parties agree. When funds are transferred, they can either be used within the original agency or shifted to a different one.

State Taxes

14.3 Differentiate among the major sources of tax revenue in Texas.

I f you were to consider state revenue alone, the $94 billion brought in by Texas in 2011 appears to be a huge increase over the $54 billion the state had garnered a decade earlier. It may give rise to the illusory idea that the state was awash with money. The reality, however, was far different. Dig a little deeper and you find that state **tax revenue** had dropped, due to a foundering economy, from its peak a few years before. Total revenue remained high because of an enormous boost from the Obama stimulus plan, a onetime injection that, in a way, would make the coming economic reckoning even harder to tackle. Plus, with inflation, $94 billion just didn't go as far as it did in 2001. That's compounded even more for a state government, where medical costs, which increased faster than the broader rate of inflation, account for a larger proportion of its costs.

If we look, for a moment, at the spending side, realizing that revenue and spending essentially even out over the long run, the picture comes more clearly into focus. When adjusted for both inflation and population growth, which amounts to the current services budget that we discussed earlier, the all funds budget for 2012–13 has increased by a biennial average of only 1.5% since 1992–93; the general funds current services budget has actually decreased over the same period.[4]

When the tax portion of revenue dropped in 2009 and 2010, Texas leaders realized the magnitude of the shortfall they were about to encounter. In January 2010, Governor Perry, Speaker Straus, and Lt. Governor Dewhurst ordered all state agencies—with the exception of Medicaid and public education—to cut their budgets by 5% for the remaining 20 months of the budget cycle. The comptroller had already amended her previous revenue estimate to indicate a $4 billion shortfall. In December, the trio asked the agencies to reduce their 2011 budgets by an additional 2.5%. Even with the big budget areas of public education and Medicaid exempted, the reductions cut over $1 billion from the 2010–11 deficit; the remainder was drawn from the state's Economic Stabilization Fund, commonly referred to as the "Rainy Day Fund."

That still left the 2011 legislature with a current services deficit of $17 billion as they began crafting the 2012–13 budget. By the time the legislature met, it was clear that the state tax revenues were finally rising, as the Texas economy recovered, but federal funding was about to drop dramatically, as the Obama stimulus expired against the backdrop of increasing federal debt. The legislature took a multifaceted approach to balancing the budget. First, it had to cut spending. Real cuts were made to public

TABLE 14.1 EFFECTS OF A REGRESSIVE SALES TAX ON TWO FAMILIES

	FAMILY A	FAMILY B
Total income	$10,000	$100,000
Sales tax rate	8%	8%
Family spending	$9,259	$80,000
Tax paid	$741	$6,400
Percent of income paid in taxes	7.4%	6.4%

regressive tax
A system of taxation whereby the tax rate increases as income decreases.

progressive tax
A system of taxation whereby the tax rate increases as income increases.

14.1

14.2

14.3

14.4

14.5

education and Medicaid. Public schools received almost $3 billion less than they had the previous biennium. The current services cut was closer to $4 billion. Cost containment measures brought Medicaid spending down by more than $1 billion. The state made cuts to colleges and universities, aid to local government, student financial aid, and state government employee retirement and health care programs.

The budget was still some $6.5 billion short of balanced. So the legislature resorted to smoke and mirrors to close the rest of the gap. Despite how it sounds, that is not necessarily a bad thing. Remember that raising taxes is not only politically risky, it can also damage a weak or recovering economy. If you are reasonably certain that the economy will recover, playing accounting games can alleviate short-term adversity. If you guess wrong, though, you may create much greater problems down the road. Texas's 2011 gamble appears to have been the correct move. Here is what the legislature did: First, it left more than $4 billion in Medicaid obligations unfunded. That meant the 2013 legislature would have to make up the gap with a supplementary appropriations bill. Second, it moved the last monthly state payments to public schools from August 2013 to September, making it part of the next biennium. Fortunately, revenues improved enough to cover the difference.

☐ Tax Collection

The Texas sales tax has often been criticized for its alleged regressive tendencies. We argue that this viewpoint is, at best, incomplete. First, let's define some terms. A **regressive tax** places a higher burden on the poor than the wealthy. In other words, the poor would pay a higher percentage of their income in taxes. A **progressive tax**, on the other hand, places a higher burden on the wealthy. Table 14.1 shows the effect of a flat sales tax on two families of four, one that makes $10,000 a year and the other, $100,000 a year.

In this simplistic model—*which is not how the Texas system operates*—the sales tax applies to all purchases, including housing, food, utilities, and medicine. The presumption is that the low-income family must spend all of its money in order to make ends meet. The wealthier family, meanwhile, saves and invests a portion of its income. It does not pay sales tax on this portion. Therefore, although Family B pays $5,659 more in sales tax than Family A, the economically challenged family actually pays a higher percentage of its income in taxes than the wealthier family does: 7.4 percent to 6.4 percent. The fact that wealthier people find other uses for a portion of their income makes an all-inclusive sales tax regressive. But the Texas sales tax is nothing like this.

An example of a progressive tax is a graduated income tax. Look at the same families in Table 14.2. This presumes a tax system under which no deductions are allowed. The 8 percent paid by Family B is, of course, a higher percentage than the 1 percent paid by Family A. The $8,000 in total taxes is also much more than the $100 incurred by the poorer family. This tax system is progressive, placing a higher burden on the wealthier family.

TABLE 14.2 EFFECTS OF A PROGRESSIVE TAX ON TWO FAMILIES

	FAMILY A	FAMILY B
Total income	$10,000	$100,000
Income tax rate	1%	8%
Tax paid	$100	$8,000

sales tax
Tax paid on goods and services; collected at the point of sale and forwarded to the state treasury.

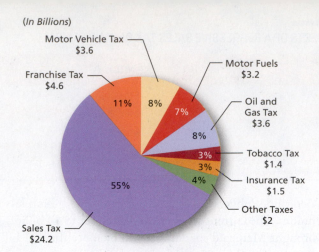

(In Billions)

Motor Vehicle Tax $3.6

Franchise Tax $4.6

Motor Fuels $3.2

Oil and Gas Tax $3.6

Tobacco Tax $1.4

Insurance Tax $1.5

Other Taxes $2

Sales Tax $24.2

11% 8% 7% 8% 3% 3% 4% 55%

FIGURE 14.2 Tax Collections by Major Tax, 2012.

SALES TAX The state **sales tax** is the largest single component of tax revenue, as shown in Figure 14.2. It generates about a quarter of the state's total income. It brought in $24.19 billion in fiscal year 2012, a 12.6 percent increase over 2011, which was itself a 9.4 percent increase over 2010. Sales tax income hit a low point in 2010 at just $19.63 billion during the depth of the recession. The increase in 2011 essentially returned sales tax revenues to where they had been in 2008. The sales tax revenue in 2011 and 2012 far outstripped the comptroller's estimates.

One of the highest sales tax rates in the nation, the 6.25 percent tax is on the retail price of selected goods and services sold in the state. Only Mississippi, Nevada, Rhode Island, and Washington have higher actual rates. Rates appear higher in Minnesota, but a portion of that rate must be distributed to the local governments. In Texas, cities can assess their own 1 percent tax, which is added to the state levy. Special districts, such as those for parks, crime control, or sport facility construction, often add another penny to the actual tax rate. In 2012, at the behest of Mayor Julian Castro, the San Antonio tax payers approved an additional one-eighth of a cent tax to help fund full-day pre-K programs, a service usually funded by public school districts.

The combined local and state tax rate can range as high as 8.25 percent. Texas lawmakers realize that they can't realistically raise the rate much higher. Already, it discourages spending, which has a negative impact on both jobs and the economy. No one has seriously proposed raising the rate since the last increase in 1990. A future legislature might tweak another quarter of a percent out of the tax, but that is about all the room that is left.

Texas is one of 28 states that exempt nonprepared food. Texas does tax prepared food, however. There is no sales tax on meat, lettuce, tomatoes, and bread, but the person who purchases a sandwich already prepared does pay the tax. Therefore, a meal prepared at a restaurant incurs the sales tax, but one prepared at home does not. Some states tax prepared food at higher than their standard rate.

What dampens the regressivity of the Texas sales tax is the fact that many of the expenses of a financially disadvantaged family are sales tax–exempt. In addition to food and prescription and nonprescription drugs, medical services, housing, and utilities are all free from the state portion of the sales tax. Most states that have a sales tax apply it to prescription drugs, and almost all apply it to nonprescription drugs. The family earning more money would be likely to eat out more often, incurring a sales tax on a higher-priced meal. If you consider the motor vehicle sales tax—see p. 334—to be a part of the broader tax, the system becomes even less regressive.

One of the more controversial aspects of the state sales tax is in the area of services. Some are taxable; others are not. If you hire an engineer to create computer software or a lawn service to cut your yard, you are required to pay a sales tax. On the other hand, if you hire a lawyer or an accountant, you don't pay a sales tax on the services provided. It is worth remembering that within the Texas Legislature, the most prevalent occupation is attorney. As such, they use their power to protect their own interests.

In 1999, the legislature added electronic data processing, nonprescription drug sales, and Internet access to the list of exemptions. Additionally, a back-to-school sales tax holiday creates a three-day period each August, during which most clothing and shoes priced under $100 per item are tax-free. Daily newspapers are tax-exempt as well.

THE FRANCHISE TAX From the inception of the latest version of the **franchise tax**—the major tax on businesses in the state of Texas—critics of the new tax maintained that it would prove to be insufficient, that it would bring in between one-third and one-quarter less revenue than its proponents project. Early reports indicated that the opponents might be dead on. In 2009, the tax brought in just $4.3 billion, a full 29.7 percent below what lawmakers had expected.[5]

Texas adopted this version of the franchise tax in reaction to a sharp shove from the Texas supreme court, which had declared the state's method of financing public education unconstitutional. Texas has long had a constitutional prohibition against a statewide property tax. Previous school financing law, however, had left 90 percent of the state's districts taxing within pennies of $1.50 per $100 of property value. State recapture of dollars from property-rich districts had created a situation where practically all districts had to tax at the maximum. The state supreme court ruled that the system had created a *de facto* statewide property tax and ordered the legislature to fix the financing structure before schools opened in the Fall of 2006. Under the gun, with elections approaching, the legislature opted for the creation of a Property Tax Relief Fund, partially paid for through a restructuring of the franchise tax. The General Revenue Fund would continue to receive an amount equal to what it received under the old franchise tax, but all additional revenue would be diverted to property tax relief.

In its original incarnation, the franchise tax was levied on a business's inventory. In 1991, however, the legislature changed the tax so that a business would pay either $2.50 per $1,000 of taxable capital or 4.5 percent of its earned surplus, whichever is greater. ("Earned surplus" meant income; the legislature simply chose to employ a more politically acceptable phrase.) From a business standpoint, the franchise tax was worse than a true income tax, because businesses paid taxes even if they failed to make money. The earned surplus tax almost doubled franchise tax revenue. Still, many profitable entities avoided the franchise tax altogether. Corporations paid the tax, but limited partnerships and professional associations—like doctors and lawyers—did not. Although limited partnerships like the Texas Rangers, the Houston Texans, and the San Antonio Spurs did contribute state revenue through sales tax on their tickets and concessions, most law firms and medical associations escaped state business taxes altogether. In 1997, Governor Bush tried and failed to extend business taxes to these entities, despite his then-ownership interest in the Rangers. The lawyer-laden legislature opposed this proposal. Many corporations turned themselves into partnerships in the ensuing years. However, in the 2006 special session, the specter of facing angry voters and closed schools was enough to make legislators opt for broader business taxes.

The new franchise tax is a **margin tax**, assessed on the lesser of the following:

- 70 percent of a business's total revenue;
- a business's revenue minus its cost of goods sold;
- a business's revenue minus employee compensation.

Businesses engaged primarily in wholesale or retail trade pay a 0.5 percent tax on that marginal rate. Other businesses pay 1 percent on the margin rate. Sole proprietorships are exempt from the tax, but professional associations, partnerships, and corporations all pay. Businesses with total revenue less than $1 million are exempt from the tax through 2013, at which point the threshold drops to $600,000, unless the legislature opts to extend it again.

The broad question that remains is whether the new margin tax will ever generate the amount of revenue that its advocates promised in 2006. After a 2 percent increase in 2011 and a much larger 16 percent increase in 2012, which generated $4.56 billion in the latter year, revenue was still about 20 percent below initial estimates. That is a sizable gap, but a significant narrowing from the first year of full implementation in

franchise tax
A specific tax paid by businesses operating in Texas.

margin tax
A tax on the marginal income of a business.

14.1

14.2

14.3

14.4

14.5

motor fuels tax

A tax on gasoline, diesel, and other motor fuels.

"sin" taxes

Taxes levied on selected goods and services, such as alcoholic beverages and tobacco products.

2009. And 2012 franchise tax revenue did little more than surpass margin tax collections in 2008, the first year most Texas businesses were subject to most of the provisions of the tax revision. As more businesses fall under the limits of the tax, revenue will rise even more, but some tweaking of the tax may eventually be required if both the property tax fund and the general revenue obligations are to be completely fulfilled.

☐ Motor Vehicle Sales and Rental Tax

The motor vehicle sales tax is identical to the broader state sales tax, at 6.25 percent. In reality, this portion of the tax is simply an extension of the sales tax. Vehicle rentals of fewer than 30 days are taxed at 10 percent, but longer term rental reverts to 6.25 percent. Manufactured homes fall under the scope of this tax, with the levy just over 3 percent. In 2012, the tax brought $3.56 billion into state coffers, the second consecutive year of double-digit percentage increase.

☐ Motor Fuels Tax

Texas taxes both gasoline and diesel fuel at 20 cents per gallon. Liquefied gas is taxed at 15 cents per gallon. In 2012, these **motor fuels taxes** generated $3.17 billion. Fuels revenue is among the least volatile of all Texas taxes.

☐ Oil and Gas Production Taxes

On the other hand, oil and gas production taxes are among the most volatile. Instead of setting a tax based on barrels of oil or cubic feet of natural gas produced, Texas taxes extractions as a percentage of their value: 4.6 percent for oil and 7.5 percent for natural gas. The market price of each is directly correlated with production in Texas. The higher the price, the more is produced. Texas oil fields that fell silent when oil prices were below $30 per barrel—a close approximation of the lowest limit for profitability in the state—are now in full production. Newer methods to tap previously unextractable oil and gas deposits have opened more productive fields, and further technological advances will release greater resources. The Eagle Shale Field in south Texas, for instance, may ultimately yield 10 billion barrels of oil; it produced almost 22 million in 2011.[6]

In 2012, the oil production tax brought $2.1 billion into the state coffers, a 43 percent increase over 2011, which was itself a 46 percent increase over 2010. That's an amazing jump from the $338 million generated a decade before. Given the ups and downs of oil prices during the previous two decades, it should not come as a surprise that Texas oil producers were conservative about committing full bore to production again. The natural gas production tax collected $1.5 billion in 2012, up 38 percent from 2011, which was a 53 percent rise from 2010. That's significantly lower than the peak revenue year of 2006, when natural gas prices averaged more than five times what they would in 2012. Still, production was up enough to make up for most of the devaluation.

☐ "Sin" Taxes

Taxes levied on those habits that are seen as detrimental by many are often dubbed **"sin" taxes**. The most significant of these are the taxes on cigarettes, tobacco products, and alcoholic beverages.

Tobacco tax revenue was one of the few taxes to drop in 2012, falling to $1.43 billion. Part of that is due to deadlines the state uses to collect the tax, which almost always ensures that an even-numbered year will produce slightly less revenue than the odd-numbered year before it, but part of it is the result of a long-term decline in the sales of cigarettes in Texas. The increased price of cigarettes, as a result of higher federal and state taxes and higher production costs that followed successful lawsuits against tobacco companies, has driven smokers away. At $1.41 a pack, Texas has one of the highest cigarette taxes in the country, although it is nowhere near New York's $4.25 per-pack tax. Price on loose tobacco has risen as well. The portion of the

An analogy for the rejuvenated Texas oil industry: A pump jack at sunrise. Increased revenue from oil and gas production taxes have helped provide a much needed boost into the state's 'Rainy Day' Fund, which has been tapped to build highways, and, somewhat ironically, as hedge against future drought as part of the state's Water Plan.

tobacco tax above the base number under the old levy, which was just $0.41 a pack, is dedicated to the property tax reduction, just like the franchise tax. Oddly (and we say that sarcastically), lawmakers have seen fit to increase taxes on all tobacco products except cigars, which many have been known to enjoy upon occasion. Go figure.

Alcoholic beverage taxes, the only taxing category that never decreased during the recession, raised $930 million in 2012. The tax rate ranges from $6 a barrel for beer to $2.40 a gallon for liquor. The state also receives 14 percent of the gross receipts from mixed-drink sales. Legislators opted not to increase alcohol taxes during the 2006 revenue realignment either.

In 2007 the legislature did, however, enact a new a sin tax on patrons of adult entertainment establishments. This $5 entry fee was dubbed the "pole tax" by political pundits and is not to be confused with the now unconstitutional "poll tax" on voting. The Texas pole tax was initially struck down by a state appeals court on the grounds that it discriminatorily infringed on a single form of free expression. The state appealed to the Texas supreme court, and collection of the tax was suspended in the interim.[7] The court found for the state, saying that the fee was not unreasonable and the clubs could avoid it by not serving alcohol. The U.S. Supreme Court refused to hear the appeal, leaving the state law in force. Illinois has followed Texas's lead and adopted a similar tax; other states are considering it as well.

Insurance and Utility Taxes

Insurance taxes produced just under $1.5 billion in 2012, continuing a sharp upward revenue trend. The tax rate varies due to the type of insurance involved and the amount of the individual insurance company's investment within the state. Likewise, utility taxes are based on a company's gross receipts. Utility taxes brought in $451 million in 2012.

income tax
A tax based on a person's income, usually progressive.

☐ Other Taxes

Hotel and motel taxes brought in just over $400 million in 2012. The inheritance tax, which is tied to the federal rate, brought in nothing. If the federal tax is reinstated, state tax liability will return unless the legislature takes action. Other taxes like amusement fees, cement taxes, and the $200 annual tax on attorneys generated about a quarter of a billion dollars during that year.

☐ Tax Notes

Although this chapter is about state taxes, Texans pay a variety of other taxes as well. It is important to differentiate among the state taxes discussed earlier, the local taxes discussed in the local government chapter, and federal taxes, such as the income and social security taxes deducted from an individual's paycheck. Alcohol, tobacco, and gasoline are subject to both federal and state taxes.

The most important note on the tax system is that, unlike 43 other states, Texas does not have a personal **income tax**. There are positives and negatives associated with that, and one's view may be colored by one's political orientation, but it is, at the very least, a starting point for any discussion of Texas taxes. The absence of an income tax makes it more difficult for the state to raise tax rates. Many Texans see that as a good thing. Common sense dictates that the current state sales tax, especially in tandem with local government add-ons, is so high that raising it would likely have a negative impact on the state economy. As it is, only eight states have a higher sales tax than Texas,[8] but that may be a little misleading because of the state's broad sales tax exemptions that we discussed earlier. In fact, sales tax revenue as a percentage of per capita income is only 13 percent higher than the average state, most of which have income taxes.[9]

Without a major rewriting of the tax code—or a major influx of revenue from some other source—state government is restrained. With revenue constrained by the tax structure, tax-based expenditures are essentially limited to current revenues plus increases that result from economic growth, plus whatever tweaking of the franchise tax that might occur. Conservatives might see this positively because, when coupled with the balanced budget provision, it limits the growth of government.

Conservatives fear that an income tax rate would be too easy to raise. The only defense to such a tax is to never let it occur. Many liberals, on the other hand, argue that the current system is far too restrictive. Some government programs, such as education, are so vital that they deserve more government funding even if nontraditional forms of financing, such as an income tax, are needed.

Since 1993, the Texas constitution has prohibited the state from instituting an income tax unless voters give their approval. Even then, the uses for income tax revenue are restricted. Two-thirds would go to provide school property tax relief, and the other third would be dedicated to education. Such a system would worsen the dedicated funds restrictions with which the state has grappled for decades. The provision requires voter approval for any rate increase.

Historically, one of the best arguments put forward by income tax advocates was that state income tax, unlike the sales tax, was deductible from federal taxes. Texans were leaving money in the federal treasury because of an inefficient taxing mechanism. In 2004, the U.S. Congress made sales tax deductible for Texans who itemize. That legislation was scheduled to expire in 2005, but has been extended through successive sessions of Congress until at least 2013. If it is permanently renewed—and that is possible, but by no means certain—it would undercut one of the arguments for a state income tax. Realistically, though, a state income tax is not politically viable in the foreseeable future.

☐ Taxation Summary

Of the 15 most populous states, Texas ranks second in lowest per capita state tax rate. Only Georgia ranks lower. Of those most populous, only Florida and Washington join Texas as states without a personal income tax.

When you include local taxes, however, Texas tax rates rise considerably. It is a consequence of low state taxes that many government responsibilities are pushed to the local level. For instance, many states heavily fund education construction programs. In Texas, most funding is local. In fact, local school district debt had risen to a level sufficient to trigger a special report from Comptroller Susan Combs in October 2012. Combs said that public school debt had risen to $63.6 billion, a 155 percent increase over the past decade.[10] Almost half of the total state and local tax burden on Texans goes to local governments, not the state.[11] Texas has the 13th highest property tax rate, which flows to cities, counties and education districts, which are not part of the state system. Texans pay 5 percent more of their personal income in sales taxes than citizens in the average state. But in overall state tax burden per $1,000 of personal income, Texas ranks 47th, and its $41.37 rate is well below the national average of $57.02.[12]

☐ Reforming Texas Taxes

After the major restructuring of the franchise and cigarette taxes in 2006, the legislature has left the Texas tax code essentially unchanged. Even in the face of the 2011 $27 billion current services deficit, the legislature didn't take a shot at what many considered low hanging fruit: legalized casino gambling. With the Speaker directly involved in the horse racing business, which would benefit from legalization for reasons we will discuss next, it may have seemed like a good bet in the last session, but with Republicans holding over two-thirds of the seats in the house, a bill never got out of the gates. Another factor that seems to point in favor of legalized gaming is that the largest horse track in Texas is now owned by the same holding company that runs the Winstar casino across the Oklahoma border, and they'd love to see slot machines at the track. The last time casino-style gambling received serious legislative consideration, Winstar was one of the biggest interests fighting *against* legalization, fearing that it would cut into their Oklahoma profits. Finally, Norquist, the instigator of the "no new taxes" pledge, has explicitly stated that he would not consider a vote for legalized gaming to be a violation of that promise.

☐ The Casino Option

Saturday, October 30, 2004 was a day filled with promise for the horse racing industry in Texas. Lone Star Park in Grand Prairie hosted the equine equivalent of the Super Bowl—the Breeder's Cup. In many ways, it is more like eight Super Bowls, with championships being determined in eight different divisions. The Cup brought over 53,000 fans and an estimated economic impact of over $35 million. Since that day, however, Texas horse racing has been in a steep and steady decline.

As an industry, horse racing is in trouble. It's no secret that Americans like to gamble. Until a few years ago, most Americans could legally gamble only in Vegas, Atlantic City, or at the racetrack. After a brief period of legalization during the Depression, Texans could not legally bet on horses until the late 1980s. Even then, opponents of gambling promised that this was only the beginning. Parimutuel betting today, slot machines tomorrow. Horsemen said they had no interest in slots, just horses. So why, 25 years later, are the same horse forces begging for casinos?

The nature of the racing game has changed. When gambling options were limited, a full 40 percent of America's legally wagered dollars were bet on horses. Now it's less than 3 percent. As more states have approved casinos, more betting money—and tax revenue—has gone other places. In other states, tracks—with the approval of state legislatures—have been able to supplement their track purses with slot money. Slots are a losing proposition for the gambler. Over the long term, the casino always wins. With a portion of those winnings, some "racinos" have added to their purses—the payout to the owners of the winning horses. Bigger payouts attract better horses and more bettors. And we are talking about a lot of money. Casino supplements to race purses in Louisiana alone topped $60 million in the 2011 fiscal year. And most Louisiana bets are placed by out-of-state bettors, which means that the state receives revenue from

Ghostzapper, shown here in the lead, won the Breeder's Cup Classic at Lone Star Park in 2004. Since then, the Texas racing industry has faced tough competition from surrounding states that supplement their purses with 'racino' money. Without a similar influx, the thoroughbred racing industry in Texas is destined to be confined to the minor leagues.

people who put no burden on the state's services.[13] Oklahoma, Louisiana, New Mexico, and Arkansas all allow tracks to supplement purses with slot income. But not Texas.

It is a tough proposition for Texas racing, with all of the surrounding states supplementing purses and Louisiana supplementing breeding programs as well. "The purses being offered at Louisiana tracks compared to Texas in some instances are three times larger and the incentive money to breed horses in Louisiana is 10 times more than it is here in Texas," stated David Hooper, executive director of the Texas Thoroughbred Breeders Association. "As a result, we've lost half of our breeding stock."[14] In 2012, Lone Star Park took the controversial step of ending its Lone Star Millions Memorial Day spectacular by eliminating several graded stakes races that attracted top horses from around the country. This followed a trend of reducing stakes races and the larger wagers that they attract.

Of course, the racing industry is just part of this story. Slot machines in Texas could bring upward of $1.5 billion a year into state coffers. That means a billion and a half dollars that doesn't come from cutting spending or raising the sales tax or other fees. Cross the Oklahoma border, visit the Winstar Casino, and try to find a car that doesn't have Texas plates. Good luck. Or head east to Shreveport for a more realistic comparison. Visit the racino at Louisiana Downs. Ninety percent of the cars are from Texas.

And that's where this controversy plays out in its starkest terms. A decade ago, Louisiana Downs was all but dead. No one went to the races. Betting totals were down; therefore, purses were in freefall. But LA Downs has had slots since May 2003. By 2005, they had extended their race season and upped their purses. Lone Star Park, on the other hand, has cut purses, then cut them again. Horse owners follow the money; horse players follow the horses. As a result, owners are taking their best horses, if not their entire stables, out of Texas. Wagering money follows. Together, they put a major strain on the Texas racing industry and provide a major boon to Louisiana state coffers. By 2013, daily average purses at Lone Star Park were about $140,000. Meanwhile, 2013 purses at Arkansas's Oaklawn Park, with racino supplements, were expected to average between $350,000 and $370,000 per day.[15] A decade ago, Lone Star Park and Oaklawn were considered comparable tracks.

Going forward, one should keep in mind that Pinnacle Entertainment obtained a three-quarters interest in a secondary Texas horse track, Retama Park, located just outside San Antonio, late in 2012. Pinnacle, which owns casinos in Louisiana and throughout the Midwest as well as a horse track in Ohio, purchased the foundering track in which Speaker of the House Joe Straus's family formerly had a significant stake for some $22 million in cash and debt acquisition. Whether this signaled a serious effort to lobby for gaming in Texas, or simply a hedging of its bets on its properties in Louisiana should gaming be legalized, remained unclear as this edition went to print.

nontax revenue
Revenue derived from nontax sources, such as the lottery and fees paid to the state.

☐ Other Revenue-Raising Options

Any single tax increase in a $173.5 billion biennial budget—or about $87 billion a year—will have only a marginal impact on revenue. But let's look at some revenue options. A nickel increase in the gas tax would generate over a half a billion dollars a year. Adding a dollar a gallon tax on beer and wine would bring in $400 million. Sales taxes on doctors and lawyers would generate about $1 billion a year. Doubling utility taxes would bring in an additional quarter billion. A full-penny sales tax increase, which would be politically unpopular, would garner almost $2 billion annually. There are other choices, of course, but keep in mind that almost any tax increase is going to generate significant opposition.

Nontax Revenue

14.4 Explain how nontax revenue has surpassed tax revenue.

O f all of the numbers on the revenue side of the equation, perhaps the most significant is this: Since fiscal year 2002, **nontax revenue** has outstripped tax revenue every year, as illustrated in Figure 14.3. Federal grants are the largest sources of nontax revenue, but significant income also comes from licenses and fees, interest income, and the lottery. In 2012, nontax revenue comprised just over 53 percent of total state revenue.

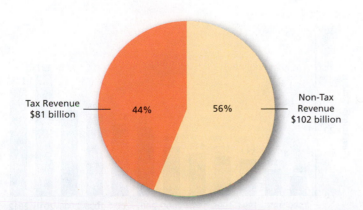

Tax Revenue
$81 billion   44%   56%   Non-Tax Revenue
$102 billion

FIGURE 14.3 Tax Revenue By Source 2012–2013 Budget.

federal income
Revenue distributed to states from the federal government.

□ Federal Income

Texas received $32.9 billion in **federal income** in 2012, as shown in Figure 14.4, a 14 percent decrease from the previous year, which was the largest grant in state history. Federal funding is the largest single source of revenue for the state, comprising almost 35 percent of the total budget. Even if you factor out the one-time bump provided by the Obama stimulus plan, federal monies have become an increasingly important portion of the state's revenue stream. Federal income in 2012 was larger than the entire state budget in 1993. It is a 1,645 percent increase in federal money since 1977. Increased Medicaid and Children's Health Insurance Program funding accounts for much of the federal increase over the last two decades.

Another significant factor was the state's restructuring of existing programs in order to qualify for matching funds. Former comptroller John Sharp deserves much of the credit for this as it was his performance reviews that made the changes possible. Over the 1994–1995 biennium, restructuring of existing programs raised an additional $1.23 billion in federal Medicaid funding alone without additional state expenditures, a base the state has built on ever since. Still, Texas receives less federal aid than most states. One reason for that is the state's failure to fully participate in all federal matching programs, which we will discuss later. Another is that congressional funding programs have traditionally been more generous to northeastern and midwestern states. Finally, per capita federal spending ranks 42nd out of 50 in Texas, leaving the state at only 88 percent of the national average.[16]

Because of the expiration of the Obama stimulus plan, federal funds decreased by almost $18 billion in the 2012–2013 budget, representing the bulk of the state's current services shortfall. In the latter biennium, however, federal funding still provides 56.8 percent of the state's health and human services spending, 20 percent of education spending, and 15.5 percent of business and economic development spending.[17]

□ Licenses, Fees, Permits, Interest, and Investment Income

Licenses, fees, permits, and fines brought in $7.6 billion in 2012, making them the second largest source of nontax revenue. The category covers everything from driver's licenses to hunting licenses to professional licenses. Interest and investment income generated revenue of about $1.1 billion in 2012.

□ The Lottery

The Texas Lottery delivers about $1 billion a year in net revenue to the state. Although the state generates far more than that in ticket sales, 63 percent of every dollar in ticket sales goes back to players in the form of prizes. Retailers receive about 5 percent of the sales, and state administrative costs are a little less than 5 percent.

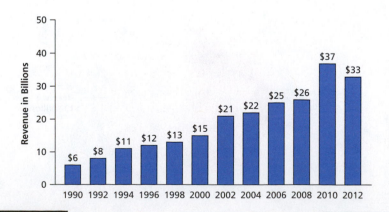

FIGURE 14.4 Federal Income in Texas.

Inside the Federalist System

Left on the Table

As you know from our discussion of federalism, federal grants come with strings attached. Usually, state governments bite the bullet and accept the requirements that come with the cash. And certainly, that's what happened with more than $12.1 billion that Texas took from the 2009 federal stimulus package. Texas did not, however, take everything it was offered.

Governor Perry turned down some $555 million in additional unemployment benefits that would have gone to out-of-work Texans. Although the funds would have provided a significant and immediate boost to the Texas economy, Perry thought the residual costs were too high. His objections were both economic and philosophic. Accepting the stimulus would require Texas to change its standards, extending benefits to part-time employees who were not looking for full-time work. In order to pay for this, since unemployment is funded by employers, businesses would have their employment taxes raised, in effect adding another tax on new employees. With Texas at the height of the recession, Perry believed that any employment disincentive was a bad policy. Furthermore, accepting the package would obligate future legislatures to abide by the agreement,

a constraint Perry was unwilling to impose. Perry was not alone, with the governors of South Carolina, Mississippi, Alabama, and Louisiana also rejecting the unemployment funds.

Not all Texans agreed with Perry's call to reject the funds, with even a significant number of Republicans voicing their objections. There were, in fact, enough votes in the legislature to pass a bill accepting the funds, but there would not have been enough votes to override the governor's inevitable veto, so the effort died in the legislature.

Unemployment wasn't the only portion of the stimulus package that Perry rejected; in addition, he turned down a much smaller energy grant that also came with strings. Although the rejections drew the press coverage, Texas took more than 95 percent of the stimulus plan money, along with all the strings that came wrapped around that package.

1. Should Congress use federal grants to shape state behavior? Why or why not?

2. Under what circumstances, if ever, should a state turn down federal money because of strings that are attached?

The **lottery** has always had a strange place in Texas politics. Often referred to as a fee on the mathematically challenged because the odds of winning are so poor, some of its biggest critics in the legislature have worked to keep it from becoming more successful. At its inception, the lottery was very successful, quickly becoming the largest in the nation. Soon thereafter, under the guise of raising more state revenue, the legislature got greedy. They cut the payout on scratch-off tickets to as low as 53 cents on the dollar and cut the Lottery Commission's advertising budget. For comparison, slot machines in Nevada and Louisiana generally pay back between 88 and 96 cents for each dollar gambled, with higher denomination machines providing a greater return. The takeout at horse and dog tracks is generally between 18 and 25 percent, with exotic bets returning less per dollar wagered. The net take on sports bets, only legal in Nevada, is 4.54 percent. The lottery is a bad gamble, and the legislature made it worse.

Some legislators were foolish enough to believe that cutting the players' share and advertising budget would result in higher net revenue. Others were stealth opponents, who intended to slash revenue to "prove" that the lottery provided an unreliable revenue stream. Neither was successful, as lottery revenue dropped, but not enough to kill off the games completely. Later, legislators did what outside experts had initially urged and cut the state's take. Revenue slowly recovered, aided by Texas's decision to join the multistate lottery in 2003. Net lottery revenue has increased slightly each year since 2008.

lottery
Revenue-raising method of the state involving games of chance.

☐ Other Sources

All other revenue sources, which include land income, sales of goods and services, tobacco settlement revenue, and settlement claims, produce another $5.4 billion to state coffers in 2012.

The Big Three Expenditures

14.5 Describe the top three areas of expenditure in Texas.

If you wish to understand a government's priorities, examine its spending habits. Spending levels show priorities, even when these priorities are mandated by politicians in Washington, DC, rather than in Austin. After decades of almost unfettered growth, the Texas Legislature contracted the state's budget in real dollars because of economic recession and structural constraints. Prior to this contraction, however, government spending had been rising steadily ever since government started providing services. Both social and technological factors have been responsible for most of these increases. Social considerations include labor–management relations, urbanization, and an expansion of the notion that government should provide, or at least regulate, basic social services. Technological advances, such as air and ground transportation and mass communication, have necessitated some degree of governmental intervention. Highway and air safety, privacy rights, and environmental concerns are among the relatively modern issues faced by government. Social and technological changes have ushered in a host of regulatory agencies that have sent state government expenditures higher.

It is vital to note, however, that Texas spends much less on government services, per person, than the average state. Texas ranks 47th among the states in total per capita government expenditures, 44th on public welfare, and 33rd on education.[18]

Texas spends more on education than any other single function of government, as demonstrated by Figure 14.5. In the 2012–2013 budget, education comprised 42 percent of state spending, with 70 percent of that going to public education—K–12—and the rest going to colleges and universities. Another 31.9 percent of state expenditures flow to the various programs that comprise health and human services. 13.6 percent of state funding is devoted to business and economic development, the largest portion of that going to transportation. Taken together, these "Big Three" consume 87.5 percent of the state's budget, leaving everything else the state does scraping for that last 12.5 percent. And criminal justice consumes half of the remainder, so funding for anything else is pretty slim.

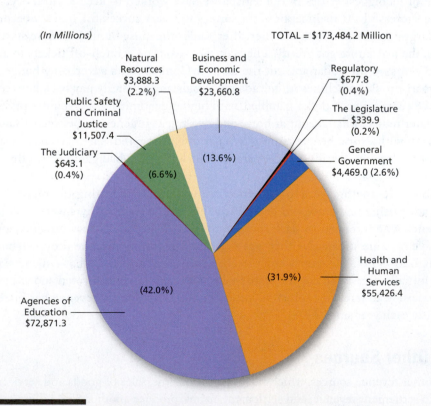

FIGURE 14.5 Texas Expenditures, 2012–2013.

□ Education

Funding public education has been one of the most contentious issues faced by the Texas government for decades. Questions of adequacy, equality, and efficiency have been constantly addressed by education agencies, the legislature, a series of governors, local school boards, and the Texas supreme court. It showcases how public policy can be shaped by many actors, often working at cross-interests to each other and establishing contradictory regulations. Its enormous costs are somewhat masked by the Texas budget, as total public and higher education expenditures in the state are much higher than the line item totals in the state appropriations bill.

□ Public Education

When we talk about the public education system, we are talking about schools that receive funding from state, federal, and local sources while providing educational services from pre-kindergarten through the twelfth grade. The state's portion of funding is just under $24 billion per year, which does not include the state's share of teacher retirement programs. Total pre-K through 12 spending averaged about $43 billion in 2012 and 2013, with most of the difference coming from local school taxes, and a much smaller portion—less than $5 billion a year—coming from federal sources. A sizable portion of federal aid is administered through the Child Nutrition Program.

Texas has 1,029 independent school districts, 201 charter schools, and 13 state-run districts. The majority of districts have less than 1,600 students, while 18 have 50,000 or more.[19] Although state education spending rose steadily over most of the previous decade, it leveled off after 2011 and dropped slightly in 2012 and 2013, due to cuts in both state revenue and income from deflated property tax values.

When schools were primarily funded through local property taxes, there were vast differences in funding per student. Some districts with high property values spent as much as nine times per student what some property poor districts did. Although the legislature made an effort to send more money to poor districts, it wasn't enough to satisfy the Texas supreme court, which ruled that these funding discrepancies violated the state constitutional provision mandating an "efficient" public education system. It took several years and two more supreme court rulings before the state finally arrived at the so-called Robin Hood plan, which took property tax money raised by wealthy districts and transferred it to poor districts. Because of this, by 2006 Texas had a *de facto* state property tax, and the state restructured the franchise and cigarette taxes to create the Property Tax Relief Fund, lowering school district property taxes and increasing the state's share of education funding.

Still, Texas spends about $1,300 per year less per student than the average state. Nonetheless, the Texas student–teacher ratio is below the national average (this is like golf; the lower number is better), despite the fact that the state's student population has increased 20 percent from a decade ago. Many of the states with better teacher ratios have fewer students than they did a decade ago, the opposite of the explosive growth Texas has experienced.

In February 2013, State District Court Judge John Deitz ruled that the state's education funding system violated the state constitution requirement that Texas operate "an efficient system of public schools." Central to the ruling was the judge's finding that the state had elevated standards while allowing funding to fall far behind the current services budget. He noted that, once again, unconstitutional per-student spending gaps had developed and that the state had lapsed into another *de facto* statewide property tax, which also violates the state constitution. The judge ruled against the state and for the schools on each of the major issues brought by the lawsuit filed by a partnership of more than 600 independent Texas public school districts. Cost for complete compliance may exceed $10 billion in each two-year budget cycle. The state appealed the decision, which will ultimately be determined by the supreme court of Texas.

Higher Education

Texas has over 1,300,000 students enrolled in public institutes of higher education, with 125,000 more in private institutions. More than half of the total is enrolled in one or more of the state's 50 community college systems. The state appropriates just under $10 billion a year for higher education, not including health care and retirement plans. Tuition, deregulated in 2003, generates another $2.5 billion a year, roughly two and a half times what it did a decade ago. Significant increases in tuition have been controversial at the state's four-year universities. Elected officials began pressuring state schools to, at the very least, lock tuition for incoming students for four years, thus establishing cost certainty and encouraging on-time graduation, as late graduators add significant expense to state colleges. The implicit threat was that legislation would follow if the institutions did not act on their own. For most community colleges in the state, property tax revenue is the largest single component of the budget.

Health and Human Services

On a per-person basis, Texas spends less on health and human services (HHS) than practically any other state. Relatively few qualify for any public assistance, and those who do generally receive much lower benefits than their counterparts in other states. Despite this, health and human services spending increased dramatically from the mid-1980s to the mid-1990s, and again through the first decade of the 21st century. Through most of that decade, in fact, Texas spent more on social services than it did on education.

Medicaid, or health services for the poor, has been the biggest driver in social service spending over the past several years and may prove the single biggest challenge for state budget-makers moving forward. As the legislature prepared the 2012–2013 budget, it took numerous steps to contain the ever-rising costs of the program, including reducing payments for some procedures and establishing stricter guidelines for others. Although almost 75 percent of Medicaid recipients are children, a significant portion of program spending flows to aging and disability services. Health and human services bore the brunt of the 2012–2013 budget cuts, as total spending dropped by more than $10 billion from the previous biennium.

Although the Health and Human Services Commission (HHSC) oversees all social service spending, the administration of Medicaid is divided between the Department of Aging and Disability Services (DADS) and the Health and Human Services Commission. The primary focus of DADS is on delivering long-term care for the elderly and disabled. Fifty-eight percent of DADS funding comes from federal funds, with 93 percent of the federal money flowing from Medicaid.[20] Although 70 percent of clients are in community-based settings, 70 percent of DADS spending goes to institutions, like nursing homes and hospice facilities. Texas has moved a large percentage of clients from institutional to community services over the past decade. The 2012–2013 budget for aging and disability is just under $10 billion, a 27 percent cut from 2010–2011 levels.

HHSC administers the remainder of the Medicaid program, which consists primarily of providing health care for the poor. The commission's 2012–2013 budget of just under $35 billion is a $6 billion reduction from the previous budget. Fifty-seven percent of HHSC appropriations are from federal funding.[21] Medicaid is available to people poor enough to receive Temporary Assistance for Needy Families (TANF) and their children, children aged 1–5 whose parents make less than 133 percent of the federal poverty level (FPL), children 6–18 whose parents live at or below the FPL, Social Security recipients whose income is less than 74 percent of the FPL, and pregnant women and infants whose income is less than 185 percent of FPL. Additionally, persons in nursing homes qualify for Medicaid with incomes up to 218 percent of FPL. Finally, children in foster care are eligible. Texas has made a concerted effort to cut Medicaid costs by moving many recipients into managed-care programs.

Additionally, almost 600,000 Texans are enrolled in the **Children's Health Insurance Program** (CHIP), which provides health care coverage to those 18 and under whose parents make too much to qualify for Medicaid, but less than 200 percent of FPL. That is a significant policy reversal from the 2003 legislative session, which slashed CHIP recipients during a time of fiscal hardship. Enrollees dropped from 500,000 to 300,000. CHIPS is one of the best federal matching fund deals available, as the national government chips—pun intended—in 71 cents for every 29 cents provided by the state. For Medicaid, the shares are 58 and 42 cents; respectively.

In the mid-1990s, massive welfare reform began in Texas. What was once called Aid to Families with Dependent Children became Temporary Assistance for Needy Families (TANF). The emphasis here is on the word "temporary," because the purpose was to wean long-term recipients off the welfare rolls. This transition has been a joint state and federal effort. Texas began the move toward restricting welfare eligibility during the 1995 legislative session by setting time limits for physically able recipients to find jobs. The federal government, which provides most of the funding for public assistance in Texas, imposed more stringent requirements in 1996, which Texas adopted in 1997. Maximum TANF payments amount to about $263 a month for a parent and two children.[22] In July 2012, about 104,000 Texans, comprising 43,000 families, received TANF assistance from the state. Compare that to the fully federal-funded food stamp program, which enrolled approximately 3.5 million Texans.[23]

The state spends much smaller amounts for child and adult protective services, child care regulation, and foster care payments. Texas also funds programs for community youth development services and intervention programs with at-risk youths. The state spends about $60 million a year on consumer protection programs and about $5 million a year on the management of violent sex offenders.

Business and Economic Development

Business and Economic Development is the third largest area of government spending, with total appropriations of about $12 billion a year. The Texas Department of Transportation (TxDot) receives the bulk of these funds, about $10 billion per year. The agency oversees the budget and operation of transportation planning, highway design, the purchase of right-of-way, public transportation systems, aviation safety, motor vehicle registrations, and a host of other functions related to transportation. Texas is a large state, so it requires many miles of highways. In recent years, more than 90 percent of the TxDot budget has gone to the construction, and maintenance of 80,000 miles of state highways. Just Dot's funding comes from federal grants. TxDot was one of the saw a budget increase from the previous biennium, a health

Other offices funded through Busine pment included the Lottery Commission and the Departm ment. Only the Texas Workforce Commission, which help has an annual budget of over a billion dollars. The Texas D and Community Affairs took an 87 percent cut from the previous bu to a federal funding cut of over $2 billion over the two-year appropriation.

Other Expenditures

After accounting for education, health and human services and business and economic development, 87.5 percent of the Texas budget is spoken for. This means that everything else that the state does has to be accomplished with about $11 billion a year. More than half of the remainder, 6.6 percent of the total budget, goes to public safety and criminal justice, with the bulk of funds flowing to the Texas Department of Criminal Justice. Texas has more than 150,000 felony inmates, and that population is expected to exceed prison capacity in 2013.[24] An additional 250,000 Texans are under some sort of community supervision. Some 70,000 inmates are serving time in county jails on any given day.

The offices of the governor, attorney general, comptroller, and other state executive officials constitute the budgetary item "general government." Together with spending for legislative operations, these items take up about 2.8 percent of the budget.

Review the Chapter

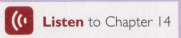 **Listen** to Chapter 14

Constraints on Budgeting

14.1 Analyze the constraints on the budget process in Texas.

The most significant constraint on budgeting in Texas is the balanced budget provision. Other noteworthy limitations include the biennial budget cycle and the public and legislative sentiment against raising taxes. Furthermore, a sizable portion of state appropriations are influenced by dedicated funds and congressional and court mandates.

The Budget-Making Process

14.2 Explain the role of the Legislative Budget Board.

The Legislative Budget Board carries the greatest weight in the budget-making process. The Speaker of the house and the lieutenant governor have significant power over the board. In addition to serving as co-chairs of the LBB, they appoint, either directly or indirectly, all the members of the board. The LBB gives guidance to individual agencies as they develop their Legislative Appropriations Request. The board's final plan, heavily influenced by its full-time professional staff, is introduced in the house and senate and serves as the blueprint for the state's budget.

State Taxes

14.3 Differentiate among the major sources of tax revenue in Texas.

The major source of tax revenue in Texas is the sales tax. The sales tax brings in more revenue than all other tax revenue combined. The second largest tax source is the motor vehicle sales tax, which is a close cousin of the general sales tax. The franchise tax, the state's primary tax on business, was significantly reformed and expanded in 2006. It has thus far failed to meet its initial projections, but a strengthening economy has narrowed the gap. Oil and gas production taxes have rebounded significantly over the last several years, adding unanticipated revenues to the state's Rainy Day Fund. The motor fuels tax produces significant revenue, as do the cigarette and alcoholic beverage taxes. Several smaller taxes provide a comparatively insignificant amount of income.

Nontax Revenue

14.4 Explain how nontax revenue has surpassed tax revenue.

For more than a decade, nontax revenue has provided the majority of the state's revenue. The biggest driver of nontax revenue has been federal grants, which account for more than a third of the state's appropriations. Within federal grants, the largest area of growth has been that associated with Medicaid.

The Big Three Expenditures

14.5 Describe the top three areas of expenditure in Texas.

The largest category of appropriations in Texas is education. About two-thirds of state education spending is devoted to K–12, with the remainder flowing to the state's public colleges and universities. The second largest area of expenditure is health and human services, although its portion of state spending dropped significantly with the adoption of a more austere budget. The third largest area, business and economic development, is comprised primarily of transportation spending. Taken together, the big three account for seven-eighths of the state's spending.

Learn the Terms

 Study and **Review** the **Flashcards**

balanced budget, p. 325
Children's Health Insurance
    Program (CHIP), p. 344
current services budget, p. 324
dedicated funds, p. 327
federal income, p. 340
federal mandates, p. 327

franchise tax, p. 333
income tax, p. 336
Legislative Budget Board
    (LBB), p. 328
lottery, p. 341
margin tax, p. 333
Medicaid, p. 344

motor fuels tax, p. 334
nontax revenue, p. 339
progressive tax, p. 331
regressive tax, p. 331
sales tax, p. 332
"sin" taxes, p. 334
tax revenue, p. 330

14.1 Analyze the constraints on the budget process in Texas.

The biggest constraint on Texas budget makers is

a. the biennial budget.
b. lax attitudes toward taxes.
c. the balanced budget provision.
d. dedicated funds.
e. federal mandates.

14.2 Explain the role of the Legislative Budget Board.

The Legislative Budget Board is

a. an interest group.
b. an independent agency.
c. the organization responsible for estimating revenue.
d. under the exclusive jurisdiction of the lieutenant governor.
e. the primary budget-making organization in Texas.

14.3 Differentiate among the major sources of tax revenue in Texas.

The biggest component of Texas tax revenue is the

a. sales tax.
b. franchise tax.
c. income tax.
d. motor fuels tax.
e. oil production tax.

14.4 Explain how nontax revenue has surpassed tax revenue.

The biggest single factor in nontax revenue increases has been

a. the lottery.
b. TANF grants.
c. CHIPS grants.
d. Medicaid grants.
e. increased collections of fines and penalties.

14.5 Describe the top three areas of expenditure in Texas.

Which of the following is not true about Texas spending?

a. Texas spends more on public education than on higher education.
b. Most health and human service spending comes from federal grants.
c. Texas spends more on prisons than on highways.
d. Texas spends more on education than on prisons.
e. Texas spends more on education than on human services.

Explore Further

Fiscal Size-Up: 2012–13 Biennium, Legislative Budget Board, 2012
Budget 101 at http://www.senate.state.tx.us/SRC/pdf/Budget_101-2011.pdf
Center for Public Policy Priorities at http://www.cppp.org/
Texas Budget Source at the Legislative Budget Board http://tbs.lbb.state.tx.us/

The Texas Public Policy Foundation www.texasbudgetsource.com
Texas House Research Organization at http://www.hro.house.state.tx.us/
Texas Senate Research Center at http://www.senate.state.tx.us/src/index.htm

Glossary

"one person, one vote" A principle of representation that means the vote of one citizen should be worth no more or no less than the vote of another citizen; districts with equal population ensure this.

"sin" taxes Taxes levied on selected goods and services, such as alcoholic beverages and tobacco products.

"tagging" A senate rule that allows a senator to postpone committee consideration of a bill for 48 hours in hopes of killing it.

"The Team" Unofficial term for those legislators who are supporters and allies of presiding officers and who form the leadership core of the legislature.

1876 constitution The current Texas constitution, written after Reconstruction.

abatement A financial incentive offered by governments to business and commercial concerns as a means of luring them to set up operations within the borders of a particular city.

access The ability of an interest group to contact policy makers in an attempt to enlist their help. Access is crucial, for without it an interest group's information is largely useless.

ad valorem A system of taxation that is assessed "according to value," whereby the more a property is worth, the higher the tax to be paid on it.

agenda setting The first stage of the public policy-making model.

Amber Alert A program enabling media and public safety agencies to immediately broadcast information in the event of a child abduction.

amendments Additions or deletions to the constitution; passed in a prescribed manner.

amorphous interest group One with tenuously connected membership and often unclear interest focus.

appellate court Courts that hear appeals from lower courts.

apportionment Dividing the population into districts for purposes of election and representation.

at-large system A method of electing representatives where there are no districts or wards drawn, and the candidate may draw votes from the entire area to be governed.

attorney general The state's lawyer; elected.

bail A cash deposit or other security given by the accused as a guarantee that he or she will return to court when summoned.

balanced budget A means to keep the government from spending more than it receives in revenues.

bench trial A criminal trial that is held without jury, as requested by the person charged.

beyond a reasonable doubt Burden of proof on the state in a criminal case.

Bill of Rights The portion of the Constitution limiting the government and empowering the individual.

Black Codes Post–Civil War laws restricting the freedom of African Americans.

bureaucracy Executive branch departments that carry out the law.

cabinet A form of government whereby the chief executive appoints other major executive department heads.

capital improvements Long-term infrastructure improvements, such as roads, that are often built with bond money

Castle Law A policy establishing a person's home as his or her personal domain and allowing for reasonable force, up to and including deadly force, to defend it.

centralized interest group One with decision making concentrated near the top among a relatively small leadership group.

change/termination The final stage of the public policy-making model.

Children's Health Insurance Program Subsidized health insurance for children whose parents make too much for Medicaid but who earn less than 200 percent of the poverty level.

city manager Professional political appointee who oversees city operations on a day-to-day basis

civil law Law that deals with private rights and seeks damages rather than punishment.

civil service Merit-based system of selecting government employees.

clemency power Power to pardon, commute, or parole.

coalitional Alliances consisting of a variety of individuals and groups in support of a particular candidate for elected office.

committee Division of a legislative body charged with initial deliberations on legislative proposals.

comptroller The state's chief accountant and financial officer.

conference committee Joint committee of house and senate members whose purpose is to iron out the differences between house and senate versions of a bill.

constable County-level elected official who provides services to the justice of the peace.

conventions Formal party meetings to select leadership, delegates, and create a platform.

cooperative federalism Era of expanded national government power, mandates, and funding.

council of government (COG) A regional voluntary cooperative with no regulatory or enforcement powers; consists of local governments and assesses the needs of the area as a whole.

criminal law Laws that regulate individual conduct and seek to protect society by punishing criminal acts.

current services budget Budget adjusted for increases in population and inflation.

decentralized interest group One with decision making widely dispersed among the membership.

dedicated funds Revenues set aside for specific expense categories.

defendant The person charged with a crime or the subject of a civil suit.

Democrats of Texas A liberal faction of Democrats formed in the 1950s.

devolution The transfer of government programs from the national to the state level.

disenfranchised Persons who cannot vote, or who believe their votes don't count.

distributive policies Public policies that are generally regarded as revenue-neutral and without winners and losers.

double jeopardy A criminal defendant's due process right to be protected from being tried a second time (after receiving a not-guilty verdict the first time).

down-ballot races Statewide races below the level of president, U.S. senator, or governor.

dual federalism Well-defined divisions between national and state powers and responsibilities.

due process Constitutionally protected rights of persons accused of committing criminal acts.

E. J. Davis The Republican governor of Texas during the era of Reconstruction.

election burnout Occurs when citizens believe there are too many elections and, thus, fail to vote.

en banc When an appellate court convenes all of its members to hear an appeal.

evaluation The fourth stage of the public policy-making model.

exclusionary rule A due process right that makes it illegal for the government to use evidence gathered during an unlawful police search.

factions Divisions within a political party.

Fairness Doctrine A federal law that required radio and broadcast television stations to devote equal time to opposing viewpoints. It was repealed in 1987.

FCC A federal agency that regulates publicly broadcasted radio stations.

federal income Revenue distributed to states from the federal government.

federal mandates Regulations set by Congress that state and local government must meet.

filibustering The practice of delaying or killing a bill by talking at great length; grows out of the senate's rule allowing unlimited debate.

formal powers Powers granted by the constitution or statutes.

formulation The second stage of the public policy-making model.

franchise tax A specific tax paid by businesses operating in Texas.

general election The process through which officeholders are elected from among party nominees.

general law A highly restrictive, and the most fundamental type of, legal status for municipal government.

general obligation bond A bond issued by a local government for the purpose of making capital improvements and, like a mortgage, are paid off in small, yearly payments.

gerrymandering The act of drawing representative districts in order to help or hinder a person, or a political party, to win an election.

Golden Age of Radio The era in which radio reached its peak in popularity, generally in the 1930s–1940s.

government Public institutions acting with authority to levy taxes and to allocate things for society.

governor The state's highest elected executive official.

grand jury A panel composed of 12 citizens who determine whether enough evidence exists to charge a person with a felony and make him or her stand trial.

Grange A populist farmers' alliance influential in the creation of the 1876 constitution.

gubernatorial election The election for governor and other executive offices.

hierarchy Chain of command.

hired gun A professional, outside lobbyist employed by an interest group to represent its interests on a particular issue. The relationship lasts until the issue is settled.

home rule A legal status that gives municipalities more autonomy in establishing tax rates and providing services; must be approved by a majority of the voters in municipalities consisting of 5,000 or more persons.

hung jury Term describing the failure to render a verdict in a criminal case.

ideological Characterizing a group or party built around a unifying set of principles.

implementation The third stage of the public policy-making model.

income tax A tax based on a person's income, usually progressive.

independent school district Local-level limited-purpose government that determines public school policy.

index crimes Eight categories of crime used for statistical study by the federal and state governments.

indictment A finding by the grand jury that the case will proceed to the trial stage; also called a true bill.

informal powers Powers not specifically granted in the constitution or statutes.

information dissemination The process whereby an interest group representative makes information about issues available to policy makers.

interest group A collection of individuals who share a common set of ideas or principles and who attempt to advance those ideas or principles by influencing public-policy makers.

interim committee A special committee formed to study a topic or problem between sessions of the legislature.

interim oversight Various actions by an interest group aimed at protecting its gains and promoting its goals between sessions of the legislature.

judicial activism A philosophical approach dictating that the purpose of the courts is to take an active role in public policy making.

judicial review The power of the courts to strike down laws that violate the state or national constitution.

jurisdiction The power of a court to hear a case.

land commissioner State official responsible for overseeing the leases and uses of state-owned land; elected.

Legislative Budget Board A body made up of members of the house and senate, including the two presiding officers, which oversees a staff responsible for preparing the basic working budget for the legislature's consideration.

legislative law Law passed by the legislature.

limited seniority system A method of committee selection used in the house that limits the Speaker to appointing half the members of most standing committees (plus the chairs); the other members gain their seats by seniority.

line item veto The governor's ability to delete individual items in the appropriations bill.

lobbyist A person who works on behalf of an interest group and who serves as a point of contact between the group and policy makers.

long ballot A system under which many officials are up for election at the same time.

lottery Revenue-raising method of the state involving games of chance.

mandates Regulations set by Congress that state and local government must meet.

margin tax A tax on the marginal income of a business.

martial law The power to impose military rule during a crisis.

Medicaid Government-sponsored health care for the poor.

membership mobilization The act of enlisting the rank-and-file members of an interest group in attempting to sway policy makers; often includes massive letter-writing and e-mail efforts and may also include marches and demonstrations.

mosaic The joining of small pieces of material, varied in shape and color, to produce a whole image; often used to describe the social and cultural diversity that defines Texas.

motor fuels tax A tax on gasoline, diesel, and other motor fuels.

new federalism Greater discretion to state governments in the use of federal grants.

new media Forms of delivering instant communications in a digitized or electronic format.

nonfiscal policies Public policies that have little or no impact on the budget or budgetary process.

nontax revenue Revenue derived from nontax sources, such as the lottery and fees paid to the state.

Obnoxious Acts The derisive name given to the legislation included in E. J. Davis's agenda.

ordinances Laws enacted by incorporated cities and towns; violations punishable by fine only and heard in municipal court.

original jurisdiction The authority of a court to try a case for the first time.

overlapping terms Terms of appointed board members that are staggered to ensure continuity of experience.

paradigm Models used by social scientists to explain and understand abstract concepts.

partisan press Newspapers and other media that reported a single viewpoint in an effort to persuade readers.

peace bond A court order providing a jail sentence issued by a justice of the peace against a person who had threatened another person.

penny press Inexpensive newspapers characterized by sensational stories to attract public readership.

pigeonholing The act of a setting aside a bill in committee and refusing to consider it, thereby "killing" it.

place system A system of electing local government leaders whereby the candidates must campaign for a particular seat on the city council.

plaintiff The person or entity that initiates a civil lawsuit.

platform The statement of principles passed by a political party's convention.

plea bargaining A process in which the accused receives a lighter sentence than could be expected from a trial verdict in exchange for a guilty plea.

plural executive A political system whereby major executive officers are elected independent of the governor.

plurality Exists when a candidate has more votes than any other candidate, even if the total is less than 50 percent.

political action committee (PAC) A voluntary association of individuals who band together for the purpose of raising and distributing money for political campaigns.

political culture The attitudes, beliefs, and behavior that shape an area's politics; often a product of various historical and social factors unique to that area.

political party A group of people who share common goals and attempt to control government by winning elections.

politics Who gets what, when, and how.

poll tax A tax paid for registering to vote (this tax no longer exists).

polling A measure of the public's opinion, intensity, and direction about government and politics.

post-adjournment veto A veto administered after the legislature has adjourned; in Texas, it cannot be overridden.

precinct convention The basic or grassroots level at which delegates are selected to the county party convention.

precinct A political subdivision through which elections are carried out.

preponderance The majority of evidence in a civil case.

primary election The process through which major parties choose their nominees for the general election.

probable cause The total set of facts and circumstances that would lead a reasonable person to believe that an individual committed a specific criminal act.

Progressive Era A period of time (1890–1910) during which Texas enacted numerous laws designed to protect ordinary citizens and to prevent their being taken advantage of by large monopolies such as the railroads.

progressive tax A system of taxation whereby the tax rate increases as income increases.

prosecutor A government employee who initiates criminal cases against individuals.

public policy Any act, law, legislation, or program enacted by a public entity.

Public Utility Commission (PUC) Agency that regulates utility companies; appointed.

push polling A tactic intended to persuade respondents, disguised as a poll.

Reconstruction Post–Civil War period (1865–1877) during which former Confederate states had restrictive laws applied to them by the federal government; it (and E. J. Davis) led to Texas becoming a one-party Democratic state.

redistributive policies Public policies that reallocate funds from the haves to the have-nots.

redistricting The process of redrawing district lines to maintain the concept of "one person, one vote."

regressive tax　A system of taxation whereby the tax rate increases as income decreases.

regular session　The constitutionally scheduled, biennial session of the legislature limited to 140 days.

regulatory policies　Public policies intended to regulate activity and provide public order.

Republic of Texas　The independent nation created by Texans that lasted from 1836 to 1846; its status as an independent country has contributed to (and continues to influence) an independent spirit in its politics.

resolutions　Proposed planks in the party platform; formed and submitted through the convention system.

revenue bond　Issued by local governments for the purpose of capital improvements and repaid by revenue generated by the improvement; examples include sports arenas and public facilities for which there is an admission charge.

reverse and remand　The high court overturns the lower court and orders a new trial.

reverse and render　The high court overturns the lower court and enacts a final verdict.

sales tax　Tax paid on goods and services; collected at the point of sale and forwarded to the state treasury.

secretary of state　The state's chief election officer; appointed by the governor.

senatorial courtesy　A discretion allowing senators to derail a governor's nomination from within their home district.

sheriff　The county's chief law enforcement officer; elected to four-year term.

single-issue groups　Interest groups, such as the NRA and MADD, that devote their energies to pursuing a single, narrowly defined policy goal.

single-member district　A specific geographic area with a population equal to that of other districts that elects one person (a single member) to represent that area.

Smith v. Allwright　U.S. Supreme Court case that overturned the white primary.

special committee　A temporary committee formed by the legislature for limited or nonroutine purposes.

special district　A type of local government established for a specific geographic area and for a specific purpose such as education, flood control, or public utility service.

special election　An election held to fill a vacancy, ratify a state constitutional amendment, or approve a local bond issue.

special sessions　Extra legislative sessions called by the governor and limited to 30 days.

spoils system　A system in which elected officials provide jobs and promotions to personal affiliates; see civil service.

staff　The governor's aides; not subject to legislative approval.

standing committee　A deliberative body formed each time a legislature meets that deals with topics of recurring interest.

State Board of Education (SBE)　Elected board that oversees the Texas Education Agency.

state senatorial district convention　Midlevel party meeting between precinct and state; same level as county convention.

straight ticket　selection at the top of the ballot that allows a voter to pick every candidate of a chosen party.

Sunset Advisory Commission　Appointed joint commission that reviews state agencies.

superintendent　The appointed manager of a public school system.

tax revenue　Funds generated through the tax system.

Texas Legislative Council　The legislature's research and bill-drafting service.

Texas Penal Code　The state's definitions and categorizations of crimes and punishments.

Texas Railroad Commission (TRC)　State commission that oversees oil and gas production; elected.

Texas Rangers　An elite division of the Department of Public Safety that investigates major crimes and allegations of police misconduct.

Texas Regulars　A conservative faction of the Democratic Party during the 1940s.

tracking polls　Polls that trace public opinion over time.

trial de novo　Cases that are retried by the county court after being heard in lower courts of nonrecord.

turnout　Percentage of registered voters who cast ballots.

unfunded mandates　Congressional directives that are issued without corresponding federal funding.

universal suffrage　The concept that holds that virtually all adult citizens (felons and illegal aliens are excluded) have the right to vote.

uphold　Higher court leaves ruling intact.

user fees　Monies paid to local governments by citizens who utilize a particular government service (e.g., tuition at a state school or fees at a public boat ramp).

veto power　The ability of the governor to strike down legislation, subject to override.

voir dire　Trial jury selection process conducted by attorneys for both sides.

Voting Rights Act of 1965　National act protecting minorities from discrimination in the voting or the registration process.

white primary　The practice of allowing only whites to vote in the Democratic primary (discontinued).

Endnotes

Chapter 1

1. Harold Lasswell, *Politics: Who Gets What, When, How* (New York: Meridian Books, 1958). This is the classic definition of politics given by Professor Lasswell, one of the giants of the 20th century-American political science.
2. "Alvar Nuñez Cabeza de Vaca," in Ron Tyler, Editor-in-Chief, *The New Handbook of Texas* (Austin: The Texas State Historical Association, 1996), Vol. I, pp. 882–883. All *Handbook of Texas* articles may now be accessed at the *Handbook of Texas Online,* http://www.tshaonline.org/handbook/online.
3. "Coronado Expedition," in Tyler, *The New Handbook of Texas*, Vol. II, pp. 328–329.
4. "René-Robert Cavelier, Sieur de La Salle," in Tyler, *The New Handbook of Texas*, Vol. IV, p. 82.
5. William C. Davis, *Lone Star Rising: The Revolutionary Birth of the Texas Republic* (New York: Free Press, 2004), pp. 58–59.
6. Ibid., pp. 202–203.
7. Ibid., pp. 270–272.
8. "Annexation," in Tyler, *The New Handbook of Texas*, Vol. I, pp. 192–193.
9. "Civil War," in Tyler, *The New Handbook of Texas*, Vol. II, p. 121.
10. "Edmund Jackson Davis," in Tyler, *The New Handbook of Texas*, Vol. II, pp. 526–527.
11. "Ranching," in Tyler, *The New Handbook of Texas*, Vol. V, pp. 430–431.
12. "James Stephen Hogg," in Tyler, *The New Handbook of Texas*, Vol. III, pp. 652–653.
13. "Spindletop Oilfield," in Tyler, *The New Handbook of Texas*, Vol. VI, pp. 29–30.
14. The most thorough account of the Ferguson impeachment and conviction can be found in Bruce Rutherford, *Ferguson: The Impeachment of Jim Ferguson* (Austin, TX: Eakin Press, 1983).
15. "Lyndon Baines Johnson," in Tyler, *The New Handbook of Texas*, Vol. III, pp. 958–959.
16. A meticulous presentation of the Sharpstown Scandal and its aftermath can be found in Charles Deaton, *The Year They Threw the Rascals Out* (Austin, TX: Shoal Creek Publishers, 1973).
17. "Republican Party," in Tyler, *The New Handbook of Texas*, Vol. V, p. 535.
18. Following discussion of Texas geography is based on Keene Ferguson, *The Texas Landscape: The Geographic Provinces of Texas* (Austin: Texas Mosaics Publishing, 1986).
19. The population figures in this section are derived from U.S. Census Bureau, *State and County Quick Facts* (2011). http://quickfacts.census.gov/qfd/states/48000.html and from the Texas State Data Center and Office of the State Demographer, *2012 Population Projections by Migration Scenario* (San Antonio: University of Texas at San Antonio, 2012). http://txsdc.utsa.edu/Data/TPEPP/Projections/Data.aspx#pnl_Output0. The model used in these latter projections reflects growth rates that occurred between 2000 and 2010. This is a relatively conservative growth projection.
20. Daniel J. Elazar, *American Federalism: A View from the States*, 3rd ed. (New York: Harper and Row, 1984).
21. U.S. Bureau of Labor Statistics, *Union Members in 2008* (January 28, 2009).

Chapter 2

1. *The Book of the States, 2011* (Lexington, KY: Council of State Governments, 2011), p. 12.
2. Ibid.
3. Ibid.
4. Rupert N. Richardson, Adrian Anderson, and Ernest Wallace, *Texas: The Lone Star State* (Englewood Cliffs, NJ: Prentice Hall, 1993), p. 110.
5. Ibid., p. 151.
6. Ibid.
7. *Seymour* v. *Conner, Texas: A History* (Arlington Heights, IL: Harlan Davidson, 1971), pp. 216–217.
8. Richardson, p. 227.
9. Ibid., p. 294.
10. Carl H. Moneyhon, *Republicanism in Reconstruction Texas* (Austin: University of Texas Press, 1980), pp. 123–124.
11. Ibid., p. 139.
12. Richardson, p. 236.
13. Moneyhon, pp. 184–185.
14. Ibid., pp. 192–193.
15. John Walker Mauer, "State Constitutions in a Time of Crisis: The Case of the Texas Constitution of 1876," *Texas Law Review* 68 (1990):1625–1626.

16. J. E. Ericson, "The Delegates to the Convention of 1875, A Reappraisal," *Southwestern Historical Quarterly* 67 (1963):22.
17. Mauer, p. 1624.
18. Ibid., pp. 1625–1626.
19. Arvel Ponton, "Sources of Liberty in the Texas Bill of Rights," *St. Mary's Law Journal* 20 (1988):97.
20. *Texas* v. *U.S. EPA*, Slip. Op. No. 10-60614 (5th Cir. Aug. 13, 2012)
21. "EPA Smack-Down Number Six," *The Wall Street Journal*, August 21, 2012. http://online.wsj.com/article/SB10000872396390443989204577603462733432478.html.
22. Ponton, pp. 102–107.

Chapter 3

1. Carl H. Moneyhon, *Republicanism in Reconstruction Texas* (Austin: University of Texas Press, 1980), p. 194.
2. *Smith* v. *Allwright*, 321 U.S. 649 (1944).
3. Rupert N. Richardson, Adrian Anderson, and Ernest Wallace, *Texas: The Lone Star State* (Englewood Cliffs, NJ: Prentice Hall, 1993), p. 394.
4. *Texas* v. *United States*, 384 U.S. 155 (1966).
5. Stephen Power, "'Motor Voter' Law Tied to Registration Climb," *Dallas Morning News*, April 9, 1995, p. 31A.
6. Office of the Secretary of State of Texas, *Election History, 1992–current*. http://elections.sos.state.tx.us/elchist.exe.
7. Ibid.
8. Office of the Secretary of State of Texas, http://www.sos.state.tx.us/elections/forms/enrrpts/2012gen.pdf.
9. Office of the Secretary of State of Texas, http://www.sos.state.tx.us/elections/forms/enrrpts/2010gen.pdf.
10. Ryan Murphy, "Interactive: Cost Per Vote for Texas Candidates for State Office," *The Texas Tribune*, November 9, 2012. www.texastribune.org.
11. Ibid.
12. Ibid.
13. Ibid.
14. Ibid.

Chapter 4

1. James Madison, *Letter to Henry Lee,* June 25, 1824.
2. Rupert N. Richardson, Adrian Anderson, and Ernest Wallace, *Texas: The Lone Star State* (Englewood Cliffs, NJ: Prentice Hall, 1993), p. 393.
3. John R. Knagg, *Two-Party Texas* (Austin, TX: Eakin Press, 1986), p. 9.
4. Ibid., pp. 12–15.
5. Ibid., p. 107.
6. Ibid., pp. 174–176.
7. *The Texas Almanac, 1992–93* (Dallas, TX: *Dallas Morning News*, 1991), p. 424.

Chapter 5

1. *United States Constitution*, Amendment One, Clause 1.
2. *Texas Constitution*, Article I, Section 27.
3. Will Rogers, "Breaking into the Writing Game," *Illiterate Digest* (New York: A. & C. Boni, 1924), pp. 25–36.
4. To learn more about this interest group, visit http://www.texasgoodroads.org/.
5. You can find out more about this powerful interest group and examine some of its policy goals by accessing its website at http://www.ttara.org/.
6. If you're curious to see labor's perspective on the issues confronting Texans today, go to http://www.texasaflcio.org/. Then compare that view with the one found on the Texas Taxpayers and Research Association site noted above.
7. You can check the pulse of the Texas Medical Association at http://www.texmed.org/, see what the trial lawyers are arguing at http://www.ttla.com/, and review TSTA activities at http://www.tsta.org/.
8. You can examine the issues important to this civil rights interest group at http://texasnaacp.org/.
9. You can find out more about this interest group, which was organized in San Antonio in 1968, if you go to http://www.maldef.org/.
10. You can check out the group's ideas and issues at http://home.nra.org/#/nraorg.
11. You can obtain information on MADD by going to their website, http://www.madd.org/.
12. Explore the values of the Nature Conservancy at the group's web site, http://www.nature.org/ourinitiatives/regions/northamerica/unitedstates/texas/index.htm.
13. Take a look at the information provided by the League of Women Voters at http://www.lwvtexas.org/ or read about Common Cause and its goals at http://www.commoncause.org/states/texas.

14. Learn more about the issues and ideas of these morality/lifestyles interest groups by navigating to their websites. Access the Texas Parent-Teacher Association at http://www.txpta.org/. Check out the Christian Life Commission of the Baptist General Convention of Texas at http://christianlifecommission.com/08/. You can see very different views on abortion by contrasting the ideas of Texas Right to Life at http://www.texasrighttolife.com/ and with those of Pro-Choice Texas at http://www.prochoicetexas.org/. Finally, explore the issues important to Texas's gay and lesbian communities at http://www.equalitytexas.org/.

15. You can view the entire legislative agenda of the TMA by clicking on this link: http://www.texmed.org/template.aspx?id=26153. Compare that to the advocacy list for the AMA that can be found at: http://www.ama-assn.org/ama/pub/advocacy.page.

16. You can examine the statutes, legal opinions, and TEC rules at the web site of the Texas Ethics Commission, http://www.ethics.state.tx.us/

17. Ibid.

18. *Citizens United* v. *Federal Election Commission*, 558 U.S. 50 (2010).

Chapter 6

1. Pew Research Center Data Bank, *65%—Internet Now Main Source of News for Young Adults*, October 11, 2012. http://www.people-press.org/2011/01/04/internet-gains-on-television-as-publics-main-news-source/.

2. Norris G. Davis, "RURAL ELECTRIFICATION," *Handbook of Texas Online* (http://www.tshaonline.org/handbook/online/articles/dpr01), accessed October 11, 2012. Published by the Texas State Historical Association.

3. Louise C. Allen, Ernest A. Sharpe, and John R. Whitaker, "NEWSPAPERS," *Handbook of Texas Online* (http://www.tshaonline.org/handbook/online/articles/een08), accessed October 11, 2012. Published by the Texas State Historical Association.

4. Ibid.

5. Ibid.

6. P. L. Cox, *The First Texas News Barons* (Austin: University of Texas Press, 2005), p. 30.

7. Allen.

8. Cox, p. 74.

9. Carl H. Moneyhon, *Republicanism in Reconstruction Texas* (Austin: University of Texas Press, 1980), p. 134.

10. Ibid., p. 174.

11. Daphne Dalton Garrett, "GIDDINGS DEUTSCHES VOLKSBLATT," *Handbook of Texas Online* (http://www.tshaonline.org/handbook/online/articles/eeg09), accessed October 12, 2012. Published by the Texas State Historical Association.

12. Ibid.

13. Cox, p. 68.

14. Cox, p. 69.

15. Cox, p. 86.

16. Cox, p. 96.

17. Cox, pp. 98–99.

18. Cox, pp. 56–57.

19. Judith Segura, *Belo: From Newspapers to New Media* (Austin: University of Texas Press, 2008), p. 51.

20. Ken Case, "Is Justice Blind?" *Texas Monthly*, May 1987, p. 137.

21. Case, p. 138.

22. Case, p. 190.

23. Case, p. 198.

24. E-mail exchange with Vincent Giardino.

25. Amy Mitchell, Tom Rosentiel, and Leah Christian. *The State of the News Media 2012*. The Pew Research Center's Project for Excellence in Journalism. Retrieved from http://stateofthemedia.org/2012/mobile-devices-and-news-consumption-some-good-signs-for-journalism.

26. *Texas Exit Poll: 2010 election*, http://www.cnn.com/ELECTION/2010/results/polls/#TXG00p1.

27. Ibid.

Chapter 7

1. Texas Constitution, art. 3.

2. Ibid. The specific amount provided in each session is established by the Texas Ethics Commission.

3. Ibid.

4. Ibid.

5. Legislative Reference Library of Texas, *81st Legislature (2009)–Statistical Profile*. http://www.lrl.state.tx.us/legis/profile81.html.

6. "Republicans' Grip on Legislature Will Slip," *Fort Worth Star Telegram*, November 7, 2012, p. 5AA.

7. Texas Secretary of State.

8. Texas House of Representatives, *Office of the Chief Clerk*.

9. Texas Senate, *Office of the Secretary of the Senate*.

10. Legislative Reference Library of Texas, *Membership Statistics for the 82nd Legislature*. http://www.lrl.state.tx.us/legeLeaders/members/memberStatistics.cfm.

11. Texas Constitution, art. 3.

12. *Reynolds* v. *Sims*, 377 U.S. 533 (1964).

13. *Kilgarlin* v. *Martin*, 252 F. Supp. 404 (1966).

14. Texas Constitution, art. 3.

15. The contemporary poster boy for wandering in the political wilderness as a result of openly opposing the election of a speaker would have to be Representative Lon Burnam of Fort Worth. Burnam resolutely voted against the election of Tom Craddick as House Speaker, and this open defiance of the speaker resulted in Burnam being sentenced to service on committees whose jurisdiction only rarely coincided with the interests and concerns of his constituents. Moreover, Burnam routinely was unable to get even a hearing in committee on most of the bills that he proposed and almost never succeeded in passing legislation. Obviously, openly opposing the Speaker comes at a tremendous price.

16. Bob Bullock was one of the most colorful and controversial figures in Texas politics. His life and legacy are brilliantly treated in Dave McNeely and Jim Henderson, *Bob Bullock: God Bless Texas* (Austin, TX: University of Texas Press, 2008).

17. Texas Legislature Online, *Senate Committees, 82st Legislature*. http://www.capitol.state.tx.us/Committees/CommitteesMbrs.aspx?Chamber=S.

18. Texas Legislature Online, *House Committees, 81st Legislature*. http://www.capitol.state.tx.us/Committees/CommitteesMbrs.aspx?Chamber=H.

19. Legislative Reference Library of Texas, *81st Legislature (2009)–Bill Statistics*. http://www.lrl.state.tx.us/sessions/billStatistics.cfm.

20. House Research Organization, *Major Issues of the 82nd Legislature, Regular Session and First Called Session*.

Chapter 8

1. The Rick Perry Primer, *Texans for Public Justice*, July 2011. www.tpj.org.

2. "Bush Trails Richards in Naming Minorities to State Boards and Agencies, Review Finds," *Dallas Morning News*, June 12, 1998, p. 22A.

3. R. J. Ratcliffe, "Perry Works with Texas Lawmakers to Salvage Bad Year," *Houston Chronicle*, May 14, 2009, http://www.chron.com/disp/story.mpl/headline/metro/6439800.html.

4. Keith J. Mueller, "Explaining Variation and Change in Gubernatorial Powers, 1960–1982," *Western Political Quarterly* (September 1985): 42–47.

5. *Vetoed Bills, 1860–2011*, Legislative Reference Library of Texas. http://www.lrl.state.tx.us/legis/vetoes.

6. Sylvia Moreno, "Conference Committee Toughens Welfare Bill," *Dallas Morning News*, May 24, 1995, p. 20A.

7. *Fiscal Size-Up: 2012–13 Biennium*, Legislative Budget Board, p. 122.

8. Ibid., p. 123.

Chapter 9

1. "Shivers Asks Delay in Plan to Abandon Fixed Price Supports," *Wichita Falls Record News*, April 27, 1954.

2. David Dewhurst, *The Water Event*, November 16, 2009, retrieved from http://www.h2o4texas.org/dewhurstvideo.html.

3. *Legislative Budget Board Fiscal Size-Up*, Texas Legislative Budget Board, 2012, p. 77.

4. Ibid., p. 89.

5. Susan Combs, *The Impact of the 2011 Drought and Beyond* (Austin: Office of the Comptroller, 2012).

6. Brian Wellborn, "Water for Power," *Fiscal Notes*, May 12, 2012. http://www.window.state.tx.us/comptrol/fnotes/fn1205/water-power.php.

7. Ibid.

8. Ibid., p. 228.

9. Terrence Henry, "Unsalting the Earth: Jerry Patterson's Desalinization Ambitions," *StateImpact*, July 9, 2012. Stateimpact.npr.org.

10. Ibid., p. 378.

11. Ray Leszcynski, "Agriculture Commissioner Unveils Water Conservation Coalition Plan," *Dallas Morning News*, April 2, 2012. dallasnews.com.

12. Ibid., p. 474.

13. Ibid., p. 19.

14. Ibid., p. 61.

15. Gerald R. Ford, *A Time to Heal* (New York: Berkeley, 1980), p. 265.

16. Texas Education Agency Division of Charter Schools Summary of Charter Awards and Closure, p. 1.
17. *Water for Texas: 2012 State Water Plan*, Texas Water Development Board, 2012, p. iii.
18. *Fiscal Size-Up*, p. 451.
19. *Guide to the Texas Sunset Process*, Sunset Advisory Commission, January 2012, p. 12.

Chapter 10

1. *Annual Report for the Texas Judiciary*, Office of Court Administration, Fiscal Year 2011, March 2012, p. 3.
2. Texas Bar Association.
3. *Annual Report for the Texas Judiciary*, Office of Court Administrator, Fiscal Year 2011, March 2012, p. 3.
4. Ibid.
5. Ibid.
6. Office of Court Administration, "The Judicial System," Pamphlet published June 2009, p. 3.
7. Ibid, p. 2.
8. Ibid, p.6.
9. Ibid, p. 7.
10. *Annual Report for the Texas Judiciary*, Office of Court Administrator, Fiscal Year 2011, March 2012, p. 113.
11. Ibid.
12. Ibid.
13. Texas Government Code 2001.171 Trial de Novo.
14. *Annual Report for the Texas Judiciary*, Office of Court Administrator, Fiscal Year 2011, March 2012, p. 9.
15. Texas Constitution, art. 5, sec. 32-a.
16. Texas Justice Courts Training Center.
17. *Annual Report for the Texas Judiciary*, Office of Court Administrator, Fiscal Year 2011, March 2012, p. 9.
18. Ibid., p. 10.
19. Amir Efrati, "Nobody . . . Is Ever Going to Plead Guilty Again," *The Wall Street Journal*, June 29, 2009.

Chapter 11

1. *FY2010 Operating Budget Schedule*. http://www.houstontx.gov/budget/index.html.
2. *Texas in Focus: A Statewide View of Opportunities*. Texas Comptroller of Public Accounts Publication, http://www.window.state.tx.us/specialrpt/tif/population.html.
3. Alphabet Soup: Types of Texas Cities, Presented by: Monte Akers Akers & Boulware-Wells, Austin, Texas. Updated by: Laura Mueller, Texas Municipal League Legal Department. Tenth Annual TCAA Riley Fletcher Basic Municipal Law Seminar, February 13, 2009, Austin, Texas.
4. "Local Governments in Texas," *Texas Town and City*, January 2009 (http://www.tml.org/HCW/LocalGovernmentsinTexas.pdf).
5. Ibid.
6. *Municipal Law 101: Basic Municipal Laws and Issues for Texas City Officials*, By Monte Akers, Barbara Boulware-Wells, and Jason D. King, Akers & Boulware-Wells, LLP. Made available at the 2009 Riley Fletcher Basic Municipal Law Seminar, February 13, 2009, Austin, Texas.
7. Bradley R. Rice, "Commission Form of City Government," *Handbook of Texas Online* (http://www.tshaonline.org/handbook/online/articles/moc01), accessed August 18, 2012. Published by the Texas State Historical Association.
8. Amanda Ripley, "The 1900 Galveston Hurricane," *Time Magazine*, September 15, 2008.
9. "Local Governments in Texas," *Texas Town and City*, January 2009 (http://www.tml.org/HCW/LocalGovernmentsinTexas.pdf).
10. *Texas constitution*, as amended, art. xi, sec. 4–5.
11. *Texas vonstitution*, art. 11, sec. 4.
12. Josh Goodman, "Dallas 'Strong Mayor' Vote Fails Narrowly," *Governing the States and Localities*, November 8, 2005.
13. *Texas Tribune*, http://www.texastribune.org/library/data/government-employee-salaries/titles/city-manager/3651.
14. Texas Comptroller of Public Accounts, 2012.
15. Amanda Ripley, "The 1900 Galveston Hurricane," *Time Magazine*, September 15, 2008.
16. *Texas in Focus: A Statewide View of Opportunities*, Texas Comptroller of Public Accounts Publication, http://www.window.state.tx.us/specialrpt/tif/population.html.
17. Kevin Welch, "Reality of Single-member Districts Complex," *Amarillo Globe News*, April 25, 2011.
18. Anthony Giardino, "Membership Has Its Privileges," *Texas Police Star* (Spring 1992), p. 55.
19. Federal Election Commission, 2012.

20. Mitchell Schnurman, "Eminent Domain Not a Threat Locally," *Fort Worth Star-Telegram,* June 29, 2005.
21. "El Paso Refuses Limits on Eminent Domain," *American City and County,* June 14, 2006.
22. Texas Constitution, art. 11, sec. 4.
23. Sheriffs Association of Texas.
24. Ibid.
25. From the Texas Comptroller of Public Accounts, *Your Money and the Taxing Facts.*

Chapter 12

1. Executive Order 13513.
2. Bryan Sperry, "Sperry: Preserve Funding for Children's Hospitals," *Austin American Statesman,* January 17, 2013.
3. http://www.mysanantonio.com/news/local_news/article/1-in-4-kids-now-living-in-poverty-3461771.php#ixzz23ZBSc2N0.
4. http://amarillo.com/news/local-news/2012-02-10/hud-awards-650k-public-housing. HUD awards $650K for public housing. February 10, 2012, *Amarillo Globe-News,* by Aziza Musa.
5. Thomas C. Hayes, "Gunman Kills 22 and Himself in Texas Cafeteria," *The New York Times,* October 17, 1991. http://query.nytimes.com/gst/fullpage.html?sec=travel&res=9C04E3D8113 BF934A25753C1A967958260.
6. The Prosecutorial Remedies and Other Tools to end the Exploitation of Children Today (PROTECT) Act, signed into law on April 30, 2003.
7. Senate Bill 378 took effect September 1, 2007.
8. http://www.txdot.gov/driver/share-road/work-zones.html.
9. http://www.austintexas.gov/news/central-texas-move-over-law-initiative.
10. http://www.texas811.org.
11. Ibid.
12. http://www.austintexas.gov/news/central-texas-move-over-law-initiative.
13. Chris Tomlinson, "Perry Officially Rejects Texas Insurance Exchange," *Houston Chronicle,* November 15, 2012.
14. Elizabeth Shogren, "House Votes to Repeal 55-M.P.H. Speed Limit : Roads Bill gives states authority to set standards. Californians are expected to see more 65-m.p.h. signs," *Los Angeles Times,* September 21, 1995.
15. http://www.texasclickitorticket.com/whats_new/?cat=3.
16. http://www.policeone.com/Motorcycle-Patrol/articles/3737352-Texas-Click-It-or-Ticket-campaign-saving-lives/.
17. Daniel Bonevac, Ph.D., and Michael D. Weiss, "Tort Reform: Has Texas Ended Its Lawsuit Lottery?" *Texas Public Policy Foundation,* October 15, 1995.

Chapter 13

1. "Texans of the Year: Christopher Scott and Michael Morton," *Dallas Morning News* (Editorial), December 29, 2012. http://www.dallasnews.com/opinion/sunday-commentary/20121229-2012-dallas-morning-news-texans-of-the-year-christopher-scott-and-michael-morton.ece.
2. Elliot Cochran, "Crime in State, County Down," *Courier of Montgomery County,* June 15, 2009.
3. Uniform Crime Reports, http://www.fbi.gov/ucr/ucr.htm.
4. Texas Family Code, 261.001.
5. Texas Family Code, 71.0021.
6. Ibid.
7. *Kennedy* v. *Louisiana,* 554 U.S. 407 (2008).
8. Michelle Deitch, "Prison Statistics Should Make Texans Feel Uneasy," *Dallas Morning News,* September 8, 2002, p. 5J.
9. Herbert H. Haines, *Against Capital Punishment: Anti-Death Penalty Movement in America, 1972–1994* (Oxford University Press, 1996). ISBN 9780195088380
10. *Hererra* v. *Collins,* 506 U.S. 390 (1993).
11. Texas Department of Criminal Justice.
12. *Roper* v. *Simmons,* 543 U.S. 551 (2005).
13. *Atkins* v. *Virginia,* 536 US 304 (2002).
14. Texas Department of Criminal Justice.
15. Texas Commission on Law Enforcement Officers Standards and Education.
16. Ibid.
17. Texas Department of Public Safety, Texas Rangers.
18. Walter Prescott Webb, *The Story of the Texas Rangers* (Austin, TX: Encino Press, 1971), p. 8.
19. Texas Alcoholic Beverage Commission pamphlet: Who We Are and What We Do.
20. Texas Sheriff's Association.
21. *Texas constitution,* sec. 5, art. 18.14.
22. Ibid.

23. Houston Police Department.

24. Texas Police Chiefs Association.

25. *Texas House Speakers Oral History*, The Dolph Briscoe Center for American History. http://www.cah.utexas.edu/projects/speakers_lewis.php.

26. Texas Government Code § 62.106. Exemption from Jury Service.

27. Ibid.

28. Nita Thurman, "Woman Wins Battle over Juror's Right to Privacy," *Dallas Morning News*, June 18, 1995, p. 37A.

Chapter 14

1. *Fiscal Size-Up: 2012–13 Biennium*, Legislative Budget Board, 2012, p. 9.

2. *Fiscal Size-Up,* p. 10.

3. Mike Reissig, "Revenues on a Roll," *Fiscal Notes* (January 1995), p. 11.

4. *Fiscal Size-Up*, p. 16.

5. *Fiscal Size-Up*, p. 30.

6. Clint Shields, "Boom in the Shale," *Fiscal Notes* (May 2012). http://www.window.state.tx.us/comptrol/fnotes/fn1205/boom.php.

7. Jim Vertuno, "Texas Appeals to Keep Pole Tax," *Houston Chronicle*, June 12, 2009. http://www.chron.com/disp/story.mpl/metropolitan/6473888.html.

8. *Fiscal Size Up*, p. 49.

9. *Fiscal Size Up*, p. 56.

10. Susan Combs, "Your Money and Education Debt," *Texas Comptroller of Public Accounts,* October 2012.

11. *Fiscal Size Up*, p. 53.

12. *Fiscal Size Up*, p. 52.

13. Martha Sills, "New Life for Old Sport," *The Advocate,* July 17, 2012. http://theadvocate.com/news/3248677-123/new-life-for-old-sport.

14. Sills.

15. Mary Rampellini, "Oaklawn Park: Gaming Revenue Boosts Purses to a Record $350,000 per Day," *Daily Racing Form*, January 9, 2013. http://www.drf.com/news/oaklawn-park-gaming-revenue-boosts-purses-record-350000-day.

16. *Fiscal Size Up*, p. 59.

17. *Fiscal Size Up*, p. 37.

18. *Fiscal Size Up*, p. 58.

19. *Fiscal Size Up*, p. 234.

20. *Fiscal Size Up*, p. 160.

21. *Fiscal Size Up*, p. 200.

22. *Fiscal Size Up*, p. 212.

23. "TANF Statistics," Texas Health and Human Services Commission, July 2012.

24. *Fiscal Size Up*, p. 339.

Photo Credits

Index

Page numbers followed by *f* or *t* indicate material in figures or tables, respectively.